T0367223

Abraham Lincoln

Abraham Lincoln

A Life

Michael Burlingame

Edited and Abridged by

Jonathan W. White

Johns Hopkins University Press

Baltimore

Printed in the United States of America on acid-free paper
2 4 6 8 9 7 5 3 1

Johns Hopkins University Press
2715 North Charles Street
Baltimore, Maryland 21218
www.press.jhu.edu

Library of Congress Cataloging-in-Publication Data

Names: Burlingame, Michael, 1941– author. |
White, Jonathan W., 1979– editor, abridger.
Title: Abraham Lincoln : a life / Michael Burlingame ;
edited and abridged by Jonathan W. White.
Description: [Abridged edition] | Baltimore : Johns Hopkins
University Press, 2023. | First published in 2 volumes by Johns Hopkins
University Press in 2008. | Includes bibliographical references and index.
Identifiers: LCCN 2022011929 | ISBN 9781421445557 (hardcover) |
ISBN 9781421445564 (ebook)
Subjects: LCSH: Lincoln, Abraham, 1809-1865. |
Presidents—United States—Biography.
Classification: LCC E457 .B95 2023 | DDC 973.7092 [B]—
dc23/eng/20230127
LC record available at https://lccn.loc.gov/2022011929

A catalog record for this book is available from the British Library.

For Lewis E. Lehrman
Lincolnian extraordinaire

Contents

Introduction

In the introduction to the one-volume abridgment of Carl Sandburg's six-volume Lincoln biography, the poet-author observed: "Every biographer of Lincoln is under compulsion to omit all or part of Lincoln's letters and speeches that he would like to include," for authors "must choose and decide what sentences or paragraphs shed the light needed for the Lincoln portrait and story."*

In writing the original version, I had the help of innumerable others whose contributions are listed in the acknowledgments section of that work. Special thanks are due to Lewis E. Lehrman, dedicatee of this book, whose exceptional generosity made possible not only the original work but this abridgment as well. Special thanks are also due to Lois McDonald, beloved soulmate who has enriched my life immeasurably for over three decades.

Not all the words included here appeared in the original version, for during the years since its publication in 2008 much new information has come to light, some of which has been added. Moreover, mistakes that were found have been corrected. The interpretive framework, however, remains the same, as does the chapter structure.

Readers interested in fuller explorations of Lincoln's marriage or his interactions with Black Americans, as well as his views on race, may wish to consult two books of mine published in 2021, *An American Marriage: The Untold Story of Abraham Lincoln and Mary Todd* and *The Black Man's President: Abraham Lincoln, African Americans, and the Pursuit of Racial Equality*, as well as Jonathan W. White's

*In choosing what sentences and paragraphs to omit in condensing my two-volume, 1.2-million-word biography for this 300,000-word abridgment, I have had the invaluable assistance of Jonathan W. White, a widely published, prizewinning Lincoln scholar and Civil War historian of the first rank. He performed the difficult original round of extensive surgery, suggesting cuts that I then reviewed and tweaked, occasionally restoring some passages. The result is this book, whose words are mine but the indispensable "creative destruction" involved in the abridgment process is the joint work of us both, especially Professor White, to whom I am profoundly grateful.

A House Built by Slaves: African American Visitors to the Lincoln White House, which appeared in 2022.

The notes in both letterpress versions of the biography are strictly limited to identifying the sources of directly quoted material. More elaborate notes can be found in the online version of the book at https://www.knox.edu/about-knox/lincoln-studies-center/burlingame-abraham-lincoln-a-life. I am grateful to Knox College and to Johns Hopkins University Press for allowing the more complete version of the book, with extensive documentation, to be made available online.

Michael Burlingame

Abraham Lincoln

1.

"I Have Seen a Good Deal of the Back Side of This World"

Childhood in Kentucky (1809–1816)

One day in the middle of the Civil War, Abraham Lincoln carved time from his busy schedule to pen some wise paternal advice to a young Union captain who had been squabbling with his superiors. Quoting from *Hamlet*, the president wrote that a father's injunction to his son—"Beware of entrance to a quarrel, but being in, bear it that the opposed may beware of thee"—was good counsel, "and yet not the best." Instead, Lincoln enjoined the captain: "Quarrel not at all." The reasons he gave were practical: "No man resolved to make the most of himself, can spare time for personal contention. Still less can he afford to take all the consequences, including the vitiating of his temper, and the loss of self-control. Yield larger things to which you can show no more than equal right; and yield lesser ones, though clearly your own. Better give your path to a dog, than be bitten by him in contesting for the right. Even killing the dog would not cure the bite."[1] Born into emotional and economic poverty, Lincoln early on "resolved to make the most of himself," and he did so, adhering to those precepts.

Ancestry

Like many another exceptional child of unexceptional parents, Lincoln was quite curious about his ancestors, especially his grandfathers, neither of whom he knew. So intrigued was he that he planned to conduct genealogical research after finishing his presidency. In two brief autobiographical sketches written for the campaign of 1860, he devoted much space to his lineage.

His father's father was known as Captain Abraham, a rank he attained by 1776 while serving in the Virginia militia. It is not clear why the captain departed the Old Dominion in 1780 with his wife and children on a 250-mile trek to the remote and dangerous Indian hunting grounds of Kentucky while the Revolutionary War still raged and attacks on settlers were common. He died a violent death on the "dark and bloody ground" of frontier Kentucky. As a boy, the future president often heard this harrowing tale, which he referred to as "the legend more strongly than all others imprinted upon my mind and memory."[2] Working his farm one spring day in 1786, 42-year-old Grandfather Abraham was ambushed by an Indian, who shot him dead before the eyes of his terrified young son Thomas (father-to-be of the sixteenth president). As the Indian prepared to kidnap the lad, his older brother Mordecai ran back to the family cabin, grabbed a rifle, aimed at the silver ornament dangling from the Indian's neck, and squeezed the trigger. Luckily for Thomas, his brother's aim was true, and the boy escaped unharmed, at least physically.

It is hard to say what Lincoln knew about his other grandfather, whom he described as "a Virginia planter, a large farmer."[3] This "nobleman" took sexual advantage of a poor, credulous young woman named Lucey Hanks. The fruit of that union was Nancy Hanks, mother of the sixteenth president. From this aristocratic progenitor Lincoln believed that he inherited "his power of analysis, his logic, his mental activity, his ambition, and all the qualities that distinguished him from the other members and descendants of the Hanks family."[4]

Lincoln's remarks about his aristocratic grandsire represent a variation of the "family romance" phenomenon, which causes some children to speculate that they are actually the offspring of more exalted parents than the ones who raised them. Most people outgrow these fantasies, but some adults—including exceptional people or men with very distant fathers—will long maintain an unusually powerful family romance. Lincoln fits the latter category on both counts.

Parents

Lincoln's father, Thomas, was quite undistinguished. Born around 1776 in Virginia's Shenandoah Valley, he moved with his parents and four siblings to Kentucky in 1780. The documentary record reveals little about Thomas's activities in the decade after his father was killed. Under the law of primogeniture, his eldest brother, Mordecai, inherited everything from their father's estate. In 1795, Thomas served in the Kentucky militia for a month, and the following year he worked on a milldam in Hardin County. While laboring there, he lived with Hananiah Lincoln, a cousin of his father's and a resident of Elizabethtown, forty-five miles southwest of Louisville. Thomas and Hananiah remained in that village only till 1798, when they evidently headed south to Cumberland County. For a time, Thomas shuttled back and forth between Washington and Cumberland Counties. In 1802, he moved to Hardin County, where his name appeared on the tax lists for the next fourteen years. In 1803, he purchased a 238-acre farm on Mill Creek, where he lived while working in nearby Elizabethtown. How Thomas could afford to buy that farm is unclear. His brother Mordecai may have shared some of his patrimony with him after Thomas attained his majority.

On June 12, 1806, shortly after returning from a trip to New Orleans, Thomas married Nancy Hanks in a ceremony that took place near Poortown in Washington County. Following a brief honeymoon, the newlyweds moved to Elizabethtown, where their first child, Sarah, was born less than eight months after her parents' wedding. At the end of 1807, Thomas moved fourteen miles to a rock-strewn spread in the "Barrens," on the South Fork of Nolin Creek, known as the Sinking Spring farm. It was near the homestead where Thomas and Betsy Sparrow, who had raised Nancy, lived with their foster child, Dennis Hanks. Thomas gambled when he chose that site, for rather than a deed, he purchased a title bond (an assignment of someone's contested right to the land). He would possess the property only if others met their financial obligations. On February 12, 1809, in a cabin that an observer called "a miserable habitation," Nancy delivered a baby boy, who was named Abraham after Thomas's father.[5]

There are abundant descriptions of Thomas Lincoln, who in a few superficial ways resembled his son. But the qualities that were to make Abraham Lincoln famous—his intellectual power, his ambition, his idealism, his eloquence, his spirituality, his integrity, his political wisdom, his judgment, his leadership—were lacking in Thomas. Few of Thomas's neighbors could remember anything special about him, only that he was "a plain unpretending plodding man," a "good average man," who "attended to his work" and was "among the very commonest of the plain pioneers," "honest and harmless," "illiterate, yet always truthful, conscientious and religious," and "peaceable good."[6] Thomas evidently could read a little but was unable to write anything other than his signature.

Unlike his tall, rangy son, Thomas was thick, weighing between 180 and 200 pounds. He was a bit stoop-shouldered, somewhat clumsy as he walked, and strong. He was indifferent to clothes, and his taste in food was simple—two traits he shared with his son. "His whole appearance," said one neighbor, "denoted a man of small intel[l]ect and less ambition, and such he was."[7] If Thomas lacked intellectual power and driving ambition, he impressed people favorably as honest and sociable, slow to take offense, with a great deal of common sense. When William G. Greene visited him in 1836, he found Thomas's manners "Back[w]oodsish," but he was "charmed" by his wit and humor and thought him "mighty hospitable, and a very entertaining host."[8]

For all his humor, Thomas could be taciturn and moody. He often became depressed and withdrew into himself. He would wander out in the barrens for hours on end. Bouts of depression would hardly be surprising in a man who, as a boy, had witnessed his father's murder and then suffered poverty and knew hard labor. Other losses—recurring financial setbacks and the deaths of his second son in 1813, his wife in 1818, and his daughter in 1828—deepened his depression. He frequently said that "everything that I ever teched either died, got killed or was lost."[9] Thomas's susceptibility to depression may have been in part genetic; many other members of the family had "moody spells."[10]

Thomas Lincoln prospered neither as a carpenter nor as a farmer. Dennis Hanks, a cousin who spent three years living with the Lincolns during Abe's youth, reported that Thomas "couldn't make a living by his trade [carpentry]; there was scarcely any money in the country. So Tom took up some land—mighty poor land, but the best he could get when he hadn't much to trade for it."[11] He learned woodworking and made his living as a "Cabinet and House Carpenter" until he wed. Thereafter he supplemented his income by farming. His carpentry skills were rudimentary, leading people to call him a "rough" and "cheap carpenter" who could "put doors, windows, and floors in log houses" and do a "tolerable" job of joining.[12] He continued practicing carpentry after he moved to Indiana, making rough tables, coffins, doors, and window casings. He worked when jobs came to him but would not seek them out.

If little more than a rough, tolerable carpenter, Thomas was even less successful as a farmer, partly because he chose unpromising land to till. The Nolin Creek property—birthplace of the future president—had poor soil except in a few small patches. In 1811, Thomas moved to equally unpromising terrain on Knob Creek, nine miles away. With a fresh start in Indiana in 1816, he unwisely selected 160 heavily timbered acres and built his cabin more than a mile from a reliable water source. In Illinois in the 1830s and 1840s he showed similarly bad judgment.

Even if he had appraised land more shrewdly, Thomas lacked the industry, ambition, and intellectual power to prosper. As Dennis Hanks put it, Thomas "was a man who took the world Easy" and "never thought that gold was God." Hanks's son-in-law was more blunt: Thomas, he declared, "was v[er]y careless about his business, a poor Manager, at time[s] accumulated considerable property which he always managed to make way with about as fast as he made it, and was what is generally called an unlucky Man in business."[13]

Several times Thomas took boatloads of pork and other goods to New Orleans, usually making little money. In one particularly unfortunate transaction, he was cheated out of the entire load. Thomas also lost money buying and selling farms, especially in Kentucky, where an archaic surveying system—permitting claims to be identified by trees, stones, creek bends, and other such imprecise landmarks—produced chaos leading to innumerable lawsuits. Kentucky law did not require a qualifying examination for surveyors, who reportedly were never correct except by accident.

Thomas made scant use of the land he occupied, usually clearing only a few acres for a garden and a corn patch. At Knob Creek, he cultivated only six acres. He worked enough to sustain life and no more. For the most part, Thomas avoided the market economy, remaining a subsistence farmer. He did, however, grow a little tobacco, which he peddled for ten cents a pound. (Lincoln later told a friend that his father raised tobacco in the family garden "and was a great lover of it," though Lincoln himself never used it because "he knew that he must be made sick by it before he could enjoy it, and did not want to get sick."[14] Similarly, Lincoln explained that he was a teetotaler because liquor made him feel "flabby and undone.")[15]

According to one of Thomas's stepsons-in-law, John J. Hall, "Thomas Lincoln did not improve with age nor with increasing responsibilities. He was still the same kind and genial 'fellow,' but grew more and more shiftless and good for nothing as the years rolled on." At the rocky Nolin Creek farm, Hall reported, Thomas "did not cultivate the soil nor 'fix up' the old shanty."[16] Like many poor settlers on the Midwestern frontier, he preferred hunting to farming. Dennis Hanks recalled, "We hunted pretty much all the time, Especially so when we got tired of work—which was very often I will assure you."[17] Ida Tarbell interviewed John D. Wickliffe of Bardstown, who "had the impression that Tom Lincoln never amounted to much." She also reported that Thomas Fortune of Indiana, who spoke with several Hoosiers who knew the Lincolns, "insisted that he [Thomas] was no account."[18] Nathaniel Grigsby, an Indiana neighbor of the Lincolns, called Thomas "a piddler—always doing but doing nothing great. . . . He wanted few things and Supplied them Easily."[19]

Thomas Lincoln's indolence, lack of ambition, and disdain for education put him at odds with his smart, enterprising son. Thomas, Abraham said, "grew up litterally [*sic*] without education" and "never did more in the way of writing than to bunglingly sign his own name."[20] This patronizing language lends credence to the testimony of Dennis Hanks, who doubted "whether Abe loved his farther Very well or Not" and concluded, "I Dont think he Did."[21] The feeling was mutual. According to Hanks's son-in-law, Thomas "never showed by his actions that he thought much of his son Abraham when a Boy. He treated him rather unkind" and "always appeared to think much more of his stepson John D Johnston than he did of his own Son Abraham."[22] This preference is not surprising, for Thomas shared much in common with his improvident stepson.

Lincoln's aversion to his father persisted into adulthood. He never once invited Thomas to visit him in Springfield and rarely lent money to his cash-strapped sire. When his law practice took him near his father's home in Coles County, Lincoln stayed with Dennis Hanks rather than under the paternal roof. As Thomas lay dying in 1851, his 42-year-old son refused his deathbed appeal for a visit but icily enjoined his stepbrother to tell their father "that if we could meet now, it is doubtful whether it would not be more painful than pleasant."[23] Lincoln did not attend the funeral, nor did he have a tombstone placed on his father's grave, and he did not name a son after his father until after Thomas's death. He belittled his father when, referring to one of Thomas's brothers, he told a friend, "I have often said that Uncle Mord had run off with all the talents of the family."[24]

Lincoln's estrangement stemmed not just from Thomas's emotional reserve, painful though that may well have been. More deeply wounding was "his father's cold & inhuman treatment of him."[25] Dennis Hanks recalled that Thomas would whip young Abe for minor indiscretions. "Sometimes Abe was a little rude," Hanks testified. "When strangers would ride along & up to his fathers fence Abe always, through pride & to tease his father, would be sure to ask the stranger the first question, for which his father would sometimes knock him a rod [sixteen feet]." Thomas "would pick up a big clod and knock little Abe off the fence, crying: 'Let older people have the first say, will you boy?'" Whenever he was "whipped by his father" he "never bawled but dropt a kind of silent unwelcome tear, as evidence of his sensations—or other feelings."[26] Hanks's son-in-law deplored Thomas's "great barbarity" in dealing with his boy.[27]

Thomas avoided whipping or scolding his son in front of visitors but would take him off after they left and punish him. Lincoln's cousin Sophie Hanks "always said that the worst trouble with Abe was when people was talking—if they said something that wasn't right Abe would up and tell them so. Uncle Tom had a hard time to break him of this."[28] She also recalled how Lincoln "very often would correct his father in talking when his father was telling how anything happened and if he didnt tell it jest right or left out any thing, Abe would but[t] in right there and correct it."[29] Thomas would then slap the lad.

Lincoln's father regarded physical strength as enough to make a manly man and thought time spent on schooling was wasted. He would "slash" Abe "for neglecting his work by reading."[30] Five years after Lincoln, aged 22, left his father's home, Thomas scoffed: "I suppose that Abe is still fooling hisself with eddication. I tried to stop it, but he had got that fool idea in his head, and it can't be got out. Now I hain't got no eddication, but I get along far better than ef I had." Thomas then showed how he kept his accounts by marking a rafter with a piece of coal and proudly declared: "That thar's a heap better'n yer eddication." He added that "if Abe don't fool away all his time on his books, he may make something yet."[31]

Nancy Hanks

Lincoln's estrangement from his father is well documented, but little is known about his relationship with his mother, who died when Abe was 9 years old. In fact, little is known about her at all. She was born in Virginia around 1783 or 1784. Accounts of her appearance differ significantly: her complexion was variously described as "dark," "sandy," "pale," and "exceedingly fair," while her hair was deemed light by some and dark by most. Her eyes were evidently hazel. Although one observer described her as "a heavy built Squatty woman," most people remembered her as taller than average (one estimate placed her at six feet). She had "a spare delicate frame," weighed "about 120 pounds," and was "not at all good looking," with a face "Sharp and angular," "high forehead," and "rather Coarse" features, all of which gave her "the appearance of a laboring woman."[32] A minister who interviewed people who had known the Lincolns in Indiana said she was "about five feet ten inches" tall, "bony," "angular," and "lean," with "long arms," large ears, nose, and mouth, small grey-blue eyes, and a big head on a long, stringy neck. Her cheekbones were high, and her chest sunken.[33]

Nancy Hanks was evidently an intelligent, kind woman. Her son described her as "intellectual," "a woman of genius," and "by nature a great woman."[34] Dennis Hanks agreed, praising her "quick perception," and good memory.[35] Nathaniel Grigsby said she was noted throughout the family for her strong mind and was "a brilliant woman" far "superior to her husband in Every way."[36] She was also notably affectionate and displayed "tenderness—charity & love to the world."[37] Her "cheerful disposition and active habits were a dower" to the pioneers with whom she lived.[38] She also enjoyed a reputation for outdoing all the local women at spinning flax. At camp meetings, the deeply religious Nancy shouted in an attempt to get others to repent.

She was not very sociable, however. She did not talk much, nor did she call on her neighbors; they, in turn, stopped going to see her because she did not return their visits. Her lack of sociability may have been linked to her apparent sadness, even depression. Neighbors remembered her "sad appearance" and that she was "rather gloomy."[39] A Kentuckian attributed her depression to gossip: "People talked about her sometimes, and that depressed her, hurt her."[40] Those hurtful rumors perhaps concerned the unchaste ways of Nancy's mother, Lucey Hanks, who bore Nancy out of wedlock in Virginia and was later charged with fornication in Kentucky. At first, Lucey turned baby Nancy over to her own parents; later the youngster was raised by her childless aunt and uncle, Thomas and Elizabeth Sparrow. She also lived for a time with Richard Berry and his wife Polly Ewing Berry, friends of

Thomas Lincoln. Her mother's lack of interest in her may well have predisposed Nancy to depression.

Questions were raised about Nancy Hanks's chastity as well as her mother's. Polly Richardson, a neighbor of the Lincolns in both Kentucky and Indiana, told her daughter "that not only was Nancy Hanks an illegitimate child herself but that Nancy was not what she ought to have been," that she was "Loose."[41] Others described her as "of low character," a woman who "did not bear a very virtuous name."[42] Lincoln's law partner and biographer William H. Herndon believed that Nancy Hanks "*fell* in Kentucky about 1805—*fell* when unmarried—*fell* afterward."[43] According to Herndon, the "reputation of Mrs. Lincoln is that she was a bold—reckless—dare devil kind of a woman, stepping to the very verge of propriety."[44]

Nancy's courtship with Thomas Lincoln raised some eyebrows. She lived in the home of a woman on South Fork Creek, where Thomas Lincoln often visited. The young couple would take extensive trips to attend camp meetings and stayed out quite late, scandalizing the neighborhood. Finally, the woman with whom Nancy was living scolded Thomas for such nocturnal adventures. This reprimand may have prompted Nancy to move temporarily to Washington County and later to marry Tom there, instead of in her adopted home. Other sources testify that Nancy lived with various families in Bourbon County, sewing, weaving, and doing domestic work, and that while there she was courted by Thomas, "whose shiftless character caused her friends to think him not worthy of her." One neighbor grew upset because Nancy "got herself 'talked about' from allowing this 'shiftless Linkhorn' to wait on her."[45] Some felt that Nancy was not a wanton woman but rather a victim of idle gossip. Nancy Lincoln Brumfield, Thomas Lincoln's sister, asserted that Nancy Hanks "was more sinned against than sinning." Mrs. Brumfield explained that Nancy visited Elizabethtown when Tom was absent, causing tongues to wag. Country folk in that era believed that women should remain at home and work.[46]

Stories about Nancy's unsavory reputation, accurate or not, evidently reached the ears of her son Abe and may have made him ashamed of her and her family. Herndon ascribed Lincoln's melancholy in part to his sensitivity about "the origin & chastity of his near & dear relations" and speculated that Lincoln might have felt suicidal because of "the knowledge of his mother's origin."[47] Lincoln "was informed of all this," Herndon believed; "probably it was thrown up to him in Indiana." Herndon reported that "Lincoln remembered the scorn of her neighbors."[48] Lincoln described his grandmother Lucey as "a halfway *prostitute*" and acknowledged "that his relations were *lascivious*, *lecherous*, not to be trusted."[49] Lucey Hanks's sister Nancy had a bastard (Dennis Hanks), and Lucey's daughter Sarah bore six illegitimate children. It was no wonder that in Indiana the Hankses were known as "a peculiar people—not chaste."[50]

Herndon contended that although Lincoln was ashamed of his mother and other Hankses, he did praise her one day around 1850 as the two men were riding in a buggy: "All that I am or hope ever to be I get from my mother—good [God] bless her." Often interpreted as a sentimental paean to Nancy Hanks, that statement was in fact a tribute to the genes she passed on to Abraham from her aristocratic father. Herndon said that Lincoln confided that his mother was "a bastard," the "daughter of a nobleman—so called[—]of virginia. My mother's mother was poor & credulous, &c. and she was shamefully taken advantage of by the man. My mother inherited his qualities and I hers."[51] Herndon explained that when "Lincoln spoke to me as he did he had reference to his mother's *mind*—nothing else."[52] Whatever the accuracy of Herndon's account, which some scholars doubt, the great weight of the evidence supports the conclusion that Nancy Hanks was illegitimate, that her son knew it, and that he most likely knew the identity of his maternal grandfather. Little is known about Nancy Hanks Lincoln's treatment of her son. Like other frontier mothers, she dealt out corporal punishment. When young Abe fell into Knob Creek one summer day and nearly drowned, his fear was that his mother might find out and thrash him. To escape punishment, he dried his wet garments in the sun.

Like many of her neighbors Nancy Hanks Lincoln seems to have been an indifferent housekeeper. The typical Midwestern frontier cabin was described by an English traveler as a "miserable little log-hole."[53] The Lincolns' Sinking Spring abode fit this description. It had a dirt floor and was scantily furnished, with rough stools serving for chairs. Four legs inserted into a hewed puncheon formed the table. Beds were fashioned from planks placed atop poles that were inserted into holes bored in the wall. The dishes were of pewter and tin, and the sole cooking utensils were a Dutch oven and a skillet. Only when Thomas Lincoln's second wife, Sarah Bush Johnston, arrived in 1819 did life become less crude for Abe. She brought a bureau, a bed, knives, forks, cooking utensils, and other amenities, and she was determined to see that a floor was laid, that windows were cut into the walls and covered with greased paper, that the ceiling was painted, and that other improvements were made. If she could persuade Thomas Lincoln to spruce up their abode, one wonders why Nancy had not. Nancy Hanks Lincoln was content to live in the primitive manner that Thomas favored, never opposing him on any matter. Catering to his simple taste in food, she would walk miles to the nearest mill to have corn ground or to purchase bacon, which, along with cornmeal mush or johnnycake, formed the staples of the family's diet.

Nancy may have been casual in her approach to childrearing. A Kentuckian who grew up near Lincoln recalled that in pioneer days "boys were men; their mothers turned them out to go when they got their diapers off and they had to 'root hog or die,' and they got so they could take care of themselves pretty soon."[54] Lincoln might have felt neglected, even abandoned, if his mother raised him in this manner. He almost certainly felt abandoned when she died in 1818, leaving the 9-year-old with his sister and his unsympathetic father.

Frontier Poverty

Lincoln was ashamed not only of his Hanks family background but also of the poverty in which he grew up. When John Locke Scripps interviewed him in 1860, Lincoln expressed reluctance "to communicate the homely facts and incidents of his early life. He seemed to be painfully impressed with the extreme poverty of his early surroundings—the utter absence of all romantic and heroic elements" and even questioned the proposal to have a biography written. "Why Scripps," said Lincoln,

> it is a great piece of folly to attempt to make anything out of my early life. It can all be condensed into a single sentence, and that sentence you will find in Gray's Elegy
>
> "The short and simple annals of the poor."
>
> That's my life, and that's all you or any one else can make of it.[55]

To a close friend Lincoln described his family's "stinted living" in Kentucky and "pretty pinching times" in Indiana.[56] In 1846 he referred to the "very poor neighborhood" where he had grown up in Indiana.[57] In 1860 he was asked to speak to some homeless and friendless boys in New York. While describing this event, he recalled his own youth: "I thought of the time when I had been pinched by terrible poverty. And so I told them that I had been poor; that I remembered when my toes stuck out through my broken shoes in winter; when my arms were out at the elbows; when I shivered with the cold."[58]

Lincoln did not exaggerate the deprivation of his childhood. In Kentucky his family's neighbors regarded them as "quite poor," in fact among "the very poorest people."[59] It was the same in Indiana, where one of the Lincolns' sympathetic neighbors, Elizabeth Crawford, invited Abraham's sister, Sarah, to live in her home, where the girl could pay for her board by performing house work. When Mrs. Crawford called at the Lincoln home they had little to offer guests other than raw sweet potatoes, which surprised her, for it was not in keeping with the hospitable customs of the frontier. Elizabeth's husband, Josiah Crawford, hired Thomas Lincoln and young Abe to do chores, even though they were "poor help," because he took pity on them.[60]

Other stories survive of the Lincolns' poverty in Indiana. Abe was not invited to Elizabeth Ray Grigsby's wedding feast because, unlike other neighbors, he lacked appropriate clothing. At the age of 20, when he tried to buy ready-made shoes on credit, he was mortified to be told to come back when he could pay for them. Joseph D. Armstrong, who during the 1860s and 1870s gathered information about the Lincolns' time in Indiana, concluded that Thomas "was a very poor man" and that Abe's life "was one of hard labor, and great privation."[61] Given the economic and emotional poverty he endured in his early years, it is no wonder that Lincoln "felt very strongly that there was more of discomfort than real happiness in human existence under the most favorable circumstances."[62] To an Illinois neighbor he confided, "I have seen a good deal of the back side of this world."[63]

Old Kentucky Homes

Cut off by a seventy-five-mile-long escarpment misleadingly named Muldraugh Hill, the isolated area of Kentucky where Lincoln spent his first seven years was exceedingly provincial, with few towns, only primitive churches, and virtually no schools. In those backwoods, social life was crude, marred by excessive drinking and savage fighting.

Lincoln was born at Sinking Spring farm, an unpromising homestead of infertile ground nestled among unproductive ridges. It was "a place for a poet," in the opinion of a leading Kentucky historian, but not for "a practical farmer who had to grub a living for a growing family from the soil."[64] The neighborhood was thinly settled; the thirty-six-square-mile tax district where the Lincoln farm was located contained eighty-five taxpayers, forty-four slaves, and 392 horses. When Abe was 2, his family moved a few miles northeast to a valley that penetrated Muldraugh Hill. This Knob Creek spread was not ideal farmland, with its bottomless hollows, deep ravines, and steep, conical hills called "knobs." Remote, small, and subject to flooding, it was much less desirable than the farm they were leaving.

Little is known of Lincoln's Kentucky years. One of his earliest memories was of the Knob Creek farm. Reminiscing in 1864, he recalled:

> Our farm was composed of three (3) fields. It lay in the valley surrounded by high hills and deep gorges. Sometimes when there came a big rain in the hills the water would come down through the gorges and spread all over the farm. The last thing that I remember doing there was one Saturday afternoon, the other boys planted the corn in what we called the big field; it contained seven (7) acres, and I dropped the pumpkin seeds. I dropped two seeds every other hill and every other row. The next Sunday morning there came a big rain in the hills, it did not rain a drop in the valley, but the water coming down through the gorges washed ground, corn, pumpkin seeds and all clear off the field.[65]

This episode may have been memorable because it represented in miniature the futile farming career of Thomas Lincoln.

Abe's First Seven Years

Abe had a reputation as a quiet, bashful, polite boy who liked solitude and was "rather noted for Keeping his clothes cleaner longer than any others."[66] He was also described as the "shyest, most reticent, most uncouth and awkward-appearing, homeliest and worse dressed" lad in the neighborhood.[67] He often served as a peacemaker, helping other children settle disagreements. Abe was also regarded as a good wrestler, though he would not fight unless he had to.

In Kentucky, Abe briefly attended a school taught by Zachariah Riney, a pious Roman Catholic who was popular with students and respected for his character and education. In later years, Lincoln always spoke of him "in terms of grateful respect," and he remembered that Riney had made no effort to proselytize his young scholars.[68] The windowless, dirt-floored schoolhouse was made of rough logs forming little niches where the youngsters played hide-and-seek.

Later Abe was a pupil of his neighbor Caleb Hazel, a young man with a rudimentary education who ran a school four or five miles from the Lincolns' cabin. A friend of his said he "could perhaps teach spelling reading & indifferent writing & perhaps could Cipher to the rule of three—but had no other qualifications of a teacher except large size & bodily Strength to thrash any boy or youth that came to his School."[69] This last quality was necessary on the frontier, where schoolboys occasionally assaulted their teachers. Hazel used only a spelling book, and when the more advanced pupils finished it, he would start them over again on one-syllable words. Lincoln went to Hazel more to keep his sister company than to learn much himself, but he did manage to master his letters and a little spelling.

Years later, Lincoln wrote of the educational system he had known, "There were some schools, so called; but no qualification was ever required of a teacher, beyond '*readin, writin, and cipherin*,' to the Rule of Three. If a straggler supposed to understand latin, happened to sojourn in the neighborhood, he was looked upon as a wizzard."[70] Lincoln's schooling, at least in the alphabet, may have begun at home. Nancy Hanks Lincoln could not write but was able to read. To her children she often read from the Bible, much to Abe's delight.

In backwoods Kentucky, the churches and preachers were as primitive as the schools and their teachers. There were three major denominations: "very ignorant Baptists, very noisy Methodists, and very dogmatic Presbyterians."[71] The two Baptist ministers whom the Lincoln family knew best, William Downs and David Elkin, hardly served as models of Christian decorum. The bibulous, disorderly, lazy, and slovenly Downs founded the Little Mount church only after being expelled by the Rolling Fork congregation. Elkin was indolent, hard-drinking, ignorant, and impoverished.

Nancy and Thomas belonged to Baptist churches in Kentucky and Indiana, and their home library contained a Bible as well as a catechism. According to John Locke Scripps, evidently reporting what Lincoln told him, the pioneers "were glad of an opportunity to hear a sermon, whether delivered by one of their own religious faith or not. Thus it was at least with the father and mother of young Lincoln, who never failed to attend, with their family, upon religious worship." They "gladly received the word, caring less for the doctrinal tenets of the preacher than for the earnestness and zeal with which he enforced practical godliness."[72]

In 1816, Thomas Lincoln decided to relocate to Indiana, where several kin already lived. He joined a chain migration from the Rolling Fork of the Salt River in Kentucky to Little Pigeon Creek in southwestern Indiana. Migrants from all over Kentucky poured into Indiana after the War of 1812. Troubles besetting Thomas in Kentucky strengthened the lure of Indiana. In February 1816, an ejectment suit filed against him threatened to force him off his rented Knob Creek acres. In May, a court instructed him to ascertain that the road from Muldraugh Hill through Knob Creek valley was maintained properly. That order may have helped persuade him to leave. Later in the year, unusually bad weather might also have influenced Thomas. Winter came early to Hardin County in 1816, with frost appearing in late July and August. By September, ice a quarter inch thick covered the ground. The temperature did not rise above freezing in October, and November was bitterly cold. The eruption of an Indonesian volcano spewed so much ash into the atmosphere that global temperatures plummeted, and 1816 became known as the year without a summer.

Thomas cobbled together a flatboat, loaded it with his tools and barrels of whiskey, left Nancy and the children at Knob Creek, and shoved off for the Ohio River. Before he reached the river, his raft capsized, pitching whiskey, tools, and sailor into the Rolling Fork. After salvaging some of his cargo with the help of friendly onlookers, Thomas continued his journey, crossing the Ohio River at Thompson's Ferry. He hacked his way through an Indiana forest choked with grapevines and underbrush. The vines were so dense that a knife could be driven into the tangle all the way up to the handle. At one point it took several days to chop through just eighteen miles of forest. Thomas, whose whole life was a struggle, said "that he never passed through a harder experience than he did going from Thompson's Ferry to Spencer County, Indiana."[73] Thomas was uncertain where to stake his claim. A friendly pioneer named William Wood recommended the site that Thomas chose for his cabin and then promised to guard Thomas's possessions while he fetched his family.

In an 1860 autobiographical sketch, Lincoln declared that his family's move had been "partly on account of slavery; but chiefly on account of the difficulty in land titles in Ky."[74] Some have inferred from this statement that Thomas Lincoln ardently opposed slavery, but that seems improbable. Dennis Hanks scoffed at the idea that Tom left Kentucky because of slavery, saying that he moved "to better his Condition. . . . Slavery did not operate on him."[75] In Kentucky, Thomas had served without apparent qualms on a slave patrol, a kind of informal police squad headed by a captain empowered to whip slaves found away from their owners' property without a pass. Lincoln's campaign-year remark that "this removal was partly on account of slavery" may have been designed for political consumption. It may also have referred to Thomas's dislike of a social system that afforded little upward mobility to poor Whites like himself. Many such settlers in Indiana, harboring no moral objections to slavery, actively—and ultimately successfully—campaigned to keep free Blacks from moving into their state.

Before leaving Kentucky, Lincoln and his mother visited the grave of his brother, Thomas, who had died in infancy around 1812. As he crossed the Ohio with his sister and parents, the 7-year-old Abraham did not seem destined for greatness. Dennis Hanks thought that "Abe Exhibited no special traits in Ky, Except a good kind—somewhat wild nature."[76] Another Kentuckian remembered him simply as the "gawkiest, dullest looking boy you ever saw," unremarkable except for his powerful memory.[77] In that cold autumn, the Lincoln family packed up and plunged into the wilderness of southwestern Indiana, seeking a new beginning in the "wild and desolate" Hurricane Township.[78]

2.

"I Used to Be a Slave"

Boyhood and Adolescence in Indiana (1816–1830)

The family's journey from Kentucky was arduous, with nothing to soften the rigors of camping out on cold winter nights. They brought with them little more than clothes, bedding, a Dutch oven, a skillet, and some tinware. Upon reaching their homesite they began a new life with these few household possessions and no domestic animals, separated by miles from their nearest neighbors.

Hardships in Frontier Indiana

They quickly erected a "half-faced camp," a temporary expedient commonly thrown up by pioneers. In that structure the family lived for several months. It would be relatively comfortable in warm, dry weather, but when winter storms raged and the south wind blew rain and smoke into the faces of the inhabitants, it proved nearly intolerable. Those who knew the Lincolns at that time testified that young Abe lived "amid want, poverty and discomfort that was . . . about on the plane of the slaves he was destined to emancipate" and that the winter of 1817–18 was "a veritable childhood Valley Forge of suffering."[1] Lincoln portrayed the Little Pigeon Creek neighborhood as a "wild region" of "unbroken forest" where "many bears and other wild animals" roamed.[2] Less menacing fauna also abounded near the Lincolns' lean-to, from which 7-year-old Abe shot a wild turkey. He later recalled that act with regret. If game was readily at hand, water was not. With a pet cat tagging along, young Abe often trudged back and forth to fetch clean water from a spring one mile away.

The social environment of Little Pigeon Creek was as primitive as the physical setting. One resident recalled that the early settlers were quite sociable, kind, and accommodating, but that "there was more drunkenness and stealing on a small scale, more immorality, less Religion, less well placed Confidence."[3] Ignorance and superstition prevailed among those early Hoosiers, and although Lincoln eventually shed many of the qualities of backwoods Indiana, he remained superstitious throughout his life.

The most pressing challenge facing the Lincolns in their primitive home was clearing the land. Large for his age, Abe set to work with an axe, and he remembered later that for the next fifteen years he was "almost always handling that most useful instrument."[4] He felled trees, chopped them into logs, cleared undergrowth, dug stumps, and grubbed up roots for drying and burning. When not so engaged, he was harrowing, planting, hoeing, plowing, weeding, harvesting, or butchering.

Once the family had cleared enough land and planted a small crop, Thomas built a log cabin that his family occupied for the next thirteen years. A windowless, one-story structure measuring eighteen by twenty feet, it was tall enough to accommodate an overhead bedroom reached by a ladder of pegs driven into the log walls. There Lincoln and Dennis Hanks slept. Thomas fashioned a few pieces of crude furniture, including a pole bedstead and a slab table and stools. Thirteen people would eventually crowd together in this abode, with little semblance of privacy.

Death of Nancy Hanks

No sooner had the Lincoln family abandoned the half-faced camp in 1817 than Nancy's aunt and uncle Thomas and Betsy Sparrow arrived from Kentucky to occupy it. They brought with them their foster child, Dennis Hanks, bastard son of Mrs. Lincoln's aunt Nancy. Dennis became a kind of surrogate older brother to his second cousin Abe, a decade his junior. The Sparrows had in effect adopted Nancy when she was quite young; she and everyone else in the Little Pigeon Creek area regarded them as her virtual if not biological parents.

In 1818, within months of the Sparrows' arrival, an epidemic of "milk sickness" swept through southwestern Indiana. Cows contracted the malady by eating weeds that contained the toxic substance tremetol; the disease killed not only the cows but also the humans who drank their infected milk. Doctors at that time knew neither the cause of nor a cure for the disease, which struck down Mrs. Peter Brooner, a neighbor of the Lincolns, and then Thomas and Betsy Sparrow. Nancy Lincoln nursed all three of them as they sickened and died. In late September, she too contracted the disease.

If Nancy Hanks died the way most victims did, her husband and children in the small cabin must have been horrified as her body was convulsed with nausea, her eyes rolled, and her tongue grew large and turned red. After a few days, as death approached, she probably lay in pain, her legs spread apart, her breath growing short, her skin becoming cool and clammy, and her heart beating ever more irregularly. Before her final coma, she urged Abe and Sarah to be good to one another and to their father and to "reverence and worship God."[5] On October 5, 1818, a week after her symptoms first appeared, she died, unattended by a physician. Young Abe helped his father construct a coffin. Nancy's body was conveyed on a homemade sled to a gravesite near the cabin, where Betsy and Thomas Sparrow were buried. No tombstone marked her final resting place.

No witnesses described Lincoln's reaction to his mother's death, nor did he say anything directly about its effect on him. Many years later, however, he indirectly revealed something of his emotions when he consoled a young woman whose father had been killed in the Civil War: "It is with deep grief that I learn of the death of your kind and brave Father; and, especially, that it is affecting your young heart beyond what is common in such cases. In this sad world of ours, sorrow comes to all; and, to the young, it comes with bitterest agony, because it takes them unawares." And then he added, "I have had experience enough to know what I say."[6] The wound that Lincoln sustained as a 9-year-old boy was deep.

In 1861, Lincoln spoke of "the sad, if not pitiable condition" of his family after Nancy died.[7] His sister, Sarah, only 11 years old, assumed the domestic responsibilities of cooking, cleaning, washing, mending clothes, and spinning wool. But she could hardly replace her mother in the household even with the help of kindly neighbors. The gloom that settled over the Lincoln cabin would not lift for more than a year, until Thomas remarried.

The "profound agony" caused by the loss of his mother left its mark on Abe. As the literary biographer Leon Edel observed, "There is no hurt among all the human hurts deeper and less understandable than the loss of a parent when one is not yet an adolescent."[8] Psychologists have found that bereavement in childhood "is one of the most significant factors in the development of depressive illness in later life" and that "a depressive illness in later years is often a reaction to a present loss or bereavement which is associated with a more serious loss or bereavement in childhood."[9] If a parent dies, the quality of the child's relationship with the surviving parent is critically important; inadequate care of the child seems to be an important cause of later depressions.

Lincoln's unsympathetic father did not provide him adequate care in the wake of Nancy's death, for Lincoln was to be plagued with depression as an adult. At one point Thomas left his two children with their cousin Sophie Hanks (who had come to live with the Lincolns around 1818) to fend for themselves while he drifted down the Ohio River to sell pork. He again left the children when he wooed Sarah Bush Johnston in Kentucky, where, according to family tradition, he spent more time than he had intended to. One source alleged that the children, having given him up for dead, became "almost nude for the want of clothes and their stomachs became leathery from the want of food."[10] By the time their stepmother arrived at the end of 1819, she found Sarah and Abe "wild—ragged and dirty."[11]

The year and a quarter that separated Nancy Lincoln's death and Sarah Bush Johnston Lincoln's arrival was miserable for Tom's son and daughter and left enduring scars. Children often regard the early death of a parent as a deliberate abandonment. Throughout his life Lincoln feared being abandoned and was inclined to attack those who forsook their party or their principles. He also harbored an abiding wariness of women in general; his mother's death evidently taught him that women are unreliable and untrustworthy.

Stepmother

It is easy to see why Thomas would find the 30-year-old widow Sarah Bush Johnston attractive. She was handsome and tall, with good posture and a light complexion; she was sprightly, talkative, proud, kind, and charitable. Although her family were "rough, uncouth, and uneducated," they occupied rungs much higher on the social and economic ladder than did the Hankses.[12] William Herndon said she "was far above Thomas Lincoln—somewhat cultivated and quite a lady."[13]

Arriving in Indiana with her three children, Sarah was taken aback by the quasi-ursine condition of the Lincoln cabin and its inhabitants. She proceeded to improve both forthwith. "I dressed Abe & his sister up—looked more human," she recalled. She soaped and scrubbed and washed them until they were "well & clean." She eliminated the lice that had taken up residence in Abe's unruly hair. After replacing the crude puncheon tables and stools, she swiftly effected other improvements: a floor was laid down, and doors and windows were installed. She dressed Sarah and Abe in some of the abundant clothing she had brought from Kentucky. In a few weeks she revolutionized the Lincolns and their house, so that everything was "snug & comfortable."[14]

Sarah Bush Lincoln was a good cook, though her culinary skill was wasted on Abe, whom she described as "a moderate Eater" who obediently "ate what was set before him, making no complaint." She tended to Abraham's intellectual as well as physical needs, encouraging him to study. She recognized that he was "a Boy of uncommon natural Talents," which she did all she could to foster. She even moderated Thomas Lincoln's reluctance to let Abe read. "I induced my husband to permit Abe to read and study at home as well as at school," she recalled.[15]

She and her stepson became close. "Abe never gave me a cross word or look and never refused in fact, or Even in appearance, to do any thing I requested [of] him," she said. In turn, she "never gave him a cross word." The two were kindred souls, she thought: "His mind & mine—what little I had[—]seemed to run together—move in the same channel." He "was dutiful to me always—he loved me truly I think." She compared Abe favorably to her own son John: "Both were good boys, but I must Say . . . that Abe was the best boy I Ever Saw or Ever Expect to see."[16]

Lincoln reciprocated the love of his stepmother, whom he called "mama." In 1861, he told Augustus H. Chapman that "she had been his best Friend in this world & that no Son could love a Mother more than he loved her." To Herndon and others, Lincoln said she was "considerate and attentive," a "kind, tender, loving mother" and a "noble woman."[17]

Just as Sarah Bush Lincoln seemed to prefer her stepson to her own boy, Thomas Lincoln favored his stepson John D. Johnston over Abe. Yet little stepsibling rivalry developed between them. A year younger than Abe, Johnston was a handsome, kindhearted, lazy, generous, hospitable fellow whose major defect was a quarrelsome streak. After Lincoln became a successful lawyer and politician, Johnston "would tell with much relish how he once thought Abe a fool, because, instead of spending his evenings sporting with the young folks, he seemed to care for nothing but some old musty books." To Johnston and his contemporaries, such behavior "was clear proof of Abe's insanity. 'But, now,' said he, 'Abe is a great and wise man, and I am a fool still.'"[18] Lincoln spoke of John "in the Most affectionate Manner" and said that he and his stepbrother "were raised together, slept together, and liked each other as well as actual brothers could do."[19]

In time, though, Lincoln became impatient with Johnston's indolence, and though he extended himself to help John's children, he was reluctant to subsidize him. Still, Dennis Hanks concluded, "I think Abe Dun more for John than he des[er]ved. . . . Abe treated John well."[20]

Education

Lincoln's own education continued fitfully in Indiana, where he attended primitive ABC schools for brief stretches. Later in life he laconically referred to his education as "defective" and estimated the aggregate of his time spent in school to have been less than a year.[21] Even though there "was absolutely nothing to excite ambition for education" in frontier Indiana, by the age of 21 "somehow I could read, write, and cipher to the Rule of Three; but that was all."[22] Lincoln's earliest surviving composition is a bit of doggerel scribbled in an arithmetic notebook:

> Abraham Lincoln
> his hand and pen
> he will be good
> god knows when.[23]

The Indiana school available to young Abe was a low-ceilinged, flea-infested cabin with a floor of split logs, a chimney of poles and clay, and a window of greased paper. Pupils sat on uncomfortable benches without backs but with splinters aplenty. The young scholars usually studied aloud in such a "blab school" so that the teacher could tell that they were not daydreaming. Such schooling probably accounts for Lincoln's tendency to read aloud, which irritated his law partner William Herndon. To justify that annoying habit, Lincoln explained: "I catch the idea by 2 senses, for when I read aloud I *hear* what is read and I *see* it; and hence 2 senses get it and I remember it better, if I do not understand it better."[24]

Frontier teachers boarded with families in the neighborhood. Preoccupied with enforcing order, making quill pens, and other chores, they hardly had time, even if they had the inclination, to encourage independent thought and understanding. Instructional technique involved rote memorization, so fast learners stagnated while waiting for slower schoolmates to master a lesson. Along Little Pigeon Creek, Lincoln's teachers were Andrew Crawford, James Swaney, and Azel Dorsey. Only Dorsey left reminiscences of Lincoln, recalling that the boy came to school in buckskins and a raccoon cap, clutching an old arithmetic book, and was remarkable for his "diligence and eagerness."[25] In one of his early bouts of schooling, Lincoln wrote an essay about the mistreatment of animals, a matter about which he cared deeply. In adolescence he upbraided John D. Johnston for smashing the shell of a land turtle against a tree, leaving the suffering animal defenseless. When his mother urged him to kill a snake, Abe said, "No, it enjoys living just the same as we do."[26] One of his stepsisters remembered Abe insisting that "an ants life was to it, as sweet as ours to us."[27] Lincoln's concern for animals persisted into adulthood. On various occasions he rescued a pig, a lamb, piglets, a cat, and birds from danger.

Lincoln composed essays on other subjects as well, including temperance and national politics. Although his command of spelling was imperfect, he was far ahead of his schoolmates, whom he often helped out. Spelling became a lifetime preoccupation for Lincoln. Even as president he would unhesitatingly admit when he did not know how to spell a word and ask for guidance. Words such as *very*, *maintenance*, *opportunity*, and *missile* perpetually stumped him. Some fretted that public confessions of lapses in learning from an important man like Lincoln were "a spectacle," but Joshua Speed thought it admirable that Lincoln "was never ashamed . . . to admit his ignorance upon any subject, or the meaning of any word no matter how ridiculous it might make him appear."[28]

Astronomy would remain a lifelong interest of Lincoln's, as would mathematics. His passion for math, which led him in his forties to master the first six books of Euclid, was initially stimulated by his teachers, by several textbooks, and by a neighbor, James Blair. His math education enabled Lincoln in his early twenties to learn surveying speedily; it also sharpened his keenly analytical mind. In contests and games with his schoolmates he excelled when he could use his exceptional strength to advantage. He could sink an axe deeper into a tree and strike a heavier blow with a maul than anyone in the neighborhood. For all his enjoyment of sports and games, Lincoln possessed a streak of introversion and a fondness for solitude. He disliked crowds and often preferred to be alone. After Nancy Hanks died in 1818, he matured quickly and had less time for playmates. David Turnham recalled that "he seemed to change in appearance and action." He "began to exhibit deep thoughtfulness, and was so often lost in studied reflection we could not help noticing the strange turn in his actions. He disclosed rare timidity and sensitiveness, especially in the presence of men and women, and although cheerful enough in the presence of boys, he did not appear to seek out company as earnestly as before."[29]

Lincoln outshone his schoolmates. He arrived at school early, paid close attention to his studies, read and reread his assignments, made swift progress, and always stood at the head of his class. Lincoln devoted most of his leisure time to study, quickly getting ahead of his classmates and even his instructors. His stepmother recalled that "Abe read all the books he could lay his hands on, and when he came across a passage that Struck him he would write it down on boards if he had no paper & keep it there till he did get paper—then he would re-write it—look at it repeat it—He had a copy book—a kind of scrap book in which he put down all things and this preserved them. He ciphered on boards when he had no paper or no slate and when the board would get too black he would shave it off with a drawing knife and go on again."[30] While John D. Johnston attended dances, Abe sat reading by the fire. When working at Josiah Crawford's farm, he read during lunchtime rather than joining the other hands as they chatted, smoked, or chewed tobacco. Crawford's wife recollected that Abe would "work out his sums" on a shovel blade and "wipe off and repeat till it got too black for more: then he would scrape and wash off and repeat again and again."[31] On other jobs too he always carried a book to read during breaks. On Sundays he devoted his free time to reading. Walking to and from school, he read aloud at such a decibel level that his voice could be heard at a great distance. In the evenings he would lie before the fireplace so that he could read, sometimes until midnight or later.

Reading helped liberate Lincoln from his backwoods environment, and books helped "immancipate" his mind.[32] To supplement his meager schooling, he practiced writing the letters of the alphabet whenever and however he could, carving those letters on slabs of wood, tree trunks, even on the stools and table in his family's cabin. When he did not have charcoal to hand, he wrote in dust, in sand, in snow. Neighbors came to regard him as "a marvel of learning" and called upon him to write for them. John Locke Scripps wrote that Lincoln's greatest asset was "his ability to express the wishes and feelings of those for whom he wrote in clear and forcible language."[33] Lincoln regularly visited William Wood's house to read newspapers aloud for the edification of the unlettered. He had a knack for making his listeners understand what they heard. When in a puckish mood, he would often invent stories while pretending to read from the paper he was holding. Sometimes he memorized items in the press. J. Rowan Herndon said Lincoln "had the Best memory of any man I Ever Knew," for he "Never forgot any thing he Read."[34]

Young Lincoln admired Lindley Murray's *English Reader*, an anthology of poetry and prose that contained some antislavery sentiments. He called it "the greatest and most useful book that could be put in the hands of a child at school."[35] In addition to his family Bible, he read volumes borrowed from neighbors, including *The Arabian Nights*, *Aesop's Fables*, John Bunyan's *Pilgrim's Progress*, Daniel Defoe's *Robinson Crusoe*, James Riley's *Authentic Narrative of the Loss of the American Brig Commerce*, William Grimshaw's *History of the United States*, a biography of Henry Clay, Mason Weems's life of George Washington, and William Scott's *Lessons in Elocution*. It is not possible to say just what Lincoln derived from these volumes, but he may have been affected by their discussion of such issues as human bondage and fatalism.

In the late 1820s, Lincoln began reading newspapers, from which he developed an interest in politics. He originally supported Andrew Jackson's Democratic Party but soon switched his allegiance to the National Republicans, whose leader, Henry Clay, would found the Whig Party in the 1830s. Influencing this decision was a prosperous merchant, William Jones, who greatly admired Clay. Jones employed young Lincoln in his store and served as a friendly, encouraging mentor to him. Lincoln hung around the store, where he could read the Louisville *Journal* and discuss politics. Eager to escape rural backwardness, he probably associated the Democrats with shiftless frontiersmen like his Democratic father, while the National Republicans represented enterprising lawyers and merchants like Jones.

Lincoln did not rely solely on the printed word or the classroom for his education. He queried travelers who stopped at Jones's store. With Dennis Hanks and other friends, he attended political meetings and discussed issues of the day. Lincoln insisted on digesting thoroughly whatever he read or heard. His stepmother recollected that "Abe, when old folks were at our house, was a silent & attentive observer—never speaking or asking questions till they were gone and then he must understand Every thing—even the smallest thing—Minutely & Exactly."[36] This passion for gaining a clear understanding of things never left him. In 1860, he told a Connecticut clergyman that he remembered "how, when a mere child, I used to get irritated when anybody talked to me in a way I could not understand. I don't think I ever got angry at anything else in my life." If he overheard his father in conversation with a neighbor and did not grasp what they had said, he would lie awake late at night "trying to make out what was the exact meaning" of what he had heard. "I could not sleep, though I often tried to, when I got on such a hunt after an idea, until I had caught it; and when I thought I had got it, I was not satisfied until I had repeated it over and over, until I had put it in language plain enough, as I thought, for any boy I knew to comprehend."[37]

Religion

It is not clear how diligently Lincoln perused the Bible. Some recalled that he read it often. In the 1850s he told an Illinois lawyer that his boyhood library had comprised "66 books of which he was very fond" (i.e., the Bible) and that he had "studied it with great care."[38] In his mature years Lincoln often referred to the Bible, which he described as "the richest source of pertinent quotations" and "the best gift God has given to man." "All the good the Saviour gave to the world," he said, "was communicated through this book. But for it we could not know right from wrong."[39] He told his best friend, Joshua Speed, to "take all of this book [the Bible] upon reason that you can, and the balance on faith, and you will live and die a happier and better man."[40] The Bible, Noah Brooks reported, "was a very familiar study with the President, whole chapters of Isaiah, the New Testament, and the Psalms being fixed in his memory."[41]

Dennis Hanks recalled that "the Bible puzzled him, especially the miracles."[42] Lincoln's stepmother testified that "Abe read the bible some, though not as much as [is] said: he sought more congenial books—suitable for his age."[43] Lincoln's youthful attitude toward the Bible, as described by his stepmother and Dennis Hanks, may reflect disenchantment with the ignorant preachers and hypocritical churchgoers he observed both in Kentucky and at the Little Pigeon Baptist Church, with which his parents affiliated in 1823 but which Abe did not join. That congregation seethed with personal feuds, quarrels over the proper credentials for those who administered baptism, opposition to benevolent missionary work, and disputes over creeds. The primitive worship, heavy emphasis on arcane doctrinal matters, and ignorant, even drunken preachers probably repelled young Lincoln.

After hearing sermons or speeches, Lincoln repeated them nearly verbatim to his friends, mimicking the gestures and the accents of the speakers. Because this interfered with farmwork, Thomas Lincoln frequently scolded Abe and made him quit. A strain of irreverence remained with Lincoln all his life. He relished humorous stories about ignorant preachers, including one that involved a Baptist minister in Indiana who had a lizard climb up his pant leg during a sermon. But although Lincoln delighted in mocking backwoods clergymen, something of what they preached embedded itself in his psyche, for he remained a Calvinistic fatalist throughout his life. He repeatedly said "that what is to be will be and no prayers of ours can arrest or reverse the decree."[44] Lincoln also retained a fondness for the frontier ministers' theatrical style. In 1861 he said that "when I hear a man preach, I like to see him act as if he were fighting bees!"[45]

Relations with the Opposite Sex

Lincoln's great height and sartorial taste did not endear him to the opposite sex, nor did his physical and social awkwardness. He was thin, swarthy, rawboned—"gawky" in one person's estimation. Although he was "very careful of his person" and "tolerably neat and clean," his clothes were typically rough and suited to the frontier—tow linen pants in warm weather, buckskin pants in cool weather, flax shirts, linsey-woolsey jackets, short socks, low shoes, and caps fashioned from animal skins. But they fit him poorly; his pants often exposed six to twelve inches of shin. This did not bother him, for he cared little about fashion.[46]

Lincoln got along well enough with neighborhood girls, kidding and chatting, but they found him "too green and awkward" to interest them romantically.[47] One Indiana maiden recalled that "he was so tall and awkward" that all "the young girls my age made fun of Abe. They'd laugh at him right before his face, but Abe never 'peared to care. He was so good and he'd just laugh with them. Abe tried to go with some of them, but no sir-ee, they'd give him the mitten every time, just because he was . . . so tall and gawky, and it was mighty awkward I can tell you trying to keep company with a fellow as tall as Abe was."[48] Another young woman, who thought him "too big, awkward & ugly," further objected that he "just cared too much for books."[49] Lincoln would attend parties but refused to dance. Instead he would gather several boys and tell stories, which upset the girls, for they would have trouble finding partners for dancing. Lincoln, for his part, returned the girls' indifference. His friend Anna Roby was one of many who noted that Abe "didn't like girls much" and found them "too frivolous."[50] Dennis Hanks called Lincoln the "bashfullest boy that ever lived," and John D. Johnston said he "didn't take much truck with the girls" because "he was too busy studying."[51]

Quasi Slavery as a Rented Laborer

Lincoln was indeed busy, but he was not always studying. He worked hard on his father's farm and also for neighbors to whom Thomas rented him out. Around 1825, Thomas Lincoln found himself in greater financial trouble than usual when a friend defaulted on a loan that he had endorsed. To pay off that note, Thomas removed the adolescent Abe from school and hired him out to neighbors, something he continued to do for the next few years. As a hireling, Lincoln was virtually a slave, toiling as a butcher, ferry operator, riverman, store clerk, farm hand, woodchopper, distiller, and sawyer, earning anywhere from 10¢ to 31¢ a day. These meager wages he handed over to Thomas, in compliance with the law and custom stipulating that children's labor was the property of their father and that any money they earned belonged to him. Locked in this quasi bondage, Abraham felt as if he were a chattel on a Southern plantation. "I used to be a slave," he declared in 1856.[52] This painful experience led him to identify with the slaves and to denounce human bondage even when it was politically risky to do so.

While working at a farm by the Ohio River, Lincoln built a small boat. One day two gentlemen in a hurry saw the craft and asked Lincoln to row them and their luggage out to a steamer on the river. He gladly agreed. While boarding it, the men dumbfounded Lincoln by pitching two silver half-dollars into his vessel. Recounting this episode many years later, he said that "it was a most important incident in my life. I could scarcely credit that I, the poor boy, had earned a dollar in less than a day; that by honest work I had earned a dollar. The world seemed wider and fairer before me; I was a more hopeful and thoughtful boy from that time."[53] When the merchant James Gentry offered to hire Lincoln to accompany his son Allen on a cargo boat trip to Louisiana, he accepted eagerly. The two young men spent weeks constructing a flatboat for their corn, pork, potatoes, hay, and kraut—all destined for Deep South sugar plantations. In late December 1828, they shoved off from Rockport on a twelve-hundred-mile, seven-week excursion down the Ohio and Mississippi Rivers, with Lincoln manning the bow oars and Gentry the tiller.

As they floated down the Mississippi, they stopped frequently to peddle their wares, trading foodstuffs for cotton, tobacco, and sugar. One night, while tied up at a plantation a few miles below Baton Rouge, they were attacked by seven slaves. The Blacks, noting that only two young men manned the boat, attempted to rob it. During the fierce struggle that ensued, Allen had the presence of mind to shout, "Lincoln get the guns and Shoot" (even though they had no firearms), which finally caused the slaves to run off, but not before the two boys were badly hurt.

After selling all their wares along the banks of the Mississippi, they proceeded to New Orleans. As they strolled about, Lincoln saw something that left an indelible impression: a slave auction at which scantily clad young women were exhibited on the block and pinched and ogled by prospective buyers. Revolted, Lincoln said, "Allen, that's a disgrace."[54] It was the first time, but not the last, that he would be repelled upon observing slavery firsthand.

If the trip to New Orleans persuaded Lincoln that chattel slavery was disgraceful, it also intensified his desire to escape his own quasi slavery. Soon after his return home, Lincoln asked a neighbor, William Wood, to help him find a job on a riverboat. Wood told him, "Abe—your age is against you—you are not 21 yet." "I know that," protested Lincoln, "but I want a start." Wood refused, counseling Lincoln to stay with his father until 1830. Reluctantly, Lincoln took that advice.[55]

Lincoln may have been eager to escape his home for some time. An interviewer who spoke with those who knew him concluded that "Mr. L does not appear *to have cared for home after the death of his mother*."[56] At 13 he worked away from his father for the first time, cutting wood on the banks of the Ohio. Thereafter he frequently absented himself from the paternal cabin. In 1825 he stayed several months with the Taylor family on Anderson Creek. After his sister, Sarah, wed Aaron Grigsby in the summer of 1826, Lincoln spent much time with them. In the spring of 1827, he lived with John Jones's family at Dale, returning home only on Saturday nights. That same year Lincoln and John D. Johnston went to Louisville, where they found employment on the Louisville and Portland Canal. In the fall of 1828, while helping Allen Gentry construct a flatboat, Lincoln stayed for weeks with the family of Daniel Grass in Rockport. Lincoln lived with William Jones when he worked on his farm and at his Gentryville store.

Lincoln heartily disliked farm chores, admitting that "his father taught him to work but never learned him to love it." Longing to escape the toilsome world of subsistence farming and make something of himself, he prophetically told Elizabeth Crawford, "I don't always intend to delve, grub, shuck corn, split rails, and the like." She remembered that "Abe was ambitious, sought to outstrip and override others."[57]

Upon his return from New Orleans, after months of freedom as a flatboat man, Lincoln grudgingly resumed the uncompensated toil imposed on him by his father. The contrast seemed to curdle Lincoln's good nature; in 1829 the dark side of his personality emerged as he became testy, belligerent, spiteful, and vindictive. This transformation became especially obvious when he attacked the neighboring Grigsby clan. Although Nathaniel Grigsby was one of his best friends, Abe detested Nathaniel's older brother, Aaron, who had married Abe's sister in 1826. Lincoln believed that the prosperous Grigsby family mistreated her and looked down upon her because she had been "hired help."[58]

A year and a half after her wedding, Sarah died in childbirth. Upon hearing the news, Lincoln "sat down on a log and hid his face in his hands while the tears rolled down through his long bony fingers. Those present turned away in pity and left him to his grief."[59] Repeatedly he asked himself, "What have I to live for?" Henry C. Whitney, who thought that "Abraham's inner life was a desert of sorrow," speculated plausibly that Sarah's passing reawakened painful memories of his mother's death.[60] Lincoln and his father blamed Sarah's fate on the neglectful conduct of the Grigsby clan.

Lincoln had a further falling out with the Grigsbys when everyone in the neighborhood except his family was invited to celebrate the double wedding of Reuben and Charles Grigsby to Elizabeth Ray and Matilda Hawkins, respectively. "Miffed, mortified, insulted," Abraham vowed revenge for the slight.[61] With his highly developed knack for mimicry and sarcasm, Lincoln penned a satire in biblical language titled "The Chronicles of Reuben," which described grooms inadvertently bedding the wrong brides. That document, Nathaniel Grigsby recalled, was so "sharp" and "cutting" that "it hurt us."[62]

Not content with the wounds inflicted on Reuben and Charles, Lincoln wrote a bawdy poem questioning the sexual preference of their brother William, which opened:

> I will tell you a Joke about [Josiah?] & Mary
> Tis neither a joke nor a story
> For Reuben & Charles have married 2 Girls
> But Billy has married a boy[63]

Thirsting for revenge, William Grigsby challenged Lincoln to a fight, but the larger and stronger Lincoln protested that it would hardly be a fair match. So a compromise was reached: Grigsby would battle Lincoln's stepbrother, John D. Johnston. As John Gentry recalled it, the fight became a much-anticipated spectacle. Johnston and Grigsby pummeled each other until the former was seriously hurt. At that point, "Abe burst through, caught Grigsby—threw him some feet—stood up and swore he was the big buck at the lick." A general melee then broke out.[64]

This uncharacteristically boastful intervention in a fight that he himself had caused suggests that Lincoln at age 20 was not entirely a paragon of virtue, despite his reputation as a sociable, cheerful, good-natured, and gentle fellow. The Bolins of Perry County thought that "the young Lincoln of Pigeon Creek, like all his Indiana cronies, was pretty much of a rowdy, and, certainly, was not of a saintly nature."[65] The "reprehensible trait of character" he showed in cruelly satirizing the Grigsbys would mar him for years to come; not until midlife did he abandon his habit of wounding people with his ridicule.[66]

Lincoln showed his frontier crudeness in other ways. He began to develop a taste for alcohol. In 1858, he told a friend that "he had never taken a drink of any alcoholic beverage in the past twenty years," clearly implying that he had stopped drinking in 1838, at the age of 29.[67] Nathaniel Grigsby testified that Lincoln was a "*temperate drinker*" who "drank his dram as well as all others did, preachers & Christians included."[68] In Indiana, Lincoln developed a lifelong taste for off-color humor. Dennis Hanks said he liked to sing "Little Smuty Songs," but Hanks refused to recite their lyrics for it "would Not Look well in print."[69] Hanks also noted that young Lincoln could be "a kind of forward boy," a "little rude," and "stubborn."[70]

Move to Illinois

In 1830, Thomas Lincoln moved his family to a site near the hamlet of Decatur, in Macon County, Illinois. Dennis Hanks had taken the lead in migrating west, removing his wife, Elizabeth (Mrs. Lincoln's daughter), and their four children from Indiana because of an outbreak of milk sickness. Not wanting to be separated from her grandchildren, Sarah Bush Lincoln prevailed upon Thomas to join Dennis and Elizabeth in Illinois. Thomas sold his farm, corn, and pigs to Indiana neighbors, and on March 1, 1830, with his wife, son, stepson, stepdaughters, and their families—eight adults and five children all told—set out for Illinois.

Although the weather was generally clement, the roads were so wet that Abe found himself slogging through mud several inches deep for long stretches. The Kaskaskia River overflowed its banks, almost washing out the corduroy road. Following some debate, the party decided to press on, and for a few miles Abraham led the team through water so high that it threatened to sweep away wagon, oxen, and all. After two weeks, they reached John Hanks's spread on the Sangamon River, four miles northwest of Decatur, where they received a hearty welcome. As of February 12, 1830, Lincoln was at last legally free to go his own way, but he did not. His sense of duty overruled the desire of his heart, and so he postponed his self-emancipation in order to help his family as they settled into a new home. Abraham assisted Hanks and Thomas Lincoln in erecting a cabin, fencing it in, and clearing several acres.

Because he often stayed with the families who hired him as a laborer, Lincoln spent little time in this new cabin. For Macon County sheriff William Warnick and William Miller, among others, he broke prairie, raised crops, and split rails. One cold day, when Miller's wife (John Hanks's sister Nancy) noticed that Lincoln's pants were worn out, she offered to make him new ones. Replying to his protest that he had no money, she said that he could chop wood for her instead of paying cash. In both Macon and Sangamon Counties, Lincoln and John Hanks cut innumerable cords of wood and divided the profits equally. (Lincoln's later reputation as a rail-splitter was no fanciful invention of political publicists.) Joining them in some of these labors was George Close, who described Lincoln as "the toughest looking man I ever saw," a "poor boy" wearing "pants made of *flax and tow*, cut tight at the ankle—*his knees were both out*." Close recalled that they had a "hard time to get work. All a man could do was to keep himself in clothes." Lincoln trudged "5, 6, and 7 miles to his day's work."[71] Henry C. Whitney, to whom Lincoln described his year in Macon County, called that period one of the "three eras of unusual hardship and misery" in Lincoln's "melancholy journey of life."[72] (The other two unusually painful times, according to Whitney, were those following the deaths of Nancy Hanks Lincoln in 1818 and Ann Rutledge in 1835.)

Lincoln's introduction to Illinois politics occurred in the summer of 1830, when he was working for William Butler as a plowman at Island Grove, near Springfield. There he heard a speech by Peter Cartwright, a popular Methodist circuit rider then campaigning for public office. Butler recalled that Lincoln, though "awkward and shabbily dressed," challenged the speaker for being too dogmatic. "My first special attention was attracted to Lincoln," Butler said, "by the way in which he met the great preacher in his arguments, and the extensive acquaintance he showed with the politics of the State—in fact he quite beat him in the argument."[73]

Later that season, Lincoln employed the speaking skills he had been cultivating for years as a mimic. He attended a debate in Decatur between two candidates for the state legislature, William L. D. Ewing and John F. Posey. When George Close urged Lincoln to abuse Posey, he said he would do so if his friends promised not to laugh at him. Nervous when he began speaking, Lincoln quickly warmed up and delivered a respectable speech. Instead of attacking Posey, he spoke well of both candidates and offered a vision of the future of Illinois. After he finished, Ewing complimented him as being "a bright one."[74] Then Posey took Abe aside and asked him where he had learned so much. When Abe described his program of reading, Posey "encouraged him to persevere."[75]

Thomas Lincoln did not wish to persevere in Illinois. In the summer of 1830, he and all the others in the Decatur area were attacked by disease-bearing mosquitoes whose bite transmitted malaria. Thomas and his family were seriously afflicted. Miserable, Thomas vowed "that as soon as he got able to travel he would 'git out o' thar.'"[76] Eventually frost killed off the mosquitoes, but the relief was short-lived, for a December blizzard dumped three feet of snow on central Illinois. Soon thereafter, a freezing rain encrusted the snow with a layer of ice, followed by more snow. In the annals of Illinois history, this season became immortalized as "the winter of the deep snow." For two miserable months the Lincolns and their neighbors huddled in their cabins while livestock froze and starved outside.

Discouraged by mosquitoes and snowstorms, Thomas Lincoln retreated toward Indiana in the spring of 1831. En route, he stopped at the Coles County home of his sister-in-law, where she and other relatives persuaded him to settle in their neighborhood. Thomas and his family built a cabin in nearby Buck Grove, where they stayed until 1834, when they moved to Muddy Point, also in Coles County. Three years later they migrated to yet another location in that county, Goosenest Prairie, near Farmington; there Thomas remained for the rest of his life. His wife Sarah, unhappy with such a nomadic existence, told the neighbors "that they moved so often that it reminded her of the children of Israel trying to find the Promised Land." When Thomas suggested yet another move, she refused.[77]

Lincoln did not accompany his family as they headed back to Indiana. In March 1831 his stepmother bundled up his meager possessions, which he slung over his shoulder, and he struck out on his own. No longer could Thomas rent him out to neighbors and attach the wages he earned in the abundant sweat of his brow. Although he did not know exactly what he wanted to do, young Lincoln was certain that he did not wish to lead the crude life of a subsistence farmer, mired in poverty, superstition, and ignorance. He had had his fill of primitive backwoods agriculture and culture. Later, as a politician, he would not pander to farmers. Despite his enthusiasm for measures promoting economic growth and opportunity, he paid little attention to homestead legislation offering people free farms on government land, a policy that many of his fellow Republicans considered the best means to end poverty.

Fleeing the drudgery of farm life and what he called "parental tyranny," Lincoln strove to distance himself from the world of his father, who embodied the indolence, ignorance, and backwardness that repelled his son.[78] Lincoln's adult life represented a flight from the frontier and from his father. Once he left his paternal home, Lincoln would never invite Thomas to visit him. Never would he give Thomas the satisfaction of knowing that his name would be carried on by a grandson. Never would Thomas see his grandchildren or his daughter-in-law. Never would Lincoln perform Thomas's work as a farmer and carpenter. Never would he pursue Thomas's favorite forms of recreation, hunting and fishing. As he stepped from the Macon County cabin, Lincoln was free at last, free at last.

3.

"Separated from His Father, He Studied English Grammar"

New Salem (1831–1834)

In 1848, the 39-year-old Lincoln offered some sage advice to his law partner, William H. Herndon, who had complained that young Whigs were being discriminated against by older Whigs. In denying the allegation, Lincoln urged him to avoid thinking of himself as a victim: "The way for a young man to rise, is to improve himself every way he can, never suspecting that any body wishes to hinder him. . . . There may sometimes be ungenerous attempts to keep a young man down; and they will succeed too, if he allows his mind to be diverted from its true channel to brood over the attempted injury."[1]

By his own account, Lincoln began his emancipated life "a strange, friendless, uneducated, penniless boy."[2] After escaping from his paternal home, he spent three years preparing himself for a way of life far different from the hardscrabble existence that he had been born into. As he groped his way toward a new identity, he improved himself every way he could.

Frontier Boatman, Humorist, and Jack-of-All-Trades

To earn some pennies, Lincoln accepted an offer from a Kentucky entrepreneur named Denton Offutt to take a flatboat to New Orleans. In February 1831, when Offutt proposed to John Hanks, a skilled riverman, that he run a flatboat of agricultural goods to New Orleans, Hanks took Offutt to meet his cousin Abraham. "I am seeking employment," Lincoln reportedly said. "I have had some experience in boating and boat building, and if you are in want of hands I think I can give you satisfaction."[3] Hanks, Lincoln, and John D. Johnston struck a deal to make the trip south as soon as the snow melted.

The first task confronting the three young men was to build a flatboat. They hiked five miles north to the mouth of Spring Creek, felled trees, floated the logs to a sawmill near Sangamotown, and with the help of a knowledgeable carpenter managed to construct a serviceable vessel. During the weeks it took to build the boat, Lincoln impressed the villagers with his agreeable wit, which made him a celebrity in Sangamotown. Residents would sit on a log as Lincoln regaled them with stories, and when he ended one in an unexpected fashion, they would laugh so hard they fell off. Lincoln's humor was distinctly crude, and his lifelong fondness for off-color stories became legendary. In 1859, when asked, "Why do you not write out your stories & put them in a book?," Lincoln replied, "Such a book would Stink like a thousand privies."[4]

Enough of Lincoln's humor has survived to illustrate why his Sangamotown colleagues found him hilarious. In one joke, Ethan Allen visited England shortly after the American Revolution. While he was there, "the English took Great pleasure in teasing him, and trying to Make fun of the Americans and General Washington in particular." One day the English put a picture of Washington in the privy. When they asked Allen if he had seen it, he said no, but that "he thought that it was a very appropriate [place] for an Englishman to Keep it" because there was "Nothing that will Make an Englishman Shit So quick as the Sight of Genl Washington."[5]

Lincoln favored stories that illustrated a point but disliked vulgarity for its own sake. William Herndon explained that even though "Lincoln's jokes were *vulgar—indecently so*," he "was not a dirty foul mouthed man by any means." He "was raised among a peculiar people—an ignorant but good people—honest ones. Hence Mr Lincoln preferred jokes to fables or maxims as they, for his people, had the pith—point & force about them to make the point luminous—clear—plain."[6]

In April 1831, Lincoln, Hanks, Johnston, and Offutt set out for New Orleans. After only a few miles the boat ran aground on a milldam at the village of New Salem. Townspeople watched curiously as Lincoln jumped off the boat into the river and took charge. After he and his crewmates transferred the cargo to another vessel, Lincoln borrowed an augur to drill a hole in the bow of the flatboat, which hung precariously over the dam. After the water drained out, he plugged the hole, freed the boat, and the journey continued. Struck by Lincoln's ingenuity, Offutt declared that he would have a steamboat built to navigate the Sangamon, and "by thunder, she'd have to go" because Lincoln would be its captain.[7] Lincoln nearly abandoned the trip when Johnston and Hanks went on a spree at Beardstown. Offutt had to track Lincoln down and persuade him to continue. Thereafter, the journey was uneventful.

When they reached New Orleans in May, Lincoln was once again appalled when he observed slavery firsthand. John Hanks alleged that he and Lincoln "saw Negroes Chained—maltreated—whipt & scourged." Lincoln's "heart bled," though he "said nothing much" and "was silent from feeling—was Sad—looked bad—felt bad—was thoughtful & abstracted." Hanks further averred that "it was on this trip that he [Lincoln] formed his opinions of Slavery; it ran its iron in him then &

there—May, 1831. I have heard him say—often & often."[8] Historians doubt Hanks's assertion since Lincoln stated that Hanks had not proceeded all the way to New Orleans but "had turned back from St. Louis."[9] It is possible that Hanks reported accurately what Lincoln later told him rather than what he (Hanks) saw with his own eyes. It is also possible that Lincoln's memory was faulty. Herndon alleged that Lincoln often related this story, and it squares with the reminiscences of Allen Gentry's wife about Lincoln's remarks made during his earlier New Orleans trip.

As the venture continued, Denton Offutt grew ever more impressed with Lincoln. "Lincoln can do any thing," he marveled. "I really believe he could take the flat-boat back again up the river."[10] Upon Lincoln's return from New Orleans, Offutt gave him a job running a store and mill at New Salem. Offutt had dreamed up the plan for a New Salem store while traveling back from Louisiana. Passing through St. Louis, he ordered goods shipped to New Salem.

In late July, Lincoln headed for the village where he was remembered for his ungainly appearance and his exploits on the milldam. Many New Salemites hailed from the Rolling Fork area of Kentucky, near Lincoln's boyhood home on Knob Creek. New Salem was considered an important small town, with its two dozen families, a grain and saw mill, three stores, a saloon, and a blacksmith shop. It served as a trading center for residents of nearby settlements.

New Salem was a rough and primitive place where violence was common and even religion reflected the crudeness of the frontier. The transplanted Kentuckians were Hardshell Baptists who opposed Sunday schools and Bible societies. They devoted Saturdays to shooting matches, card games, horse racing, cock and dogfights, drinking sprees, and fisticuffs. Combatants gouged, bit, kicked, and did anything else they could to prevail. On Sunday men were seen with bruised faces or, worse still, missing fingers, eyes, or ears. Womenfolk placed bets on the outcome of the fights. Strangers incautious enough to play cards regularly lost all their money and then got beaten up.

New Salem's living conditions were as rough as its people. One resident described the village's cabins to his New England family as "not half so good as your old hogs pen and not any larger."[11] Drunkenness was common, even among children. Looking back on his early years, Lincoln recalled that "intoxicating liquor [was] recognized by every body, and repudiated by nobody. It commonly entered into the first draught of the infant, and the last draught of the dying man."[12] Some New Englanders in the village, led by the pious Dr. John Allen, tried to civilize it by establishing a temperance society, but its advocates in New Salem faced ridicule and stiff opposition. (Lincoln allegedly once said, while pointing to Allen: "There stands the man who, years ago, was instrumental in convincing me of the evils of trafficking in and using ardent spirits.")[13]

For all its drawbacks, New Salem offered residents a chance to rise on the basis of their talent, ability, and industry. As Lincoln entered the village in the summer of 1831, he thought of himself as "a sort of floating Drift wood," swept along by the floods that inundated the region after the "winter of deep snow."[14] Because neither Offutt nor his goods had arrived yet, Lincoln had to postpone his debut as a merchant. With nothing much to do in the meantime, Lincoln "rapidly made acquaintances and friends."[15] The genial personality that had won him popularity at Sangamotown did the same in New Salem. One new friend, schoolteacher Mentor Graham, was clerking at the polls on August 1, an election day, when Lincoln entered to vote for the pro–Henry Clay candidate for Congress—an unpopular choice in that heavily Democratic precinct. In need of an assistant, Graham asked the rangy newcomer if he could write. "I can make a few rabbit tracks," Lincoln replied.[16] Graham pressed him into service and later testified that Lincoln "performed the duties with great facility—much fairness and honesty & impartially."[17] During lulls, Lincoln delighted his colleagues and voters with jokes and stories. Soon the penniless newcomer "*had nothing only plenty of friends*," as George Close put it.[18]

In September 1831, Lincoln finally began his career as Offutt's store clerk in a rented log storehouse, dispensing coffee, tea, gunpowder, liquor, tobacco, and other commodities. Offutt hired two assistants for Lincoln, Charles Maltby and William Greene, a 19-year-old Tennessean who, like Lincoln, was a highly entertaining storyteller. The three young men bunked at the store. Greene recalled that he and Lincoln "slept on the same cott & when one turned over the other had to do likewise."[19]

Lincoln became a popular store clerk. His integrity made him especially appealing to women customers, who trusted him to give an accurate assessment of the wares. One woman bought a dress for which she paid $2.37. Later that day, Lincoln realized he had overcharged her six and a quarter cents, which he refunded that very evening. Another woman asked for a pound of tea, which he measured out on a scale, inadvertently using the half-pound weight rather than the pound. When he discovered his error, he promptly went to her home and gave her another half pound of tea. Such episodes earned him the sobriquet "Honest Abe."

While he usually treated his customers kindly, Lincoln could on occasion lose patience with them. He took umbrage at one Charlie Reavis, who used profanity around women in the store. When Reavis ignored warnings to stop, Lincoln accosted him. "I have spoken to you a number of times about swearing in this store in the presence of ladies," he said angrily, "and you have not heeded. Now I am going to rub the lesson in so that you will not forget again." Lincoln grabbed Reavis by the arm, hustled him out of the store, threw him to the ground, and rubbed his face with smartweed.[20]

Lincoln, Maltby, and Greene assumed new responsibilities when Offutt rented the grain and saw mill whose dam had obstructed the flatboat earlier that year. The mill brought in a great deal of business. There Lincoln helped unload wheat, measure it out, tie up bags, and collect payments. Despite these added duties, Lincoln had a fair amount of free time. The store was busy on Saturdays, when many farmers came to town, but the rest of the week was quieter. Lincoln therefore could devote most of his time to the mill, while Greene and Maltby minded the store. Most business was transacted between 9:00 a.m. and 3:00 p.m. After the store closed, Lincoln would usually devote an hour to wrestling or other physical exercise.

One day, Denton Offutt bet a rival storekeeper, Bill Clary, that Lincoln could outwrestle any challenger, including Jack Armstrong, leader of the Clary's Grove Boys. Lincoln was irritated by Offutt's challenge. He had become popular in New Salem and did not wish to lose the goodwill of anybody. Moreover, he was by nature a peacemaker, not a fighter. But Lincoln knew he could not back down from Offutt's challenge to the Clary's Grove Boys without being shunned as a coward. On the day of the match a large crowd gathered near Offutt's store. Although Armstrong was an exceptionally powerful and clever wrestler, he found it difficult to cope with Lincoln's great reach and height. As the contest went on, the newcomer was getting the better of it. Just as it seemed that Lincoln would prevail, Bill Clary shouted to his man, "Throw him anyway, Jack." Breaking the rules of wrestling with a hold permissible only in scuffling, Armstrong instantly threw Lincoln, who angrily "said that if it ever came right, he would give Bill Clary a good licking."[21]

John Todd Stuart, Lincoln's friend, mentor, and first law partner, called this contest "the turning point in Lincoln's life."[22] His courage, strength, and good-natured acceptance of Armstrong's violation of the rules impressed New Salemites, especially the Clary's Grove Boys. They honored him with invitations to referee their horse races, where he further cemented his reputation for fairness. Armstrong became his fast friend and admirer. The popularity he thus gained would help lay the foundation for his political career. As long as Lincoln remained in New Salem, the Clary's Grove Boys supported him at election time. That Lincoln won such support without sharing their enthusiasm for drinking, gander pulling, and general mayhem was a tribute to his remarkable capacity for making and keeping friends.

Self-Education

Once established as a promising young man in New Salem, Lincoln began steadily bettering himself in preparation for a career in politics. Most nights after he closed the store, Lincoln would settle into reading and study from 8:00 to 11:00, then review what he had done. At first Lincoln concentrated on English grammar, for he did not want to seem like an uneducated bumpkin. He borrowed a copy of Samuel Kirkham's *English Grammar in Familiar Lectures* and "then turned his immediate & almost undivided attention to English grammar."[23] He mastered the subject quickly, obtaining a working knowledge in a few weeks, but he never completely overcame his primitive linguistic background. Even in his presidential years his speech (not his grammar) betrayed his frontier roots. He began his celebrated 1860 Cooper Union address by saying, "Mr. Cheerman."[24] As president he said *unly* for *only*, *own* for *one*, *waal* for *well*, *thar* for *there*, *was* for *were*, *git* for *get*, *ye* for *you*, *rare* for *rear*, and *one on 'em* for *one of them*. In his antebellum career as a lawyer, Lincoln used *ain't* freely, greeting friends in court with a jocular: "Ain't you glad to see me?"[25]

Settled in New Salem, Lincoln became a bookworm. He occasionally indulged in sports and games, but never to the neglect of his work or studies. If he had a few minutes to spare at the store, he would crack open a book. He read while walking to dinner at the boardinghouse or strolling about New Salem. When he took his meals with the family of the village cooper, Henry Onstot, Lincoln would read after work lying down before the fireplace. When Mrs. Onstot, busy preparing supper, complained that he was in her way, he replied: "Just step over me, Susan."[26]

In New Salem, Lincoln devoured newspapers, just as he had done in Indiana. He looked forward to the weekly arrival of the Louisville *Journal*, whose politics and wit he relished. He also regularly perused the *Sangamo Journal*, a Whig paper from nearby Springfield, which served as his political bible. Lincoln especially enjoyed the poetry of Burns, Cowper, Gray, Pope, Byron, and Shakespeare. In New Salem he would sit on the banks of the Sangamon and quote the Bard of Avon with Jack Kelso, a sometime handyman and devotee of poetry. He and Jack were constant companions, frequently seen conversing and arguing. After he left New Salem, Lincoln would regularly carry a copy of Shakespeare with him when traveling. He liked above all political figures like Richard III, Hamlet, Macbeth, Julius Caesar, and Coriolanus. His favorite plays were *Hamlet* and *Macbeth*. As president, he told an actor that he had read and reread Shakespeare "perhaps as frequently as any unprofessional reader."[27]

Lincoln's course of self-improvement drew him into the meetings of the Literary and Debating Society in New Salem, presided over by the warm, generous, and sociable James Rutledge. When Lincoln first spoke before the group in the winter of 1831–32, everyone expected him to tell a funny story. To their amazement, he instead focused seriously on the question before the society. As he proceeded, he awkwardly gestured to emphasize his points, which were so convincing that they astonished his largely uneducated audience. After the meeting, Rutledge told his wife that "there was more in Abe's head than wit and fun, that he was already a fine speaker; that all he lacked was culture to enable him to reach the high destiny which he Knew was in store for him."[28] As Lincoln spoke at more and more such meetings, he displayed the logic, intelligence, and spontaneity that would make him the most formidable debater in the New Salem area. Daniel Green Burner recalled that arguments "seemed to come right out of him without study or long preparation."[29] No records of Rutledge's debating club survive, but some do for nearby equivalents. In Illinois, debate topics from this period included what should be done with free Blacks if slavery were abolished and whether slavery had been beneficial or not. There were also debates on public works, temperance, banking, public land policy, marriage, and female voting and education. In time, Lincoln as an officeholder would address many of these issues.

While Lincoln's studies progressed well at New Salem, his career as a store clerk did not. The flighty Offutt neglected the store, which failed in early 1832, leaving Lincoln and Maltby unemployed. Soon, however, Vincent A. Bogue, who owned a store and mill near Springfield, announced that he would bring a steamboat, *The Talisman*, to Springfield. On it, farmers could ship their crops cheaply to St. Louis and New Orleans; merchants, mechanics, and professional men also stood to gain. Lincoln and Maltby, sensing an opportunity to make New Salem a shipping point for the new steamer, bought on credit a large log building that they planned to use for storing and forwarding merchandise and crops. Bogue hired Lincoln and others to clear the channel of the Sangamon. In March the little vessel reached New Salem, where part of its cargo was stored at Lincoln and Maltby's warehouse, and then proceeded upriver as far as Portland Landing, a few miles from Springfield.

Just as things seemed propitious, the water level began to drop, forcing *The Talisman*, on which Lincoln served as assistant pilot, to turn back. The boat retreated slowly, and trees overhanging the sluggish river severely damaged its cabin and upper portions. The crew repaired ignominiously to Beardstown, their mission a failure. After pocketing his forty-dollar fee, Lincoln trudged back to New Salem, where his warehousing business met the same melancholy fate as Offutt's store.

Black Hawk War Service

When Lincoln returned to New Salem that spring, he found the village astir with excitement over brewing trouble. Chief Black Hawk had led eight hundred members of the "British Band" of Sauk and Mesquakie (or Fox) tribes across the Mississippi to repossess lands in northern Illinois that they had earlier ceded to the U.S. government. To repel those forces, Governor John Reynolds called for volunteers. Before the Black Hawk War ended in August, ten thousand volunteers, aided by one-third of the U.S. Regular Army, would spend $2 million to chase several hundred Indian warriors from Illinois. Seventy-two Whites and anywhere from six hundred to a thousand Indians were killed.

On April 21, 1832, Lincoln and sixty-seven others from the New Salem area responded to the governor's call-up. Lincoln's unit, the Fourth Illinois Regiment of Mounted Volunteers, included some members of the Clary's Grove Boys. The would-be soldiers chose their own officers, and a prosperous sawmill owner, William Kirkpatrick, assumed that he would be elected captain. To his intense disappointment, however, the volunteers chose Lincoln. Although Lincoln was reluctant to stand for the office, his friends grabbed him, pushed him forward, and lined up behind him to indicate their preference; few lined up behind Kirkpatrick. Lincoln gleefully exclaimed to William G. Greene, "I'll be damned, Bill, but I've beat him!"[30] This first electoral victory of his life was, Lincoln wrote later, "a success which gave me more pleasure than any which I have had since."[31] Lincoln's toughness, fairness, and native ingenuity made him an effective officer; however, not everything went smoothly. When he issued his first order as captain, he was told, "Go to the devil, sir!"[32] He may have had some rudimentary militia training in Indiana, but he knew little of military practice and terminology.

Lincoln served three brief tours of duty from late April to mid-July, but to his disappointment, he saw no combat. He had occasion, however, to observe its horrors. On May 15, during his first tour, Lincoln and his men found eleven soldiers' corpses, "all scalped," some "with the heads cut off," some "with their throats cut and otherwise Barbourously Mutilated."[33] A week later, near Ottawa, Illinois, they discovered the mutilated bodies of women and children hanging upside down. In this charged atmosphere, Lincoln showed courage when his company grew alarmed at a threat posed by a large force of Indians. He was riding a borrowed horse at the time, and although it was more dangerous to march along with his men, he returned the horse to its owner and took his chances on the ground.

At the end of May, after a month's service, the fourteen-hundred-man volunteer army disbanded. Lincoln was among the three hundred veterans who reenlisted because, as he put it, "I was out of work, and there being no danger of more fighting, I could do nothing better."[34] He was mustered into U.S. service by Lieutenant Robert Anderson, who in 1861 would be in command of Fort Sumter when it fell to the Confederacy. The company formed part of a cavalry force charged with protecting the frontier until a new army could be formed. They scouted in northern Illinois, reassuring settlers and menacing Black Hawk as best they could. While undertaking a risky mission to Galena, they paused to bury the victims of yet another massacre.

On June 20, Lincoln volunteered for his final tour as a private in Dr. Jacob Early's Independent Spy Company, a thirty-six-man outfit that primarily conveyed messages and conducted reconnaissance. The men came upon the corpses of several troops killed at Kellogg's Grove and buried them. Lincoln described the scene vividly: "The red light of the morning sun was streaming upon them as they lay [with their] heads towards us on the ground. And every man had a round red spot on the top of his head about as big as a dollar, where the redskins had taken his scalp. It was frightful, but it was grotesque; and the red sunlight seemed to paint everything all over."[35]

Army life had its sociable moments for Lincoln and his mates. When not marching, they held foot races, swam, wrestled, played checkers, chess, and cards, and listened to Lincoln tell stories. They baked bread on ramrods, ate fried meat off of elm bark, and ground coffee in tin cups with their hatchet handles. Of a ration of chickens Lincoln said, "They are much like eating saddle bags," then added, "but I think the stomach can accomplish much today." During his three-week stint with the spy battalion, he and John Todd Stuart joined others in search of feminine companionship at Galena. Stuart, who came to know Lincoln well in the Black Hawk War, recollected that they "went to the hoar houses. . . . All went purely for fun—devilment—nothing Else."[36]

Lincoln's cheerful, agreeable nature stood him in good stead. According to Stuart, "Lincoln had no military qualities whatever except that he was a good clever fellow and kept the esteem and respect of his men. He made a very good Captain."[37] When a Regular Army officer insisted that his own troops must enjoy preferment in rations and pay and then ordered Lincoln to perform an unauthorized act, he reluctantly obeyed. But he protested: "Sir . . . resistance will hereafter be made to your injust orders. & further my men must be Equal in all particulars in rations—arms—camps &c to the regular Army."[38] Acknowledging that Lincoln's complaint was legitimate, and realizing that he was resolved to have his men treated justly, the officer thereafter saw to it that the volunteers received the same treatment as the regulars. Lincoln's action endeared him to most of his men. Lincoln was not popular with everyone, however. His superiors disciplined him for firing his pistol near the camp and for allowing his troops to become drunk. In the first instance, he was arrested for a day; in the second, he was made to carry a wooden sword for two days.

On occasion, Lincoln defied his men. Once an old Indian entered the camp bearing a note signed by Lewis Cass attesting to his good character. Several troops menaced him, swearing that they had volunteered to fight Indians and they intended to do so. Lincoln interposed himself between them and the Indian, saying, "Men, this must not be done—he must not be shot and killed by us." When some accused the man of being a spy, Lincoln would not budge.

"This is cowardly on your part Lincoln," a comrade charged.

"If any man thinks I am a coward let him test it," Lincoln replied, drawing himself up to his full height.

One member of the regiment protested, "Lincoln—you are larger and heavier than we are."

"This you can guard against—Choose your weapons," Lincoln retorted.

This challenge abruptly ended all charges of cowardice. This episode was one of the first times William Greene ever witnessed Lincoln's righteous anger. "He would do justice to all though the heavens fell," Greene noted.[39]

Lincoln's military service ended in mid-July, when he was mustered out in Wisconsin. He would later poke fun at his service record, saying, "I had a good many bloody struggles with the musquetoes; and, although I never fainted from loss of blood, I can truly say I was often very hungry."[40] Despite this self-mockery, Lincoln was proud of his service in the Black Hawk War, which proved valuable financially and politically. He received $175 and forty acres of public land; gained popularity among both soldiers and civilians; and made friendships that would prove important for his future careers in politics and the law. Although he saw no combat, he did get a taste of war, and his selection as captain whetted his appetite for future electoral contests.

First Bid for Elective Office

Upon returning to New Salem, Lincoln threw himself into the political campaign that he had entered back in March. After his debut at the literary society, James Rutledge had urged him to run for the legislature. At first, Lincoln balked, fearing he had no chance, but Rutledge suggested that "a canvass of the County would bring him prominently before the people and in time would do him good."[41] Lincoln finally agreed to run and issued a lengthy announcement of his candidacy, a document that John McNamar helped him compose. Like many other frontier merchants, Lincoln was a Whig. But as soon as he announced his intention, the Black Hawk War broke out. By the time it ended that summer, he had only a few days to campaign.

With the election looming on August 6, Lincoln's chances seemed poor, for he was a little-known Whig in a Democratic district. His formal campaign announcement, published in March, made his principles clear. He rejected the Jacksonian creed, which *the Democratic Review* summarized in 1838: "As little government as possible; that little emanating from, and controlled by, the people; and uniform in its application to all."[42] Democrats in general believed that the only assertive action the federal government should undertake was aggressive foreign expansionism. Whigs, on the other hand, favored positive government. A leading Whig spokesman, Horace Greeley, of the New York *Tribune*, explained in 1845 that the "great fundamental principle" of Whiggery was that government "is bound to do all that is fairly within its power to promote the welfare of the people."[43]

Lincoln shared the Whig vision. He later wrote that the "legitimate object of government is 'to do for the people what needs to be done, but which they can not, by individual effort, do at all, or do so well, for themselves.' There are many such things—some of them exist independently of the injustice in the world. Making and maintaining roads, bridges, and the like; providing for the helpless young and afflicted; common schools; and disposing of deceased men's property, are instances."[44] In his 1832 campaign announcement, Lincoln above all championed government support for internal improvements that would enable subsistence farmers to escape rural poverty by participating in the market economy. Lincoln wanted to spare others the ox-like drudgery that rural isolation had imposed on him and his family. To that end, he recommended affordable projects, primarily to facilitate navigation of the Sangamon River. For reasonable sums, he predicted, the river could be straightened and its channel cleared. Desirable as other improvements, such as canals and railroads, might be, their high cost produced "a heart appalling shock."

Lincoln suggested another technique for liberating people from rural poverty: usury laws, because the poor could not escape poverty without access to loans at reasonable interest rates. Yet another means for emancipating frontiersmen won Lincoln's approval: public education, which he deemed "the most important subject that we as a people can be engaged in." The kind of superstitious, primitive ignorance that surrounded him in Kentucky and Indiana could be banished by education, which would in turn promote "morality, sobriety, enterprise, and industry." He longed to see the day when the world of backwoodsmen—the world of his father—would disappear.

In the final paragraph of his campaign statement, Lincoln went beyond policy matters to reveal his personal feelings:

> Every man is said to have his peculiar ambition. Whether it be true or not, I can say for one that I have no other so great as that of being truly esteemed of my fellow men, by rendering myself worthy of their esteem. . . . I am young and unknown to many of you. I was born and have ever remained in the most humble walks of life. I have no wealthy or popular relations to recommend me. My case is thrown exclusively upon the independent voters of this country, and if elected they will have conferred a favor upon me, for which I shall be unremitting in my

> labors to compensate. But if the good people in their wisdom shall see fit to keep me in the background, I have been too familiar with disappointments to be very much chagrined.[45]

Lincoln's ambition, like that of many other politicians, was rooted in an intense craving for deference and approval. But unlike many power seekers, Lincoln was expansive and generous in his ambition. He desired more than ego-gratifying power and prestige; he wanted everyone to have a chance to escape the soul-crushing poverty and backwardness that he had experienced as a quasi slave on the frontier. From first to last, Lincoln's political goal was to free the oppressed, starting with the kind of frontier people whose conditions he knew firsthand; in time, the scope of his sympathies would broaden.

To forward these principles, Lincoln had to campaign hard in late July and early August. He stumped the huge county, delivering speeches and socializing with the voters. His first campaign address was given at Pappsville, a hamlet eleven miles southwest of New Salem. An auditor remembered that it went something like this: "Fellow citizens, I suppose you all know who I am. I am humble Abraham Lincoln. I have been solicited by many friends to become a candidate for the Legislature. My politics are short and sweet, like the old woman's dance. I am in favor of a national bank. I am in favor of the internal-improvement system and a high protective tariff. These are my sentiments and political principles. If elected I shall be thankful; if not it will be all the same."[46]

Lincoln poked fun at his own odd appearance. On one occasion he mockingly observed, "Fellow Citizens: I have been told that some of my opponents have said that it was a disgrace to the County of Sangamon to have such a looking man as I am stuck up for the Legislature. Now, I thought this was a free country. That is the reason that I address you today. Had I known to the contrary I should not have consented to run."[47] In addition, Lincoln used logical, thoughtful, and engaging speeches to offset the effect of his unprepossessing appearance.

Campaigning in the 1830s could be grim and tiresome. Local candidates often spoke to audiences of no more than twenty to thirty at social events like house raisings. Lincoln, a political newcomer and a long shot, declared that if he were defeated he would try and try again: "When I have been a candidate before you some 5 or 6 times and have been beaten every time I will consider it a disgrace and will be sure never to try it again."[48] And in his first try for office he did lose, finishing eighth in a field of thirteen where only the top four vote-getters won legislative seats. It was, he remarked in 1859, "the only time I ever had been beaten by the people."[49]

Because Sangamon County was huge, Lincoln could not begin to cover it in the short time he had to campaign. On election day, few voters outside New Salem knew who he was. Still, his respectable showing boded well for the future. In New Salem, he was astonishingly successful, winning 277 of 300 votes cast even though his candidate for president, Henry Clay, lost that precinct by 115 votes. Lincoln was so popular that several pro-Jackson partisans voted for him because he seemed so honest and worthy. Moreover, he pleased New Salemites who were keen to separate from sprawling Sangamon County and form a new county. Since Lincoln was their local candidate, they counted on him to help achieve that end. Also swelling Lincoln's vote in New Salem was a long-standing enmity between one of his rivals, the Methodist minister Peter Cartwright, and Samuel Hill, the village's leading merchant. Hill, a staunch Democrat, detested Cartwright so much that he not only voted for Lincoln, the Whig, but also worked for him.

Lincoln was quite gratified despite the outcome, for his showing amazed many, including his strongest backers. His skeptical comrades discovered that he "knew what he was about and that he had running qualities."[50] And John Todd Stuart believed that Lincoln's candor, honesty, and effective speeches had laid the foundation for future campaigns. "He ran on the square," said Stuart, "and thereby acquired the respect and confidence of everybody."[51]

Frontier Merchant, Postmaster, Surveyor

Two years had to pass before Lincoln could run for office again. In the meantime, though jobless and broke, he resolved to stay in New Salem, where people had been exceptionally kind and where he had many friends. He thought about studying law but feared that his educational background was inadequate for that challenge. He also considered becoming a blacksmith. But before long, Lincoln found himself working in a store once again, this time as a co-owner.

Early in 1832, William Franklin Berry, the son of a Cumberland Presbyterian minister, bought half interest in a store from James Herndon. Berry's partner, J. Rowan Herndon, soon sold his half to Lincoln on credit. Shortly after the August election, Berry, Lincoln's junior by two years, and Lincoln opened their emporium with the stock on hand, supplemented by goods, including whiskey, purchased from Henry Inco and James A. Rutledge after their store had failed.

Frontier village merchants like Lincoln and Berry were general factotums for everyone and thus came to know what was happening in their neighborhoods. Stores were gathering places, often contained the post office, and usually had a whiskey barrel in a back room with a tin cup dangling from its side. In January 1833 the new storekeepers bought up the stock of a competitor, Reuben Radford, whose store had been demolished by the Clary's Grove Boys. They had become incensed when the clerk refused to serve them more than two drinks. William G. Greene, who owned the building, bought the surviving merchandise from the agitated Radford for $400. Greene began to fret that he had overpaid, but his friend Lincoln said, "Cheer up, Billy, it's a good thing; we will take an inventory." Not understanding exactly what an inventory was, and fearing that the Clary's Grove Boys had committed one, Greene replied: "No more inventories for me."[52] Greene gladly accepted a $650 promissory note from Lincoln and Berry for the goods and the store, a more substantial building than the one they already had. That same month, Berry and Lincoln applied for a license to sell liquor by the glass. Daniel Green Burner, who clerked in the store, dispensed drinks for 6¢ apiece. Then, in April, the partners bought even more goods from a Beardstown firm. All this expansion left the entrepreneurs, as Lincoln put it, "deeper and deeper in debt," and eventually the business "winked out."[53]

The store failed not just because the partners were overextended but also because Berry was an undisciplined, hard-drinking fellow. He neglected the store and died in 1835, apparently of tuberculosis caused by his dissolute ways. Making matters worse, Lincoln was too softhearted to deny credit to anyone, no matter how impecunious. Nor could he pressure customers to pay their bills or sue them. Moreover, he lacked enthusiasm for the job and was far too likely to interrupt a transaction with a long story. He also erred in letting the bibulous Berry wait on women and in candidly warning good customers that the whiskey he sold would ruin them and that the tobacco was of poor quality. If he did not know much about some goods in the store, he would frankly acknowledge his ignorance. He and Berry extended too much credit, bought and sold goods unwisely, and invested so much money in slow-selling merchandise that their stock became an unappealing hodgepodge.

When Berry died in 1835, Lincoln's debts amounted to approximately eleven hundred dollars. "That debt was the greatest obstacle I have ever met in life," he told a friend. "I had no way of speculating, and could not earn money except by labor, and to earn by labor eleven hundred dollars, besides my living, seemed the work of a lifetime." So Lincoln told his creditors that if they "would let me alone, I would give them all I could earn, over my living, as fast as I could earn it." As late as 1860, Lincoln was still being dunned for payment of these New Salem debts. According to Herndon, "The debt galled him and hastened his wrinkles."[54]

While struggling to pay back what he owed, Lincoln had few expenses, for his rent was minimal. At first he slept for free in Offutt's store and took his meals with John M. Camron, who charged him one dollar per week. Later he paid the same fee for room and board to Isaac Burner. He lodged in the second Lincoln-Berry store even after it folded. When he roomed with James Short, Lincoln paid two dollars a week. Meals and laundry were cheap. During his five and a half years in New Salem, Lincoln stayed in a half dozen homes.

In May of 1833, as he struggled to eke out a living, Lincoln was delighted to be named postmaster of New Salem, a job he would hold until that post office closed three years later. The position had been held by the storekeeper Samuel Hill, who had neglected his postal patrons in favor of customers for his merchandise, including liquor. Several New Salem women, indignant that they had to wait while tipplers were served their whiskey, got up a petition to replace Hill with Lincoln. Ossian M. Ross, the postmaster at Havana, reviewed the petition, noted that it had been signed by leading citizens, and forwarded it with his endorsement to Washington. Lincoln's Whiggery did not hurt his chances with the Democratic administration because, as he explained, the "office was too insignificant, to make . . . politics an objection."[55] Besides, Lincoln was one of the few people in New Salem who could manage the paperwork. He was greatly pleased, not only because he would be able to earn some money but also because he gained access to newspapers to which he did not subscribe.

When business took him out of the village, Lincoln delivered letters to homes, using his hat as a mailbag. He kept his accounts carefully. After the New Salem post office closed in 1836, he had a surplus of about sixteen dollars, which he took with him when he moved to Springfield the following year. A few months later, an agent approached Lincoln's friend Anson G. Henry about the outstanding balance. Henry feared that the cash-strapped young man might not have it on hand, so he offered to help Lincoln. But it proved unnecessary, for the erstwhile postmaster had in his room all the money—in fact, the very coins—that he had received in New Salem, which he turned over to the government agent with a simple explanation: "I never make use of money that does not belong to me."[56]

But the postmastership paid little, and his debts weighed him down so much that he often struggled to pay his modest board bill. So he took every odd job he could, serving as an election clerk, a rail splitter, a mill operator, a store clerk, and a farm hand. All together they yielded just enough to make ends meet. Lincoln's economic situation improved considerably, however, when John Calhoun, the Democratic surveyor of Sangamon County, offered to hire him as an assistant. Business was heavy in the northern part of the county, where New Salem was located, because the voyage of the *Talisman* had prompted many landowners to have their property surveyed for town lots. The townsite craze lasted from 1832 to 1838. Speculators filed on lands at $1.25 an acre and resold them for more. Consequently surveyors' stakes covered the vacant prairies. Calhoun knew Lincoln from the Black Hawk War, and friendship trumped politics. When he was approached about the position, Lincoln asked, "Do I have to give up any of my principles for this job? If I have to surrender any thought or principle to get it I wouldn't touch it with a ten foot pole." Assured that he would not have to abandon his Whig convictions, Lincoln gratefully accepted.[57] In later years, the two men would clash in political debates, but they remained friends.

Lincoln went about his surveying duties with characteristic industriousness. He procured a compass and surveyor's chain and began to study textbooks. Having mastered the basics, he set out with his compass, chain, marking pins, range poles, plumb bobs, stakes, and ax to pursue his new calling. He borrowed a horse from Jack Armstrong for a time before eventually buying one, along with a bridle and saddle, on credit. When he finally recorded his first survey on January 6, 1834, Lincoln's friends and neighbors helped him celebrate his good fortune. He quickly gained an enviable reputation as a skilled surveyor, becoming the preferred expert for determining survey lines in the dense forest. Whenever settlers disagreed about property boundaries, Lincoln refereed the dispute to the satisfaction of all.

From 1834 to 1836, Lincoln surveyed homesites, roads, school sections, and towns. It was rugged work, hard on men, equipment, and clothes. Surveyors lived outdoors in all conditions while trying to impose order on a wild, untracked land. Elizabeth Abell, at whose home Lincoln lodged while he was surveying the hills between New Salem and Petersburg, recalled that he often returned at night "ragged and scratch[ed] up with the Bryers." He "would laugh over it and say that was a poore mans lot."[58]

Despite his success as a surveyor, Lincoln continued to have financial troubles. The man who sold him the horse on credit sued him for payment in April 1834. That same month, other creditors also won judgments against Lincoln. To satisfy the debts, Lincoln's surveying tools and horse were sold at a sheriff's auction. A friend from Sandridge, James Short, saw that Lincoln was "very much discouraged" and heard him say "he would let the whole thing go by the board." Generously, Short bought Lincoln's possessions for $120 and returned them. Trying to express his gratitude, Lincoln said simply, "Uncle Jimmy, I will do as much for you sometimes."[59] (During the Civil War, Lincoln appointed Short to supervise an Indian agency.)

Election to the State Legislature

While surveying land in Sangamon County, Lincoln also surveyed his political prospects, which seemed encouraging. As a veteran of the Black Hawk War, a merchant, humorist, surveyor, and handyman, and an honest, helpful friend, he had made himself well known and well liked. He was a Whig with a host of Democratic friends and admirers, among them Bowling Green, who persuaded Lincoln to make a second run for the legislature. In March 1834, Green and Lincoln presided over a meeting called to endorse a gubernatorial candidate. Afterward, Green and other Democrats approached Lincoln and offered to remove two of their own nominees in favor of his candidacy. Lincoln immediately recognized that this might hurt the chances of his friend John Todd Stuart, and he informed Stuart of the scheme. Stuart appreciated that Lincoln had "acted fairly and honorably." Confident of his own strength, Stuart told Lincoln "to go and tell them he would take their votes—that I would risk it."[60]

An important issue in 1834 was a proposal to lop off the New Salem area from Sangamon County and form a new county. Travel to the county seat, Springfield, imposed hardships on jurors, witnesses, litigants, land filers, and all others who had public business there. Between New Salem and Springfield lay twenty miles of rough country traversed by bad roads. In addition to their desire to avoid the perils of travel to Springfield, voters in New Salem hoped their town would become the seat of the new county. New Salemites and their neighbors began petitioning for their own separate county in 1830. Lincoln pledged that he would attempt to get New Salem detached and incorporated into a new county. That pledge won Lincoln nearly unanimous support in the New Salem area, while he secured at least the Whig vote elsewhere in the county.

Lincoln issued no principled manifesto in 1834, focusing instead on the county-separation issue during what he called "more of a hand-shaking campaign than anything else." At Island Grove, when he approached some thirty men harvesting crops, they declared that they would support no man unless he could lend them a hand. Lincoln replied, "Well, boys if that is all I am sure of your votes." He grabbed a cradle, pitched in heartily, and won the votes of them all.[61]

Lincoln's personal qualities appealed to the voters, especially his geniality and humor. He talked to the families about their hopes and prospects, about schools, farms, crops, and livestock. People felt "they had met a friend—one near as a brother." He paid attention to the children, gave them candy and nuts, and it was clear that all this "came from the natural impulses of his heart." While other home-visiting candidates immediately talked politics, Lincoln would propose a tour of the farm while supper was cooking. After the meal he would eventually involve the women and children and regale the family with tales of his own childhood. He was folksy and congenial, and he made people feel he was one of them—a smart one of them, to be sure, but one of them nonetheless.[62] Lincoln's family-friendly campaign style worked because it was no affectation.

A potential threat to Lincoln's electoral chances was his reputation as a religious skeptic. When he told a political backer, Samuel Hill, that he intended to publish a heretical essay about Christianity, Hill snatched the manuscript and tossed it into the fire, for many voters took religion seriously. Lincoln often discussed religious topics with his friends, pointing out contradictions or logical lapses in the Bible. In New Salem, and later in Springfield, he shocked residents with views bordering on atheism. When Samuel Hill's devout wife asked Lincoln, "Do you really believe there isn't any future state?," he replied: "Mrs. Hill, I'm afraid that when we die that is the last of us."[63]

Despite his unorthodox religious views, in 1834 Lincoln won election to the Illinois legislature. Democratic crossover votes helped him finish among the top four in a twelve-man contest, even though he was unyielding in his devotion to Whig principles. In the two years since his first try for office, he had become much better known and appreciated. Lincoln was overjoyed. Not only was election an honor but members of the legislature were paid four dollars a day, a sum that he told a friend was "more than I had ever earned in my life."[64] By the end of 1834, the piece of human driftwood who three and a half years earlier had washed up on the banks of the Sangamon River at New Salem had been transformed. Although still known as "a mighty rough man," he had acquired a sense of direction.[65] Having chosen his career as a politician, he would pursue it single-mindedly, distancing himself ever further from the backward, provincial, isolated, ignorant world of Thomas Lincoln.

4.

"A Napoleon of Astuteness and Political Finesse"

Frontier Legislator (1834–1837)

Surrogate Father

After leaving his paternal home, Lincoln found in New Salem a surrogate father, Bowling Green, a rotund, easygoing, humorous, jovial "reading man" from North Carolina known as a gifted spinner of yarns. Twenty-two years Lincoln's senior, Green served at various times as justice of the peace, canal commissioner, doorkeeper of the Illinois House of Representatives, judge of elections, county commissioner, sheriff, and candidate for the state senate. In Lincoln's early days at New Salem, he boarded at Green's house, which attracted many visitors, for Green was famously hospitable.

Abner Y. Ellis reported that Lincoln "Loved Mr Green" as "his allmost Second Farther." Green, in turn, "looked on him with pride and pleasur[e]" and "Used to Say that Lincoln Was a Man after his own heart." Green told Ellis "that there Was good Material in Abe and he only Wanted Education." Undertaking to fill that gap, Green nurtured his protégé, lending him books, encouraging him to study, and fostering his political career. Lincoln confided to Ellis "that he owed more to Mr Green for his advancement than any other Man."[1] Green stimulated Lincoln's interest in the law by inviting him to attend sessions of his court. Lincoln also learned some law from books that Green lent him, which he read in 1832 and 1833. Because few lawyers lived in the New Salem area, the would-be attorney was often asked to try suits in Green's court. He accepted the challenge but turned down any remuneration. Initially the judge, who enjoyed Lincoln's humor, allowed him to practice for amusement's sake. Green's fat sides would shake as he laughed at the young man's laconic presentation of cases. Soon realizing that Lincoln was more than just a comedian, Green came to respect his intellect.

Lincoln grew close to Green and his wife, the former Nancy Potter, an unusually maternal, hospitable woman. In 1835, while suffering from depression, Lincoln repaired to the Greens' cabin, where for three weeks they nursed him back to psychological health. When apoplexy killed Green in 1842, his widow asked Lincoln to speak at the memorial service. He agreed to do so, but when "he arose he only uttered a few words and commenced choking and sobbing" and acknowledged that he was "unmanned" and could not proceed.[2]

Law Student

In 1832, Lincoln had considered studying law formally but hesitated because of his meager education. By 1834 Lincoln was far less intimidated by the prospect, in part because of his experience in Springfield in April 1833, when he served as a witness in two cases and a juror in three others. More than half of the members of the bar whom he might have observed had attended neither college nor law school. With his powerfully analytical mind, Lincoln might well have been drawn to lawyers as a class, for they were reputedly the most intelligent members of frontier society and usually owned the largest and best houses. Lawyers also had an advantage over non-lawyers in the political arena, and after his 1834 electoral victory Lincoln's appetite for politics grew.

Further stimulating Lincoln's ambition to become a lawyer was encouragement from a sophisticated, dignified, college-educated attorney, John Todd Stuart. The tall, slender Stuart enjoyed a reputation as one of the best jury lawyers in the state. A Kentuckian like Lincoln, he had graduated from Center College and studied law with Judge Daniel Breck. Soon thereafter he had settled in Springfield, where in 1833 he formed a partnership with Henry E. Dummer. The previous year he had run successfully for the state legislature, quickly rising to become a Whig leader in the house of representatives. There he was known as "Jerry Sly" for his mastery of legislative intrigue. Political opponents denounced him as "indolent and inefficient" and condemned his "low cunning."[3] In the Black Hawk War, Stuart came to admire Lincoln so much that he decided to take him under his wing. Whenever Lincoln expressed anxiety about the difficulties standing in his way or doubts about entering the legal profession, Stuart reassured him. Without such encouragement, Lincoln probably would not have been a lawyer.

Although Stuart became Lincoln's mentor, unlike Green he did not play the role of surrogate father. (He was only a year older than Lincoln.) Jesse W. Fell, who observed the two men during the legislative session of 1834–35, called them "congenial spirits not only boarding at the same house but rooming and sleeping together. Socially and politically they seemed inseparable." Indeed, Fell said, they were "boon companions," though totally different in temperament and appearance. Stuart, who had "all the adornments of a polished gentleman," provided a startling contrast to the rough-hewn Lincoln.[4]

Under Stuart's guidance, Lincoln began his legal studies by wading through Blackstone's *Commentaries*. He went at his task industriously, claiming to have mastered forty pages on his first day. Years later he recalled, "I began to read those famous works, and I had plenty of time; for, during the long summer days, when the farmers were busy with their crops, my customers were few and far between. The more I read the more intensely interested I became. Never in my whole life was my mind so thoroughly absorbed. I read until I devoured them."[5]

When Lincoln began to "go at" the law "in good earnest" following the 1834 election, he once again "studied with nobody," save Stuart. He followed a regimen that he would prescribe twenty-four years later to a young man who asked him how to gain "a thorough knowledge of the law." Lincoln replied: "The mode is very simple, though laborious, and tedious. It is only to get the books, and read, and study them carefully. Begin with Blackstone's Commentaries, and after reading it carefully through, say twice, take up Chitty's Pleadings, Greenleaf's Evidence, & Story's Equity &c. in succession. Work, work, work, is the main thing."[6] Once Lincoln devoted himself to legal studies, he became a different man, much to the consternation of friends and neighbors. When Russell Godbey initially noticed him with a law book in hand, he asked, "Abe—what are you Studying?" "Studying law," Lincoln replied, leading Godbey to exclaim, "Great God Almighty!"[7]

For the first time since his arrival in New Salem, Lincoln became antisocial. In the summer he often sought solitude in the woods in order to read and study undisturbed. Some New Salemites thought him deranged. Henry McHenry remembered that when Lincoln "began to study law he would go day after day for weeks and sit under an oak tree on a hill near Salem, and read—moved round the tree to keep in shade—was so absorbed that people said he was crazy. Sometimes he did not notice people when he met them."[8] McHenry and others joshed Lincoln for walking all the way to Springfield for books. When they also teased him about his first name, he began signing letters and documents "A. Lincoln."

In 1836, Lincoln took some necessary formal steps to become a lawyer. In March he obtained a certificate of good moral character from the attorney Stephen T. Logan, and six months later he received his license from the Illinois Supreme Court. After another six months, a clerk of that court officially enrolled him as an attorney. No record survives of the required examination that Lincoln took, but a judge probably asked him questions about various aspects of the law for about half an hour.

Freshman Legislator

In December 1834, legislative duties interrupted Lincoln's self-education in the law. Until taking his seat in the General Assembly, he had been indifferent about clothing, but the freshman legislator decided to purchase new garments. He approached his friend Coleman Smoot and asked, "Smoot, did you vote for me?" When Smoot said yes, Lincoln replied: "Well, you must loan me money to buy suitable clothing for I want to make a decent appearance in the Legislature." Smoot obliged with a generous loan, which Lincoln used to purchase "a very respectable looking suit of jeans."[9]

In the capital city of Vandalia, a primitive village of about eight hundred souls located seventy-five miles south of Springfield, Lincoln and three dozen other newcomers joined nineteen returning veterans in the house of representatives. Three-quarters of the legislators were, like Lincoln, Southern-born. The second-youngest member of that chamber, he belonged to the minority anti-Jackson contingent, which numbered only about eighteen in the lower house; the Democrats were more than twice as numerous. The factions had not yet become formal parties, and legislative business was conducted primarily through personal influence. The anti-Jackson forces in Illinois did not officially coalesce to form the Whig Party until 1838.

The Illinois House of Representatives that Lincoln entered was a rudimentary body. Most of his colleagues were farmers, many of them unsophisticated. The state capitol where Lincoln first served was also unprepossessing. One legislator called the decade-old building with its falling plaster, sagging floors, cracked and bulging walls, and crumbling bricks "manifestly inconvenient for the transaction of public business."[10] Some members of the General Assembly thought the town "the dullest, dreariest place," and the governor complained that "there is no young ladies in Vandalia."[11] The sleepy hamlet, which one of its founders described as "a most dull and miserable village" when the legislature was not in session, came to life when the lawmakers arrived.[12] Primitive as it was, Vandalia—with its bookshop, jewelry store, furniture emporium, and other businesses—must have seemed glamorous to the rough young legislator from New Salem. Parties, dances, and receptions enlivened society during sessions of the General Assembly.

Lincoln struck up a close friendship with Senator Orville H. Browning of Quincy and his wife, Eliza, a proud, friendly, ambitious, charming, and witty woman. Browning told an interviewer: "Lincoln had seen but very little of what might be called society and was very awkward, and very much embarrassed in the presence of ladies. Mrs. Browning very soon discovered his great merits, and treated him with a certain frank cordiality—which put Lincoln entirely at his ease. On this account he became very much attached to her."[13]

During the ten-week legislative session in 1834–35, Lincoln, under the tutelage of John Todd Stuart, remained inconspicuous, quietly observing his colleagues grant petitions for divorce, pass private bills to relieve individual citizens, appeal to Congress for money, declare creeks navigable, lay bills on the table, and listen to committee reports. On roll calls, Lincoln sided with Stuart 101 times but voted against him on 26 occasions. On votes for public officials, Lincoln agreed with Stuart every time save one. As he laid plans for a congressional race in 1836, Stuart groomed Lincoln to take over his leadership role in the General Assembly.

Lincoln's first bill sought to limit the jurisdiction of justices of the peace; much amended, it won approval in the house but not in the senate. Two weeks into the session he introduced a measure that did pass, authorizing the construction of a toll bridge over Salt Creek. Appreciating his literary skill, colleagues pressed him to draft legislation for them; he also wrote reports for the Committee on Public Accounts and Expenditures. In addition, he composed anonymous dispatches about legislative doings for the *Sangamo Journal*, an influential Whig newspaper in Springfield that over the years would publish many of his unsigned articles. James Matheny, who was to be a groomsman at Lincoln's wedding, recalled that while serving as deputy postmaster in Springfield in the mid-1830s, he had come to recognize Lincoln's handwriting and estimated that he delivered scores of editorials from him to the editor, Simeon Francis. Lincoln's political opponents took note that he was contributing to the *Journal*. The Democratic *Illinois State Register* of Springfield charged that the "writers of the *Journal* have had a *late* acquisition (Lincoln)—a chap rather famous not only for throwing filth, but for *swallowing it afterwards*."[14] Lincoln's journalism is not easy to identify with certainty, but dozens of pieces from the 1830s, including dispatches from an unnamed Whig legislator, seem clearly to be his handiwork. At first those dispatches simply offered terse accounts of legislative activity; in time they grew longer and more partisan.

In the first session of his initial term as a legislator, Lincoln made no formal speeches and only two brief sets of remarks. Economic issues dominated the session. The most important bill dealt with a much-discussed proposal to dig a canal from Chicago to La Salle, connecting the Great Lakes with the Illinois River, which fed into the Mississippi. Lincoln, who wanted to be known as "the De Witt Clinton of Illinois," voted with the majority to finance that internal improvement.[15] The most controversial national issue involved the Second Bank of the United States, on which President Andrew Jackson had declared well-publicized war. Another was the distribution of funds generated by the sale of federal public lands. Lincoln introduced an unsuccessful resolution calling for the U.S. government to remit to the state at least one-fifth of such proceeds collected in Illinois. In fulfillment of a campaign pledge, he also submitted a petition of "sundry citizens of the counties of Sangamon, Morgan and Tazewell, praying the organization of a new county out of said counties." The Committee on Petitions reported against it.[16]

That winter of 1834–35, the General Assembly passed 191 laws, chiefly dealing with roads, corporations, schools, and acts to relieve individuals. A state bank was chartered; the Illinois and Michigan Canal received vital funding; public roads were encouraged; the state was divided into judicial districts; and four colleges were incorporated. Lincoln voted on 131 of the 139 roll calls and was present for at least fifty-nine of the sixty-five days when the legislature met. Some observers felt that Lincoln had achieved little during the session. He did virtually nothing to implement the three main proposals of his 1832 platform—expanding public education, improving navigation of the Sangamon, and curbing high interest rates. Despite this meager record, contemporaries recalled Lincoln's legislative debut positively. John Locke Scripps wrote in 1860 that Lincoln "acquired the confidence of his fellow-members as a man of sound judgment and patriotic purposes, and in this manner he wielded a greater influence in shaping and controlling legislation than many of the noisy declaimers and most frequent speakers of the body."[17]

If Lincoln achieved little renown, he learned a great deal: he had met legislators, lobbyists, judges, and attorneys from around the state and assessed their strengths and weaknesses, and he had seen firsthand how legislation was framed and passed. In addition, he had made friends, in part through his legendary skill at storytelling. Those ten weeks in Vandalia sharpened Lincoln's already keen desire to escape the backwoods world of his father. He wanted to belong to this new realm, peopled with ambitious and talented men, and so he returned to New Salem resolved not only to continue studying law but also to smooth some of his rough edges.

Romance

In Illinois as in Indiana, the bashful Lincoln paid little attention to young women. When he boarded with John M. Camron, he took no romantic interest in his host's attractive daughters, one of whom described him as "thin as a beanpole and as ugly as a scarecrow!"[18] From 1831 to 1834, when Daniel Burner and Lincoln both lived in New Salem, Burner never saw Lincoln with a girl. Because he could not sing "any more than a crow," Lincoln avoided the singing school, where on weekends young men and women received elementary musical instruction and also courted. When he did attend social occasions where the sexes mingled, he "never danced or cut up."[19]

Women who claimed that Lincoln was drawn to them testified that he was socially backward and not a particularly eligible bachelor. A New Salem woman remembered that he "seemed to prefer the company of the elderly ladies to the young ones."[20] Those more mature women (in effect surrogate mothers) included Mrs. Bennett Abell, who encouraged Lincoln's ambition. While boarding at Bowling Green's, Lincoln came to know the Abells, who lived nearby. In time, Lincoln boarded with them. William Butler thought that "it was from Mrs. Able he first got his ideas of a higher plane of life—that it was she who gave him the notion that he might improve himself by reading &c."[21] Hannah Armstrong, another surrogate mother, remembered that he "amused himself by playing with the children, or telling some funny story to the old folks."[22]

Romantic love finally entered Lincoln's life in the person of Ann Rutledge, the daughter of one of his early New Salem landlords, James Rutledge. Four years younger than Lincoln, she was by all accounts attractive, intelligent, and lovable. She weighed approximately 120 pounds, stood five feet, three inches tall, and had large blue eyes. Her mother "said she had been noted for three things, her skill with the needle, being a good spinner and a fine cook."[23] She also possessed a kind nature, which one observer described as "angelic," and a modesty that left her "without any of the airs of your City Belles."[24]

Lincoln described Ann as "a handsome girl," "natural and quite intellectual, though not highly educated," who "would have made a good loving wife."[25] He may have been smitten with her when boarding at her father's tavern in 1831, but she was then engaged to the successful merchant John McNamar (who used the alias McNeil), partner of Samuel Hill. The women of New Salem considered McNamar "the catch of the village," for he had accumulated between $10,000 and $12,000 by the time he began courting Ann.[26] But Ann's father disapproved of him, perhaps because he was twelve years Ann's senior, unattractive, and cold. Around the time that Lincoln returned from the Black Hawk War, McNamar left New Salem to fetch his family from New York; he did not return for three years. During that period he wrote to Ann so seldom that she believed he had broken their engagement. Meanwhile, she had moved with her family to Sandridge, a few miles from New Salem. Lincoln began to court her, visiting Sandridge several times a week.

Few details of that courtship survive. Parthena Nance Hill recalled that when McNamar stopped writing to his fiancée, "some of the girls lorded it over Ann who sat at home alone while we other young people walked and visited." Lincoln, who thought highly of Ann and "felt sorry for her," began escorting her on evening walks.[27] When visiting her family, Lincoln would cheerfully, if awkwardly, help Ann with household chores. They also studied together, poring over a copy of *Kirkham's Grammar* that he had given her. Eventually, according to Ann's sister Nancy, "he declared his love and was accepted for she loved him with a more mature and enduring affection than she had ever felt for McNamar. No one could have seen them together and not be convinced that they loved each other truly."[28]

In early 1835, Abe and Ann evidently became engaged but decided to postpone their wedding for a year because she wished to further her education and Lincoln wanted to prepare for the bar. She also desired to wait until she could honorably break her engagement to McNamar. While awaiting McNamar's return, she became sick, probably with typhoid fever, and lingered for several weeks. Lincoln was distraught. One stormy night he braved the foul weather to walk to Sandridge.

En route he stopped at the cabin of Parson John M. Berry, who invited him in. After protesting that he must get to Ann, Lincoln finally accepted Berry's offer to spend the night. Rather than sleeping, he paced the floor for hours and decamped early the next morning.

According to her sister Sarah, Ann "had brain fever and was out of [her] head all the time till about two days before she died, when she came to herself and called for Abe." Bowling Green fetched Lincoln. When he arrived, "everybody left the room and they talked together." Emerging from that room, Lincoln "stopped at the door and looked back. Both of them were crying."[29] Dr. John Allen, who had been attending Ann, took the devastated Lincoln to his house for the night.

Ann's death on August 25, 1835, crushed Lincoln. So grief-stricken was he that many friends worried that he might lose his mind. William G. Greene testified that "after this sudden death of one whom his soul & heart dearly lov[e]d," Lincoln's friends were "compelled to keep watch and ward over Mr Lincoln," for he was "from the sudden shock somewhat temporarily deranged. We watched during storms—fogs—damp gloomy weather Mr Lincoln for fear of an accident. He said 'I can never be reconciled to have the snow—rains & storms to beat on her grave.'"[30] He did not quickly recover. "Long after Anne died," Greene reported, "Abe and I would be alone perhaps in the grocery on a rainy night, and Abe would sit there, his elbows on his knees, his face in his hands, the tears dropping through his fingers."[31] Elizabeth Abell, who witnessed the depth of Lincoln's grief, recalled that "he was staying with us at the time of her death," which "was a great shock to him and I never seen a man mourn for a companion more than he did for her." The "community said he was crazy," she recollected, but "he was not crazy," though "he was very disponding a long time."[32]

In great despair, Lincoln thought of killing himself. Samuel Hill "had to lock him up and keep guard over him for some two weeks . . . for fear he might Commit Suicide." Henry Sears and his wife remembered that Lincoln "strolled around the neighborhood for the next three or four weeks humming sad songs and writing them with chalk on fences and barns. It was generally feared that the death of Ann Rutledge would drive him insane."[33]

This was not the only time Lincoln considered suicide. He told Mentor Graham "that he felt like Committing Suicide often."[34] To Robert L. Wilson he confided "that although he appeared to enjoy life rapturously, Still he was the victim of terrible melancholly. He Sought company, and indulged in fun and hilarity without restraint." Yet, "when by himself, he told me that he was so overcome with mental depression, that he never dared carry a knife in his pocket."[35] On the third anniversary of Ann's death, an unsigned poem about suicide, probably by Lincoln, appeared in the newspaper for which he regularly wrote anonymous pieces.

Decades later, when asked by Isaac Cogdal if he "ran a little wild" after Ann's death, Lincoln replied: "I did really—I run off the track: it was my first. I loved the woman dearly & sacredly: . . . I did honestly—& truly love the girl & think often—often of her now."[36] The depth of Lincoln's sorrow and the severe depression he suffered after her demise were probably a result, at least in part, of his unresolved grief at the death of his mother and siblings. He was unconsciously reminded by Ann's death of those old wounds, which began to suppurate once again, causing him to reexperience "the bitter agony" he had endured as a youth. Such intense depression can lead to suicide, even among young and physically healthy people like Lincoln.

While recuperating from the devastating effect of Ann's death, Lincoln neglected his duties at the post office. He often started out for a destination but returned without having reached it; instead he would wander about, absorbed in his thoughts, recognizing no friends or neighbors. Three weeks after she died, a New Salem resident complained that the "Post Master (Mr. Lincoln) is very careless about leaving his office open & unlocked during the day—half the time I go in & get my papers &c without any one being there as was the case yesterday."[37] Years later, when his friend Joshua Speed suffered from depression, Lincoln suggested an antidote: "avoid being idle; I would immediately engage in some business, or go to make preparations for it."[38]

In the fall of 1835, Lincoln took this cure, focusing on the study of law, which he had begun the previous summer. By December he had managed to pull himself together enough to attend a special session of the legislature that the governor had called to modify the Illinois and Michigan Canal Act and to reapportion the General Assembly. During his six weeks in Vandalia, Lincoln won approval for the incorporation of the Beardstown and Sangamon Canal Company, a pet project of his. He bought stock in that corporation and at a public meeting urged others to do so; he even purchased land on the Sangamon a mile from the eastern terminus of the proposed canal, which was never dug.

During the 1835–36 special session of the General Assembly, Lincoln answered all but 11 of the 130 roll calls. He spent three days writing the report of the Committee on Public Accounts and Expenditures. By supporting the state bank and the canal, he remained true to his Whig principles. His most important contribution was the steadfast encouragement he gave to the Illinois and Michigan Canal, which was begun in 1836 and completed twelve years later.

Sophomore Legislator

In June 1836, two months after the Ninth General Assembly adjourned, Lincoln announced that he would stand for reelection in a campaign statement far more breezy and succinct than the one he had issued four years earlier. He began by stating, "I go for all sharing the privileges of the government, who assist in bearing its burthens. Consequently I go for admitting all whites to the right of suffrage, who pay taxes or bear arms, (by no means excluding females.)"[39] This was rather startling, not only because the Illinois Constitution placed no property or militia-service qualifications on adult White male suffrage but also because it made no provision of any kind for female suffrage.

At that time, the exclusion of Blacks from the franchise was hardly controversial in Illinois, a state full of Southerners devoted to White supremacy. Indeed, hostility to Black voting prevailed throughout the Old Northwest. The Illinois constitution of 1818 limited voting rights to "white male inhabitants" at least 21 years of age. Membership in the militia was open to "free male ablebodied persons, negroes, mulattoes, and Indians excepted." Between 1819 and 1846, the General Assembly outlawed interracial marriage and cohabitation, forbade Blacks to testify in court against Whites, and denied them the right to attend public schools. In 1848, the Illinois electorate adopted a new constitution banning Black suffrage and prohibiting Black immigration. With that, Illinois became the only Free State forbidding Blacks to settle within its borders. (Oregon and Indiana soon followed suit.)

Lincoln's suggestion that women be enfranchised, however, was hardly a campaign cliché. His proto-feminist endorsement of women's suffrage may have been inspired by participation in debating and literary societies that addressed that question. At a meeting of such an organization in Springfield, he contributed some verses about the sexual double standard:

> Whatever spiteful fools may say,
> Each jealous ranting yelper,
> No woman ever went astray
> Without a man to help her.[40]

Lincoln's support for women's suffrage and his opposition to the sexual double standard reflected his sense of fair play, the bedrock of his political philosophy.

Throughout his life, Lincoln took strong measures against men who physically harmed women. In 1839, he warned a hard-drinking Springfield cobbler to stop abusing his spouse. When this admonition went unheeded, Lincoln and some friends became vigilantes, as one of them later remembered: "It was late at night and we dragged the wretch to an open space back of a store building, stripped him of his shirt and tied him to a post. Then we sent for his wife, and arming her with a good stout switch bade her to 'light in.'" She was "a little reluctant at first" but "soon warmed up to her work, and emboldened by our encouraging and sometimes peremptory directions, performed her delicate task lustily and well. When the culprit had been sufficiently punished, Lincoln gave the signal 'Enough,' and he was released; we helped him on with his shirt and he shambled ruefully toward his home."[41]

In the public letter announcing his candidacy for reelection in 1836, Lincoln also promised that as a legislator he would be guided by the wishes of his constituents insofar as he knew what those wishes were and otherwise by his own judgment. The only policy issue he addressed was internal improvements, which he said should be funded by proceeds from the sale of federal lands rather than by state taxes and borrowing.

During the campaigns of 1832 and 1834, Lincoln had been reserved and stumped only in rural areas. In 1836 he grew bolder and spoke in towns as well as villages, winning the respect of friends and the fear of opponents. One legislative colleague said that "he was the best versed and most captivating and trenchant speaker" for the Whigs and that he "used the weapons of sarcasm and ridicule, and always prevailed."[42] His new style made him the leading Whig of the district. On the stump he almost always kept his temper; a week after he declared his candidacy, however, he found it difficult to do so. When Colonel Robert Allen, a prominent Democrat known as a dishonest blowhard, told New Salemites that he could destroy the young politician by revealing information that he had but would forbear releasing, Lincoln charged that Allen would be "a traitor to his country's interest" if he refused to make public his supposedly damaging facts.[43] Later in the campaign, Lincoln called an anonymous critic "a liar and a scoundrel" and threatened "to give his proboscis a good wringing."[44]

When angry, Lincoln often resorted to ridicule. In July, at a Springfield event, he "skinned" Richard Quinton, and at a meeting in Mechanicsburg he "peeled" another Democrat. Such tactics could be dangerous, for violence was not unknown in Illinois politics. What Lincoln said as he "peeled" and "skinned" his victims is unrecorded, but he was almost certainly the author of many abusive, insulting, heavy-handed anonymous and pseudonymous attacks on Democrats that appeared in the *Sangamo Journal*. In 1835 and 1836, that Whig paper ran satirical letters ostensibly written by prominent Democrats, making their authors look ridiculous. In all likelihood, Lincoln wrote them, and they shed harsh light on the politics of that time and place.

Some of the satirical letters focused on voting rights for Blacks. Vice President Martin Van Buren, then running for president, had endorsed limited suffrage for free Blacks in New York fifteen years earlier. To embarrass Van Buren and his supporters, Whigs in the 1835–36 special session of the Illinois legislature introduced a resolution condemning several Democratic policies, slyly including as one of them, "Colored persons ought not to be admitted to the right of suffrage." When, as expected, the Democrats voted against that omnibus resolution, Whigs, including Lincoln, taunted them for implicitly endorsing Black voting rights. The *Sangamo Journal* protested that Illinois "is threatened to be overrun with free negroes" and suggested that such undesirables be sent to Van Buren's home state of New York. As election day drew near in 1836, the *Journal* asked: "If Mr. Van Buren be made the president, is it not reasonable to suppose that before his term of service expires, free negro suffrage will prevail throughout the nation? . . . If these men be elected, how long before poor white girls will become the waiting maids of sooty wenches? How long before we shall have a negro president?"[45]

When not engaged in race baiting, Lincoln condemned the Democrats' newly established convention system, which Ebenezer Peck and Stephen A. Douglas had introduced in December 1835. Previously any Democrat who wished to run for office had simply announced his intention and entered the race; now candidates must win endorsement at a nominating convention. Lincoln called adherents of this innovation "slaves of the magician [Van Buren]" and "eastern trading politicians," whereas Democrats opposing it were men "born and raised west of the mountains" and "south of the Potomac."[46]

Lincoln assailed members of the "Monster party" for delaying construction of the Illinois and Michigan Canal until they could vest the legislature with the power to appoint canal commissioners. He caustically observed that "there are men hanging on here who are bankrupt in principle, business habits, and every thing else who have the promises of these offices as soon as they shall be made elective."[47] He referred to Democratic supporters of Van Buren as "ruffle-shirted Vannies" and "locofocos," a derogatory term originally applied to the most radical faction of the party, which was accused of abandoning Jeffersonian and Jacksonian principles. When opponents denounced that tactic, Lincoln responded with a story about a farmer who captured a skunk in his henhouse. Reacting to the varmint's insistence that he was no polecat, the farmer remarked: "You look like a polecat, . . . act like one, smell like one and you are one, by God, and I'll kill you, innocent & friendly to me as you say you are." The locofocos, Lincoln continued, "'claim to be true democrats, but they are only locofocos—they look like locofocos, . . . act like locofocos,' and turning up his nose and backing away a little . . . as if the smell was about to smother him, 'are locofocos by God.'" Members of the audience "nearly bursted their sides laughing."[48]

In the 1836 campaign, Lincoln emerged as a prominent and effective Whig spokesman. One of his fellow Whig candidates for the legislature, Robert L. Wilson, praised him for "manifesting Skill and tact in offensive and defensive debates, presenting his arguments with great force and ability, and boldly attacking the questions and positions taken by opposing Candidates."[49] On August 1, he handily won reelection, finishing first in a field of seventeen. In New Salem he ran well ahead of the victorious Whig ticket. Lincoln was among the few veteran members of the enlarged and reapportioned legislature; of the ninety-one members (thirty-six more than in its immediate predecessor) fewer than a quarter were incumbents. During the 1836–37 session, Lincoln became the leading Whig in the house, where he regularly squelched Democrats with clever stories. Robert L. Wilson thought him "a natural debater" who "was always ready and always got right down to the merits of his case, without any nonsense or circumlocution." To Wilson, Lincoln "seemed to glide along in life without any friction or effort."[50]

In fact, Lincoln was not exactly gliding along. Shortly after the General Assembly convened, he wrote from Vandalia to a friend: "My spirits [are] so low, that I feel I would rather be any place in the world than here. I really can not endure the thought of staying here ten weeks."[51] Downcast or not, Lincoln gathered himself in time to help shape important legislation. He championed the state bank with special vehemence. On January 11, 1837, he defended that institution against an attack by Democrat Usher F. Linder. Sarcastically acknowledging that Linder was his superior in "the faculty of entangling a subject, so that neither himself, or any other man, can find head or tail to it," Lincoln dismissed his opponent's arguments as "silly" and harshly declared that if Linder were unaware of Illinois's usury statute, "he is too ignorant to be placed at the head of the committee which his resolution proposes." Lincoln went on to denounce "capitalists," who "generally act harmoniously, and in concert, to fleece the people," and politicians, "a set of men who . . . are, taken as a mass, at least one long step removed from honest men."[52]

Lincoln's speech rested on the sound notion that economic growth required banks and an elastic money supply. His political opponents, with their agrarian fondness for a metallic currency, failed to understand this fundamental point. Banks, he knew, had a vital role to play in financing the canals and railroads essential for ending rural isolation and backwardness, a goal he cared about passionately. In addition, he wanted to protect the assets earned by ordinary people by the sweat of their brows; he predicted that the destruction of the bank would "annihilate the currency of the State" and thus "render valueless in the hands of our people that reward of their former labors."[53] Banks also allowed the "honest, industrious and virtuous" poor to get ahead through loans. Without internal improvements and banks, argued the *Sangamo Journal*, the poor would remain "hewers of wood and drawers of water" for the rich "as long as they live." By making credit difficult to obtain, the Democrats forced the "industrious poor" to accumulate capital on their own before starting a business, a process that might take decades.

The Whigs, by making the surplus capital of the rich available through banks, aimed to expand economic opportunity for the poor.[54]

Lincoln's chief goal in the winter of 1836–37 was to have Springfield chosen as the new state capital. Vandalia's claim to that honor expired in 1839 and was not likely to be continued, for the town seemed inadequate and too remote. Moreover, critics protested, it not only offered inferior lodgings and food but was also notorious for its lawlessness. Many towns aspired to become the new state capital. In an 1834 statewide referendum on relocating the seat of government, Alton had received 7,511 votes; Vandalia, 7,148; and Springfield, 7,044. Three years later, Lincoln led the Springfield forces in the legislature even though he was the youngest of the nine members from Sangamon County. That delegation, made up of men whose average height was slightly over six feet, was contemptuously labeled by the Springfield *Republican* "the Long Nine," after a type of cheap cigar. To win support for Springfield, Lincoln and his colleagues did what legislators usually do: they cut deals. In 1839, David Davis described the legislature's "barter, trade & intrigue—'You vote for my measure, & I will vote for yours.'"[55] In the first session of the General Assembly held in the new capitol, a journalist reported: "Log rolling is now in most successful operation; and that party which understands the art of *buying* and *selling* votes the best will succeed."[56]

Under Lincoln's direction, the Long Nine promised to support various internal improvements throughout the state in return for endorsement of Springfield's aspirations. Since Sangamon County's delegation was the largest in the General Assembly, it had significant leverage when its members voted as a bloc. While legislative business was grinding along in December and January, the Long Nine relentlessly accumulated friends by promising support for internal-improvement projects tailored to needs of each county. It was difficult work, and progress came hard. As Lincoln remarked later, the subject of internal improvements was fraught with problems because it was impossible to please everyone: "One man is offended because a road passes over his land, and another is offended because it does not pass over his."[57]

On December 13, 1836, a serious threat confronted the Long Nine when John Taylor of Springfield submitted a petition to divide Sangamon County. Taylor and his lieutenant, John Calhoun, had speculated in land that they hoped would become county seats and thus appreciate in value. In addition, Taylor and others had bought up acreage at the geographical center of the state, a locale they named Illiopolis, and hoped to make the capital. Lincoln, not wanting to see the delegation reduced in size while it was seeking votes for Springfield, adopted delaying tactics, urging that the question be postponed until Springfield had achieved its goal. When signatures on a petition favoring division of the county proved fraudulent, the measure failed. In late January 1837, another attempt to divide the county was condemned at a mass meeting in Springfield. Soon thereafter that city's champions submitted a remonstrance bearing more signatures than the original petition, thus killing the proposal.

At one point in the long, tedious process Lincoln succumbed to despair. Jesse K. Dubois, a fellow legislator who became Lincoln's neighbor and good friend, recalled that he "came to my room one evening and told me that he was whipped—that his career was ended—that he had traded off everything he could dispose of, and still had not got strength enough to locate the seat of government at Springfield." Yet, he said, "I cant go home without passing that bill. My folks expect that of me, and that I cant do—and I am finished forever."[58] In "these dark hours," Lincoln "collect[ed] his Colleagues to his room for consultation" and with them developed a plan.[59] Somehow he managed to rally his troops. The bill to move the capital to Springfield won approval on February 28. Its passage "was felt to be one of the greatest of political triumphs, and its credit was freely ascribed to Lincoln." Robert L. Wilson said flatly that "had Lincoln not been there, it would have failed."[60]

Lincoln's most important maneuver may have been an amendment he offered stipulating that the legislature "reserves the right to repeal this act at any time hereafter."[61] This tautological measure won over the support of four legislators who had previously been in opposition. As amended, the bill was adopted that same day, facilitating Springfield's victory. Helping expedite that choice was another amendment suggested by Lincoln, one requiring the town selected as the capital to donate two acres of land and pay fifty thousand dollars to help cover the cost of a new statehouse. This measure, which virtually eliminated the smaller towns from competition, passed 53–26.

The internal-improvements bill and the transfer of the capital to Springfield had lasting implications, not all of them salutary. Most of the men appointed to the board of public works were "party leaders who had never been conspicuous for any thing but their blind devotion to the dominant party." None "had the least experience in the important duties assigned them," but because "they had done something for 'the party,'" they "had to be provided for, and if they knew nothing else, they knew that they got good salaries, and that was of course satisfactory."[62] A case in point was the Democrat John A. McClernand, who broke with his party to support the measure and as a reward was named treasurer of the Illinois and Michigan Canal.

Lincoln acknowledged openly that he had engaged in logrolling, and his sense of honor demanded that the commitments he and others had made be respected. Unfortunately, the internal-improvements scheme was far too ambitious for the meager resources of the new state and was therefore doomed to fail. Indeed, the bargain crafted by Lincoln wound up benefiting Springfield at the expense of Illinois. Governor Thomas Ford called the internal improvements scheme "the most senseless and disastrous policy which ever crippled the energies of a growing country." In 1832, Lincoln had sensibly warned voters about the "heart-appalling" costs of railroads and canals. Four years later he cavalierly ignored his own good counsel and helped saddle Illinois with a $14 million system of internal improvements that its population of five hundred thousand could ill afford. Among the approved projects were laying thirteen hundred miles of railroad tracks, deepening the channels of five rivers, constructing a mail route from Vincennes to St. Louis, and awarding $200,000 to compensate the counties through which neither a canal nor a railroad would pass. The interest on the necessary loans exceeded the entire revenue raised by the state in 1836. When the economy collapsed in 1837, any slight chance that the state could pay for the many projects went glimmering. Illinois suspended interest payments on its debt, and for years thereafter its credit rating was poor and its treasury strapped. The state "became a stench in the nostrils of the civilized world."[63] Illinois did not finally pay off the loans incurred for the internal improvements until 1880.

When at the same session the General Assembly voted to increase its members' pay from three dollars per day to four, protests deluged the statehouse. One indignant constituent, "a blunt, hard-working yeoman," berated Lincoln, for he "could and would not understand why men should be paid four dollars per day for 'doing nothing but talking and sitting on benches,' while he averaged only about one [dollar] for the hardest kind of work." To his angry question "What in the world made you do it?" Lincoln replied: "I reckon the only reason was that we wanted the money."[64] In addition to passing the internal-improvements bill, the statute removing the capital to Springfield, and the pay hike, the legislature continued its routine work of incorporating businesses, schools, and towns; authorizing roads and declaring streams navigable; and defining the boundaries of counties. Lincoln participated in these matters, answering all but 17 of the 220 roll calls taken during the first session of the Tenth General Assembly.

Between the time that he declared his candidacy in 1832 and his triumph as the champion of Springfield's bid to become the state capital in 1837, Lincoln had become an adept partisan, renowned for logrolling and scourging Democrats, but little more. The day before the General Assembly adjourned, however, he took a step that foreshadowed the statesmanship of his later career. On March 3, 1837, he and another member of the Long Nine, Dan Stone, filed a protest against antiabolitionist resolutions that the legislature had adopted six weeks earlier by the lopsided vote of 77–6 in the house and 18–0 in the senate. Lincoln and Stone were part of the tiny minority who opposed the resolutions. The overwhelmingly popular resolutions had been introduced at the behest of Southern state legislatures outraged by the American Anti-Slavery Society's pamphlets depicting slave owners as cruel brutes. Equally objectionable in the legislators' eyes was the society's massive petition drive calling for the abolition of slavery in the District of Columbia. The resolutions that the Illinois General Assembly passed declared that its members "highly disapprove of the formation of abolition societies, and of the doctrines promulgated by them," that "the right of property in slaves is sacred to the slave-holding States by the Federal Government, and that they cannot be deprived of that right without their consent," and that "the General Government cannot abolish slavery in the District of Columbia, against the will of the citizens of said District."[65]

Lincoln wrote a protest against these resolutions and circulated it among his colleagues. None would sign except Stone, a native of Vermont who was not seeking reelection (he would soon become a judge). Lincoln declared in the document, which he and Stone entered into the journal of the house of representatives, "that the institution of slavery is founded on both injustice and bad policy"—a remarkably bold gesture for 1837, when antislavery views enjoyed little popularity anywhere in the Midwest. Several months after Lincoln and Stone issued their protest, the governor of Illinois, Joseph Duncan, speaking for the clear majority of his constituents, denounced all "wicked and sinful" efforts "to agitate the question of abolishing slavery in this country, for it can never be broached without producing violence and discord," even in the Free States.[66] Seven months after the Lincoln-Stone protest, Springfield residents publicly condemned abolitionism. While the Presbyterian synod was meeting there, citizens banded together to disrupt the proposed delivery of an antislavery sermon. Mob violence was averted, but some townspeople met on October 23 and adopted the following resolutions: "the doctrine of immediate emancipation in this country, (although promulgated by those who profess to be christians,) is at variance with christianity, and its tendency is to breed contention, broils and mobs, and the leaders of those calling themselves abolitionists are designing, ambitious men, and dangerous members of society, and should be shunned by all good citizens."[67] Simeon Francis's newspaper rejoiced "that public opinion in the frontier states is likely to check at once the perfidy of these fanatical men [abolitionists]."[68]

Francis was right; the antislavery movement had difficulty taking root in Illinois. An Urbana newspaper observed that *abolition* is "considered synonymous with treason, . . . disunion, civil war, anarchy and every horror [of] which an American can conceive."[69] From 1817 to 1824, some Illinoisans had waged a successful battle against the introduction of slavery into their state constitution, but thereafter enthusiasm for the antislavery cause dramatically waned. Before 1837, only one county in the state—Putnam—had an auxiliary of the American Anti-Slavery

Society. Simeon Francis noted that *abolitionist* "is an odious epithet among us; and we do not believe that there are a dozen men to be found in Sangamon county to whom it can be properly applied."[70]

In such a region at such a time, Lincoln could scarcely expect criticism of slavery, even that which stopped short of abolitionism, to win him popularity. Yet he clearly had come to loathe slavery by 1837. Two decades later he said that "I have always hated slavery, I think as much as any Abolitionist." He had not emphasized the slavery issue before 1854, he explained, because until then support for the peculiar institution had seemed to be ebbing. In 1858, he said that "the slavery question often bothered me as far back as 1836–1840. I was troubled and grieved over it."[71] A friend remembered that in 1837 a man had asked Lincoln "if he was an abolitionist. Mr. Lincoln in reply, reached over and laid his hand on the shoulder of Mr. [Thomas] Alsopp who was a strong abolitionist and said, 'I am mighty near one.'"[72] In 1860, Lincoln stated that the protest he and Stone had issued in 1837 "briefly defined his position on the slavery question; and so far as it goes, it was then the same that it is now."[73]

Lincoln and Stone, while condemning slavery, also criticized abolitionists, asserting that "the promulgation of abolition doctrines tends rather to increase than to abate its [slavery's] evils." In this, they faintly echoed the committee report to which they were objecting. That document asserted that abolitionists "have forged new irons for the black man," have "added an hundred fold to the rigors of slavery," have "scattered the fire brands of discord and disunion," and have "aroused the turbulent passions of the monster mob." The committee could not "conceive how any true friend of the black man can hope to benefit him through the instrumentality of abolition societies."[74] This view that uncompromising abolitionism was detrimental to the true welfare of slaves was common, even among foes of slavery. Elijah P. Lovejoy, the antislavery editor who would die a martyr's death at Alton, Illinois, in 1837, had three years earlier denounced abolitionists as "the worst enemies the poor slaves have" and charged that their efforts were "riveting the chains they seek to break."[75]

Abolitionists' tactics and rhetoric could be inflammatory as they pursued what they termed "the duty to rebuke which every inhabitant of the Free States owes to every slaveholder."[76] To critics of his approach, William Lloyd Garrison said in the famous lead editorial of his Boston newspaper, *The Liberator*, "I am aware that many object to the severity of my language; but is there not cause for severity? I *will be* as harsh as truth, and as uncompromising as justice. On this subject, I do not wish to think, or speak, or write, with moderation."[77]

Such an approach to reform was diametrically opposed to Lincoln's. In a temperance address delivered in 1842, he criticized hectoring crusaders: "It is an old and true maxim, that a 'drop of honey catches more flies than a gallon of gall.' So with men. If you would win a man to your cause, first convince him that you are his sincere friend." Previous temperance efforts had failed, Lincoln said, because they were led by "Preachers, Lawyers, and hired agents" whose lack of "approachability" had proved "fatal to their success." They "are supposed to have no sympathy of feeling or interest, with those persons whom it is their object to convince and persuade." They had indulged in "too much denunciation against dram sellers and dram drinkers," a strategy that had proved "impolitic, because, it is not much in the nature of man to be driven to any thing; still less to be driven about that which is exclusively his own business; and least of all, where such driving is to be submitted to, at the expense of pecuniary interest, or burning appetite." To expect denunciation to bring about reform "was to expect a reversal of human nature. . . . When the conduct of men is designed to be influenced, persuasion, kind, unassuming persuasion, should ever be adopted." He doubtless felt the same way about those abolitionists whose vituperative, intolerant style alienated potential recruits to their worthy cause. In fact, Lincoln may have been trying to persuade abolitionists to exercise more tact. Clearly the abolition of slavery was on his mind, for in the peroration of his temperance address appeared a seeming non sequitur: "When the victory shall be complete—when there shall be neither a slave nor a drunkard on the earth—how proud the title of that Land, which may truly claim to be the birth-place and cradle of both those revolutions, that shall have ended in that victory."[78]

The Lincoln-Stone protest further declared that "the Congress of the United States has the power, under the constitution, to abolish slavery in the District of Columbia; but that power ought not to be exercised unless at the request of the people of said District." Lincoln had unsuccessfully tried to amend the original resolution to permit abolition in the District "if the people of said District petition for same." (Twelve years later, as a member of Congress, he would frame legislation to rid the District of slavery with such consent.) Unlike the committee report to which Lincoln and Stone responded, their protest clearly asserted that the Constitution empowered Congress to abolish slavery in the District, a question that was hotly debated at the time and became a litmus test for distinguishing the friends of slavery from its foes.

The boldness of the Lincoln-Stone protest is notable but uncharacteristic of Lincoln in his twenties and thirties. When in March 1837 he moved to Springfield from the dying hamlet of New Salem, he was essentially a clever partisan whose promise of future statesmanship would long remain unfulfilled.

5.

"We Must Fight the Devil with Fire"

Slasher-Gaff Politico in Springfield (1837–1841)

Lincoln began his new life as a lawyer and legislator in the "straggling" and "irregular village" of Springfield (population 1,300), which visitors described as "a very unattractive, sickly, unenterprising town." In the 1830s its dirty, dusty, unpaved streets and sidewalks were flanked by log cabins and shabbily constructed frame houses. The city's mud was notorious. When wet, the black loam of central Illinois became knee-deep "prairie gumbo," rendering the sidewalks, such as they were, impassable. The streets were even worse; in foul weather they "approached the condition of a quagmire with dangerous sink-holes where the boatmen's phrase 'no bottom' furnished the only description." Garbage and refuse made the muddy streets even more repellant. They became "the dumping ground for the community rubbish so that the gutters were filled with manure, discarded clothing and all kinds of trash, threatening the public health with their noxious effluvium." Roaming livestock compounded matters. Throughout the antebellum period, hogs and cattle moved freely throughout the town.[1] When the summer sun beat down on privies, sinkholes, stables, abattoirs, and the like, the stench became overwhelming.

Springfield's business structures were arranged haphazardly and slapped together in the cheapest possible manner. Its hotels and livery stables were few in number, small, badly managed, and expensive. Its stores were meagerly stocked, and the concert hall was so dirty and shabby that renowned soprano Adelina Patti refused to sing there after she had taken the stage and beheld its appearance. The capitol was considered an eyesore, with an interior that impressed one visitor as "the most shabby, forlorn, dirty, dilapidated specimen of a public edifice which we have ever seen."[2]

Lincoln enjoyed telling a story about Springfield that he had heard from his friend Jesse K. Dubois, the Illinois state auditor. In that capacity, Dubois had once been asked by an "itinerant quack preacher" for permission to use the Hall of Representatives for a religious lecture. When Dubois had inquired what it was about, the minister replied, "The second coming of Christ." "Nonsense," the auditor had retorted. "If Christ had been to Springfield once, and got away, he'd be damned clear of coming again."[3]

Settling Down in Springfield

A few weeks after moving from New Salem to the new capital-designate, Lincoln gloomily confided to a friend that "living in Springfield is rather a dull business after all, at least it is so to me. I am quite as lonesome here as [I] ever was anywhere in my life." Beyond the drawbacks of Springfield itself, he felt embarrassed about his poverty. Calling the town a "busy wilderness," he noted that there was "a great deal of flourishing about in carriages," a form of transportation that he could not afford because of his debts.[4] Allegedly Lincoln was so depressed at that time that he told friends that he "wished he never saw the light of day."[5]

He may have been lonesome for female companionship, but kind male friends helped Lincoln settle in Springfield. One of them, William Butler, recalled that as he, Lincoln, and two others rode to the town from Vandalia after the legislative session in March 1837, they "stopped overnight down here at Henderson's Point, and all slept on the floor. We were tired, and the rest slept pretty well." Butler noticed, however, "that Lincoln was uneasy, turning over and thinking, and studying, so much so that he kept me awake."

Finally Butler asked, "Lincoln what is the matter with you?"

"Well," came the reply, "I will tell you. All the rest of you have something to look forward to, and all are glad to get home, and will have something to do when you get there. But it isn't so with me. I am going home, Butler, without a thing in the world. I have drawn all my pay I got at Vandalia, and have spent it all. I am in debt— . . . and I have nothing to pay the debt with, and no way to make any money. I dont know what to do."

When they reached Springfield, Butler sold Lincoln's horse "without saying anything to him," paid off his debts, and took the saddlebags to his home, where his wife washed the clothes they contained. When Lincoln learned that Butler had disposed of his horse, he "was greatly astonished" and asked, "What in the world did you do that for?"[6] For the next five years Lincoln took his meals, without charge, at Butler's home, a large boardinghouse. Butler may have been prompted by Ninian W. Edwards, who considered the impoverished newcomer a promising young man who, with a little help, might flourish. Butler was probably grateful to Lincoln for his recent successful effort to have Springfield named the state's capital.

Equally generous assistance was proffered by the Kentucky-born merchant Joshua F. Speed, who became Lincoln's closest friend. Speed remembered that Lincoln rode into town "with no earthly goods but a pair of saddle-bags, two or three law books, and some clothing which he had in his saddle-bags. He took an office, and engaged from the only cabinet-maker then in the village, a single bedstead." Lincoln asked Speed, a silent partner in the general merchandise store James Bell & Company, how much he would have to pay to furnish the bed. When the young businessman, nearly five years Lincoln's junior, calculated that a mattress, blankets, pillow, sheets, and coverlid would cost seventeen dollars, Lincoln replied: "It is probably cheap enough: but I want to say that, cheap as it is, I have not the money to pay. But if you will credit me until Christmas, and my experiment here as a lawyer is a success, I will pay you then. If I fail in that I will probably never be able to pay you back at all." Speed reported that the "tone of his voice was so melancholy that I felt for him."

"The contraction of so small a debt seems to affect you so deeply," Speed remarked, "I think I can suggest a plan by which you will be able to attain your end, without incurring any debt. I have a very large room, and a very large double-bed in it; which you are perfectly welcome to share with me if you choose." He explained that "my partner and I have been sleeping in the same bed for some time. He is gone now, and if you wish, you can take his place." After inspecting the room above the store, Lincoln, "with a face beaming with pleasure," said, "Well, Speed, I'm moved."[7] From 1837 to 1841 Lincoln bunked with Speed in the room above the store, where Speed's clerks, William H. Herndon and Charles R. Hurst, also slept. There was no partition and hence no privacy. Such sleeping arrangements were not uncommon in frontier Illinois.

Neophyte Lawyer

The generosity that Speed and Butler extended to Lincoln was matched by John Todd Stuart, his law partner. On September 9, 1836, the justices of the Illinois Supreme Court licensed the young attorney to practice throughout the state. Seven months later, he moved to Springfield, where in April the firm of Stuart and Lincoln was formally established in a small, second-floor office near the town square.

Most of Stuart and Lincoln's business involved debts in one form or another, though the two men also dealt with various matters in the criminal, common, and chancery branches of the law. Many of the cases were of small importance, challenging Lincoln to determine who owned a litter of pigs or who was responsible for the death of sheep owing to foot rot. Lincoln and Stuart could not make ends meet if they confined their practice to Springfield, so like most of their colleagues at the bar, they rode the First Judicial Circuit, encompassing ten counties. In 1839, when Sangamon County was included in the newly created Eighth Judicial Circuit, Lincoln traveled its nine counties but did the bulk of the firm's work in Sangamon, Tazewell, Logan, and McLean.

Lincoln handled much of the business of the firm, for politics monopolized Stuart's attention. Lincoln's first law case, *Hawthorn v. Wooldridge*, which began in 1836, involved a farmer charged with trespass and breach of contract. David Woolridge, Lincoln's client, allegedly "assaulted, struck, beat, bruised and knocked down" James Hawthorn.[8] The case, involving three separate actions, was argued before a jury, which awarded Hawthorn damages of thirty-six dollars and costs. The other two actions were settled out of court, with Hawthorn paying the costs of one and Woolridge those of the other. No record indicates how the settlement was reached, but Lincoln may well have urged the parties to compromise. Years later he advised lawyers to "discourage litigation" and to "persuade your neighbors to compromise whenever you can. Point out to them how the nominal winner is often a real loser—in fees, expenses, and waste of time. As a peacemaker the lawyer has a superior opportunity of being a good man."[9]

Lincoln and Stuart usually charged five to ten dollars for their services, dividing those modest fees equally. The only large sum they received was five hundred dollars for a sensational murder trial in 1838.

Special Legislative Session

In July 1837, Governor Joseph Duncan summoned the legislature for a special session to address the consequences of the financial panic that had struck that spring, drying up the market for Illinois bonds. The state bank was in danger of losing its charter, a development that might delay construction of the Illinois and Michigan Canal. In response to this crisis, Duncan recommended that the legislature scrap the internal-improvements scheme it had passed earlier that year.

Ignoring this advice, the General Assembly first turned its attention to a bill repealing the other major piece of legislation passed at the last session, the capital-removal statute. The champion of repeal, William L. D. Ewing, an able, ambitious, conceited politico, denounced "the arrogance of Springfield," maintaining that "its presumption in claiming the seat of government—was not to be endured." To respond, the Whigs chose Lincoln, who "retorted upon Ewing with great severity; denouncing his insinuations in imputing corruption to him and his colleagues, and paying back with usury all that Ewing had said." Onlookers feared that Lincoln "was digging his own grave; for it was known that Ewing would not quietly pocket any insinuations that would degrade him personally." Ewing then asked the Sangamon County delegation: "Gentlemen, have you no other champion than this coarse and vulgar fellow to bring into the lists against me? Do you suppose that I will condescend to break a lance with your low and obscure colleague?" Observers expected that Ewing might issue a formal challenge, but cooler heads prevailed and no duel took place. Ewing's bill was referred to a special committee, chaired by Lincoln, who amended it to have Springfield pay the fifty thousand dollars it had pledged before work could begin on the statehouse. The measure as amended passed in the house but died in the senate.

In the short 1837 session, the General Assembly bristled with hostility toward banks because of the financial panic. With the help of some Democrats, Lincoln and his fellow Whigs thwarted attempts to repeal the 1835 charter of the Bank of Illinois. Under that law, if the bank suspended specie payments (redemption of its notes in gold and silver on demand) for more than sixty days, it must disband. The bank did suspend such payments on May 27, 1837, in response to the financial panic. The Whigs managed to persuade the General Assembly to allow the bank to continue operations temporarily.

Politics, 1838–1840

In the following year's election campaign, the county-division issue dominated Sangamon County politics, with the Democrats favoring the proposed change and the Whigs opposing it. Lincoln went to work in the press. Writing from "Lost Townships," an author signing himself "Rusticus"—probably Lincoln—attacked the proposal in a series of articles in the *Sangamo Journal.* In one, Rusticus denounced the editor of Springfield's *Illinois Republican* for plotting "to benefit certain speculators who own town lots in Allenton, Pulaski and Petersburg" and "to gratify a few men who want offices."[10]

In 1838, Lincoln campaigned not only for his own reelection but also for his law partner, John Todd Stuart, who tried once again to win the congressional seat he had unsuccessfully sought two years earlier. The hard times, widely blamed on the Democratic administration in Washington, improved Whig chances and aroused the public to pay closer attention than usual to politics. Lincoln attacked Stuart's opponent, Stephen A. Douglas, in letters by "A Conservative," which the *Sangamo Journal* ran in January and February 1838. In one of these missives, Lincoln called Douglas a radical, accused him of striking a corrupt bargain to win his nomination, and mocked him as a "towering genius" who had at the age of twenty-four achieved greater fame than Napoleon at that stage of his career and also as a man destined to become president who might deign to serve a term in Congress as a preliminary step on the road to the White House.

Douglas furiously denied the charges and condemned the "vindictive, fiendish spirit" of Conservative. With some justice, he protested that "my *private* and *moral,* as well as public and political character [has] been assailed in a manner calculated to destroy my standing as a man and a citizen."[11]

The day that Lincoln's satirical belittling of Douglas appeared in the *Sangamo Journal,* he delivered a significant speech to the Young Men's Lyceum in Springfield titled "The Perpetuation of Our Political Institutions." In this address, Lincoln added his voice to the Illinois Whig chorus denouncing the upsurge in mob violence and also struck a blow against Douglas. He warned that a new Caesar, someone "of ambition and talents," would ruthlessly pursue fame and power while overthrowing democratic institutions to achieve his ends. "Many great and good men sufficiently qualified for any task they should undertake, may ever be found, whose ambition would aspire to nothing beyond a seat in Congress, a gubernatorial or a presidential chair; *but such belong not to the family of the lion, or the tribe of the eagle.*" Rhetorically, Lincoln asked if such a person would be content to follow traditional paths to distinction, then answered, "What! think you these places would satisfy an Alexander, a Caesar, or a Napoleon? Never! Towering genius disdains a beaten path." Clearly, the "towering genius" who was compared to Caesar and Napoleon was Douglas. (This was probably a slighting reference to Douglas's diminutive stature—he stood five feet, four inches).[12] Since the rules of the Lyceum forbade political speeches, Lincoln could not directly attack Douglas, but because his audience was doubtless aware of Conservative's letter in that day's paper, he could assume that they understood that Douglas was the target of his remarks. It was a clever maneuver to circumvent the ban on partisanship at the Lyceum.

The speech could be construed as an attack not only on Douglas but also on the Democratic Party, which Whigs denounced for championing "mobocracy."[13] With some justice, this florid address was criticized as "highly sophomoric in character" and a prime example of "'spread eagle' and vapid oratory."[14] The moral Lincoln drew from his survey of recent mob violence in Mississippi, Missouri, and Illinois was that "every American, every lover of liberty, every well wisher to his posterity" should "swear by the blood of the Revolution never to violate in the least particular, the laws of the country; and never to tolerate their violation by others." He portrayed reverence for the law as the "political religion" of the nation.[15]

Beneath the surface, Lincoln's address constituted a bold commentary on slavery and race, couched so as to give little offense but nevertheless to prick the conscience of his audience. In part, the speech was inspired by the recent murder of the abolitionist Elijah P. Lovejoy, whom Missouri slaveholders had driven from their state. When Lovejoy had transferred operations from St. Louis to Alton, Illinois, he encountered an even more hostile reception. Mobs twice destroyed his printing presses, dumping them into the Mississippi River. On November 7, 1837, as he brandished firearms in an attempt to protect yet another press from mob violence, he was killed. His death aroused indignation throughout the North, where he was regarded as a martyr to freedom of expression.

In the Lyceum speech, Lincoln, who several months earlier had denounced slavery as an institution based on "injustice and bad policy," clearly alluded to Lovejoy's murder in a passage condemning mobs that "throw printing presses into rivers" and "shoot editors." Lincoln's central theme was the danger that mob violence posed to democracy. Although the speech did not mention Lovejoy by name, its application to his murder was obvious. Lincoln's audience might also have been reminded of the Springfield mob that had forced the cancellation of an abolitionist sermon the previous October.

If it took courage in the Springfield of 1838 to express sympathy for an abolitionist like Lovejoy, it took even more nerve to speak compassionately of a Black man who in April 1836 had stabbed two White men. Lincoln nonetheless did so, referring to a "highly tragic" and "horror-striking scene at St. Louis," where a "mulatto man, by the name of McIntosh, was seized in the street, dragged to the suburbs of the city, chained to a tree, and actually burned to death; and all within a single hour from the time he had been a freeman, attending to his own business, and at peace with the world." Moreover, Lincoln condemned Mississippi mobs for lynching "negroes, suspected of conspiring to raise an insurrection," "white men, supposed to be leagued with the negroes," and "strangers, from neighboring States, going thither on business." Within the bombast of the Lyceum address, Lincoln thus subtly embedded attacks not only on Stephen A. Douglas but also on anti-abolitionists and racial bigotry.[16]

Lincoln continued to attack Douglas in new installments of the letters from Conservative in the *Sangamo Journal*, ostensibly written by unhappy Democrats but probably composed by Lincoln. He and Stuart also confronted Douglas in person, both on the stump and in the courtroom. In one encounter, Stuart grew incensed at Douglas's allegations, grabbed his smaller opponent by the neck, and walked about with him. In response, Douglas bit Stuart's thumb, scarring it for life. Realizing that the race between his partner and Douglas would be close, Lincoln worked hard and urged other Whigs to follow suit. "If we do our duty we shall succeed in the congressional election," he told a friend, "but if we relax an *iota* we shall be beaten."[17] His concern proved justified on election day, when Stuart narrowly prevailed, receiving 18,254 votes to Douglas's 18,218. Lincoln easily won a third legislative term, running ahead of the fifteen other candidates, even though some of his old friends in New Salem and Petersburg voted against him because his party opposed the division of Sangamon County.

When the Eleventh General Assembly convened in December 1838, Lincoln again found himself pitted against William L. D. Ewing, who had run for the legislature that year promising to "be a *thorn* in the side of the 'long nine' should we again see them."[18] As the most prominent Whig, Lincoln was his party's obvious choice for speaker of the house. Ewing managed to win that post after several ballots, making Lincoln in effect minority leader of the lower chamber. Although

Lincoln reportedly "did not seem to be seriously disappointed," he declared that Ewing "is not worth a damn."[19] Thus began what one representative called "a stormy session & a very unpleasant one."[20] Instead of responding to the financial panic and recession by sensibly reducing expenditures for canals and railroads, the General Assembly, with Lincoln's approval, unaccountably appropriated more funds for such purposes. In December, acknowledging that "his own course was identified with the system," Lincoln said Illinois "had gone too far to recede, even if we were disposed to."[21] To meet the costs of the internal-improvements system, he proposed that Illinois buy twenty million acres of public land within the state from the federal government for 25¢ per acre, then sell it for $1.25 per acre. If implemented, the plan would generate enough revenue to pay off the debt. Resolutions endorsing Lincoln's scheme passed the legislature but were ignored by Congress.

Lincoln also voted to impose a modest levy on land and to change the formula used to compute property taxes. He argued that the old system, which relied almost exclusively upon taxes levied on the property of out-of-state landowners, had failed to produce enough revenue. Moreover, it had valued all land at either three dollars or four dollars per acre, allowing owners of valuable property to pay less than their fair share of taxes. Lincoln claimed that the new system "does not increase the tax upon the 'many poor'; but upon the '*wealthy few*' by taxing the land that is worth $50 or $100 per acre, in proportion to its value, instead of, as heretofore, no more than that which was worth but $5 per acre." If the wealthy did not like it, there was little reason to worry, for "*they* are not sufficiently numerous to carry the elections."[22]

The Eleventh General Assembly addressed the touchy subject of county divisions, with Lincoln fighting a rearguard action to prevent the balkanization of Sangamon County. It was clear, however, that some kind of division was inevitable. Lincoln pragmatically sought to ensure that Sangamon would be reconfigured into three small counties and one large one instead of four counties of equal size. Thus Springfield would not be disadvantaged. As a member of the Committee on Counties, he drafted a bill creating three small new counties. When it was reported on January 16, 1839, the house referred it to a special committee (among whose members was Lincoln), which amended the bill (all of the amendments being in Lincoln's hand). On February 2, the house debated the measure, with Lincoln arguing against four equal counties. The bill as amended passed, establishing the counties of Logan, Dane, and Menard. Sangamon remained large, with five representatives; Lincoln preserved for it six townships that would have been lost if the county had been divided into quadrants of equal size. As the *Sangamo Journal* noted, "Old Sangamon, though considerably shorn of territory, will still remain among the most extensive and populous counties in the State."[23] In protecting the interests of the county, Lincoln employed the same skills he had used in Springfield's campaign to become the state's capital.

The General Assembly also addressed the issue of slavery. On January 5, 1839, the Judiciary Committee moved two resolutions, the first condemning the governor of Maine for his refusal to extradite Georgia men who had helped runaway slaves, the second declaring that citizens of the Free States "ought not to interfere with the property of slaveholding States; which property has been guarantied unto them by the Constitution of the United States, and without which guaranty, the Union, perhaps, would never have been formed."[24] Lincoln initially concurred but on second thought said he wanted more time for deliberation; finally, he concluded that it was "best to postpone the issue indefinitely."[25]

The subject would not go away, however; on February 1, it came up again when John Calhoun, in reply to abolitionist petitions, introduced resolutions urging Congress to ignore pleas for the abolition of slavery in both Washington, D.C., and the territories and for the prohibition of slave trading among the states. He added that attempts to grant Illinois Blacks fundamental rights were "not only unconstitutional, but improper, inexpedient, and unwise."[26] The house defeated Calhoun's motion 44–36, with Lincoln joining the majority. In March 1839, the General Assembly adjourned. Lincoln had as usual been conscientious, answering 157 of the 181 roll calls and serving on eleven select committees.

The legislature reconvened the following December at the urging of Governor Thomas Carlin. Meeting in Springfield for the first time, the General Assembly had to deliberate in churches, for the statehouse stood unfinished on the public square, surrounded by stagnant pools in which many of the city's free-roaming hogs wallowed. Governor Carlin wanted the legislature to modify the internal-improvements system, for the state could not pay the interest on the debt needed to support it. He also recommended an investigation of the state bank. The legislators complied by establishing a special committee, with Lincoln as one of its members. Although he initially thought there was "but verry little disposition to resuscitate it," he soon came to see that the "Bank will be resuscitated with some trifling modification."[27] He was right; the investigating committee defended the bank in a report that Lincoln signed. The General Assembly permitted that institution to suspend specie payments until the close of the next legislative session.

The removal of the state capital came up yet again, because the citizens of Springfield, suffering from the economic hard times, had difficulty raising the fifty thousand dollars to help pay for the new statehouse. Some legislators were ready to introduce a bill relieving the townspeople of that burden, but Lincoln "objected, and, though fully appreciating the kindly feelings that prompted the proposal, insisted that the money should and would be paid."[28] The legislature adjourned on

February 1, 1840, after reviving the state bank, continuing support for the Illinois and Michigan Canal (but otherwise cutting back on internal improvements), and incorporating the town of Springfield, while leaving unchanged its new status as state capital. Characteristically, Lincoln had answered 145 of 169 roll calls.

Well before adjournment, Lincoln and other Whigs girded themselves for the presidential election. Thanks to the hard times caused by the Panic of 1837, they had a good chance to win. Illinois Whigs had at first opposed the convention system adopted by the Democrats, believing it to be "a Yankee contrivance, intended to abridge the liberties of the people by depriving individuals, on their own mere motion, of the privilege of becoming candidates, and depriving each man of the right to vote for a candidate of his own selection and choice."[29] Eventually, however, defeat at the polls forced them to reconsider. David Davis told a fellow Whig in 1839: "The longer I live the more I am convinced that unless the Whigs of this State organize through Conventions they will be beaten at the next General election. Candidates show themselves as plenty as blackberries."[30] In September 1839, the Whigs of Sangamon County urged their counterparts throughout Illinois to send representatives to a state convention the following month. At that conclave, delegates to the Whig national convention were chosen, resolutions passed, a plan for organizing the state adopted, and an address to the people drafted. Lincoln was named one of the five Whig presidential electors and placed on the Whig State Central Committee, which the Democrats derisively called the "Junto." The delegates endorsed the presidential candidacies of both Henry Clay and William Henry Harrison.

Although Lincoln deeply admired Clay, he supported Harrison for expediency's sake. A letter in the *Sangamo Journal*, probably by Lincoln, argued that Harrison was more electable than Clay. In December 1839, delegates to the first Whig national convention agreed with Lincoln, passing over Clay and the other conspicuous leader of the party, Daniel Webster, to nominate the popular, colorless Harrison and send him forth unencumbered by a platform. When a Democratic newspaper sneered at Harrison's simple ways—"Give him a barrel of hard cider and settle a pension of two thousand a year upon him, and our word for it, he will sit the remainder of his days content in a log cabin"—the Whigs made a virtue of them.[31]

Instead of principles, Harrison would run on his military record, his humble log-cabin origins, and his fondness for egalitarian hard cider rather than elitist champagne. The Whigs ridiculed Van Buren as an aristocrat who ate with gold cutlery, wore silk hose and ruffled shirts, scented himself with perfume, and primped before immense mirrors. By contrast, they championed Harrison as a true man of the people, content with homespun clothes and log-cabin rusticity. When Lincoln's friend Albert Taylor Bledsoe expressed "intense mortification that the

Whig Party, which had claimed a monopoly of all the intelligence and decency of the country, should descend to the use of such means," Lincoln replied: "It is all right; *we must fight the devil with fire; we must beat the Democrats, or the country will be ruined*."[32]

Lincoln took charge of the Harrison campaign in traditionally Democratic Illinois. During the fall and winter of 1839–40 he helped organize debates with Democrats. The first one took place on November 19, with Cyrus Walker making the Whig case and Douglas presenting the Democratic response; Lincoln had the final word. In the course of his remarks, he called the Democratic editors of the Springfield *Register* "liars" for alleging that he supported John Bennett instead of his old friend Bowling Green for a legislative seat. In response, the *Register* chided Lincoln for the "*assumed clownishness* in his manner which does not become him."[33] The next night, Douglas and Lincoln debated the Bank of the United States. Lincoln evidently did badly. The *Register* ridiculed his efforts and said that even Lincoln's friends thought he had been whipped.

In a second round of debates, which attracted an audience of about five hundred, Lincoln redeemed himself. According to his friend Joseph Gillespie, he "begged to be permitted to try it again and was reluctantly indulged and in the next effort he transcended our highest expectations[.] I never heard & never expect to hear such a triumphant vindication as he then gave of Whig measures or policy."[34] On December 18, Lincoln branded the Democrats' subtreasury plan a "scheme of fraud and corruption."[35] Douglas responded in a manner that caused Lincoln to remark that he "is not now worth talking about."[36]

The day after Christmas, Lincoln gave such a powerful address that it became the Illinois Whig Party's 1840 textbook. He offered a sober analysis of President Van Buren's independent subtreasury scheme for government funds, a deflationary plan that, he argued, would create "distress, ruin, bankruptcy and beggary" by removing money from circulation. Hardest hit would be poor people in states with large tracts of public land. "Knowing, as I well do, the difficulty that poor people *now* encounter in procuring homes, I hesitate not to say, that when the price of the public lands shall be doubled or trebled . . . it will be little less than impossible for them to procure those homes at all." The Bank of the United States had performed this service cheaply, while the subtreasury would cost more and do less to restore prosperity. In addition, government money was safer in a Bank of the United States than it would be in the hands of government officials like those who had recently embezzled large sums.

As he proceeded, Lincoln abandoned his didactic exposition of economic theory and history and began to attack the Jackson and Van Buren administrations in earnest for their extravagant spending. At length, he rebutted Douglas's attempt to explain the unusual expenses incurred by the federal government in 1838. Lincoln was occasionally harsh: he ridiculed arguments of the Bank of the United States' opponents as "absurd"; he called Douglas "stupid" and "deserving of the world's contempt" and deemed one of his arguments "*supremely ridiculous.*"

Warming to the task, Lincoln became almost hysterical as he savaged the Van Buren administration: "Many free countries have lost their liberty; and *ours may* lose hers; but if she shall, be it my proudest plume, not that I was the *last* to desert, but that I *never* deserted her. I know that the great volcano at Washington, aroused and directed by the evil spirit that reigns there, is belching forth the lava of political corruption, in a current broad and deep, which is sweeping with frightful velocity over the whole length and breadth of the land, bidding fair to leave unscathed no green spot or living thing, while on its bosom are riding like demons on the waves of Hell, the imps of that evil spirit, and fiendishly taunting all those who dare resist its destroying course, with the hopelessness of their effort; and knowing this, I cannot deny that all may be swept way."[37]

Although such rhetorical bombast marred this speech, Lincoln made some legitimate economic points. The independent treasury scheme would have been deflationary, if not so badly as Lincoln predicted. He sensibly praised the useful regulatory function that the Bank of the United States had served, something like the role to be played later by the Federal Reserve System. The speech was widely published in the Whig press and issued as a campaign document in pamphlet form.

Lincoln stumped for Harrison throughout Illinois, spending much time in the southern part of the state, known as "Egypt," chief stronghold of the Democratic Party. There his speaking style, accent, and folksy approach to politics seemed more suitable than in northern Illinois. The hardships of campaigning in such a primitive region were compounded by illness. As Edward D. Baker and Lincoln traversed Egypt, they found themselves "shaking with the ague one day, and addressing the people the next." In the absence of railroads and stage lines, they had to ride on horseback with their clothes jammed into saddlebags. They covered vast distances through swamp and over prairie, all the while enduring miserable accommodations. But "no matter how tired, jaded and worn the speaker might be, he was obliged to respond to the call of the waiting and eager audiences."[38] Lincoln's oratorical skills proved a valuable weapon in the Whig arsenal, for many Westerners seldom read newspapers and thus obtained political information solely from stump speakers.

Negrophobia loomed large in the campaign. The few extant examples of Lincoln's speeches show that he indulged in the same race baiting that he had so freely employed four years earlier. For their part, the Democrats labeled Harrison an "Abolitionist of the first water" and a hypocrite who would "make slaves of White men" while making "free men of black slaves."[39] Responding in kind, Lincoln and other Whigs reiterated their earlier charges about Van Buren's support for Black suffrage in 1821.

In a March 1840 debate with Douglas at Jacksonville, Lincoln ambushed the Little Giant on the abolition issue. While preparing for that event, Lincoln had his "headstrong and vengeful" friend Dr. William H. Fithian, a skilled practitioner of political dirty tricks, write to Van Buren asking if William M. Holland's biography of the president accurately described Van Buren's support for Black suffrage in 1821. Van Buren confirmed Holland's account. While debating Douglas, Lincoln asserted that Van Buren "had voted for Negro Suffrage under certain limitations."[40] When Douglas denied it, Lincoln read aloud from Holland's life of the president. Douglas called it a forgery, whereupon Lincoln produced Van Buren's letter to Fithian. Douglas angrily seized the biography, damned it, and flung it out into the audience.

Addressing a Whig rally in heavily Democratic Belleville, Lincoln charged that "Van Buren had always opposed the interests of the West—was in feeling and principle an Aristocrat—had no claims upon the people on the score of Democracy, and was unworthy of their confidence and support." Lincoln analyzed Van Buren's rise to power "in a manner which drew forth bursts of applause and peals of laughter from the assemblage."[41] In justifying his tactics, Lincoln told James Matheny that Douglas "was always calling the Whigs Federalists—Tories—Aristocrats" and alleging that "Whigs are opposed to liberty—Justice & Progress. This is a loose assertion I suppose to Catch votes. I don't like to *catch votes by* cheating men out of their judgment, but in reference to the whigs being opposed to Liberty &c let me Say that that remains to be seen & demonstrated in the future. The brave don't boast. A barking dog don't bite."[42]

Lincoln's oratory in 1840, like that of other Harrison campaigners, tended to pander to popular taste. Insult and ridicule were common in frontier politics, but Lincoln deployed them so mercilessly that they constituted a form of cruelty that reflected his primitive background. Not until midlife would he change his ways and earn a justified reputation for infinite forbearance and goodwill. If in 1864 he could declare that as president he had "not willingly planted a thorn in any man's bosom," during his youth and early adulthood he positively delighted in planting such thorns.[43]

Lincoln skinned Colonel Dick Taylor, a Democratic candidate for the state senate, whose assaults on Whig elitism nettled him. The "showy, bombastic" Taylor was "a talkative, noisy fellow" and "a consummate fop" who "never appeared in public without a ruffled shirt, a blue coat and brass buttons, and a gold-headed cane." When Taylor denounced Whigs as aristocrats, Lincoln replied that while Taylor "was riding in a fine carriage, wore his kid gloves and had a gold headed cane, he [Lincoln] was a poor boy hired on a flat boat at eight dollars a month, and had only one pair of breeches and they were of buckskin." He explained to the audience, "If you know the nature of buckskin when wet and dried by the sun they would shrink and mine kept shrinking until they left several inches of my legs bare between the top of my Socks and the lower part of my breeches—and whilst I was growing taller they were becoming shorter: and so much tighter, that they left a blue streak around my leg which you can see to this day—If you call this aristocracy I plead guilty to the charge." Lincoln then unbuttoned Taylor's vest and out cascaded his "ruffled shirt like a pile of Entrails," causing the crowd to "burst forth in a furious & uproarious laughter."[44]

In late May, the Quincy, Illinois, *Whig* reported that the Democrats "have not been able to start a man that can hold a candle to him in political debate,—All of their crack nags that have entered the lists against him, have come off the field crippled or broken down."[45] In late October, a Jacksonian legislator, Dr. William G. Anderson, repeatedly interrupted Lincoln's speech at Lawrenceville, charging that the speaker was "falsifying the acts and record of the Democratic party."[46] Lincoln's response must have been heated, for Anderson declared that it "imported insult" and ominously demanded an explanation. A duel seemed likely, but Lincoln disarmed that threat with a conciliatory reply: "I entertain no unkind feeling to you, and none of any sort upon the subject, except a sincere regret that I permitted myself to get into such an altercation."[47] What Lincoln said in his many other speeches may be inferred from contributions in the *Sangamo Journal* and the *Old Soldier*, a campaign paper he helped edit. Many of the opinion letters signed "A Looker-on," "An Old Jackson Man," and the like, were evidently Lincoln's handiwork. Some excoriated Democrats for attacking the Illinois state bank, calling them "would-be dictators," while others condemned the Van Buren administration for abusing the patronage power.

In November, Harrison swamped Van Buren, carrying nineteen of the twenty-six states. The president did manage to eke out a victory in Illinois, capturing 51 percent of the vote. But hard times, Van Buren's bland personality, and the vogue for egalitarianism combined to doom the incumbent's bid for reelection. David Davis, who narrowly lost a race for the state senate, complained that "if the *Irish* did not vote more than *3 times* we could easily carry the State."[48] Like Davis, Lincoln was angered by such irregularities. On election day, when he heard that an Illinois railroad contractor had brought a construction gang to take over the polls, Lincoln told him menacingly: "You will spoil & blow if you live much longer." That night Lincoln confided to Joshua Speed, "I intended to knock him down & go aw[a]y and leave him a-kicking."[49] On a similar occasion in Springfield, Lincoln stymied a group of Democrats who had threatened to seize the polls and prevent their opponents from voting. Armed with an ax handle, he scared off the obstructionists. When the legislature convened soon after the November elections, Lincoln proposed an investigation of electoral fraud. Nevertheless, he was jubilant over Harrison's victory. At a raucous celebration, he "made a great deal of sport with his speeches, witty sayings and stories" and "even played leap-frog."[50]

In 1840, Lincoln sought a fourth legislative term, though in March he told Stuart that "I think it is probable I shall not be permitted to be a candidate."[51] Many Sangamon County Whigs outside the capital had resisted the convention system and objected to the "Springfield Junto" that supported it. That "Junto" had further alienated voters by opposing the division of Sangamon County. Despite all this, the county's Whigs did nominate Lincoln at their convention that March, although they rejected all other Springfield residents save Edward D. Baker, whom they chose to run for the state senate. Lincoln reported that Ninian W. Edwards "was verry much hurt at not being nominated" and added that for his own part he "was much, verry much, wounded myself at his [Edwards] being left out. The fact is, the country delegates made the nominations as they pleased; and they *pleased* to make them all from the country, except Baker & me, whom they supposed necessary to make stump speeches."[52] On election day in August, Lincoln retained his seat in the General Assembly, coming in fifth in a field of ten, with 1,844 votes.

Shortly after election day, Governor Thomas Carlin summoned the legislature to a special session, beginning two weeks before the constitutionally stipulated date for the regular session, in order to deal with the mounting state debt. It seemed unlikely that Illinois could meet the interest payments due on January 1. Because the new capitol was still not quite ready for occupancy, the legislators again met in Springfield churches. They elected William L. D. Ewing Speaker of the house, and after some vigorous but futile attempts to have Vandalia restored as the state capital, they prepared to convene the regular session on December 7.

The Democrats tried to seize the moment for some mischief. Since a recent law provided that the Bank of Illinois would have to resume specie payments at the end of the "next session" of the legislature, Democrats argued that it must meet that burdensome requirement as of December 5, when the special session closed. The Whigs, hoping to have the regular session combined with the special session and thus postpone the bank's day of reckoning, boycotted the legislature, thereby preventing the necessary two-thirds quorum for adjournment *sine die*. When the representatives gathered on December 5, the Whigs stayed away, except for Lincoln, Joseph Gillespie, and Asahel Gridley, who were to observe the proceedings and demand roll call votes. The frustrated Democrats, eager to hurt the state bank by adjourning, instructed the sergeant at arms to round up absent Whigs. When that tactic failed, the Democrats managed to bring in enough of their own previously absent members to create a quorum. Lincoln and his two Whig colleagues bolted for the door, which was locked. Because the sergeant at arms had received no instruction to unlock the door, he refused to do so. Lincoln then opened a window and stepped through, followed by Gillespie and Gridley.

This unconventional departure drew laughter from the Democratic members, who derisively shouted: "He who fights and runs away, lives to fight another day."[53] The *Register* sneered at the "gymnastic performance of Mr. Lincoln and his flying brethren" and recommended that the statehouse be raised "in order to have the House set in the *third story!* so as to prevent members from *jumping out of the windows!*" That way, "Mr. Lincoln will in future have *to climb down the spout!*"[54] For his part, Lincoln found this episode embarrassing; in later years, whenever the matter came up, he would change the subject.

When the regular session began on December 7, 1840, the house of representatives, meeting for the first time in the new capitol, wrangled over the debt crisis. Lincoln managed, after much cajoling, to persuade his colleagues to raise the general land tax and issue special bonds to cover the pending interest obligations. That tax hike, however, yielded insufficient revenue to solve the problem, and in July 1841 the state defaulted on its interest payments, causing the price of Illinois bonds to plunge. In 1842, Illinois took in revenues of less than $100,000, while interest payments approached $800,000.

A struggle over the Whig-dominated supreme court convulsed the legislature. The justices had angered Democrats by overruling Governor Carlin's decision to remove Alexander P. Field, a partisan Whig, from his post as secretary of state. When the court also seemed likely to weaken the Democrats' electoral base by denying aliens the right to vote, the General Assembly entertained a motion to pack the supreme bench by adding five justices. The ensuing debate was, in the words of a state senator, "vehement & exciting, partaking much of party abuse & personal crimination."[55] Although the main battleground of this war was in the house, Lincoln scarcely took part; he had prepared remarks, but he could not deliver them because Speaker Ewing allowed the Democrats to cut off debate. On February 1, when the bill cleared the house by a 45–43 vote, the *Sangamo Journal* published a letter by a member of that body (probably Lincoln) indignantly protesting that the "Judiciary of Illinois is to be assailed, and the constitution in its spirit, if not in the letter, violated, and the members who would have raised a voice in its defence, are to be gagged into silence!"[56]

When Ewing rejected this protest as "gratuitous and unfounded," Lincoln replied in a statesmanlike fashion, remarking that there was "no reason we should wound each other's feelings, or that those civilities and kindnesses which mark the character and intercourse between gentlemen, should be violated and endangered."

He maintained that the "official conduct, or decisions of public officers is public property, and are fair and legitimate subjects of criticism, so that facts are correctly stated, and inferences fairly drawn."[57] Lincoln was not so conciliatory in late February, when he and thirty-four other Whig representatives denounced the court-packing statute as "a party measure for party purposes" that manifested "supreme contempt for the popular will," undermined "the independence of the Judiciary, the surest shield of public welfare and private right," and set a "precedent for still more flagrant violations of right and justice."[58]

In the 1840–41 session, Lincoln once again fought on behalf of the Illinois and Michigan Canal, moving that the state increase the land tax and issue bonds to complete the project. Much as they admired Lincoln's wit, his fellow legislators rejected his argument that "to prosecute the work now was in fact the most economical plan that could be adopted: to stop it, would involve the State in much more debt and ruin."[59]

Lincoln clashed with Democrat John A. McClernand over the state bank. From southern Illinois, McClernand hated all banks. Vain and overbearing, he was an effective if unscrupulous speaker, always ready for a political fight. McClernand and Lincoln held an especially heated debate over the question whether the state bank should be the fiscal agent for Illinois. Lincoln, with asperity, accused Democrats of underhanded dealing. He declared that there was "a manifest disposition on the part of some of the Van Buren men to prop up the Bank" and later "throw the odium of suspension upon the Whigs."[60] Lincoln's attempt to protect the interests of the bank proved futile, and it was compelled to shut its doors the following year.

When the legislature adjourned in March, Lincoln found himself out of office for the first time in seven years. He had chosen not to seek reelection, for he wished to obtain the Whig nomination for Congress, and thus he closed the apprentice phase of his political career. Since entering the legislature in 1834, he had gained stature. In December 1840, a member of "the lobby"—a kind of shadow legislature that met in the capitol after the General Assembly sessions adjourned for the day—called him "emphatically a man of *high standing*," a "self-made man, and one of the ablest, whether as a lawyer or legislator, in the State."[61]

In 1840, Lincoln's ambition had grown more intense, fueled by his new status as a presidential elector, Whig campaign manager, chief stump speaker and organizer, and Whig floor leader in the state house of representatives. He told William H. Herndon "that his ideas of [becoming] something—burst on him in 1840."[62] He now felt ready to advance from the state to the national legislature. In the General Assembly he had learned how to build coalitions, how to persuade his colleagues to do his bidding, and how to roll logs. According to Lyman Trumbull, a colleague in the Illinois House, Lincoln was viewed "by his political friends as among their shrewdest and ablest leaders, and by his political adversaries as a formidable opponent."[63]

But for all his growing sense of strength and competence, there was, as his friend Samuel C. Parks noted about the Lincoln of 1841, "nothing to indicate the future reformer, either in religion, or morals, or politics."[64] His greatness as a moral statesman in years to come would have been hard to predict, given his legislative record, which showed him to be likable and clever but little more. He understood the nuts and bolts of lawmaking and excelled at ridiculing Democrats. In his leadership role, however, he had little to do with framing legislation. Of the 1,647 bills passed during Lincoln's four terms, he directly introduced only 10 and offered only 8 resolutions and 14 petitions. It is no wonder that fellow Whig leaders observed that during his years in the legislature Lincoln "never gave any special evidence of that masterly ability for which he was afterward distinguished."[65]

Lincoln by the age 32 had proved himself to be an ambitious, talented partisan who exhibited few signs of true statesmanship.

6.

"It Would Just Kill Me to Marry Mary Todd"

Courtship and Marriage (1840–1842)

In 1842, Lincoln wed Mary Todd, a woman who was to make his domestic life "a burning, scorching hell," as "terrible as death and as gloomy as the grave," according to one who knew him well.[1]

Courting Mary Owens

Lincoln's courtship of Mary Todd is poorly documented, but indirect light is shed on it by his earlier, well-recorded romance with Mary S. Owens. Born in Kentucky a few months before Lincoln, Mary Owens received a good education at the home of her wealthy father, a planter in Green County. She was older, bigger, and better educated than Ann Rutledge. Raised in a relatively sophisticated society, she dressed more elegantly than women in New Salem. Her clothes may have been more attractive than Ann Rutledge's, but her features and figure were not. Standing five feet, five inches tall, she was plump, weighing between 150 and 180 pounds, and considered "not pretty," "matronly," "muscular," with a "massive, angular, square, prominent, and broad" forehead, "fair skin, deep blue eyes," and "dark curling hair." If less comely than Ann Rutledge, however, Mary Owens was more intellectually gifted and accomplished—"quick & strong minded," "very intellectual," a "good conversationalist," "a splendid reader." She was "jovial," "social," "good natured," as well as "kind and considerate."[2]

In the fall of 1833, Mary Owens spent a month at New Salem with her sister, Mrs. Bennett Abell, who was eager to have Lincoln as a brother-in-law. He found Mary Owens intelligent and "agreeable."[3] She, in turn, recalled that they "were congenial spirits" who saw "eye to eye" on political matters.[4] Three years later, Lincoln accepted a startling proposition made by Betsy Abell: that she bring her sister Mary back from Kentucky for him to wed. Lincoln agreed, and Mary returned to New Salem for a year and a half, to be courted by Lincoln.

The first known photograph of Lincoln, ca. 1846. When this image first appeared in published form in 1895, the noted geologist and author John Wesley Powell expressed his delight. Lincoln's pictures, he said, "have never quite pleased me, and I now know why. I remember Lincoln as I saw him when I was a boy; after he became a public man I saw him but few times. This portrait is Lincoln as I knew him best: his sad, dreamy eye, his pensive smile, his sad and delicate face, his pyramidal shoulders, are the characteristics which I best remember; and I can never think of him as wrinkled with care, so plainly shown in his later portraits. This is the Lincoln of Springfield, Decatur, Jacksonville, and Bloomington." Robert Todd Lincoln later stated that this "daguerreotype was on the walls of a room in my father's house from my earliest recollection," along with one of his mother. Daguerreotype probably by Nicholas H. Shepherd, Springfield. Abraham Lincoln Presidential Library and Museum, Springfield, Illinois.

Mary Todd Lincoln, photograph probably by Nicholas H. Shepherd ca. 1846 and likely the companion mentioned by Robert Todd Lincoln. Library of Congress.

After the relationship ended, Lincoln wryly told his close friend Eliza Browning that he had seen "no good objection to plodding through life hand in hand with her." But the courtship did not go well. In 1836 Lincoln found her less attractive than he had remembered. "I knew she was over-size," he confided to Mrs. Browning, "but she now appeared a fair match for Falstaff." In addition, she looked old: "When I beheld her, I could not for my life avoid thinking of my mother; and this, not from withered features, for her skin was too full of fat, to permit its contracting in to wrinkles; but from her want of teeth, weather-beaten appearance in general, and from a kind of notion that ran in my head, that *nothing* could have commenced at the size of infancy, and reached her present bulk in less than thirty five or forty years." He tried to convince himself "that the mind was much more to be valued than the person." Despite his reservations, Lincoln felt honor-bound to follow through on his pledge: "I had told her sister that I would take her for better or for worse; and I made a point of honor and conscience in all things, to stick to my word, especially if others had been induced to act on it, which in this case, I doubted not they had, for I was now fairly convinced, that no other man on earth would have her." Understandably, he hesitated before marrying such a woman. "Through life I have been in no bondage, either real or immaginary from the thraldom of which I so much desired to be free," he told Mrs. Browning.

After procrastinating as long as possible, he finally proposed. To his surprise, she turned him down. As he related to Mrs. Browning, "My vanity was deeply wounded by the reflection, that I had so long been too stupid to discover her intentions, and at the same time never doubting that I understood them perfectly; and also, that she whom I had taught myself to believe no body else would have, had actually rejected me with all my fancied greatness." Ruefully he conceded that others "have been made fools of by the girls; but this can never be with truth said of me. I most emphatically, in this instance, made a fool of myself." He resolved "never again to think of marrying," for "I can never be satisfied with any one who would be block-head enough to have me."[5]

This account of the courtship is misleading, for Lincoln's correspondence with Mary Owens indicates that he had become quite fond of her and backed away only after she wounded him repeatedly. A letter he wrote her in December 1836 from Vandalia suggests that he really was in love; in it, he complained of "the mortification of looking in the Post Office for your letter and not finding it." The prospect of spending ten weeks with the legislature in Vandalia was intolerable, he lamented, for he missed her. "Write back as soon as you get this, and if possible say something that will please me, for really I have not [been] pleased since I left you."[6] Such language was hardly that of an indifferent suitor.

The romance ended largely because of the couple's incompatibility. With good reason she thought his manners oafish. As she explained, "Mr. Lincoln was deficient in those little links which make up the great chain of womans happiness, at least it was so in my case; . . . his training had been different from mine, hence there was not that congeniality which would have otherwise existed." Lincoln had behaved in ways that she understandably considered thoughtless and insensitive. One day, while riding with other New Salem young women and their swains, they came to a creek, which all the men save Lincoln gallantly helped their companions cross. Mary Owens chided her escort: "You are a nice fellow! I suppose you did not care whether my neck was broken or not." Lincoln replied that he reckoned she was "plenty smart enough to care for herself."[7]

A similar incident provoked her to tell Lincoln that she thought he was not promising husband material. One day he accompanied her and Mrs. Bowling Green on a walk. As they climbed a steep hill, he offered no help to Nancy Green, who was struggling to carry "a great big fat child—heavy & crossly disposed." After reaching their destination, Mary suggested that Lincoln should have helped "carry a baby that weighs nearly forty pounds." Lincoln replied: "Why, she never asked me." The two got into a tiff, with Lincoln saying, "Why, I never thought of it. I always supposed she would be afraid to let a fellow like me touch the baby for fear he might break it or something. I'd carry a bushel of them for you, Mary."[8] Lincoln laughed the incident off, but it was a turning point in their relationship, which began to cool.

Soon after this contretemps, Lincoln spent a few weeks on a surveying expedition. When he returned to New Salem, he asked one of the Abells' sons if Mary Owens was at their home. When the lad said she was, Lincoln asked him to tell her that he would visit later that day. But she had made plans to dine with her cousin Mentor Graham. When she heard that Lincoln would call, she regarded the occasion as an opportunity to test his devotion: "She thought a moment and Said to herself if I can draw Lincoln up there to Grahams it will all be right. . . . She wanted to make L bend."[9] When he dropped by the Abells' home to see Mary Owens, Betsy Abell informed him that she was at Mentor Graham's, a mile and a half distant. Lincoln asked if Mary had known he was coming to call. When Mrs. Abell said no, one of her children corrected her, insisting that he had informed her. His feelings hurt, Lincoln returned to New Salem without stopping at Graham's.

Lincoln's hypersensitivity about the differences in their social class was manifested in a letter he wrote to Mary in May 1837, shortly after he had moved to Springfield. They had considered the possibility of her joining him there, evidently as Mrs. Abraham Lincoln. He discouraged her, saying, "I am afraid you would not be satisfied. There is a great deal of flourishing about in carriages here, which it would be your doom to see without shareing in it. You would have to be poor without the means of hiding your poverty." For this reason he believed that they should not wed. He said he would "do all in my power" to make her "happy and contented," but he urged her to consider the prospect carefully before deciding. "My opinion is that you had better not do it. You have not been accustomed to hardship, and it may be more severe than you now immagine." But, he hastened to add, "I am willing to abide your decision."[10]

Three months later, in his final surviving letter to Mary Owens, Lincoln discussed the prospect of marriage lukewarmly: "I want in all cases to do right, and most particularly so, in all cases with women. I want . . . more than any thing else, to do right with you, and if I knew it would be doing right, as I rather suspect it would, to let you alone, I would do it." To make "the matter as plain as possible," he told her that she "can now . . . dismiss your thoughts (if you ever had any) from me forever, and leave this letter unanswered, without calling forth one accusing murmur from me. . . . If you feel yourself in any degree bound to me, I am now willing to release you, provided you wish it; while, on the other hand, I am willing, and even anxious to bind you faster, if I can be convinced that it will, in any considerable degree, add to your happiness."[11] Unsurprisingly, she rejected this halfhearted proposal, returned to Kentucky, and eventually married her brother-in-law. A few months after her departure, Lincoln remarked to Betsy Abell: "Tell your Sister, that I think she was a great fool, because she did not stay here and marry me."[12]

The Mary Owens courtship reveals an aspect of Lincoln's character that helps explain his intense political ambition: a deep-seated inferiority complex. Some political psychologists maintain that such ambition is often rooted in "an intense and ungratified craving for deference." Many aspiring politicos expect, as Lincoln did, power "to overcome low estimates of the self." The compensatory psychological benefits of political power and fame strongly appeal to those with damaged self-esteem, especially "the 'provincial' or the 'small-town boy' or the 'country boy'" who wants "to succeed against the stigma of rusticity."[13] Lincoln is a good example of such a "provincial." As noted earlier, he "seemed to be painfully impressed with the extreme poverty of his early surroundings."[14] Moreover, he regretted his "undistinguished" ancestry and meager schooling.

The psychologist G. Stanley Hall speculated that Lincoln's ambition was rooted in his feelings about his appearance: "His height, long limbs, rough exterior, and frequent feeling of awkwardness must have very early made him realize that to succeed in life he must cultivate intrinsic mental and moral traits, which it is so hard for a handsome man or women to excel in. Hence he compensated by trying to develop intellectual distinction."[15] In his initial political campaign, Lincoln declared candidly: "I have no other [ambition] so great as that of being truly esteemed of my fellow citizens."[16] That thirst for admiration lasted a lifetime; only political success would slake it and permit relief from a nagging sense of inferiority.

Emotional as well as material and educational poverty seems to have plagued the young Lincoln. Neither parent met his most basic psychological needs. Nancy Hanks Lincoln may have provided her young son with love and support during his first nine years, but he evidently viewed her death as an act of abandonment. In later life, he seldom mentioned her; one of the few times he did so, in his letter to Eliza Browning about his love life, it was in unflattering terms. His father offered little nurturance. Perhaps the best thing Thomas Lincoln ever did for his son was to marry Sarah Bush Johnston, but by the time she arrived in Indiana the boy's psyche had endured much. Suffering from emotional malnutrition, Lincoln thought himself unloved and unlovable. To compensate, he sought in public life a surrogate form of the love and acceptance he had not known at home; by winning elections he would prove to himself that he was lovable.

Lincoln's conduct toward Mary Owens may have been affected by his distrust of women, stemming from the death of his mother. The "bitter agony" that he experienced as a 9-year-old in Indiana seems to have crippled his capacity for trusting and loving women lest they abandon him as his mother had done. Throughout life, he harbored irrational fears of abandonment. When Joshua Speed married, Lincoln plaintively told the newlyweds, "I feel som[e]what jealous of both of you now; you will be so exclusively concerned for one another, that I shall be forgotten entirely."[17]

Courting Mary Todd

The Mary Owens affair also reveals Lincoln's extraordinary passivity in dealing with women and his scrupulous determination to carry out promises, even bad ones. These traits resurfaced when he became involved with the temperamental, headstrong, volatile Mary Todd. Two years after Mary Owens disappeared from Lincoln's life, he met Miss Todd, another well-educated Kentuckian from a prosperous family. Her cousin John Todd Stuart was his law partner and political mentor. Evidently she believed that if her much-admired cousin had chosen Lincoln as a law partner, that young attorney might make a good life partner. Mary was short and plump, and though not pretty, she had striking blue eyes and a fine complexion. Friends recalled that she was "impulsive & made no attempt to conceal her feeling, indeed it would have been an impossibility had she desired to do so, for her face was an index to every passing emotion." In addition, she had "an unusual gift of sarcasm."[18]

While in Springfield to visit her eldest sister, Elizabeth, who had married Ninian W. Edwards, son of a former governor, Mary Todd met eligible bachelors aplenty at the Edwards' home, a social center for the city's elite. She was "the very creature of excitement," a Springfielder reported in 1840; she "never enjoys herself more than when in society and surrounded by a company of merry friends."[19] One such friend was Joshua Speed, who brought Lincoln along to events at the Edwards home. Lincoln began seeing Mary in the winter of 1839–40. According to a relative of Ninian Edwards, Lincoln admired her "naturally fine mind and cultivated tastes," for she was "a great reader and possessed of a remarkably retentive memory," and her "brilliant conversation, often embellished with apt quotations," made her "much sought after by the young people of the town."[20]

Initially, her sister Elizabeth encouraged the romance, for she realized that Lincoln was a man on the way up in the world and she therefore wanted Mary to wed him. In time, however, she came to recognize his social deficiencies: he "Could not hold a lengthy Conversation with a lady—was not sufficiently Educated & intelligent in the female line to do so." Mrs. Edwards withdrew her earlier support for Lincoln and prophetically told her sister that they were not "Suitable to Each other."[21]

Elizabeth Edwards realized, as did others in Springfield, that Lincoln was "a mighty rough man," "uncouth," "moody," "dull in society," "careless of his personal appearance," "awkward and shy."[22] At social gatherings, young ladies avoided him, perhaps in part because of his ineptitude on the dance floor. When asked why he did not dance, he explained that "my feet weren't made that way."[23] At a party in Jacksonville, Lincoln reportedly approached Mary Todd saying: "I want to dance with you in the worst way." Afterward she told him: "Mr. Lincoln I think you have literally fulfilled your request—you have danced the worst way possible."[24]

Early on, Mary became aware of Lincoln's gaucheries, which irritated her. When she criticized him for a social indiscretion, he seemed unable to understand why she cared so much about something so unimportant. Her cousin Stephen T. Logan warned Mary that Lincoln was "much too rugged for your little white hands to attempt to polish."[25] In fact, Mary never reconciled herself to Lincoln's lack of polish, even after years of marriage. A Springfield resident said that "it hurt her that Lincoln was so plain and dressed so plain," and Mary's half-sister Emilie reported that "she complained because L. would open [the] front door instead of having [a] servant do so and because L. would eat butter with his knife she raised 'merry war.'"[26]

Just how Lincoln courted Mary Todd is unclear. When in Springfield, he regularly spent Sundays at the Edwards home. But Lincoln could not have visited that home often in the winter and spring of 1840, for politics and his law practice frequently took him out of town. He would not have seen much of Mary Todd in the summer, which she spent with relatives in Missouri. When she returned, Lincoln was busily campaigning throughout southern Illinois. Joshua Speed said that they courted through the mails that fall while Lincoln was stumping for William Henry Harrison: "He first wrote his *Mary*—She darted after him—wrote him."[27] But Lincoln did not mention her in any of the surviving letters he wrote in 1840, nor does her correspondence or that of their friends refer to any romance between them that year. Others confirmed Speed's observation that Mary Todd took the initiative in the courtship. In 1875, Orville H. Browning told an interviewer that "Mary Todd did most of the courting" and added that she "was thoroughly in earnest [in] her endeavors to get Mr. Lincoln."[28]

Despite their differences and their inability to spend much time together, Lincoln and Mary evidently became engaged sometime in the fall of 1840. Lincoln's matrimonial impulsiveness recalls his abrupt acceptance of Betsy Abell's 1836 proposition that he wed Mary Owens. Why he and Mary Todd decided to marry is difficult to understand, for they were, as Elizabeth Edwards and many others noted, quite different. Their backgrounds could hardly have been more dissimilar. The Todds lived in a very different Kentucky from the one inhabited by Thomas Lincoln, occupying as they did a prominent social position in Lexington, self-identified as "the Athens of the West." In contrast to young Abe's all-too-brief formal schooling, Mary Todd was sent to Lexington's best private schools, where she spoke French and studied social graces like conversation, dancing, and letter writing.

Abraham Lincoln and Mary Todd did share an important childhood experience in common: the premature death of their mothers. Mary was 6 when Eliza Parker Todd succumbed to a post-birth bacterial infection; Lincoln was 9 when the milk sickness cut short Nancy Hanks's life. From these painful losses, both children sustained debilitating psychological wounds that contributed to the marital problems they would face later.

Mary Todd called her privileged childhood "desolate" not only because of the actual death of her mother but also because of the metaphorical death of her father.[29] After the passing of his first wife, Robert Smith Todd paid little attention to Mary and her siblings. A scant few weeks after his wife's burial, he traveled to nearby Frankfort and courted young Elizabeth Humphreys, whom he wed a year later, and with whom he would sire nine half-siblings for Mary over the next fifteen years. Mary evidently felt betrayed, abandoned, and rejected by her "impetuous, high-strung, sensitive" father, who apparently withdrew from Mary emotionally to please his new wife.[30] Deep-seated anger at him and her stepmother seemingly smoldered in Mary Todd's unconscious. According to Elizabeth Todd, she "left her home in Kentucky to avoid living under the same roof with a stepmother."[31] As a married adult, Mary continued to have difficulties with Betsy Humphreys, and she likely harbored a rage that she was unable to vent directly. It also suggests that she might have sought a surrogate father; indeed, she may have married Lincoln in part because she needed a benevolent paterfamilias who would indulge her and fill the void created in her life when Robert Smith Todd began a second family. More than a foot taller and nearly ten years Mary's senior, Lincoln radiated the positive qualities of elderhood.

Conversely, Mary Todd's youthful qualities may have appealed to Lincoln. Mary also certainly needed a great deal of protection, or at least looking after, for she had mental problems, including manic depression. Orville H. Browning, who thought her "demented," recalled that she "was subject to . . . spells of mental depression" and "was always 'either in the garret or cellar.'"[32] Manic depression is not the only diagnosis that seems to fit Mary Lincoln's condition; she also exhibited many symptoms associated with narcissism and with borderline personality disorder. In late 1840, Lincoln broke the engagement. According to a friend, he had concluded that they "were not congenial, and were incompatible" and "ought not to marry."[33]

Another powerful consideration gave Lincoln pause as he contemplated wedding Mary Todd: in the autumn of 1840 he fell in love with Matilda Edwards, a beautiful 18-year-old cousin of Ninian Edwards who had come to Springfield from Alton and stayed with Mary Todd at the Edwards home. Like many other young women, she visited the capital during the legislative session to attend the numerous parties given at that time. The "very bright" Matilda Edwards was "something of a coquette" and "a most fascinating and handsome girl, tall, graceful, and rather reserved."[34] Her "gentle temper, her conciliatory manners, and the sweetness of her heart made her dear to all who knew her."[35] Lincoln was among the many young men holding her dear, including Joshua Speed, who described her thus: "Two clear blue eyes, a brow as fair as Palmyra marble touched by the chisel of Praxatiles. Lips so fresh, fair and lovely that I am jealous even of the minds that kiss them. A form as perfect as that of the Venus de Medicis. A Mind clear as a bell, a voice bewitchingly soft and sonorous, and a smile so sweet, lovely, and playful, and a countenance and soul shining through it."[36]

In the winter of 1840–41, Matilda and Mary Todd "seemed to form the grand centre of attraction. Swarms of strangers who had little else to engage their attention hovered around them, to catch a *passing smile*."[37] In January 1841, Lincoln declared that "if he had it in his power he would not have one feature in her face altered, he thinks she is so perfect." According to one acquaintance, he and Joshua Speed "spent the most of their time at [the] Edwards [home] this winter," and "Lincoln could never bear to leave Miss Edward's [*sic*] side in company" because "he fell desperately in love with her."[38] Yet he was too shy to approach the young beauty, who informed Elizabeth Edwards that Lincoln "never mentioned Such a Subject to me: he never even Stooped to pay me a Compliment."[39] After becoming enamored of Matilda Edwards, Lincoln confided to John J. Hardin "that he thought he did not love" Mary Todd "as he should and that he would do her a great wrong if he married her."[40] To Mrs. William Butler, Lincoln declared that "it would just kill me to marry Mary Todd."[41]

And so Lincoln felt compelled to break his engagement, but just how he did so is unclear. According to Joshua Speed, he wrote Mary Todd "a letter saying he did not love her," but Speed persuaded him not to deliver it. Instead, he urged Lincoln "to go and see her and Speak to her what you say in that letter." Acting on Speed's advice, Lincoln visited her and, again according to Speed, "told her that he did not love her—She rose—and Said 'The deciever shall be decieved wo is me.'; alluding to a young man She fooled." Speed reported that "Lincoln drew her down on his Knee—Kissed her—& parted—He going one way & She another—Lincoln did Love Miss [Matilda] Edwards—'Mary' Saw it—told Lincoln the reason of his Change of mind—heart & soul—released him."[42] It is not known what Mary Todd said to Lincoln when he asked to be released. Perhaps she deliberately manipulated his conscience to win him back. Her sister Elizabeth recalled that "She wrote a letter to Mr L Stating that She would release him from his Engagements," with the understanding "that She would hold the question an open one—that is that She had not Changed her mind, but felt as always."[43] She thus left him the option of renewing the engagement if he so desired; she clearly hoped he would do so.

Under these circumstances, it is little wonder that, as Ninian Edwards put it, Lincoln "in his Conflicts of duty—honor & his love went as Crazy as a *Loon*."[44] In late January 1841, Jane D. Bell reported that Lincoln "is in rather a bad way," for the "doctors say he came within an inch of being a perfect lunatic for life."[45] In fact, Lincoln went "crazy for a week or so" and was nursed back to health at the Butlers' home, where Orville H. Browning was staying. Browning said his friend "was so much affected as to talk incoherently, and to be delirious to the extent of not knowing what he was doing." This "aberration of mind resulted entirely from the situation he . . . got himself into—he was engaged to Miss Todd, and in love with Miss Edwards, and his conscience troubled him dreadfully for the supposed injustice he had done, and the supposed violation of his word which he had committed."[46] Many friends feared that Lincoln might kill himself. According to Speed, they "had to remove razors from his room—take away all Knives and other such dangerous things."[47]

In despair, Lincoln turned to his physician friend Anson G. Henry, with whom he spent several hours each day between January 13 and 18. Shortly thereafter, Lincoln wrote to John T. Stuart: "I have, within the last few days, been making a most discreditable exhibition of myself in the way of hypochondriaism [depression] and thereby got an impression that Dr. Henry is necessary to my existence." Three days later he elaborated: "I am now the most miserable man living. If what I feel were equally distributed to the whole human family, there would not be one cheerful face on the earth. Whether I shall ever be better I can not tell; I awfully forebode I shall not. To remain as I am is impossible; I must die or be better, it appears to me."[48]

In the General Assembly, Lincoln behaved oddly that January. With unwonted testiness he lashed out at a fellow legislator who had chided him for his earlier "jump" from the church window. Lincoln "said that as to jumping, he should jump when he pleased and no one should hinder him." A few days later, on the floor of the house of representatives, he alluded to his lack of appeal to the opposite sex: "If any woman, old or young, ever thought there was any peculiar charm in this distinguished specimen . . . I have, as yet, been so unfortunate as not to have discovered it."[49] Shortly thereafter, he stopped attending sessions of the General Assembly, just when his leadership was needed to combat the Democrats' court-packing scheme. He answered only one roll call between January 13 and 20. On January 21, he resumed casting votes regularly. Such absenteeism was unusual for Lincoln, who in four legislative terms missed only 180 of 1,334 roll calls; more than half of those absences occurred during this session.

On January 24, Lincoln appeared to James C. Conkling to be "reduced and emaciated," with barely enough strength "to speak above a whisper." But by late January he seemed to have recovered. On the twenty-sixth, Mrs. John J. Hardin told her husband: "I am glad to hear Lincoln has got over his cat fits[.] we have concluded it was a very unsatisfactory way of terminating his romance[.]"[50]

In March, after the legislature adjourned, Turner R. King saw Lincoln in Springfield "hanging about—moody—silent." King believed that the "question in his mind was 'Have I incurred any obligation to marry that woman.'"[51] Although Lincoln had broken the engagement, he was still tormented by the thought that he really should have wed Mary Todd, not because he loved her but because his tyrannical conscience nagged him unmercifully. Conkling reported that Lincoln would probably "now endeavor to drown his cares among the intricacies and perplexities of the law."[52]

New Law Partner

Conkling was right. The following month, Lincoln amicably ended his partnership with John Todd Stuart and joined forces with Stephen T. Logan, a better lawyer and worse politician than Stuart. Logan, displeased with the ethical obtuseness of his partner Edward D. Baker, sought to replace him. He had observed young Lincoln in three cases where they opposed each other; Lincoln had won all three. Lincoln probably also hoped to find a mentor in Logan, a Kentuckian nine years his senior. In 1843 the *Sangamo Journal* observed that Logan "is regarded as perhaps the best lawyer in the State, and has undoubtedly a fine logical mind," even though his appearance made him seem "the very personification of carelessness."[53] Logan also lacked a winning personality, for he had a volatile temper and was notoriously tightfisted.

Logan and Lincoln became close friends personally and politically despite their different values. Logan cared a great deal about money and made lots of it, while Lincoln was little concerned about it and made comparatively little. Logan revered the law, while Lincoln took up the law primarily to facilitate a political career. For three years Lincoln worked with Logan, who taught his young partner a great deal about the preparation of cases. The older man also shared Lincoln's natural inclination to act as a peacemaker, for Logan discouraged litigation and tried to resolve controversies amicably.

Under Logan's tutelage, Lincoln expanded his legal horizons to include practice in the federal courts and the Illinois Supreme Court, both of which had transferred operations to Springfield from Vandalia in 1839. Of the 411 state supreme court cases that Lincoln appeared in during his twenty-four-year legal career, a substantial number were tried during his brief partnership with Logan. In response to the hard times following the Panic of 1837, Congress enacted a short-lived bankruptcy law in 1841 to relieve debtors, many of whom enlisted the services of Logan and Lincoln. They handled seventy-seven such cases, more than any other firm in Springfield. Of the roughly 850 cases they were involved in, 70 percent related to debt collection. Logan stopped riding the circuit when he joined forces with Lincoln, who traveled not only the Eighth Judicial Circuit but also many other counties, among them Coles, where his stepmother and father resided.

In the winter and spring of 1841, Lincoln avoided Mary Todd, much to her distress. He may even have considered leaving the country; on March 5, John Todd Stuart recommended him for the post of chargé d'affaires at Bogotá, Colombia. In June, Mary lamented to a friend that Lincoln "deems me unworthy of notice, as I have not met *him* in the gay world for months." She consoled herself with the knowledge "that others were as seldom gladdened by his presence as my humble self." Yet, she confessed, "I would that the case were different, that he would once more resume his Station in Society, that 'Richard should be himself again,' much, much happiness would it afford me."[54] According to a cousin, Mary wanted Lincoln back because she had "made up her mind that he should marry her at the cost of her pride to show us all that she was not defeated."[55]

While ignoring Mary Todd, Lincoln sometime in 1841 briefly courted Sarah Rickard, the sister of Mrs. William Butler (née Elizabeth Rickard). He had often seen Sarah at the Butlers' house, where he boarded from 1837 to 1842. She was only 12 years old when they first met; four years later he seriously paid her court and proposed marriage, remarking that since she was named Sarah, she was destined to wed Abraham. She rejected the offer, later explaining that "his peculiar manner and his General deportment would not be likely to fascinate a young girl just entering the society world."[56] She thought of him as a big brother, not a potential mate.

In the summer of 1841, Lincoln spent six weeks in Kentucky with Joshua Speed at his family's stately home, Farmington, near Louisville. There his spirits revived as he enjoyed the Speeds' gracious hospitality, the luxurious appointments of a house far grander than any he had lived in, the companionship of his closest friend, the maternal warmth of Speed's mother, the playfulness of Speed's older half-sister Mary, and the intellectual stimulation provided by Speed's brother James, whom Lincoln in 1864 would appoint U.S. attorney general. When it came time to leave, Speed's mother gave Lincoln an Oxford Bible, which she called "the best cure for the 'Blues.'"[57] In late October 1841, Joshua Speed reported that since Lincoln's return to Springfield "he has been eminently successful in his practice" and "is in fine spirits and good health."[58] Three months later, Lincoln cheerfully told Speed that he recently had "been quite clear of the hypo."[59]

Lincoln soon found an opportunity to return the Speeds' kindness, for just as he was recovering from his romantic misadventures with Mary Todd, Joshua Speed, who was highly susceptible to Cupid's arrows, found himself tormented by an affair of the heart. He had fallen in love with a young neighbor, Fanny Henning, and impulsively proposed to her. When she accepted, however, Speed experienced "immense suffering" instead of joy because he doubted that he really loved her. Now Lincoln played counselor to Speed, reversing their earlier roles, writing him several letters that reveal as much about their author as they do about their recipient. He assured Speed that his anxiety was groundless, rhetorically asking his doubt-torn friend:

> How came you to court her? . . . You say you reasoned yourself into it. What do you mean by that? Was it not, that you found yourself unable to reason yourself out of it? Did you not think, and partly form the purpose, of courting her the first time you ever saw or heard of her? What had reason to do with it, at that early stage? There was nothing at that time for reason to work upon. Whether she was moral, amiable, sensible, or even of good character, you did not, nor could not then know; except perhaps you might infer the last from the company you found her in. All you then did or could know of her, was her personal appearance and deportment; and these, if they impress at all, impress the heart and not the head. Say candidly, were not those heavenly black eyes, the whole basis of all your early reasoning on the subject?[60]

This document suggests indirectly that Lincoln had several doubts about wedding Mary Todd: that he persuaded himself that he loved her because she wanted and expected him to do so; that he feared he was interested in her wealth and social status; and that he had allowed his head to rule his heart. When Speed expressed deep concern about his fiancée's health, Lincoln poignantly referred to his own experience as he tried to comfort his friend: "Why, Speed, if you did not love her, although you might not wish her death, you would most calmly be resigned to it." Alluding to doubts he harbored about Mary Todd, he added: "You know the Hell I have suffered on that point, and how tender I am upon it."[61]

To help Speed cope with his depression, Lincoln offered some advice: "Let me urge you, as I have ever done, to remember in the dep[t]h and even the agony of despondency, that verry shortly you are to feel well again. I am now fully convinced, that you love her as ardently as you are capable of loving. . . . I incline to think it probable, that your nerves will fail you occasionally for a while; but once you get them fairly graded now, that trouble is over forever. I think if I were you, in case my mind were not exactly right, I would avoid being *idle*; I would immediately engage in some business, or go to making preparations for it, which would be the same thing."[62] Lincoln evidently was trying to persuade himself not to take seriously his doubts about Mary Todd and to immediately busy himself with some project should he succumb to them.

On February 15, 1842, despite his misgivings, Speed married Fanny Henning. Lincoln reassured him that "no woman could do more to realize them [his dreams], than that same black-eyed Fanny. If you could but contemplate her through my immagination, it would appear ridiculous to you, that any one should for a moment think of being unhappy with her. My old Father used to have a saying that 'If you make a bad bargain, *hug* it all the tighter'; and it occurs to me, that if the bargain you have just closed can possibly be called a bad one, it is certainly the most *pleasant one* for applying that maxim to."[63] Here Lincoln seemed to be telling himself that he should not be disappointed if Mary Todd did not measure up to his unreasonable ideal and that he should marry her even if the engagement was a "bad bargain."

In March 1842, when Speed wrote that he was much happier than he had anticipated being, Lincoln rejoiced with him but confessed that his own pleasure in the newlyweds' bliss was diminished by his guilty conscience, which continued to torment him about Mary Todd. Referring cryptically to "that fatal first of Jany. '41," he asserted that since that time, "it seems to me, I should have been entirely happy, but for the never-absent idea, that there is *one* still unhappy whom I have contributed to make so. That still kills my soul. I can not but reproach myself, for even wishing to be happy while she is otherwise."[64]

In July, Lincoln again confided to Speed misgivings about his broken engagement to Mary Todd. He said he could not follow Speed's (unidentified) advice yet: "I must regain my confidence in my own ability to keep my resolves when they are made. In that ability, you know, I once prided myself as the only, or at least the chief, gem of my character; that gem I lost—how, and when, you too well know. I have not yet regained it; and until I do, I can not trust myself in any matter of such importance." With characteristic fatalism and passivity in matters of the heart, he declared that his own course was now to obey the injunction of Moses: "Stand *still* and see the salvation of the Lord."[65]

Near Duel

While awaiting a sign from the Almighty, Lincoln accepted a challenge to fight a duel. In August and September 1842 the *Sangamo Journal* ran three letters signed by "Aunt Rebecca of Lost Townships" ridiculing the Democratic leader James Shields. In August 1842, Shields, the state auditor, announced that his office would no longer accept in payment of taxes any notes issued by Illinois's state bank. Written the day after this order was published, the second "Rebecca" letter, which Lincoln was to acknowledge as his handiwork, ridiculed Shields as a "conceity dunce" and "a fool as well as a liar." The letter also poked fun at Shields's manliness and vanity, having him say to a group of young women, "Dear girls, *it is distressing*, but I cannot marry you all. Too well I know how much you suffer; but do, *do*, remember, it is not my fault that I am so handsome and *so* interesting."[66]

Enraged, Shields demanded the author's identity. When Lincoln confessed, the feisty Irishman insisted on a retraction and apology, alleging that "I have become the object of slander, vituperation and personal abuse, which were I capable of submitting to, I would prove myself worthy of the whole of it."[67] Indeed, he had become such a laughingstock in Springfield that people on the street teased him about it. His law partner, Gustav Koerner, thought that nobody "of the least spirit could have taken those insults without seeking satisfaction, even by arms, if necessary."[68]

For guidance, Lincoln turned to his friend Dr. Elias Merryman, who had once fought a duel and had, as a physician, witnessed several others. Lincoln told Merryman that "he was wholly opposed to duelling, and would do any thing to avoid it that might not degrade him in the estimation of himself and friends; but, if such *degradation* or a *fight* were the only alternative, he would fight."[69] The notoriously combative Merryman relished the prospect of a duel between Lincoln and Shields. Acting on Merryman's advice, Lincoln formally replied to Shields that "there is in this so much of assumption of facts, and so much menace as to consequences, that I cannot submit to answer that note."[70] When Shields responded with a more temperate and specific letter of complaint, Lincoln again refused to answer until the auditor withdrew his first note. Frustrated by such maneuvers, Shields without further ado issued a challenge.

Perplexed, Lincoln consulted his fellow Whig leader Albert Taylor Bledsoe, who recalled that Lincoln came to his office one night "with somewhat more than the usual gloom seated on his melancholy face" and said: "That fool letter which I wrote for the *Sangamo Journal* has made Shields mad, and he has challenged me. I have accepted the challenge, and, *without thinking*, I have chosen Dr. Merryman for my second. I believe he would rather see a fight than not; if I have to fight, I will fight; but I don't care about fighting just to gratify Dr. Merryman." Lincoln then asked Bledsoe to "make Dr. Merryman do right" so that "the whole difficulty may be settled." When Bledsoe asked about Merryman's role, Lincoln replied: "The friend of Shields says that if I will explain or apologize he will withdraw the challenge, and the quarrel can be settled honorably to both parties. But Dr. Merryman says, if Shields will first withdraw the challenge, then I will explain or apologize, and the quarrel may be settled honorably to both parties. And there they have come to a deadlock. Now I don't see, if both things have to be done, that it makes much difference which is done first. It seems to me that Dr. Merryman is disposed to stand upon niceties, and I don't think he ought to stand upon niceties in a case of life and death."

Bledsoe recommended to Lincoln, who had the choice of weapons, that he select cavalry broadswords. "I know Shields well," Bledsoe said, "and his courage is not of the truest stamp; there is altogether too much of bluster and bravado about the man . . . he is trying to make you back out, and you can make him back out very easily . . . if you will choose broadswords." Bledsoe assured Lincoln that Shields "will never fight you in the world. You are at least seven inches taller than Shields, and your arms are three or four inches longer than his; so that you could cut him down before he could get near enough to touch you. I know you will never do this; because he will never fight you with broadswords. He will show the white feather first."[71]

Following Bledsoe's advice, Lincoln stipulated that the weapons be broadswords "of the largest size" and that the field of honor be divided into two contiguous rectangular zones, each ten feet wide and six feet deep, which the combatants would occupy during the fight. Separating the two zones would be a plank set on edge, which neither duelist could cross over. When Shields's second protested that broadswords were "barbarous weapons for the nineteenth century" and insisted that the duelists use pistols or rifles, Lincoln replied: "Yes, they are barbarous; so is dueling, for that matter. It is just as well to have the whole thing of a piece."[72] Lincoln explained his choice of broadswords to Usher F. Linder: "I did not want to kill Shields, and felt sure that I could disarm him . . . ; and furthermore, I didn't want the d—d fellow to kill me, which I rather think he would have done if we had selected pistols."[73]

Because dueling was illegal in Illinois, the affair of honor, scheduled for September 22, was to take place on Missouri soil across the Mississippi River from Alton. On his way thither, Lincoln cracked a joke. The situation reminded him, he said, of a Kentuckian who had volunteered for service in the War of 1812. As he was about to leave home, his sweetheart presented him with a bullet pouch and belt bearing the embroidered motto "Victory or Death." In expressing his gratitude, the young man asked, "Isn't that rather too strong? Suppose you put 'Victory or Be Crippled.'"[74] When Lincoln and his entourage arrived and unloaded a bundle of huge broadswords, onlookers became curious and began speculating. After breakfast at the hotel, Lincoln and Shields, with their seconds and surgeons, boarded a ferry.

Word spread quickly, drawing hundreds of excited residents. Many, including the town constable and some would-be peacemakers, clambered aboard the ferry. The dueling parties sat at opposite ends of the boat. After the ferry reached Bloody Island, the seconds prepared a field of honor while Lincoln sat silent, looking quite sober. He slowly removed from its scabbard a saber resembling a fence rail (cavalry sabers were three and a half feet long and weighed nearly five pounds), and like a man testing a knife or scythe he had just sharpened, he lightly ran his thumb along the edge. He then arose, lifted the sword high, and sliced a twig from the overhanging branch of a willow tree.

Meanwhile, peacemakers sought a compromise. The leading role was taken by the brusque, loud-voiced Dr. Thomas M. Hope, a local Democratic editor. After vainly begging Shields to compromise, Hope grew angry and declared that the auditor "was bringing the Democratic party of Illinois into ridicule and contempt by his folly." Impatiently he blurted out: "Jimmy, you——little whippersnapper, if you don't settle this I will take you across my knee and spank you."[75]

That seemed to break the deadlock. Shields's seconds thereupon agreed to withdraw his notes, and in return Lincoln acknowledged:

> I did write the "Lost Township" letter which appeared in the Journal of the 2nd. inst but had no participation, in any form, in any other article alluding to you. I wrote that, wholly for political effect. I had no intention of injuring your personal or private character, or standing as a man or a gentleman; and I did not then think, and do not now think that that article could produce or has produced that effect against you, and had I anticipated such an effect I would have forborne to write it. And I will add, that your conduct towards me, so far as I knew, had always been gentlemanly; and that I had no personal pique against you, and no cause for any.[76]

All participants in the near duel took the ferry back to Alton, where a crowd awaited them. A humorist on the boat draped a sheet over a log, making it look like a human body, and fanned it vigorously as if caring for an injured duelist. Shields and Lincoln debarked together, pleasantly conversing as if nothing untoward had happened.

The Democratic press lashed out at Lincoln, derisively calling him "Aunt Becca," rebuking him for his "most unwarrantable and unprovoked attack" on Shields.[77] Even the Whig editor George T. M. Davis attacked him for getting involved in a near duel. Davis scolded the would-be combatants, pointing out that they were lawyers, legislators, and leaders of their communities who had nonetheless blatantly violated the law. Dueling, Davis insisted, "is the calmest, most deliberate and malicious species of murder."[78] The affair embarrassed Lincoln terribly. The following year, the Whig Party rejected his bid for a congressional nomination in part because, as he put it, he "had talked about fighting a duel."[79] After a participant in the near duel later attempted to discuss it with him, Lincoln said that he "seems anxious to revive the memory of an affair that I am trying to forget."[80] His embarrassment prompted Lincoln to stop writing abusive anonymous and pseudonymous letters, though he kept on ridiculing political opponents in speeches.

Marriage

Five days after helping Lincoln reconcile his differences with Shields, John J. Hardin assisted him in effecting another reconciliation, this time with Mary Todd. Hardin and his wife, who fancied herself a matchmaker, invited both Lincoln and Mary individually to attend the wedding of Hardin's sister Martinette at their home in Jacksonville on September 27. When the young people who were assembled there went for a ride, they left Mary Todd behind because she had no escort. As she sadly watched their carriage depart, she was astonished to see Lincoln ride up. According to the wife of John Todd Stuart, Mary "went down & he said he had come for her to join the party."[81] Off they went and soon were reconciled. Thereafter they met clandestinely at the house of Simeon Francis, courting secretly because, as Mary later explained somewhat obscurely, "the world—woman & man were uncertain & slippery and [we thought] that it was best to keep the secret Courtship from all Eyes & Ears."[82]

A week after that wedding in Jacksonville, Lincoln asked Joshua Speed a pointed question: "Are you now in *feeling* as well as *judgement*, glad you are married as you are?"[83] Lincoln believed he could not wed Mary Todd unless Speed had found happiness in matrimony. In reply, Speed advised him "not to hesitate or longer doubt that happiness would be the result of his marriage to Miss Todd," and he assured Lincoln that he found contentment once "he and Miss Henning had finally made up and determined to risk their happiness in each other's keeping."[84]

Taking this advice, Lincoln wed Mary Todd on November 4 with virtually no advance notice. That morning, the bride-to-be announced to her sister that "she and Mr. Lincoln would get married that night."[85] Similarly, Lincoln informed Charles Dresser, an Episcopal minister, "I want to get hitched tonight."[86] When Lincoln also told Ninian Edwards of their plans to wed that evening at Dresser's home, he responded: "That will never do. Mary Todd is my ward. If the marriage is going to take place, it must be at my house."[87] His wife Elizabeth also insisted that the ceremony take place in their home, admonishing Mary: "Do not forget that you are a Todd. But, Mary, if you insist on being married today, we will make merry, and have the wedding here this evening. I will not permit you to be married out of my house."[88]

A handful of people, including the two groomsmen, James H. Matheny and Beverly Powell, and the two bridesmaids, Julia Jayne and Ann Rodney, gathered in the Edwards' home that evening, where the Reverend Mr. Dresser performed the ceremony. Matheny recalled, "I could not help noticing a certain amount of whispering and elevation of eyebrows on the part of a few of the guests, as if preparing each other for something dramatic or unlooked-for to happen." That "something" was provided by the rotund, crude state supreme court justice Thomas C. Browne, who habitually blurted out whatever was on his mind. Unfamiliar with the Episcopal service, Browne was nonplussed when the groom turned to the bride and said, "With this ring I thee endow with all my goods and chattles, lands and tenements." At that point the judge exclaimed: "Lord Jesus Christ, God Almighty, Lincoln, the Statute fixes all that."[89] Startled and amused by this outburst, Dresser paused to stifle the impulse to burst out laughing; after a minute or so he managed to regain his composure and pronounce the couple man and wife.

In commenting on his marriage a week after the ceremony, Lincoln told Samuel D. Marshall: "Nothing new here, except my marrying, which to me, is matter of profound wonder."[90] After the ceremony, the newlyweds did not take a honeymoon but moved into a no-frills hostelry, the Globe Tavern, a large, ugly frame structure that Lincoln thought "very well kept" and economical, with room and board costing a mere four dollars per week.[91]

A Loveless Match?

From the outset, people wondered why Lincoln and Mary Todd wed. A guest at their wedding, Mrs. Benjamin S. Edwards, later wrote: "I have often doubted that it was really a love affair."[92] Close friends thought that honor and obligation, not love, impelled Lincoln to marry. According to Orville H. Browning, Lincoln "undoubtedly felt that he had made [a mistake] in having engaged himself to Miss Todd. But having done so, he felt himself in honor bound to act in perfect good faith towards her—and that good faith compelled him to fulfill his engagement with her, if she persisted in claiming the fulfillment of his word."[93]

On his wedding day, Lincoln, appearing and acting "as if he were going to the slaughter," said to one of his groomsmen, James Matheny, "I shall have to marry that girl." Matheny reported that Lincoln "often" confided "directly & indirectly" that "he was driven into the marriage."[94] While dressing for the ceremony, he was asked where he was headed. Lincoln replied, "I guess I am going to hell."[95] All this, coupled with the fact that Mary gave birth slightly less than nine months after the wedding, tends to confirm Wayne C. Temple's hypothesis that she seduced Lincoln the night before and made him feel obliged to wed her immediately in order to preserve her honor. She could not, of course, have known whether she was pregnant, but she might have been, and this knowledge could have constrained a man with an exceptionally tender conscience and highly developed sense of honor to marry her, despite strong misgivings.

This explanation is plausible, if not provable. It helps explain why the wedding took place on such short notice; why Lincoln looked like an animal en route to the slaughter; why he said he was "going to hell"; why he married someone whom he did not love; why Orville H. Browning believed that Lincoln was not "entirely free to act upon his own impulses"; why Herndon claimed that Lincoln "self-sacrificed himself rather than to be charged with dishonor"; and why Lincoln told Matheny that he "had to marry that girl" and that he "was driven into the marriage."[96]

Neither Lincoln nor Mary Todd seems to have been undersexed. Herndon considered her "the most sensual woman" he ever knew.[97] Similarly, despite his social awkwardness with girls in his youth, Lincoln was "a Man of strong passions for woman," according to his good friend David Davis.[98] Herndon recollected that Lincoln had "terribly strong passions for women" and "could scarcely keep his hands off them." Lincoln once confessed to Herndon that in the mid-1830s he had succumbed to "a devilish passion" for a girl in Beardstown.[99] Long after his wedding, Lincoln while on the circuit made improper advances to a young woman sleeping in a bed near his. He told companions that while spending the night at the home of a friend he had been awakened by the foot of his host's grown daughter, which inadvertently "fell on Lincoln's pillow. This put the *devil* into Lincoln at once, thinking that the girl did this of a purpose. Lincoln reached up his hand and put it where it ought not to be. The girl awoke, got up, and went to her mother's bed and told what had happened." Fortunately for Lincoln, who hurriedly departed the next morning, the mother urged her daughter to keep quiet.[100] In early adulthood Lincoln may have also patronized prostitutes. As a married man he continued to show signs of a robust sexuality, though Herndon said he "was true as steel to his wife, during his whole married life."[101] Thus it seems reasonable to conclude that if Mary Todd did try to seduce Lincoln in November 1842, she likely succeeded.

It is possible that Lincoln knew that Mary Todd would make his life miserable when he married her, but Herndon believed that she changed dramatically after the wedding. Before marriage, he asserted, she was "rather pleasant—polite—civil—rather graceful in her movements—intelligent, [and] witty." Indeed, she could be "affable and even charming in her manners." But "after she got married she became soured—got gross—became material—avaricious—insolent—mean—insulting—

imperious; and a she wolf." Herndon thought that the wolf "was in her when young and unmarried, but she unchained it."[102] (When she was First Lady, the two main presidential secretaries referred to her as "the Hell-Cat" and "her Satanic Majesty.")[103]

Mary Lincoln abused her husband both physically and verbally. When a farmer peddling apples door-to-door approached Lincoln, "Mrs. Lincoln came out and demanded of her husband why he was purchasing apples and set upon him with such violence that he feared Lincoln was in actual physical danger from his wife."[104] Lincoln got a taste of her temper shortly after their wedding. One morning at the Globe Tavern she arrived late for breakfast, as usual, inconveniencing the other guests. Boardinghouse etiquette dictated that in the morning no one could eat until all the guests were seated at the table. Lincoln, evidently irritated and embarrassed, gently chided her as she entered the room. She instantly threw a cup of hot coffee at him and fled in hysterics. Lincoln "sat there in humiliation and silence" while Mrs. Jacob Early helped clean him up.[105]

Now and then Mary Lincoln physically attacked her husband. One day, absorbed in his newspaper, he permitted the fire in the parlor to die down and then ignored several requests to add some fuel. Thereupon his wife struck him with a piece of firewood, declaring: "I'll make you hear me this time."[106] The next day, he appeared in court with a bandaged nose. On other occasions she hit him with a broomstick, cutlery, vegetables, and a package of meat he had purchased from a butcher in Springfield. Once in the mid-1850s, a knife-wielding Mary Lincoln chased her husband through their yard. When he realized that they were being observed, he suddenly wheeled about, grabbed his wife, and marched her back, saying: "There d—n it, now Stay in the house and don't disgrace us before the Eyes of the world."[107]

Mary behaved similarly toward her sons. Neighbors recalled that she was "always yelling at children . . . saying many things that were sharp and caustic, and which she afterward usually regretted."[108] She once "held a private-strapping party" with her youngest son, Tad, after he had fallen into a mud puddle.[109] Occasionally Lincoln would intervene to protect his children from their mother's wrath. One summer afternoon she accused Tad of stealing ten cents, flew into a rage when he denied it, and beat his legs with a switch. The punishment ceased when Lincoln entered the room, where the boy cringed in fright as his mother stood over him. When Lincoln asked what had happened, she replied incoherently. Lincoln solved the crisis by having the boy empty his pockets, then turned to his wife and said tenderly, "Mary! Mary!"[110]

Occasionally these roles were reversed: Lincoln would use corporal punishment, and his wife would object. Once he found young Robert and his friends putting on a play with dogs. The boys fastened a rope around one canine's neck, tossed the rope over a beam, and tugged hard to make the dog rise up. When the animal-loving Lincoln beheld the scene, he grabbed a barrel stave "and immediately began plying it indiscriminately on the persons of such boys as were within reach." Mary Lincoln reportedly "was very angry, and reproached her husband in language that was not at all adapted to Sunday School."[111]

Throughout his married life, Lincoln would regularly flee the house in search of peace and quiet. Herndon recalled that after marital squabbles Lincoln often would come to their office quite early, accompanied by his young son Robert. There Lincoln, "full of sadness," would sit quietly, "driven from home, by a club—knife or tongue."[112] To enable him to sleep over at the office "on nights of domestic discord," Lincoln purchased a couch six and a half feet long.[113] He would leave Springfield altogether whenever Mary was "having one of her spells." He told a neighbor: "I have found that when Mrs. Lincoln gets one of these nervous spells, it is better for me to go away for a day or two."[114] One evening Abner Y. Ellis, postmaster of Springfield, swapped stories with Lincoln at the post office until nearly midnight. Finally Lincoln sighed, "Well I hate to go home." When Ellis invited him to stay at his house, he accepted.[115]

In Springfield, men like William Herndon and Milton Hay understandably called Lincoln "woman whipt," "woman Cowed," and "hen pecked."[116] Mary was angry at her husband in part because he made comparatively little money. One acquaintance recalled that she "was very desirous of having a carriage to take herself and packages home, but was unable to persuade Mr. Lincoln to purchase one." Intent on shaming him, one day she called at his office and informed him that she had arranged for a vehicle to carry him home. Giving no signs of surprise, he calmly descended the stairs and beheld "an old fashioned one-horse dray," to which Mrs. Lincoln pointed and said, "There is your carriage."[117] He smiled and clambered aboard, urging her to follow his lead. She did not appreciate the joke and refused his offer. Lincoln then instructed the driver to convey him to their home.

Mary Lincoln was as tightfisted as her husband was generous. The Lincolns quarreled about the wages of servants, including a young woman who wanted a raise from $1.25 per week to $1.50. Mary refused, telling the girl to leave if she could not accept the smaller salary. Lincoln wanted the servant to stay, so when he failed to persuade his spouse, he tried to make a clandestine deal with the girl to feign accepting the $1.25 on the condition that he would surreptitiously make up the difference. Mary overheard this and barged in, exclaiming, "What are you doing—I heard Some Conversation—Couldn't understand it—I'm not going to be deceived—Miss you Can leave and as for you Mr L I'd be ashamed of myself."[118]

Herndon reported that Lincoln usually paid his wife no heed when she was enraged but that occasionally he would flare up. Remorsefully, Lincoln admitted to Herndon one Monday that the previous day, when his wife "had annoyed him to the point of exasperation," he had "lost his habitual self-control." She "was in a tirade so fierce" that he grabbed her, "pushed her through the door," and exclaimed: "If you can't stop this abuse, damn you, get out." Lincoln told Herndon "that he was deeply sorry for this act. He was not accustomed to lose his temper," and "he was greatly depressed that he had permitted himself to do and say what he had done and said."[119]

Mary Lincoln suffered from many anxieties. When her husband was out of town, she would become frightened and turn to neighbors for relief. James Gourley recalled one such occasion: "Mrs Lincoln had a bad girl [servant] living with her: the boys & men used to Come to her house in L[incoln']s absence and scare her: She was crying & wailing one night—Called me and said—'Mr Gourly—Come—do Come & Stay with me all night—you can Sleep in the bed with Bob and I.'"[120] She would hire neighborhood boys to stay with her when Lincoln was away. One of them recollected, "I spent many a night at the house, sleeping usually in the same room which Robert had occupied."[121] Mary once screamed "Murder!" because an old, bearded umbrella-repair peddler was on the back porch waiting for her. On departing, the umbrella man mumbled, "I wouldn't have such a fool for my wife!"[122]

For all the misery she caused Lincoln, creating what his law partner aptly called "a domestic hell on earth," Mary Todd proved a useful goad to his ambition.[123] John Todd Stuart told an interviewer that she "had the fire—will and ambition—Lincolns talent & his wifes Ambition did the deed." Joshua Speed thought "Lincoln needed driving—(well he got that.)"[124] Mary badly wanted her husband to become president. In the late 1840s she predicted to Ward Hill Lamon that Lincoln "is to be President of the United States some day; if I had not thought so I never would have married him, for you can see he is not pretty."[125]

In another way Mary Lincoln indirectly stimulated her husband's political career. According to Milton Hay, she made "his home tolerably disagreeable and hence he took to politics and public matters for occupation. If his domestic life had been entirely happy, I dare say he would have stayed at home and not busied himself with distant concerns."[126] A close friend of Lincoln's maintained that his domestic misery "operated largely in his favor; for he was thereby kept out in the world of business and politics. Instead of spending his evenings at home," he "was constantly out with the common people, was mingling with the politicians, discussing public questions." His spouse, "therefore, was one of the unintentional means of his promotion." If Lincoln had married Ann Rutledge or some other woman more agreeable than Mary Todd, "the country would never have had Abraham Lincoln for its President."[127]

Lincoln's friend and political ally Carl Schurz, who spent time with Mary Lincoln during the Civil War, summed up the feelings of many when he wrote that "it was no secret to those who knew the family well, that his domestic life was full of trials. The erratic temper of his wife not seldom put the gentleness of his nature to the severest tests; and these troubles and struggles, which accompanied him through all the vicissitudes of his life from the modest home in Springfield to the White House at Washington, adding untold private heartburnings to his public cares, and sometimes precipitating upon him incredible embarrassments in the discharge of his public duties, form one of the most pathetic features of his career."[128] In an interview, Schurz put it even more strongly, calling the marriage "the greatest tragedy of Mr. Lincoln's existence."[129]

7.

"I Have Got the Preacher by the Balls"

Pursuing a Seat in Congress (1843–1847)

In 1843, Mary Lincoln, eager and anxious to get to Washington, urged her husband to run for Congress. He required little goading, for his ambition was strong. Because voters in the Sangamon region had sent a Whig, John Todd Stuart, to Congress in the two previous elections, whoever secured that party's nomination would probably win. But Lincoln faced some very formidable challengers, most notably his friends Edward D. Baker and John J. Hardin.

During the winter of 1842–43, just after his wedding, Lincoln began a quest for the congressional nomination, to be decided at a convention in May. On February 14, he told a fellow Whig leader, "If you should hear any one say that Lincoln don't want to go to Congress, I wish you as a personal friend of mine would tell him you have reason to believe he is mistaken. The truth is, I would like to go very much."[1] Soon thereafter, at a meeting of Whigs in Springfield, he drew up a party platform endorsing protective tariffs, a national bank, distribution to the states of proceeds from federal land sales, and the convention system of choosing candidates.

In a circular elaborating on those points, he indulged in mild demagoguery, implausibly arguing that a protective tariff would burden "the wealthy and luxurious few, while the substantial laboring men . . . go entirely free." Only those "whose pride, whose abundance of means, prompt them to spurn the manufactures of our country, and to strut in British cloaks and coats and pantaloons, may have to pay a few cents more on the yard for the cloth that makes them." Whigs must adopt the convention system, Lincoln argued, for "while our opponents use it, it is madness in us not to defend ourselves with it." Nominating conventions united the faithful behind one candidate. To illustrate the point, Lincoln employed a scriptural aphorism that he would famously use again in 1858: "He whose wisdom surpasses that of all philosophers has declared that 'a house divided against itself cannot stand.'"[2]

Baker and Lincoln battled strenuously for the endorsement of the Sangamon County Whigs. When the local convention met, it chose Baker, mortifying Lincoln and angering his wife, who berated him for not working hard enough to win. Over his protest, the Sangamon County Whigs chose him as a delegate to the congressional district convention, where he was obliged to vote for Baker. When that convention assembled at Pekin and chose Hardin, Lincoln persuaded the delegates to pass a resolution supporting Baker for the following congressional term. This "Pekin agreement" seemed to establish a principle of one-term congressmen who would cede the post to a successor in regular rotation, with Lincoln as the obvious heir apparent to Baker.

In mid-May, Lincoln declared that he would cheerfully abide by the results of the Pekin convention. Even though he campaigned for Hardin extensively, Lincoln apparently begrudged him the nomination, for he did not vote for Hardin, who won the district handily. Instead, he cast ballots only for justice of the peace and constable, refusing to express any preference for congressional or county office candidates. Such uncharacteristically spiteful behavior suggests the intensity of his disappointment, which was shared by his wife, who wept copiously on the day that Hardin left to take his seat in Congress.

Domestic Life

The Lincolns' marriage had gotten off to a rocky start in the Globe Tavern, as Mary's flinging coffee in Lincoln's face indicates. She regularly complained about her husband's failure to come to bed on time; when she retired for the night, he often excused himself to fill a water pitcher, and while downstairs doing so, he would sit on the porch and relate stories to anyone who cared to listen. She would cough to signal that she wanted him to return to their room; sometimes he ignored her summons till after midnight. She would occasionally retaliate by entertaining gentlemen callers in their room with the door locked, hoping to annoy her neglectful spouse.

Things at the boardinghouse worsened after August 1, 1843, when Robert Todd Lincoln was born. Mrs. Albert Taylor Bledsoe, who was then staying at the Globe, did not like Mary Lincoln; nevertheless, each day for several weeks she helped wash and dress baby Robert. Mrs. Bledsoe's 6-year-old daughter, Sophia, who was fond of infants, also helped care for him. Lincoln would occasionally tend to Robert. One day as the baby was shrieking, his father picked him up and carried him around the room while his mother sat by, quietly weeping. The proprietress of the Globe assured the couple that their child merely had colic and was in no danger. But Robert's wailing so displeased other guests that they threatened to leave if the Lincolns didn't.

And so Abraham and Mary rented a small cottage on South Fourth Street. She, having grown up in a prosperous home with slaves to mind children, cook, and clean, felt that such duties were beneath her. While washing dishes one day in the mid-1840s, she was heard to sigh: "What would my poor father say if he found me doing this kind of work?"[3] According to a neighbor, she "was quite disposed to make a servant girl" of Lincoln, compelling him "to get up and get the breakfast and then dress the children, after which she would join the family at the table, or lie abed an hour or two longer as she might choose."[4]

Mary Lincoln found herself overwhelmed by the demands of motherhood as she gave birth to three more sons (Edward in 1846, William in 1850, and Thomas, better known as Tad, in 1853). If anything untoward happened to her children, she became hysterical. One day in 1844 she overreacted when young Robert became ill; she sent the maid to fetch a doctor, shouting after her, "Charity! Charity! run for your life and I'll give you fifty dollars when you get back."[5] Mrs. Frederick S. Dean, who lived across the street from the Lincoln home, took pity on the distracted newcomer and gently quieted her down when her hysterics threatened to disturb the peace of the neighborhood.

Maria Biddle, one of their neighbors, disapproved of the treatment Lincoln received at the hands of his wife, who "seemed to take a special delight in contradicting her husband, and humiliating him on every occasion."[6] Among other things, she criticized his appearance, often asking him, "Why don't you dress up and try to look like somebody?" She felt embarrassed because he "was so plain and dressed so plain."[7] Dale Carnegie, who interviewed people in Illinois whose ancestors had known Lincoln, wrote that Mary Lincoln "was always complaining, always criticizing her husband; nothing about him was ever right: He was stoop-shouldered, he walked awkwardly and lifted his feet straight up and down. She complained that there was no spring to his step, no grace to his movements; and she mimicked his gait and nagged at him to walk with his toes pointed down, as she had been taught at Madame Mentelle's [Academy in Lexington]. She didn't like the way his huge ears stood out at right angles from his head. She even told him that his nose wasn't straight, that his lower lip stuck out, that he looked consumptive, that his feet and hands were too large, his head too small."[8]

On January 16, 1844, the Lincolns purchased a one-and-a-half-story, six-room cottage at Eighth and Jackson Streets, where they spent the next seventeen years. The Lincolns' unpretentious home seemed too small for Mary Lincoln's taste. In the mid-nineteenth century, a house with a two-story back was a status symbol that she longed to have and could do so by expanding the upstairs of the house into a full second story. Lincoln, who opposed the idea, allegedly conspired with local carpenters to have an inflated estimate of the cost prepared so that he could reasonably claim that it was too expensive. In 1856, while he was away on the circuit, Mary had the job done anyway, evidently using money that her father had left her.

She decided on the addition soon after a successful tailor acquired an impressive house in their neighborhood; she was displeased that a mere tailor should have a more handsome residence than one of the city's more eminent lawyers. The alteration did make the twelve-room house stand out, dwarfing adjacent homes.

Lincoln avoided that house as much as possible because, according to William Herndon, "his home was *Hell*" and "absence from home was his *Heaven*."[9] Rather than return to Springfield on weekends like the other circuit riders, he stayed over in the little county seats by himself. Herndon remembered that "while all other lawyers, Every Saturday night after court hours, would start for home to see wife & babies," Lincoln, "poor soul, would grow terribly sad at the sight, as much as to

The house in Springfield where the Lincolns lived from 1844 to 1861 and the only one they ever owned. Charles Dresser, the Episcopalian minister who presided at the Lincolns' wedding in 1842, sold it to them. A modest six-room cottage when Lincoln bought it, it was expanded in 1856 into the twelve-room home depicted here. The photograph, taken by John Adams Whipple in 1860, shows Lincoln and his son Willie behind the front fence. Mary's sister Frances said that neither of the Lincolns "loved the beautiful—I have planted flowers in their front yard myself to hide nakedness—ugliness &c. &c. have done it often—and often—Mrs L never planted trees—Roses—never made a garden, at least not more than once or twice." Abraham Lincoln Presidential Library and Museum, Springfield, Illinois.

say—'I have no wife and no home.' None of us on starting home would say to Lincoln—'Come, Lincoln, let's go home,' for we knew the terrors of home to him."[10]

Presidential Politicking

In 1844, Lincoln campaigned passionately for the Whig presidential standard-bearer, Henry Clay, whom he said he "almost worshipped."[11] Lincoln could easily identify with Clay, for, as he observed at the Kentucky statesman's death in 1852, he—like Lincoln—had been born to "undistinguished parents" in "an obscure district," had only a "comparatively limited" formal education, and "added something to his education during the greater part of his whole life." His political philosophy, as Lincoln interpreted it in his eulogy for the Great Compromiser, reflected Lincoln's own views. Like Lincoln, Clay "loved his country partly because it was his own country, but mostly because it was a free country." He "burned with a zeal for its advancement, prosperity and glory, because it thus promoted the cause of liberty." Like Lincoln, Clay "desired the prosperity of his countrymen partly because they were his countrymen, but chiefly to show to the world that freemen could be prosperous." Like Lincoln, Clay was "in principle and feeling, opposed to slavery."[12] Whigs entertained high hopes for Clay's success in 1844. Throughout the campaign they concentrated on the tariff, while Democrats focused on expansionism in Texas and Oregon. The tariff of 1842—the chief accomplishment of the Whig-dominated Twenty-seventh Congress—had been designed to restore prosperity, encourage foreign investment, improve the balance of trade, and enhance government revenues.

During the winter of 1843–44, Lincoln joined Edward D. Baker, Stephen T. Logan, and John Todd Stuart in speaking nightly throughout Sangamon County. Several times during the spring, Lincoln debated John Calhoun, the Democratic congressional nominee in the Seventh District and the Democrat with the best intellect. An admiring Jesse W. Fell reported that Lincoln "evinced a thorough mastery of the principles of political economy which underlie the tariff question, and presented arguments in favor of the protective policy with a power and conclusiveness rarely equaled, and at the same time in a manner so lucid and familiar and so well interspersed with happy illustrations and apposite anecdotes, as to secure the delighted attention of his auditory."[13]

By 1844, the rising tide of immigration was beginning to roil American politics. When the Democrats tried to blame the Whigs for bloody anti-Catholic riots in Philadelphia, Lincoln and his party forcefully denied that there was any "hostility of the Whig party in general of *foreigners and Catholics*." At a Springfield public meeting in June, the Whigs adopted resolutions, presented by Lincoln, condemning the riots and asserting that foreigners who showed "fidelity to our country and institutions" should be admitted to citizenship" in "as convenient, cheap, and expeditious [a way] as possible." Moreover, they resolved that "the guarantee of the rights of conscience, as found in our Constitution, is most sacred and inviolable, and one that belongs no less to the Catholic, than to the Protestant."[14]

By October, Lincoln acknowledged that Clay would probably lose in Illinois, so he crossed the Wabash River and spoke several times in southwestern Indiana. That November, Clay received only 105 electoral votes to James K. Polk's 170. In Illinois, where enthusiasm for the annexation of Texas and for the American claim to all of the Oregon Territory was especially strong, the expansionist Polk swamped Clay, 54 percent to 42 percent. Lincoln, who was "not only disappointed but disgusted," regarded Clay's defeat "as a great public calamity and a keen personal sorrow."[15] He blamed the outcome on New York antislavery Whigs, who had voted for the Liberty Party candidate, James G. Birney, thus ensuring that Polk would carry the Empire State, and with it the nation. In 1845, he told a Liberty Party supporter that if the "whig abolitionists of New York had voted with us last fall, Mr. Clay would now be president, whig principles in the ascendent, and Texas not annexed; whereas by the division [of the Liberty and Whig forces], all that either had at stake in the contest, was lost." An antislavery Whig had declared to Lincoln that he could not vote for the slaveholder Clay because people of conscience "are not to do *evil* that *good* may come." Plaintively, Lincoln asked: "If by your votes you could have prevented the *extension*, &c. of slavery, would it not have been *good* and not *evil* so to have used your votes, even though it involved the casting of them for a slaveholder? By the *fruit* the tree is to be known. An *evil* tree can not bring forth *good* fruit. If the fruit of electing Mr. Clay would have been to prevent the extension of slavery, could the act of electing [him] have been *evil*?"[16]

Third Law Partnership

A month after the election, Lincoln amicably ended his partnership with Stephen T. Logan, who wanted to take into the firm his bibulous son. To replace Logan, Lincoln selected an inexperienced, erratic, impulsive attorney nearly ten years his junior, William H. Herndon, who described himself at that time as "a young, undisciplined, uneducated, wild man."[17] During an election campaign, Lincoln spotted him in Springfield urging a crowd of young men to vote for Whig candidates. By that time Herndon had come to hate the Democrats' proslavery inclinations. Lincoln halted, called Herndon over, asked his name, and said: "So you are a good Whig, eh? How would you like to study law with me?" Thereafter Lincoln regularly discussed politics with Herndon and took him into the Logan-Lincoln law office to prepare for the bar. A year and a half later, Lincoln went a step further, asking his apprentice: "Billy do you want to enter into partnership with me in the law business?" Herndon, who thought Lincoln was joking, replied: "Mr Lincoln this is something unexpected by me—it is an undeserved honor; and yet I say I will gladly & thankfully accept the kind and generous offer." He then broke down crying, for, as he later stated, Lincoln "picked me out of the gutter and made a man of me. I was a drunkard till he took me in hand and kept me straight."[18] Lincoln's sense of pity may have been aroused by Herndon's relative poverty and by the shabby treatment he had suffered at the hands of his father, conditions to which Lincoln could easily relate.

Lincoln viewed Herndon as a surrogate son, a role for which the young man was well suited. Lincoln, Herndon said, was "truly paternal in every sense of the word" and was "the best friend I ever had or expect ever to have except my wife & mother."[19] Estranged from his hard-drinking, proslavery sire, Herndon went to live at the Springfield store of Joshua Speed, where Lincoln also roomed. In time, Herndon became a temperance zealot, perhaps as a gesture of rebellion against his father, and later spoke of Lincoln as though he were a surrogate parent, calling him "the great big man of our firm" and himself "the little one," and remarking that the "little one looked naturally up to the big one."[20] Once, when the junior partner lay sick for three months, some of Lincoln's friends urged him to end the partnership. Lincoln "exclaimed vehemently: 'Desert Billy! No, never! If he is sick all the rest of his days, I will stand by him.'"[21] Herndon, perhaps recalling this episode, said that at one point he "had become so dissipated that some of Lincoln's friends thought proper to advise a separation, but Lincoln, with great dignity, declined their counsel, and the manner of the act so moved Herndon as to sober him and endeared him to Lincoln forever."[22] Lincoln stood by Herndon for sixteen years, dividing fees equally with him. Only after the election of 1860 did the partnership end. The firm of Lincoln and Herndon would handle approximately thirty-four hundred cases, of which half involved debt collection, and argued on average fifteen cases annually before the Illinois Supreme Court. At first, Herndon was, as he later recalled, "inclined to lawyers['] tricks false pleas—and so on. Lincoln strictly forbade it."[23]

Election to Congress

Lincoln quietly launched a campaign for the 1846 congressional nomination eight months before the district convention. If Baker and Hardin would abide by the Pekin understanding of 1843, Lincoln seemed to have the nomination sewed up. In keeping with its terms, Hardin had stepped down in 1844 in favor of Baker, who won the seat. But Hardin was not so accommodating in 1846; despite the Pekin agreement, he intended to run for Congress once again. To preempt Hardin, who delayed announcing his candidacy, Lincoln obtained pledges from Whigs as he traveled the legal circuit that fall. He also urged leading Whig editors not to support Hardin. In the Seventh District, only one Whig paper—the *Morgan Journal* (in Hardin's hometown)—rejected his appeal.

In February 1846, Lincoln did some politicking throughout the northern half of the district. Among the counties he targeted was Putnam, where hostility to slavery was strong. When two Free Soilers, Thomas Alsop and Franklin King, asked Lincoln about slavery, they were, as King recalled, "so well pleased with what he said on the subject that we advised that our anti-slavery friend[s] throughout the district should cast their vote for Mr. Lincoln: which was genirally done."[24] King, Alsop, and their friends significantly helped Lincoln win the district. Once in Congress, Lincoln had King's brother appointed register of the Springfield land office, much to the dismay of William Butler and some other Whigs.

Lincoln effectively argued that the Pekin understanding should be interpreted to mean that Hardin ought not be nominated because he had already served his term in Congress. Lincoln declared that "turn about is fair play" and asked for "a fair shake."[25] The influential Robert Boal, of Lacon, agreed, and when Hardin tried to enlist his support, that good doctor replied that while he admired the former congressman, "I do not see how we can avoid adopting the maxim that 'turn about is fair play.'"[26] Discouraged that many Whig voters were persuaded by that argument, Hardin tried to sow animosity between Lincoln and Baker by misrepresenting to each man what the other had said. But eventually Baker withdrew after Lincoln expressed reluctance to abandon his dream of a congressional seat.

Desperate to counter the turn-about-is-fair-play argument, Hardin proposed that the convention system be scrapped in favor of a preferential primary election. Lincoln, sensing that the "movement is intended to injure me," urged Whig editors to take "strong ground for the old system under which Hardin and Baker were nominated."[27] On January 19, 1846, Lincoln calmly and firmly told Hardin that the primary scheme was unfair. In his usual accommodating fashion, Lincoln said: "I have always been in the habit of acceeding to almost any proposal that a friend would make; and I am truly sorry I can not in this."[28] In reply, Hardin denounced the convention system as "anti-republican," criticized Lincoln for trying to derail his congressional candidacy by having him nominated for governor, and belittled the Pekin agreement for its assumption that "the District is a horse which each candidate may mount and ride a two mile heat without consulting any body but the grooms & Jockeys."[29] Although nettled by Hardin's failure to abide by the Pekin accord, Lincoln insisted that "nothing be said" against him.[30] When Lincoln's law student Gibson Harris proposed that he respond in kind to Hardin's tactics, Lincoln said, "Gibson, I *want* to be nominated. I should like very much to go to Congress; but unless I can get there by fair means I shall not go."[31]

On January 31, the Whigs of Athens named Lincoln as their choice for Congress. Two weeks later, on the eve of other precinct meetings, Hardin, despairing of his prospects, withdrew from the race. Although bitter, he graciously refused to run as an independent candidate or otherwise injure Lincoln's chances. Lincoln, fearful of Whig defections, did his best to salve the wounded feelings of Hardin and his followers. By May 1, when the Whig district convention assembled in Petersburg, Lincoln's nomination was a foregone conclusion. He may well have worried that Hardin might thwart his future aspirations. In 1847, however, Hardin was killed in the Mexican War, thus clearing the political field for Lincoln. Baker, who also might have posed a threat to Lincoln's political future, moved to Oregon.

In late May, Democrats nominated the well-known Methodist circuit-riding preacher Peter Cartwright to run against Lincoln. Almost a quarter century older than his Whig opponent, the colorful, energetic, combative, ambitious Cartwright was an imposing man and a formidable foe. Little is known about the Lincoln-Cartwright campaign, for the press virtually ignored it. The only extant newspaper report of an appearance by Lincoln merely noted that at Lacon he "gave us a good speech" on the tariff that concluded "with some general observations on the Mexican war, annexation of Texas, and the Oregon question."[32] Those observations may have resembled what Lincoln told Williamson Durely in 1845: "I never was much interested in the Texas question," but insofar as the annexation of Texas might strengthen slavery, "I think annexation an evil."[33] It was later alleged that Lincoln initially supported the Mexican War in 1846 before changing his mind and criticizing it in 1847, but in all likelihood, he was agnostic about the war rather than a strong supporter.

Lincoln campaigned relentlessly, traversing the district often, though spending little money. Prominent Whigs collected a two-hundred-dollar campaign fund, of which he used less than 1 percent. "I did not need the money," Lincoln said as he returned the balance of the cash. "I made the canvass on my own horse; my entertainment being at the houses of friends, cost me nothing; and my only outlay was 75 cents for a barrel of cider, which some farmhands insisted I should treat them to."[34] Eighteen years later Lincoln described the 1846 campaign as the least acrimonious of his political career. It was, however, not without its ugly side. Cartwright avoided meeting Lincoln in public discussion and instead launched a whispering campaign against his opponent, describing him as an infidel. As a result, many pious Christian Whigs were reluctant to vote for Lincoln.

Such attacks angered Lincoln. When the president of Illinois College wished him success, Lincoln replied, "I do not know. We are dealing with men that would just as soon lie as not."[35] At Postville, where Cartwright had accused Lincoln of being a "skeptic," the Whig candidate responded by reading to his audience a passage from the Illinois Constitution stipulating that "no religious test shall ever be required as a qualification to any office or public trust under this state." Lincoln then added: "Brother Cartwright may be well posted in theology but he is not informed as to the constitution of his own state which he has several times sworn to maintain."[36]

Lincoln decided to meet the charge of atheism head-on. On July 31, he issued a handbill protesting that he was no "open scoffer at Christianity." To be sure, he acknowledged that he was "not a member of any Christian church" but asserted that he had "never denied the truth of the Scriptures" and had "never spoken with intentional disrespect of religion in general, or of any denomination of Christians in particular." At one time, he admitted, he "was inclined to believe in what . . . is called the 'Doctrine of Necessity'—that is, that the human mind is impelled to action, or held in rest by some power, over which the mind itself has no control." He had even defended this proposition in private discussions—never publicly—but had given up doing so five years earlier. That doctrine, he asserted, was "held by several of the Christian denominations." He concluded by declaring that "I do not think I could myself, be brought to support a man for office, whom I knew to be an open enemy of, and scoffer at, religion." No man, he said, "has the right thus to insult the feelings, and injure the morals, of the community in which he may live. If, then, I was guilty of such conduct, I should blame no man who should condemn me for it; but I do blame those, whoever they may be, who falsely put such a charge in circulation against me."[37]

Some residents of the Seventh District found Lincoln's "lawyer like declaration" less than forthcoming. One said of it that in "war, politics and religion, a *ruse* is admissible."[38] The criticism has some merit, for in this document Lincoln seemed to make two different claims: that he never believed in infidel doctrines and that he never publicly espoused them. If the former were true, the latter would be superfluous; if the former were untrue, the latter would be irrelevant. Moreover, his reference to the doctrine of necessity was a dodge, for he was accused of infidelity, not fatalism. In addition, Lincoln's assertion that he had "never denied the truth of the Scriptures" is belied by the testimony of friends, as is the implication that he was skeptical only in his early years. After moving to Springfield in 1837, Lincoln continued to express the irreverent views he had proclaimed in New Salem. John Todd Stuart recalled that "he was an avowed and open Infidel—Sometimes bordered on atheism" and that he "always denied that Jesus was . . . the son of God."[39]

Lincoln's 1846 handbill may seem a clever attorney's ingenious exercise in obfuscation, but it is more than that. The "doctrine of necessity," as Lincoln understood it, was a kind of determinism akin to that of psychologists who maintain that acts and thoughts are dictated by forces beyond the control of the rational, conscious ego. Lincoln believed that no act was unselfish. For example, when he aided birds or animals in distress, he was not behaving altruistically; he selfishly wished to avoid the pain that his hypersensitive conscience would cause him if he did not so act. This belief inclined Lincoln to be unusually charitable, forbearing, nonjudgmental, compassionate, and forgiving, especially in his later years. Yet Lincoln found determinism hard to square with the fundamental principles of law and morality. He told his good friend Joseph Gillespie "that he could not avoid believing in predestination although he considered it a very unprofitable field of speculation because it was hard to reconcile that belief with responsibility for ones act[s]."[40]

Cartwright's whispering campaign availed him little in those localities where he and Lincoln were well known, but in the northern part of the district it proved effective, undermining support for Lincoln, who nevertheless captured 56 percent of the vote, topping Hardin's 53 percent in 1843 and Baker's 52 percent in 1844. Many Democrats probably supported Lincoln, for in the Seventh Congressional District the Whig nominee for governor received only 426 more votes than his Democratic opponent, while Lincoln won 1,511 more votes than Cartwright. Some of the men who voted for both Lincoln and the Democratic gubernatorial candidate may have objected to Cartwright's profession. During the campaign, one Democrat told Lincoln, "Such is my utter aversion to the meddling of preachers in politics, that I will vote for you Even at the risk of losing cast with my party, if you think the contest doubtful." Lincoln responded: "I would like your vote, but I fully appreciate your position, and will give you my honest opinion on the morning of Election day." When that day arrived, Lincoln confidently told this Democrat: "I am now satisfied that I have got the preacher by the [balls], and you had better keep out of the ring."[41]

Lincoln felt little elation upon achieving the goal that he had strenuously pursued; he confided to Joshua Speed that his election to Congress "has not pleased me as much as I expected."[42] Such a letdown is not unusual among the compulsively ambitious, for the attainment of power satisfies only temporarily the hunger for approval rooted in a damaged sense of self-worth. Another reason for the lack of euphoria on Lincoln's part may have been the peculiar congressional timetable: the Thirtieth Congress would not meet until December 1847. Wishing to avoid conflict with fellow Whigs, he refused to fill the unexpired term of his friend Edward D. Baker, who in January 1847 quit his seat to participate in the Mexican War.

Poet

While waiting for his congressional term to begin, Lincoln indulged his poetical muse, writing verses inspired by his 1844 campaign swing through Indiana. The sight of old haunts that he had not visited for fourteen years prompted him to compose what he called "poetry, or doggerel" about his youth.[43] In 1846 and 1847 he submitted to attorney Andrew Johnston a few poems, some of which Johnston published anonymously in the Quincy *Whig*. (Lincoln did not want his authorship revealed, for, as he told Johnston, "I have not sufficient hope of the verses attracting any favorable notice to tempt me into risk being ridiculed for having written them.")[44] Their most striking feature is morbidity, reflecting Lincoln's obsession with death, rooted in his childhood experiences of loss.

Lincoln sent Johnston not only his own verses but also a copy of his favorite poem, William Knox's "Mortality." "I would give all I am worth, and go into debt, to be able to write so fine a piece as I think that is," he told Johnston.[45] Lincoln discovered "Mortality" in a newspaper in 1845, shortly after his campaign trip to Indiana. The memories thus awakened made him susceptible to the appeal of Knox's dirge-like quatrains:

> Oh why should the spirit of mortal be proud!
> Like a swift flying meteor—a fast flying cloud—
> A flash of lightning—a break of the wave,
> He passeth from life to his rest in the grave.

Various stanzas of that poem may have brought back images of loved ones who had died in his youth—Nancy Hanks, her aunt and uncle, his infant brother, his sister, and Ann Rutledge.

Lincoln's own 1846 poem, "My Childhood Home I See Again," is similarly obsessed with "loved ones lost." The first canto clearly deals with Lincoln's own family and friends.

> My childhood-home I see again,
> And gladden with the view;
> And still as mem'ries crowd my brain,
> There's sadness in it too.
> O memory! thou mid-way world
> 'Twixt Earth and Paradise,
> Where things decayed, and loved ones lost
> In dreamy shadows rise.

After two decades' absence, Lincoln noted, "Where many were, how few remain / Of old familiar things!" Now half of his old friends were dead and gone.

> I hear the lone survivors tell
> How nought from death could save,
> Till every sound appears a knell,
> And every spot a grave.
> I range the fields with pensive tread,
> And pace the hollow rooms;
> And feel (companions of the dead)
> I'm living in the tombs.[46]

Another psychological concern appears in a poem he composed after his 1844 visit to Indiana: fear of insanity. His schoolmate Matthew Gentry, three years older than Lincoln, had at the age of 19 become "a howling, crazy man" and tried to kill his parents. Thereafter, he was locked up as a madman. Lincoln's verses reveal the horror he felt as he observed Gentry:

> But here's an object more of dread
> Than aught the grave contains—
> A human form with reason fled,
> While wretched life remains.

In this poem Lincoln reflects on his fear of madness—of "pangs that killed the mind!" of "reason dead and gone," and of losing "the power to know."[47] His reaction to Gentry's insanity suggests that he may have feared that he might lose his own mind. In the opinion of his neighbors, he had gone crazy at least twice—following the death of Ann Rutledge in 1835 and after breaking his engagement to Mary Todd in 1841. Perhaps he feared that such an attack would recur. He may also have feared that his wife was insane. She behaved irrationally, starting early in their marriage. According to William Herndon, Lincoln "held his wife partly insane for years, and this shows his toleration of her nature—his great forbearance of her outlandish acts."[48]

Lincoln's Old-Man Archetype

In 1847, while attending a conference in Chicago, Lincoln first became known as "Old Abe," though he was only 38. Elihu B. Washburne recalled that one day "several of us sat on the sidewalk under the balcony of the Sherman House," and a member of that group, S. Lyle Smith, exclaimed, "There is Lincoln on the other side of the street. Just look at 'Old Abe.'" Washburne recollected that "from that time we all called him 'Old Abe.'" Washburne thought his colleague's remark peculiar: "Old Abe, as applied to him, seems strange enough, as he was then a young man."[49] Nonetheless, others sensed what Smith did. Even Lincoln, at 39, declared to Herndon: "I suppose I am now one of the old men."[50]

Why he should be deemed old when he betrayed few physical signs of aging cries out for explanation. The psychologist Carl Jung maintained that everyone is dominated by an archetypal figure, a condition unrelated to the experiences of childhood. Lincoln's archetype seems to have been the Old Man, combining the qualities of the Wise Elder and the Great Father. Regardless of physical appearance, the mature Lincoln seemed to radiate the positive qualities of being old. Accordingly, many Illinoisans regarded him with filial reverence. A train conductor in Illinois recalled, "We couldn't exactly make him out. . . . There was something about him that made plain folks feel toward him a good deal as a child feels toward his father."[51] That "something" was Lincoln's Old Man/Great Father archetype. During his presidency, it would play a vital role in sustaining Union morale, for many Northerners trusted him as one would trust a benevolent, wise father.

Defending a Slave Owner

Lincoln had not dealt with the slavery issue during his congressional campaign, but he confronted it in the fall of 1847 when a Kentucky slaveholder, Robert Matson, employed his legal services to help recover a slave family. Matson cultivated a farm in Coles County, Illinois, with slaves imported from Kentucky, where he also owned a farm. At first, when he began this pattern, after each harvest he would send them back across the Ohio River, and then the following spring he would import a new gang from Kentucky. This practice was legal in Illinois, where the law only forbade a slaveholder from domiciling bondspeople. Matson nonetheless permanently retained a slave in Illinois, Anthony Bryant, as an overseer, thus technically freeing him. Bryant, however, did nothing to assert his free status until the spring of 1847, when his wife, Jane, and their children, who had arrived in Illinois two years earlier, seemed in danger of being permanently separated from him. (In 1845, Matson evidently feared that if he returned the slaves to Kentucky, they would be seized by his creditors.) Matson's hot-tempered, jealous housekeeper-mistress, known as "a vicious negro hater," suspected that he was sexually involved with Jane Bryant and demanded that she and her children be sold.[52] To thwart that possibility, Anthony Bryant enlisted the help of two local abolitionists, Hiram Rutherford, a Pennsylvania-born physician, and Gideon Ashmore, a hotel-keeper known as "a wide-awake business man" whom "nothing pleased so well as a stiff legal fight." A "strong anti-slavery man," Ashmore sheltered Jane Bryant and her offspring.[53] Matson sued for possession of his slaves, who at the direction of a justice of the peace were temporarily jailed in Charleston, Illinois.

Soon thereafter, Lincoln arrived in Coles County, where he had suits pending in the circuit court. There he was approached by his friends Usher F. Linder and Thomas Marshall, attorneys for Matson, who wanted to sue Rutherford and Ashmore for damages. That conversation turned out to be important, for subsequently Dr. Rutherford asked Lincoln to serve as his lawyer. Rutherford told Lincoln of the situation, emphasized that they had seen eye to eye on political issues, and requested that he defend him in court. Rutherford remembered that as he described the case to Lincoln, "a peculiarly troubled look came over his face now and then, his eyes appeared to be fixed in the distance beyond me and he shook his head several times as if debating with himself some question of grave import." Lincoln responded "with apparent reluctance" that he must refuse for "he had already been counseled with in Matson's interest and was therefore under professional obligations to represent the latter unless released." Rutherford became angry at Lincoln, who tried his best to explain that "as a lawyer, he must represent and be faithful to those who counsel with and employ him." Lincoln then went to Linder and Marshall and obtained a release. When, however, he informed Rutherford that he was now free to represent him in court, his offer was spurned. Later the hot-tempered Rutherford admitted, "I was a little too hasty."[54] So it was that Lincoln came to represent a slave owner in court. Had Rutherford been less petulant, Lincoln would have represented the Blacks and their protectors. He could, of course, have simply refused to participate in the case, but he was specially importuned by Linder and Marshall, both of them friends and political allies of his. He evidently agreed to support them more for friendship's sake than anything else.

However reluctant Lincoln may have been to act on Matson's behalf, he argued his client's case forcefully. That case was weak, for Jane Bryant had been in Illinois for two years and clearly was not just a seasonal worker. Lincoln's client therefore lost. With the aid of Dr. Rutherford, the Bryant family was able to immigrate to Liberia, where they were observed the following year living "truly in a deplorable condition."[55]

Lincoln's agreement to represent Matson has been called "one of the greatest enigmas of his career," the "most profound mystery ever to confound Lincoln specialists," and "one of the strangest episodes in Lincoln's career at the bar."[56] Six years earlier, in the case of *Bailey v. Cromwell*, he and John Todd Stuart had successfully defended a Black woman who sued for her freedom. They convinced the Illinois Supreme Court that the sale of the woman, who had been purchased in Illinois, was invalid, for she was free under the provisions of both the Northwest Ordinance of 1787 and the Illinois Constitution.

Lincoln's behavior in the Matson case was hardly inexplicable; it demonstrated his acceptance of the advice of Judge George Sharswood, a well-known mid-nineteenth-century American commentator on legal ethics who urged lawyers "not to pass moral judgments on potential clients, but to rely on the legal process itself to determine the merits of the claim." Sharswood believed that an attorney "is not morally responsible for the act of the party in maintaining an unjust cause, nor for the error of the court, if they fall into error, in deciding in his favor." A lawyer "who refuses his professional assistance because in his judgment the case is unjust and indefensible, usurps the function of both judge and jury."[57] So, despite his antislavery convictions, Lincoln accepted the Matson case in keeping with what became known in England as the "cab-rank" rule (that lawyers must accept the first client who hails them) and with the prevailing Whig view that lawyers should try to settle disputes in an orderly fashion through the courts, trusting in the law and the judges to assure that justice was done.

Ideological neutrality characterized Lincoln's law practice in general, not just in slave-related cases. In malpractice suits he would represent doctors and patients alike; he represented railroads being sued by boat owners whose vessels crashed into their bridges and also boat owners suing railroads for obstructing navigation with their bridges; he represented stock subscribers reneging on their pledges and corporations suing such stock subscribers. At least three times he was defeated because of a precedent that he had helped establish earlier. On the stump he defended the Whig economic program favoring banks, corporations, and internal improvements like railroads, but in court he showed no hesitancy in representing clients suing those banks, corporations, and railroads. Like other members of the bar, Lincoln could ill afford to be finicky about clients; there were simply too many lawyers and too few clients.

Some attorneys did view slave cases from a principled position and not, as Lincoln did, neutrally, as just another piece of necessary business. Known as the "Attorney General for Runaway Negroes," Ohio's Salmon P. Chase often represented Blacks fleeing from bondage and never defended a slaveholder. He became a leader of the more radical political antislavery forces. Lincoln, by contrast, avoided fugitive slave cases, as one friend explained, "because of his unwillingness to be a party to a violation of the Fugitive Slave Law, arguing that the way to overcome the difficulty was to repeal the law."[58]

Journey to Washington

In October 1847, Congressman-elect Lincoln rented his Springfield house and with his wife and children set out to assume his new post in Washington. On their circuitous journey, the family passed from St. Louis to Frankfort, where they caught a train for Lexington, intending to spend three weeks with the Todds. On the last leg of their trip, 4-year-old Robert and his 18-month-old brother, Eddy, irritated their fellow passengers, including Joseph Humphreys, nephew of Mary Lincoln's stepmother. Arriving at his aunt's home before the Lincolns, young Humphreys exclaimed: "I was never so glad to get off a train in my life. There were two lively youngsters on board who kept the whole train in a turmoil, and their long-legged father, instead of spanking the brats, looked pleased as Punch and aided and abetted the older one in mischief."[59]

As this anecdote suggests, Lincoln was notoriously indulgent to his sons. William Herndon observed that Lincoln was "so blinded to his children's faults" that if "they s[hi]t in Lincoln's hat and rubbed it on his boots, he would have laughed and thought it smart. . . . He worshipped his children and what they worshipped; . . . disliked what the[y] hated, which was everything that did not bend to their . . . whims." Herndon complained that when the boys came to the office with their father, they "would take down the books—empty ash buckets—coal ashes—inkstands—papers—gold pens—letters etc., etc. in a pile and then dance on the pile."[60]

The visit with Mary's family went smoothly in part because Robert Smith Todd was fond of his son-in-law, whom he had met at Springfield in 1843. To help the newlyweds out, Todd gave them eighty acres of land near Springfield, provided annual gifts for the remaining six years of his life (totaling more than eleven hundred dollars), and assigned to them notes of various Illinois merchants who owed him money. These funds were doubtless much appreciated by Lincoln, who in 1843 told Joshua Speed that he could not come to Kentucky because of "poverty."[61]

Arriving at the Todd house shortly after the irate Joseph Humphreys, the Lincolns were warmly received. During this vacation, Lincoln spent much time reading periodicals like *Niles' Register* and a poetry anthology that included William Cullen Bryant's "Thanatopsis," which he committed to memory. Lincoln also had ample opportunity to observe the cruelties of slavery. He doubtless saw the public square, with its slave auction block and whipping post, and may have observed slave coffles filing by the Todd house, for Lexington was the state's principal slave market. The noisome holding pens of a slave dealer practically abutted the home of Mary Lincoln's grandmother, the redoubtable Elizabeth R. Parker. Lincoln perhaps witnessed auctions there or at the public square.

On November 13, Lincoln heard Henry Clay launch his fourth attempt to win the presidency with a speech about James K. Polk's actions precipitating the war with Mexico, a conflict still under way at the time. "This is no war of defence," Clay charged, "but one unnecessary and of offensive aggression. It is Mexico that is defending her fire-sides, her castles and her altars, not we." He emphatically opposed the extension of slavery into any territory acquired from Mexico: "I have ever regarded slavery as a great evil, a wrong, for the present, I fear, an irremediable wrong to its unfortunate victims. I should rejoice if not a single slave breathed the air or was within the limits of our country."[62]

With these words ringing in his ears, Lincoln soon left Kentucky to take his seat in Congress, where he would denounce President Polk's Mexican War policy and try to abolish slavery in the District of Columbia. Accompanying him was a wife who aspired "to loom largely" at the nation's capital.[63]

8.

"A Strong but Judicious Enemy to Slavery"

Congressman Lincoln (1847–1849)

Lincoln's entire public service on the national level before his election as president was a single term in the U.S. House. Although he had little chance to distinguish himself there, his experience proved a useful education in dealing with Congress and patronage. He also had to grapple with the slavery issue head-on.

Washington, D.C.

Arriving in Washington on December 2, 1847, the Lincolns found themselves in "an ill-contrived, ill-arranged, rambling, scrambling village" of approximately forty thousand souls.[1] For a few days, the newly arrived Lincolns resided at the Indian Queen, a shabby hotel. Soon thereafter, they settled at one of the city's numerous boardinghouses, the one known as "Abolition House," located across from the Capitol and operated by Mrs. Ann Sprigg. Theodore Dwight Weld, a prominent abolitionist who had roomed at Mrs. Sprigg's in 1842, explained that his Virginia-bred landlady was "*not* a slaveholder, but hires slaves. She has eight servants all colored, 3 men, one boy and 4 women. All are free but 3 which she hires and these are buying themselves."[2] The Illinoisans admired Mrs. Sprigg; during the Civil War, Lincoln called her "a most worthy and deserving lady."[3]

Eight of Lincoln's fellow congressmen lived at Mrs. Sprigg's, including James Pollock of Pennsylvania, who described Lincoln as "full of good humor, ready wit and with an unlimited fund of anecdote, which he would relate with a zest and manner that never failed to bring down the 'Mess', and restore harmony & smiles, when the peace of our little community was threatened by a too earnest or heated controversy on some of the exciting questions of the hour."[4] Another messmate was Joshua R. Giddings of Ohio, the most radical antislavery representative, who during the Thirtieth Congress would help shape Lincoln's views. Six feet, two inches tall, courageous and self-assured, he stood ever ready to battle for righteousness.

When intemperate debates about slavery erupted at Mrs. Sprigg's table, Lincoln defused the tension with humor. Although he had strong feelings about slavery, he was careful to express them in such a way as to offend no one, not even proslavery colleagues. At mealtime, when he was preparing to share an anecdote, he would set down his utensils, place his elbows on the table, cup his face in his hands, and preface his remarks with, "That reminds me." His fellow diners keenly relished the prospect of a hilarious recitation. They liked him not only for his sense of humor but also for his amiability, kindness, and unpretentious manners. Lincoln often relaxed at a nearby bowling alley. Although he was quite awkward at the sport, he enjoyed it and played with gusto. Whenever it was known he was at the alley, people would drop by to listen to his stories.

Popularity

Lincoln's humor won him friends all over Capitol Hill. Around Christmas of 1847, he began to frequent the small post office of the House of Representatives, where members often gathered to swap yarns. After diffidently remaining silent for a while, once he began to tell stories he quickly outstripped all competitors. His tales of the Black Hawk War were especially popular.

Colleagues in the House admired more than Lincoln's humor; his character and personality also earned their esteem. In May 1848, a Washington correspondent reported that "no member of whom I have any knowledge, possesses in a higher degree the respect and confidence of the House" than Lincoln—heady praise for a newcomer.[5] A few months later, another journalist called Lincoln a "universal favorite here—an entirely self-made man, and of singular and striking personal appearance."[6] His colleagues praised his warmth, generosity, magnanimity, practical common sense, and oratorical prowess. One observer reported that whenever the Illinois Whig "addressed the House, he commanded the individual attention of all present."[7] This was no small accomplishment in a chamber whose notoriously poor acoustics made it difficult for speakers to be heard.

Unlike her husband, Mary Lincoln enjoyed little popularity, and by April 1848 she had returned to her father's home in Lexington. She may have been lonely, for there were few congressional wives with whom to socialize. At Abolition House, where she rarely appeared save at mealtime, some boarders found her disagreeable. Lincoln had mixed feelings about his wife's absence. "In this troublesome world of ours," he told her, "we are never quite satisfied. When you were here, I thought you hindered me some in attending to business; but now, having nothing but business—no variety—it has grown exceedingly tasteless to me. I hate to sit down and direct documents, and I hate to stay in this room by myself."[8]

Life of a Freshman Representative

Like many of his colleagues, Lincoln found routine congressional work unrewarding. Representatives usually began their day by answering correspondence, visiting government offices on behalf of constituents, attending committee meetings, and conning newspapers. House sessions customarily ran from noon till early evening, when caucuses were often held. As a lowly freshman, Lincoln occupied an undesirable seat at the back of the House chamber. He also was assigned to unimportant committees (those on expenditures in the War Department and on post offices and post roads). The chairman of the latter said that "no man on that Committee worked more industriously than he did."[9]

The House teemed with activity. The representatives' desks made the lower chamber a convenient place for them to take care of their correspondence and other business, much to the annoyance of speechifying colleagues. Even more annoying was the cacophony generated by members clapping their hands to summon ubiquitous page boys for various chores. To many representatives, however, their colleagues' inattention made little difference, for speeches were designed for home consumption, while the real business of the House was transacted in committees and private consultations.

Speeches

Much as Lincoln enjoyed the popularity that his humor and personality won him, he aspired to do more than merely ingratiate himself with his colleagues, a slight majority of whom were Whigs. Lincoln's brief initial speech, given on January 5, was not his magnum opus. It dealt with a government mail contract and was not a conspicuous success. He presented his argument like a legal pleading and was interrupted at the beginning of his remarks, admonished that he must not reveal in debate what had taken place in committee deliberations.

The Whigs, who had been critical of the Mexican War since it began in May 1846, intended to make President Polk's conduct of hostilities a centerpiece of the presidential campaign. Those plans were scotched by the peace treaty that arrived in Washington in February 1848 and won Senate ratification the following month. Attention shifted to the president's justification for going to war in the first place.

Lincoln anticipated that change. On December 22, 1847, he introduced a series of resolutions asking the administration to supply information about the commencement of hostilities. In his annual message earlier that month, the president had insisted that the conflict began as a result of Mexican soldiers "invading the territory of the State of Texas, striking the first blow, and shedding the blood of our citizens on our own soil."[10] In eight legalistic interrogatories, which became known as "spot resolutions," Lincoln clearly intimated that the soil where blood had first been spilled was not American and that in the spring of 1846 Polk had dispatched troops to Mexico in order to provoke an attack. Lincoln was particularly graphic in inquiring whether "the People of that settlement [where hostilities began] did, or did not, flee from the approach of the United States Army, leaving unprotected their homes and their growing crops, *before* the blood was shed."[11] Polk ignored those interrogatories. In Illinois, Whig journals applauded Lincoln's resolutions as "direct to the point" and "based on facts which cannot be successfully controverted."[12] The Democratic Chicago *Times*, by contrast, claimed that Lincoln "made himself ridiculous and odious . . . in giving aid and comfort to the Mexican enemy."[13]

On January 3, 1848, Lincoln provoked further Democratic criticism by voting for Representative George Ashmun's amendment asserting that the Mexican War had been "unnecessarily and unconstitutionally begun by the President."[14] Pointing out that one thousand young men from Illinois's Seventh District were fighting in Mexico, the Springfield *Register* asked rhetorically: "What will these gallant heroes say when they learn that their representative has declared in the national councils that the cause in which they suffered and braved everything, was 'unconstitutional,' 'unnecessary,' and consequently infamous and wicked?"[15]

Nine days later, Lincoln delivered a major hour-long speech on the war. He would have remained quiet, he said, if Polk had not stated that the Mexican government was solely responsible for provoking the war. Moreover, the president had asserted that Congress endorsed his interpretation of the war's origin by voting to supply troops in the field. Lincoln, who always voted for such supplies, could not let those assertions go unchallenged. Calling the president's discussion of the issue in his recent message "the sheerest deception," he denied Polk's assumption that either the Nueces River or the Rio Grande formed the southern boundary of Texas; he thought that boundary was located somewhere in the "stupendous deserts" between the two.[16]

Lincoln urged Polk to respond to the interrogatories he had earlier propounded. If the president could "show that the soil was ours, where the first blood of the war was shed—that it was not within an inhabited country, or, if within such, that the inhabitants had submitted themselves to the civil authority of Texas, or of the United States, . . . then I am with him for his justification." But if Polk could not prove his case, "then I shall be fully convinced, of what I more than suspect already, that he is deeply conscious of being in the wrong—that he feels the blood of this war, like the blood of Abel, is crying to Heaven against him." Lincoln maintained that the chief executive had deliberately provoked a war while "trusting to escape scrutiny, by fixing the public gaze upon the exceeding brightness of military glory—that serpent's eye, that charms to destroy."[17]

Reaction to the speech was predictably partisan. William Schouler, a Massachusetts Whig leader, reported that Lincoln "speaks with rapidity and uses a good deal of gesture, some of which is quite new and original. He was listened to, however, with great attention, and made a sound, sensible and manly speech."[18] Lincoln's opponents were less pleased. Representative John Jameson of Missouri expressed astonishment that the congressman from a district that had sent into battle such heroes as John J. Hardin, Edward D. Baker, and James Shields could "get up here and declare that this war is unconstitutional and unjust, and thereby put so many of his brave constituents in the wrong, . . . committing moral if not legal murder."[19] Meanwhile, back in Illinois, some Democrats called Lincoln the "Benedict Arnold of our district," who would "be known here only as the Ranchero Spotty of one term."[20]

Lincoln was doubtless unsurprised by Democratic criticism, though he may have been nonplussed when William Herndon, a strong Whig, challenged his partner's support of the Ashmun amendment and his denunciation of Polk. In response, Lincoln emphatically declared: "I will stake my life, that if you had been in my place, you would have voted just as I did [on the Ashmun amendment]." Rhetorically he asked, "Would you have voted what you felt you knew to be a lie? I know you would not. Would you have gone out of the House—skulked the vote? I expect not."[21]

Herndon's contention, as Lincoln paraphrased it, was "that if it shall become *necessary, to repel invasion*, the President may, without violation of the Constitution, cross the line, and *invade* the territory of another country; and that whether such *necessity* exists in any given case, the President is to be the *sole* judge." After denying the relevance of such an argument to the case against Polk, Lincoln declared: "Allow the President to invade a neighboring nation, whenever *he* shall deem it necessary to repel an invasion, and you allow him to do so, *whenever he may choose to say* he deems it necessary for such purpose—and you allow him to make war at pleasure. Study to see if you can fix *any limit* to his power in this respect, after you have given him so much as you propose." Lincoln contended that Herndon's interpretation differed from that of the Founding Fathers: "The provision of the Constitution giving the war-making power to Congress, was dictated, as I understand it, by the following reasons. Kings had always been involving and impoverishing their people in wars, pretending generally, if not always, that the good of the people was the object." But the framers of the Constitution believed that such an abuse of power was "the most oppressive of all Kingly oppressions," and they therefore made sure that "*no one man* should hold the power of bringing this oppression upon us." But Herndon's "view destroyed the whole matter, and places our President where kings have always stood."[22]

As this letter suggests, Lincoln was truly outraged by Polk's conduct. The Polk administration had, in his view, played the bully, and he hated bullies. In addition, Lincoln may have denounced Polk because he came to realize that the war might expand the realm of slavery. Most Midwesterners who opposed the war did so because of their antislavery convictions. The passion behind Lincoln's invective was striking, for it was among the bitterest antiwar speeches delivered in the House up to that time.

The presidential election of 1848 dominated the first session of Lincoln's congressional term. No sooner had he arrived in Washington than he was accosted by "the great Kentucky Kingmaker," Senator John J. Crittenden, champion of General Zachary Taylor's candidacy. The influential Democratic leader Duff Green, a boarder at Mrs. Sprigg's, told Lincoln that Taylor would have the support not only of Whigs but also of Calhounites like himself. (Green's nephew was Ninian W. Edwards, Mary Lincoln's brother-in-law.) Lincoln agreed with these veteran politicians. Fearing realistically that his "beau ideal of a statesman"—the septuagenarian Henry Clay, a three-time loser in presidential contests—was unelectable, Lincoln had already decided to support Taylor, a hero of the Mexican War. The traditional Whig issues—banks, tariffs, and internal improvements—had lost their popular appeal, as had Clay, who after his defeat in 1844 forswore a further race for the White House. But the Great Compromiser changed his mind and came to Washington in January 1848 to enlist support for a fourth bid for the presidency.

The Sage of Ashland was still eloquent, but his time had passed. As early as the spring of 1847, after Taylor's electrifying victory at Buena Vista in February over Santa Anna's much larger army, Whig leaders had realized that the modest, unassuming, successful general was their most eligible standard-bearer. In Congress, Lincoln struck up a pro-Taylor partnership with the tiny, frail, sickly, brilliant Alexander H. Stephens of Georgia, who was eager to nominate the slaveholding general in order to protect Southern interests. Those interests seemed ominously threatened by the introduction of the 1846 Wilmot Proviso, prohibiting slavery in any territory acquired from Mexico. (It passed the House but failed in the Senate.) As enthusiastic backers of the Hero of Buena Vista, they formed the first congressional Taylor Club, dominated by Southerners. Calling themselves "the Young Indians," they corresponded with Whigs in all regions as they organized the Taylor movement.

Stephens admired Lincoln; in turn, Lincoln thought highly of the charming, kind, fiercely individualistic Stephens. On February 2, 1848, Lincoln reported to Herndon that the Georgia representative, "a slim, pale-faced, consumptive man, with a voice like [Stephen T.] Logan's has just concluded the very best speech, of an hour's length, I ever heard. My old, withered, dry eyes, are full of tears yet."[23] In December and January, Lincoln worked behind the scenes with Stephens to promote Taylor's candidacy. He supported Old Rough and Ready "because I am satisfied we can elect him, that he would give us a whig administration, and that we can not elect any other whig." Lincoln predicted that with Taylor heading the ticket, the Whigs would gain one more House seat in Illinois and probably win the state's electoral votes. To an Illinoisan who feared that Clay supporters could not be induced to back Taylor, Lincoln explained that he sided with Taylor "not because I think he would make a better president than Clay, but because I think he would make a better one than [Democrats like] Polk, or [Lewis] Cass, or [James] Buchanan, or any such creatures, one of whom is sure to be elected, if he is not." Clay, Lincoln believed, had "no chance at all."[24]

In June, the Whig national convention assembled at Philadelphia, with Lincoln in attendance, and chose Taylor to run against the bland Michigan senator Lewis Cass, whom the Democrats had nominated the previous month. Though many Northern Whigs were outraged by the nomination of a slaveholder who had never been a true backer of the party or its principles (some were also disillusioned by the party's failure to adopt a platform), Lincoln reported on June 12 that such disaffected elements "are fast falling in" and predicted that "we shall have a most overwhelming, glorious, triumph."[25]

En route back to Washington from Philadelphia, Lincoln stopped in Wilmington, Delaware, where he attacked Polk's "high-handed and despotic exercise of the veto power, and the utter disregard of the will of the people."[26] Lincoln, like many other Whigs, charged that Polk had started the war with Mexico to distract public attention from his failure to gain all of the Oregon Territory from Great Britain despite his belligerent campaign rhetoric about "fifty-four forty or fight." Ten days later, on the floor of the House, Lincoln denounced Polk's veto of an internal-improvements bill and Cass's hostility to federal support for such legislation. Although that subject had been debated early in the session, Lincoln may have refrained from speaking on traditional Whig economic policies until Taylor, whose views on those matters were sketchy, was safely nominated. He also probably realized that with the earlier ratification of a treaty ending the Mexican War, criticism of the administration's conduct in provoking that conflict would no longer yield political dividends.

On July 27, Lincoln treated the House to a partisan stump speech on the presidential question. Prompted by criticism of Taylor's pledge to use the veto power sparingly, it commanded the attention of his colleagues and gallery onlookers. Lincoln praised the general's willingness to defer to Congress, for that accorded with the "principle of allowing the people to do as they please with their own business." He admitted that he did not know if Taylor would join him in supporting the Wilmot Proviso. (Lincoln voted for the proviso or its equivalent at least five times during his congressional term.) As "a Western free state man, with a constituency . . . against the extension of slavery," Lincoln hoped and trusted that Taylor would sign a bill containing the controversial proviso. Lincoln may have learned that in May, Taylor had privately given assurances that he would not veto Wilmot's measure. Since Cass would definitely support slavery expansion and veto the proviso, it was better to vote for a candidate who might not do so. Moreover, under a Cass administration, the country would probably embark on "a course of policy, leading to new wars, new acquisitions of territory and still further extensions of slavery."

With his customary sarcasm and ridicule, Lincoln lampooned Cass's military record, comparing it wryly to his own experience in the Black Hawk War. He mocked Cass's "wonderful eating capacities," which enabled him to consume "ten rations a day in Michigan, ten rations a day here in Washington, and near five dollars worth a day on the road between the two places!" Everyone, Lincoln remarked, has "heard of the animal standing in doubt between two stacks of hay, and starving to death. The like of that would never happen to Gen: Cass; place the stacks a thousand miles apart, he would stand stock still midway between them, and eat the both at once; and the green grass along the line would be apt to suffer some too at the same time."[27] Throughout the final half hour of his idiosyncratic speech, Lincoln was so genial and humorous that his colleagues laughed uproariously several times.

After Congress adjourned on August 14, Lincoln remained in Washington for nearly a month, helping the Whig Executive Committee of Congress organize the national campaign. Like a benign mentor, he urged young Whigs in Sangamon County to take an active role in the campaign and not passively look for instructions from their elders. When Herndon complained that the older Whigs were discriminating against the younger ones, Lincoln responded with paternal wisdom, urging him not to wallow in jealousy, suspicion, or a feeling of victimhood: "The way for a young man to rise, is to improve himself every way he can, never suspecting that any body wishes to hinder him. Allow me to assure you, that suspicion and jealousy never did help any man in any situation. There may sometimes be ungenerous attempts to keep a young man down; and they will succeed too, if he allows his mind to be diverted from its true channel to brood over the attempted injury. Cast about, and see if this feeling has not injured every person you have ever known to fall into it."[28]

Lincoln stumped vigorously for Taylor, spending eleven days in Massachusetts, where dissatisfaction with the general ran especially deep. "Conscience Whigs" like Charles Sumner, Henry Wilson, and Anson Burlingame denounced Taylor and his "Cotton Whig" allies. In August, antislavery militants met at Buffalo, where they formed the Free Soil Party, selected as their presidential candidate Martin Van Buren (who in November would win 14 percent of the Northern popular ballots but no electoral votes), adopted a vigorous antislavery platform, and chose as their motto "Free Soil, Free Speech, Free Labor, and Free Men." The new party's gubernatorial candidate predicted that Van Buren would siphon off twenty-five thousand Massachusetts votes from Taylor. Although they had no expectation that Van Buren could win, some Free Soilers hoped that his candidacy would throw the election into the House of Representatives. Just as Joshua Giddings had four years earlier campaigned to persuade antislavery Whigs not to vote for the Liberty Party's James Birney, now Lincoln sought to persuade antislavery Whigs not to support the Free Soiler Van Buren. Searching for help, the Massachusetts Whigs looked west.

On September 13, the Bay State's Whig convention took place in Worcester, where Lincoln argued that a vote for Van Buren was in effect a vote for Cass. To the Illinois congressman it seemed "absurd and ridiculous" for opponents of slavery to "unite with those [Democrats] who annexed the new territory" in order "to prevent the extension of slavery in that territory." He criticized purists who intended to "do their duty and leave the consequences to God."[29] Lincoln was invited to speak in Boston, Taunton, New Bedford, Dedham, Dorchester, Cambridge, Chelsea, and Lowell. While at the Massachusetts capital, he shared a platform with William Henry Seward, who declared that "all Whigs agree—that Slavery shall not be extended into any Territory now free" and that "it shall be abolished" in Washington, D.C.[30] The following day, Lincoln told the New York senator: "I have been thinking about what you said in your speech. I reckon you are right. We have got to deal with this slavery question, and got to give much more attention to it hereafter than we have been doing."[31]

In late September, while returning to Illinois, Lincoln stopped in Albany to visit Seward's alter ego, Thurlow Weed, an influential Whig journalist and political operative who introduced him to the Whig vice presidential candidate, Millard Fillmore. Then, as he sailed from Buffalo to Chicago, Lincoln observed a steamboat aground on a Detroit River sandbar. The sight inspired him to devise plans for a boat with an apparatus like water wings allowing it to float over such obstacles. After the November elections, he worked on his idea, for which he obtained a patent.

Lincoln spent the latter part of October extensively canvassing his district in Illinois, where he continued urging Free Soilers to vote for Taylor. On election day, the general defeated Cass by a margin of 45 percent to 42 percent in the popular vote and 163 to 127 in the Electoral College. Taylor carried Massachusetts with 61,070 votes to Van Buren's 38,058 and Cass's 35,281. The Hero of Buena Vista also won the

Seventh District of Illinois by a majority of 1,481 but lost statewide to Cass, 45 percent to 42 percent, even though he received 7,009 more ballots than Clay had in 1844.

Dealing with the Slavery Issue

Upon returning to Washington for the brief second session of the Thirtieth Congress, Lincoln participated in a fierce legislative struggle over slavery. Both major parties, sobered by the electoral showing of the Free Soilers, hoped to neutralize those upstarts somehow. The slavery debates had actually begun in earnest during the first session, in 1848, and Lincoln's awareness of the issue increased significantly before his term ended. In fact, slavery was by far the most frequently discussed topic in that congress, and Lincoln paid special attention to the subject during the second session (December 1848–March 1849).

During the previous session, he had done little about slavery other than voting with the antislavery bloc. In the summer of 1848, the debate over slavery in the territories grew intense, posing the gravest threat to national unity since the South Carolina nullification crisis of 1832–33. By the time Congress adjourned in mid-August, Oregon had finally become a territory, one without slavery. The attempt to fasten the peculiar institution on California and New Mexico had been thwarted, and those territories remained unorganized. A journalist called such developments "the only signal defeat the slave power has ever experienced under this government."[32] On just three occasions during the long first session did Lincoln vote against Giddings and the other antislavery militants.

Although doing little about the peculiar institution in 1848 other than voting with the antislavery forces, Lincoln that year expanded his knowledge of slavery through firsthand observation, as he had done in Kentucky the previous autumn. In the late 1840s, Washington was a predominantly Southern town that John Randolph of Virginia had called "a depot for a systematic slave market."[33] In 1854, with obvious distaste, Lincoln would speak about Washington's slave pens: "in view from the windows of the capitol" was the Georgia Pen (also known as Robey's Pen), "a sort of negro-livery stable, where droves of negroes were collected, temporarily kept, and finally taken to Southern markets, precisely like droves of horses."[34] Lincoln also observed slavery up close when, in January 1848, slave traders seized a Black waiter at Mrs. Sprigg's boardinghouse, clapped him in irons, and dragged him off to a slave prison. The unfortunate victim had been buying his freedom for three hundred dollars, all but approximately sixty dollars of which had been paid at the time he was abducted. In response, Giddings introduced a resolution, supported by Lincoln, calling for an investigation of the matter and for the abolition of slave trading in the District.

In April 1848, more than seventy slaves in the District of Columbia boldly tried to escape aboard the schooner *Pearl*, which had been chartered by an abolitionist sympathizer, Daniel Drayton. Betrayed by a Black man, the fugitives, after traveling 140 miles, were overtaken, imprisoned, promptly sold, and removed further south. The capital was in a frenzy of excitement as hundreds of incensed Whites marched on the office of an antislavery newspaper, *The National Era*, demanding that its editor, Gamaliel Bailey, leave the District. When Bailey refused, the mob began to stone the building, but police, assisted by leading citizens, restored order before significant damage was done or blood was shed. When Joshua Giddings visited the District jail to assure Drayton and Edward Sayers, who were accused of helping the runaway slaves, that they would receive legal counsel, a mob threatened the Ohio congressman's life. Doubtless this episode reminded Lincoln and many others of the fatal attack on Elijah Lovejoy's newspaper in Alton, Illinois, a decade earlier.

In the House, Giddings and John G. Palfrey of Massachusetts introduced resolutions of inquiry, which touched off an angry debate. An antislavery congressman reported that "we have had threats, insults, the invocation of mob-rule & lynch law, &, indeed, all the whole Southern armory has been exhausted upon us. Their orators . . . begin as tho' they were calling up a herd of slaves from a distant cotton-field" and "gesticulate, as tho' they had the lash in hand, & were cutting into the flesh, before & behind."[35] One such Southerner, Andrew Johnson, who in 1865 would become president, tauntingly asked Palfrey if he would like his daughter to marry a Black man. In the upper chamber, Henry S. Foote of Mississippi invited John P. Hale of New Hampshire, a leading antislavery spokesman, to visit his state and promised that his constituents, with the assistance of their senator, would lynch him. Lincoln had been a silent observer of these episodes and debates during the first session. They forced him to think about the peculiar institution more seriously than he had done since 1837, when he condemned slavery as an institution "founded on both injustice and bad policy."[36]

During the second session of the Thirtieth Congress, Lincoln acted on his increased sensitivity to the slavery issue. In December, Palfrey had asked leave to submit a bill abolishing slavery in Washington, D.C. Because it contained no provision for compensating owners, Lincoln voted against it. That same day he voted twice to support a motion by Joseph Root instructing the Committee on Territories to propose legislation excluding slavery from California and New Mexico. The resolution passed 108–80, a vote that Palfrey called "very encouraging."[37] On December 18, Lincoln again voted in favor of Root's measure. That day Giddings introduced legislation to allow District residents, including Blacks, to express their opinion on abolishing the peculiar institution; it was tabled by a vote of 106–79, with Lincoln and nine other Northern Whigs siding with the majority.

On December 21, when Daniel Gott of New York submitted a resolution calling for the abolition of slave trading in the District, Lincoln, for unclear reasons, joined three other Northern Whigs in an unsuccessful bid to table it. Giddings condemned this vote by Lincoln and others as "direct support of the slave trade."[38] But Lincoln thought the resolution's preamble—which stated that slave trading in the District was "contrary to natural justice" and "notoriously a reproach to our country throughout Christendom and a serious hindrance to the progress of republican liberty among the nations of the earth"—was too abrasive.[39] Resolutions like Gott's had been offered many times, but without such a controversial preamble. Perhaps Lincoln opposed Gott's resolution not only because he objected to its inflammatory wording but also because he himself was preparing a stronger measure. Later that day, when Gott's resolution was adopted 98–87, Lincoln and only two other Northern Whigs sided with the minority.

That voting took place amid great excitement, for it represented the first congressional action limiting the domestic slave trade. This dramatic gesture struck fear into the hearts of Southern congressmen, who warned that their region might withdraw from the Union if the Free States did not back down. Intimidated by the prospect of disunion, the House on January 10 voted (with Lincoln and fifteen other Northern Whigs in the 119–81 majority) to reconsider the Gott resolution, thus effectively consigning it to oblivion. These votes on Gott's resolution caused Horace Greeley to term Lincoln "one of the very mildest type of Wilmot Proviso Whigs from the free States" and Indiana congressman George W. Julian to conclude that the Illinoisan's "anti-slavery education had scarcely begun."[40]

But in fact Lincoln's antislavery education was well advanced, as he demonstrated the very day that he voted to reconsider the Gott resolution: he announced that he would offer a substitute for that measure, a bill more advanced than the New Yorker's resolution, calling for the abolition of *slavery itself*—not merely slave trading—in the District of Columbia. Lincoln proposed that starting in 1850 all children born to slave mothers in the District would be free; that their mothers' owners would be responsible for supporting and educating those children; that the children in return "would owe reasonable service, as apprentices, to such owners . . . until they respectively arrive at the age of ____ years when they shall be entirely free"; that if owners emancipated slaves in the District, Congress would compensate them at full market value; and that fugitive slaves reaching the District would be extradited by municipal authorities. The bill was to take effect only if a majority of the voters of the District approved it. Lincoln announced "that he was authorized to say, that among fifteen of the leading citizens of the District of Columbia to whom this proposition had been submitted, there was not one but who approved of the adoption of such a measure."[41]

When colleagues shouted out "Who are they?" and "Give us their names!" Lincoln did not reply. Two were Joseph Gales, coeditor of the *National Intelligencer*, and his partner, William S. Seaton, the mayor of Washington. A day earlier, Giddings and Lincoln had called on Seaton. Years later Lincoln told an interviewer: "I visited [the] Mayor, Seaton, and others whom I thought best acquainted with the sentiment of the people, to ascertain if a bill such as I proposed would be endorsed by them. . . . Being informed that it would meet with their hearty approbation I gave notice in Congress that I should introduce a bill. Subsequently I learned that many leading southern members of Congress, had been to see the Mayor and the others who favored my bill and had drawn them over to their way of thinking. Finding that I was abandoned by my former backers and having little personal influence, I *dropped* the matter knowing it was useless to prosecute the business at that time."[42] Lincoln's measure suffered the fate of earlier such proposals; from 1805 to 1862 none ever reached a vote.

Some Southerners condemned Lincoln as an abolitionist. At the opposite end of the political spectrum, the antislavery purist Wendell Phillips regarded Lincoln's proposal to end slavery in the District as "one of the poorest and most confused specimens of pro-slavery compromise."[43] Joshua Giddings, however, praised Lincoln's bill, which he had helped draft. On January 8, 1849, the Ohio antislavery militant recorded in his diary: "I believe it as good a bill as we could get at this time, and am willing to pay for slaves in order to save them from the Southern market."[44]

Horace Greeley decried Lincoln's provision to require that the electorate of the District vote on emancipation, writing that "it seemed to me much like submitting to a vote of the inmates of a penitentiary a proposition to double the length of their respective terms of imprisonment."[45] But in fact many citizens of the District had long opposed slavery and slave trading in their midst. In 1828, nearly six hundred Washingtonians had petitioned Congress to abolish slavery there. Moreover, because Congress controlled the District, and since no senators or representatives were elected by its residents, some argued that it would be unjust to deny the voters there a say in the matter. In offering compensation to slave owners, Lincoln had majority opinion on his side. A New York *Herald* reporter who opposed slavery declared that it would be "dishonorable in the extreme" to "free at once all slaves, without compensating their owners."[46] In like manner, the Washington correspondent of the New York *Tribune* praised Lincoln's effort: "He is a strong but judicious enemy to Slavery, and his efforts are usually very practical, if not always successful."[47]

In 1860, Wendell Phillips triggered a lively debate by denouncing Lincoln as "the slave hound of Illinois" because his 1849 emancipation bill included a fugitive slave clause.[48] In a public letter to Phillips, Joshua Giddings defended Lincoln, saying that the Illinoisan was "laboring in the cause of humanity." Chiding Phillips, Giddings added: "You speak of that act with great severity of condemnation. I view it as one of high moral excellence, marking the heroism of the man. He was the only member among the Whigs proper [as opposed to the handful of advanced antislavery Whigs] of that session, who broke the silence on the subject of those crimes."[49] William Herndon in 1860 similarly affirmed that when Lincoln was in Congress "he was then a strong Anti-Slavery man and is now the same. This I know, though he wishes and will act under the Constitution: he is radical in heart, but in action he must Conform to Law & Constitution as Construed in good old times."[50]

Patronage Scramble

In the wake of Taylor's victory, Lincoln was, as a constituent wrote, "harast to deth by applicants for the various offices."[51] Aggressive Whigs besieged members of Congress, clamoring for government jobs, including posts as diplomats, customs collectors, postmasters, judges, attorneys, marshals, census takers, clerks, as well as land office registers and receivers. Lincoln conscientiously tended to the requests of office seekers, just as he had dutifully answered constituents' mail and regularly voted on the floor of the House. But as a lame-duck freshman, he wielded little influence. "Not one man recommended by me has yet been appointed to any thing, little or big, except a few who had no opposition," he acknowledged in May 1849.[52]

Many Illinois Whigs were indignant at the shabby treatment his recommendations received from the Taylor administration. Although he later would say during his own presidency that "he did not regard it as just to the public to pay the debts of personal friendship with offices that belonged to the people," Lincoln tried to procure jobs for some close personal and political friends, including Anson G. Henry, Jesse K. Dubois, and Simeon Francis.[53] For Henry he won an Indian agency and for Dubois the receivership of public monies in Palestine, Illinois, but he failed to secure a position for Francis, who wanted to move to Oregon. With more supplicants than jobs to satisfy them, Lincoln had to make choices, some of which were not popular back home.

Would-Be Bureaucrat

At first, Lincoln had not planned to ask for an office for himself, because, as he explained to Joshua Speed, "there is nothing about me which would authorize me to think of a first class office; and a second class one would not compensate me for being snarled at by others who want it for themselves." He could, he said, "have the

Genl. Land office [a position in the Department of the Interior] almost by common consent," but he did not wish to antagonize other Illinoisans who sought that lucrative post.[54] In due course, though, Lincoln did become a candidate for that job and thereby found himself embroiled in a complicated and often mean-spirited struggle.

The General Land Office, whose commissioner supervised several dozen clerks, was considered one of the more important government bureaus. Illinois residents thought their state was entitled to that commissionership. Initially, Lincoln backed Cyrus Edwards for the job. Although some Illinois party members were unenthusiastic about Edwards, when the governor and the legislature of Kentucky also endorsed him and he appealed for Lincoln's help in February, Lincoln agreed to press his candidacy. Meanwhile, Edward D. Baker supported Colonel James L. D. (Don) Morrison, and Elihu B. Washburne backed Martin P. Sweet. Thus a three-way contest developed, pitting Edwards, Morrison, and Sweet against one another.

On April 6, worried that Illinois was not fielding a strong enough candidate, Anson G. Henry and four other Prairie State Whig leaders urged Lincoln to seek the commissionership himself, lest an out-of-stater win it. On April 7, Lincoln, who had returned to Springfield a week earlier, cautiously replied to Henry, saying that "if the office can be secured to Illinois by my consent to accept it, and not otherwise, I give that consent." He insisted that he "must not only be chaste but above suspicion." If offered the job, he insisted, "I must be permitted to say 'Give it to Mr. Edwards, or, if so agreed by them, to Col. Morrison, and I decline it; if not, I accept.'"[55] Edwards said that he did not wish to burden his friends or to play the role of dog in the manger and wanted Lincoln to feel "entirely untrammelled" to do what he thought best in order to defeat Baker's candidate, whoever that might be.[56]

A few days later, yet another formidable candidate entered the contest, Justin Butterfield, an able, witty attorney from Chicago. On April 12, Josiah M. Lucas, an Illinois Whig journalist, alerted his longtime friend Lincoln that "Butterfield is trying his best for the place, although not here in person, he is operating through friends," among them Interior Secretary Thomas Ewing, Congressman Truman Smith, and Senator Daniel Webster.[57] Like some other Whigs, Lincoln believed that Butterfield had not earned a patronage reward, for in 1848 he had supported Clay for the presidency and done little for the party during the subsequent campaign. Butterfield's chances looked good, however, because the president granted cabinet members control over appointments in their departments, and Secretary of the Interior Ewing insisted on the Chicago attorney. Just as the final decision was about to be made, Anson G. Henry prevailed on Taylor to postpone the matter for three weeks. "I told him Butterfields appointment would ruin us in Ills.," Henry confided to a friend. Secretary of the Navy William B. Preston informed Henry that "Lincoln is the only man in Illinois that can beat Butterfield" but added that the commissionership could be his only "if he comes on, & his friends back him up."[58] Other Illinois Whig leaders implored Taylor to postpone the decision until Lincoln could reach Washington, and they urged Lincoln to press his claims in the capital: "Pocket your *modesty*, as the preacher did his religion," Lucas counseled.[59] On May 21, Lucas spoke with Taylor, who "expressed great partiality for Lincoln" and was "astonished" to learn from letters Lucas showed him that Butterfield was not the choice of most Illinois Whigs. According to Lucas, the president had been misled by Ewing, Caleb B. Smith, and Truman Smith. Taylor said he would delay his decision until he heard more from the people of the Prairie State.[60] Lincoln then implored Illinois friends as well as congressional colleagues to write on his behalf.

Casting a wider net than Lincoln, Butterfield secured endorsements from the legislatures of Iowa, Michigan, and Wisconsin; from many bar associations; and from northern Illinois, his home base. He also attacked Lincoln downstate, especially in Springfield, where he circulated two petitions, one of which contained the signatures of twenty-eight "Whig mechanics of the City of Springfield," who declared that they were "dissatisfied with the course of Abraham Lincoln as a member of Congress" and supported Butterfield's application.[61] It is hard to know what to make of these petitions. Anson G. Henry alleged that nearly all the signatures on one of them had been obtained under false pretenses. Some of the signers, however, may have been dissatisfied with Lincoln's work in Congress. James W. Singleton, who lobbied against Lincoln's appointment, reported in August 1849 that the former congressman had two years earlier been "a strong and popular man" but since then had become "the most unpopular one in Illinois. His political dishonesty and double dealing with his friends has brought upon him the contempt of all classes."[62]

In mid-June, both Lincoln and Butterfield hastened to Washington. Upon arriving, Lincoln discovered that Taylor planned to name Butterfield because he came from northern Illinois. Lincoln appealed to the president, arguing that both he and Butterfield were equally qualified and that "if it appears that I am preferred by the Whigs of Illinois," he (Lincoln) should be appointed, for the Prairie State deserved recognition and other Midwestern states already had received their fair share of patronage. He further maintained that central Illinois had been neglected in the allotment of offices.[63]

In early June, others called on Taylor to plead Lincoln's case, arguing that he was the choice of three-fourths of the people of Illinois and "is loved by her people—a self made man, and now stands at the head of the bar in his state."[64] But it was to no avail; Butterfield won the contest on June 21. Upon learning the bad news,

Lincoln returned to his room and lay down in a fit of depression. He later declared: "I hardly ever felt so bad at any failure in my life."[65] The following day, when he called on Ewing to retrieve his papers, the secretary told him that if Lincoln had applied for the commissionership when the administration first came to power, instead of maintaining his support of Cyrus Edwards, he would have won it. To placate Edwards, Lincoln asked the secretary to give him a letter stating those facts. Ewing did so, but Edwards was not mollified. Believing that Lincoln had acted in bad faith, Edwards broke off their friendship. To Edwards's confidant and protégé Joseph Gillespie, Lincoln lamented: "The better part of one's life consists of his friendships; and, of these, mine with Mr. Edwards was one of the most cherished." He claimed that he had "not been false to it." At any time before June 2, he had been ready to step aside for Edwards; only after that date, when he was reliably informed that Edwards had withdrawn and that Butterfield and he were the sole Illinoisans in the running, had he decided to become "an applicant, *unconditionally*."[66] Edwards finally agreed to "bury the hatchet" in 1860.[67] Two weeks after his defeat, Lincoln had recovered his good spirits. On July 9, he informed David Davis that "I am less dissatisfied than I should have been, had I known less of the particulars." With characteristic magnanimity, he added: "I hope my good friends every where will approve the appointment of Mr. B[utterfield] in so far as they can, and be silent when they can not."[68]

In fact, Ewing may have employed underhanded tactics while championing Butterfield. Evidence suggests that some of Lincoln's letters of recommendation were suppressed. While it cannot be proven that Ewing ordered someone to tamper with Lincoln's file, justifiable suspicion arose that he had done so. On July 8, when Lincoln inspected the sealed file of his endorsements that Ewing had provided two weeks earlier, he was surprised to find missing two of the most important documents, letters from Indiana congressmen Richard W. Thompson and Elisha Embree. Indignantly, Lincoln asked Ewing to explain the absence of those missives, which might have spelled the difference between victory and defeat. He told the secretary: "I relied upon, and valued, them more than any other two letters I had, because of the high standing of the writers, because of their location within the Public Land states, and because they did (what few other members of Congress could) speak of my character and standing *at home*."[69]

Lincoln decided against making a public protest about the letters, even though Ewing's response did not satisfy him. In 1850, he said privately that he could have revealed the "piece of villainy" that denied him the commissionership and filled him "with indignation." But, he added, "my high regard for some of the members of the late cabinet; my great devotion to Gen: Taylor personally; and, above all, my fidelity to the great whig cause, have induced me to be silent." Much as he would like to "confound the guilty," he feared that such a public exposure of the story "might also injure some who are innocent," "disparage a good cause," and "reflect no credit upon me."[70]

Why did Lincoln want the position? Some thought his dogged pursuit of a patronage job resulted from the pressure of economic necessity. More importantly, perhaps, Lincoln may have had little desire to return to provincial Springfield after consorting with eminent lawyers and politicians in sophisticated Washington. Parties and soirees for three hundred to nine hundred guests were a regular occurrence in the capital. Lincoln's own strong ambition had been fortified by his two years there, where conversation was brilliant and he could mingle with eminent men with impeccable manners and great wit. One of the giants of the Senate, Daniel Webster, now and then invited Lincoln to his Saturday breakfasts, where the Illinoisan's humor and geniality charmed the other guests.

To restore peace and forestall attacks on Butterfield's appointment, the administration tried to appease Lincoln by offering him the secretaryship of the Oregon Territory, which he promptly declined, urging that it be given instead to his friend Simeon Francis. Soon thereafter, as Lincoln was attending court in Bloomington with John Todd Stuart, a special messenger arrived with an offer to appoint him governor of Oregon at a salary of three thousand dollars a year. Truly tempted, Lincoln asked Stuart if he should accept. His former law partner said he "thought it was a good thing: that he could go out there and in all likelihood come back from there as a Senator when the State was admitted." Lincoln, according to Stuart, "finally made up his mind that he would accept the place if Mary would consent to go." But she had no wish to live on the remote frontier and did not consent.[71] During her husband's presidency she liked to remind him that she had kept him from "throwing himself away" by accepting the governorship of Oregon.[72] And so Lincoln returned to Springfield. Not long after his defeat by Butterfield, he told a friend: "I have a little property and owe no debts; it is perhaps well that I did not get this appointment. I will go home and resume my practice, at which I can make a living—and perhaps some day the people may have use for me."[73]

This setback may have been a blessing in disguise. Richard W. Thompson believed that Lincoln's failure to win the commissionership of the General Land Office was "most fortunate both for him and the country." If he had been successful, he would have stayed on in Washington, "separated from the people of Illinois," sinking "down into the grooves of a routine office, so that he would never have reached the eminence he afterwards achieved as a lawyer, or have become President of the United States."[74]

Five years would pass before Lincoln sought public office again. During that political hiatus he underwent a painful introspective ordeal from which he emerged a different man. At the age of 40 he was an accomplished partisan politician of limited scope; by 45 he had somehow transformed himself into the statesman the world came to revere. Signs of that statesmanship had appeared in his congressional term (when he denounced the president's conduct in provoking the Mexican War and when he framed an emancipation bill for the District of Columbia) and during his tenure as an Illinois legislator (when he declared that slavery was based on "injustice and bad policy"). But only after he had passed through a fiery psychological trial at midlife was he to fulfill the promise foreshadowed in those gestures.

9.

"I Was Losing Interest in Politics and Went to the Practice of Law with Greater Earnestness Than Ever Before"

Midlife Crisis (1849–1854)

A colleague at the bar maintained that Lincoln's life from 1849 to 1854, although outwardly "uneventful and even unimportant," was really a time "in which by thought and much study he prepared himself for his great life work."[1] Indeed, Lincoln matured remarkably during those years, passing through a highly successful midlife crisis. Semiretired from public life (he campaigned sporadically and desultorily for others but ran for no office himself), the slasher-gaff politico who reveled in sarcasm and excelled at ridicule somehow developed into a statesman, a principled champion of the antislavery cause who rose far above the narrow partisanship of his earlier years. To be sure, the 1837 Lincoln-Stone protest and his 1849 proposed statute abolishing slavery in the District of Columbia showed Lincoln's interest in the slavery issue, but only as a secondary matter in his political consciousness. Believing "that God will settle it, and settle it right, and that he will, in some inscrutable way, restrict the spread of so great an evil," he had concluded that "it is our duty to wait."[2] After 1849, Lincoln focused closely on his legal career for half a decade. He later wrote that he was then "losing interest in politics" and "went to the practice of law with greater earnestness than ever before." By 1854, he said, the legal profession "had almost superseded the thought of politics" in his mind.[3]

Looking back on his legal career, Lincoln considered that it had two distinct stages, separated by his term in Congress. Before serving in the House of Representatives, he handled petty cases of debt collection, property damage, land titles, negligence, trespassing livestock, divorce, and slander, from which he earned little money, even though he and his partners had an extensive practice. To make ends meet, Lincoln and other lawyers in Springfield traveled the circuit during the spring and fall, when rural counties held court. In the winter and summer, the attorneys would remain in Springfield, appearing before the Illinois State Supreme Court, the Sangamon County Court, and the federal district court, as well as justices of the peace.

When Lincoln returned from Washington, Illinois was changing rapidly. In 1848, the adoption of a new state constitution, the completion of the Illinois and Michigan Canal, the launching of a rail line connecting Chicago with Galena, and the arrival of a presidential message via the telegraph for the first time all heralded the end of the frontier era. During the 1850s, the state's rail network expanded rapidly and its population doubled. Illinois's transformation changed the lives of the state's lawyers. Because they found more and more business in their own towns, they no longer spent weeks and months traveling from one county seat to another. Simultaneously, night sessions became more common, reducing the opportunities for convivial gatherings after dark. Rather than petty cases tried under the common law, more and more commercial causes filled the dockets, especially those involving railroads. The law became less a means of resolving local disputes and promoting community harmony than an impersonal mechanism for dealing with the booming industrial and commercial revolutions. Lincoln found the new climate more profitable but less congenial than the old one.

Law Practice

It must have been a letdown for Lincoln to exchange the glamorous world of Washington for his simple Springfield law office, which contained only a plain small desk and table, a couch, a rusty antique stove, a bookcase, and a few wooden chairs. The floors were so seldom cleaned that plants took root in the accumulated dirt. (As a congressman, Lincoln had distributed seeds to his farmer constituents; from some of the packets that he had brought home from Washington the contents leaked out and sprouted in the office corners.) Little light penetrated the filthy windows, and the upper and center panels of the office door leading to the hallway were missing. In the crude bookcase were copies of Blackstone, Kent's *Commentaries*, Chitty's *Pleadings*, and a few other volumes. Outside hung a small, weather-beaten sign by the staircase leading to the office. In these crude surroundings Lincoln spent many monotonous hours dealing with what he called "the drudgery of the law."[4]

Much of that office drudgery was performed by Herndon, who in 1857 described Lincoln as a "*hoss*" and added that "I am the runt of the firm and no 'hoss.'"[5] As the runt, he "'*toted books*,' and '*hunted up authorities*' for Lincoln," who "detested the mechanical work of the office."[6] Herndon drafted pleadings and other papers for cases in the district courts, while Lincoln wrote them for supreme court cases. In addition to composing wills, mortgages, contracts, deeds, and other documents requiring no litigation, Herndon managed the office. Lincoln did most of the interviewing and litigation, as well as zealously drumming up business for the firm.

The Lincoln-Herndon partnership, formed in 1844 and lasting until Lincoln departed Springfield as president-elect in 1861, was harmonious. The two men, according to Herndon, "never had a cross word—a quarrel nor any misunderstandings—however small." When other lawyers tried to supplant Herndon, Lincoln rebuffed their overtures. Herndon's fondness for liquor often landed him in trouble and embarrassed his partner, who characteristically overlooked this foible. Herndon acknowledged that "in his treatment of me Mr. Lincoln was the most generous, forbearing, and charitable man I ever knew. Often though I yielded to temptation he invariably refrained from joining in the popular denunciation which, though not unmerited, was so frequently heaped upon me. He never chided, never censured, never criticized my conduct."[7]

The tolerant, humane, evenhanded treatment Lincoln accorded his junior partner also characterized his approach to clients and their disputes. He often sought to resolve matters at a personal level, out of court. He believed that "it is better to get along peaceably if possible" than to litigate.[8] If potential clients were merely carrying on a community quarrel, or had a weak case, or were acting out of avarice, hate, ill will, or malice, Lincoln would tell them frankly, "My friend you are in the wrong—You have no justice and no equity with you—I would advise you to drop the matter."[9] He often told would-be clients, "You have no case; better settle."[10] About one-third of Lincoln's cases were dismissed, most of them doubtless because of such counsel. Lincoln viewed the role of peacemaker the lawyer's principal function. Characteristically he told a client in Menard County: "By settling, you will most likely get your money sooner; and with much less trouble & expense."[11] When another client who wished to sue for a trivial sum rejected advice to drop the matter, Lincoln told him: "My friend, if you are going into the business of showing up every rascal you meet, you will have no time to do anything else the rest of your life."[12]

Lincoln actively promoted social harmony in dealing with slander cases. He often mediated these suits, sometimes persuading a defendant to admit guilt if the plaintiff would agree to remit the monetary settlement, minus court costs. On other occasions he persuaded his client to acknowledge the plaintiff's good character and reputation or got the plaintiff to drop charges. Slander was traditionally a common-law offense; in addition, the Illinois legislature had made it punishable by fines up to a thousand dollars. The statute specifically deemed actionable false accusations of adultery and fornication, and several of Lincoln's eighty-nine slander cases involved such charges.

Racial prejudice exacerbated tension in some cases. One client, William Dungey, alleged that Joseph Spencer had wrongfully accused him of being a Black man. In presenting this case to the jury, Lincoln was, as one of the opposing counsel recalled, "both entertaining and effective. A dramatic and powerful stroke was his direct reference to Spencer's accusation that Dungey was a 'nigger.' It had a curious touch of the ludicrous by his pronunciation of a word which, instead of detracting, seemed to add to the effect. I hear him now as he said: 'Gentlemen of the jury, my client is not a negro, though it is no crime to be a negro. His skin may not be as white as ours, but I say he is not a negro, though he may be a Moor.'" On Spencer's defense team was Clifton H. Moore, a resident of the town where the case was being tried.[13]

Lincoln also tried to promote social harmony in handling divorces, which he found a disagreeable branch of the law. Toward the end of his life he said: "I learned a great many years ago, that in a fight between man and wife, a third party should never get between the woman's skillet and the man's ax-helve."[14] He and his partners participated in 145 divorce actions, two-thirds of which were brought by females. Lincoln's willingness to take on so many cases illustrates his solicitude for women, for usually male defendants would not contest a divorce. His motive could hardly have been mercenary, for there was little money to be made. Deserter husbands were hard to find and dun for fees.

Most of Lincoln's colleagues at the bar saw him as an adept trial lawyer, especially before a jury. Isaac N. Arnold said Lincoln could "compel a witness to tell the truth when he meant to lie. He could make a jury laugh, and, generally, weep, at his pleasure." A "quick and accurate reader of character," Lincoln "understood, almost intuitively, the jury, witnesses, parties, and judges, and how best to address, convince, and influence them. He had a power of conciliating and impressing every one in his favor." He could "disentangle" a complicated case "and present the turning point in a way so simple and clear that all could understand." His "wit and humor, and inexhaustible stores of anecdote, always to the point, added immensely to his power as a jury-advocate."[15] According to Hiram W. Beckwith, Lincoln rarely referred to notes, instead relying on "his well-trained memory that recorded and indexed every passing detail," and skillfully kept the jury focused on the main issues.[16] A juryman before whom Lincoln conducted a case recalled that he "knew nearly every juror, and when he made his speech he talked to the jurors, one at a time, like an old friend who wanted to reason it out with them and make it as easy as possible for them to find the truth."[17]

Fellow attorneys admired Lincoln's way with a jury. He "had few equals and no superiors," according to Leonard Swett. "He was as hard a man to beat in a closely contested case as I have ever met." Lincoln "was wise as a serpent in the trial of a case, but I tell you I have got too many scars from his blows to certify that he was harmless as a dove."[18] Lack of egotism, a quality at the core of Lincoln's personality, won over many juries, colleagues, and judges. Lincoln also employed his legendary talent as a storyteller with great effect. He was most inclined to resort to humor when he and his client stood on shaky ground.

Herndon reported that Lincoln before a jury "used his head a great deal in speaking, throwing or jerking or moving it now here and now there—now in this position and now in that, in order to be more emphatic—to drive the idea home." He "never beat the air—never sawed space with his hands—never acted for stage effect." As he proceeded, Lincoln "gently and gradually warmed up—his shrill—squeaking—piping voice became harmonious[,] melodious—musical." His face began to glow, "his form dilated—swelled out and he rose up a splendid form, erect, straight and dignified."[19]

As a general tactic, Lincoln shrewdly conceded much to opposing counsel. Attorney James C. Robinson recalled that he "had the manner of treating his antagonist with such perfect fairness, as to make the jury and bystanders think that he could not be induced to take advantage of him—a manner which was the hell-firedest lie that was ever acted, because the very fairness he assumed was an ambuscade to cover up a battery, with which to destroy the opposing counsel, and so skillfully laid, too, that after it had done its work, only occasionally would the defeated party, and almost never would the uninitiated, discover the deception."[20] Lincoln had difficulty persuading a jury, however, when he was not sure his client was in the right. Samuel C. Parks averred that "when he thought he was wrong he was the weakest lawyer I ever saw." In one case, Lincoln told his co-counsel: "If you can say any thing for the man do it—I cant—if I attempt it the Jury will see that I think he is guilty & convict him of course."[21]

When Lincoln first began riding the Eighth Judicial Circuit in 1839, jury trials took place in modest courtrooms that were vacant most of the year. When roads became passable in the spring, and again when the summer heat abated in the fall, lawyers teamed up with the state's attorney and the presiding judge, mounted horses or clambered into buggies, and began the five-hundred-mile, three-month trek through the circuit's many county seats, located mostly in primitive hamlets scattered throughout central Illinois. In each of these, the cavalcade would spend anywhere from three days to two weeks, depending on the volume of business. The judge and his entourage reminded one attorney "of a big schoolmaster with a lot of little boys at his heels."[22]

Lincoln's old, odd-looking horse, his decrepit buggy, and his ill-fitting garments combined to give him an unusual appearance. His brown, high-crowned hat lacked nap, his trousers were too short, and his coat and vest seemed to flap like garments on a scarecrow. He carried a carpetbag and a faded green umbrella. Like other circuit riders, he used his hat as a briefcase, tucking all kinds of papers into the inside band. On windy days his headgear would sometimes blow off, scattering important documents about the streets.

From 1848 to 1862, Lincoln's good friend David Davis presided over the Eighth Circuit. Born in Maryland in 1815, Davis attended Kenyon College and Yale Law School before settling in Bloomington, Illinois. There he quickly acquired a reputation as an outstanding business lawyer. A faithful Whig, he was only modestly successful in politics. Both his body and his personality were large. He weighed around three hundred pounds and had a forceful character and executive talent. Ambitious, vain, fun-loving, industrious, and genial, he eagerly acquired friends and money. After court adjourned for the day, Davis would usually gather the attorneys in his room for a merry evening of storytelling and scintillating conversation. Efficiently he promoted harmony among the lawyers on the circuit, authoritatively settling minor disputes. His manners and sense of propriety were exemplary. He could be a good friend as well as an outspoken enemy. His strong acquisitive streak and keen business sense made him rich. Davis's principal weakness was vanity, rendering him unusually susceptible to flatterers. But while he insisted on deference from some, he gave it to others, above all to Lincoln. In dealing with his flock of attorneys, Davis strove to be impartial, never intending to display favoritism to any lawyer. Of the eighty-seven cases Lincoln tried before the judge without a jury, he won only forty.

Sessions of the circuit court enlivened the dull life of rural Illinois, in effect providing farmers with the equivalent of the entertainment that city dwellers enjoyed in theaters, opera houses, and lecture halls. Arriving in town, the dust-covered lawyers would immediately be accosted by potential clients needing assistance in preparing pleas, filing demurrers, or defending themselves from litigious neighbors or officers of the law. Amid such confusion, the legal crew had to be quick-witted and flexible. Sometimes they would find themselves enlisted to try a case on very short notice, even as the jury was being impaneled. When not in court, they would amuse themselves by taking walks, playing cards, drinking whiskey, fighting, wrestling, racing, and even holding dances. Egalitarianism prevailed, for the sociable attorneys put on no airs in their dealings with colleagues or townspeople.

In the early years of the circuit, most cases involved assault and battery, unpaid debts, minor squabbles, slander, horse trades, petty larceny, and occasionally manslaughter. During the 1830s and 1840s Illinois was lightly populated, society relatively uncomplicated, land plentiful, employment widespread, and litigation quite simple, requiring little sophistication on the part of the lawyers. Such cases yielded modest financial rewards. Cash-strapped pioneers would usually pay a little and write IOUs for the remainder, or else give some livestock in lieu of money. Personal comfort was scarce for circuit lawyers, and accommodations were primitive, with poorly cooked and badly served food; the rooms seldom contained more than a bug-filled bed, a chair or two, and a spittoon. When taverns were unavailable, lawyers would stay at a farmer's home. Two attorneys often had to sleep in the same bed, and there would be as many as eight staying in one room. Lincoln frequently shared a bed with Usher Linder or Leonard Swett.

Unlike his colleagues, Lincoln bore these hardships without complaining. Herndon recalled that his partner cared little about food. He was a "*most perfect gentleman*" to his hosts and their families and servants. "Others would growl—complain—become distressed, and distress others—with the complaints and whine about what they had to eat—how they slept—and on what and how long—and how disturbed by fleas, bed bugs or what not."[23] Only rarely would Lincoln voice displeasure with the food. He once remarked wryly, "Well—in the absence of anything to Eat I will jump into this Cabbage."[24]

Lincoln complained so little because he loved life on the circuit. David Davis believed that Lincoln was "as happy as *he* could be, when on this Circuit—and happy no other place. This was his place of Enjoyment. As a general rule when all the lawyers of a Saturday Evening would go home and see their families & friends at home Lincoln would refuse to go home."[25] Even after railroads connecting Springfield with most of the county seats were completed by the mid-1850s, Lincoln seldom returned to Springfield on weekends. He was also one of the very few attorneys who traveled the entire circuit each spring and fall. While most of his colleagues at the bar stayed close to home, attending only circuit courts in counties adjacent to their own, Lincoln, Swett, Lamon, and Davis covered it all, becoming in effect a family. "We journeyed together along the road," said Swett, "slept in the same cabin or small hotel at night, breakfasted, dined, and supped together every day, and lived as intimately and in a manner as friendly as it is possible for men to live."[26]

Lincoln's intelligence, geniality, and humor made him exceptionally popular on the circuit; few of his friends, however, were truly close. One of those few was David Davis. Their friendship flourished despite their many differences in appearance, temperament, values, and social background. Davis was five inches shorter and a hundred pounds heavier than Lincoln and had an assertive personality, while Lincoln's was more passive. Lincoln was indifferent to money and lived modestly; Davis was a shrewd investor who became rich. Davis had attended college and law school; Lincoln had spent less than twelve months in frontier blab schools. The two did share some things in common: they were both devoted to the Whig party; each had rock-ribbed integrity; and both were excellent storytellers and exceedingly affable. Davis, Lincoln, and Leonard Swett were known as "the great triumvirate" on the circuit. Swett, one of the foremost criminal lawyers of his era, enjoyed immense popularity, for he was charming, magnetic, eloquent, generous, unselfish, entertaining, and a devoted friend.

The only thing like a formal partnership Lincoln had outside Springfield was with Ward Hill Lamon, a tall, stout, hard-drinking, humorous, earthy Virginian who practiced in Danville. Friends described him as "chivalrous, courageous, generous," and "a reckless, dashing, pleasant, social, good looking fellow."[27] In Vermilion County, Lincoln teamed up with Lamon, eighteen years his junior, on more than 150 causes. Lamon drummed up business, and Lincoln tried the cases. Their quasi partnership lasted from 1852 to 1857, when Lamon won election as prosecutor of the Seventeenth Judicial Circuit and moved to Bloomington. Each day after court adjourned, Lamon entertained Lincoln and the other attorneys, supplying a pitcher of liquor to slake their thirst. When he had drunk enough to loosen up, Lamon could be persuaded to sing off-color ditties. During his presidency, Lincoln appointed Lamon marshal of the District of Columbia and enlisted him as an informal bodyguard.

Lincoln charged notoriously low fees. In 1856 he wrote a client saying: "I have just received yours of the 16th, with check on Flagg & Savage for twenty-five dollars. You must think I am a high-priced man. You are too liberal with your money. Fifteen dollars is enough for the job. I send you a receipt for fifteen dollars, and return to you a ten-dollar bill."[28] In notes he wrote for a law lecture, Lincoln counseled that an "exorbitant fee should never be claimed." Nor should an attorney take any more than a small retainer. "When fully paid beforehand, you are more than a common mortal if you can feel the same interest in the case as if something were still in prospect for you, as well as for your client. And when you lack interest in the case the job will very likely lack skill and diligence in the performance."[29]

It is impossible to determine just how much Lincoln earned from the practice of law, but a fee book that he kept while in partnership with John Todd Stuart and another one kept by Herndon for the years 1845–47 indicate that most cases yielded ten dollars for circuit and supreme court work and twenty dollars for cases in the U.S. courts. With Stuart and Herndon, Lincoln split fees evenly; with Logan, he received one-third of the fees. In partnership with Stuart from 1837 to 1841, he averaged about one thousand dollars annually; with Logan as a partner, his income rose by approximately 50 percent. By the late 1850s, he earned roughly four thousand to five thousand dollars a year. Compared with other lawyers in Springfield, Lincoln was not especially prosperous. According to the census of 1860, he ranked twelfth of the seventeen attorneys in terms of assets. (Of the 414 Springfield households listed in the census, the Lincolns ranked 127th.) The five lawyers who owned less than he did—including Herndon—were much younger, with an average age of 32; Lincoln was then 51.

Although Lincoln seemed relatively insouciant in setting fees, he was not careless about collecting them. After winning a case for a client, Lincoln wrote him: "As the Dutch justice said when he married folks, 'Now, vere ish my hundred tollars.'"[30] At least half a dozen times he sued for unpaid fees. Once, in 1857, he had to sue the Illinois Central Railroad for a fee of five thousand dollars. When Lincoln presented his bill to George B. McClellan, the latter replied, "Why that is as much as a first-class city lawyer would charge."[31]

For all his acknowledged skill as a jury-trial lawyer, Lincoln was even more successful on the appellate level. For cases in the federal courts and the Illinois Supreme Court, he had time enough to prepare extensively and master the facts and the law. Lawyers from afar regularly asked him to handle cases on appeal to the Illinois Supreme Court. In the 1840s he averaged about forty supreme court cases annually until the fall of 1847, when he left Illinois to serve in Congress. In the 1850s he had fewer cases, but they involved higher stakes. Of the 5,173 documented cases that he and his partners participated in, 411 were tried in the Illinois Supreme Court. All of them were civil rather than criminal, primarily involving the ownership of horses and other animals.

The most lucrative cases involved iron horses, though railroads were involved in only about 4 percent of his total caseload. Lincoln represented the Illinois Central, the Alton and Chicago, and the Tonica and Petersburg, among others. On behalf of individuals, he sued the Alton and Chicago, the Illinois River, the Northern Cross, and the Chicago, Burlington, and Quincy lines. The only corporation that gave him a regular retainer was the Illinois Central, which he represented in several dozen cases. Most of them concerned simple questions and were tried in lower courts. As part of his retainer agreement, he pledged not to represent anyone suing the Illinois Central.

Lawyers and courts in antebellum Illinois blazed trails, for there were few precedents to guide them. The challenge was especially marked in railroad cases. Lincoln helped establish important precedents in suits involving railroad stocks, insurance of freight, and other novel aspects of transportation. The most lucrative case Lincoln tried, *Illinois Central Railroad v. McLean County, Illinois and Parke*, better known as the McLean County tax case, involved the power of counties to tax the corporation. In 1851, the General Assembly had granted the railroad a charter stipulating that its property would be exempt from taxation; in return, it would pay the state a percentage of its gross receipts. Some counties regarded the state's action as an unconstitutional usurpation of their authority to tax. In the summer of 1853, Champaign County officials discussed the matter with Lincoln, who was subsequently approached by the corporation, which was already being taxed by McLean County. The stakes were high for both the counties and the corporation; the former anticipated a large tax windfall, and the latter dreaded the prospect of having to pay property taxes in each of the two dozen counties through which its rails passed, above and beyond its levy to the state government. If the county would pay him roughly what the corporation would, then Lincoln would feel obliged to work for it. The judge of the Champaign County Court urged that "no time is to be lost in securing the services of Mr. Lincoln," but nothing came of his initiative.[32] In October Lincoln therefore accepted the offer of the corporation, which gave him a two-hundred-dollar retainer. In cooperation with several other attorneys and the general counsel of the Illinois Central, Lincoln filed suit to block McLean County's attempt to tax the corporation. The county agreed to have the case dismissed by the circuit court in order to appeal it to the supreme court expeditiously. There in 1856, Lincoln and his colleagues prevailed after arguing the case twice. It ranks as one of the most persuasive and complex briefs he ever penned.

Of the many cases Lincoln handled in his twenty-four years at the bar, none was more important than *Hurd v. The Rock Island Bridge Company*, better known as the *Effie Afton* case, tried in September 1857 before the U.S. circuit court in Chicago, Justice John McLean presiding. The previous year a river packet, the *Effie Afton*, had crashed into a pier of the first railroad bridge thrown across the Mississippi River. Both the ship and the draw span of the bridge caught fire and were destroyed. Alleging that the bridge had materially obstructed navigation, the ship's owner, Jacob S. Hurd, sued the bridge company. The case became a cause célèbre, pitting the river towns, principally St. Louis, against rail hubs, notably Chicago. The future of Western railroads was jeopardized by the suit, which might lead to the prohibition of all bridge construction over the Mississippi.

Norman B. Judd, a leading railroad attorney who was engaged by the bridge company, suggested that it also hire Lincoln, who spent months in preparation, carefully inspecting the bridge site and the relevant documents. In his closing speech to the jury, he demonstrated a formidable command of the details of the case. He argued that "the current of travel" flowing east and west had as much right to protection as that flowing north and south; that a substantial amount of traffic crossed the bridge; that the rail line, unlike the river, was an all-weather highway for commerce; that the pilot of the ship had not exercised reasonable skill and care; that one of the ship's two paddle wheels had stopped working as it passed through the draw; and that it was unreasonable to expect railroad companies to dig tunnels beneath the Mississippi or to erect costly suspension bridges high above it. An observer recollected that Lincoln "went over all the details with great minuteness, until court, jury, and spectators were wrought up to the crucial points. Then drawing himself up to his full height, he delivered a peroration that thrilled the courtroom and, to the minds of most persons, settled the case."[33] After splitting nine to three in favor of the bridge company, the jury was dismissed. (In 1862 the case ended when the U.S. Supreme Court overturned a lower court order to remove a portion of the bridge.)

Lincoln practiced extensively in the federal courts in Illinois once he was admitted to do so in 1842. (In 1849 he also argued one highly technical case before the U.S. Supreme Court.) About 7 percent of his total caseload consisted of trials at the federal level, where he, not Herndon, did virtually all the litigating. The federal courts handled disputes between citizens of different states. Residents of other states trying to collect sums larger than five hundred dollars from Illinoisans would often hire Lincoln to bring suit in federal court. The extent of his practice before that court is impossible to determine, for the Chicago fire of 1871 consumed most of the Illinois federal records prior to 1855. The surviving documents indicate that Lincoln was involved in 332 federal cases, in addition to the 77 bankruptcy actions he and Logan handled in the brief period when the federal bankruptcy law was in effect (1842–43). Many of those cases, like most of the ones he dealt with in the state court system, involved debt collection. Debt litigation accounted for 55 percent of Lincoln's total caseload. The sums involved in federal cases were often large and therefore yielded handsome fees.

In federal court, Lincoln and his partners handled two dozen patent cases, one of which took him to Cincinnati in 1855 for a major trial that would affect his future. The McCormick Reaper Company sued the John H. Manny Company of Rockford, Illinois, for infringing its patent. Because the case was originally scheduled to be tried in Illinois before Judge Thomas Drummond, the Manny Company hired Lincoln as associate counsel, paying him a retainer of a thousand dollars to keep McCormick from employing him. Lincoln's name was suggested because he knew Judge Drummond and because the firm wanted to have local talent on the legal team. But the lead attorney for Manny, George Harding of Philadelphia, was unenthusiastic about Lincoln; his choice for co-counsel was a Pittsburgh attorney, Edwin M. Stanton. Reluctantly, Harding dispatched an associate, Peter Watson, to consult with Lincoln. When Watson knocked on the door of the house at Eighth and Jackson Streets, Mary Lincoln poked her head out of a window and asked, "Who is there?"

Watson explained that he had come from Philadelphia to see her husband.

"Business or politics?" she queried.

"When told it was business, she (Mrs. Lincoln) indicated her satisfaction by the modified tone in which she shouted, 'Abe, there is a man wants to see you on business.'"

Dressed casually, Lincoln opened the door and invited Watson into the parlor, which his guest found unprepossessing. As Harding related, "Watson was satisfied that he was not the associate we wanted, but, after some conversation, concluded that Lincoln had qualities which might be rather effective in that community, that it would be unwise to incur his hostility by turning him down after consulting him, and paid him a retainer (at which he seemed much surprised), arranged for quite a substantial fee to be paid at the close of the litigation, and left him under the impression that he was to make an argument and should prepare himself for it."

When Watson reported back to Harding, however, they agreed that Lincoln would not in fact help present the argument but that Stanton would be hired to do so. Lincoln would be sidetracked, but he was not informed of this altered plan. When the trial was moved from Chicago to Cincinnati to suit the convenience of Justice John McLean, who was to preside instead of Drummond, the need for Lincoln's services as local talent disappeared. Instead of letting him go, Harding and Watson allowed him to continue writing his brief. As Lincoln worked away, he looked forward to jousting with some of the finest legal minds in the country.

When he arrived in the Queen City, Lincoln was surprised to discover that he would not help present the argument. The sophisticated Stanton and Harding, for their part, were taken aback when they first beheld their co-counsel, whose clothes fit him badly. After being introduced, Lincoln suggested that they proceed to the court "in a gang." Stanton drew Harding aside and said, "Let that fellow go with his gang. We'll walk up together." And so they did, snubbing Lincoln. At the courthouse, Stanton emphatically announced that only he and Harding would be arguing their client's case.[34]

Throughout the trial, Harding and Stanton continued to ignore their Illinois associate. When Lincoln asked Watson to present Harding a copy of the argument he had laboriously prepared, the Philadelphia attorney returned it unopened. Harding remembered that "in all his experience he had never seen one man insult another more grossly, and that too without reason, than Stanton insulted Lincoln on that occasion." Stanton "conducted himself toward Lincoln in such a way that it was evident that he, Stanton, thought Lincoln was of no importance, and deserved no consideration whatever from himself, and he refused to talk with him, and told Harding that it was shameful that such a low-down country lawyer should be sent to associate with them." In court, Stanton "even refus[ed] to take from Lincoln's hands one of the models used in the case."[35] Stanton, who referred to Lincoln as a "giraffe" and a "long-armed baboon," once rudely jerked him by the coattails and told him to step aside as lawyers examined the reapers on display.[36] Thereafter, Stanton "did not attempt to conceal his unkind feelings" toward Lincoln until he was appointed secretary of war in 1862.[37] Later Stanton said, "What a mistake I made about that man when I met him in Cincinnati."[38]

Understandably Lincoln felt so mistreated that he told Ralph Emerson, an officer of the Manny Company, that he planned to quit. Only persistent lobbying by Emerson and Watson persuaded him to stay on. As Lincoln sat closely observing the proceedings, he looked depressed but was fascinated by the dueling high-powered attorneys. Upon leaving town, he told his hostess, "You have made my stay here most agreeable, and I am a thousand times obliged to you; but in reply to your request for me to come again I must say to you I never expect to be in Cincinnati again. I have nothing against the city, but things have so happened here as to make it undesirable for me ever to return here."[39] Although 95 percent of the documented cases that Lincoln and his partners handled were civil, they participated in some trials for murder and assault with intent to murder. In his best-known murder case, the "Almanac Trial," Lincoln defended William "Duff" Armstrong, the 24-year-old son of his good friends from New Salem days, Hannah and Jack Armstrong. In September 1857, the defendant was accused of killing James Preston "Pres" Metzker, a 28-year-old father of three. Along with several other young men, including Armstrong, Metzker had been drinking on the outskirts of a camp meeting near Hiawatha in Mason County. Around 10:00 p.m., the drunken Armstrong lay down to sleep not far from the impromptu bars that were a common feature at camp meetings. Suddenly the much taller and stronger Metzker, also intoxicated, awoke him and picked a fight. After they battled, Metzker similarly provoked 27-year-old James Norris. Not long thereafter, Armstrong and Norris attacked him. The latter clubbed Metzker from behind, fracturing his skull. Armstrong was accused of hitting Metzker in the eye with a kind of blackjack called a slung-shot. Somehow Metzker managed to mount his horse and ride home, where he died three days later.

Norris and Armstrong were arrested, jailed in nearby Havana, and indicted for murder. Armstrong's family hired the local firm of Dilworth & Campbell, which successfully moved for a change of venue. Unfortunately for Norris, his court-appointed attorney failed to do the same; in November he was swiftly tried, convicted of manslaughter, and sentenced to eight years at hard labor. It seemed likely that Armstrong would meet a similar fate when tried in Beardstown that same month. Public sentiment ran strongly against Armstrong, who was known for his rather wild behavior. The possibility of a lynching hung heavy in the air. Compounding the woes of the Armstrongs, Jack suddenly died in November, leaving Hannah a poor widow.

In November, while in Beardstown representing a client, Lincoln called on Armstrong's lawyer, Caleb J. Dilworth, who filled him in on the facts of the case. To Dilworth's delight, Lincoln volunteered to help defend the lad. That night they interviewed some witnesses. When the prosecution won a continuance, Lincoln had more time to prepare his defense. He visited Hannah at her home in Mason County, traversed the scene of the crime, inspected records of the Norris trial, and interviewed witnesses. One of those witnesses, Nelson Watkins, had been drinking with the others on the fatal night. He owned the homemade slung-shot that

Ambrotype dated May 7, 1858, the day Lincoln won the Duff Armstrong case. After the acquittal, 22-year-old Abraham M. Byers stopped Lincoln on the street and asked him to pose in his studio. At first Lincoln protested, insisting that his white linen suit was too dirty, but eventually he yielded, leading to one of the few images showing him looking directly into the camera. Abraham Lincoln Presidential Library and Museum, Springfield, Illinois.

Armstrong allegedly had used to strike and kill Metzker; it had been discovered near the scene of the crime. Armstrong denied ever having possession of it.

Armstrong's trial began in Beardstown on May 7, 1858. Two witnesses testified that while Armstrong had occasionally behaved like a rowdy, he had never done anything vicious. Lincoln summoned other witnesses, who stated that Armstrong had used only his fists against Metzker. Lincoln also called an expert witness, Dr. Charles E.

Parker, who stated that both of Metzker's skull injuries could have been caused by the blow Norris had administered to the back of the victim's head. Nelson Watkins swore that he owned the slung-shot and that Armstrong had never possessed it. Then Charles Allen, the prosecution's chief witness, took the stand. According to the jury foreman, Milton Logan, the questioning went something like this:

Q. Did you see Armstrong strike Metzker?
A. Yes.
Q. About how far were you from where the affair took place?
A. About forty feet. I was standing on a knoll or hill looking down at them.
Q. Was it a light night?
A. Yes, it was.
Q. Any moon that night?
A. Yes, the moon was shining almost as bright as day.
Q. About how high was the moon?
A. About where the sun would be at 10 o'clock in the day.
Q. Are you certain there was a moon that night?
A. Yes, sir; I am certain.
Q. You are sure you are not mistaken about the moon shining as brightly as you represent?
A. No, sir; I am not mistaken.
Q. Did you see Armstrong strike Metzker by the light of the moon and did you see Metzker fall?
A. I did.
Q. What did Armstrong strike him with?
A. With a sling shot.
Q. Where did he strike Metzker?
A. On the side of the head.
Q. About what time did you say this happened?
A. About 11 o'clock at night.[40]

Another juror remembered that "Lincoln was very particular to have him [Allen] repeat himself a dozen or more times during the trial about where the moon was located" and "was very careful not to cross Mr. Allen in anything, and when Allen lacked words to express himself, Lincoln loaned them to him."[41] The prosecutor, who had gone over the same ground, eliciting the same testimony, felt confident that he would win. But then Lincoln sprang a trap, producing an 1857 almanac showing that the moon, instead of being high overhead at 11:00 p.m., when Metzker was attacked, had been low on the horizon and due to set within an hour. This flummoxed Allen and led the prosecutor to object strenuously. Judge James Harriott examined the volume, as did the prosecutor and the jurymen. This move shattered Allen's credibility.

Lincoln's closing speech was, by all accounts, a tour de force. Because of the sultry heat on that summer day, he removed his coat, tie, and vest. As he proceeded, one of his suspenders slid from his shoulder. A juror recollected that Lincoln began by "saying he appeared before us without any expectation of reward; that the prisoner's mother, Hannah Armstrong, had washed and mended his worn shirts and clothes and done for him when he was too poor to pay her, and that he stood there to but partially try and pay the debt of gratitude he owed her."[42] Lincoln wept, for his "sympathies were fully enlisted in favor of the young man, and his terrible sincerity could not help but arouse the same passion in the jury," according to the assistant prosecutor. "I have said it a hundred times, that it was Lincoln's *speech* that saved that criminal from the Gallows." But, curiously, when the jury withdrew, nine of its members voted to find Armstrong guilty. As the deliberations went on, however, the effect of Lincoln's speech and the damaged credibility of the chief prosecution witness eventually led to a unanimous verdict of not guilty.[43]

Lincoln was not in court when the verdict was announced. Upon his return, the jurors shook his hand as if they were old friends. Hannah Armstrong, who had withdrawn to await the outcome, was overjoyed. When informed of the good news, she hurried to thank the jury, the court, and Lincoln. "We were all affected," she recalled, "and tears streamed down Lincoln's Eyes." He told her, "I pray to God . . . that this lesson may prove in the End a good lesson to him and to all."[44] He instructed Duff to return home "and be a good boy, and don't get into any more scrapes. That is all I ask of you."[45] When Hannah offered to pay him, Lincoln replied "that at the time he boarded with her she had spent more time mending his stockings and clothes than he had in defending her son and he considered himself amply paid."[46] Soon thereafter, Lincoln helped Hannah Armstrong fend off attempts to take from her the land she had inherited from her husband.

Mentor

In dealing with his fellow attorneys, Lincoln was unfailingly courteous to all, especially to young members of the bar. Gibson W. Harris recalled that Lincoln "was never more gracious than when he was the opposing counsel. He had a happy knack of setting them at ease and encouraging them to put forth their best efforts. In consequence they all liked him."[47] Lincoln did not seek popularity with young attorneys, but he won their affection, and they came to him often.

In 1851, tyro attorney James Haines was startled when Lincoln, his co-counsel on a case, urged him to make the opening speech in defense of their client. Nervous, Haines suggested that Lincoln take the lead. Tactfully the older man placed his hand on Haines's shoulder and said: "No, I want you to open the case, and when you are doing it talk to the jury as though your client's fate depends on every word you utter. Forget that you have any one to fall back upon, and you will do justice to yourself and your client."[48] When attorney Joe Blackburn was starting out as a nervous 19-year-old, he began his presentation in a such a confused fashion that he was tempted to let the case go by default. But Lincoln, who had been paying close attention, rose and made Blackburn's point for him so effectively that the judge granted his demurrer. When the opposing counsel complained about this meddling, Lincoln replied "that he claimed the privilege of giving a young lawyer a boost when struggling with his first case, especially if he was pitted against an experienced practitioner."[49] Like Herndon, these young men were surrogate sons to Lincoln, whose paternal streak ran deep. Gibson W. Harris recollected that he "took undisguised pleasure in fathering many of us younger persons, including some already in their thirties."[50]

Anger

For all Lincoln's equanimity, he could erupt in terrible anger, as he did in the 1843 case *Regnier v. Cabot and Taylor*. Lincoln's client, Eliza Cabot, sued Francis Regnier, charging that he had publicly declared that one Elijah Taylor "has Rogered her" and that he "has got skin there [from Eliza] as much as he wanted." When Lincoln took the floor, he bitterly denounced Regnier for slandering a friendless schoolteacher. His tirade was, a colleague recalled, "as bitter a Philippic as was ever uttered." Eliza Cabot won a judgment of sixteen hundred dollars.[51] Seven years later, defending an orphan girl who had been seduced and abandoned, Lincoln reacted to defamatory testimony against his client by pouring upon the witness "a torrent of invective and denunciation of such severity as rarely ever falls from the lips of an advocate at the bar." Turning to his client, he abruptly shifted gears, becoming mild and tender as he spoke on her behalf.[52]

Lincoln's indignation knew no bounds in the case of Rebecca Thomas, a poor widow of a Revolutionary War veteran. Her agent, Erastus Wright, had in Lincoln's view charged too much for winning her a pension. Lincoln took the case gratis. The notes for his speech to the jury included the following words: "Describe Valley Forge privations.—Ice—Soldier's bleeding feet.—Pl'ffs husband.—Soldier leaving home for army. *Skin Def't.*—Close." In speaking of this trial, David Davis recollected that when Lincoln "attacked Meanness & littleness—vice & fraud—he was most powerful—was merciless in his Castigation."[53]

Lying witnesses also provoked Lincoln's wrath. "Woe be to him," wrote Herndon, "if Mr. Lincoln took the notion in his head that the man was swearing to a willful lie. Whips of scorpions in a man's conscience could be no worse."[54] According to Leonard Swett, any attorney "who took Lincoln for a simple-minded man would very soon wake [up] with his back in a ditch." When lawyers "went at him to joust him from his position and take away his weapons," Lincoln "arose like a lion wakened from his lair."[55] Usher Linder once interrupted Lincoln repeatedly as he was presenting his client's case, and the judge refused to stop the disruptions. Lincoln grew exasperated, shook his fist at his opponent, and declared angrily: "I did not bother you in your plea, and if the court cannot protect me I can protect myself. Now, sir, we'll have no more of this."[56]

Reputation

Lincoln was a highly capable lawyer but not outstanding, and he offered characteristically modest estimates of his own stature as an attorney. Likening himself to swine scavenging acorns in a forest, he said: "I'm only a *mast-fed* lawyer." In general, he was conscientious. Preparing for trial, he anticipated what opposing counsel might do. He told a friend that "he habitually studied the opposite side of every disputed question, of every law case, of every political issue, more exhaustively, if possible, than his own side. He said that the result had been that in all his long practice at the bar he had never once been surprised in court by the strength of his adversary's case—often finding it much weaker than he had feared."[57]

It is hard to assess the importance of Lincoln's legal career in shaping his political life. Certainly his widespread practice on the Eighth Circuit helped acquaint him with many voters, and his uncanny ability to read public opinion was enhanced by that experience. The friends he made on the circuit lent invaluable assistance in promoting his political fortunes. His work as a legal draftsman doubtless contributed to his ability to write terse, precise prose and to think through such difficult legal subjects as emancipation and habeas corpus. His knowledge of human nature was deepened by widespread contact with all sorts of people in court and out, and his powers of persuasion were enhanced. His God-given talent as a logician was honed during his twenty-four years at the bar. In his practice, he helped settle innumerable disputes, a task he performed regularly in the White House. In all these ways, Lincoln's legal career helped prepare him for greatness as president. But that greatness rested largely on his moral vision, which was little fostered by an adversarial legal system in which he acted as a hired gun. Such a system can easily produce a kind of ethical agnosticism. Fortunately for the nation, it did not do so in Lincoln's case.

Political Dabbling

From 1849 to 1854, Lincoln retained some interest in politics, though nothing like what he had shown in the previous seventeen years or the subsequent eleven. In June 1850, he refused to sign a call for a rally in support of the fateful compromise measures pending in Congress. In 1852, however, he did inject some political content into his eulogy on Henry Clay. After quoting the Great Compromiser's eloquent defense of the American Colonization Society, Lincoln offered his own biting commentary on slavery: "Pharaoh's country was cursed with plagues, and his hosts were drowned in the Red Sea for striving to retain a captive people who had already served them more than four hundred years."[58]

During the presidential campaign of 1852, Lincoln spoke occasionally on behalf of the Whig standard-bearer, Winfield Scott. As he observed in his 1860 autobiographical sketch, however, "he did something in the way of canvassing, but owing to the hopelessness of the cause in Illinois, he did less than in previous presidential canvasses."[59] He compared the Democratic presidential nominee, Franklin Pierce, to a Springfield militia leader who rode at the head of his men "with a pine wood sword, . . . cod-fish for epaulets, . . . [and] bologna sausages for a sash," while holding a "spy-glass; with BUT labeled on some appropriate part of his person."[60]

Midlife Crisis

That anti-Pierce address is notable as the last such crude partisan speech that Lincoln would deliver. In the years 1849 to 1854, while sitting on the political sidelines and devoting himself outwardly to the practice of law, Lincoln inwardly was undergoing a profound transformation, successfully wrestling with the challenges of midlife. Little documentation of his inner life survives; he kept no diary, seldom wrote revealing personal letters, and confided few of his innermost thoughts to anyone. Yet he was clearly trying to come to grips with the questions that many men address, consciously or unconsciously, as they pass from the first half of life to the second during their early forties: What do I really want from life? What kind of legacy do I wish to leave? Have I paid too much attention to the demands of the outer world and conformed too much to its pressures? What do I hope to accomplish with the rest of my days? What are my basic beliefs? Have I suppressed parts of my personality that now need to be developed? How shall I deal with the uglier aspects of that personality? How have I behaved in a destructive fashion, and how have I in turn been affected by the destructiveness of others? Have I chosen the right career and the right spouse?

Introspection of this sort is often triggered by a sense of failure, which Lincoln painfully experienced. In 1857, a Democratic newspaper contemptuously observed that "Lincoln is undoubtedly the most unfortunate politician that has ever attempted to rise in Illinois. In everything he undertakes, politically, he seems doomed to failure. He has been prostrated often enough in his political schemes to have crushed the life out of any ordinary man."[61] In his mid-forties he lamented, "With *me*, the race of ambition has been a failure—a flat failure."[62] Reflecting on his legal career, he said: "I am not an accomplished lawyer. I find quite as much material for a lecture, in those points where I have failed, as in those wherein I have been moderately successful."[63]

Lincoln worried about his legacy. In 1851 he told Herndon: "How hard—oh how more than hard, it is to die and leave one's Country no better for the life of him that lived and died her child."[64] Joshua Speed recalled Lincoln uttering a similar lament: "He said to me he had done nothing to make any human being remember that he had lived—and that to connect his name with the events transpiring in his day & generation and so impress himself upon them, as to link his name to something that would redound to the interest of his fellow man was what he desired to live for."[65]

Lincoln's obsession with death, which dated back to his youth, became even more acute in his early forties. A heightened awareness of mortality is common among men at that stage of life. In Lincoln's case it became especially acute when his 3-year-old son Eddy died in 1850. Lincoln told a friend that if he "had twenty children he could never cease to sorrow for that one."[66] The lad's funeral was conducted by the Reverend Dr. James Smith, who gave the Lincolns a copy of his 676-page book, *The Christian's Defense*, which (according to Smith) Lincoln found convincing. Mary Lincoln said her husband's "heart, was turned towards religion" following Eddy's death.[67] Soon after the funeral, the Lincolns rented a pew in the First Presbyterian Church, where Smith served as pastor.

The following year, Lincoln's father passed away. As Thomas lay dying near Charleston, a day's journey from Springfield, Lincoln rejected his deathbed appeal for a visit. Coldly Lincoln instructed his stepbrother, John D. Johnston, to tell their father "that if we could meet now, it is doubtful whether it would not be more painful than pleasant."[68] Lincoln neither attended Thomas's funeral nor arranged for a tombstone to mark his grave.

In some men, the painful questioning that often occurs at midlife can lead to despair; in others it produces stagnation. But it can also be a creative if turbulent period during which inner psychological growth takes place and leads to profound maturity. Out of the crucible of midlife introspection can emerge an awareness of one's own identity and uniqueness that breeds self-confidence and inspires confidence in others. A hallmark of such psychological progress is an ability to overcome egotism, to avoid taking things personally, to accept one's shortcomings and those of others with equanimity, to let go of things appropriate for youth and accept gladly the advantages and disadvantages of age. People able to meet these challenges successfully radiate a kind of psychological wholeness and rootedness. Lincoln was such a person after this period of retreat from politics. As he came to be more fully himself, Lincoln resembled the archetypal Kentuckian described by Ralph

Waldo Emerson in a lecture that the future president heard and remembered. The Sage of Concord said that men from the Bluegrass State proclaim by their manners, "Here I am, if you don't like me, the worse for you."[69]

During the final eleven years of his life, Lincoln impressed people with what Herndon called "that peculiar nature . . . which distinguishes one person from another, as much to say 'I am myself and not you.'"[70] Joshua Speed, his closest friend, similarly remarked that "if I was asked what it was that threw such charm around him, I would say it was his perfect naturalness. He could act no part but his own. He copied no one either in manner or style."[71] Lincoln "had no affectation in any thing," Speed reported. "True to nature[,] true to himself, he was true to every body and every thing about and around him—When he was ignorant on any subject no matter how simple it might make him appear he was always willing to acknowledge it—His whole aim in life was to be true to himself & being true to himself he could be false to no one."[72]

Others echoed the observations of Herndon and Speed. In 1859, a perceptive friend noted that what Lincoln "does and says is all his own. What Seward and others do you feel that you have read in books or speeches, or that it is a sort of deduction from what the world is full of. But what Lincoln does you feel to be something newly mined out—something above the ordinary."[73] Admiral David Dixon Porter, who knew Lincoln in the Civil War, thought he "had an originality about him which was peculiarly his own."[74] John Littlefield recalled that Lincoln "was a very modest man in his demeanor, and yet gave you an impression of strong individuality. In his freedom of intercourse with people he would seem to put himself on a par with everybody; and yet there was within him a sort of reserved power, a quiet dignity which prevented people from presuming on him, notwithstanding he had thrown down the social bars. A person of less individuality would have been trifled with."[75] John W. Forney, an influential newspaper editor who saw Lincoln often during his presidency, recalled that he "was a man of the most intense individuality, so that his capacity to stand alone, and, in a measure, outside of others, was one of the hidden forces of his character."[76]

Lincoln's highly evolved sense of his own identity lent him what some called "psychic radiance." His good friend and political ally Joseph Gillespie observed that "there was some magnetic influence at work that was perfectly inexplicable, which brought him & the masses into a mysterious correspondence with each other."[77] Like others, Henry C. Whitney was hard put to identify Lincoln's special quality. Although Lincoln was "awkward and ungainly," Whitney said, "there nevertheless was in his *tout ensemble* an indefinable *something* that commanded respect."[78] In 1863, Jane Grey Swisshelm, a Radical critic of Lincoln's administration, called on him in Washington "with a feeling of scorn for the man who had tried to save the Union and slavery." But quickly she was "startled to find a chill of awe pass over me as my eyes rested upon him. It was as if I had suddenly passed a turn in a road and come into full view of the Matterhorn. . . . I have always been sensitive to the atmosphere of those I meet, but have never found that of any one impress me as did that of Mr. Lincoln, and I know no word save 'grandeur' which expresses the quality of that atmosphere."[79] That sense of grandeur impressed an Illinois railroad conductor, who often observed leading politicians on his train. He considered Lincoln "the most folksy of them. He put on no airs. He did not hold himself distant from any man." Yet "there was something about him which we plain people couldn't explain that made us stand a little in awe of him. . . . You could get near him in a sort of neighborly way, as though you had always known him, but there was something tremendous between you and him all the time."[80]

The modesty that accompanied Lincoln's grandeur was genuine. Like most people who have truly come to grips with their own dark side—and Lincoln possessed a cruel streak that had marred his conduct toward political opponents in earlier years—he cherished no exalted self-image. "I am very sure," he told a friend one day in the White House, "that if I do not go away from here a wiser man, I shall go away a better man, for having learned here what a very poor sort of a man I am."[81] To a delegation of clergy who called at the Executive Mansion, he declared, "I know I am not a great man."[82] This lack of egotism, a hallmark of psychological maturity, impressed many observers. It is an especially noteworthy quality in a politician, for seekers of political preferment often have exceptionally needy egos.

Thus it was that when Lincoln reentered the political world wholeheartedly in 1854, he was a changed man. No more would he ridicule and belittle his opponents. No more would he travel the political low road of narrow partisanship. Summoned by a grave national crisis, the partisan politico was about to emerge from his semiretirement as a true statesman.

10.

"Aroused as He Had Never Been Before"

Reentering Politics (1854–1855)

By 1854, Lincoln recalled, the practice of law "had almost superseded the thought of politics in his mind, when the repeal of the Missouri compromise aroused him as he had never been before."[1] He and hordes of other Northerners were outraged by the Kansas-Nebraska Act, which threw open to slavery millions of acres in the West that had long been set aside for freedom. That legislation, introduced in January 1854 by Stephen A. Douglas, allowed settlers in the central plains territories to decide for themselves whether slavery should exist there. The statute, which its author said rested on the principle of "popular sovereignty," raised "a hell of a storm," as Douglas had predicted it would, because it repealed the 1820 Missouri Compromise, which forbade slavery in the northern portion of the Louisiana Purchase territory.[2]

Indignation swept the Free States, where voters had been relatively indifferent to the slavery issue since the Compromise of 1850. Some antislavery Democrats in Congress denounced Douglas's bill "as a gross violation of a sacred pledge, as a criminal betrayal of precious rights, as part and parcel of an atrocious plot" to transform free territory into "a dreary region of despotism, inhabited by masters and slaves," and condemned Douglas for sacrificing the peace of the nation to gratify his insatiable ambition.[3] Such anger was so widespread that when Douglas returned to Illinois, he said of his trip: "I could travel from Boston to Chicago by the light of my own [burning] effigy at night."[4]

Whigs in Illinois, Lincoln observed, "were thunderstruck and stunned; and we reeled and fell in utter confusion." But quickly they arose in a fighting mood, each one "grasping whatever he could first reach—a scythe—a pitchfork—a chopping axe, or a butcher's cleaver."[5] Lincoln's weapon of choice was the pen, which he used to write editorials condemning the Kansas-Nebraska Act and urging voters to elect opponents of that law. When some fellow Whigs seemed unwilling to act, Lincoln reportedly "said if we hold these opinions in regard to the outrages upon the black man why should we fear to avow them and say what we think and do what we can in behalf of right and justice?"[6]

Lincoln did not, however, call at this time for a new party. Throughout the Free States, Whigs in 1854 hoped to reunite their party's Northern and Southern wings for the next presidential contest. Only in 1856 would Lincoln and other antislavery Whigs in the Prairie State form a party to combat the expansion of slavery and thus fulfill the prophesy of the New York *Tribune* that the "passage of the Nebraska bill will arouse and consolidate the most gigantic, determined and overwhelming party for freedom that the world ever saw."[7]

Northern Racism

Diving once again into the political waters, Lincoln found himself swimming in a sea of Negrophobia. Illinois Democrats blatantly attacked him and other opponents of Douglas's legislation as "nigger worshippers," "nigger agitators," and "nigger-stealers."[8] The Quincy, Illinois, *Herald* claimed that there "are hundreds of abolitionists that wouldn't hesitate a minute . . . to marry nigger women."[9] Negrophobia was strong in almost every segment of American society outside of New England, and Illinoisans were among the most bigoted of all Northerners—some of them doubted that Blacks "were altogether human beings."[10] One antislavery journalist noted that the Black man in Illinois "has no rights, except the right of being taxed; he has no privileges, except the privilege of paying."[11] To combat their opponents' demagoguery, many opponents of slavery expansion felt compelled to insist that they truly championed the interests of Whites. The New York *Times* defended Republicans, arguing that they had insisted "always and everywhere, that they aimed at the good of the *white men* of the country, and had nothing to do with negroes."[12]

Attacking the Kansas-Nebraska Act

Lincoln eschewed racial arguments in his attacks on the Kansas-Nebraska Act, focusing attention most closely on Douglas. From 1854 to 1860 the two men conducted an ongoing political and moral contest, of which their celebrated debates in 1858 formed only a part. Douglas proved a formidable, immensely popular opponent, as Lincoln acknowledged. From 1852, when Henry Clay and Daniel Webster died, until 1860, Douglas loomed larger than any other American politician, presidents included. He was pugnacious, arrogant, vituperative, and ferociously ambitious, with a knack for genially convincing everyone he met that he was their good and true friend, interested in what they cared about. They, in turn, felt drawn to him and disposed to support him. Though short (five feet, four inches), he had broad shoulders, a muscular frame, a huge head, bright eyes, and a firm mouth, which gave him a most imposing presence. Lincoln referred to him as Judge Douglas, for he had served briefly on the Illinois Supreme Court, where he scandalized older members of the bar with his lack of dignity. Douglas's detractors called him egotistical, quarrelsome, demagogic, unscrupulous, brash, impudent, vindictive, vulgar, and morally obtuse. John Russell Young deplored his "insane yearning for immediate success" and his willingness to truckle to Southern slaveholders.[13] Even the Little Giant's friends lacked "confidence in his moral principle."[14]

In debate, Douglas could be abusive. According to Carl Schurz, "He would, with utter unscrupulousness, malign his opponents' motives, distort their sayings, and attribute to them all sorts of iniquitous deeds or purposes of which he must have known them to be quite guiltless." His "style of attack was sometimes so exasperatingly offensive, that it required, on the part of the anti-slavery men in the Senate, a very high degree of self-control to abstain from retaliating."[15] Lincoln said that he found it virtually "impossible to get the advantage" of Douglas, for "even if he is worsted, he so bears himself that the people are bewildered and uncertain as to who has the better of it."[16] In 1854, Lincoln analyzed Douglas's debating style: "It was a great trick among some public speakers to hurl a naked absurdity at his audience, with such confidence that they should be puzzled to know if the speaker didn't see some point of great magnitude in it which entirely escaped their observation. A neatly varnished sophism would be readily penetrated, but a great, rough *non sequitur* was sometimes twice as dangerous as a well polished fallacy."[17]

Douglas treated the 1854 Illinois electoral campaigns as a referendum on both the Kansas-Nebraska Act and his leadership. In January, he had accurately predicted that Northerners would assail him "without stint or moderation."[18] To vindicate himself, he returned from Washington late in the summer to speak on behalf of Democratic candidates, especially Thomas L. Harris, challenger to Lincoln's friend Congressman Richard Yates. When Lincoln took to the hustings in August shortly after the announcement of Yates's candidacy, he was no longer the fierce Whig partisan. As Yates's campaign manager, he tried to marshal support for the incumbent congressman, reaching across party lines to seek the help of anti-Nebraska Democrat John M. Palmer. "You know how anxious I am that this Nebraska measure shall be rebuked and condemned every where," Lincoln wrote Palmer on September 7. He added that if the Democrats had nominated Palmer instead of Thomas L. Harris, Lincoln would not have opposed him: "I should have been quiet, happy that Nebraska was to be rebuked at all events. I still should have voted for the whig candidate; but I should have made no speeches, written no letters. And you would have been elected by at least a thousand majority."[19]

To counter rumors that Yates was a nativist bigot, Lincoln drafted a letter for him to circulate. Yates ignored the advice and later acknowledged that his failure to heed it probably cost him the election. Antiforeign, anti-Catholic sentiment was sweeping the North, in some states becoming the dominant theme in 1854. Supporters of this movement, called Native Americans or Know-Nothings, adopted the slogan "Americans must rule America." They believed that Catholicism was incompatible with America's democratic, individualistic values; that established political parties and professional politicians were corrupt and unresponsive to the popular will; that both slavery and liquor were evil; and that immigrants were the source of crime, corruption, pauperism, wage reductions, voter fraud, and the defeat of antislavery candidates.

When Know-Nothings in Springfield approached Lincoln asking if they could run him for the state legislature, he flatly turned them down, stating "that he had belonged to the old Whig party and must continue to do so until a better one arose to take its place." He asked "who the native Americans were. 'Do they not,' he said, 'wear the breech-clout and carry the tomahawk? We pushed them from their homes and now turn upon others not fortunate enough to come over as early as we or our forefathers. Gentlemen of the committee, your party is wrong in principle.'" The following year, Lincoln condemned the Know-Nothings in an eloquent private letter to his old friend Joshua Speed, who had asked where Lincoln stood politically now that the Whigs were defunct. "I am not a Know Nothing," he declared. "That is certain. How could I be? How can any one who abhors the oppression of negroes, be in favor of degrading classes of white people? Our progress in degeneracy appears to me pretty rapid. As a nation, we began by declaring that '*all men are created equal*.' We now practically read it 'all men are created equal, except negroes, *and foreigners, and catholics*.' When it comes to this I should prefer emigrating to some country where they make no pretence of loving liberty—to Russia, for instance, where despotism can be taken pure, without the base alloy of hypocracy."[20]

One day when he was out of town, Springfield Whigs nominated Lincoln for the General Assembly, much to his surprise and his wife's dismay. Upon reading a press account indicating that he was being put forward for the state house of representatives, Mary rushed to the newspaper's office and ordered her husband's name stricken from the list of candidates. Later, when William Jayne called seeking permission to reinstate Lincoln's name, he found the potential candidate "the saddest man I ever saw—the gloomiest." Lincoln, nearly in tears, paced the floor, resisting Jayne's blandishments by saying, "No—I can't—you don't know all. I say you don't begin to know one half and that's enough."[21] Henry C. Whitney explained that it "was Mrs. Lincoln's opposition which so much disturbed him. She insisted in her imperious way that he must now go to the United States Senate, and that it was a degradation to run him for the Legislature."[22] But despite his wife's opposition, Lincoln remained on the ballot, explaining to a friend, "I only allowed myself to be elected, because it was supposed my doing so would help Yates."[23]

The First Great Speech

For the campaign he prepared a long, masterful speech arraigning Douglas, the Kansas-Nebraska Act, and slavery with a passionate eloquence that heralded the emergence of a new Lincoln. Abandoning his earlier "slasher-gaff" style, he began to speak with authority as a principled, articulate, high-minded champion of the antislavery cause. He dissected Douglas's popular sovereignty doctrine with surgical precision, forceful logic, and deep moral conviction. Lincoln had planned to debate Douglas just as he had done on earlier occasions. In September, the Little Giant was to speak in Bloomington, where a leading Whig, Jesse W. Fell, proposed that he share time with Lincoln. "No, I won't do it!" Douglas exclaimed.[24] Fear of Lincoln's ability as a debater may have led Douglas to reject Fell's suggestion. In October the Little Giant called Lincoln "the most difficult and dangerous opponent that I have ever met" in debate.[25]

That same month, Lincoln responded to Douglas in Springfield, where thousands of Illinoisans had flocked to attend the State Fair. There the Little Giant defended his record and asserted that the defection of anti-Nebraska Democrats could not defeat his party. Sitting directly before Douglas, Lincoln listened with close attention, obviously planning to offer a rejoinder. At the close of the speech, he announced to the crowd that Trumbull might reply to it the following day, but in case the senator could not do so, he himself would. When a friend opined that it would be hard to respond to the Little Giant's speech, Lincoln replied: "No, it won't. Douglas lied; he lied three times and I'll prove it!"[26] The next afternoon, in Trumbull's absence, he did just that before an unusually large crowd at the statehouse. He repeated this address twelve days later in Peoria and wrote it out for publication. Even though he had delivered virtually the same remarks earlier at Springfield, it became known as the Peoria Speech.

Lincoln prepared his address with special care. In this, his first oratorical masterpiece, he offered a comprehensive analysis and denunciation of slavery and its apologists. Before getting to the substance of his speech, he graciously pledged "that he should not assail the motives and not impeach the honesty of any man who voted for the Nebraska Bill, much less, his distinguished friend, Judge Douglas." He gave Douglas "credit for honesty of intention and true patriotism—referring whatever of wrong he might happen to find among his actions, entirely to a mistaken sense of duty."

After a few preliminary remarks, Lincoln traced the course of the slavery issue in American politics, showing how the Kansas-Nebraska Act was "wrong in its direct effect, letting slavery into Kansas and Nebraska—and wrong in its prospective principle, allowing it to spread to every other part of the wide world, where men can be found inclined to take it." He quoted from an 1849 speech in which Douglas had lauded the Missouri Compromise of 1820 for "allay[ing] all sectional jealousies and irritations growing out of this vexed question." He described that address as "powerful and eloquent; the language is choice and rich. I wish I was such a master of language as my friend, the Judge." Douglas interjected: "A first-rate speech."[27]

After sketching the historical background of the current crisis, Lincoln displayed intense moral conviction as he excoriated Douglas's popular sovereignty doctrine. The senator had nothing to say about the morality of slavery, proclaiming, "I do not know of any tribunal on earth that can decide the question of the morality of slavery or any other institution. I deal with slavery as a political question involving questions of public policy."[28] With unwonted vehemence, Lincoln denounced Douglas's neutrality on such a burning moral issue: "This *declared* indifference, but as I must think, covert *real* zeal for the spread of slavery, I can not but hate." *Hate* was a word Lincoln rarely used, but he repeated it in this address: "I hate it because of the monstrous injustice of slavery itself. I hate it because it deprives our republican example of its just influence in the world—enables the enemies of free institutions, with plausibility, to taunt us as hypocrites—causes the real friends of freedom to doubt our sincerity, and especially because it forces so many really good men amongst ourselves into an open war with the very fundamental principles of civil liberty—criticizing the Declaration of Independence, and insisting that there is no right principle of action but *self-interest*."

Lincoln found slavery "monstrous" because, among other things, it represented the systematic theft of the fruits of hard labor, a kind of institutionalized robbery. But Lincoln then balanced his repeated use of the word *hate* with a conciliatory gesture toward slaveholders. "I think I have no prejudice against the Southern people," he said. "They are just what we would be in their situation. If slavery did not exist amongst them, they would not introduce it. If it did now exist amongst us, we should not instantly give it up."

Lincoln confessed that he saw no easy solution to the problem of slavery. His "first impulse would be to free all the slaves, and send them to Liberia,—to their own native land." Yet that was impractical and could be deadly for American immigrants. Moreover, "there are not surplus shipping and surplus money enough in the world to carry them there in many times ten days." If colonization was not feasible, what alternatives remained? "Free them all, and keep them among us as underlings?" It was not clear "that this betters their condition." Still, Lincoln said, "I think I would not hold one in slavery." What else could be done? "Free them, and make them politically and socially, our equals?" Lincoln confessed that "my own feelings will not admit of this; and if mine would, we well know that those of the great mass of white people will not." In a democracy, he added, a "universal feeling, whether well or ill-founded, can not be safely disregarded. We can not, then, make them equals." Here he did not say that Blacks *were not* the equals of Whites; rather he implied that while they might be equal to Whites, Negrophobia would prevent African Americans from being *made* equals, that is to say, given equal rights by a government responsive to the wishes of the overwhelmingly White electorate.

In dealing with the controversial Fugitive Slave Act of 1850, which outraged many Northerners, Lincoln conceded that when White Southerners "remind us of their constitutional rights, I acknowledge them, not grudgingly, but fairly; and I would give them any legislation for the reclaiming of their fugitives, which should not, in its stringency, be more likely to carry a free man into slavery, than our ordinary criminal laws are to hang an innocent one." Here Lincoln implicitly endorsed the "personal liberty laws" adopted by several Northern states in response to the Fugitive Slave Act. Those statutes provided African Americans accused of being runaway slaves with the legal rights enjoyed by Whites accused of a felony, including a jury trial, the right to appeal, the right to counsel, and the like.

After conceding that the Fugitive Slave Act should be faithfully enforced, Lincoln insisted that "all this, to my judgment, furnishes no more excuse for permitting slavery to go into our own free territory, than it would for reviving the African slave trade by law." To Lincoln's mind, the statute "which forbids the bringing of slaves *from* Africa; and that which has so long forbid the taking them *to* Nebraska, can hardly be distinguished on any moral principle."

Lincoln indignantly argued that the abrogation of the Missouri Compromise was "manifestly unjust." Both the South and the North had made concessions in 1820; now the South wanted to renege on its end of the bargain while enjoying the benefits of the North's concession. To illustrate this point, Lincoln employed one of his favorite images, a man unfairly taking food from another man who deserves it: "It is as if two starving men had divided their only loaf; the one had hastily swallowed his half, and then grabbed the other half just as he was putting it to his mouth!"

Lincoln dismissed as an "inferior matter" and a "*lullaby*" the contention of Douglas and many others that slavery would never spread into Kansas and Nebraska even if popular sovereignty were applied there. He pointed out that more than 860,000 slaves—fully one-fourth of the nation's unfree population—lived north of the Missouri Compromise line (in Delaware, Maryland, Missouri, Virginia, Kentucky, and the District of Columbia). Moreover, slavery flourished in western Missouri, abutting Kansas. The best way to keep Kansas free was to prevent the peculiar institution from entering it in the first place. By allowing slaves to be brought into that territory as soon as it was thrown open to settlement, Douglas would guarantee that slavery fastened itself on Kansas in perpetuity. Slavery had never sunk deep roots in Illinois, he said, because the Northwest Ordinance of

1787 had specifically banned the peculiar institution there. But neighboring Missouri, with no such ban, had become a Slave State.

Lincoln's fundamental point—which distinguished his position from Douglas's—was that African Americans were fully human and thus entitled to certain basic rights. The popular sovereignty doctrine—resting on the assumption that if settlers in Kansas and Nebraska were allowed to take their swine with them, they should also be allowed to take their slaves—was, Lincoln contended, "perfectly logical" only "if there is no difference between hogs and negroes." He flatly refused "to deny the humanity of the negro" and argued that White Southerners showed by their actions, if not their words, that they agreed with him. In both the North and the South there lived few "natural tyrants," he said; most people in both sections "have human sympathies" that made them hostile to slavery. White Southerners revealed their own antislavery feelings in many ways. In 1820, Southern senators and representatives had joined with Northerners to declare African slave traders pirates subject to the death penalty. Addressing the citizens of the South, Lincoln asked: "Why did you do this? If you did not feel that it was wrong, why did you join in [providing] that men should be hung for it? The practice was no more than bringing wild negroes from Africa, to sell to such as would buy them. But you never thought of hanging men for catching and selling wild horses, wild buffaloes or wild bears." Why did respectable White Southerners "utterly despise" slave dealers, refusing to socialize with them, befriend them, or even touch them? Lincoln asked. "You do not so treat the man who deals in corn, cattle or tobacco." The presence in the United States of more than 430,000 free Blacks, worth more than $200 million if enslaved, further showed that White Southerners realized that slaves were human beings, not mere chattel. "How comes this vast amount of property to be running at large?" The freedpeople were slaves liberated by their masters or descendants of slaves who had been so liberated. What had induced their owners to free them? "In all these cases," Lincoln concluded, "it is your sense of justice, and human sympathy, continually telling you, that the poor negro has some natural right to himself—that those who deny it, and make mere merchandise of him, deserve kickings, contempt and death." Rhetorically he queried White Southerners, "Why will you ask us to deny the humanity of the slave? And estimate him only as the equal of the hog? Why ask us to do what you will not do yourselves?"

If Blacks were humans and not chattel, then Douglas's argument that the Missouri Compromise violated "the sacred right of self government" was false. Lincoln agreed with the Little Giant's basic premise: "The doctrine of self government is right—absolutely and eternally right," but whether that doctrine was relevant in the current debate over Kansas and Nebraska depended "upon whether a negro is *not* or *is* a man. If he is *not* a man, why in that case, he who *is* a man may, as a matter of self-government, do just as he pleases with him. But if the negro *is* a man, is it not to that extent, a total destruction of self-government, to say that he too shall not govern *himself*?" Like an Old Testament prophet, Lincoln declared, "When the white man governs himself, that is self-government; but when he governs himself, and also governs *another* man, that is *more* than self-government—that is despotism. If the negro is a *man*, why then my ancient faith teaches me that 'all men are created equal;' and that there can be no moral right in connection with one man's making a slave of another." To Douglas's contemptuous assertion that antislavery forces argued that the "white people of Nebraska are good enough to govern themselves, *but they are not good enough to govern a few miserable negroes*,"[29] Lincoln replied that "no man is good enough to govern another man, *without that other's consent*. I say this is the leading principle—the sheet anchor of American republicanism." After quoting the Declaration of Independence, Lincoln called the relationship between master and slave a "total violation" of its central principle: "The master not only governs the slave without his consent; but he governs him by a set of rules altogether different from those which he prescribes for himself. Allow ALL the governed an equal voice in the government, and that, and that only is self-government."

Lincoln explained that he was not advocating equal political rights for Blacks, but was rather "combating what is set up as [a] MORAL argument" for permitting slaves "to be taken where they have never yet been—arguing against the EXTENSION of a bad thing, which where it already exists, we must of necessity, manage as best we can." Douglas was wrong, said Lincoln, in asserting that the extension of slavery into Kansas and Nebraska concerned only settlers in those territories: "The whole nation is interested that the best use shall be made of these territories. We want them for the homes of free white people. This they cannot be, to any considerable extent, if slavery shall be planted within them." Here Lincoln was not making the argument that some Free Soilers did: that they wanted slavery kept out of the territories because they disliked African Americans and had no desire to live near them. Instead, he emphasized something that his own family had acted on three decades earlier: "Slave States are places for poor white people to remove FROM; not to remove TO. New free States are the places for poor people to go to and better their condition." Lincoln objected not to the presence of Blacks but to the presence of slave owners and their hierarchical social system. In asserting that Republicans wanted the territories to become "homes of free white people," Lincoln was adopting what the Chicago *Tribune* called "a narrow method" for appealing to White voters. It was necessary to appeal to White self-interest because, said the *Tribune*, "it is far easier to convince the multitude that Slavery is a baleful evil to them than to possess them with the idea that it is a cruel wrong to the enslaved."[30]

Northern Whites also had a stake in the outcome of the debate over slavery expansion, Lincoln averred, because of "constitutional relations between the slave and free states, which are degrading to the latter." Free State residents did not wish to help catch runaway slaves, as the Fugitive Slave Act mandated. Moreover, Northern Whites did not want more Slave States because the Constitution's three-fifths clause permitted them to have representation of their unfree population in the U.S. House and the Electoral College. Offering an argument that had been made repeatedly since 1789, Lincoln protested that it was grossly unfair for South Carolina, where 274,567 Whites lived, to have the same number of representatives in Congress as Maine, with a White population of more than 580,000. The three-fifths rule, Lincoln calculated, gave the Slave States twenty more representatives in the House and twenty more votes in the Electoral College than they would have had in the absence of such a rule. Without those extra congressmen, the Kansas-Nebraska Act, which passed the House by a seven-vote margin, might never have been adopted. Lincoln insisted "that whether I shall be a whole man, or only, the half of one, in comparison with others, is a question with which I am somewhat concerned; and one which no other man can have a sacred right of deciding for me."

To those claiming that opposition to the Kansas-Nebraska Act posed a threat to the Union, Lincoln replied that it was Douglas and his supporters who had imperiled national unity by needlessly reviving the slavery controversy, which had been defused by the Compromise of 1850. Speaking again with the moral passion of a biblical prophet, Lincoln declared: "Slavery is founded in the selfishness of man's nature—Opposition to it, in his love of justice. These principles are in eternal antagonism; and when brought into collision so fiercely, as slavery extension brings them, shocks, and throes, and convulsions must ceaselessly follow." Supporters of slavery might repeal the Missouri Compromise, the Declaration of Independence, and "all past history," but "you still can not repeal human nature." Paraphrasing Jesus, he said, "It still will be the abundance of man's heart, that slavery extension is wrong; and out of the abundance of his heart, his mouth will continue to speak." Lincoln agreed that the Union was indeed worth preserving: "Much as I hate slavery, I would consent to the extension of it rather than see the Union dissolved, just as I would consent to any GREAT evil, to avoid a GREATER one." (By 1861 he had changed his mind on this question.)

Lincoln pointed out a basic flaw in the popular sovereignty argument: its failure to specify at what point in the development of a territory its residents could forbid slavery. "Is it to be decided by the first dozen settlers who arrive there? Or is it to await the arrival of a hundred?" And just who would be empowered to take action against the peculiar institution—the territorial legislature or the people in a referendum?

To those Whigs who opposed the Kansas-Nebraska Act but who hesitated to demand the restoration of the Missouri Compromise lest they be seen as pro-abolitionist, Lincoln counseled: "Stand with anybody that stands RIGHT. Stand with him while he is right and PART with him when he goes wrong. Stand WITH the abolitionist in restoring the Missouri Compromise; and stand AGAINST him when he attempts to repeal the fugitive slave law. In the latter case you stand with the southern disunionist. What of that? You are still right. In both cases you oppose the dangerous extremes." That, he said, "is good old whig ground. To desert such ground, because of any company, is to be less than a whig—less than a man—less than an American."

Scouting Douglas's attempt to enlist the Founding Fathers as supporters of popular sovereignty, Lincoln quite rightly pointed out that the "argument of 'Necessity' was the only argument they ever admitted in favor of slavery; and so far, and so far only as it carried them did they ever go. They found the institution existing among us, which they could not help; and they cast blame upon the British King for having permitted its introduction." In 1787 they forbade slavery from expanding from the original states into the Old Northwest. In writing the Constitution, "they forbore to so much as mention the word 'slave' or 'slavery' in the whole instrument." So "the thing is hid away, in the constitution, just as an afflicted man hides away a wen or a cancer, which he dares not cut out at once, lest he bleed to death; with the promise, nevertheless, that the cutting may begin at the end of a given time." The early Congresses followed suit, passing several laws to restrict the slave trade between 1794 and 1807 and declaring the African slave trade to be piracy in 1820. So the Founders showed "hostility to the principle" of slavery "and toleration, ONLY BY NECESSITY."

But, Lincoln argued, Douglas was forsaking the Founding Fathers by placing slavery "on the high road to extension and perpetuity." Warming to his task, Lincoln deplored this betrayal of the Framers' vision: "Nearly eighty years ago we began by declaring that all men are created equal; but now from that beginning we have run down to the other declaration, that for SOME men to enslave OTHERS is a 'sacred right of self-government.' These principles can not stand together. They are as opposite as God and mammon." He was especially incensed at Indiana senator John Pettit, who, in supporting the Kansas-Nebraska bill, referred to the Declaration of Independence as "a self-evident lie." None of his colleagues in the Douglas camp had rebuked Pettit for that statement. Passionately Lincoln remarked that if such words had been spoken "to the men who captured [British spy John] Andre, the man who said it, would probably have been hung sooner than Andre was. If it had been said in old Independence Hall, seventy-eight years ago, the very door-keeper would have throttled the man, and thrust him into the street." ("The applause that followed was continued for some minutes.")[31] The new cynicism about the Declaration was "a sad evidence that, feeling prosperity we forget about right—that liberty as a principle we have ceased to revere."

In his heartfelt peroration, Lincoln urged North and South alike to reconsider their views: "In our greedy chase to make profit of the negro, let us beware, lest we 'cancel and tear to pieces' even the white man's charter of freedom." Paraphrasing a biblical reference to washing robes in the blood of the lamb, he added: "Our republican robe is soiled, and trailed in the dust. Let us repurify it. Let us turn and wash it white, in the spirit, if not the blood, of the Revolution. Let us turn slavery from its claim of 'moral right,' back upon its existing legal rights, and its arguments of 'necessity.' Let us return it to the position our fathers gave it; and there let it rest in peace. Let us re-adopt the Declaration of Independence, and with it, the practices, and policy, which harmonize with it. Let north and south—let all Americans—let all lovers of liberty everywhere—join in the great and good work. If we do this, we shall not only have saved the Union; but we shall have saved it, as to make and keep it, forever worthy of the saving. We shall have so saved it, that the succeeding millions of free happy people, the world over, shall rise up and call us blessed, to the latest generations."[32]

This statesmanlike speech, delivered with the utmost conviction, "attracted a more marked attention," Lincoln observed, than had his earlier addresses and was published in the *Illinois State Journal*.[33] Significantly, Lincoln devoted little attention to nativism, the temperance crusade, or any issue other than slavery. The Springfield *Register* thought it noteworthy that "Lincoln spoke of Judge Douglas in a less denunciatory manner than is the custom on such occasions."[34] He had come a long way since the 1830s and 1840s, when he heaped ridicule on his political opponents.

Horace White recalled the occasion in Springfield vividly: "It was a warmish day in early October, and Mr. Lincoln was in his shirt sleeves when he stepped on the platform." Although he started off in a "slow and hesitating manner," it became immediately clear that "he had mastered his subject, that he knew what he was going to say, and that he knew he was right." Sweat "would stream from his face, and each particular hair would stand on end." At that point "the inspiration that possessed him took possession of his hearers also. His speaking went to the heart because it came from the heart."[35] White said Lincoln's address "left Douglas's edifice of 'Popular Sovereignty' a heap of ruins."[36]

Immediately after Lincoln finished, Douglas "took the stand actually quivering," complaining that "he had been grossly assailed though in a perfectly courteous manner," that Lincoln had handled him "without mercy or gloves," and that Lincoln and other critics aimed "to agitate until the people of the South would, from fear of their slaves, set them free."[37] Other Democrats attacked the speech for alleging that "the white man had no right to pass laws for the government of the black man without the nigger's consent."[38]

On October 16, Lincoln delivered substantially the same speech in Peoria that he had given at Springfield, adding a response to Douglas's most recent criticism of the October 4 address.

Senate Bid

In November, Democrats lost badly throughout the Free States, including Illinois. Opponents of the Kansas-Nebraska Act dominated both the legislature and the congressional delegation, gratifying antislavery newspapers like the New York *Tribune*, which deemed the election a referendum on Douglas: "No Senator of the United States ever before received such a withering repudiation."[39] Douglas's Illinois colleague in the Senate, James Shields, ascribed the defeat in their state to the Little Giant's dictatorial insistence that all Democratic candidates support the unpopular Kansas-Nebraska Act. Democrat John M. Palmer deeply resented the high-handed tactics of the Little Giant, whom he called "this miniature negro driver, this small sample of a Carolina overseer who speaks to us as if we were slaves."[40]

Despite the Democrats' poor showing, Yates lost his bid for reelection, largely because of redistricting and because he was labeled a Know-Nothing. Democrats also denounced him as a friend to Blacks. The Springfield *Register* stated that "those who are in favor of repealing all laws making distinctions between whites and blacks, and are willing to let the negroes vote, sit on juries and give evidence in court against the white man, and that whites and blacks marry indiscriminately, just let them vote for Mr. Yates."[41]

If Yates bemoaned his defeat, Lincoln regretted his own victory in the legislative contest, for, as he soon learned, it rendered him ineligible for the U.S. Senate seat that he had hoped to win when the newly elected General Assembly, with a slim majority of anti-Nebraska members, convened in January. It is uncertain just when the prospect of the senatorship first tickled Lincoln's ambition, but as election day approached, it seemed clear that he might attain such a high office. And following the election, it was also clear that James Shields would likely lose his seat.

Three days after the November election, Lincoln began lining up support for his Senate bid. To Joseph Gillespie, for example, he wrote: "I have really got it into my head to try to be United States Senator; and if I could have your support my chances would be reasonably good."[42] In late November, belatedly realizing that his status as a member-elect of the General Assembly might doom his bid to win a Senate seat. Lincoln formally declined election as a state representative. Although this step helped pave the way for his elevation to the Senate, it was risky, for anti-Nebraska forces enjoyed only a slim majority in the legislature and were divided by old party animosities. In the special election called to replace Lincoln, the Democratic candidate, Jonathan McDaniel, surprisingly defeated Republican Norman Broadwell.

The anti-Nebraska forces in the legislature were understandably angry at Lincoln and other Sangamon County Whigs for losing that seat. David Davis told Lincoln that voters would say "Damn Springfield—the Whigs have behaved so shamefully that they ought to be punished & Lincoln should not be elected."[43] Lincoln also alienated antislavery radicals by failing to make common cause with them when they gathered in Springfield to form the Illinois Republican Party. At that meeting, held on October 4 and 5, they elected Lincoln, without his knowledge, to their central committee. In November he declined that honor, saying: "I was not consulted on the subject; nor was I apprized of the appointment, until I discovered it by accident two or three weeks afterwards. I supposed my opposition to the principle of slavery is as strong as that of any member of the Republican party; but I had also supposed that the *extent* to which I feel authorized to carry that opposition, practically, was not at all satisfactory to that party."[44] Zebina Eastman, an abolitionist editor in Chicago, advised Republicans not to support "Lincoln, or any of the moderate men of his stamp," for the Senate. "He is only a Whig, and the people's movement is no whig triumph."[45]

To help combat such opposition, Lincoln enlisted the aid of Congressman Elihu B. Washburne. In December, Lincoln told him: "I have not ventured to write all the members [of the legislature] in your district, lest some of them should be offended by the indelicacy of the thing—that is, coming from a total stranger. Could you not drop some of them a line?"[46] Washburne jumped in to help, writing not only to legislators but also to Eastman, urging him to reconsider. The abolitionist editor would not yield and retorted that many anti-Nebraska Democrats "have a repugnance at voting for Lincoln," who "did not give entire satisfaction to the Republicans in his speech in Chicago. Did not take high ground enough."[47] In response, Washburne implored Eastman to be flexible and magnanimous: "I am afraid our friends will be so impracticable that we may lose the fruits of our splendid victory. We must be yielding and liberal all round. I mentioned Lincoln, not because he had been a whig, but because he is a man of splendid talents, of great probity of character, and because he threw himself into the late fight on the *republican platform* and made the greatest speech in reply to Douglas ever heard in the State. *I know he is with us in sentiment*, and in such times as these, when we want big men and true men in the Senate, it seems cruel to strike him down. I thought, also he could combine more strength than any other man in the State. He has great personal popularity, and the entire confidence of all men of all parties."[48]

Eastman consulted with the more vocally antislavery Herndon, who converted him with assurances that Lincoln was "all right."[49] With Eastman in the fold, Lincoln managed to win over other antislavery leaders with the assistance of friends like Joshua Giddings and David Davis. When the legislature convened in early January, Lincoln's hard work lining up the antislavery members paid dividends; Washburne, Giddings, Davis, and others had overcome the objections of most abolitionists. As the General Assembly gathered, Lincoln was understandably confident of his prospects for the senatorship. A majority of the one hundred legislators opposed the Kansas-Nebraska Act. Lincoln estimated that in the house of representatives the Whigs and anti-Nebraska Democrats outnumbered the regular Democrats forty-four to thirty-one; their majority in the Senate was only thirteen to twelve.

The chief business before the legislature was choosing a U.S. senator, a high-stakes contest that both sides desperately sought to win. The Democrats justly feared that if an anti-Nebraska candidate won the senatorship, the nation would interpret it as a repudiation of Douglas and popular sovereignty. Accordingly, they circulated letters among themselves that stated: "They *outnumber* us, but we must *outmanage* them. Douglas must be sustained. We must elect the Speaker; and we must elect a Nebraska U.S. Senator, or elect none at all."[50] Upon convening, the General Assembly filled all its offices save one with Democrats. Many lesser-known Whigs hoped to become a U.S. senator as a result of such partisan magnanimity. On January 6, Lincoln informed Washburne that other contenders' prospects were poor, for he himself was the front-runner, with twenty-six commitments; no one else had more than ten. He began to make personal appeals to legislators once they assembled in Springfield. He would say, in essence: "Gentlemen, this is rather a delicate subject for me to talk upon; but I must confess that I would be glad of your support for the office, if you shall conclude that I am the proper person for it."[51]

The Democrats anticipated that if the incumbent, James Shields, were unable to prevail, the legislature would adjourn without choosing his successor, thus leaving the seat vacant temporarily. Shields had injured his reelection chances by supporting the Kansas-Nebraska Act despite his opposition to it in principle. Anti-Nebraska Democrats like William H. Bissell and Lyman Trumbull were regarded as possibilities, though Bissell's poor health seemed to disqualify him. Douglas insisted that the party must "*stand by Shields to the last and make no compromises*." If the Irishman were to lose, then the Democrats could denounce their opponents as nativist bigots who opposed Shields simply because he had been born abroad.[52]

By refusing to meet with the House of Representative, senate Democrats postponed the vote. On January 17, James W. Sheahan, editor of Douglas's organ (the

Chicago *Times*), wrote in alarm to Charles Lanphier at Springfield: "I think that all hope of electing Shields is gone: that the postponement of the election is a hazardous matter. . . . A new man should be talked of at once; and before the election, let a caucus be held, at which *Shields' declination* should be read by some one."[53] But who should that new man be?

Governor Joel Matteson, a wealthy, corrupt anti-Nebraska Democrat who could appeal to both factions of his party, worked industriously to line up votes. He won the support of seven legislators (at least some of whom were bribed) and then assured the pro-Nebraska Democrats that he could win if he had their support. Matteson's appeal led them to abandon Shields. Democrats had meanwhile gained control of the state senate with the defection of Whig Don Morrison and anti-Nebraska Democrat Uri Osgood, who was allegedly "bought outright."[54] The senate then refused to hold a joint session with the house to elect a senator until Matteson had rounded up the necessary votes. And so it was not until February 8 that the joint session took place.

That day, the statehouse galleries and lobby were packed as the balloting began. Lincoln received forty-five votes on the first round, a mere five short of victory. Those five votes could have been provided by Norman B. Judd, Burton C. Cook, Henry Baker, George T. Allen, and John M. Palmer, anti-Nebraska Democrats all. But adamant in their refusal to vote for a Whig, they united behind Lyman Trumbull, an antislavery Democrat from Alton who had just won a seat in the U.S. House. Those five liked Trumbull personally and regarded his election to the Senate as essential to uniting the opponents of Douglas's popular sovereignty dogma, for it would lure thousands of Democrats to support the anti-Nebraska party who would balk at the choice of Lincoln.

Although it was speculated that Trumbull could have as many as eighteen votes on the initial ballot, in fact he received only five, while Lincoln's closest competitor, Shields, had forty-one. Over the next five ballots, Lincoln's vote decreased, Shields's held steady, and Trumbull's grew. When it became clear that Lincoln could not win, Stephen T. Logan moved for adjournment until the morning, but the anti-Nebraska Democrats teamed up with their estranged party colleagues to defeat the motion. The seventh ballot created great excitement, as the pro-Nebraska Democrats suddenly switched from Shields to Matteson, who received forty-four votes. On the eighth ballot the governor picked up two more votes, while Lincoln's total dwindled to twenty-seven and Trumbull's swelled to eighteen. The following ballot showed Lincoln with fifteen, Trumbull with thirty-five, and Matteson with forty-seven. Fearing that the governor would win on the next round, Lincoln and his allies threw their support to Trumbull, who won on the tenth ballot, receiving fifty-one votes to Matteson's forty-seven.

Jubilation reigned among the anti-Nebraska forces at Trumbull's election. A tremendous roar rang out in the lobby of Representatives Hall, which overflowed with well-wishers. The New York *Tribune* hailed the "glorious result" as "a fitting finale to the Repeal of the Missouri Compromise by Douglas & Co."[55] Zebina Eastman crowed that of "all the candidates named for the station, the successful one was the most obnoxious to the aspiring leader [Douglas], and whose election is the most mortifying to him personally and politically."[56] If Matteson and his friends did resort to bribery, which seems highly probable, then it is easy to understand why Lincoln rejoiced at thwarting the governor's scheme. "I regret my defeat moderately," he told Washburne, "but I am not nervous about it. I could have headed off every combination and been elected, had it not been for Matteson's double game—and the governor's defeat now gives me more pleasure than my own gives me pain." Lincoln was not gloating or being vindictive; he was genuinely offended by Matteson's tactics and regarded the governor's defeat as a triumph for antislavery principles and a rebuke to Democrats who had supported the Kansas-Nebraska Act—not to mention a triumph over corruption. "On the whole," he mused to Washburne, "it is perhaps as well for our general cause that Trumbull is elected. The Neb[raska] men confess that they hate it worse than any thing that could have happened. It is a great consolation to see them worse whipped than I am. I tell them it is their own fault—that they had abundant opertunity to choose between him & me, which they declined, and instead forced it on me to decide between him & Matteson."[57] Lincoln correctly gauged the level of discomfort in the Douglas camp. Trumbull reported that the pro-Nebraska Democrats "are exhibiting towards me a great deal of ill natured & malignant feeling."[58]

Although pleased that he had delivered a blow to the Douglas forces, Lincoln acknowledged that it "was rather hard for the 44 to have to surrender to the 5—and a less good humored man than I, perhaps would not have consented to it—and it would not have been done without my consent. I could not, however, let the whole political result go to ruin, on a point merely personal to myself."[59] In fact, his failure to win the Senate seat plunged him into depression. Washburne thought that "no event in Mr. Lincoln's entire political career . . . brought to him so much disappointment and chagrin as his defeat for United States Senator in 1855."[60] When Samuel C. Parks, a pro-Lincoln legislator, tried to console him by saying he would surely be elected senator in 1858, Lincoln predicted that "the taste for the senatorship would get out of his mouth" by then.[61] Joseph Gillespie, another legislator active on Lincoln's behalf, accompanied him home after the election and later recalled that he "could bear defeat inflicted by his enemies with a pretty good grace; but it was hard to be wounded in the house of his friends."[62] However dejected he may have been, at a party in honor of the senator-elect, Lincoln cheerfully responded to a query about his disappointment by saying he was "not *too* disappointed to congratulate my friend Trumbull."[63] To young Shelby Cullom, who offered condolences, he replied, "My boy, don't worry; it will all come right in the end."[64] When asked if he were bitter about Judd's failure to support him, Lincoln replied: "I can't harbor enmity to any one; it's not my nature."[65] Mary Lincoln, by contrast, denounced Trumbull's "cold, selfish treachery." She even turned on her old friend and bridesmaid Julia Jayne, now Mrs. Lyman Trumbull, calling her "ungainly," "cold," "unsympathizing," and "unpopular."[66] Shortly after the election, she snubbed Julia Trumbull as the two women emerged from a church service; when Mrs. Trumbull tried to catch her eye, Mary Lincoln looked away. Julia persuaded her mother to invite Mrs. Lincoln to a party, but the invitation was declined. When the two politicians' wives met by chance, Mary Lincoln was singularly ungracious. Julia reported that "I have shaken hands with Mary, her lips moved but her voice was not audible[.] I think she was embarrassed."[67] Mrs. Lincoln continued to hold a grudge against her former bridesmaid and friend until Julia Trumbull's death in 1868.

Norman Judd, one of the five anti-Nebraska Democrats whose obstinacy spoiled Lincoln's chances, appreciated that "Lincoln never joined in that clamor" against them. "He had the good sense to see that our course was the result of political sagacity," Judd explained. "If we had voted for him, we should simply have been denounced by our own papers as renegades who had deserted the democrats and gone over to the Whigs."[68]

Disappointing though his defeat was to both him and his spouse, Lincoln could derive satisfaction from having laid the foundation for the Illinois Republican Party, which would mature into a full-blown organization in 1856. By magnanimously throwing his support to Trumbull, he had helped cement the coalition of former Whigs and former Democrats. He might also have taken heart from the pledge made by John M. Palmer that he and his Democratic friends would "stand by him in the next fight" against Douglas.[69] Lincoln's statesmanlike reaction to his loss illustrated the truth of Richard J. Oglesby's observation that he "submitted to adversity and injustice with as much real patience as any Man I Ever knew—because he had an abiding belief that all would yet come out right or that the right would appear and Justice finally be awarded to him."[70] And so it would.

11.

"Unite with Us, and Help Us to Triumph"

Building the Illinois Republican Party (1855–1857)

"You enquire where I now stand," Lincoln wrote to Joshua Speed in the summer of 1855. "This is a disputed point. I think I am a Whig; but others say there are no whigs, and that I am an abolitionist." That was not the case, he averred, for "I now do no more than oppose the *extension* of slavery."[1] To unite all who shared that goal was now Lincoln's principal aim. As he helped build a new antislavery party to replace the defunct Whig organization, he little imagined that he would soon become its standard-bearer. In this endeavor, he displayed the statesmanlike qualities that would characterize his presidency: eloquence, shrewdness, industry, patience, selflessness, diplomacy, commitment to principle, willingness to shoulder responsibility, and a preternatural sense of timing. While many joined the Republican ranks out of hostility to the South, the tolerant Lincoln played down sectional antagonism and focused on the evils of the peculiar institution itself.

Difficulty in Forming a New Party

Of all the obstacles Lincoln faced in rallying Illinoisans against slavery expansion, none was more formidable than an upsurge of nativism. In 1855, the Know-Nothings of Illinois united to form a branch of the American Party, which denounced Catholicism, immigrants, and slavery expansion. Their bigotry alienated many other antislavery advocates, making it difficult to keep the anti-Nebraska coalition intact. Antagonizing the foreign-born, who constituted 20 percent of Illinois's population, would be politically ruinous, but so, too, would be any move that offended nativists.

In the summer and fall of 1855, abolitionists campaigned throughout Illinois to enlist support for their cause and lay the groundwork for a Republican victory in 1856. When Owen Lovejoy proposed that a state antislavery convention meet in Springfield that autumn, Lincoln replied that although he was ready to endorse the abolitionists' antislavery principles, the time was not yet ripe for a new party.

The main problem was that the Know-Nothing organization had "not yet entirely crumbled to pieces," and until the anti-Nebraska forces could win over elements of it, "there is not sufficient materials to successfully combat the Nebraska democracy with." Lincoln hoped the nativists' "organization would die out without the painful necessity of my taking an open stand against them." Of course, he deplored their principles: "Indeed I do not perceive how any one professing to be sensitive to the wrongs of the negroes, can join in a league to degrade a class of white men." He was not squeamish about combining with "any body who stands right," but the Know-Nothings stood wrong.[2] In 1855, he, like many other Whigs, still nursed a hope that their party might continue as a viable organization.

Lincoln's doubts about launching a new party that year were as great as his skepticism about the chances for nonviolent abolition. Writing to the Kentucky attorney George Robertson, who in 1820 had predicted the peaceable elimination of slavery, Lincoln said: "Since then, we have had thirty six years of experience" that "demonstrated, I think, that there is no peaceful extinction of slavery in prospect for us." Lincoln bemoaned the decline of American virtue since 1776, when the nation "called the maxim that 'all men are created equal' a self evident truth." Now, he said, "we have grown so fat, and have lost all dread of being slaves ourselves, we have become so greedy to be *masters* that we call the same maxim 'a self-evident lie.'" Sarcastically he observed: "The fourth of July has not quite dwindled away; it is still a great day—*for burning fire crackers*!!!" The idealism of the Revolutionary era, which had prompted several states to abolish slavery, "has itself become extinct," he lamented. He predicted that the "Autocrat of all the Russias will resign his crown, and proclaim his subjects free republicans sooner than will our American masters voluntarily give up their slaves." Foreshadowing a speech that would help make him famous three years later, Lincoln told Robertson: "Our political problem now is 'Can we, as a nation, continue together *permanently—forever—* half slave, and half free?'"[3]

To another Kentuckian, Joshua Speed, Lincoln also unbosomed himself on the vexed question of slavery. Speed had criticized Northerners for agitating the slavery issue; they should mind their own business. In response, Lincoln argued that Speed ought to applaud the restraint shown by Free State residents who were willing to honor constitutional provisions concerning fugitive slaves and states rights. Lincoln reminded Speed of a steamboat trip they had taken on the Ohio River in 1841, during which "there were, on board, ten or a dozen slaves, shackled together with irons. That sight was a continual torment to me; and I see something like it every time I touch the Ohio or any other slave-border. It is hardly fair for you to assume, that I have no interest in a thing which has, and continually exercises, the power of making me miserable."

Shifting from old memories to current affairs, Lincoln expressed outrage at events in Kansas, where proslavery forces, led by Missourians, ran roughshod over Free Soilers, stealing elections by fraud and violence, expelling antislavery legislators, and passing statutes that forbade criticism of slavery and imposed the death penalty on anyone assisting runaway slaves. In response to Speed's professed willingness to dissolve the Union if the rights of slaveholders were violated, Lincoln said that he would not attempt to do so if the tables were turned and Kansas were admitted as a Slave State. Echoing his 1854 Peoria address, Lincoln told his longtime friend that "slave-breeders and slave traders, are a small, odious and detested class, among you; and yet in politics, they dictate the course of all of you, and are as completely your masters, as you are the masters of your own negroes." Although dubious about the prospects for a free Kansas, Lincoln said he would work for "the restoration of the Missouri Compromise."[4]

Shortly after the 1855 elections, a small group of antislavery newspapermen launched another attempt to unify the foes of slavery. On February 22, twelve hardy journalists braved a snowstorm to meet in Decatur for that purpose. Lincoln participated in the meeting as an informal guest. He had grown more optimistic about the chances for successful fusion because hostility to slavery and to the South was mounting throughout the North, largely in response to the outrages in Kansas and the rendition of fugitive slaves. In Decatur, he helped draft a platform containing an antinativist plank. One editor, German-born George Schneider of the Chicago *Staats-Zeitung*, who came to Decatur "with his war paint on," had prepared a declaration sharply condemning Know-Nothingism.[5] Because it provoked strong opposition, Schneider turned in desperation to Lincoln, who, after reading it, told the assembled editors: "The resolution introduced by Mr. Schneider is nothing new. It is already contained in the Declaration of Independence and you cannot form a new party on proscriptive principles." Lincoln's intervention, according to Schneider, "saved the resolution" and "helped to establish the new party on the most liberal democratic basis."[6] Lincoln composed the "States Rights Plank," which condemned demands to protect slave owners' right to expand as "an invasion of our rights, oppressive and unjust, [that] must be resisted."[7] The preamble and other resolutions called for the restoration of the Missouri Compromise and endorsed the principle that slavery was local and freedom national. But they also affirmed that the Fugitive Slave Act must be obeyed and that the federal government was not authorized to tamper with slavery in the states where it existed. After adopting this declaration of principles and naming a central committee, the editors called for a state convention of antislavery forces to meet in Bloomington on May 29. They did not, however, formally endorse a gubernatorial candidate, though some wanted to run Lincoln. Meanwhile, he had been trying to woo the popular antislavery

Democrat and Mexican War hero William H. Bissell, who seemed the most electable of all the anti-Nebraska leaders. In 1850 as a congressman, Bissell had achieved national renown by accepting Jefferson Davis's challenge to a duel. An eloquent speaker, Bissell suffered from poor health, which made his availability problematic. At the dinner following the editors' convention, Lincoln announced his support for Bissell. When toasted as "our next candidate for the U.S. Senate," Lincoln replied that if he were nominated, "the Democrats would say, it was nothing more than an attempt to resurrect the dead body of the old Whig party. I would secure the vote of that party and no more, and our defeat will follow as a matter of course. But, I can suggest a name that will secure not only the old Whig vote, but enough Anti-Nebraska Democrats to give us the victory. That man is Colonel William H. Bissell."[8]

The editors' convention had in effect launched the Republican Party of Illinois. Under Lincoln's leadership, it steered a moderate course to avoid alienating potential allies, especially conservative Whigs and Know-Nothings, yet at the same time forcefully condemned the expansion of slavery. The editors had carefully avoided using the name Republican, which, as antislavery congressman John Wentworth of Chicago observed, connoted to many voters "a sort of Maine Law, Free Love, Spiritual Medium &c. &c. concern."[9]

First Republican Convention

The gubernatorial nomination would be formally considered at the convention that the editors set for May 29, 1856, at Bloomington. Moderation was the watchword that spring. Most important, the anti-Nebraska forces needed to select the right gubernatorial candidate. As Lincoln had suggested, William Bissell was the obvious choice. In January, Bissell had indicated a willingness to run for governor, saying that although his health was shaky, he would do whatever the party thought best. By early May, however, he had changed his mind, fearing that the anti-Nebraska organization would not be successful. Bissell's reluctance now placed the entire movement in jeopardy. Through Herndon, Lincoln indirectly conveyed the optimism needed to dispel Bissell's gloom. Two weeks after Bissell expressed his reluctance to run, Herndon told Trumbull of an upbeat discussion he had just had with his partner: "Lincoln and myself had a long talk in reference to affairs, and I have never seen him so sanguine of success, as in this election—*he is warm*."[10] Prospects brightened four days later, when Bissell announced that he would in fact accept the gubernatorial nomination.

En route to Bloomington, Lincoln told his colleagues of "his hopes and fears of the results of the coming convention, and of his earnest wish that the old Whig element from Southern Illinois might be well represented there."[11] He did not "attempt to conceal fears and misgivings entertained by him as to the outcome of the gathering. He was well assured that the radical element of the northern counties would be there in force, and feared the effect upon the conservative element of the central and southern parts of the State."[12] The next day, as their train rolled northward toward Bloomington, Lincoln anxiously inquired of fellow passengers if they were delegates from southern Illinois, where antislavery sentiment was weak. He was jubilant upon discovering two trainmates from Egypt (i.e., southern Illinois) who would attend the convention. Arriving in Bloomington the next day, Lincoln eagerly sought out Whig friends from that region. Lincoln's goal was to persuade them to unite with the abolitionists of the north and the moderates of central Illinois.

Energetically but discreetly, holding no official position other than that of chairman of the nominations committee, Lincoln was the master spirit of the convention, managing through some political alchemy to persuade former enemies to set aside their differences and cooperate for the greater good. He helped craft the main slavery plank in the platform, which held that "congress possesses full power to prohibit slavery in the territories; and that while we maintain all constitutional rights of the south, we also hold that justice, humanity, the principles of freedom as expressed in our Declaration of Independence, and our national constitution and the purity and perpetuity of our government, require that that power should be exerted to prevent the extension of slavery into territories heretofore free."[13] In justifying this stance to radical anti-Nebraska Democrats, Lincoln said: "Your party is so mad at Douglas for wrecking his party that it will gulp down anything; but our party [Whig] is fresh from Kentucky and must not be forced to radical measures; the Abolitionists will go with us anyway, and your wing of the Democratic party the same, but the Whigs hold the balance of power and will be hard to manage, anyway."[14]

Intervening to settle further disputes between radicals and conservatives, Lincoln approved the other platform planks, which denounced the violence in Kansas, called for the restoration of the Missouri Compromise, urged the admission of Kansas as a Free State, professed devotion to the Union, pledged to "support the constitution in all its provisions," criticized nativist bigotry, and attacked the administration of Governor Joel Matteson.[15] The convention adopted that platform unanimously and chose a slate of presidential electors headed by Lincoln and Frederick Hecker, a German-born antislavery leader who persuaded many of his fellow countrymen to support the Republican Party. Lincoln was also named a delegate to the Republican national convention, scheduled to meet in June at Philadelphia.

Uniting the conventioneers was their indignation at events in Kansas, where on May 21 proslavery militia had sacked the Free Soil town of Lawrence, and in

Washington, where on May 22 Congressman Preston Brooks of South Carolina had cudgeled abolitionist senator Charles Sumner of Massachusetts into insensibility at the Capitol. Those violent acts created an unparalleled rage that swept the North. In the subsequent election campaign, Republicans aroused the Free States with an appeal to remember "bleeding Kansas and bleeding Sumner." Fueling the anger in Bloomington were refugees from Kansas, including Governor Andrew H. Reeder, who on the night of May 28 described to a crowd the violence he had observed in that territory before being compelled to flee for his life. The people who heard Reeder speak called for Lincoln, who briefly compared the abrogation of the Missouri Compromise to the destruction of a fence, thus allowing one man's cattle to eat the crops belonging to his neighbor, and spoke of the outrages in Kansas, including the destruction of newspaper offices and the dismissal of government employees for political reasons.

The next day those Kansas outrages were portrayed by another fugitive from that territory, James S. Emery of Lawrence, who described the sacking of his town and the destruction of its newspaper office. When Emery finished, he watched Lincoln stride to the podium with a giraffe-like gait. His hair was tousled, his clothes were not neat, and his shoulders were stooped. But his appearance was scarcely noticed by the delegates, whose attention was arrested by his intensely serious look. Emery recalled that Lincoln "at once held his big audience and handled it like the master he was before the people, pleading in a great and just cause."[16]

Incredibly, what Lincoln said on that occasion has not survived, and so this oration, believed to be one of his masterpieces, has become known as the "lost speech." Reporters were allegedly so carried away that they dropped their pencils and listened, spellbound. Although many journalists were present, only two brief newspaper accounts of the speech's substance are extant. According to the Alton *Courier*, Lincoln "enumerated the pressing reasons of the present movement," said he "was here ready to fuse with anyone who would unite with him to oppose the slave power," and referred to "the bugbear of disunion which was so vaguely threatened." It "must be remembered," he said, "that the *Union must be preserved in the purity of its principles as well as in the integrity of its territorial parts.*" Lincoln also rejected Douglas's contention that his doctrine of popular sovereignty squared with the teachings of Henry Clay. He further maintained that a "sentiment in favor of white slavery now prevailed in all the slave state papers" except in some Border States.[17]

The only other contemporary account of Lincoln's remarks appeared in the Belleville, Illinois, *Advocate*, which reported: "Abraham Lincoln by his wonderful eloquence electrified the audience of two thousand men . . . and excelled himself. Men who had heard him often said he never spoke as well before. . . . He paid his respects to those 'National Whigs,' as they call themselves, who are all the time stepping about to the *music of the Union*! He had no doubt but that the music of an overseer's lash upon a mulatto girl's back would make some of them dance a Virginia hornpipe. 'Let them step,' said he, 'let them dance to the music of the Union, while we, my old Whig friends, stand fast by Principle and Freedom and the Union, together.'"[18] In a dispatch written that day, John Locke Scripps described the delivery and reception of Lincoln's speech: "For an hour and a half he held the assemblage spell-bound by the power of his argument, the intense irony of his invective, and the deep earnestness and fervid brilliancy of his eloquence. When he concluded, the audience sprang to their feet, and cheer after cheer told how deeply their hearts had been touched, and their souls warmed up to a generous enthusiasm."[19]

The failure of newspapers to report the content of Lincoln's remarks may have resulted from a deliberate political decision. According to Joseph Medill, party leaders "strongly urged" Lincoln "to write out his speech to be used as a campaign document," but he declined, saying "it would be impossible for him to recall the language he used on that occasion, as he had spoken under some excitement." It was more likely, Medill speculated, that Lincoln thought "it was too radical in expression on the slavery question for the digestion of Central and Southern Illinois at that time, and that he preferred to let it stand as a remembrance in the minds of his audience."[20]

1856 Campaign

With Bissell heading their state ticket, anti-Nebraskaites had reason to be optimistic. "If we can save pretty nearly all the whigs, we shall elect him, I think by a very large majority," Lincoln predicted. But saving the Old Line Whigs would not be easy. Nationally, Democrats reacted to the public revulsion against the Kansas-Nebraska Act and the turmoil in Kansas by rejecting both Stephen A. Douglas and the incumbent president, Franklin Pierce. Instead they chose as their standard-bearer James Buchanan of Pennsylvania, who had recently been in London serving as U.S. minister to the Court of St. James's and thus was untainted by the Kansas-Nebraska Act and its consequences. This move alarmed Lincoln, who observed that "a good many whigs, of conservative feelings, and slight pro-slavery proclivities, withal, are inclining to go for him, and will do it, unless the Anti-Nebraska nomination be such as to divert them."[21]

Lincoln, who had worked so hard to ensure that Illinois Republicans avoided taking a radical antislavery stance, hoped his party's national convention, in mid-June at Philadelphia, would follow suit. His favorite candidate was Supreme Court justice John McLean, whose nomination, he said, "would save every whig, except those who have already gone over hook and line." The mainstream Whigs might, however, flee to Buchanan if the Republicans chose a radical like Salmon P. Chase of

Ohio, Nathaniel P. Banks of Massachusetts, William Henry Seward of New York, Francis P. Blair of Missouri, or John C. Frémont of California. The latter two might be acceptable to Illinois Whigs for vice president, but not for president. Although he was chosen as a delegate to the Republican national convention, Lincoln did not attend. At Bloomington he had declined the honor "on account of his poverty and business engagements," but when Jesse W. Fell offered to pay his expenses, Lincoln said he might be able to go after all. At the last minute, however, he wired Fell that he could not accept, so Jesse's brother Kersey went as his replacement.

At Philadelphia, the Republicans did not choose a conservative candidate. To Lincoln's dismay, John C. Frémont, a former Democrat known as "the Pathfinder," for his celebrated explorations in the West, secured the presidential nomination. William L. Dayton of New Jersey was named as his running mate. Although chagrined by the selection of Frémont, Lincoln doubtless found some consolation in the 110 votes he himself received for vice president. (The Illinois delegation had supported McLean for president; when he lost, a leading Prairie State delegate, Congressman William B. Archer, resolved to nominate Lincoln for the second spot on the ticket.) When the news arrived of his near nomination for vice president, Lincoln modestly shrugged it off, saying the candidate being discussed was probably Levi Lincoln of Massachusetts. When friends showed him that indeed he was the one who had almost won the vice presidential nomination, he remained seemingly unmoved, but Henry C. Whitney believed that "from that time Lincoln trimmed his sails to catch the breeze which might waft him to the White House."[22]

Lincoln threw himself into the presidential campaign, delivering more than fifty speeches around Illinois in an unusually bitter contest. His principal concern was to woo disaffected Whigs, a class well represented by his old friend Joseph Gillespie, who still resented the anti-Nebraska Democrats who had refused to support Lincoln's Senate bid the previous year. To enlist Whigs opposed to the expansion of slavery, Lincoln had to battle the taint of abolitionism and fears of disunion. He responded to the challenge energetically. With Herndon, he stumped throughout southern Illinois, where his services were in demand. This was disagreeable, discouraging labor. Frequently crowds failed to turn out because there were simply too few Republicans in the area. In rural counties, Republican processions, headed by some frantic marshals leading a brass band and a carriage full of local dignitaries, were often pitiful because the shy farmers would not fall in behind them. The result was a poor excuse for a parade.

No full text of his many Illinois addresses that year has survived, but in a draft fragment of his Galena speech, he rejected the charge of sectionalism leveled against the Republicans, a charge he called "the most difficult objection we have to meet." The "naked issue" that divided the Democrats from his party he summarized briefly: "*Shall slavery be allowed to extend into U.S. territory, now legally free*?" Appealing to fair-minded voters, he asked, "How is *one* side of this question, more *sectional* than the other?" If the parties were divided along sectional lines, as most other institutions were, how should the problem be solved? The answer was simple, he declared: one side must yield. Republicans "boldly say, let all who really think slavery ought to spread into free territory, openly go over against us." But why, he asked, should anyone who opposed slavery vote Democratic? "Do they really think the *right* ought to yield to the *wrong*? Are they afraid to stand by the *right*? Do they really think that by right surrendering to wrong, the hopes of our constitution, our Union, and our liberties, can possibly be bettered?"

Lincoln pointed out that White Southerners "have an immediate and palpable and immensely great pecuniary interest" in the question of slavery expansion, while for Northerners "it is merely an abstract question of moral right, with only *slight*, and *remote* pecuniary interest added." The value of Southern slaves, which Lincoln estimated at $3 million, would double if slavery were allowed to expand, whereas it would be reduced if slavery were bottled up. This consideration "unites the Southern people, as one man. But it can not be demonstrated that the *North* will gain a dollar by restricting it." It was a pity, Lincoln observed, that moral principle constituted "a looser bond, than pecuniary interest." He excoriated Northern Democratic presidential aspirants for selling out to the South. Scornfully, he noted that the party lash and personal ambition led them to auction off their principles and abandon "their own honest impulses, and sense of right."[23]

Echoing his Bloomington remarks and foreshadowing his first inaugural address, Lincoln boldly asked critics who called the Republicans disunionists: "Who are the disunionists, you or we? We, the majority, would not strive to dissolve the Union; and if any attempt is made it must be by you, who so loudly stigmatize us as disunionists. But the Union, in any event, won't be dissolved. We don't want to dissolve it, and if you attempt it, *we won't let you*. With the purse and the sword, the army and navy and treasury in our hands and at our command, you *couldn't do it*. This Government would be very weak, indeed, if a majority with a disciplined army and navy, and a well-filled treasury, could not preserve itself, when attacked by an unarmed, undisciplined, unorganized minority. All this talk about the dissolution of the Union is humbug—nothing but folly. *We* WON'T dissolve the Union, and *you* SHAN'T."[24]

In early August, Lincoln stumped throughout southeastern Illinois. With characteristic modesty, he said that since there were only sixteen registered Republicans in Shelby County, "however poorly I may defend my cause, I can hardly harm it, if I do it no good."[25] Later that month, he spoke in Kalamazoo, Michigan. Alluding to Stephen A. Douglas's reluctance to specify just how and when the people of

Kansas could, under his popular sovereignty doctrine, prohibit slavery in their midst, Lincoln sarcastically referred to the Little Giant as "a great man—at keeping from answering questions he don't want to answer." Cogently, Lincoln argued that once slavery managed to take root in Kansas, attempts to expel it would fail: "Suppose that there are ten men who go to Kansas to settle. Nine of these are opposed to slavery. One has ten slaves. The slaveholder is a good man in other respects; he is a good neighbor, and being a wealthy man, he is enabled to do the others many neighborly kindnesses. They like the man, though they don't like the system by which he holds his fellow-men in bondage." Over time, Lincoln argued, the nine antislavery men would "look upon slavery with complacency." Thus, slavery would be "planted" there.

Lincoln protested against the Richmond *Enquirer*'s assertion that "slaves are far better off than freeman." In response he exclaimed: "What a mistaken view do these men have of Northern laborers! They think that men are always to remain laborers here—but there is no such class. The man who labored for another last year, this year labors for himself, and next year he will hire others to labor for him." He denied that Frémont and his party were abolitionists, and he movingly appealed to Democrats to honor the principles they had espoused before the introduction of the Kansas-Nebraska Act. Their party, he said, "has ever prided itself, that it was the friend of individual, universal freedom." Now, to support Douglas's handiwork, Democrats had abandoned their idealism. In closing, he implored Democrats to "come forward. Throw off these things, and come to the rescue of this great principle of equality."[26]

Returning to Illinois, Lincoln repeated his warning about the inevitable conflict between slavery and freedom. At Bloomington in September he addressed a large crowd: "It is my sincere belief that this government can not last always part slave and part free.—Either Slavery will be abolished—or it must become equally lawful everywhere—or this Union will be dissolved. There is natural incompatibility between the institutions incident to Slave-holding States—so irreconcilable in their character, that they can not co-exist perpetually under the same Government." When T. Lyle Dickey warned him that preaching such a doctrine would hasten the outbreak of a bloody civil war, Lincoln reluctantly agreed to stop.[27]

In August, Lincoln and Herndon felt optimistic. "We are gaining on the nigger Democracy every day," Herndon informed Lyman Trumbull.[28] Lincoln told the senator that "we shall ultimately get all the Fillmore men who are real[l]y anti-slavery extension—the rest will probably go to Buchanan, where they rightfully belong." The "great difficulty" in persuading antislavery Fillmore supporters to back Frémont "is that they suppose Fillmore as good as Fremont" on slavery expansion.[29] Indeed, the Fillmore men proved hard to move. On September 8, Lincoln wrote a form letter to the supporters of the American Party's candidate arguing that Fillmore could only win if the election were thrown into the House of Representatives, where the former president might prevail as a compromise candidate. But that would never happen if Buchanan carried Illinois, whose electoral votes, when combined with those of the South and of the Democratic standard-bearer's home state of Pennsylvania, would assure his election. Therefore Fillmore backers in Illinois should vote for Frémont because Fillmore had no chance of carrying the state. "This is as plain as the adding up of the weights of three small hogs," Lincoln declared. He sent this letter, marked "confidential," to many "good, steady Fillmore men" throughout the state.[30]

In mid-September, Lincoln spent another week stumping southern Illinois. The unpopularity of the Frémont-Dayton ticket there meant that "my efforts are more needed" there than elsewhere, he lamented.[31] The following month, he addressed a rally in Ottawa, where he was introduced as "Our next United States Senator."[32] In Belleville, the largest city in Egypt and home to many German Americans, including the lieutenant governor, Gustave Koerner, Lincoln "referred to the Germans and the noble position taken by them in just and dignified terms. When he called down the blessings of the Almighty on their heads, a thrill of sympathy ran through this whole audience."[33] Soon thereafter, a campaign encounter with another German won Lincoln a lifelong devotee. In Pittsfield to deliver a speech, he called at the office of the *Pike County Free Press* to have some materials printed. The paper employed a young journalist, John G. Nicolay, who had helped arrange a political rally for Lincoln. Later that evening, as a member of the Republican committee, Nicolay was introduced to the speaker; that introduction changed his life. The young man became an enthusiastic admirer even before hearing the eloquent speech, which further strengthened his devotion to Lincoln. Four years later he would become Lincoln's chief personal secretary.

Nicolay's fellow Germans struggled to balance their hatred of slavery with their revulsion against nativism. Traditionally Democrats, they despised the Kansas-Nebraska Act but loved its author, Douglas, for his opposition to the Know-Nothings. The Republicans' choice of William Bissell (who had a Catholic wife) as their gubernatorial candidate sat well with the Germans, however. To woo Illinois Germans, Lincoln urged the widespread dissemination of antislavery German newspapers and helped raise funds for the relief of Friedrich Hecker, a prominent German campaigner whose house had burned down that summer. In November, the Republicans captured more than half the German vote.

The Democratic press denounced Frémont supporters as "nigger-worshippers," a tactic that worked. Buchanan carried Illinois handily, winning 105,528 votes to Frémont's 96,278 and Fillmore's 37,531. Frémont received 74 percent of the vote in northern Illinois, 37 percent in the central part of the state, and 23 percent in Egypt (mostly from Germans living near St. Louis). Nationwide, the Democratic nominee garnered 174 electoral votes to Frémont's 114 and Fillmore's 8. In the popular vote Buchanan won 45 percent of the ballots cast; Frémont, 33 percent; and Fillmore, 21 percent. Like Republicans throughout the North, the Frémonters of Illinois had failed to gain the support of both the conservative Whigs, who feared disunion, and the Know-Nothings, who believed the false charge that Frémont was a Catholic, as well as the allegation that he was too radical on the slavery issue. Bissell, a moderate opponent of slavery who could not plausibly be accused of nativism, did far better than Frémont. He won the governor's race with 111,466 votes to his opponent's 106,769. "This is glory enough for Ill[inoi]s," Herndon crowed. "We Frémont men feel as if victory perched on our banner."[34]

Lincoln accurately ascribed Buchanan's success both to a lack of cooperation among his opponents and to the Democrats' racist appeals. Republicans, Lincoln told his political allies, "were without party history, party pride, or party idols," merely "a collection of individuals, but recently in political hostility, one to another; and thus subject to all that distrust, and suspicion, and jealousy could do." The Democrats enjoyed a significant advantage, for their ranks contained "old party and personal friends, jibing, and jeering, and framing deceitful arguments against us" while dodging the real issue. Moreover, Lincoln said, "We were constantly charged with seeking an amalgamation of the white and black races; and thousands turned from us, not believing the charge (no one believed it) but *fearing* to face it themselves."[35]

Taking a longer view, Lincoln hailed the election result as a milestone on the road to equal rights. "Our government rests in public opinion," he told Republican banqueters in December. "Public opinion, on any subject, always has a '*central idea*,' from which all its minor thoughts radiate. That 'central idea' in our political public opinion, at the beginning was, and until recently has continued to be, 'the equality of men.' And although it always submitted patiently to whatever of inequality there seemed to be as matter of actual necessity, its constant working has been a steady progress towards the practical equality of all men." Lincoln called the recent presidential contest "a struggle, by one party, to discard that central idea, and to substitute for it the opposite idea that slavery is right, in the abstract, the workings of which, as a central idea, may be the perpetuity of human slavery, and its extension to all countries and colors." To promote the ideal of equality, the solid majority who opposed Buchanan must unite. Warming to his theme, Lincoln said, "Let every one who really believes, and is resolved, that free society is not, *and shall not be*, a failure, and who can conscientiously declare that in the past contest he has done only what he thought best—let every such one have charity to believe that every one can say as much. Thus let bygones be bygones. Let past differences as nothing be; and with steady eye on the real issue, let us reinaugurate the good old 'central ideas' of the Republic. We *can* do it. The human heart *is* with us—God is with us. We shall again be able not to declare, that 'all States as States, are equal,' nor yet that 'all citizens as citizens are equal,' but to renew the broader, better declaration, including both these and much more, that 'all *men* are created equal.'"[36]

This eloquent address helped clinch Lincoln's reputation as the leader of Illinois's Republicans. A correspondent for the *Illinois State Journal* declared: "There is no man upon whom they would so gladly confer the highest honors within their gift, and I trust an opportunity may not long be wanting which will enable them to place him in a station that seems to be by universal consent conceded to him, and which he is so admirably qualified by nature to adorn."[37]

Throughout the winter of 1856–57, Lincoln continued to help strengthen the Republican Party in Illinois, often attending legislative caucuses. When in doubt about how to deal with the Democrats, Norman B. Judd would say: "I will go round and bring in Old Abe tomorrow night."[38] Lincoln regularly obliged, amazing the lawmakers with his shrewd analysis of their opponents' thinking and offering much-appreciated advice about political strategy, particularly in combating a reapportionment law that would have ruined the Republicans' electoral prospects.

Attacking the Dred Scott Decision

As 1857 dawned, the tide of political unrest seemed to be ebbing. On New Year's Day, the *Illinois State Journal* announced that the mood "throughout our Republic is buoyant and encouraging. The prospect before the nation is well calculated at once to induce gratitude to Divine Providence."[39] Most importantly, the violence in Kansas had finally been quelled, thereby cooling off both Southern disunionism and Northern antislavery zeal.

Then the U.S. Supreme Court abruptly shattered the calm.

On March 6, 1857, that tribunal handed down its decision in the case of *Dred Scott v. Sandford*, ruling that Congress could not prohibit slavery from entering the Western territories and that Blacks, both slave and free, were not American citizens. The Chicago *Tribune* spoke for millions when it called the majority opinion of Chief Justice Roger B. Taney and six colleagues "sudden, unexpected and shocking to the sensibilities and aspirations of lovers of freedom and humanity," reversing "the current of progressive ideas and christian humanity."[40]

In June at Springfield, Lincoln denounced the court in one of his most eloquent speeches, prompted by Stephen A. Douglas's address there two weeks earlier. The Little Giant had declared that the "history of the times clearly shows that our fathers did not regard the African race as any kin to them, and determined so to lay the foundations of society and government that they should never be of kin to their posterity." Douglas also denounced Republican criticism of the Dred Scott decision, insisting that anyone who "resists the final decision of the highest judicial tribunal aims a deadly blow to our whole republican system of government" and is "an Amalgamationist."[41]

In reply, Lincoln stated that the Republicans "offer no *resistance*" to the Dred Scott decision, for the court might change its mind. He conceded that it would be "revolutionary" not to "acquiesce in it as a precedent" if—and only if—it "had been made by the unanimous concurrence of the judges, and without any apparent partisan bias, and in accordance with legal public expectation, and with the steady practice of the departments throughout our history, and had been in no part, based on assumed historical facts which are not really true; or, if . . . it had been before the court more than once, and had there been affirmed and re-affirmed through a course of years." But because the decision satisfied none of those requirements, it was "not resistance," "not factious," "not even disrespectful" to regard it "as not having yet quite established a settled doctrine."

Lincoln challenged Taney's claim that the condition of African Americans had improved since the adoption of the Constitution. Pointing out that in 1857 fewer states allowed Blacks to vote, or masters to manumit their slaves, than had done so seventy years earlier, Lincoln described the plight of the Black man in America as though he were hopelessly "bolted in with a lock of a hundred keys, which can never be unlocked without the concurrence of every key; the keys in the hands of a hundred different men and they scattered to a hundred different and distant places; and they stand musing as to what invention, in all the dominions of mind and matter, can be produced to make the impossibility of his escape more complete than it is."

Lincoln protested vehemently against Douglas's racial demagoguery. Conceding that there was "a natural disgust in the minds of nearly all white people, to the idea of indiscriminate amalgamation of the white and black races," Lincoln scornfully criticized Douglas for suggesting that because "the Republicans insist that the Declaration of Independence includes ALL men, black as well as white" they therefore "want to vote, and eat, and sleep, and marry with negroes!" Bosh! said Lincoln. "I protest against that counterfeit logic which concludes that, because I do not want a black woman for a *slave* I must necessarily want her for a *wife*. I need not have her for either, I can just leave her alone. In some respects she certainly is not my equal; but in her natural right to eat the bread she earns with her own hands without asking leave of any one else, she is my equal, and the equal of all others." Cleverly, Lincoln showed that Douglas's complaint about the Republicans' desire to promote racial mixing was better directed at Whites in the South, where the mixed-race population of 405,751 dwarfed that of the North (56,649). These figures demonstrated that "slavery is the greatest source of amalgamation." If Douglas were sincere in his desire to prevent racial amalgamation, he should oppose expansion of the peculiar institution.

Lincoln was especially indignant at the way Douglas made "a mere wreck—mangled ruin" out of the Declaration of Independence—which "contemplated the progressive improvement in the condition of all men everywhere"—by insisting that it "referred to the white race alone, and not the African." The authors of that "glorious" document, Lincoln averred, "intended to include *all* men," Black as well as White, "but they did not intend to declare all men equal *in all respects*. They did not mean to say all were equal in color, size, intellect, moral developments, or social capacity. They defined with tolerable distinctness, in what respects they did consider all men created equal—equal in 'certain inalienable rights, among which are life, liberty, and the pursuit of happiness.'" They "did not mean to assert the obvious untruth, that all were then actually enjoying that equality, nor yet, that they were about to confer it immediately upon them." Rather, they "meant to set up a standard maxim for free society, which should be familiar to all, and revered by all; constantly looked to, constantly approximated, and thereby constantly spreading and deepening its influence, and augmenting the happiness and value of life to all people of all colors everywhere." The Declaration's statement about equality was intended to be "a stumbling block to those who in after times might seek to turn a free people back into the hateful paths of despotism." Its authors "knew the proneness of prosperity to breed tyrants, and they meant when such should re-appear in this fair land and commence their vocation they should find left for them at least one hard nut to crack."

In closing, Lincoln drew a distinction between the two parties: "The Republicans inculcate, with whatever ability they can, that the negro is a man; that his bondage is cruelly wrong; and that the field of his oppression ought not to be enlarged. The Democrats deny his manhood; deny, or dwarf to insignificance, the wrong of his bondage; so far as possible, crush all sympathy for him, and cultivate and excite hatred and disgust against him; compliment themselves as Union-savers for doing so; and call the indefinite outspreading of his bondage 'a sacred right of self-government.'" Economic self-interest helped explain the Democrats' views, Lincoln argued: "The plainest print cannot be read through a gold eagle [coin]; and it will be ever hard to find many men who will send a slave to Liberia, and pay his passage while they can send him to a new country, Kansas, for instance, and sell him for fifteen hundred dollars."[42]

A striking feature of this speech was Lincoln's compassionate description of the plight of Blacks. Usually he shied away from expressing concern for the suffering of the slaves, probably because Illinois voters would be unresponsive to such antislavery appeals. But when Julian M. Sturtevant commented to him that St. Louis opponents of slavery seemed to care only for the well-being of Whites, Lincoln replied: "I must take into account the rights of the poor negro."[43] Curiously, Lincoln dwelt at much greater length on the Supreme Court's denial of Black citizenship than he did on the overthrow of the Missouri Compromise. Politically it would have been safer to focus on the latter rather than on the former, given the intense Negrophobia of the Illinois electorate. Moreover, he did not attempt to show how the decision might affect Douglas's popular sovereignty doctrine; that task he postponed for a year. Given the weak reasoning of the court's majority and concurring opinions, the vigorous dissents of Justices Benjamin R. Curtis and John McLean, and the significance of the slavery issue in American life, Lincoln was justified in maintaining that *Dred Scott* did not definitively settle the question of slavery in the territories.

The speech attracted attention in the press, including brief mentions in the New York *Times* and the New York *Tribune*. The *Southern Illinoisan* called it an "able and masterly refutation of Douglas' slanders."[44] In the Chicago *Tribune*, Herndon praised it for giving "utterance to the heart inspiration, clothed in the eternal maxims of purest reason."[45] Herndon told friends in Massachusetts that "Lincoln 'bursted Douglas wide open' as we say [in the] west" with his "gentlemanly—strong—powerful and conclusive speech," which contrasted sharply with the Little Giant's "low, gutter, rabble-rousing" effort.[46]

In commenting on Lincoln's address, one Democratic paper sneered at him as a failure in whatever he turned his hand to. He probably would not have disagreed, at least not strenuously. Around that time he wrote a private memo comparing his lack of success with Douglas's many accomplishments: "Twenty-two years ago Judge Douglas and I first became acquainted. We were both young then; he a trifle younger than I. Even then, we were both ambitious; I, perhaps, quite as much so as he. With *me*, the race of ambition has been a failure—a flat failure; with *him* it has been one of splendid success. His name fills the nation; and is not unknown, even, in foreign lands. I affect no contempt for the high eminence he has reached. So reached, that the oppressed of my species, might have shared with me in the elevation, I would rather stand on that eminence, than wear the richest crown that ever pressed a monarch's brow."[47]

In 1858, the comparatively obscure Lincoln would challenge the internationally famous Douglas in what became known as the Lincoln-Douglas debates, not the Douglas-Lincoln debates. They would raise Lincoln to national prominence and fatally injure the Little Giant's chances to win the presidency. In time, most people would remember Douglas only as Lincoln's debate opponent, while the name of Lincoln would "fill the nation" and reverberate around the world.

12

"A House Divided"

Lincoln versus Douglas (1857–1858)

Throughout 1857 and the first half of 1858, Lincoln devoted himself to his law practice. When asked to speak publicly on behalf of the Republicans, he replied in May 1858: "It is too early, considering that when I once begin making political speeches I shall have no respite till November. The *labor* of that I might endure, but I really can not spare the time from my business."[1]

"Discoveries And Inventions"

Lincoln did carve out time to deliver a lecture on discoveries and inventions. Like his 1838 Lyceum address, it was ostensibly nonpolitical but in fact contained a thinly disguised put-down of Stephen A. Douglas. At the time, the Little Giant was championing a program of bumptious, expansionistic nationalism known as Young America, a title that distinguished it from the creed of "old fogy" Whigs and senior Democratic leaders. The term applied to a faction of the Democratic Party that was eager to revive the jingoistic spirit of Manifest Destiny that had prevailed in the mid-1840s; to promote the expansion of the United States southward and westward; to express sympathy for gallant, unsuccessful European revolutionaries of 1848; and to repudiate the stuffy conservatism of superannuated officeholders like Lewis Cass. Douglas was widely regarded as Young America's chief spokesman. In his lecture, Lincoln discussed Young America as if it were a person—obviously Douglas, though not actually so identified—rather than a movement or a slogan. "Some think him conceited, and arrogant," Lincoln remarked, adding that Young America (i.e., Douglas) had reason "to entertain a rather extensive opinion of himself." Lincoln poked fun at Young America (Douglas) for coveting Cuba and other territory. Young America also lusted after political office (in Douglas's case, the presidency). Mocking the senator's popular sovereignty doctrine as well as his expansionism, Lincoln said: "He is a great friend of humanity; and his desire for land is not selfish, but merely an impulse to extend the area of freedom." Lincoln alluded to Douglas's well-known fondness for liquor and cigars: "His horror is for all that is old, particularly 'Old Fogy'; and if there be any thing old which he can endure, it is only old whiskey and old tobacco."

Turning from political satire, Lincoln became serious, asserting that "the discovery of America, and the introduction of Patent-laws" ranked among the most significant of all modern developments. He lauded not only patents like the one he himself held but the cast of mind that produced them. He deemed written language "the great invention of the world" and called printing "the *better* half of writing." The ignorance of the Dark Ages he considered "slavery of the mind," which he said Gutenberg's printing press had abolished, creating a "habit of freedom of thought." Such imagery came easily to a man who had emancipated himself from rural ignorance and backwardness through the written and printed word and who strove to end slavery of the body as well as of the mind.[2] (In his list of modern inventions he alluded to "the negro," by which he meant the African slave trade.)

Douglas's Bid for Republican Support

While devoting himself to law and his lecture, Lincoln also followed closely the high political drama unfolding in Washington, where Douglas had declared war on the Buchanan administration. During the autumn of 1857, proslavery Kansans, though a distinct minority of the territory's population, had managed to dominate the constitutional convention held in the town of Lecompton, largely because Free Soilers, regarding the election for delegates as fraudulent, shunned the polls. When the territory applied for statehood under the proslavery constitution adopted at Lecompton, Buchanan in a special message on December 8 urged Congress to accept this outcome and admit Kansas, even though impartial observers regarded the constitution as woefully unrepresentative of majority opinion among the settlers. Northerners were outraged by what they considered yet another example of Southerners' high-handed, arbitrary behavior. Douglas, suffering from hurt pride, fearful that if he supported the Lecompton Constitution he would doom his chances for reelection in 1858, resentful toward Buchanan for ignoring his patronage requests, and incensed by the administration's support for a clear miscarriage of popular sovereignty, immediately denounced the president's message. The Little Giant's impulsive revolt cheered his party colleagues back home. Even some Illinois Republicans applauded his anti-Lecompton stand and considered backing him for reelection. Lincoln counseled his allies to "stand clear" of the fight, for "both the President and Douglas are wrong" and Republicans "should not espouse the cause of either, because they may consider the other a little the farther wrong of the two."[3]

Douglas's rebellion shook the political world. Many Eastern Republicans regarded his bolt as providential, splitting the Democrats and smoothing the way for a Republican victory in 1860. Douglas met with Horace Greeley, editor of the influential New York *Tribune*, who believed that the senator might well join the Republican Party. He therefore urged Illinoisans to support the Little Giant for reelection. Lauding Douglas's "fidelity and courage," Greeley told his many readers that the senator's "course has not been merely right—it has been conspicuously, courageously, eminently so."[4] Although privately he called the Illinoisan "a low and dangerous demagogue" with "enormous self-conceit," the *Tribune* editor was convinced that he could not be beaten.[5] Other leading papers in the East and some prominent Massachusetts Republicans (such as Senator Henry Wilson, Congressman Anson Burlingame, and Governor Nathaniel P. Banks) seconded Greeley's motion that Republicans should support Douglas. These actions by Eastern Republicans infuriated their counterparts in Illinois. Lincoln, the obvious candidate to challenge the Little Giant, indignantly asked Trumbull, "What does the New-York Tribune mean by it's constant eulogising, and admiring, and magnifying [of] Douglas? Does it, in this, speak the sentiments of the republicans at Washington? Have they concluded that the republican cause, generally, can be best promoted by sacraficing us here in Illinois?" Bitterly he added, "If so we would like to know it soon; it will save us a great deal of labor to surrender at once."[6] Douglas later denied consorting with the Republicans, though abundant evidence suggests that he did. Anson Burlingame, Schuyler Colfax, and Frank Blair often met with the Little Giant at his house, where he inveighed against Southern high-handedness.

Herndon, evidently speaking for his law partner, protested to Elihu B. Washburne about rumors "that Illinois was to be chaffered for, and *huckstered* off without our consent, and against our will." Herndon insisted that Illinoisans "want to govern ourselves 'in our own way.' We want the man *that* we want, and have him, and *him alone. . . . Illinois is not for sale.*" If the Republicans of the Prairie State were to run Douglas for the Senate, "the masses would drag us from power and grind us to powder." The Little Giant's "abuse of us as Whigs—as Republicans—as men in society, and as individuals, has been so slanderous—dirty—low—long, and *continuous*, that we cannot soon forgive, and *can never forget.*"[7]

Lincoln could not share some Republicans' enthusiasm for Douglas. To him it appeared obvious that the Little Giant, though opposing Buchanan on the Lecompton Constitution, continued to side with the president on matters of general policy. In May, Lincoln told a friend that "there remains all the difference there ever was between Judge Douglas & the Republicans—*they* insisting the Congress *shall*, and *he* insisting that congress *shall not*, keep slavery out of the Ter[r]itories *before & up to the time* they form State constitutions." By making common cause to fight the Lecompton Constitution, neither the Illinois senator nor the Republicans "conceded anything which was ever in dispute between them."[8]

While some of Lincoln's friends dismissed Douglas's rebellion as an election-year gimmick, others were truly tempted to ally with anti-Lecompton Democrats. When Ozias M. Hatch and Jesse K. Dubois asked Lincoln about overtures being made by Douglas's friends, he urged them to resist the senator's siren song: "We must never sell old friends to buy old enemies. Let us have a State convention, in which we can have a full consultation; and till which, let us all stand firm, making no committals as to strange and new combinations."[9]

In December 1857, Lincoln prepared a speech warning Republicans not to flock to Douglas's banner, no matter how much they might admire his attacks on the Buchanan administration. He scorned Douglas's demagoguery, calling him "the most dangerous enemy of liberty, because the most insidious one."[10] Douglas's indifference to the evils of slavery, which contrasted starkly with the Republican view that the peculiar institution was "not only morally wrong, but a 'deadly poison' in a government like ours, professedly based on the equality of men," aroused Lincoln's ire. Republicans, he advised, should not "oppose any measure merely because Judge Douglas proposes it." Indeed, they ought to join him in assaulting the Lecompton Constitution, which "should be throttled and killed as hastily and as heartily as a rabid dog." But the "combined charge of Nebraskaism, and Dred Scottism must be repulsed, and rolled back. The deceitful cloak of 'self-government' wherewith 'the sum of all villanies' [i.e., slavery] seeks to protect and adorn itself, must be torn from it's hateful carcass."[11]

Most Illinois Republicans agreed that Douglas was hardly a fit champion of their cause, no matter how vehemently he denounced the Lecompton Constitution. Moreover, many of the party faithful believed that Lincoln deserved the senatorial nomination. They regarded him as their most capable leader and felt that it was only fair to reward the magnanimity he had shown by bowing to Trumbull in the 1855 Senate contest. A Chicago Republican told Greeley, "We all think more highly of Douglas than we did a year ago, but still we hope to be pardoned for preferring one of the 'truest and most effective advocates of Republican principles' [i.e., Lincoln] to the Little Giant."[12]

While Lincoln professed a liking for Greeley, he was personally "dejected" by the influential editor's support of Douglas, saying (in substance) that Greeley "is not doing me . . . right. He is talking up Douglas, an untrue and an untried man." Lincoln wished "that someone would put a flea" in the ear of Greeley and other Eastern Republicans.[13] And so Herndon packed his bags and headed east to act as his partner's emissary and observer. In Washington, Herndon met with Douglas, who told him: "Give Mr. Lincoln my regards when you return, and tell him I have crossed the river and burned my boat." He added "that he and the Republicans would be together soon." From Trumbull, Herndon learned that some Eastern Republicans were scheming to betray their Illinois counterparts by supporting Douglas's reelection bid. Rumor had it that Greeley, Seward, Weed, Henry Wilson, and Douglas had struck a bargain whereby the Little Giant pledged to support Seward for president in 1860 if the editor of the *Tribune* would back Douglas's reelection in 1858. In New York, Herndon called on Greeley, who "talked bitterly . . . against the papers in Ill[inoi]s—and said they were fools." When Herndon referred to the Little Giant as one who had "abused and betrayed" the North, Greeley replied, "Forget the past and sustain the *righteous*." The "Republican standard is too high," the editor declared; "we want something practical."[14]

After returning home, Herndon informed Greeley that Illinois Republicans could not possibly support Douglas. Three months later, Herndon scoffed at Greeley's belief that Douglas might join the Republicans: "Did Douglas ever give an inch in his whole political life?" he asked. "He is the most imperious and selfish man in America. He is the greatest liar in the world."[15] Herndon doubtless wrote in consultation with Lincoln, who did not directly communicate with Greeley in 1858.

On April 21, fear that Douglas might seduce Illinois Republicans all but evaporated as a result of the Democratic state convention in Springfield. There delegates endorsed the party's 1856 platform calling for popular sovereignty, berated Republicans harshly, and failed to denounce the Buchanan administration for its support of the Lecompton Constitution. These acts alienated those antislavery men whom the Little Giant might have won over. Republicans rejoiced at the "hard blows, and withering strokes" that the pro-Buchanan and pro-Douglas factions administered to each other. "Oh what a sight!" Herndon exclaimed. "Plunderers of the People now at bloody war with each other over the spoils." Douglas "cut his own throat with his own hands," Herndon observed; "he cut himself loose from the Southern Democracy, and . . . tore loose from, all Republican sympathy."[16] The disaffected pro-administration delegates, constituting roughly one-tenth of the total and calling themselves National Democrats, bolted the convention and resolved to hold a conclave of their own in June.

The evening of the Democrats' turbulent convention, Lincoln met in Springfield with two dozen leading Republicans to discuss strategy. Everyone in attendance made it clear that they had no intention of supporting Douglas. They expressed great indignation at the course of Anson Burlingame and deplored the wavering of some Illinois congressmen, including Washburne. When some voiced concern that ex-Democrats in their party would desert Lincoln, George T. Brown reassured them that he had spoken with several Democrats-turned-Republicans throughout the state, all of whom vowed their determination to back Lincoln. Brown added that Trumbull's election in 1855 had made it morally imperative that he and other former Democrats in the party support Lincoln, who rejoiced that the badly divided Democrats were "in not a very encouraged state of mind."[17] The following day, the Republicans agreed to hold their convention on June 16 at Springfield.

Lincoln denied that he and his colleagues were plotting to make common cause with the National Democrats in order to defeat Douglas. "Of course the Republicans do not try to keep the common enemy from dividing; but, so far as I *know*, or *believe*, they will not unite with either branch of the division," he said. He added that "it is difficult for me to see, on what ground they could unite; but it is useless to spend words, there is simply nothing to it. It is a trick of our enemies to try to excite all sorts of suspicions and jealousies amongst us."[18]

In fact, the Republicans did work behind the scenes to promote discord within the Democratic ranks. Herndon freely acknowledged that the *Illinois State Journal* "and each and every Republican, is trying to create the split" between the Douglas and Buchanan forces and "make it wider and deeper—hotter and more impassable." Lincoln was kept ignorant of such machinations. Herndon reported to Trumbull that his partner "does not know the details of how we get along. I do, but he does not. That kind of thing does not suit his tastes, nor does it suit me, yet I am compelled to do it—do it because I cannot get rid of it."[19] Since Herndon's father and brother staunchly supported the administration, he was unusually well placed to learn the doings of the National Democrats.

Preserving Republican Unity

As the date for the Republican state convention approached, Lincoln grew optimistic. "I think our prospects gradually, and steadily, grow better," he told Washburne on May 15. "There is still some effort to make trouble out of 'Americanism.' If that were out of the way, for all the rest, I believe we should be 'out of the woods.'"[20] Less sanguine Republicans feared that many of Illinois's 37,351 Fillmore voters might make common cause with Douglas on a "Union-saving" platform. Lincoln, though generally optimistic, did worry about Douglas's attempts to woo Republicans while still holding on to Democrats by playing down his differences with the Buchanan administration. The National Democrats were slated to hold a convention in Springfield in the second week of June. "Possibly," Lincoln mused, "even *probably*—Douglas is temporarily deceiving the President in order to crush out the 8th of June convention here." But he predicted that the Little Giant's attempt to please both factions would fail: "Unless he plays his double game more successfully than we have often seen done, he can not carry many republicans North, without at the same time losing a larger number of his old friends South."[21]

To defeat Douglas's "double game" Lincoln must persuade his party colleagues that the senator was hardly a true believer in their principles. Republican leaders in Washington were still urging their Illinois counterparts to back Douglas. In private correspondence and anonymous journalism, Lincoln had for months been arguing against fusion with Douglas; at the Republican state convention, he seized the opportunity to make his case in one of his most famous speeches.

Nomination for the Senate

On June 16, Republican delegates crowded into the capitol's Hall of Representatives, where they speedily adopted a platform similar to the one passed at the 1856 Bloomington convention and nominated candidates for the two state offices to be contested that fall. In the midst of the deliberations, the Chicago delegation unfurled a banner reading "Cook County for Abraham Lincoln," which was greeted with loud shouts. When it was suggested that the text be amended to read "Illinois for Abraham Lincoln," the motion received a deafening barrage of hurrahs. The same day, Charles L. Wilson, editor of the Chicago *Journal*, unexpectedly offered a resolution that won unanimous, enthusiastic approval: "Resolved that Abraham Lincoln is the first and only choice of the Republicans of Illinois for the United States Senate, as the successor to Stephen A. Douglas."[22]

A journalist reported that "*Lincoln*! LINCOLN!! LINCOLN!!! was the cry everywhere, whenever the senatorship was alluded to. Delegates from Chicago and from Cairo, from the Wabash and the Illinois, from the north, the center, and the south, were alike fierce with enthusiasm, whenever that loved name was breathed."[23] This was an extraordinary development, for customarily state parties did not endorse a candidate for the Senate before the election of the legislature that would decide who filled that post. But so intensely did the Republicans of Illinois resent Horace Greeley and other Easterners who urged them to support Douglas that they had, in many counties, passed resolutions endorsing Lincoln for the Senate.

That evening, Lincoln addressed the delegates, uncharacteristically reading from a manuscript. He had been working steadily on his speech for over a week, taking great pains to make it accurate. He delivered it slowly and carefully, fully aware that his auditors might be startled by his arguments. Lincoln aimed to show that Douglas's rebellion against Buchanan, which rendered the Little Giant so attractive to many opponents of slavery, was merely superficial and that the senator and the president agreed on basic principles and had cooperated, either by design or coincidence, in promoting the interests of the slaveholding South.

Lincoln began, "If we could first know *where* we are, and *whither* we are tending, we could then better judge *what* to do, and *how* to do it." Since the introduction of the Kansas-Nebraska Act, a measure "with the *avowed* object, and *confident* promise of putting an end to slavery agitation," that agitation "has not only, *not ceased*, but has *constantly augmented*." Such agitation, Lincoln predicted, "*will* not cease, until a *crisis* shall have been reached, and passed." That was inevitable, he said, because a "house divided against itself cannot stand," as Jesus had warned. "I believe this government cannot endure, permanently half *slave* and half *free*. I do not expect the Union to be *dissolved*—I do not expect the house to *fall*—but I *do* expect it will cease to be divided. It will become *all* one thing, or *all* the other. Either the *opponents* of slavery, will arrest the further spread of it, and place it where the public mind shall rest in the belief that it is in course of ultimate extinction; or its *advocates* will push it forward, till it shall become alike lawful in *all* the States, *old* as well as *new*—*North* as well as *South*."

After prophesying the future, Lincoln analyzed the past, arguing that a conspiracy to expand slavery had been actively pursued in recent years. The 1854 Kansas-Nebraska Act, the 1856 annual message of President Pierce, the election of Buchanan that year, and the 1857 Dred Scott decision had all benefited the proslavery forces. Lincoln thought it noteworthy that when Douglas was asked whether "the people of a territory can constitutionally exclude slavery from their limits," the Little Giant had replied, "That is a question for the Supreme Court." Equally noteworthy was Buchanan's inaugural address, calling on all Americans to abide by whatever decision the court might reach in *Dred Scott*. Two days later (a suspiciously short time) the justices handed down their controversial decision. The behavior of Douglas, Pierce, Buchanan, and Taney had aroused Lincoln's suspicion. He continued: "We can not absolutely *know* that all these exact adaptations are the result of preconcert." Nevertheless, "when we see a lot of framed timbers, different portions of which we know have been gotten out at different times and places and by different workmen—Stephen [Douglas], Franklin [Pierce], Roger [B. Taney], and James [Buchanan], for instance—and when we see these timbers joined together, and see they exactly make the frame of a house or a mill, . . . in *such* a case, we find it impossible to not *believe* that Stephen and Franklin and Roger and James all understood one another from the beginning, and all worked upon a common *plan* or *draft* drawn up before the first lick was struck." This history had convinced Lincoln that "we may, ere long, see . . . another Supreme Court decision, declaring that the Constitution of the United States does not permit a *state* to exclude slavery from its limits." Illinoisans "shall *lie down* pleasantly dreaming that the people of *Missouri* are on the verge of making their state *free*; and we shall *awake* to the *reality*, instead, that the *Supreme* Court has made *Illinois* a *slave* State," Lincoln predicted, "unless the power of the present political dynasty shall be met and overthrown."

Reaching the central point of his address, Lincoln maintained that to achieve the overthrow of the slave power, its opponents must resist the overtures of the Douglasites. How, Lincoln asked, could Douglas "oppose the advances of slavery?

He don't *care* anything about it," and his "avowed *mission is impressing* the 'public heart' to *care* nothing about it." On the issue most dear to Republicans—prohibiting the expansion of slavery—"clearly, he [Douglas] is not *now* with us—he does not *pretend* to be—he does not *promise* to *ever* be." The Republican cause "must be intrusted to, and conducted by its own undoubted friends—those whose hands are free, whose hearts are in the work—who *do care* for the result." Optimistically he predicted that "sooner or later the victory is *sure* to come."[24]

Many others before Lincoln had charged that a conspiracy was afoot to nationalize slavery. In all likelihood, Lincoln sincerely believed his allegation. Unbeknownst to him, there was in fact good evidence of collusion between Buchanan and the Supreme Court. In February 1857, only the five Southern justices had favored overturning the Missouri Compromise. Worried that such a 5–4 decision might not sit well with Northerners, Buchanan had urged his friend Justice Robert C. Grier of Pennsylvania to side with the five justices from below the Mason-Dixon line. Grier had complied and let Buchanan know that the court would decide the case soon after his inauguration. Buchanan, who may well have seen a draft of Chief Justice Roger B. Taney's majority opinion, had prepared his inaugural address accordingly, urging the public to abide by whatever decision the court might reach.

The Republican press in Illinois hailed Lincoln's speech as "able, logical, and most eloquent."[25] Horace Greeley's New York *Tribune* ran the full text and said Lincoln "never fails to make a good speech, . . . and this is one of his best efforts."[26] It did not change Greeley's mind about Douglas, however. Douglas's supporters took heart from the "House Divided" speech because it seemed too radical for Illinois. The Democratic press reviled it as an incitement to civil war and a call for abolition. Lincoln was probably unsurprised by such attacks. Before he delivered the speech, his political confidants had warned that it was too extreme, but he had rejected their advice to tone it down. When Samuel C. Parks suggested that he modify one passage before publishing it, Lincoln asked, "Isn't it true?"

"Certainly it is true, but it is premature. The people are not prepared for it, and Douglas will beat us with it all over the state."

"I think that the time has come to say it, and I will let it go as it is."[27]

After the election, some friends told Lincoln that his defeat had been due to the radicalism of the speech. "Well Gentlemen, you may think that Speech was a mistake, but I never have believed it was, and you will see the day when you will consider it was the wisest thing I ever said."[28] He explained to Horace White that "all of his wise friends had objected to that 'house' paragraph, but he thought the people were much nearer to the belief than the politicians generally supposed"; therefore, "while he was willing to assume all the risks incident to the use of that phrase, he did not consider the risk great."[29] Lincoln insisted that his address was not an abolitionist document: "I am much mortified that any part of it should be construed so differently from any thing intended by me," he wrote to John Locke Scripps. "The language, 'place it [slavery] where the public mind shall rest in the belief that it is in course of ultimate extinction,' I used deliberately, not dreaming then, nor believing now, that it asserts, or intimates, any power or purpose, to interfere with slavery in the States where it exists." Emphatically he declared that "whether the clause used by me, will bear such construction or not, I never so intended it."[30] Nevertheless, the charge of "ultraism" would dog Lincoln throughout the campaign as he tried to woo conservative former Whigs.

The Senate Campaign Begins

Douglas and his allies tried to discredit Lincoln by claiming that as a congressman he had opposed funding supplies for the troops during the Mexican War. The Chicago *Times*, Douglas's organ, falsely claimed that Lincoln had sworn an oath to "refuse to vote one dollar to feed, clothe, or minister to the wants of the sick and dying volunteers from my own State, who are suffering in Mexico. Let them die like dogs! Let them die for want of medicine! Let the fever-parched lips of my Illinois neighbors crack in painful agony—not one drop of cooling liquid shall soothe them if I can help it."[31]

Lincoln swiftly provided Joseph Medill with an account of his congressional votes on Mexican War appropriations, which he had always supported, and protested that the Chicago *Times*, "in its' blind rage to assail me," had ascribed to him a vote that had been cast by another Illinois congressman before Lincoln had even taken his seat.[32] Medill's newspaper denounced "the intense meanness which prompted the *Times* to falsify his position, and the intenser meanness which induces it not to retract its calumnies."[33] This was not the last dirty trick that Douglas and his organ would play on Lincoln, for the Little Giant and his editor friend James W. Sheahan proved to be unscrupulous opponents, willing to make false charges, garble Lincoln's words, resort to bribery, and engage in demagoguery.

Each candidate ran scared. In July, Herndon wrote that his partner meticulously calculated Republican prospects in each county and was "gloomy—rather uncertain, about his own success."[34] In assessing Douglas's strengths, Lincoln acknowledged that the senator "knew the people of the state thoroughly and just how to appeal to the[ir] prejudices and was a very powerful opponent, both on and off the stump."[35] Douglas reciprocated the sentiment. Upon hearing of Lincoln's nomination, he told a friend: "I shall have my hands full. He is the strong man of his party—full of wit, facts, dates—and the best stump speaker, with his droll ways and dry jokes, in the West. He is as honest as he is shrewd; and if I beat him, my victory will be hardly won."[36]

On July 9, Douglas opened the campaign with a speech before a crowd of several thousand Chicagoans. He began by complimenting Lincoln, describing him as "a kind, amiable, and intelligent gentleman, a good citizen and an honorable opponent." The Little Giant then charged that in his "House Divided" speech Lincoln had "boldly and clearly" advocated "a war of sections, a war of the North against the South, of the free states against the slave states—a war of extermination—to be continued relentlessly until the one or the other shall be subdued." The senator further argued that Lincoln's policy of "uniformity" would lead to despotism, for if people did not have the right to decide for themselves whether to allow slavery in their midst, they were no longer free. The true safeguard of liberty, Douglas asserted, was "diversity," not "uniformity."

Turning to the race issue, Douglas focused on Lincoln's criticism of the Dred Scott decision. In a characteristic appeal to the intense Negrophobia of Illinois voters, he flatly asserted that "this government was made by the white man, for the benefit of the white man, to be administered by white men, in such manner as they should determine. . . . I am opposed to negro equality. I repeat that this nation is a white people—a people composed of European descendants—a people that have established this government for themselves and their posterity, and I am in favor of preserving not only the purity of the blood, but the purity of the government from any mixture or amalgamation with inferior races." He closed with a salvo against the "unholy, unnatural" alliance between the Republicans and the pro-Buchanan Democrats.[37]

Lincoln, who sat through Douglas's speech, reported that the Little Giant sought "to make it appear that he is having a triumphal entry into, and march through the country; but it is all as bombastic and hollow as Napoleon's bulletins sent back from his campaign in Russia."[38] A majority of the crowd, he estimated, consisted of Republicans, some of whom called for him to respond to Douglas then and there, but since the hour was late, it was arranged that he would speak on the morrow.

The next day, before an audience almost as large as Douglas's, the challenger responded to the Little Giant. With gentle mockery he dismissed the charge of Republican collusion with the Buchaneers. More bitingly, he maintained that "popular sovereignty" had become a meaningless concept, for thanks to the Dred Scott decision, inhabitants of a territory could only vote to exclude slavery at the very final stage of territorial settlement, when a constitution was to be adopted and an application for statehood was to be submitted. According to the Supreme Court, Lincoln noted, "if any one man chooses to take slaves into a territory, all the rest of the people have no right to keep them out." Thus popular sovereignty was, for all intents and purposes, a dead letter, and Douglas was hypocritical in proclaiming his devotion both to it and to the Dred Scott decision, which negated it.

Lincoln protested against Douglas's misinterpretation of his "House Divided" speech. "I am not [a] master of language," he confessed. "I have not a fine education." But he insisted that the senator had distorted his meaning. Obviously the nation had existed half slave and half free for more than eight decades, but it had done so only because people expected the peculiar institution to ultimately die out; the Kansas-Nebraska Act, however, had negated that expectation. Boldly Lincoln declared, "I have always hated slavery, I think as much as any Abolitionist. . . . I have always hated it, but I have always been quiet about it until this new era of the introduction of the Nebraska Bill began. I always believed that everybody was against it, and that it was in the course of ultimate extinction." The Constitution, he argued plausibly, had been framed and adopted by men who "intended and expected the ultimate extinction" of slavery.

Lincoln pleaded with Republicans not to forget Douglas's demagoguery about racial amalgamation; they should recall "all the hard names that Judge Douglas has called them by—all his repeated charges of their inclination to marry them and hug negroes." Eloquently he concluded, "Let us discard all this quibbling about this man and the other man—this race and that race and the other race being inferior, and therefore they must be placed in an inferior position. . . . Let us discard all these things, and unite as one people throughout this land, until we shall once more stand up declaring that all men are created equal."[39]

This remarkable address, with its soaring rhetoric and heartfelt idealism, was published in a number of Eastern papers, including the New York *Herald*, which referred to Lincoln as Douglas's "nigger worshipping competitor," who espoused the "most repulsive disunion nigger equality principles and doctrines."[40] The abolitionist Chicago *Congregational Herald* detected in Lincoln "a champion" who was willing to "stand by the Declaration of Independence and fight for *human* rights, for *man as man*, irrespective of country, race, creed, or other accidental circumstances."[41] The "war is begun," remarked the Chicago *Journal*. "The first fire has been exchanged," and "the Little Giant is wounded in several vital parts. In sound, manly argument, Lincoln is too much for him."[42]

Douglas and other Democrats repeatedly quoted Lincoln's peroration to illustrate the challenger's radicalism on the race issue. The *Illinois State Register* alleged that in his Chicago address, "Lincoln takes bold and unqualified ground with Lovejoy and ultra abolitionism. . . . Old Whigs can see in it the 'contemptible abolitionism' in which Mr. Lincoln desires to engulf his old whig friends."[43] The Chicago *Times* saw in it an appeal for slaves to rise up and kill their masters.

Thanks to Douglas's prominence, the attention of the country focused on the Illinois Senate race, and Lincoln began to emerge as a national figure. When the two candidates spoke in Springfield a week later, the contrast between them was highlighted by their mode of transportation and their appearance. Fashionably attired in the "plantation style," Douglas was the glass of fashion in his well-tailored broadcloth and linen garments. Traveling in imperial fashion, he and his wife, along with a large entourage, rode in a private rail coach maintained by the Illinois Central. Accompanying it was a platform car outfitted with a small cannon called "Popular Sovereignty" which heralded the Little Giant's approach. On that same train Lincoln traveled alone as a regular passenger, toting an ancient carpetbag and bulging umbrella. He wore an ill-fitting coat, vest, and trousers, all of black alpaca. On his head sat a too-large, battered, napless stovepipe hat. Like all lawyers working for the railroad, Lincoln had a free pass, which he used to campaign simply, and usually alone. Occasionally, he would even ride on freight trains.

En route to the capital, Douglas stopped in Bloomington, where he once again praised Lincoln as "a kind-hearted, amiable gentleman, a right good fellow, a worthy citizen, of eminent ability as a lawyer, and, I have no doubt, sufficient ability to make a good Senator." But he also attacked his rival as a miscegenationist.[44] When he finished, the crowd called for Lincoln, who declined to give a speech, saying: "This meeting was called by the friends of Judge Douglas, and it would be improper of me to address it."[45]

In Springfield on the afternoon of July 17, Douglas repeated his Chicago speech, laying special emphasis on Lincoln's belief that Blacks were covered by the Declaration of Independence's assertion that "all men are created equal."[46] In response that evening at the statehouse, Lincoln renewed his attack on the popular sovereignty doctrine as "the most errant humbug that has ever been attempted on an intelligent community." He acknowledged that the Declaration of Independence should not be construed literally—that it did not "mean that all men were created equal in all respects." Offering a bizarre, perhaps satirical example of one respect in which the races were unequal, he said, "Certainly the negro is not our equal in color . . . still, in the right to put into his mouth the bread that his own hands have earned, he is the equal of every other man, white or black. In pointing out that more has been given you, you can not be justified in taking away the little which has been given him. All I ask for the negro is that if you do not like him, leave him alone. If God gave him but little, that little let him enjoy." Noteworthy here is Lincoln's agnosticism about Black inferiority above and beyond the dubious category of color; the Black *might* be inferior to the White in other respects as well, but he did not identify them. Nor did he say that God gave Black people little; he insisted only that *if* God gave them little, they should be allowed to enjoy that little undisturbed.[47]

This carefully hedged treatment of the racial-inferiority argument differed sharply from Douglas's raw, unvarnished racism.

The two candidates focused their attention on central Illinois, where the legislative races would be most hotly contested. In the thick of the struggle, Douglas sometimes lost his composure. At Beardstown on August 11, he assailed Lyman Trumbull for alleging that Douglas's opposition to the Lecompton Constitution was hypocritical. The Little Giant "raved like a maniac," "tore his hair," and "shook his fists" while calling his senatorial colleague an "infamous liar" and a "miserable, craven-hearted wretch" who would "rather have both ears cut off than to use that language in my presence, where I could call him to account." On August 13 at Havana, where fistfights broke out among the boisterous drunkards clogging the streets, Douglas delivered an intemperate speech in which he called Lincoln "a liar, a coward, a wretch and a sneak." Asked why he had used such abusive language, the senator replied "that Lincoln's course has been such as to leave him no other line of argument."[48] In September, Douglas's temper grew worse. The Little Giant, whom one Republican called a "drunken demagogue," may have been intoxicated during some of these speeches (his private rail car was well stocked with liquor).[49] He drank and smoked so much that three years later throat and liver problems combined to kill him at the age of 48.

The beautiful, cultivated, tactful, well-bred Mrs. Douglas (née Adele Cutts, his second wife), a grandniece of Dolley Madison, accompanied her husband throughout the campaign, much to the consternation of Republicans, who regarded her as an effective weapon in the senator's arsenal. Wherever her husband spoke, she attended receptions. At such an event a Republican editor, Charles L. Bernays, was so taken with her beauty that he became an admirer of her husband.

In late July and early August, Lincoln attended some of his opponent's afternoon speeches, then responded in the evening. On July 27, he listened at Clinton, where Douglas finally answered Lincoln's conspiracy charge. "Unfounded and untrue," the senator said; "I never exchanged a word with Chief Justice Taney or any other member of the Supreme Court about the Dred Scott decision in my life, either before or after it was rendered. I never exchanged a word with President Pierce on the subject . . . nor did I exchange a word with President Buchanan upon it until long after it was made."[50] When Douglas "said that no man could look him in the face and say that he ever denounced the U.S. Bank decision" of the Supreme Court, Lincoln stood and stared directly into Douglas's eyes. The Little Giant averted his gaze.[51]

As he proceeded along the Illinois River in Douglas's wake, Lincoln seemed to be in high spirits. Accompanying him were many old Whig friends, who delighted in hearing his stories and political commentary. When Horace White asked why in his speeches "he did not oftener turn the laugh on Douglas," Lincoln "replied that he was too much in earnest, and that it was doubtful whether turning the laugh on anybody really gained any votes."[52] His aim as an orator was simple: "I do not seek applause, nor to amuse the people. I want to convince them."[53]

On August 17 at Lewistown, Lincoln delivered an even more ringing apostrophe to the Declaration of Independence than the one he had made earlier: the author and signers of that document "erected a beacon to guide their children and their children's children, and the countless myriads who should inhabit the earth in other ages." With "great earnestness," he told his audience: "If you have been inclined to believe that all men are *not* created equal in those inalienable rights enumerated by our chart[er] of liberty, let me entreat you to come back. Return to the fountain whose waters spring close by the blood of the Revolution. Think nothing of me—take no thought for the political fate of any man whomsoever—but come back to the truths that are in the Declaration of Independence. You may do anything with me you choose, if you will but heed these sacred principles. You may not only defeat me for the Senate, but you may take me and put me to death. While pretending no indifference to earthly honors, I *do claim* to be actuated in this contest by something higher than an anxiety for office. I charge you to drop every paltry and insignificant thought for any man's success. It is nothing; I am nothing; Judge Douglas is nothing. *But do not destroy that immortal emblem of humanity—the Declaration of American Independence.*"[54]

Although Lincoln told a friend that "my recent experience shows that speaking at the same place the next day after D[ouglas] is the very thing—it is, in fact, a concluding speech on him," some Republicans frowned on such a strategy.[55] Farmers were reluctant to neglect their chores for two consecutive days. One of his strong supporters said that "Douglas takes the crowd & Lincoln the leavings."[56] At Lewistown, Lincoln only drew an audience of about 2,000, compared with Douglas's audience of 3,000 the day before. At Havana on August 13, according to the Democratic press, Lincoln attracted only 659 people, compared with Douglas's 6,000 the previous day. After one speech, Lincoln reportedly said "that he would have to make his own appointments because Douglas, under present circumstances, has the crowd, and the people will not turn out in the evening to hear him reply."[57] Unsatisfied by the results of Lincoln's rebuttals of Douglas, Republicans in Illinois and elsewhere urged him to challenge his opponent to debate.

On July 24, when Lincoln saw the published announcement of Douglas's appointments for August, he conferred with Norman B. Judd about debating his opponent. Judd, sensing that Lincoln had already determined to challenge the senator, said he thought it would be a good idea. Lincoln then wrote a letter for Judd to deliver to Douglas, formally proposing that they "divide time, and address the same audiences." With great difficulty, Judd tracked Douglas down. When, after three days, he finally did catch up with him and presented Lincoln's note, the Little Giant angrily asked: "What do you come to me with such a thing as this for?"[58] Douglas "angrily and emphatically declined to consider on the ground that it was a childish idea and that he would be belittling himself and dignifying Lincoln."[59] Another reason for Douglas's hesitation was his respect for Lincoln's ability. As he told Joseph O. Glover, "I do not feel, between you and me, that I want to go into this debate. The whole country knows me and has me measured. Lincoln, as regards myself, is comparatively unknown, and if he gets the best of this debate, and I want to say he is the ablest man the Republicans have got, I shall lose everything and Lincoln will gain everything. Should I win, I shall gain but little."[60] Judd warned Douglas that if he refused to debate, he would seem afraid of his rival. But as Douglas noted, the underdog stands to benefit more than the favorite in political debates.

Realizing that he could not afford to look cowardly, the senator offered a counterproposal: since the Democratic State Central Committee had committed him to speak at party meetings throughout the state, he declined to share time with Lincoln at those occasions, but he would agree to debate in seven of the state's nine congressional districts, excluding the two where they had already in effect debated (Chicago and Springfield). Forwarding Douglas's response to Lincoln, Judd observed that it "is a clear dodge, but he has made the best case he could."[61] On July 29, protesting against the "attempted unfairness," Lincoln accepted Douglas's terms.

The following day, Douglas submitted a schedule for the debates: Ottawa (August 21), Freeport (August 27), Jonesboro (September 15), Charleston (September 18), Galesburg (October 7), Quincy (October 13), and Alton (October 15). Each debate would last three hours, with the time evenly divided between the two candidates, one opening for an hour, the other replying for an hour and a half, and the first speaker concluding with a half-hour rejoinder. Douglas would have the opening and closing speeches in the first, third, fifth, and seventh debates. Mildly protesting that this arrangement gave the Little Giant four openings and closes to his three, Lincoln accepted these conditions. He also pledged, "I shall be at no more of your exclusive meetings."[62]

Throughout the country, eyes turned to Ottawa, where the candidates would inaugurate what one Illinois abolitionist regarded as "no less than a contest for the advancement of the kingdom of Heaven or the kingdom of Satan—a contest for an advance or a retrograde in civilization."[63] Prophetically the New York *Times* remarked: "The battle must be close, severe, and doubtful. That it will be well fought is certain, and its results will be both important and memorable."[64] As so they would be.

13.

"A David Greater Than the Democratic Goliath"

The Lincoln-Douglas Debates (1858)

In 1860, the abolitionist Parker Pillsbury maintained that there was "no essential difference" between Lincoln and Stephen A. Douglas.[1] In fact, the two Illinois rivals disagreed fundamentally about slavery, the Declaration of Independence, the Constitution, the role of the Supreme Court, racial equality, and American history. Their epic debate battle in 1858, which proved to be a dress rehearsal for the presidential contest two years later, threw into sharp relief not only these disagreements but also the stark difference in the combatants' fundamental character.

As the Little Giant and his challenger girded for battle, oddsmakers probably favored Douglas, though he suffered some potential handicaps, including the split in his party; the reluctance of some former Whigs to back a Democrat; the growing population of the northern part of the state, where hostility to slavery was intense; and the hard times produced by the Panic of 1857, which the public blamed on the Democrats. Outweighing those disadvantages were the Little Giant's obvious strengths: he was much better known than Lincoln; his leadership in the struggle against the Lecompton Constitution had won respect among Illinoisans who had earlier lost faith in him; his forceful personality endeared him to many; his party had long dominated the state's politics; his appeals to race prejudice resonated in Negrophobic Illinois; and his skills as a debater were legendary. Helping to make Douglas formidable in debate was his lack of scruples. In addition, his verbal dexterity and self-assurance enabled him to impress audiences even though he might be uttering non sequiturs, untruths, exaggerations, and falsehoods. Moreover, the Illinois General Assembly, which would choose the next senator, was malapportioned; the heavily Democratic southern counties had more than their fair share of legislative seats, depriving the Republicans of six to ten votes that they would have had if a reapportionment had been undertaken based on the most recent census. The twenty-five-member state senate contained Democratic holdovers from districts that now had Republican majorities.

Lincoln acknowledged that Douglas's eminence benefited the Democrats. "Senator Douglas is of world wide renown," he observed. "All the anxious politicians of his party, or who have been of his party for years past, have been looking upon him as a certainty, at no distant day, to be the President of the United States." Moreover, hoping for patronage rewards, these politicos "rush about him, sustain him, and give him marches, triumphal entries, and receptions." Lincoln, on the other hand, had no such support: "nobody has ever expected me to be President. In my poor lean, lank, face, nobody has ever seen that any cabbages were sprouting out."[2]

Lincoln possessed offsetting advantages: his party was comparatively unified; the appeal of the antislavery cause was waxing; the sincerity of his commitment to that cause was palpable and persuasive; he was an effective, seasoned debater with political skills honed over the past quarter century; his psychological maturity and paternal qualities predisposed men to regard him with the affection and trust bestowed on a wise father; his self-effacing modesty and keen sense of humor made him likable; and his reputation for integrity had won him an unusual measure of respect. Nevertheless, some Republicans were nervous about the debates. The unpopularity of Lincoln's stands on the Mexican War and on racial issues, along with the opposition of prominent Eastern Republicans like Horace Greeley, boded ill.

First Debate: Ottawa

When Lincoln and Douglas took the platform for their first meeting, at Ottawa, the crowd of more than ten thousand doubled the population of that county seat. Under a fierce sun, they jammed into the unshaded public square, where they stood patiently for three hours. Douglas opened the debates by repeating many of his earlier arguments, vehemently denying that he had conspired to nationalize slavery and charging that Lincoln favored racial equality. He underscored his arguments by furiously pointing skyward, giving his head a shake, and moving forward, resembling a panther about to spring or a dog single-mindedly tugging on a root.

In his opening remarks, the senator praised his opponent's character, then abruptly asked the audience, "Are you in favor of conferring upon the negro the rights and privileges of citizenship? . . . Do you desire to turn this beautiful State into a free negro colony, in order that when Missouri shall abolish slavery, she can send us these emancipated slaves to become citizens and voters on an equality with you? If you desire negro citizenship . . . then go with Mr. Lincoln and the Black Republicans in favor of negro citizenship. For one, I am opposed to negro citizenship in any form." Blacks were hopelessly inferior, Douglas argued. Snidely he remarked, "I do not question Mr. Lincoln's conscientious belief that the negro was made his equal, and hence is his brother. But, for my own part, I do not regard the negro as my equal, and I positively deny that he is my brother, or any kin to me whatever."[3]

Douglas made several other false allegations. He mischaracterized Lincoln's record in Congress on the Mexican War and alleged that Lincoln was a drinker. One untruth in particular would significantly undermine the senator's credibility: he charged that Lincoln had helped write an antislavery platform allegedly drawn up at Springfield in October 1854. He read portions of what he wrongly identified as that document, calling for the repeal of the Fugitive Slave Act, the abolition of slavery in the District of Columbia, the elimination of the interstate slave trade, and a ban on the acquisition of more slave territory, among other things. He then posed seven interrogatories, asking if Lincoln endorsed that platform. (The document Douglas cited was actually a radical platform adopted at Aurora in 1854. He had wrongly connected Lincoln to it in the past and had been corrected.)

Lincoln responded to what he called "very gross and palpable" misrepresentations by treating them as more amusing than provoking. Because he did not recognize Douglas's mistake in attributing to Springfield Republicans the radicalism of the Aurora Republicans, he failed to call attention to it. Instead, he found himself on the defensive, protesting that he had not helped frame that platform. Lincoln rejected the charge of abolitionism and racial egalitarianism, quoting from his 1854 Peoria address to illustrate the point. He then elaborated: "I have no purpose directly or indirectly to interfere with the institution of slavery in the States where it exists.... I have no purpose to introduce political and social equality between the white and black races ... but I hold that notwithstanding all this, there is no reason in the world why the negro is not entitled to all the natural rights enumerated in the Declaration of Independence, the right to life, liberty, and the pursuit of happiness. I hold that he is as much entitled to these as the white man. I agree with Judge Douglas that he is not my equal in many respects.... But in the right to eat the bread, without the leave of anybody else, which his own hand earns, *he is my equal and the equal of Judge Douglas and the equal of every living man*." Douglas, Lincoln charged, was blowing out the candles of "moral light" and eradicating the love of liberty by proclaiming his indifference to the morality of slavery, by asserting that the Black man "has nothing in the Declaration of Independence," and by stating that he "cares not whether slavery is voted down or voted up." Once he persuaded the public to adopt his amoral attitude, "then it needs only the formality of the second *Dred Scott* decision which he endorses in advance, to make Slavery alike lawful in all the States—old as well as new, North as well as South."[4] Enraged, Douglas sprang up to deliver his half-hour rejoinder, asking Lincoln if he agreed with the Springfield (actually Aurora) platform of 1854 and denouncing his "miserable quibbles." Passionately he rejected the conspiracy charge, calling it "an infamous lie."[5]

Press reaction to the debate followed party lines. Democratic newspapers lauded Douglas for exposing Lincoln's "nigger-loving propensities" and for showing that the senator was no "nigger worshipper."[6] The senator was delighted with the outcome, believing that he now had Lincoln on the defensive, for the incumbent had ducked the seven interrogatories. Even if he were to answer them in the next debate, it would not undo the damage. Lincoln's comments in Ottawa about Black equality seemed to repudiate his Chicago speech, in which he had called for an end to "all this quibbling about . . . this race and that race and the other race being inferior." It is noteworthy that this disavowal of any intention to promote racial equality was delivered in northern Illinois, where abolitionist sentiment was far stronger than it was in the more Negrophobic central and southern counties. Nevertheless, many Republicans rejoiced over Lincoln's performance (although some thought he was too passive and defensive). Samuel Galloway of Ohio asked John Locke Scripps, "Who is this new man?" He "has completely worsted the little giant. You have a David greater than the Democratic Goliath."[7]

Casting doubt on Douglas's claim to statesmanship was the conduct of his organ, the Chicago *Times*, which ran a hopelessly garbled version of Lincoln's remarks at Ottawa. Hundreds of discrepancies exist between its version of Lincoln's words and the version published in the Chicago *Press and Tribune*, which declared that a "more cowardly and knavish trick was never undertaken by a desperate politician." The *Times*'s shorthand reporter who deliberately mangled Lincoln's remarks was a disreputable character named Henry Binmore. Just who instructed Binmore to perform that mutilation is unclear. The *Press and Tribune* alleged that it was Douglas himself, with the assistance of Chicago *Times* editor James W. Sheahan. No hard evidence corroborates this charge, though the *Press and Tribune* alleged that Binmore had "offered to do for us, for pay, in behalf of Lincoln, what he is now doing for Douglas."[8] The Little Giant's lies about Lincoln's record, his claim that Lincoln had helped write the 1854 "Springfield" Republican platform, and his general unscrupulousness make it seem likely that Douglas instructed Binmore to misrepresent Lincoln. The *Times* denied all charges and alleged that "the Republicans have a candidate for the Senate of whose bad rhetoric and horrible jargon they are ashamed."[9] The *Press and Tribune* retorted that everyone "who has ever heard Abraham Lincoln address the people . . . knows that he is forcible, agreeable and correct in his delivery, and that he never did and never can talk the nonsense which the *Times* attributes to him."[10]

Two days after the Ottawa event, Lincoln asked Ebenezer Peck and Norman B. Judd to meet him for consultation. "Douglas is propounding questions to me," he explained, "which perhaps it is not quite safe to wholly disregard." Although he had "the means to dispose of them," he nonetheless wanted his friends' advice.[11] The night before the second debate, at Freeport, Lincoln read to them his proposed replies to Douglas's queries. Judd suggested modifications to suit the strong antislavery sentiment of northern Illinois. "But I couldnt stir him," Judd recalled. "He listened very patiently to both Peck and myself, but he wouldn't budge an inch from his well studied formulas."[12]

Earlier that day, Judd and Peck had conferred in Chicago with Joseph Medill and several others. They urged Lincoln to ask the senator, "What becomes of your vaunted popular Sovereignty in [the] Territories since the Dred Scott decision?"[13] Lincoln had already anticipated Douglas's reply to such a query, accurately predicting that he would insist that while Congress had no such authority, it did not matter, for "slavery can not actually exist in the ter[r]itories, unless the people desire it, and give it protective territorial legislation." Lincoln thought the senator had calculated that while such an argument might offend the South in the long run, it was more important in the short run "to hold on to his chances in Illinois."[14]

While drawing up the questions he intended to pose, Lincoln reviewed Douglas's speech at Bloomington, where the senator had made that very argument. Lincoln therefore knew how his opponent would respond and wanted those answers published so that the entire country—especially the South—could read them. They might well undermine Douglas's support not only in Dixie but also among the pro-Buchanan forces in Illinois.

Second Debate: Freeport

On August 27, a crowd one-third larger than the one at Ottawa converged on Freeport, a Republican stronghold with a population of seven thousand. Lincoln began by answering Douglas's interrogatories, then read slowly and distinctly four questions to the Little Giant:

1. Would he favor the admission of Kansas if it did not have the population called for in the English Bill compromise (i.e., 93,000)?
2. In light of the *Dred Scott* decision, could the inhabitants of a territory lawfully "exclude slavery from its limits prior to the formation of a State Constitution" if a citizen wished to bring slaves into that territory?
3. Would he support a second *Dred Scott* decision forbidding states to exclude slavery?
4. Would he support the acquisition of new territory "in disregard of how such acquisition may affect the nation on the slavery question"?

Lincoln as he appeared on the eve of the debates with Stephen A. Douglas in 1858. The photographer, T. Painter Pearson, offered his subject a mirror so that he could tidy up. Lincoln allegedly replied: "It would not be much of a likeness if I fixed it up any." Library of Congress.

By far the most important question was the second, which placed Douglas in an awkward position. As Lincoln told a friend, "If he sticks to the Dred Scott decision, he may lose the Senatorship; if he tries to get around it, he certainly loses the Presidency."[15]

Lincoln scolded Douglas for confusing the radical Aurora platform of 1854 with the more moderate one of the Springfield Republicans. Witheringly he speculated: "I can only account of his having done so upon the supposition that that evil genius which has attended him through his life . . . has at last made up its mind to forsake him." How hypocritical of Douglas to make such a mistake, when "he is in the habit, in almost all the speeches he makes, of charging falsehood upon his adversaries." In fact, he preferred to "stand upon his dignity and call people liars" rather than answer questions.

In response to the first interrogatory, Douglas asserted that he would support the admission of Kansas with a small population even if its voters rejected the Lecompton Constitution. After reciting the crucial second question, Douglas offered what became known as the Freeport Doctrine, a proposition that he had made earlier but that now became much better known. The Dred Scott decision may have forbidden the people of a territory to formally exclude slavery, he said, but informally they could do so by refusing to pass "local police regulations" guaranteeing the rights of slaveholders. Slavery "cannot exist a day or an hour anywhere unless supported" by such regulations, which "can only be furnished by the local legislature. If the people of the Territory are opposed to slavery they will elect members to the legislature who will adopt unfriendly legislation to it."

Southern newspapers were swift to denounce this Freeport Doctrine. The *Missouri Democrat* prophetically declared that Douglas's presidential chances were doomed: "If his opposition to the Lecompton Constitution could be forgiven, his Freeport speech, equivocal as it is, would put him out of the ring."[16] Although Lincoln was not the first to expose this weakness in Douglas's popular sovereignty doctrine, at Freeport he brought it more fully into public awareness. The senator's clear statement at Freeport not only ruined his reputation in the South but also widened the breach within the Illinois Democracy. By forcing Douglas to reiterate his "unfriendly legislation" doctrine and exposing his false accusation regarding the radical Aurora platform, Lincoln won the debate and regained the initiative he had lost at Ottawa.

Third Debate: Jonesboro

In contrast to the populations of Ottawa and Freeport, the eight hundred residents of Jonesboro, site of the third debate, seemed indifferent to the event. Located 350 miles south of Chicago in the poorest, most backward, and most heavily Democratic (and pro-Buchanan) part of the state, Jonesboro did little to welcome either candidate or the fourteen hundred people who came to hear them. When trains arrived bearing Lincoln and Douglas, no one cheered.

After lunch on September 15, a desultory crowd ambled to the fairground to hear the debate. Recounting the history of the birth of the Republican Party in 1854, the Little Giant alleged that in New York antislavery forces had adopted a platform "every plank of which was as black as night, each one relating to the nigger, and not one referring to the interests of the white man." In addition to his usual arguments about "degraded races," the senator introduced a new element into the debates: overseas expansionism. Since 1843, he had been calling for the annexation of Cuba. He told the Jonesboro audience that the time "has come, when our interests would be advanced by the acquisition of the [slaveholding] island of Cuba."

Lincoln devoted much of his time to reading Democratic antislavery platforms and resolutions adopted in 1850 throughout northern Illinois, arguing that if Douglas were justified in holding him responsible for radical resolutions endorsed by Republicans in Aurora, the Little Giant should also be held responsible for the 1850 documents he quoted. Lincoln denied the central tenet of Douglas's Freeport Doctrine, that slavery could not exist without "friendly legislation" to protect it. After all, he pointed out, Dred Scott had been held in slavery in Minnesota, which had no police regulations supporting slavery. "It takes not only law but the *enforcement* of law to keep it out," he sensibly observed. He then chided the Little Giant for inconsistency. Before 1857, Douglas had maintained that the Supreme Court should decide whether the people of a territory could exclude slavery; at Freeport he asserted that the territorial settlers could make an end run around the court and were not obliged to abide by its explicit decision. Was not Douglas oath-bound to support laws protecting the right of slaveholders to take their slaves into the territories? Pointedly Lincoln asked how Douglas could swear to uphold the Constitution and simultaneously "assist in legislation *intended to defeat that right*?"

Lincoln then asked: "If the slaveholding citizens of a United States Territory should need and demand Congressional legislation for the protection of their slave property in such Territory, would you, as a member of Congress, vote for or against such legislation?" In response, the Little Giant declared that "there shall be non-interference, non-intervention by Congress in the States and Territories." Although this was a platitude that did not address the question, the audience applauded lustily. This stance would cost Douglas dearly, for, especially after Freeport, Southerners were to interpret it as an affront to their section. Lincoln's abbreviated Jonesboro speech was the weakest he made in the debates, for his reading of documents was tedious.

Fourth Debate: Charleston

On September 18, the candidates clashed at Charleston, in east-central Illinois. From surrounding villages some twelve thousand people poured in to witness the debate. Tension charged the air. Lincoln had been warned that Negrophobia was especially intense in the county. (In 1848, 95 percent of the voters there favored the constitutional provision forbidding Blacks to settle in the state.) His friend

William M. Chambers, an influential American Party leader in Charleston, told him after reading his Chicago speech of July 10 that he should give his audiences "less of the favouring of negro equality." Appeals for racial justice pleased neither Fillmore voters nor Republicans around Charleston. The town's leading Republican, Thomas A. Marshall, a good friend with whom Lincoln stayed, recommended that he "not propose to confer upon them [Blacks] any further social or political rights than they are now entitled to."[17]

Lincoln took his friend's advice to heart. "When I was at the hotel to-day," he began, "an elderly gentleman called upon me to know whether I was really in favor of producing a perfect equality between the negroes and white people." Lincoln had not planned to address that subject, which he had already dealt with at Ottawa, but since he was asked, he thought he "would occupy perhaps five minutes in saying something in regard to it." He declared bluntly: "I am not, nor ever have been, in favor of bringing about in any way the social and political equality of the white and black races; that I am not, nor ever have been, in favor of making voters or jurors of negroes, nor of qualifying them to hold office, nor to intermarry with white people; and I will say, in addition to this, that there is a physical difference between the white and black races which I believe will forever forbid the two races living together on terms of social and political equality. And inasmuch as they cannot so live, while they remain together there must be the position of superior and inferior, and I as much as any other man am in favor of having the superior position assigned to the white race." Lincoln immediately qualified this stark avowal: "I do not perceive that because the white man is to have the superior position the negro should be denied everything. I do not understand that because I do not want a negro woman for a slave I must necessarily want her for a wife. My understanding is that I can just let her alone."

In response, the Little Giant again appealed to the prejudice of the state's many Negrophobes: "I say this Government was created on the white basis by white men for white men and their posterity forever, and never should be administered by any except white men. I declare that a negro ought not to be a citizen whether he was imported into this country or born here, whether his parents were slave or not. It don't depend upon the question where he was born, or where his parents were placed, but it depends on the fact that the negro belongs to a race incapable of self-government, and for that reason ought not to be on an equality with the white man."

Democrats chastised Lincoln for inconsistency on racial matters, pointing out that his opposition to Black civil rights as expressed in the Charleston debate contrasted markedly with the peroration of his Chicago speech, in which he urged an end to "all this quibbling about . . . this race and that race and the other race being inferior."[18] They charged that in northern Illinois he talked out of one side of his mouth, while in the southern counties he spoke out of the other side. But in fact, his Charleston remarks echoed what he had said at the debate in Ottawa, far north of Coles County.

At the other end of the ideological spectrum, abolitionists deplored Lincoln's remarks about Black citizenship. "Our standard bearer has faltered thus soon," lamented the Chicago *Congregational Herald*. "Lincoln deliberately, and with repetition, declared himself to be opposed to placing colored men on a political equality with white men."[19] While that criticism was valid, it should be born in mind that Lincoln was at heart a racial egalitarian, while Douglas was a flagrant, unvarnished bigot. Lincoln was careful not to say that Blacks *were* inferior, but since they could not coexist on terms of political and social equality, thanks to intractable White prejudice, he would prefer that they be *placed* in the inferior position. As Don E. Fehrenbacher noted, Lincoln supported racial separation "on grounds of the incompatibility rather than the inequality of the races."[20] Furthermore, as George Fredrickson observed, it "is clear that no one who did not at least pay lip service to white supremacy could get elected to a statewide office in Illinois."[21] Most if not all of Lincoln's racist-sounding remarks, like his opening statements at Ottawa and Charleston, merely paid such lip service. When the journalist David R. Locke asked Lincoln why he supported the Prairie State's anti-miscegenation statute, he replied: "The law means nothing. I shall never marry a negress, but I have no objection to any one else doing so. If a white man wants to marry a negro woman, let him do it—*if the negro woman can stand it*."[22]

Lincoln's primary goal was to end slavery, which he considered a greater evil than discrimination against free African Americans. In the South lived 4,000,000 slaves, a huge number compared with the 250,000 free Blacks in the North; deplorable as the lack of civil rights for the latter was, slavery was much worse. Although it might be possible to attack both evils simultaneously in antebellum New England, it was not then politically feasible either in Illinois or in the country at large. Racial equality was an issue that Lincoln felt compelled to soft-pedal in order to win votes in Negrophobic Illinois and thus have a chance to defeat Douglas, who posed the greatest threat by far to the antislavery cause, in Lincoln's view. (Soon after the Charleston debate, he spoke at Jacksonville, where Julian Sturtevant, president of Illinois College, solicitously observed, "You must be having a weary time." Lincoln replied: "I am, and if it were not for one thing I would retire from the contest. I know that if Mr. Douglas' doctrine prevails it will not be fifteen years before Illinois itself will be a slave state.")[23]

As James Oakes put it, for Lincoln "the entire issue" of racial equality "was a distraction. He wanted questions about race moved off the table, and he needed a strategy to get rid of them."[24] That strategy involved paying lip service to Illinois's

Black Code, which outlawed interracial marriage as well as African American voting, officeholding, and jury service.

Final Debates

On October 7, the fifth debate took place on the campus of Knox College, a hotbed of abolitionism located in Galesburg, a Republican town 175 miles southwest of Chicago. Douglas opened by complaining about the Buchanan administration's efforts to defeat him through an "unholy and unnatural" alliance with the Republicans. He taunted members of the opposition party for using different names in different parts of the state; in southern and central Illinois they called themselves "Lincoln men" and the "Free Democracy" instead of using the more radical term *Republican*. Pointing out that the author and many of the signers of the Declaration of Independence owned slaves, Douglas asked how it could be inferred that they meant to include Blacks in the proposition that "all men are created equal." Lincoln replied that Thomas Jefferson, though a slaveholder, had said that "he trembled for his country when he remembered that God was just." He challenged Douglas to "show that he [Douglas], in all his life, ever uttered a sentiment at all akin to that of Jefferson." He also noted that no signers of the Declaration of Independence ever stated that Blacks were excluded from that document's statement that "all men are created equal."

In dealing with the charge that he spoke out of both sides of his mouth on the race issue, Lincoln ridiculed Douglas's logic, saying that "the Judge will have it that if we do not confess that there is a sort of inequality between the white and black races which justifies us in making them slaves, we must then insist that there is a degree of equality that requires us to make them our wives."

The central issue dividing the parties, Lincoln maintained, was the morality of slavery. Douglas and his friends denied "that there is any wrong in slavery." The Republicans disagreed. "I confess myself," stated Lincoln, "as belonging to that class in the country who contemplate slavery as a moral, social, and political evil" and who "desire a policy that looks to the prevention of it as a wrong, and looks hopefully to the time when as a wrong it may come to an end." Finally, Lincoln heatedly attacked Douglas for the "fraud" and "absolute forgery" that he had introduced at the Ottawa debate regarding the Aurora Republicans' platform. When the senator rose to reply, he seemed agitated as he paced the platform, shaking his fist in anger. Approaching his rival, he said: "I do not believe that there was an honest man in the State of Illinois who did not believe that it was an error I was led into innocently." Brazenly he maintained that the Aurora Republican platform of 1854 reflected the party's thinking throughout the state in 1858, a demonstrably untrue assertion.

Less than a week after the Galesburg event, the candidates clashed again at Quincy, a Democratic stronghold where Douglas had lived for a time. Lincoln once again made the case that slavery "is a moral, a social and a political wrong."[25] Stepping forward to respond, Douglas managed to radiate supreme confidence. Curiously, he devoted much of his rebuttal to a defense against charges leveled by the Buchanan administration's organ, the Washington *Union*. He also continued to attack Lincoln personally.

Two days later, the final debate took place at Alton, a sluggish town on the Mississippi River twenty-five miles north of St. Louis, where Lincoln and James Shields had once met for a duel and where Elijah Lovejoy had been killed by a proslavery mob two decades earlier. The event was subdued, generating so little excitement that there was no procession. When Douglas began his address, his bloated face, haggard appearance, and hoarse voice indicated that he was exhausted. In a sour temper, he rehearsed earlier arguments and roasted President Buchanan.

Lincoln replied with passionate eloquence, effectively challenging Douglas's claims to statesmanship. The agitation over slavery expansion, he argued, had not been caused by politicians' selfish desire for power; it had, after all, divided the largest Protestant denominations. Douglas urged people to stop talking about the slavery issue and let settlers in the territories decide the matter. "But where is the philosophy or statesmanship which assumes that you can quiet that disturbing element in our society which has disturbed us for more than half a century, which has been the only serious danger that has threatened our institutions . . . ? Is it not a false statesmanship that undertakes to build up a system of policy upon the basis of caring nothing about *the very thing that everybody does care the most about?*—a thing which all experience has shown we care a very great deal about?"

Lincoln then stressed the moral dimension of the antislavery cause in the most eloquent language of the campaign. "The real issue in this controversy—the one pressing upon every mind—is the sentiment on the part of one class that looks upon the institution of slavery as a wrong, and of another class that does not look upon it as a wrong." The Republicans "insist that it should, as far as may be, *be treated* as a wrong; and one of the methods of treating it as a wrong is to *make provision that it shall grow no larger*." The Democratic Party, by contrast, contained "all who positively assert that it [slavery] is right, and all who, like Judge Douglas, treat it as indifferent and do not say it is either right or wrong." The morality of slavery was the crux of the matter. Passionately he continued: "That is the real issue. That is the issue that will continue in this country when these poor tongues of Judge Douglas and myself shall be silent. It is the eternal struggle between these two principles—right and wrong—throughout the world. They are the two principles that have stood face to face from the beginning of time, and will ever continue to struggle. The one is the common right of humanity, and the other the 'divine right of kings.' It is the same principle in whatever shape it develops itself. It is the same spirit that says, 'You work and toil and earn bread, and I'll eat it.' No matter in what shape it comes, whether from the mouth of a king who seeks to bestride the people of his own nation and live by the fruit of their labor, or from one race of men as an apology for enslaving another race, it is the same tyrannical principle."

Optimistically Lincoln predicted that once the public became fully aware of this fundamental difference between the parties, and the opponents of slavery were united, then "there will soon be an end" of the controversy, and that end will be the "ultimate extinction" of slavery. With unwonted heat, Lincoln denounced the Freeport Doctrine as "a *monstrous* sort of talk about the Constitution of the United States! *There has never been as outlandish or lawless a doctrine from the mouth of any respectable man on earth.*" Logically, the notion that the people of a territory could in effect overrule the Supreme Court by "unfriendly legislation" was no different from the argument that the people of a state could effectively overrule the Fugitive Slave Act. Thus, Lincoln argued, "there is not such an Abolitionist in the nation as Douglas, after all."

Douglas concluded the debates with one final racist appeal: If a state "chooses to keep slavery forever, it is not my business, but its own; if it chooses to abolish slavery, it is its own business,—not mine. I care more for the great principle of self-government, the right of a people to rule, than I do for all the niggers in Christendom. I would not endanger the perpetuity of this Union, I would not blot out the great inalienable rights of the white men, for all the niggers that ever existed."[26]

This final debate elicited little applause, though it was certainly Lincoln's finest rhetorical hour.

Intervention by Outsiders

Four days after the Alton debate, Lincoln's campaign suffered a grievous blow when T. Lyle Dickey publicly read a pro-Douglas letter he had received months earlier from Kentucky senator John J. Crittenden. Hearing rumors that Crittenden favored the reelection of Douglas and had agreed to write friends in Illinois saying so, Lincoln asked the Kentuckian in early July if that was in fact the case and predicted that Crittenden's Illinois admirers would be "mortified exceedingly" by any such correspondence.[27] On July 29, Crittenden replied that he admired the Little Giant's opposition to the Lecompton Constitution and deplored his "persecution" by the Buchanan administration and that he had so expressed himself to several men at Washington. Now he was besieged by Illinoisans, including Dickey, for confirmation of those discussions and would answer their requests honestly. He added that he had "no disposition for officious intermeddling" and "should be extremely sorry to give offense or cause mortification to you or any of my Illinois friends."[28] Three days later, Crittenden wrote Dickey recounting the praise he had bestowed upon Douglas in April and authorizing him to repeat what he had said.

Dickey kept the letter private until October 19, when he incorporated it into a speech denouncing Lincoln as an apostate from Clay's Whiggery. The Democrats cited that document as proof positive that the Old Line Whigs should not support Lincoln, though in fact it was hardly a ringing endorsement of Douglas's bid for reelection. Crittenden, in company with many Republicans, applauded the Little Giant's attack on the Lecompton Constitution, but that document had ceased to be an issue when Kansas voters in August decisively rejected it.

Election Results

Prairie State voters trooped to the polls on November 2 to choose members of the General Assembly, a state treasurer, and a state superintendent of public instruction. When the votes were tallied, the Republicans had narrowly won the two statewide offices but failed to gain control of the legislature. The election results are difficult to interpret with precision, but generally speaking, Republican candidates for the Illinois House of Representatives won a total of 190,468 votes, their Democratic opponents won 166,374, and the Buchaneers won 9,951. If in fact all votes for Democratic legislative candidates indicate a preference for Douglas over Lincoln, and all Republican votes were deliberately cast to indicate the opposite, then the challenger beat the incumbent handily, winning 52 percent to the Little Giant's 45 percent. Similarly, in the twelve races for senate seats, Republican candidates won 54 percent of the votes cast. If U.S. senators had been popularly elected in 1858, Lincoln would have trounced Douglas. But even under the prevailing system for choosing senators, Lincoln would have won if the legislature had been fairly apportioned. Illinois Republicans seethed with anger over the conduct of Eastern leaders of their party, especially Seward and Greeley. The Chicago *Press and Tribune* ascribed Lincoln's defeat primarily to the intervention of Crittenden and the coolness of those East Coast Republicans, of whom it exclaimed, "Every effort of our friends abroad was for our enemies at home!"[29]

Lincoln had mixed emotions regarding his defeat. On January 7, he "good-naturedly" told a journalist "that he felt like the Kentucky boy, who, after having his finger squeezed pretty badly, felt 'too big to cry, and too badly hurt to laugh.'"[30] Years later he recalled that on the "dark, rainy, and gloomy" night when the election returns showed that the Democrats had won the legislature, he started to walk home. "The path had been worn hog-back & was slippery. My foot slipped from under me, knocking the other one out of the way, but I recovered myself & lit square, and I said to myself, '*It's a slip and not a fall.*'"[31] He told friends that even though he had lost, he felt "ready for another fight," predicted that "it will all come out right in the end," and remarked that "Douglas has taken this trick, but the game is not played out."[32] And yet when the legislature formally reelected Douglas on January 5, 1859, Henry C. Whitney found Lincoln alone in his office "gloomy as midnight . . . brooding over his ill-fortune." Whitney "never saw any man so radically and thoroughly depressed." With bitterness, Lincoln said: "I expect everybody to desert me."[33]

Lincoln did not commit such sentiments to paper; he was stoic when writing to people like Anson G. Henry. "I am glad I made the late race," he told his longtime friend. "It gave me a hearing on the great and durable question of the age, which I could have had in no other way; and though I now sink out of view, and shall be forgotten, I believe I have made some marks which will tell for the cause of civil liberty long after I am gone."[34] He was also confident that Douglas would eventually be crushed between the upper and nether millstones, for he could not continue to please both the South and the North.

In fact, Lincoln had accomplished much in defeat. The Illinois Republican organization survived a fateful challenge, thanks largely to his efforts. Moreover, as the Chicago *Press and Tribune* observed, he had gained "a splendid national reputation." His speeches, the editor accurately predicted, "will become landmarks in our political history."[35] The debates *were* shortly to become landmarks, for Lincoln, obviously believing that he had won those seven encounters, had the texts of both his speeches and Douglas's published in book form. When that volume appeared early in 1860, it was a bestseller that helped Lincoln secure the Republican presidential nomination.

Lincoln's admiring party colleagues began to search for a fitting next step, a leadership position that would both reward him and strengthen the Republican cause. Some began referring to him as presidential timber. In the summer of 1859, Josiah M. Lucas reported from Washington that he had heard "various prominent men lately freely express themselves to me, and in crowds also, that Lincoln is the best man that we have got to run for the next President."[36]

While the debates significantly improved Lincoln's chances for the presidency, they materially injured Douglas's. Disillusioned by the "Freeport heresy," and even more by the Little Giant's refusal to support the Lecompton Constitution and a federal slave code for the territories, Southerners turned on him. In December, his Senate colleagues deposed him from the chairmanship of the Committee on Territories. In 1860, the South refused to support his presidential bid. Indeed, Douglas's 1858 victory was Pyrrhic; hurt by his own tactics and language, he was connected irreversibly to a doctrine—popular sovereignty—whose time had come and gone. It no longer satisfied either the North or the South. Soon he would suffer decline, defeat, and an early death.

Meanwhile, Lincoln insisted that the "fight must go on. The cause of civil liberty must not be surrendered at the end of *one*, or even, one *hundred* defeats." The future looked bright, for "the Republican star gradually rises higher everywhere." He had "abiding faith that we shall beat them in the long run." Perhaps that victory might even occur in the short run because, he predicted, "it is almost certain that we shall be far better organized for 1860 than ever before."[37] And so they were.

14.

"That Presidential Grub Gnaws Deep"

Pursuing the Republican Nomination (1859–1860)

In 1863, Lincoln mused that "no man knows, when that Presidential grub gets to gnawing at him, just how deep in it will get until he has tried it."[1] The grub began seriously gnawing at Lincoln after the 1858 campaign. His astute friend Joseph Gillespie believed that the debates with Douglas "first inspired him with the idea that he was above the average of mankind."[2] While that was probably true, Lincoln pooh-poohed any talk of the presidency. During the canvass with the Little Giant he had told a reporter: "Mary insists . . . that I am going to be Senator and President of the United States, too." Then, "shaking all over with mirth at his wife's ambition," he exclaimed, "Just think of such a sucker [i.e., Illinoisan] as me as President!"[3] In December 1859, when his friend and ally Jesse W. Fell urged him to seek the Republican presidential nomination, he replied: "Oh, Fell, what's the use of talking of me for the presidency, whilst we have such men as Seward, Chase and others."[4] The following spring, he said that the idea of "seriously considering me for that position" was "absurd."[5]

But it was not absurd; the race for the nomination was wide open. Despite his modesty, between August 1859 and March 1860 Lincoln positioned himself for a presidential run by giving speeches and corresponding with party leaders in several states. At the same time, he labored to keep Republicans on a prudent middle course between Douglas's popular sovereignty and radical abolitionism.

Law Practice

Before turning his attention fully to politics, Lincoln had to replenish his depleted bank account. Shortly after the 1858 election, he told Norman B. Judd, "I have been on expences so long without earning any thing that I am absolutely without money now for even household purchases."[6] As Lincoln grudgingly devoted himself once again to the law, he found it difficult to readjust to the routine of legal work. In the late summer of 1859, he tried one of his few murder cases, defending Peachy

Quinn Harrison, a grandson of his former political adversary Peter Cartwright. Harrison allegedly had stabbed to death a young attorney named Greek Crafton. Since both the Crafton and Harrison families were well known in Sangamon County, the lengthy, complicated, and tedious trial became a cause célèbre.

Throughout that proceeding, Lincoln was thwarted by adverse rulings from the bench. When he objected, citing authorities that clearly sustained his argument, the judge, Edward Y. Rice, overruled him. According to Herndon, Lincoln grew "so angry that he looked like Lucifer in an uncontrollable rage." Careful to stay "within the bounds of propriety just far enough to avoid a reprimand for contempt of court," he was "fired with indignation and spoke fiercely—strongly [and] contemptuously" against the ruling of the judge, whom "he 'pealed' from head to toe."[7] The turning point of trial came when Peter Cartwright testified that the dying Crafton had told him that he forgave his killer and urged that Harrison not be held responsible. Cartwright's hearsay testimony, which amazingly was allowed to stand, helped sway the jury. In his closing speech, Lincoln urged the jurors to heed Cartwright's lachrymose account of Crafton's deathbed plea, which they did, finding Harrison innocent.

Combating Douglasism

In late 1858, Lincoln saw his party still tempted to unite with Douglas. He anticipated that the Little Giant might bolt the Democratic Party to oppose a federal slave code for the territories. The senator could, Lincoln thought, "claim that all Northern men shall make common cause in electing him President as the best means of breaking down the Slave power." If that should happen, Lincoln predicted, "the struggle in the North will be, as it was in Illinois last summer and fall, whether the Republican party can maintain it's identity, or be broken up to form the tail of Douglas's new kite."[8] To Thomas Corwin in Ohio he insisted that any flirtation with Douglasites would ruin the Republican Party in Illinois. "It is idiotic to think otherwise."[9] Lincoln made the same point in March 1859, reminding a Republican audience in Chicago that the fight against slavery expansion was a proxy for the struggle against slavery itself: "Never forget that we have before us this whole matter of the right or wrong of slavery in this Union, though the immediate question is as to its spreading out into new Territories and States."[10] Let us not lower our standard, he counseled.

In a public letter to Massachusetts Republicans, Lincoln argued that the current Democratic Party had deserted Thomas Jefferson by holding "the *liberty* of one man to be absolutely nothing, when in conflict with another man's right of *property*." Jefferson's Declaration of Independence had framed "the definitions and axioms of free society," which were now disowned by Democrats, who regard them as "glittering generalities," "self-evident lies," and principles applying "only to 'superior races.'" Such expressions "are identical in object and effect—the supplanting the principles of free government, and restoring those of classification, caste, and legitimacy." Forcefully he maintained that whoever "would *be* no slave, must consent to *have* no slave. Those who deny freedom to others, deserve it not for themselves; and, under a just God, can not long retain it."[11]

When asked whether Republicans should ally with other opponents of the Democrats (e.g., Know-Nothings), Lincoln said: "I am for it, if it can be had on Republican grounds; and I am not for it on any other terms."[12] To help secure the German vote, Lincoln bought a printing press and gave it to Theodore Canisius, a German American editor, with the understanding that he would publish the *Staats-Anzeiger*, a German-language Republican paper, in Springfield.

In addition to nativism, Lincoln combated the threat posed by radicalism. In Ohio, Republicans adopted a platform calling for the repeal of "the atrocious Fugitive Slave Law." Alarmed, Lincoln told Salmon P. Chase that their stand was "already damaging us here. I have no doubt that if that plank be even *introduced* into the next Republican National convention, it will explode it."[13] Turning to Indiana, Lincoln asked Schuyler Colfax to avoid issues that might split the party. "The point of danger is the temptation in different localities to '*platform*' for something which will be popular just there, but which, nevertheless, will be a firebrand elsewhere, and especially in a National convention."[14]

Through the winter, spring, and summer of 1859, whenever Lincoln received invitations to speak, he declined, pleading poverty. In September, however, he agreed to make a brief swing though Ohio, where voters were about to elect a governor and legislators. Douglas was already stumping for Democrats there. The Little Giant had just published in *Harper's Magazine* a lengthy, turgid, repetitious article, "The Dividing Line between Federal and Local Authority: Popular Sovereignty in the Territories," which in effect continued his debate with Lincoln. Inexplicably ignoring the Northwest Ordinance of 1787 and the Missouri Compromise of 1820, Douglas argued that settlers in the territories had historically been empowered to regulate "all things affecting their internal polity—slavery not excepted" without congressional interference. After reading that article, Lincoln burst into Milton Hay's adjacent law office and "without a salutation, said: 'This will never do. He puts the moral element out of this question. It won't stay out.'"[15]

At the Ohio capital on September 16, Lincoln called Douglas's article "the most maturely considered" of his opponent's "explanations explanatory of explanations explained." He challenged it on historical and constitutional grounds, citing the Northwest Ordinance of 1787. Popular sovereignty meant that "if one man chooses to make a slave of another man, neither that other man nor anybody else has a right to object." Similarly, he reduced the Freeport Doctrine to a simple proposition: "*a thing may be lawfully driven away from where it has a lawful right to be.*" The fundamental question, Lincoln maintained, was whether Douglas was correct in regarding slavery as a minor matter. "I suppose the institution of slavery really looks small to him" because his capacity for empathy was limited. "He is so put up by nature that a lash upon his back would hurt him, but a lash upon anybody else's back does not hurt him." The Little Giant's popular sovereignty doctrine would, he predicted, pave the way not only for a new Dred Scott decision but also for the reopening of the African slave trade and for a federal slave code in the territories.[16]

In Cincinnati on September 17, Lincoln aimed his remarks primarily at residents of Kentucky. Republicans, he assured them, had no plans to invade the South or tamper with slavery. "We mean to leave you alone, and in no way to interfere with your institution, to abide by all and every compromise of the Constitution, and, in a word, coming back to the original proposition, to treat you . . . according to the examples of those noble fathers—Washington, Jefferson, and Madison. We mean to remember that you are as good as we; that there is no difference between us other than the difference of circumstances. We mean to bear in mind always that you have as good hearts in your bosoms as other people, or as we claim to have, and treat you accordingly." How would Southerners react if Republicans were to capture the White House? he asked. Would they secede? How would that help them? Would they go to war? They might be at least as gallant and brave as Northerners, but they would nonetheless lose because Northerners outnumbered them.

He urged Republicans to support only those candidates who embraced the party's basic principle: unyielding opposition to the spread of slavery. Lincoln defended the free labor system against critics who claimed that slaves were better off than hired laborers. Men like himself might start off with no capital and thus be forced to work for others, but in time they could, if they were industrious and prudent, accumulate capital and hire others to work for them. "In doing so they do not wrong the man they employ, for they find men who have not their own land to work with, or shops to work in, and who are benefited by working for others, hired laborers, receiving their capital for it. Thus a few men that own capital, hire a few others, and these establish the relation of capital and labor rightfully." None are locked into the position of hired laborer forever unless they sink into vice, fall victim to misfortune, or simply choose such a life. The free institutions of the country were designed to promote social and economic mobility. "This progress by which the poor, honest, industrious and resolute man raises himself, that he may work on his own account, and hire somebody else, is that progress that human nature is entitled to, is that improvement in condition that is intended to be secured by those institutions under which we live, is the great principle for which this government was really formed. Our government was not established that one man might do with himself as he pleases, and with another man too."[17]

Back in Springfield, Lincoln penned a note to Salmon P. Chase expressing regret that they had been unable to meet during his brief foray into Ohio. Having warned Chase earlier to avoid radicalism, he now counseled Buckeyes to give no "encouragement to Douglasism."[18] On October 13, Lincoln rejoiced at the news that Republicans had won control of the Ohio legislature and that the Republican gubernatorial candidate had bested his opponent. The Ohio result damaged Douglas's prospects, while enhancing Lincoln's.

The victorious Ohio Republicans wanted to publish the 1858 Lincoln-Douglas debates, which Lincoln had unsuccessfully attempted to bring out earlier. On his September visit, Lincoln had brought along a carefully assembled scrapbook containing the Chicago *Times*'s account of Douglas's speeches and the Chicago *Press and Tribune*'s version of his own remarks. He evidently showed it to the Ohio Republican leaders with a view to having them see it into print. Back in Springfield, Lincoln entrusted the scrapbook to young John G. Nicolay to deliver to Columbus, where the firm of Follett, Foster and Company agreed to publish the volume. A week before the Republican national convention at Chicago, Lincoln received his first copies. The 268-page work would be circulated widely in the presidential campaign.

Soon after his Ohio sojourn, Lincoln filled speaking engagements in Wisconsin. At Milwaukee he delivered an ostensibly nonpolitical speech before the Wisconsin Agricultural Society attacking proslavery arguments and vindicating free labor. After recommending steps to improve agricultural productivity, he reiterated his analysis of the advantages of free labor and refuted the "'*mud-sill*' theory" propounded by Southerners like George Fitzhugh and James Henry Hammond. Labor, he argued, "is prior to, and independent of, capital," for "capital is the fruit of labor" and therefore "labor is the superior—greatly superior—of capital." Free labor economics was "the just and generous, and prosperous system, which opens the way for all—gives hope to all, and energy, and progress, and improvement of condition to all."[19]

Having bolstered his reputation in the Midwest, Lincoln looked east, especially to Pennsylvania, one of the swing states that the Republicans must carry in 1860. In December, when Jesse W. Fell urged Lincoln to supply a Pennsylvania journalist with an autobiographical sketch, he complied, saying: "There is not much of it, for the reason, I suppose, that there is not much of me. If anything be made out of it, I wish it to be modest, and not to go beyond the material. If it were thought necessary to incorporate anything from any of my speeches, I suppose there would be no objection. Of course it must not appear to have been written by myself."[20] This brief document was forwarded to Joseph J. Lewis, who used it to write a long article about Lincoln for the *Chester County Times* of West Chester. Appearing on February 11, 1860, it described the Illinoisan as "a consistent and earnest tariff man from the first hour of his entering public life," a statement endearing Lincoln to Pennsylvanians.[21] It was widely copied in the Republican press.

The October electoral victory in Ohio was encouraging, but Republican euphoria was short-lived. On the sixteenth of that month the abolitionist firebrand John Brown led an abortive raid on the federal arsenal at Harpers Ferry, Virginia, sending shock waves throughout the South. His goal was evidently to seize arms and provide them to slaves for an uprising. Republicans feared that Brown's act might injure them at the polls. Newspapers throughout the South and the Border States fumed that Brown's act was a logical consequence of Republican agitation over slavery. In Sangamon County, Lincoln worried that John M. Palmer, the Republican candidate running for the seat vacated by the death of Congressman Thomas L. Harris, would lose to Democrat John A. McClernand, which he did. "I reckon the Harpers Ferry affair damaged Palmer somewhat," Lyman Trumbull speculated plausibly.[22] That affair also damaged other Republicans, especially Radicals like William Henry Seward, the front-runner for the presidential nomination, who had acquired a reputation as an extremist for his declaration in 1850 that there was a "higher law" than the Constitution and for an 1858 speech in which he alluded to an "irrepressible conflict" between North and South, widely misrepresented as a call for civil war. "Since the Humbug insurrection at Harpers Ferry, I presume Mr Seward will not be urged," a Pennsylvanian told Lincoln.[23] The most obvious beneficiary of John Brown's raid was Lincoln, who seemed acceptably moderate compared with Seward and acceptably radical and energetic compared with Edward Bates.

In the late autumn, Lincoln expanded his political horizons westward with a visit to Kansas, where he gave speeches in several towns. Alluding to the bloody history of the Kansas Territory over the past five years, he said that "both parties had been guilty of outrages" but that ultimate blame must be assigned to the popular sovereignty doctrine. As for John Brown, that abolitionist "has shown great courage, rare unselfishness," but "no man, North or South, can approve of violence or crime."[24] On December 2, Lincoln spoke of Southern threats to pull out of the Union, declaring "that any attempt at secession would be treason." The following day, he again addressed the Harpers Ferry episode: "Old John Brown has just been executed for treason against a state. We cannot object, even though he agreed with us in thinking slavery wrong. That cannot excuse violence, bloodshed, and treason." Therefore, "if constitutionally we elect a [Republican] President, and therefore you undertake to destroy the Union, it will be our duty to deal with you as old John Brown has been dealt with."[25] Although Kansas Republicans overwhelmingly favored Seward, some talked of Lincoln for president. At Leavenworth, Able Carter Wilder grabbed him by the hand and announced, "Here comes the next President of the United States."[26] Lincoln's efforts in frigid, primitive Kansas testified to his devotion to the Republican cause. As a resident of Leavenworth observed, few politicos would "have been forced to do the work in which Abraham Lincoln *volunteered*. In dead of Winter he left the comforts of an attractive home to couple his energies with those of a young people in a distant Territory battling for the RIGHT."[27]

Boosting Lincoln's Candidacy

In late January 1860 at Springfield, Norman Judd and Lincoln attended a caucus of leading Republicans who wished to boost Lincoln's vice presidential candidacy; few of them thought he had a chance to head the national ticket. The foremost spirit at the meeting, Jackson Grimshaw, had been organizing Cameron-Lincoln clubs throughout Illinois and intended to win more backing for that effort. Judd "strongly opposed this action, saying the proper and only thing to do was to claim the Presidency for him [Lincoln] and nothing less."[28] Evidently Judd was persuasive, for Grimshaw asked Lincoln "if his name might be used at once in Connection with the Coming Nomination and election." With "characteristic modesty," Lincoln expressed doubt "whether he could get the Nomination even if he wished it and asked until the next morning to answer whether his name might be announced as one who was to be a candidate for the office of President." Leonard Swett accosted him: "Now, see here, Lincoln, this is outrageous. We are trying to get you nominated for the presidency, and you are working right against us. Now you must stop it, and give us a chance." Lincoln "laughed, and said it wasn't serious enough to make any fuss about, but he promised he wouldn't interfere if we were bound to put him forward." The following day he acceded to his friends' request, but when they inquired whether they might push for his nomination as vice president in case the presidential bid failed, he demurred: "My name has been mentioned rather too prominently for the first place on the ticket for me to think of accepting the second."[29]

Lincoln strove to avoid offending his rivals or their supporters. On February 8, after the Republican State Central Committee had met, he conferred with Orville H. Browning, who opined that Edward Bates of Missouri would be the strongest Republican presidential candidate. Lincoln tactfully replied that "it is not improbable that by the time the National convention meets in Chicago he may be of [the] opinion that the very best thing that can be done will be to nominate

Mr Bates."[30] Alarmed by this conversation, Lincoln wrote to Judd, who hoped to win the party's nomination for governor: "I am not in a position where it would hurt much for me not to be nominated on the national ticket, but I am where it would hurt some for me to not get the Illinois delegates. . . . Your discomfited assailants are most bitter against me; and they will, for revenge upon me, lay to the Bates egg in the South, and to the Seward egg in the North, and go far towards squeezing me out in the middle with nothing. Can you not help me a little in this matter?"[31]

Judd was willing to help more than a little. A week after Lincoln wrote him, the Chicago *Press and Tribune*, to which Judd had close ties, heartily endorsed Lincoln for president. In April 1860, Judd suggested to Lyman Trumbull that "a quiet combination between the delegates from New Jersey Indiana and Illinois be brought about—including Pennsylvania." Together they could stop Seward, but they must maintain a low profile. "It will not do to make a fight for delegates distinctly Lincoln," but he could get at least the unanimous backing of the Illinois delegation.[32] Let the supporters of Seward, Chase, Bates, and Cameron fight among themselves; then, at the proper time, when a strong push was to be made, he would face no embittered rivals. In a late February dispatch from Washington, Joseph Medill speculated that Lincoln would be more electable than the conservative Bates or the radical Seward: "Does not common sense whisper in every man's ear that the middle ground is the ground of safety?"[33] That article infuriated Seward, who accused Medill of "going back" on him and of preferring the "prairie statesman," as he patronizingly referred to Lincoln.[34]

Meanwhile, Judd was busy trying to persuade the Republican National Committee, on which he sat, to hold the party's national convention in Chicago. It was Lincoln's good fortune to have a man like Judd aiding his cause. Known as a shrewd manager, he was genial, personable, and popular with the men who tended to the party machinery. (In 1861, Lincoln said of Judd that "he has done more for the success of our party than any man in the State, and he is certainly the best organizer we have.")[35] Judd found the national committee divided: Seward's men wanted the convention held in New York, Chase's backers argued for Cleveland, and supporters of Bates insisted on St. Louis. Slyly, Judd suggested that since Illinois had no prominent candidate for the presidency, Chicago should be chosen as a neutral compromise site. On December 21 the committee accepted that proposal.

Cooper Union Speech

One day in October 1859, Lincoln rushed into his office brandishing an invitation to deliver a lecture at Plymouth Church in Brooklyn, where the renowned minister Henry Ward Beecher presided. The topic could be virtually anything. With this

Mathew Brady took this photo in New York on February 23, 1860, the day Lincoln delivered his Cooper Union speech. The artist-photographer George H. Story scheduled and attended the session. Afterward, Lincoln allegedly said that Brady and the Cooper Union speech made him president. The sculptor Truman H. Bartlett observed that "Lincoln's tall & well made body, vivified by his kind & undemonstrative nature" enabled him "to stand with perfect ease, unconscious & dignified force, making this portrait one of unique distinction." Bartlett thought this image of Lincoln "the only portrait of him in existence which while including the larger part of Lincoln's body produces on the observer the extraordinary effect so often described by the one word, 'presence.'" Abraham Lincoln Presidential Library and Museum, Springfield, Illinois.

opportunity Lincoln could, if successful, overcome Eastern skepticism about the wisdom of nominating an ill-educated "prairie statesman." A leading Chase operative, James A. Briggs, had extended the invitation, and Chase men, eager to stop Seward or any other rival of their hero, had earlier talked of boosting Lincoln as a way to head off a Bates movement. Seward was told that "Mr. Lincoln was brought to New York to divide your strength."[36]

To Briggs, Lincoln proposed giving a political address toward the end of February. That was too late for the lecture series, so Briggs turned Lincoln's appearance over to the Young Men's Republican Union of New York. Anti-Seward forces in that organization were employing it as a forum to showcase alternative candidates. To prepare for his New York appearance, Lincoln conducted thorough research in order to rebut Douglas's *Harper's Magazine* article.

En route to New York, Lincoln was surprised to read in a newspaper that he would be speaking at the Cooper Institute in New York instead of at the Plymouth Church in Brooklyn. Feeling the need to revise his speech to suit a Manhattan audience, Lincoln devoted himself to that task. He turned down the offer of merchant Henry C. Bowen to stay at his home, explaining that "he was afraid he had made a mistake in accepting the call to New York, and feared his lecture would not prove a success. He said he would have to give his whole time to it, otherwise he was sure he would make a failure, in which case he would be very sorry for the young men who had kindly invited him."[37]

Lincoln later recalled that the day of the speech "was one of the loneliest days of his life," for he feared that the New Yorkers who greeted him "were over critical of his entire appearance." He felt the same way "when on the platform of the hall *before* he spoke."[38] Urged to supply newspapers with a copy of his remarks, Lincoln expressed doubt that any paper would want to publish them. He visited the studio of Mathew Brady, where he had a photograph (which he called his "shadow") taken.[39] There Lincoln met the worldly George Bancroft, a model of sophistication compared with the provincial Lincoln, who apologized frequently for his unfamiliarity with city ways. He told the eminent historian that he was on his way to New England to visit his son Robert, who, he said, "already knows much more than his father."[40]

Fifteen hundred New Yorkers packed the Cooper Institute, where William Cullen Bryant, the distinguished poet and editor, introduced Lincoln as "a gallant soldier of the political campaign of 1856" and the man who had almost defeated Douglas in 1858. As Lincoln awkwardly stepped to the podium, his ill-fitting clothing, self-conscious rusticity, and ungainly manner inspired pity in some members of the audience. His opening words, which he delivered in a Kentucky accent, grated on cultivated Eastern ears. (The chairman of the meeting he addressed as

"Mr. Cheerman.") He spoke in a low, dull monotone, emphatically stressing his words. One auditor was led to think, "Old fellow, you won't do; it's all very well for the wild West, but this will never go down in New York."[41] As time passed, Lincoln straightened himself up and began gesturing with some grace, while his voice gained in volume and clarity.

The audience at first thought Lincoln's manner quite peculiar but soon found it captivating. The first portion of the address elaborately refuted Douglas's *Harper's Magazine* article "The Dividing Line between Federal and Local Authority," though it was not mentioned by name. In a brilliant piece of historical research and analysis, Lincoln examined the views of the thirty-nine signers of the Constitution as manifested in votes on the Northwest Ordinances of 1784 and 1787, a 1789 bill to enforce the latter ordinance, a 1798 bill forbidding the importation of slaves into the Mississippi Territory from abroad, an 1804 statute regulating slavery in the Louisiana Territory, and the Missouri Compromise of 1820. On those measures, twenty-three of the thirty-nine signers had expressed an opinion through their votes; of those twenty-three, twenty-one had indicated their belief that Congress could regulate slavery in the territories. Among the sixteen signers whose opinion could not be inferred from voting records were leading critics of slavery, including Benjamin Franklin, Alexander Hamilton, and Gouverneur Morris. The first Congress, which passed the fifth and tenth amendments, cited by those who denied that Congress had the power to regulate slavery in the territories, also passed legislation implementing the Northwest Ordinance of 1787. If the men who approved those amendments really believed that the Constitution did not empower the federal government to regulate slavery in the territories, why would they have reauthorized the ordinance? It would be "presumptuous," nay "impudently absurd," to maintain that the authors of those statutes and amendments were acting inconsistently. Lincoln then chastised Douglas (without naming him) for "substituting falsehood and deception for truthful evidence and fair argument."

In the second section of his hour-and-a-half-long speech, Lincoln addressed Southern Whites who would not respond to Republicans except "to denounce us as reptiles" and men "no better than outlaws." Lincoln urged them to abandon their insults and to deal rationally with Republican arguments. Would they break up the Union if the Republicans won the 1860 election? he asked. Such a rule-or-ruin approach was unjustified, for Republicans were hardly depriving the South "of some right, plainly written down in the Constitution." Indignantly he said of Southern threats to secede that "you will not abide the election of a Republican President! In that supposed event, you will destroy the Union; and then, you say, the great crime of having destroyed it will be upon us! That is cool. A highwayman holds a pistol to my ear, and mutters through his teeth, 'Stand and deliver, or

I shall kill you, and then you will be a murderer!'" Lincoln denied that the Republican Party could be held responsible for John Brown's raid, which he likened to attempted assassinations of monarchs: "An enthusiast broods over the oppression of a people till he fancies himself commissioned by Heaven to liberate them. He ventures the attempt, which ends in little else than his own execution."

In the final segment of the speech, Lincoln urged Republicans to remain calm in the face of Southern provocations. "It is exceedingly desirable that all parts of this great Confederacy shall be at peace, and in harmony, with one another," he said. "Let us Republicans do our part to have it so. Even though much provoked, let us do nothing through passion and ill temper. Even though the southern people will not so much as listen to us, let us calmly consider their demands, and yield to them if, in our deliberate view of our duty, we possibly can." But what would placate the Southerners? Only if we "cease to call slavery *wrong*, and join them in calling it *right*." Southerners would eventually demand the repeal of Free State constitutions forbidding slavery, Lincoln predicted. Republicans must stand fast by their determination to halt the spread of slavery and place it in the course of ultimate extinction.

In a mighty crescendo, he concluded: "Let us be diverted by none of those sophistical contrivances wherewith we are so industriously plied and belabored—contrivances such as groping for some middle ground between the right and the wrong . . . such as a policy of 'don't care' on a question about which all true men do care—such as Union appeals beseeching true Union men to yield to Disunionists, reversing the divine rule, and calling, not the sinners, but the righteous to repentance—such as invocations to Washington, imploring men to unsay what Washington said, and undo what Washington did. Neither let us be slandered from our duty by false accusations against us, nor frightened from it by menaces of destruction to the Government nor of dungeons to ourselves. Let us have faith that right makes might, and in that faith, let us, to the end, dare to do our duty as we understand it."[42]

The audience responded with thunderous applause. Cornelius A. Runkle shouted like a "wild Indian" and proclaimed Lincoln "the greatest man since St. Paul."[43] Richard C. McCormick of the New York *Evening Post* said he "never saw an audience more thoroughly carried away by an orator."[44] William Cullen Bryant, who thought Lincoln's address "the best political speech he ever heard in his life," singled out for special praise his analysis of the Founders' views on slavery expansion and his closing argument about the unreasonable demands of the "arrogant innovators" in the South.[45] Horace Greeley called it "the very best political address to which I ever listened—and I have heard some of Webster's grandest."[46] Several papers ran the full text of the speech.

Lincoln provided the New York *Tribune* with the manuscript of his oration and carefully examined the galleys with the proofreader, who discarded the document when he was finished. In September, a reprint was published with elaborate notes by Cephas Brainerd and Charles C. Nott. The Republican Congressional Document Committee mailed out more than one hundred thousand copies of that edition. Leaders of the New York Young Men's Republican Central Union, which published the pamphlet, boasted that it was "the most elaborate and popular campaign document ever issued."[47] The Democratic press was less enthusiastic. The New York *Herald* called Lincoln's speech a "hackneyed, illiterate composition" and "unmitigated trash, interlarded with coarse and clumsy jokes."[48]

Lincoln's triumph at Cooper Institute led to a flood of speaking invitations from Republicans in New England, Pennsylvania, and New Jersey. He had originally intended to visit his son Robert at Phillips Exeter Academy in New Hampshire and then return home promptly, but he agreed to take to the stump in Rhode Island and Connecticut as well as the Granite State; all three were to hold elections in April. During the next two weeks, Lincoln gave hastily scheduled addresses throughout those New England states. In the midst of that whirlwind tour, he complained to his wife: "I have been unable to escape this toil. If I had foreseen it I think I would not have come East at all. The speech at New-York, being within my calculation before I started, went off passably well, and gave me no trouble whatever. The difficulty was to make nine others, before reading audiences, who have already seen all my ideas in print."[49]

In most of those appearances Lincoln repeated his Cooper Institute address, but in Connecticut he added a new element: a discussion of laborers' right to strike. Endorsing that right, he ringingly declared: "I want every man to have the chance—and I believe a black man is entitled to it—in which he *can* better his condition—when he may look forward and hope to be a hired laborer this year and next, work for himself afterward, and finally to hire men to work for him! That is the true system. Up here in New England, you have a soil that scarcely sprouts black-eyed beans, and yet where will you find wealthy men so wealthy, and poverty so rarely in extremity?"[50] A Yale professor of rhetoric found Lincoln's speech so impressive that he lectured his class on its merits, and a student from the South who had come to jeer him remarked at the close, "That fellow could shut up old Euclid himself, to say nothing of Steve Douglas."[51]

At Hartford, Lincoln decried the opposition's charge that Republicans had incited John Brown to raid Harpers Ferry. Scornfully he predicted that "if they think they are able to slander a woman into loving them, or a man into voting with them, they will learn better presently." Of White Southerners he sarcastically remarked: "If a slave runs away, they overlook the natural causes which impelled him to the act; do not remember the oppression or the lashes he received, but charge us with instigating him to flight. If he screams when whipped, they say it is not caused by the pains he suffers, but he screams because we instigate him to outcrying."[52]

On his return trip to Illinois, Lincoln stopped over in New York and visited the Five Points House of Industry School in one of the poorest districts of the city. When a teacher asked him to address the children, he at first declined, but at the youngsters' insistence, he finally agreed, telling them that "the way was open to every boy present, if honest, industrious, and persevering, to the attainment of a high and honorable position."[53] When he tried to cut short his remarks, the lads clamored for more, and he obliged them.

By the time his Eastern tour ended, Lincoln had achieved a new stature and attracted a flock of presidential supporters. New England's most influential journal, the Springfield, Massachusetts, *Republican*, declared that Lincoln's "visit East has added greatly to his reputation among the republicans of this section, and they will be readily reconciled to any use of his name which the Chicago convention may propose in its selections for the national ticket."[54] A chorus of praise greeted Lincoln when he returned to Springfield in mid-March. "No inconsiderable portion of your fellow citizens in various portions of the country have expressed their preference for you as the candidate of the Republican party for the next Presidency," Milton Hay proudly told him on behalf of the capital's Republican Club. "There are those around you sir who have watched with manly interest and pride your upward march from obscurity to distinction."[55]

Girding for the Republican National Convention

Lincoln faced moral and practical dilemmas about using money to line up delegates to the Republican national convention. Mark W. Delahay had complained to Lincoln that Seward spent freely to win support in Kansas and that "we, your friends, are all very poor" and hinted that "a very little money now would do us and you a vast deal of good." Lincoln would have none of it: "I can not enter the ring on the money basis—first, because in the main, it is wrong; and secondly, I have not, and can not get, the money." Yet, he added, "for certain objects, in a political contest, the use of some, is both right, and indispensable." So saying, he agreed to give Delahay one hundred dollars to enable him to attend the Chicago convention, assuming that he would be selected as a delegate. When Delahay and all other Lincoln supporters in Kansas were defeated, Lincoln advised Delahay not to stir the Seward delegates "up to anger, but come along to the convention, and I will do as I said about expenses."[56]

News that the Republicans had won the spring elections in Connecticut and New Hampshire delighted Lincoln. The political implications, he and others thought, boded ill for Seward's nomination and well for his own, increasing his appetite for the ever-more-attainable nomination. To Lyman Trumbull he confided on April 29: "The taste *is* in my mouth a little."[57] He spelled out his strategy to a loyal booster, Samuel Galloway: "If I have any chance, it consists mainly in the fact that the *whole* opposition would vote for me if nominated. . . . My name is new in the field; and I suppose I am not the *first* choice of a very great many. Our policy, then, is to give no offense to others—leave them in a mood to come to us, if they shall be compelled to give up their first love. This, too, is dealing justly with all, and leaving us in a mood to support heartily whoever shall be nominated." He was particularly eager to avoid offending Chase, for "he gave us sympathy in 1858, when scarcely any other distinguished man did."[58] This strategy made sense, for the front-runners might well cancel each other.

As the date for the Republican national convention (May 16) drew near, Lincoln expressed guarded optimism, predicting that only the Illinois delegation would unanimously support him, though Indiana "might not be difficult to get." In the other states, "I have not heard that any one makes any positive objection to me."[59] The clear implication was that if Seward did not win, Lincoln might well do so, especially since most delegates would support a candidate who could carry Illinois, Indiana, Pennsylvania, and New Jersey. The shrewd Delahay had told him that Seward was unacceptably radical to delegates from those swing states; that Connecticut was also "a doubtful state" and therefore chary of Seward; that Ohio would go for any Republican and therefore Chase "can claim nothing in the way of availability"; that Bates was unacceptable to both the Germans and the Radicals and thus could not even carry his own state; and that Cameron, known as a corrupt wheeler-dealer, was unable to win the nomination.[60]

Delahay's astute analysis was echoed by many of Lincoln's correspondents and jibed with his own understanding. Certainly Cameron was weakened by doubts about his character. His sobriquets—"The Great Winnebago Chief" and "Old Winnebago"—referred to his conduct in 1838 when, acting as a claims commissioner, he allegedly had cheated the Winnebago Indians. Chase and Seward suffered from their prominence; having been in the spotlight for many years, they had made enemies. Lincoln looked good by comparison for he was, as Horace Greeley pointed out, "unencumbered by that weight of prejudice, and that still heavier responsibility for the sins of others, sure to be fastened upon the shoulders of every man who occupies for a long time the position of a political leader."[61] Lincoln was also more likable than the vain, hyperambitious Chase and the arrogant, dictatorial Seward. Both Cameron and Chase were also damaged by a lack of unanimity in their home-state delegations.

Complicating the picture was the stalemate reached by Democrats at their strife-torn national convention in Charleston, which opened on April 23 and adjourned on May 3 without choosing a candidate. Along with most other observers, Lincoln had expected Douglas to win there. The Democrats were scheduled to reconvene in mid-June at Baltimore, when presumably they would finally name Douglas. In the meantime, the Republicans would be meeting in Chicago in mid-May without knowing for sure whom they would face. Since Lincoln was regarded as the strongest foe against Douglas, any uncertainty about the Little Giant's becoming the Democratic standard-bearer improved Seward's chances. Meanwhile, conservative ex-Whigs, mostly proslavery Southerners, had met in Baltimore to form the Constitutional Union Party, which nominated John Bell of Tennessee for president and adopted a platform calling simply for support of the Union and the Constitution. They hoped to preempt the Republicans and force them to endorse their nominee. This move enhanced Lincoln's prospects, for it was feared that moderate Republicans might vote for Bell if the Chicago convention chose a candidate viewed as an antislavery radical, such as Seward or Chase.

Illinois Republican Convention

Lincoln predicted that he would receive unanimous support from the Illinois delegation to the impending national convention. On May 9 and 10 at Decatur, 645 Republican delegates gathered in a hastily erected structure to choose a gubernatorial candidate and adopt a platform. Shortly after the convention opened, the tall, handsome Richard J. Oglesby interrupted the proceedings by announcing: "I am informed that a distinguished citizen of Illinois, and one of whom Illinoisans ever delight to honor, is present, and I wish to move that this body invite him to a seat on the stand." Oglesby teased his auditors by refusing to name the "distinguished citizen" immediately. When he finally shouted "Abraham Lincoln," the crowd roared its approval and tried to move Lincoln, who had been sitting in the rear of the hall, through the densely packed crowd to the stage. Because he was unable to penetrate the throng, they hoisted him up and passed him forward over the heads of the multitude. Scrambling and crawling along this unsteady surface, he finally reached the platform, where half a dozen delegates set him upright. "The cheering," reported an observer, "was like the roar of the sea. Hats were thrown up by the Chicago delegation, as if hats were no longer useful." Lincoln, who "rose bowing and blushing," appeared to be "one of the most diffident and worst plagued men I ever saw." With a smile, he thanked the crowd for its expression of esteem.[62]

After the aspirants for governor had been placed in nomination but before the voting for governor began (in which Yates defeated Swett and Judd), Oglesby once again interrupted, announcing that "an old Democrat of Macon county" wanted "to make a contribution to the Convention," whereupon Lincoln's cousin John

Hanks, accompanied by a friend, entered the hall bearing two fence rails along with a placard identifying them thus: "Abraham Lincoln, The Rail Candidate for President in 1860. Two rails from a lot of 3,000 made in 1830 by Thos. Hanks and Abe Lincoln—whose father was the first pioneer of Macon County." (The sign painter was wrong about Hanks's first name and about Thomas Lincoln's status as an early settler in Illinois.) Oglesby's carefully staged gesture, conjuring up images of the 1840 log-cabin-and-cider campaign, electrified the crowd, which whooped and hollered for more than ten minutes. In response to those thunderous cheers and calls of "Lincoln," the candidate-to-be rose, examined the rails, then sheepishly told the crowd that he couldn't say whether they had been hewn by him, "but one thing I *will* say—I've made a good many better looking rails than either one of them."[63] Once again the crowd cheered Lincoln, whose sobriquet "the Railsplitter" was born that day.

The next day, when John M. Palmer introduced a resolution "that Abraham Lincoln is the first choice of Illinois for the Presidency, and that our delegates be instructed to use all honorable means for his nomination . . . and to cast their votes as a unit for him," the convention enthusiastically passed it. Obviously moved by this tribute, Lincoln briefly expressed his heartfelt thanks. The committee charged with selecting four at-large delegates, acting on Lincoln's advice, chose David Davis and Norman B. Judd. The two other at-large delegates, also selected by Lincoln, were Gustave Koerner and Orville H. Browning, a Bates supporter with close ties to the Old Whigs. Lincoln explained: "I know that old Browning is not for me . . . but it won't do to leave him out of the convention," for he "will do more harm on the outside than he could on the inside." Lincoln was "satisfied that Bates has no show. When Orville sees this he'll undoubtedly come over to me, and do us some good with the Bates men."[64] In the end, Browning did exactly that. Of the eighteen delegates chosen by congressional district, a few were pro-Seward, but operating under the unit rule, all would vote for Lincoln.

Two delegates who were staying at the same Decatur hotel as Lincoln invited him to accompany them to Chicago for the national convention. "I should like to go," Lincoln replied, "but possibly I am too much of a candidate to be there—and probably not enough to keep me away—on the whole I think I had best not go." Enthusiastically they declared that "as to that, Mr. Lincoln, we are going to nominate you," and they boarded a train for the Windy City.[65]

Though the Illinoisans were prepared to work hard for Lincoln's nomination, they did not really expect him to win. It was widely assumed that they would cast a complimentary vote for him, then turn to some other candidate. Above all they wanted to stop Seward, whose nomination would make it impossible to win the legislature, which was to choose a U.S. senator in 1861. They dreaded the prospect of a Democrat replacing Trumbull. For all his recent successes and optimistic calculations, Lincoln shared the delegation's doubts about his chances at Chicago. He cautiously guessed that he might receive around one hundred votes. "I have a notion that will be the high mark for me," he predicted.[66] To William Bross, who suggested that he should be preparing his acceptance speech, Lincoln somewhat less cautiously replied: "Well, it does look a little that way; but we can never be sure about such things."[67]

15.

"The Most Available Presidential Candidate for Unadulterated Republicans"

The Chicago Convention (May 1860)

In May 1859, Lincoln's friend Nathan M. Knapp prophetically called him "the most available" (i.e., the most electable) presidential candidate "for unadulterated Republicans."[1] By the time the party's national convention met in 1860, that view had become so prevalent that the Rail-splitter was able to capture the Republican nomination. But his success was not inevitable; he faced strong rivals, most notably New York senator William Henry Seward, the odds-on favorite.

Undermining Seward

On May 12, Lincoln's operatives met in the Windy City, where they established headquarters at the Tremont House. David Davis took command, ably assisted by Eighth Circuit lawyers like Leonard Swett, old friends like Stephen T. Logan, as well as many others. Their strategy was simple: first, stop Seward; then line up about one hundred delegates for Lincoln on the first ballot; then make sure that he had more votes on the second ballot in order to show momentum; finally, clinch the nomination on the third ballot.

Davis assigned his troops to work tactfully with the delegates, greeting them upon their arrival in Chicago, escorting them to their lodgings, and making sure that all their needs were met. These handlers engaged in no aggressive salesmanship but rather urged the delegates to consider making Lincoln their second choice, if not their first. To those favoring Seward, they quietly argued that the New Yorker, unlike Lincoln, could not carry the key swing states Illinois, Indiana, Pennsylvania, and New Jersey. A similar argument was made to Bates supporters, led by Horace Greeley, who was serving as a proxy delegate from Oregon as well as a Bates manager. The Lincoln men persuaded Bates's delegates to support the Rail-splitter as their second choice, arguing that most Westerners thought the party would surely lose the national election if Chase or Seward were its standard-bearer. The only serious objection to Lincoln was that he was as radical—and thus as unelectable—

as Seward. To combat that impression, Lincoln notified his operatives, "I agree with Seward in his 'Irrepressible Conflict,' but I do not endorse his 'Higher Law' doctrine."[2]

After helping to slow the Seward bandwagon, Davis and his coterie turned their attention to the Indiana delegation, which at first seemed divided among supporters of Bates, John McLean, and Cassius M. Clay. Strengthening Lincoln's chances was his personal acquaintance with some Indiana delegates whom he knew from his circuit court practice in counties near the Hoosier State. Helping to win over those men was the eloquence of Gustave Koerner. When he heard that Frank Blair and other Bates spokesmen were addressing the Indianans, he hurried to their conclave in order to tout Lincoln. Koerner denied that Bates could win his home state against Douglas and insisted that the Missourian, who had backed Know-Nothings in previous elections, did not deserve the support of Germans. Bates's champions Caleb B. Smith and John D. Defrees reluctantly concluded that their man could not win. David Davis evidently promised that Lincoln would appoint Smith to his cabinet, which helped persuade the delegates to support the Railsplitter. (In 1861, Lincoln named Smith secretary of the interior).

The Platform

As the convention opened, the city was so overrun with visitors that some wound up sleeping on tables at billiard parlors. The convention hall, specially built of rough timber for the occasion, was called the Wigwam because it resembled an Indian longhouse. A large, clumsy, solid, barn-like structure measuring 100 × 180 feet, with a seating capacity of twelve thousand, it was like a huge theater whose stage was reserved for delegates and journalists. The excellent acoustics allowed an ordinary voice to be easily heard throughout the building.

The first two days were devoted to routine business and to consideration of a platform that criticized attempts to limit the rights of immigrants; condemned disunionism, the popular sovereignty doctrine, and threats to reopen the African slave trade; upheld the power of states to regulate their own institutions; denounced the Buchanan administration's corruption and support of the Lecompton Constitution; maintained that the normal condition of the territories was freedom; called for the immediate admission of Kansas as a Free State; and endorsed protective tariffs, internal improvements (including a Pacific railroad), and homestead legislation.

Wooing Pennsylvania and New England

Meanwhile, behind the scenes, David Davis and his allies, having secured Indiana, turned their attention to Pennsylvania, whose favorite-son candidate, Simon Cameron, would receive almost all the state's votes on the first ballot but stood no chance of winning the nomination. Illinois gained the Pennsylvanians' support with the material aid of John A. Andrew of Massachusetts. On the eve of the convention, he headed a New England delegation that made a proposition to their Keystone State counterparts. Although ideologically sympathetic to Seward, the New Englanders wanted above all to win in November and feared that the New Yorker could not do so; along with the rest of the convention delegates, they regarded Pennsylvania, New Jersey, Indiana, and Illinois as the keys to victory. New Jersey, like Pennsylvania, was backing a favorite son, William L. Dayton, who was clearly unable to secure the nomination. Illinois and Indiana supported Lincoln. So Andrew proposed that the four swing states hold a joint caucus and try to unite on a candidate.

The delegates from those states met on May 17. Thomas Dudley of New Jersey, observing that no compromise candidate was emerging, successfully moved that a special committee of three members from each state recommend a standard-bearer. David Davis headed the Illinois contingent, Caleb B. Smith the Indianans, and Dudley the Jerseymen. That evening they all gathered in David Wilmot's rooms, where for five hours they negotiated inconclusively. Dudley then suggested that each delegation rank order its preferences. Indiana, Illinois, and New Jersey quickly determined that Lincoln was the one they could agree upon. In Pennsylvania, Cameron topped the list, and McLean, championed by Thaddeus Stevens, was second. Since neither of them could win the nomination, the choice of the third name would determine how Pennsylvania would go after casting a complimentary vote for her native son. The contest between Lincoln and Bates for that crucial third spot was close, with the Illinoisan prevailing by a few votes after a tense debate. Governor Andrew G. Curtin, along with some of Cameron's supporters who favored the selection of Congressman John Hickman or John M. Read as vice president, swung the delegation to support Lincoln. (On the first day of the convention, there had been much talk of a Lincoln-Hickman ticket.) That choice by the twelve-member committee proved to be a crucial and unexpected turning point.

The night of May 17, while Sewardites complacently swilled champagne in anticipation of their impending triumph, David Davis and his team lobbied furiously for Lincoln. Davis wanted to cut a deal with the Pennsylvanians, but the previous day Lincoln had sent a terse message via Edward L. Baker: "*Make no contracts that will bind me*." When Baker read that instruction to those gathered at the Lincoln headquarters, they erupted in laughter. Davis, who guffawed louder than anyone, said: "Lincoln ain't here, and don't know what we have to meet, so we will go ahead, as if we hadn't heard from him, and he must ratify it."[3] Davis and Swett negotiated with the leading Cameron operatives deep into the night. In the wee hours of Friday morning, Cameron was apparently offered a cabinet post in return for the votes of the Pennsylvania delegates.

In addition to slowing Seward's momentum and gaining Indiana's twenty-six votes and most of Pennsylvania's fifty-four (at least on the second ballot), Davis and his allies tried to bolster their strength at the very outset of the polling. They found crucial support in New England, which would lead off the roll call. Thurlow Weed, Seward, and many delegates assumed that at least the northern part of that region was solidly behind the New Yorker. If Seward's support there proved weak at the opening stage of the first ballot, and Lincoln's stronger than anticipated, it might have a profound psychological effect.

Gideon Welles, a Chase partisan, rallied New Englanders against Seward. Some New Hampshiremen had long been working on Lincoln's behalf. Leonard Swett, born and raised in Maine, lobbied his old friends from the Pine Tree State. He was assisted by Hannibal Hamlin, who worked behind the scenes to keep the Maine delegation from endorsing Seward. The uncommitted Maine delegates wanted to support William P. Fessenden, but when he expressed no interest, they decided to vote for Lincoln. In delegations from the South and the Midwest, David Davis's minions also trolled for votes. By the time the convention opened on May 16, Lincoln's operatives felt confident that they had secured about one hundred votes for the initial ballot, with some reserves to be added on the next one.

Victory

Thurlow Weed and his allies boasted that Seward's nomination was assured. Straw polls taken on trains pouring into Chicago indicated overwhelming support for the senator. At his headquarters the night before balloting started, champagne corks popped like firecrackers and bands played festive music. But that night, while Davis and his crew were busily securing the Pennsylvania delegation, some anti-Seward New Yorkers, led by David Dudley Field, were also hard at work lobbying against the front-runner. Weed planned to have a gigantic claque of Seward supporters infiltrate the Wigwam and stampede the convention. When the Lincolnites discovered that scheme, they persuaded a Chicago printer to run off five thousand copies of an admission ticket that were then evenly distributed between Illinois and Indiana contingents, which arrived at the Wigwam early on May 18, the day of the balloting.

That morning, while the cocksure Seward forces marched across town, the Lincoln shouters were already streaming into the Wigwam. After parading through the streets, the Sewardites were astounded to learn that they could not all enter the packed convention hall even though they held tickets. Also frustrating the Seward forces was the seating arrangement devised by Norman B. Judd, who as a member of the Republican National Committee had been assigned that task. Judd surrounded the New York delegation with other solid Seward delegations, effectively

This photograph was taken by Alexander Hesler in Chicago on June 3, 1860, less than three weeks after the Chicago convention. "That looks better and expresses me better than any I have ever seen," Lincoln allegedly said; "if it pleases the people I am satisfied." That year a journalist wrote that Lincoln was 51 years of age, "but he certainly has no appearance of being so old. His hair is black, hardly touched with gray, and his eye is brighter than that of many of his juniors." Illinois State Historical Society, Springfield, Illinois.

cordoning the New Yorkers off from the undecided states. Judd seated the Illinois and Indiana delegations close to their Pennsylvania and Missouri counterparts.

By the time Seward's name was placed in nomination, enough of his men had somehow gained admission to create a deafening roar that took Lincoln's supporters aback. Then, said Swett, "our people tested their lungs."[4] Although George Ashmun, president of the convention, banged his gavel and ordered silence, the audience "rose above all cry of order, and again and again the irrepressible applause broke forth and resounded far and wide."[5] Spectators were electrified by this sudden, vehement outburst—none more so than Seward's forces, who "turned pale and looked wild."[6] But they rallied when their man's nomination was seconded, and they outshouted the Lincolnites. "The effect was startling," reported Murat Halstead. "Hundreds of persons stopped their ears in pain. The shouting was absolutely frantic, shrill and wild."[7] The Lincoln forces then responded at an even greater decibel level, shouting and yelling for five minutes.

The shouting duel continued throughout the first ballot, with the Lincolnites winning each round. Color drained from the faces of the Sewardites at the unexpected announcement that Maine, instead of going for their champion as a unit, was awarding six votes to Lincoln. Following on the heels of that shocker came New Hampshire, which gave seven votes to Lincoln and only one to Seward. With those two states polled, Seward had fallen behind in a region where he was supposedly dominant. Many New England delegates wept while acknowledging that they had to desert Seward because of his inability to win Pennsylvania and Indiana. Of the eighty-two New England delegates, Seward received a disappointing thirty-two to Lincoln's nineteen. Another shock came when Virginia, a presumed Seward stronghold, cast fourteen votes for Lincoln and only eight for the senator.

Lincoln's backers were ecstatic when the results of the first ballot were announced: Seward had 173½ votes (only 3½ from the Lower North); Lincoln, 102; Cameron, 50½; Chase, 49; Bates, 48; with the rest scattering. The tally dealt a deathblow to Seward's chances, for clearly Lincoln, Cameron, Chase, and Bates could stop the New Yorker. On the next ballot, Vermont gave Lincoln all ten of its votes, and he picked up five more in Connecticut and Rhode Island. He now topped Seward in New England, thirty-six to thirty-three. Then came a stunning announcement: Pennsylvania cast forty-eight votes for Lincoln, a net gain of forty-four. That proved the clincher. The second-ballot totals showed Seward with 184½ votes; Lincoln with 181; Chase, 42½; Bates, 35; and the rest scattering.

As the third round of voting began, the suspense was palpable. Gains in Massachusetts, New Jersey, Pennsylvania, Maryland, Kentucky, Ohio, and Oregon gave Lincoln a total of 231½, a scant one and a half votes short of victory. Seward had slipped to 180, despite Weed's best efforts. Suddenly the Wigwam grew silent. In the stillness could be heard only pencils scratching and telegraph instruments clicking. Because Chairman Ashmun had not yet announced the result, changes could still be made. Everybody looked around to see who would put Lincoln over the top. The chairman of the Ohio delegation, David K. Cartter, suddenly sprang upon his chair, having just been told by Joseph Medill, "If you can throw the Ohio vote for Lincoln, Chase can have anything he wants."[8] Managing to catch the attention of the chairman, Cartter won recognition and declared: "I rise (eh)

Mr. Chairman (eh) to announce the change of four votes of Ohio from Mr. Chase to Mr. Lincoln."[9] After a brief moment of stillness, the Wigwam erupted. Delegates jumped on benches, screamed, cheered, and waved their hats. Atop the building, a cannon repeatedly fired announcements of the result to the immense crowd outside.

Amid this pandemonium, Thurlow Weed and several of his fellow delegates from the Empire State wept openly. Finally, a sorrowful William M. Evarts mounted a table and, with his eyes glistening, graciously moved that the nomination be made unanimous. Orville Browning responded with a speech on behalf of the Lincolnites, thus ending the morning session. Supporters of the Rail-splitter celebrated manically while Seward backers "were terribly stricken down," Murat Halstead reported.[10] At the Tremont House, Lincoln's operatives celebrated wildly, forming processions, drinking gallons of whiskey, and carrying rails through the streets. That afternoon the convention chose as Lincoln's running mate the affable and portly Maine senator Hannibal Hamlin, a longtime opponent of slavery. As a former Democrat, he lent both geographical and ideological balance to the ticket.

Some delegates believed Lincoln would have triumphed at Chicago even if no bargains with the Indiana and Pennsylvania delegations had been struck, because his 1858 debates with Douglas and his 1860 Cooper Union speech had won him respect from all factions and because he was widely viewed as the only candidate with solid antislavery credentials who could carry the swing states. While it is true that the delegates made the rational choice, political conventions are not always ruled by reason. It is not at all unthinkable that without the able leadership of Davis and Judd, the support of their indefatigable operatives, the decision to hold the convention in Chicago, and the influence of the stentorian pro-Lincoln shouters, Seward could have been the Republican nominee.

Reaction in Springfield

When news of Lincoln's victory reached Springfield, the dispatch bearer rushed into the office of the *Illinois State Journal*, where the candidate and a large crowd had been following events, and proposed three cheers. After the huzzahing died down, Lincoln took the dispatch, read it, and said: "I must go home; there is a little short woman there that is more interested in this matter than I am." En route people stopped him on the street to offer congratulations. He thanked them and jestingly said, "You had better come and shake hands with me now that you have an opportunity—for you do not know what influence this nomination may have on me. I am human, you know."[11]

Springfielders rejoiced fervently, dragging a cannon from the capitol to celebrate. Lincoln banners of all varieties waved in the breeze, and church bells hailed the victory of the local hero. In the evening, townsfolk surged to the statehouse to hear speeches, then marched to Eighth and Jackson Streets to serenade the nominee. When the crowd rushed forward to shake his hand, Lincoln invited them into his modest home. One of the revelers streaming across the threshold shouted, "We'll give you a larger house on the fourth of next March!"[12]

And so they would.

16.

"I Have Been Elected Mainly on the Cry 'Honest Old Abe'"

The Presidential Campaign (May–November 1860)

Shortly after the Chicago convention, Joshua Giddings assured Lincoln that "your selection was made upon two grounds," first that "you are an *honest* man" and second that "you are not in the hands of corrupt or dishonest men."[1] Hostility to corruption not only contributed to Lincoln's nomination in May, it also helped clinch his victory in November. The public was fed up with steamship lobbies, land-grant bribery, hireling journalists, the spoils system, rigged political conventions, and cost overruns on government projects. After winning the presidency, Lincoln told a visitor, "All through the campaign my friends have been calling me 'Honest Old Abe,' and I have been elected mainly on that cry."[2] His reputation as an honest man proved as important as his reputation as a foe of slavery.

Formal Notification

Mary Lincoln, whose childhood dream of becoming First Lady was about to come true, busily prepared for the arrival of an official delegation formally notifying her husband of his nomination. Reaching Springfield before the others was an advance party of that committee, including Ebenezer Peck, who suggested to some townspeople that Mrs. Lincoln should be informed that her presence when the committee called would be inappropriate. Too timid to do so, the townsfolk replied: "Go up and tell her yourself."[3] When Peck and Gustave Koerner called at the Lincolns' house, they were taken aback at the sight of brandy decanters, champagne baskets, cakes, and sandwiches all spread out. (The alcoholic beverages had been provided by Lincoln's neighbors, who knew he was a teetotaler.) When Mrs. Lincoln came in and asked what Peck and Koerner thought of the repast, they replied that it was not advisable, for some of the committee members might be temperance men. She protested vigorously until Koerner finally instructed a servant to remove the beverages.

When the committee did call on the evening of May 19, Mrs. Lincoln swept into the parlor wearing a fancy low-necked dress, while Lincoln had donned a new, ill-fitting black suit. When the dignitaries arrived, he greeted them with an awkward bow. After George Ashmun, head of the delegation, briefly explained their mission, Lincoln replied that he was "deeply, and even painfully sensible of the great responsibility which is inseparable from that honor—a responsibility which I could almost wish had fallen upon some one of the far more eminent men and experienced statesmen whose distinguished names were before the Convention." He promised to reply soon in writing.[4] Lincoln made a favorable impression on his visitors, most of whom felt completely at ease in his house. Upon leaving, they expressed relief and gratification. One declared: "Well, we might have done a more brilliant thing, but we could hardly have done a better thing."[5]

As he composed his acceptance letter, Lincoln heard from several leaders urging him to soft-pedal the platform's immigration plank, but he ignored such counsel and endorsed the entire platform.

Placating the Losers

Lincoln's first task after his nomination was to placate the disgruntled losers at Chicago. Chase and Bates presented no problem, for they quickly assured the candidate of their support. Cameron, however, stayed aloof, delaying ten weeks before congratulating the nominee personally.

Mollifying Seward's disappointed followers presented the most formidable challenge. While still in Chicago, Thurlow Weed met with David Davis and Leonard Swett, who urged him to call on Lincoln before returning home. On May 24, Weed met with the candidate, who reported that his visitor "asked nothing of me, at all. He merely seemed to desire a chance of looking at me, keeping up a show of talk while he was at it. I believe he went away satisfied."[6] Two days after the meeting in Springfield, Weed's newspaper praised Lincoln warmly. As for the senator himself, Weed counseled Seward that "a prompt and cheerful acquiescence in the Nomination" was "not only wise, but a duty."[7] His frustrated, embittered, and mortified friend did not comply, however. He felt humiliated and thought of abandoning politics altogether. Lincoln salved some hurt feelings by reassuring New Yorkers that they would occupy honored places at the patronage trough.

Front Porch Campaign

As word of Lincoln's nomination spread throughout the North, jubilant Republicans set off fireworks, rang bells, ignited bonfires, illuminated buildings, erected rail fences, paraded by torchlight, cheered speakers, and fired cannons. Wide Awake organizations—groups of young Republican activists best known for night-time parades during which they carried tin torches on poles that they deemed "rails"—provided much of the campaign's hoopla. Lincoln himself said he "was not particularly fond of show and parade, and personally did not care much for such demonstrations," though he acknowledged that the Wide Awakes were useful in turning out crowds for speakers.[8]

Publishers scrambled to meet the great demand for information about the little-known Republican candidate. The most informative of the thirteen campaign lives that appeared in 1860 were by William Dean Howells, a young Ohio journalist who would later achieve literary fame, and John Locke Scripps, editor of the Chicago *Press and Tribune*. For Howells, Scripps, and other authors, Lincoln prepared an autobiographical sketch in which he said little about slavery, other than to reproduce his 1837 resolution denouncing the peculiar institution as based on "injustice and bad policy" and assert that his views had not changed since then. He devoted much more space to his Mexican War stand, correctly assuming that the Democrats would once again attack his record on that conflict. When Scripps sought to interview Lincoln, the candidate was initially reluctant to cooperate, telling his would-be biographer that "it is a great piece of folly to attempt to make anything out of my early life. It can all be condensed into a single sentence and that sentence you will find in Gray's Elegy: 'The short and simple annals of the poor.' That's my life, and that's all you or any one else can make of it."[9] Nevertheless, he told Scripps much about his life, which was then incorporated into the campaign biography, making it virtually an autobiography. Hastily the busy editor churned out ninety-six pages of copy, only to be instructed by the publisher to reduce it to thirty-two. After reluctantly making wholesale cuts, he apologized to Lincoln for the "sadly botched" final section.

Lincoln wrote few letters that season, in part because friends urged him to remain silent lest he, like Henry Clay, ruin his presidential chances by seeming to modify earlier positions. The National Republican Campaign Committee recommended that he follow the traditional custom of staying quietly at home during the campaign to avoid resembling an undignified "stump candidate." Lincoln spent most of his days in the state capitol, where he occupied the governor's office used by Yates only when the legislature was in session. Furnished with a sofa, a table, and a few armchairs, it could accommodate up to a dozen people comfortably. There was also a desk where his secretary, John G. Nicolay, worked. The industrious, efficient Nicolay was a 28-year-old, German-born journalist from Pike County who since 1857 had been clerking for Secretary of State Ozias M. Hatch.

In time the correspondence grew so heavy that Nicolay needed an assistant. To the committee covering Lincoln's extra expenses, Milton Hay proposed his young nephew John Hay. The committee agreed, and the 23-year-old Hay, a suave, intelligent, sophisticated graduate of Brown University, began working with Nicolay, who had been his school chum in Pittsfield, Illinois. Both young men later accompanied Lincoln to Washington, where they served as his private secretaries.

At the governor's office Lincoln received politicians from around the country. He usually told them a story, said nothing significant, and sent them home happy. He also met ordinary people who simply wished to see him. He was especially happy to greet friends from his early days in the state. No matter how eminent a figure he was entertaining, Lincoln, when informed that such a caller wished to see him, would promptly excuse himself to make his new guest comfortable. They would then reminisce about the old days. Lincoln's office was overrun with all kinds of visitors almost every day. He made no distinction between the great and the humble. His patience, affability, and dignity impressed his callers, including a few Southerners who found to their surprise that the prejudice against him was unjustified. Some visitors annoyed him, particularly the office seekers who swarmed to Springfield.

The prominent German American Republican orator Carl Schurz called on Lincoln at his house. As they discussed the campaign, Lincoln's manner was so unpretentious that Schurz could scarcely realize that he was in the presence of a man likely to become president in a few months. Afterward, Lincoln escorted his guest to the site where he was scheduled to speak. As the two men followed a brass band to the meeting place, Lincoln showed no signs of inflated ego but rather behaved as if nothing special had happened to him in the past few months. His neighbors waved and cheered, and he greeted them unselfconsciously with his usual cordiality. He declined to sit on the platform where Schurz spoke but instead took a seat in the front row. After listening to the impassioned young campaigner hold forth, Lincoln told him: "You are an awful fellow! I understand your power now!"[10]

None of Lincoln's many visitors were clients because he had stopped practicing law, save for a handful of cases to which he attended in June. Several artists called to sketch and paint him. Capturing Lincoln's image proved challenging. Jestingly he explained that it was "impossible to get my graceful motions in—that's the reason why none of the pictures are like me!"[11] Similarly, when told that none of the photographs accurately depicted him, he "laughingly suggested that it might not be desirable to have justice done to such forbidding features as his."[12] Lincoln was pleased by J. Henry Brown's miniature portrait, which he deemed "an excellent one, so far as I can judge. To my unpracticed eye, it is without fault."[13] Brown thought that there were "so many hard lines in his face that it becomes a mask to the inner man. His true character only shines when in an animated conversation or when telling an amusing tale."[14]

Alexander Hesler took this photograph in Chicago in February 1857. Lincoln called the likeness "a very true one; though my wife, and many others, do not. My impression is that their objection arises from the disordered condition of the hair." (The photographer had mussed Lincoln's hair to make him look more natural.) After Lincoln won the Republican presidential nomination in 1860, his supporters rushed a lithograph of the photo into print. Lincoln then enjoyed telling friends that newsboys hawking it on city streets cried out: "Ere's yer last picter of Old Abe! He'll look better when he gets his *hair* combed!" Abraham Lincoln Presidential Library and Museum, Springfield, Illinois.

Ultimately, the election hinged on the Whig/American voters of 1856, especially in Indiana and Pennsylvania, where gubernatorial contests were to be held in October. Such voters might easily follow the lead of their 1856 candidate, Millard Fillmore, who supported John Bell. To prevent that from happening was Lincoln's greatest electoral challenge. He realized that he must win over men like James O. Putnam, the postmaster in Fillmore's hometown of Buffalo and a close friend of the former president. Putnam came to admire Lincoln vastly and supported him rather than Bell, whose Constitutional Union Party stood no chance of carrying a Northern state, while electing Lincoln would at least rebuke the hated Democrats and stem the tide of corruption. In the end, Republican worries about Fillmore voters casting their lot with Bell proved unfounded. This reluctance to throw away their vote affected large numbers of Bell supporters above the Mason-Dixon line. Lincoln also had to win over protectionists as well as Know-Nothings in the Keystone State. Pennsylvanians had been hit hard by the Panic of 1857, which depressed iron and coal prices and threw thousands of men out of work. The unemployed blamed low tariff rates for their misery. Republican newspapers hammered away at the tariff issue incessantly.

Surveying the political landscape, Lincoln was not discouraged about his prospects. With the Democrats split and the Constitutional Union Party weakening them further in the Border States, his election began to look more and more likely as autumn approached. Optimistic though Lincoln was, he shared Henry Wilson's belief that unglamorous organizational work deserved more attention than it was receiving. He told that Massachusetts senator that the "point you press—the importance of thorough organization—is felt, and appreciated by our friends everywhere. And yet it involves so much more of dry, and irksome labor, that most of them shrink from it—preferring parades, and shows, and monster meetings. I know not how this can be helped. I do what I can in my position; but it does not amount to so much as it should."[15]

Publicly silent, Lincoln left it to party orators and newspapers to rebut charges that he was a deep-dyed abolitionist, that he had been unpatriotic during the Mexican War, that he sought to provoke warfare between the sections, that he had betrayed Henry Clay, and that he favored equality for Blacks. By September, the New York *Times* could observe that critics had abandoned their earlier attacks on Lincoln as a Radical. Some Northern Democratic papers, however, still termed him a dangerous extremist.

On August 6, a harbinger of things to come occurred in Missouri, where Frank Blair won election to the U.S. House on the Republican ticket, reversing the outcome of 1858. "I count that day as one of the happiest in my life," Lincoln said a few weeks later.[16] Elections were held in Ohio, Indiana, and Pennsylvania in October.

Assured by Pennsylvanians that their gubernatorial candidate, Andrew G. Curtin, would win easily, and with Ohio safely in hand, Lincoln advised that all efforts be focused on Indiana, where a fusion movement of the opposition parties threatened Henry S. Lane's chances of capturing the governorship. Republicans took Lincoln's counsel and flooded Indiana with money and speakers.

Favorable dispatches rolled in on election night until finally, a little after midnight, the Republican gubernatorial victories seemed assured. As his friends whooped and hollered, Lincoln alone retained his composure. He permitted himself to rejoice only upon receipt of Simon Cameron's telegram announcing the Pennsylvania result, which prompted him to remark: "Now Douglas might learn a lesson about what happens when one tries to get people opposed to slavery to vote for slavery. It is not my name, it is not my personality which has driven Douglas out of Indiana and Pennsylvania, it is the irresistible power of public opinion, which has broken with slavery."[17]

Those victories, Lincoln told Seward, "have surpassed all expectation, even the most extravagant."[18] But his approaching success also meant that he must soon cope with formidable challenges. After visiting Springfield in mid-October, David Davis wrote that "Lincoln looked as if he had a heavy responsibility resting on him. The cares & responsibilities of office will wear on him." Mary Lincoln, on the other hand, "seemed in high feather" at her prospects, according to Davis. She was "not to my liking," he added. "I dont think she would ever mesmerise any one." His feelings were not unique, he said, for the "people of Springfield do not love Lincoln's wife as they do him." Davis's hope "that she will not give her husband any trouble" would prove vain.[19]

After the October triumphs, attention shifted to New York, which the Democrats hoped to win, thus forcing the election into the House of Representatives. In August, Lincoln had told Weed, "I think there will be the most extraordinary effort ever made, to carry New-York for Douglas. . . . it will require close watching, and great effort on the other side."[20] His prediction seemed borne out later when the Bell, Breckinridge, and Douglas forces agreed on a unified slate of presidential electors. The fusionists spent lavishly, causing some alarm, for the overconfident Empire State Republicans had exported money to New Jersey and Delaware and could not match their opponents' last-minute outlays.

To improve the Republican chance of carrying the Empire State, Joseph Medill had been trying since June to persuade James Gordon Bennett to moderate the New York *Herald*'s criticism of the Republican ticket. That paper initially dismissed Lincoln as "an uneducated man—a vulgar village politician, without any experience worth mentioning in the practical duties of statesmanship, and only noted for some very unpopular votes which he gave while a member of Congress."[21] After speaking twice with the crusty Bennett, Medill reported to Lincoln that the editor had pledged that "he would not treat you harshly," for he "thought you would make a very respectable President, if you kept out of the hands of the radicals."[22]

Secession Threats

After the Republican victories in Ohio, Indiana, and Pennsylvania, Southern threats of secession grew louder. The South's reaction to Lincoln's impending victory puzzled Northerners, who regarded the Rail-splitter as a moderate. But to Southerners, the candidate's call for the "ultimate extinction" of slavery conjured up visions of the bloody revolt in Haiti two generations earlier and Nat Turner's uprising in 1831. Like most Republicans, Lincoln failed to take those Southerners seriously, in part because they had so frequently raised the specter of secession that their minatory blustering lacked credibility.

Secession threats backfired, for Northern voters had grown weary of Southern intimidation and contempt for fair play. The Chicago *Press and Tribune* assured Southerners "that they entirely underestimate the character of the Northern people, and that their 'boo-boos' and their 'bug-a-boos,' instead of frightening any one, are really helping Lincoln." Free State residents "have become entirely satisfied that the only way to effectually stop this threat of disunion, is by the election of a Republican President."[23] In fact, that fall many Northerners did vote Republican to protest against the arbitrary, high-handed behavior of the South.

As Douglas violated conventional political norms by stumping the country, he displayed true statesmanship by warning the South against disunion. While Lincoln's election might constitute "a great national calamity,"[24] he insisted that the South must abide by the result.

Victory in November

On election day, Springfield shed its customary tranquility as cannons boomed to herald the dawn. Augmenting their din were bands blaring from wagons drawn about the city to arouse the populace. That morning at the statehouse, Lincoln showed little concern as he received visitors, including some Illinoisans who wanted to see him in the flesh. Then came a few New Yorkers, who Lincoln thought should have remained home to vote. He told one resident of the Empire State that "he was afraid there were too many of us from New York that day." When that caller asked Lincoln whether the South would secede if the Republicans captured the White House, he "said they might make a little stir about it before [the inauguration], but if they waited until after his inauguration and for some overt act, *they would wait all their lives.*"[25]

Lincoln had intended to vote late in the day to avoid crowds; in midafternoon, however, when told that there were few people at the polls, he decided to cast his ballot then. To questioners seeking to know how he would vote for president, he responded: "How vote? Well, undoubtedly like an Ohio elector of which I will tell you—by ballot."[26] As he approached the courthouse, the crowd around it started shouting wildly and parted to allow him entrance to the polling place. They then followed him down the hall and up the stairs to the jam-packed courtroom, cheering him all the while. There the huzzahing grew louder still. Before depositing his ballot, Lincoln cut off the names of the presidential electors so that he would not be voting for himself.

Lincoln spent the rest of the afternoon at the capitol, where he discussed the election prospects of local and state candidates. To Ozias Hatch's observation "that it was lucky for him that women couldn't vote, otherwise the monstrous portraits of him which had been circulated during the canvass by friends would surely defeat him," Lincoln replied smilingly, "Hatch, I tell you there is a great deal more in that idea than you suppose."[27]

About 7:00 p.m., the crowd at the statehouse flooded into the room where Lincoln awaited the returns. When someone suggested that they be cleared out, he immediately objected, saying that "he had never done such a thing in his life and wouldn't commence now." The candidate remained cool and collected until a messenger arrived from the telegraph office; his face then betrayed a touch of anxiety. That first dispatch, from Decatur, showed a significant Republican gain over the previous election. It was greeted with shouts and taken from the governor's office to the assembly chamber as if it were a trophy. At 8:00 p.m. Lincoln was greatly pleased by a dispatch from Jacksonville indicating a significant Republican gain.

An hour later Lincoln and some friends left the statehouse for the telegraph office to see the returns as they arrived. Fragmentary reports from nearby counties were like tea leaves that Lincoln was able to read cannily. He was gleeful when news arrived from Saline County, where in 1856 Frémont had received one lone vote to Buchanan's nearly two thousand; now three of its main precincts gave Lincoln a majority of nearly two hundred more than Douglas. Laughingly he called the result "a tribute from Egypt to the success of our public school fund."

As the good news rolled in, Lincoln's friends and the telegraph operators could hardly contain their enthusiasm. The nominee himself, however, remained calm. A dispatch announcing that he had won by a twenty-five-hundred-vote margin in Chicago occasioned a thrill of elation. The candidate instructed: "Send it to the boys [over at the statehouse]." He was equally delighted with good news from St. Louis, where he had bested Douglas by more than nine hundred votes. When word from Pittsburgh arrived indicating that Lincoln had carried Allegheny County by ten thousand votes, he "remarked that this was better than expected."[28]

Soon returns arrived from more distant points. Lincoln betrayed some anxiety about the result in New York, "remarking that 'the news would come quick enough if it was good, and if bad, he was not in any hurry to hear it.'" Around 10:30, in response to a hopeful message from Thurlow Weed, Lincoln said "that the news was satisfactory so far, only it was not conclusive." Then returns from New Jersey showed that the Douglas-Bell-Breckinridge slate was doing surprisingly well. Offsetting this bad news were encouraging returns from New England. When word came in that Massachusetts had gone for him by fifty thousand, Lincoln called it "a clear case of the Dutch taking Holland."[29] As expected, he carried Pennsylvania easily. Worries about New York, however, persisted.[30] As predictable results rolled in from the South, Lincoln and his friends took a break shortly after midnight, visiting the collation prepared by the women of Springfield, who lined up to kiss him on the cheek.

Back in the telegraph office, cheering news from New York thrilled Lincoln's companions, but he observed solemnly: "Not too fast, my friends. Not too fast, it may not be over yet." When even more favorable reports arrived, Jesse K. Dubois asked. "Well, Uncle Abe, are you satisfied now?" Lincoln replied with a smile, "Well, the agony is most over, and you will soon be able to go to bed." When it was learned that Bell had carried Virginia, Lincoln "suggested that this was the most hopeful return for the peace of the country he had heard and he hoped the majority was so large as to crush out the fire-eaters completely. He spoke with considerable emphasis and satisfaction about the strength shown for the conservative American [i.e., Constitutional Union] ticket in the border States."[31]

Finally, when definitive word of his victory in New York arrived, he read the fateful dispatch with obvious pleasure. The crowd at the statehouse cheered lustily, tossed their hats, and even rolled about on the floor in uncontrollable delight. Men dashed through the streets to inform the citizenry that Lincoln had won. People shouted from their houses, stores, roofs, and everywhere else. After accepting hearty congratulations, Lincoln prepared to leave. When a messenger announced that he had won Springfield by sixty-nine votes, he abandoned his reserve and exuberantly let out an expression of joy that sounded like a cross between a cheer and a croak. Then he laughed contentedly, bade everyone good night, and returned home.

Several times the next day Lincoln told friends, "Well, boys, your troubles are over now, but mine have just commenced." As callers became more numerous, he held a regular levee, shaking the hands of all, including an elderly farmer who exclaimed, "Uncle Abe, I didn't vote for yer, but I am mighty glad yer elected just the same." Lincoln responded, "Well, my old friend, when a man has been tried and pronounced not guilty he hasn't any right to find fault with the jury."[32] David Davis reported from Springfield that "Mr. Lincoln seems as he always does. You would not think that he had been elevated to the highest office in the world."[33]

Lincoln made no formal response to his victory until a grand celebration took place in Springfield two weeks later. During that interim he received advice to make a Union-saving address that might appease Southern fire-eaters, but Joseph Medill insisted that "we want no speech from Lincoln . . . on political questions. W[e] are content with the Republican platform, his letter of acceptance and his published speeches."[34]

Although Lincoln won only 39.9 percent of the popular vote (far more than Douglas's 29 percent), he captured a solid majority of the electoral votes, 180 out of 303. He swept all the Free States except New Jersey, where the Bell, Breckinridge, and Douglas forces had created a fusion ticket at the last moment and received 52.1 percent of the ballots cast. (Because some anti-Lincoln voters refused to go for the fusion slate, the Republicans got four of the state's seven electoral votes.)

The Republicans triumphed because of their party's unity and the bitter split within the Democracy; because of the rapidly growing antislavery feeling in the North, where the Lecompton Constitution and the Dred Scott decision had outraged many who had not voted Republican in 1856; because of the North's ever-intensifying resentment of what it perceived as Southern arrogance, high-handedness, and bullying; because Germans defected from the Democratic ranks; because the Republican economic program was far more appealing both to farmers (with homestead legislation) and to manufacturers and workers (with tariffs) than the Democratic economic policies adopted in response to the Panic of 1857; because the rapidly improving economy blunted fears of businessmen as they contemplated a Republican victory; and because of public disgust at the corruption of Democrats, most notably those in the Buchanan administration. Lincoln did especially well among younger voters, former nonvoters, rural residents, skilled laborers, members of the middle class, newly eligible voters, German Protestants, evangelical Protestants, native-born Americans, and most particularly former Know-Nothings and Whig/Americans.

Correspondence, newspaper commentary, and other anecdotal sources also suggest that Lincoln's victory was in part owing to his character, his biography, and his public record. Throughout the campaign, Republicans emphasized the rail-splitting image in posters, transparencies, newspapers, cartoons, and oratory. In addition, Lincoln's reputation as "Honest Abe" helped his cause immeasurably. Corruption in the Pierce and Buchanan administrations, as well as in state and local governments throughout the 1850s, had scandalized the nation. Lincoln himself interpreted his election as a rebuke to corruptionists. During an interview that summer, he had spoken of corruption "as the bane of our American politics" and said that "he could not respect, either as a man or a politician, one who bribed or was bribed."[35]

The outcome of the election pleased some Radicals, including Frederick Douglass, who exulted: "For fifty years the country has taken the law from the lips of an exacting, haughty and imperious slave oligarchy. . . . Lincoln's election has vitiated their authority, and broken their power" and "has demonstrated the possibility of electing, if not an Abolitionist, as least [a man with] an anti-slavery reputation to the Presidency."[36] At the opposite end of the political spectrum, Southern fire-eaters prepared to carry out their secession threats. Well before the election, South Carolina, Alabama, and Mississippi had provided that if a Republican won the presidency, they would hold conventions to determine their response. On November 10, the Palmetto State legislature unanimously authorized such a convention to be elected three weeks later. Georgia and the five Gulf States rapidly followed suit. When the New York *Herald* predicted that "Lincoln's troubles will begin on the first day after his election," for the "selection of his cabinet will sow the bitterest discord among his supporters," it was only partially correct.[37] Lincoln faced the formidable challenge of uniting not only his young party but also the nation; and yet he would be unable to exercise power for four long, frustrating months, during which seven Slave States pulled out of the Union and others seemed likely to join them.

It is no wonder that Lincoln remarked upon learning of his triumph, "I feel a great responsibility. God help me, God help me."[38] The weight of that new responsibility kept him awake that night. He told a friend that though "much fatigued and exhausted he got but little rest." The next morning, he "rose early, oppressed with the overwhelming responsibility that was upon him and which he had not before fully realized."[39]

17.

"I Will Suffer Death before I Will Consent to Any Concession or Compromise"

President-elect in Springfield (1860–1861)

During the period separating his election from his inauguration, Lincoln faced the ominous challenge of Southern secession. Although he would not officially take office until March 1861, his party looked to him for guidance. Like most Republicans, he was startled when the Cotton States made good their supposedly idle threat to withdraw from the Union. Should they be allowed to go in peace? Should they be forcibly resisted? Should they be conciliated or appeased? What compromise measures might preserve national unity without sacrificing the Republican Party's principles? Like most of his Northern constituents-to-be, Lincoln sympathized with hard-liners rather than with appeasers and conciliators. Although accommodating by nature, he stubbornly refused to be bullied. Truculent Southerners and timid Northerners could not make him submit to what he considered unreasonable demands. Lincoln thought that Southern hotheads had been plotting secession for years and were looking for a convenient excuse to carry out their plans. "By no act or complicity of mine, shall the Republican party become a *mere sucked egg, all shell & no principle* in it," he told a visitor in January 1861.[1] Herndon assured Wendell Phillips that his partner would "make a grave yard of the South, if rebellion or treason lifts its head."[2] Lincoln's firmness was rooted in a profound self-respect that forbade knuckling under to what he perceived as extortionate bullying. He insisted that "he did not wish to *pay* for being inaugurated."[3]

In addition, his hatred of slavery and his unwillingness to abandon the principle of majority rule made him reluctant to appease disunionists. Moreover, if secession were tolerated, the nation and the ideals for which it stood—that ordinary people should have a significant voice in their governance and be allowed to advance socially and economically as far as their talent, virtue, industry, and ability allowed—would be discredited. Practical political considerations also influenced his thinking, for he could ill afford to alienate Republicans who opposed any abandonment of the party's platform.

Answering Mail and Receiving Visitors

Lincoln was so inundated with mail that he "reads letters constantly—at home—in the street—among his friends," according to John Hay, who added: "I believe he is strongly tempted in church."[4] The sculptor Thomas D. Jones, who executed a bust of Lincoln that winter, told a friend that the president-elect "generally opened about seventy letters every morning in my [hotel] room. He *read* all the *short* ones—laid all of the long ones aside."[5] The journalist Henry Villard observed that the mail emanating "from representatives of all grades of society" included missives from impulsive Southerners containing "senseless fulminations, and, in a few instances, disgraceful threats and indecent drawings."[6]

To carve out time to answer letters as well as to devise a Southern policy, to consider cabinet appointments, and to compose his inaugural address, Lincoln restricted public visits to two hours in the morning and two and a half hours in the afternoon. (He usually arose before dawn, breakfasted around 7:00 a.m., arrived at the office by 8:00, and read mail and held private interviews until 10:00.) A typical levee began with the crowd making its way up the stairs of the statehouse to the governor's reception room, which continued to be available to Lincoln throughout November and December. (Thereafter he used a room in the nearby Johnson's Building.) Upon reaching their destination, callers were greeted by the president-elect, who shook hands with the leader of the delegation and heartily announced, "Get in, all of you." After informal introductions, he genially launched a conversation. All sorts of people availed themselves of the opportunity to call on the president-elect. Some men wore mud-caked brogans and hickory shirts, others elegant broadcloth and linen garments. Most women were attired in their Sunday best. Not all visitors behaved well. Churls with their hats on and pants tucked into their boots and reeking of the barnyard would puff away on malodorous cigars while staring at Lincoln as if he were a museum object.

The president-elect showed no signs of self-importance, remaining ever the kind, good-natured, affable neighbor that he had been since his arrival in Springfield twenty-three years earlier. All visitors, even the most irksome, received a cordial greeting. He made no distinction between rich and poor, though he did manifest an unusually strong affection for friends from his early days in Illinois. He genially set guests at ease, joking, answering questions, and reminiscing.

Secession of the Lower South

That winter the nation trembled at the prospect of secession and the possibility of war. From December to February, seven states of the Deep South withdrew from the Union. When they formed the Confederate States of America in February 1861, the vice president of that new entity, Alexander H. Stephens of Georgia, asserted that its "foundations are laid, its corner-stone rests upon the great truth, that the negro is not equal to the white man; that slavery—subordination to the superior race—is his natural and normal condition."[7] Stephens and many others maintained that White liberty (by which they evidently meant harmony between the social classes) required Black slavery, and they refused to bow to the Republicans' policy forbidding them to take slaves into the territories. The South also feared losing power. As members of a traditional society, White Southerners resented the modernizing Northerners, whose watchwords were *improvement* and *progress*. Below the Mason-Dixon line, new economic, social, intellectual, and cultural trends enjoyed little favor. The Southern revolt against the Union thus represents, among other things, a chapter in the long history of traditionalist resistance to modernization.

On election night, when a report reached Springfield that both South Carolina senators had resigned their seats, it alarmed most of Lincoln's friends but not him. An Ohio journalist recalled that the president-elect considered secession "as a sort of political game of bluff, gotten up by politicians, and meant solely to frighten the North." Lincoln predicted that they "won't give up the offices. Were it believed that vacant places could be had at the North Pole, the road there would be lined with dead Virginians."[8]

Lincoln's optimism rested not only on the information derived from visitors and newspapers but also on his interpretation of the election results. In the Slave States, John C. Breckinridge, whose candidacy was widely interpreted as pro-secession (although the nominee himself repudiated disunionism), received only 44 percent of the vote. Together, Bell and Douglas won 110,000 more Southern votes than Breckinridge. Bell carried Virginia, Tennessee, and Kentucky and nearly won North Carolina, Maryland, and Missouri. In the months following the election, Lincoln took heart from the strong Unionist sentiment in the Upper South and the Border States, where slaves were less numerous and Whiggish sentiments and organizations more persistent than in the Deep South.

Lincoln was not unrealistic in imagining that the Upper South and the Border States might remain in the Union. After all, the Deep South had threatened to secede in 1832–33, 1850–51, and 1856; and as recently as 1859–60, South Carolina, Alabama, and Mississippi had failed to win support for disunion. He assumed that reasonable people understood that nothing, including his election, had occurred to justify secession. The Southern grievance most often cited was insufficiently rigorous enforcement of the Fugitive Slave Act. But very few slaves escaped from the South; in 1860 there were only 803, constituting less than one-fiftieth of 1 percent of the slave population, and most of those fled from the Border States, not the Deep South, where disunionist sentiment prevailed. To White Southerners the psychological cost was greater than the economic. "The loss of property is felt, the loss of honor is felt still more," said Virginia senator James M. Mason.[9]

Commercial interests in New York eagerly sought to appease the South, lest they suffer financially. In the month after the election, as legislatures in the Deep South authorized secession conventions, some influential Republican editors recommended conciliatory gestures, such as compensating slaveholders for runaways, repealing personal liberty laws, toughening enforcement of the Fugitive Slave Act, allowing slavery to expand, and restoring the Missouri Compromise line. In response to such trial balloons, Lincoln expressed surprise that "*any* Republican could think, for a moment, of abandoning in the hour of victory, though in the face of danger, every point involved in the recent contest."[10]

When urged to issue a statement placating the South, Lincoln declined, stressing that he must maintain his self-respect and submit to no demands that he appease unreasonable Southerners. "I could say nothing which I have not already said, and which is in print, and open for the inspection of all," he replied. "To press a repetition of this upon those who *have* listened, is useless; to press it upon those who have *refused* to listen, and still refuse, would be wanting in self-respect, and would have an appearance of sycophancy and timidity, which would excite the contempt of good men, and encourage bad ones to clamor the more loudly."[11]

On November 20, during a jubilation in Springfield, Lincoln spoke publicly for the first time since the election. His tone was far more conciliatory than the one he had used in private. A torchlight procession of Wide Awakes led an exultant crowd to his house, where they shouted themselves hoarse. Distinctly and emphatically, he told them: "I thank you, in common with all those who have thought fit, by their votes, to endorse the republican cause. . . . Yet in all our rejoicings let us neither express nor cherish any harsh feelings towards any citizen who by his vote has differed with us. Let us at all times remember that all American citizens are brothers of a common country, and should dwell together in the bonds of fraternal feeling."[12]

While these vague remarks offered little to reassure the South, Lincoln penned a more explicit statement that Lyman Trumbull incorporated into his speech that same day in Springfield: "I have labored in, and for, the Republican organization with entire confidence that whenever it shall be in power, each and all of the States will be left in as complete control of their own affairs respectively, and at as perfect liberty to choose, and employ, their own means of protecting property, and preserving peace and order within their respective limits, as they have ever been under any administration. Those who have voted for Mr. Lincoln, have expected, and still expect this; and they would not have voted for him had they expected otherwise." Lincoln decried the secessionists' "hot haste to get out of the Union."

Naively he added this closing thought: "I am rather glad of this military preparation in the South. It will enable the people the more easily to suppress any uprisings there, which their misrepresentations of purposes may have encouraged."[13]

The Democrats' scornful reaction to this speech reportedly persuaded people in Springfield (presumably including Lincoln) that "disunion has been determined upon, and that it will be accomplished at all hazards."[14] Secessionists sneered that Lincoln was "nothing but a weak, prejudiced local politician" from "a retired country village in the interior of Illinois."[15] Lincoln determined to offer no further public statements. In hindsight, his unwillingness to do so may have been a mistake. Such a document might have allayed fears in the Upper South and the Border States and predisposed them to remain in the Union when hostilities broke out. But it might also have wrecked the Republican coalition and doomed his administration to failure before it began.

While Lincoln did not issue formal statements before departing Springfield in February, he did make known his views in other ways. He sometimes spoke about the crisis with visitors, who then leaked his remarks to the press. But he would often qualify those remarks by saying that he hoped his callers "would bear in mind that he was not speaking as President, or for the President, but only exercising the privilege of talking which belonged to him, in common with private citizens."[16] Occasionally Lincoln let down his guard. When a visitor speculated that disunionists would seize Washington before his inauguration if they were not appeased, he replied: "I will suffer death before I will consent or will advise my friends to consent to any concession or compromise which looks like buying the privilege of taking possession of this government to which we have a constitutional right."[17] This strong statement was widely published in the Northern press. To a Missourian who urged him to support a "backdown declaration," Lincoln replied with emphasis that he "would sooner go out into his backyard & hang himself."[18]

Lincoln also used journalists to broadcast his views. From November to February, Henry Villard reported almost daily from Springfield, often describing the opinion of "the men at the capitol," which doubtless reflected the president-elect's thinking. In addition, Lincoln continued his decades-long habit of writing anonymous contributions to the Springfield *Illinois State Journal*, widely regarded as his mouthpiece. Major newspapers quoted the *Journal*'s editorials as if they represented his thinking. He occasionally granted formal interviews, in which he discussed public affairs. His assistant personal secretary, John Hay, also wrote anonymous dispatches for the St. Louis *Missouri Democrat* that described Lincoln's views.

As he followed events in the South, Lincoln conscientiously searched for precedents to guide him in shaping his response. When news reached Springfield that on December 20 South Carolina had officially seceded, it shook just about everyone except Lincoln, who quipped that "he would henceforth look for 'foreign inland news' in his dailies." Henry Villard concluded that "timidity is evidently no element of his moral composition" and that "there are dormant qualities in 'Old Abe' which occasion will draw forth, develope and remind people to a certain degree of the characteristics of 'Old Hickory' [Andrew Jackson]."[19]

Events in Georgia strengthened Lincoln's hope that South Carolina's example would not be imitated. The disunionist governor, Joseph E. Brown, met stiff resistance from prominent leaders like Alexander H. Stephens. Lincoln read Stephens's November 14 pro-Union speech before the Georgia legislature with pleasure and requested a copy from its author. Stephens, who had been a friend and ally of Lincoln's during the Illinoisan's one term in the House, argued that since the Democrats would control Congress, the new president could do little harm; that his mere election was no justification for rash action; and that secession should not be undertaken unless the federal government committed an aggressive act. On November 30, Lincoln was "reported to have said that the best item of news he had received since the 6th of November was that of Mr. Stephens' election as delegate to the Georgia State Convention." If that convention were to reject secession, the disunionist movement might collapse elsewhere.

In December, Lincoln asked Stephens: "Do the people of the South really entertain fears that a Republican administration would, *directly, or indirectly*, interfere with their slaves, or with them, about their slaves? If they do, I wish to assure you, as once a friend, and still, I hope, not an enemy, that there is no cause for such fears. The South would be in no more danger in this respect, than it was in the days of Washington. I suppose, however, this does not meet the case. You think slavery is *right* and ought to be extended; while we think it is *wrong* and ought to be restricted. That I suppose is the rub. It certainly is the only substantial difference between us."[20]

Responses to Secession in Washington—Buchanan and Seward

In December, the nation turned its eyes toward Washington, where Buchanan and Congress would confront the brewing storm. The weak, vacillating president disappointed Lincoln and most other Northerners by proclaiming that while secession was unconstitutional, the federal government could do nothing legally to stop it. The lame-duck president denounced the antislavery movement and blamed the crisis on the "long-continued and intemperate interference of the Northern people with the question of slavery in the Southern states."[21] Lincoln was incensed at Buchanan's ascription of blame for the crisis to the antislavery forces rather than to the Southern fire-eaters. When the president's message was referred to a special thirty-three-member House committee, Lincoln's fear of a split between Radical and conservative Republicans grew. He thought such a committee was too big and made up of too many diverse elements. He was right; the committee, which wrangled throughout the winter, failed to reach a consensus.

Dominating Congress that winter, Seward maneuvered desperately to keep the Union intact. He viewed himself as a well-informed realist who must somehow save the nation from fire-eaters in the Deep South and naive stiff-backed Republicans like Lincoln, who failed to understand the gravity of the crisis. He paid lip service to upholding the party's principles while urging his colleagues "to practice reticence and kindness."[22] Meanwhile, behind the scenes he maneuvered to win concessions that might placate the South even if they violated the Republican platform. Privately (but not publicly) he supported the Crittenden Compromise, which would have allowed slavery to expand south of the Missouri Compromise line, latitude 36°30′. Seward was delighted to learn that the House Committee of Thirty-Three would contain pro-compromise members. On December 18, the Senate established a Committee of Thirteen, akin to that House committee, and named Seward a member. Alarmed by the ferocity of Deep South secessionists, many Republicans joined Seward in favoring conciliation.

Behind-the-Scenes Pressure by Lincoln to Resist Appeasement

In mid-December, the special House committee almost adopted a conciliatory proposal, but it failed thanks largely to Lincoln's behind-the-scenes intervention. To him, the plan contained "too great a sacrifice of principles," and he opposed it adamantly. Slavery, he insisted, must not be allowed to expand. The symbolic significance of the issue of slavery in the territories, as well as its practical implications, dominated his thinking in the winter of 1860–61. On December 6, he wrote to Congressman William Kellogg, Illinois's representative on the Committee of Thirty-Three, who had asked him for guidance: "Entertain no proposition for a compromise in regard to the *extension* of slavery. The instant you do, they have us under again; all our labor is lost, and sooner or later must be done over. Douglas is sure to be again trying to bring in his 'Pop. Sov.' Have none of it. The tug has to come & better now than later. You know I think the fugitive slave clause of the constitution ought to be enforced—to put it on the mildest form, ought not to be resisted." He wrote similar letters to Elihu B. Washburne, Lyman Trumbull, and others.[23]

While privately refusing to support the Crittenden Compromise, Lincoln continued to balk at issuing a public statement. He was doubtless correct in thinking that no statement would placate the Deep South. His legendary patience wore thin as disunionists continued to misrepresent him. He lamented that the South "has eyes but does not see, and ears but does not hear."[24] Back in Washington, Seward, aware that his original strategy of "reticence and kindness" was not working, decided to take the offensive. He dispatched Weed to Springfield to lobby the president-elect on behalf of the Crittenden Compromise. But Lincoln strenuously rejected it and gave Weed the following resolutions to pass along to Seward for submission to Congress:

> That the fugitive slave clause of the Constitution ought to be enforced by a law of Congress, with efficient provisions for that object, not obliging private persons to assist in it's execution, but punishing all who resist it, and with the usual safeguards to liberty, securing free men against being surrendered as slaves—
>
> That all state laws, if there be such, really, or apparently, in conflict with such law of Congress, ought to be repealed; and no opposition to the execution of such law of Congress ought to be made—
>
> That the Federal Union must be preserved.

Lincoln felt that these resolutions "would do much good, if introduced and unanimously supported by our friends."[25] Weed was instructed to show them to the vice president elect, Hannibal Hamlin, and Trumbull; if they approved, he was to have them introduced in Congress.

Lincoln's emphatic opposition to the Crittenden Compromise was partly responsible for its defeat in the Committee of Thirteen on December 22 and in the Senate on January 16. The day of the first vote, Charles Francis Adams observed that the "declarations coming almost openly from Mr Lincoln have had the effect of perfectly consolidating the Republicans."[26] Senator Henry Wilson reported that some congressional Republicans "are weak; most of them are firm. Lincoln's firmness helps our weak ones."[27]

It was one of Lincoln's most fateful decisions, for the Kentucky senator's scheme, though fraught with many practical problems and silent on the constitutionality of secession and the right of a legally elected president to govern, represented the best hope of placating the Upper South and thus possibly averting war, though it was a forlorn hope at best, given Southern intransigence. The House Committee of Thirty-Three might have approved Crittenden's plan, which the Conditional Unionists of the Upper South regarded as the bare minimum for remaining in the Union, if the Democrats had not insisted that slavery be protected south of latitude 36°30′ in all future acquisitions as well as in territory already belonging to the United States. Although Senate Republicans rejected the compromise, it still could have passed the upper house on January 16 if three of the six Southern senators in attendance had voted for it instead of abstaining; similarly, on December 22, if two abstaining Democratic senators on the Committee of Thirteen had voted for the compromise, it would have received the endorsement of that body.

Stiff-backed Republicans cheered Lincoln's course. Carl Schurz told his wife that the president-elect "stands firm as an oak" and that "his determination is imparted to the timorous members of the party."[28] Joshua Giddings came away from an interview with the president-elect convinced that "he intends doing *right*" and will "endeavor to carry out the doctrines of the Republican platform."[29] The leading Senate Radical, Charles Sumner, was optimistic about defeating compromise proposals because "Lincoln stands firm. *I know it*."[30]

Lincoln could not be aware that his rejection of the Crittenden plan would necessarily help pave the road to war. He believed that if he were conciliatory on all matters other than slavery expansion and secession, the Upper South and the Border States would remain in the Union and the Deep South, after a sober second thought, might well return to the fold. In retrospect, that seems like wishful thinking, but it was not unreasonable, given the size of the Bell and Douglas vote in the South and other indications that disunionism enjoyed only limited popularity there. It was widely believed that many secessionists had no intention of leaving the Union permanently but simply wanted to strengthen their bargaining position in negotiations with the North, hoping to extort concessions through a temporary withdrawal.

Lincoln doubtless shared the widespread, erroneous belief that if a war broke out, it would be short and relatively bloodless.

18.

"What If I Appoint Cameron, Whose Very Name Stinks in the Nostrils of the People for His Corruption?"

Cabinet-Making in Springfield (1860–1861)

As he struggled with the thorny problem of secession, Lincoln faced a related challenge: selecting a cabinet. Should he take a Southern Democrat or a Constitutional Unionist? Many Republican conciliators urged him to choose at least one of them. He was not averse, but who? And among the Republicans, should he select only ex-Whigs or form a coalition government including ex-Democrats? Should he favor the conservatives, the moderates, or the radicals? The day after the election he had tentatively chosen his department chiefs, but six weeks later he complained that "the making of a cabinet, now that he had it to do, was by no means as easy as he had supposed."[1] Throughout the long weeks from the election until his departure from Springfield, callers besieged Lincoln offering advice about the cabinet.

Many executives fear to surround themselves with strong-willed subordinates who might overshadow them, but Lincoln did not. When advised against appointing Salmon P. Chase because the Ohioan regarded himself as "a great deal bigger" than the president-elect, Lincoln asked: "Well, do you know of any other men who think they are bigger than I am? I want to put them all in my cabinet."[2] He was both remarkably modest and self-confident. He did not need to be surrounded by sycophants dependent on him for political preferment; instead he chose men with strong personalities, large egos, and politically significant followings whose support was necessary for the administration's success.

Initial Appointments: Secretary of State, Attorney General

Seward's stature as a leading exponent of Republican principles virtually guaranteed that he would be named secretary of state. Physically unprepossessing, he had a powerful personality and a keen intellect. One of his bitterest enemies in the Lincoln administration, Montgomery Blair, called him "a kindly man in his social relations" who "had a warm and sympathetic feeling for all that pertained to his domestic life."[3] Although he got off to a rocky start with Lincoln, the two men became close friends. The president appointed him because of "his ability, his integrity, and his commanding influence, and fitness for the place";[4] in time he came to value the New Yorker's wit, charm, and bonhomie.

Lincoln sent Hannibal Hamlin two letters to deliver to Seward, one a brief, formal offer of the State Department portfolio, the other a longer, more personal appeal. Hamlin presented the letters offering Seward the State Department post with the hope he would accept. Seward responded cautiously, promising to answer "at the earliest practicable moment."[5] Having failed to win Lincoln's backing for the Crittenden Compromise, Seward hoped to persuade him to appoint conciliators rather than stiff-backs to the cabinet. He sent his alter ego, Thurlow Weed, to Springfield to lobby the president-elect. There Lincoln politely but firmly resisted his recommendations. Disappointed by his failure to win Lincoln's support for compromise or the appointment of a cabinet to his liking, Seward nevertheless decided to accept the president's offer.

For colleagues in the cabinet, Seward desired former Whigs who would support a policy of conciliation, not former Democrats who favored a hard line in dealing with secessionists. So the Sage of Auburn urged the appointment of Southerners, including John A. Gilmer of North Carolina. And so Lincoln invited the cheerful, likable Gilmer to Springfield without revealing his purpose. "Such a visit would I apprehend not be useful to either of us, or the country," Gilmer replied, not realizing that he was being considered for the cabinet.[6] Upon returning to Washington after the Christmas recess, Gilmer was accosted by Weed and Seward, who urged him to accept a cabinet appointment. The North Carolinian agreed to think it over and eventually declined. Meanwhile, Lincoln had been sounding out other Southern leaders, among them William A. Graham of North Carolina and James Guthrie of Kentucky, neither of whom was interested. Frustrated in these bids, Lincoln told Frank Blair that "he could hardly maintain his self respect" if he were to appoint a Southern opponent to his cabinet, asserting that "he considered such a course an admission that the Republican party was incapable of governing the country & would be a rebuke by him to those who had voted for him."[7] He explained to Joshua Speed that he hesitated to name men from the Deep South for fear that "they might decline, with insulting letters still further inflaming the public mind."[8]

Lincoln next turned to Edward Bates of Missouri. When the two men met in Springfield on December 15, Lincoln offered his guest the post of attorney general. Bates had declined a similar offer from Millard Fillmore in 1850, but now that the nation "was in trouble and danger," he felt duty-bound to accept. Lincoln asked him to examine the constitutionality of secession; Bates indicated that he was "inflexibly opposed to secession, and strongly in favor of maintaining the government by force if necessary."[9] When Bates's appointment was announced, it failed to placate those wishing to reassure Southerners, for the Missourian was a prominent antislavery Republican and hailed from a Border State.

Choosing a Pennsylvanian

Causing Lincoln even greater trouble was his quest for a Pennsylvanian acceptable to the party. Since he had already appointed to his cabinet two of his rivals at Chicago, it seemed logical to pick a third, Simon Cameron. And that is what he did—and undid—and then did again.

Cameron's operatives went to work immediately after the election, deluging Lincoln with an avalanche of mail. The president-elect received few anti-Cameron letters, for the opponents of "the Chief" were complacent. Alexander K. McClure recalled that "no one outside a small circle of Cameron's friends, dreamed of Lincoln calling him to the Cabinet. Lincoln's character for honesty was considered a complete guarantee against such a suicidal act."[10] On December 5, Lincoln summoned David Wilmot to discuss Pennsylvania appointments. The veteran antislavery champion replied that his mind was "rather inclined" toward Cameron but said that "it cannot be concealed that he is very objectionable to a large portion of the Republicans of this State."[11] On Christmas Eve, Wilmot arrived in Springfield, where he had a long talk with Lincoln. Five days later Cameron himself appeared in the Illinois capital. The Chief acted coy during his two long conversations with the president-elect, who expressed concern about which post to offer his visitor. If it were the Treasury portfolio (which Cameron wanted), what should Chase receive? As a prominent Republican leader, the Ohioan had an undeniable claim to a high cabinet position.

"Let him have the War Department," said Cameron.

"Would you accept that job?" Lincoln asked.

"I am not seeking for any position, and I would not decline of course what I had recommended to another," came the reply.[12]

As the Chief prepared to leave town, Lincoln handed him a letter: "I think fit to notify you now, that by your permission, I shall, at the proper time, nominate you to the U.S. Senate, for confirmation as Secretary of the Treasury, or as Secretary of War—which of the two, I have not yet definitely decided. Please answer at your own earliest convenience."[13] Cameron triumphantly shared this document with friends and leaked its contents to the press. When the news arrived in Washington, his enemies exploded in wrath, swamping Lincoln with protests. Alarmed by these complaints, Lincoln asked Henry C. Carey of Philadelphia what Cameron had done to earn his unsavory reputation. In reply, Carey offered nineteen reasons why the Chief should not be given a seat in the cabinet, emphasizing his intellectual and ethical shortcomings. Lincoln also met with the anti-Cameron Republican Alexander McClure on January 3. After presenting remonstrances from leaders like Governor Curtin, David Wilmot, and Thaddeus Stevens, McClure urged Lincoln to appoint either Wilmot or Stevens to his cabinet. Lincoln assured his guest that he would reconsider the plan to appoint Cameron.

Stunned by the hostile reaction to Cameron, Lincoln wrote him asking him to retract his acceptance of a cabinet post. "Telegraph, me instantly, on receipt of this, saying 'All right.'"[14] Hurt and embarrassed, Cameron sent no such telegram or letter; he had already resigned his Senate seat. Trumbull reported that "Cameron is behaving very badly about the tender of an appointment. It was very injudicious for him to be exhibiting your letter about as he did, & after the receipt of your second letter he talked very badly—said to me that he would not then go into the cabinet, but that he would not decline by which I suppose he meant that he would embarrass you all he could, & he made a good many other remarks which I do not choose to repeat; but showing to me that he is wholly unfit for the place."[15]

Lincoln scrambled to find a way to soothe Cameron. One of McClure's associates suggested that Lincoln retract his abrupt January 3 letter and replace it with a gentler one. Eager to apply some salve to the wounds he had inflicted, Lincoln complied, writing Cameron on January 13 that "with much pain, I now say to you, that you will relieve me from great embarrassment by allowing me to recall the offer. This springs from an unexpected complication; and not from any change of my view as to the ability or faithfulness with which you would discharge the duties of the place." Lincoln assured Cameron that on January 3 he had written "under great anxiety" and had "intended no offense." The Chief should destroy or return that hurtful letter. Tactfully the president-elect added, "I say to you now I have not doubted that you would perform the duties of a Department ably and faithfully."[16]

Lincoln continued to wrestle with the decision. Believing that he had won the election because of his reputation for honesty, he heatedly asked one caller: "What will be thought now if the first thing I do is to appoint C[ameron], whose very name stinks in the nostrils of the people for his corruption?"[17] On January 24, he told a group of pro-Cameron Philadelphians that he would like to appoint the Chief because he had been a Democrat, while Bates and Seward were former Whigs. But Cameron's "opponents charge him with corruption in obtaining contracts, and contend that if he is appointed he will use the patronage of his office for his own private gain." Lincoln said he would have the charges investigated and that, in the unlikely event that they were proven true, Cameron would not be appointed. If, on the other hand, the charges were disproved, then the Chief would be named to the cabinet. Lincoln closed with an ominous warning: "If, after he has been appointed, I should be deceived by subsequent transactions of a disreputable character, the *responsibility will rest upon you gentlemen of Pennsylvania who have so strongly presented his claims to my consideration*."[18]

To help clarify matters, Lincoln asked Leonard Swett to visit Harrisburg. There Swett interviewed detractors of Cameron, who told him that the president-elect must abandon the Chief and support Thaddeus Stevens, for leading politicians of Pennsylvania were backing that Lancaster congressman. Torn by conflicting advice, and reluctant to appoint a spoilsman to his cabinet, Lincoln decided that once he was in Washington he would ask the Republican senators their candid opinion of Cameron. This matter, he said, had given him "more trouble than anything that he had yet to encounter," including the secession of the Lower South.[19]

Choosing a Treasury Secretary

The struggle over Salmon Chase's appointment pitted Lincoln against Seward in a battle to determine who would dominate the cabinet. When it was announced that the New Yorker had accepted the State Department portfolio, Weed's paper called him the "Premier" of the administration.[20] George G. Fogg warned the president-elect that "Seward would insist on being *master* of the administration, and would utterly scorn the idea of playing a subordinate part. He has no more doubt of his measureless *superiority to you*, than of his existence."[21]

The first scheme Seward and Weed tried to carry out was to pack the cabinet with former Whigs who would defer to the senator and agree with him that the South ought to be conciliated and the slavery issue deemphasized. Chase was anathema to the Albany Duo because he espoused radical antislavery views and fought against measures designed to appease the secessionists; in addition, the Ohioan had a strong personality and would challenge Seward for cabinet leadership. From the day he accepted the State Department portfolio in late December until inauguration day in March, Seward lobbied against Chase and for Cameron. To reconcile these contending forces would severely tax Lincoln's patience and statesmanship.

On December 31, the day he offered Cameron a cabinet post, Lincoln urgently summoned Chase to Springfield. The president-elect had received strong recommendations for the Ohioan from many political leaders who considered Chase an essential counterbalance to Seward. Some, however, presciently warned that the "supremely selfish" and "very vindictive" Buckeye governor "will use his place first and chiefly to promote his own ambition."[22]

On Friday, January 4, Chase arrived in Springfield, where he spent two days. Lincoln began their first interview by thanking him for his help in the 1858 campaign against Douglas. He then made his guest a peculiar offer: "I have done with you what I would not perhaps had ventured to do with any other man in the country—sent for you to ask you whether you will accept the appointment of secretary of the treasury, without, however, being exactly prepared to offer it to you."[23] The hyperambitious Chase replied that he was not eager for a cabinet post, especially a subordinate one, and would prefer to keep the Senate seat that he was to occupy beginning in March. But he coyly promised to think over the possibility of heading the Treasury Department, and Lincoln pledged to write him more definitely soon. Chase said their conversations "were entirely free & unreserved" and that he had "every reason to be satisfied with the personal confidence which Mr. Lincoln manifested in me."[24] Lincoln did admire Chase, though in time he would come to think less highly of the opportunistic, stately, vain, humorless, priggish, and imperious Ohioan.

Although he esteemed Lincoln, Chase deeply resented his failure to offer the Treasury portfolio unconditionally. Still, Chase said, if the tender were repeated, "I shall consider all the wishes so flatteringly if not kindly expressed, and if really satisfied that I ought to take the post I shall. But I do not now see on what grounds I could be so satisfied."[25] This coyness was disingenuous, for behind the scenes he was urging George Opdyke and others to lobby on his behalf for the cabinet post.

A Seat for Indiana

Alarmed by the appointment of Seward and Bates, Chase feared that ex-Whigs would dominate the cabinet; he regarded Cameron, though nominally a former Democrat, as a tool of Seward. When rumor suggested that another quondam Whig, Caleb B. Smith of Indiana, would be appointed, he protested to Lincoln that the Hoosier's ethics were suspect. Lincoln felt grateful to Smith for helping him win both the presidential nomination and the election. Smith's principal Indiana competitor was Congressman Schuyler Colfax of South Bend. In December, when Hoosier Republican leaders called at Springfield to lobby for Smith, they suggested that Colfax was "too inexperienced." Lincoln replied that he "could only say that he saw no insuperable objections to Indiana's having a man [in the cabinet], nor to Smith's being that man."[26] To offset opposition, Smith skillfully organized a letter-writing campaign that swelled Lincoln's mailbag. Foremost among Smith's backers were Seward and Weed, aided by David Davis and Leonard Swett. When Cyrus Allen called on Lincoln to endorse Colfax, the president-elect said that no pro-Colfax delegations had lobbied him and he therefore supposed Colfax did not enjoy earnest support.

In addition to Colfax, Smith faced competition from Norman B. Judd, whose candidacy was championed by former Democrats like Lyman Trumbull, Gustav Koerner, Joseph Medill, and the Blairs. Fierce opposition came from Illinois ex-Whigs, among them Richard Yates, Leonard Swett, William Kellogg, and David Davis, who could not forgive Judd for his failure to support Lincoln during the senatorial contest six years earlier. Mrs. Lincoln opposed Judd's candidacy for the same reason. Lincoln, ever magnanimous, said: "I can not understand this opposition to Judd's appointment. It seems to me he has done more for the success of our party than any man in the State, and he is certainly the best organizer we have."[27] He would have liked to appoint Judd but feared that such a move would alienate too many allies. He had only seven cabinet positions to fill and wished to use them to strengthen the Republican Party in key states like Indiana, Ohio, Pennsylvania, and New York, as well as important regions like the South and New England; Illinois did not need a representative in the cabinet, for it already had one in the White House. As a consolation prize, Lincoln offered Judd the lucrative post of minister to Prussia, which he accepted.

A Seat for New England

To Hannibal Hamlin, Lincoln delegated the task of choosing a New Englander for the cabinet. Two days after the election, the president-elect invited his running mate to confer with him in Chicago, where in late November they discussed cabinet matters at some length. After asking the vice president elect to negotiate with Seward and discussing candidates for the various posts, Lincoln mentioned some possible nominees for the Navy Department portfolio, including Charles Francis Adams and Nathaniel P. Banks of Massachusetts, Gideon Welles of Connecticut, and Amos Tuck of New Hampshire.

As Hamlin proceeded to carry out his assignment, Lincoln met with Thurlow Weed on December 20 and expressed partiality for Welles, a quondam Democrat who edited the Hartford *Evening Press*. "Lord Thurlow" ridiculed the bearded, bewigged leader of the Connecticut Republicans, facetiously suggesting that Lincoln could, while traveling to Washington for his inauguration, stop at an Eastern seaport, buy a ship's figurehead, "to be adorned with an elaborate wig and luxuriant whiskers, and transfer it from the prow of a ship to entrance of the navy department." It would, Weed gibed, "be quite as serviceable" as Welles, and cheaper. "Oh," replied Lincoln, "'wooden midshipmen' answer very well in novels, but we must have a live secretary in the navy."[28] In fact, Weed's pressure backfired, for it strengthened Lincoln's inclination to appoint Welles.

On Christmas Eve, Lincoln instructed Hamlin to recommend "a man of Democratic antecedents from New England." He explained that he could not "get a fair share" of the Democratic element in the cabinet without appointing a Democrat from that region.[29] Lincoln had by this time decided on two former Whigs (Seward and Bates) and was leaning toward one more (Smith), as well as three former

Democrats (Chase, Montgomery Blair, and Cameron). If he picked one more former Democrat, at cabinet meetings the number of ex-Whigs (including himself) would equal that of ex-Democrats.

Welles was the front-runner. Months earlier he had impressed Lincoln during his campaign visit to Hartford, and the president-elect knew of the helpful role Welles had played at the Chicago convention. The Connecticut editor also enjoyed strong backing from Hamlin, Horace Greeley, John A. Andrew, and others. Thus when Lincoln left Springfield for Washington in February, Welles stood the best chance of occupying the New England seat in the cabinet.

A Seat for the Border States

Eager to keep the Upper South and the Border States in the Union, Lincoln resolved to appoint a Marylander to his cabinet. The two leading candidates were Montgomery Blair, the scholarly, quarrelsome, socially awkward West Point graduate and son of the longtime political insider Francis P. Blair Sr., and the Whig/American congressman Henry Winter Davis, a combative, self-righteous, vain cousin of David Davis. The former had support from influential senators like Trumbull and Hamlin, but Weed and Seward supported Davis and opposed Blair, for he was a former Democrat who, along with his father and brother, had worked hard at Chicago to defeat the Sage of Auburn. On Christmas Eve, Lincoln told Trumbull that he expected "to be able to offer Mr. Blair a place in the cabinet; but I can not, as yet, be committed on the matter, to any extent whatever."[30]

Lincoln postponed a final decision on the five unfilled cabinet positions until he could meet with congressional leaders in Washington. He determined to remain in Springfield until February 11, when he would begin a circuitous, two-week train journey to the capital. He understandably feared that after reaching Washington "he could have no time to himself."[31]

Dealing with Compromise Proposals and Seward

Since Lincoln was not at the center of power during the crucial weeks when the Cotton States were pulling out of the Union, Seward took it upon himself to keep the country intact at least until inauguration day. To those urging him to openly back the Crittenden Compromise, he replied that it would be politically suicidal and insisted that "you must let me save the Union in my own way."[32] He viewed himself as indispensable, predicting that if he were away from Washington for only three days, "this Administration, the Congress, and the District would fall into consternation and despair. I am the only *hopeful, calm, conciliatory* person here."[33] When Seward spoke in favor of conciliation, the public assumed that he reflected Lincoln's views. But, as the president-elect told a visitor in early February, "Seward made all his speeches without consulting him."[34] Instead of acting as Lincoln's agent, the senator served as an independent negotiator between the president-elect and representatives of both the Upper South and the Border States.

Seward calculated that time would heal the sectional wounds. In late December, he introduced four resolutions in the Committee of Thirteen, but they were not the ones that Lincoln had asked Weed to pass along to him. Unlike the president-elect, Seward called for a guarantee of slavery in the states where it already existed. Moreover, he failed to include Lincoln's affirmation that the Union must be preserved, as well as his support for federal enforcement of the fugitive slave provision of the Constitution. Seward reported to the president-elect that his Republican colleagues on the Committee of Thirteen objected to Lincoln's resolutions because "the ground has already been covered" and that they "would divide our friends, not only in the committee, but in Congress," many of whom believed that the rendition of fugitive slaves was a state and not a federal responsibility.[35] Compromise seemed doomed in the Senate.

In a major speech on January 12, Seward shocked Radical Republicans by urging immediate concessions to keep the Upper South in the Union and offering a long-range proposal to settle outstanding differences between the sections. The atmosphere in the packed Senate chamber was tense. Three days earlier, South Carolina authorities had fired on an unarmed ship, the *Star of the West*, laden with supplies for Charleston's Fort Sumter garrison, forcing the vessel to abandon its mission. The country seemed to teeter on the brink of war. Could Seward keep the peace? After extolling the advantages of the Union for all sections, including the South, the senator in conciliatory tones endorsed the creation of two huge new states, one slave and one free, out of the existing Western territories; a constitutional amendment guaranteeing slavery where it already existed; a modification of the Fugitive Slave Act exempting bystanders from any role in the pursuit of runaways; and a law forbidding invasions of one state by residents of another. He also recommended a cooling-off period of two or three years, to be followed by a national constitutional convention. Although Lincoln allegedly was "not overpleased with Seward's speech," he told the senator that it "is well received here; and, I think, is doing good all over the country."[36]

Lincoln indirectly backed Seward's call for a national convention to revise the Constitution when he drafted resolutions to be introduced in the Illinois legislature. Norman B. Judd objected that it was too early to move, for it might appear that Lincoln was applying undue pressure to have a peace conference assemble. Lincoln disagreed but gave the resolutions to his friend state senator Thomas A. Marshall with instructions to introduce them whenever Judd thought it advisable. The first resolution recommended that Congress "call a Convention . . . to propose amendments to the Constitution of the U.S." To balance this conciliatory gesture, Lincoln added a firm Unionist resolution: "Resolved that until the people of the United S[tates] shall otherwise direct, the present Federal Union must be preserved as it is; and the present Constitution and laws must be administered as they are; and to secure these objects the whole resources of the State of Illinois are hereby pledged to the Federal authorities."[37] The Illinois legislature adopted the resolutions in February.

Although the reaction to Seward's address was generally positive, the New Yorker knew that he must win Lincoln over before there could be any compromise. To this end he enlisted the aid of Illinois congressman William Kellogg, who visited Springfield on January 20. To Kellogg's appeal for concessions on the territorial issue, Lincoln emphatically replied that he would endorse no measure betraying the Chicago platform, but he did indicate that if the American people wished to call a convention dealing with Southern grievances, he would not object. During his meeting with Kellogg, Lincoln received a dispatch from Trumbull urging him to do nothing until he had received letters that the senator was forwarding from Washington. The president-elect informed Kellogg that he would honor Trumbull's request and then write to Seward explaining his position on compromise measures.

Frustrated yet again, Seward sank into depression. In late January, he warned Lincoln that compromise was necessary to prevent the Upper South from seceding. Moreover, the senator cautioned, the "resort to force would very soon be denounced by the North, although so many are anxious for a fray. The North will not consent to a long civil war. . . . For my own part I think that we must collect the revenues—regain the forts in the gulf and, if need be maintain ourselves here—But that every thought that we think ought to be conciliatory forbearing and patient, and so open the way for the rising of a Union Party in the seceding states which will bring them back into the Union."[38] Seward's admonition was well taken, for he accurately gauged Southern public opinion. But, ironically, he misjudged the mood in his own section. The North, he feared, would shatter into bickering factions once war broke out, making it impossible to restore the Union by force; hence everything must be done to prevent hostilities. Lincoln may have overestimated the depth and extent of Southern Unionism, but he understood Northern opinion better than Seward did.

Despite Seward's desperate plea, Lincoln refused to budge. Reiterating his earlier opposition to compromise, he told the New Yorker that "on the territorial question—that is, the question of extending slavery under the national auspices,—I am inflexible. I am for no compromise which *assists* or *permits* the extension of the institution on soil owned by the nation." Changing his tone, he closed with a startling concession: "As to fugitive slaves, District of Columbia, slave trade among the slave states, and whatever springs of necessity from the fact that the institution is amongst us, I care but little, so that what is done be comely, and not altogether outrageous. Nor do I care much about New-Mexico, if further extension were hedged against."[39] This rather casual statement about New Mexico represented a momentous policy shift. It is hard to know why Lincoln reversed his stance on New Mexico. Perhaps he believed that slavery could never take root in that huge territory, which included the later state of Arizona as well as New Mexico. The 1860 census showed that no slaves lived there. Lincoln's change of heart could perhaps have averted bloodshed if Seward had exploited it, and if Southern Unionists would have accepted the New Mexico scheme. Radicals viewed that as the most dangerous compromise proposal, for it might pass. If Lincoln's approval had been made known, many Republicans would have backed the measure. But nothing came of it, for Seward failed to act on Lincoln's new position regarding New Mexico statehood. The senator's behavior on this matter is one of the great mysteries of the secession crisis.

The stunning victories achieved by anti-secessionists in Virginia and Tennessee elections on February 4 and 9, respectively, led Henry Winter Davis to crow that there the "back of the revolution is broken."[40] (In Virginia, far more moderates than disunionists won election to a secession convention. In Tennessee, voters rejected a proposal to hold a secession convention.) With this turn of events, Seward may well have felt that his job was over and he could calmly await Lincoln's arrival without further efforts on behalf of compromise. "At least," said he, "the danger of conflict, here or elsewhere, before the 4th of March, has been averted. Time has been gained." Seward wrote his wife in mid-February as Lincoln's train wended its circuitous way toward the capital: "I am, at last, out of direct responsibility. I have brought the ship off the sands, and am ready to resign the helm into the hands of the Captain whom the people have chosen."[41] Seward deserves credit, for he, with the help of others, had managed to keep the Upper South in the Union, at least temporarily.

Peace Conference

By early February, Seward may have felt that the initiative for compromise could now be assumed by the peace conference that Virginia had summoned to meet in Washington. He hoped that the conclave, which opened on February 4, would last for weeks and thus postpone any violent sectional clash. All states were invited to send delegates to consider a peaceful solution to the crisis, one based on a variation of the Crittenden Compromise.

When the invitation to send delegates to that conclave arrived at Springfield, Lincoln suggested that the legislature take no immediate action. Employing morbid imagery yet again, he said "that he would rather be hung by the neck till he was dead on the steps of the Capitol, before he would buy or beg a peaceful inaugeration."[42] Lincoln drafted resolutions calling for the governor to appoint representatives to the Peace Conference, making it clear that such action was not to be construed as endorsing any form of the Crittenden Compromise. When Norman B. Judd advised that it would be premature to submit those resolutions to the General Assembly, Lincoln agreed. After Ohio and New York decided to send delegates, the Illinois legislature followed suit, passing Lincoln's resolutions in order to help keep weak-kneed appeasers from dominating the convention. The president-elect feared that the conclave might do more harm than good. He predicted to Orville H. Browning that "increased excitement would follow when it broke up without having accomplished any thing," and that "no concession by the free States short of a surrender of every thing worth preserving, and contending for would satisfy the South, and that Crittendens proposed amendment to the Constitution in the form proposed ought not to be made."[43] In fact, the Peace Conference deliberated for weeks before recommending a variation of the Crittenden Compromise, which Congress rejected. During their deliberations, Republican leaders in Washington awaited Lincoln's arrival impatiently. At least the Peace Conference helped postpone the start of the war until after the inauguration.

The Southern Forts

Worried about Southern forts, Lincoln turned to Winfield Scott, commander in chief of the U.S. Army. In late October, the general had recommend that all unmanned or undermanned U.S. forts be garrisoned and expressed the hope that a moderate but firm policy would thwart the secessionists. Lincoln thanked Scott and instructed Congressman Elihu B. Washburne to tell him "to be as well prepared as he can to either *hold*, or *retake*, the forts, as the case may require, at, and after the inaugeration."[44] On December 26, Major Robert Anderson in Charleston caused a sensation when he abandoned Fort Moultrie, which he rightly feared the secessionists would overrun, and moved his troops to Fort Sumter, which was in the middle of the harbor, thus far less vulnerable to attack. Hard-liners in the North cheered this bold action. Assessing events in the Palmetto State, Lincoln approved Anderson's conduct "in the most emphatic terms" and indicated that if "Buchanan should dismiss Major Anderson he would be reinstated the moment Mr. Lincoln comes into power, and probably promoted."[45]

Lincoln asked Simon Cameron to consult with Scott about assuring a safe inauguration. On January 4, Scott told the president-elect that all would be well.

Composing the Inaugural Address

By late January, Lincoln was devoting much time to his inaugural address and to the speeches he would deliver en route to Washington. To concentrate on that task and avoid distracting visits, he squirreled himself away in a small, little-used room in the store owned by his wife's brother-in-law Clark M. Smith. He also took refuge in the hotel room of Thomas D. Jones, a Cincinnati sculptor who was executing a bust of the president-elect. Lincoln, who had only "his law books and the few gilded volumes that ornamented the centre-table in his parlor at home, comparatively no library," asked William Herndon "to furnish him with Henry Clay's great speech delivered in 1850; Andrew Jackson's proclamation against Nullification; and a copy of the Constitution," as well as Webster's reply to Hayne and George Washington's farewell address. With these few books and documents at his fingertips, Lincoln secluded himself at Smith's store and drafted his inaugural.[46]

At Lincoln's request, William Bailhache of the *Illinois State Journal* secretly printed a few copies of the inaugural address and kept them under lock and key. Before leaving Springfield, Lincoln showed one copy to a firm opponent of concessions to the South, Carl Schurz, who approved its insistence that the revenues be collected, that federal facilities be retaken, and that the laws be enforced.

In preparation for his departure, Lincoln rented out his house, sold his furniture, threw an elaborate farewell party, reminisced with old friends, and arranged his itinerary. The day he left, he affixed simple identification tags to his trunks reading "A. Lincoln / White House / Washington, D.C." On January 30 he took affectionate leave of Sarah Bush Lincoln, whom he visited at her home near Charleston. Lincoln was also affectionate with Herndon when he said goodbye. "Billy," he asked on the eve of his departure for Washington, "how long have we been together?"

"Over sixteen years."

"We've never had a cross word during all that time, have we?"

"No, indeed we have not."

After reminiscing about various cases, Lincoln pointed to the firm's sign outside the office and said: "Let it hang there undisturbed. Give our clients to understand that the election of a President makes no change in the firm of Lincoln and Herndon. If I live I'm coming back some time, and then we'll go right on practicing law as if nothing had ever happened."[47] When Republicans throughout the North urged him to speak in their cities as he made his way to the nation's capital, Lincoln remarked that if he were to accept them all, "he would not get to Washington until the Inauguration was over."[48] He did agree, however, to make addresses in Indiana, Ohio, New York, Pennsylvania, and New Jersey.

Struggling with cabinet selections, his inaugural address, and compromise schemes, Lincoln suffered agony as Buchanan allowed the Cotton States to seize federal forts, arsenals, custom houses, mints, post offices, and courthouses. The sculptor Thomas Jones observed that in late January "a deep-seated melancholy seemed to take possession of his soul."[49] A month earlier, upon hearing a rumor that the president would surrender Fort Moultrie in Charleston harbor, Lincoln snapped, "If that is true, they ought to hang him."[50] A visitor reported that Lincoln's "Kentucky blood is up, he means *fight*."[51] In fact, Lincoln's anger was widely shared in the North, where the secessionists' takeover of government facilities was regarded as outrageous theft on a massive scale. Such wholesale robbery undermined support for compromise measures.

On New Year's Day 1861, the president-elect lamented to his old friend Joseph Gillespie that "every hour adds to the difficulties I am called upon to meet, and the present Administration does nothing to check the tendency toward dissolution." Speaking with more bitterness than Gillespie had ever heard him express, he added: "Secession is being fostered, rather than repressed, and if the doctrine meets with general acceptance in the border States it will be a great blow to the Government."[52]

On February 11, Lincoln boarded the train that would take him to the nation's capital, where he would strive to prevent those states from leaving the Union.

19.

"The Man Does Not Live Who Is More Devoted to Peace Than I Am, but It May Be Necessary to Put the Foot Down Firmly"

From Springfield to Washington (February 11–22, 1861)

The ever-obliging Lincoln agreed to take a circuitous, 1,904-mile train journey from Springfield to Washington to accommodate Republican friends who had invited him to speak. There were obvious drawbacks to such a trip. It would be tiring, he would be exposed to potential assassins, and such a journey would not suit Lincoln's taste for simplicity and his aversion to pomp and circumstance. Moreover, though he would have to speak often, he could say little, for he wanted to postpone revealing his plans for dealing with the secession crisis until his inauguration. Because the route would be indirect—Indianapolis, Cincinnati, Columbus, and Pittsburgh, then a detour through Cleveland, Buffalo, Albany, New York, Trenton, Philadelphia, Harrisburg, and Baltimore—it would consume twelve days. The trip would divert attention away from the secession crisis and might enhance Lincoln's legitimacy if huge crowds turned out to welcome him. Moreover, it would allow him to meet leading Republicans outside Illinois and consult with them about patronage and policy matters.

Originally Lincoln had intended to have his wife and younger sons join him in New York for only the final leg of the trip. He evidently wanted to spare them the fatigue of the longer, more indirect journey. On February 9, he changed plans, apparently because General Scott had advised that Mrs. Lincoln's "absence from the train might be regarded as proceeding from an apprehension of danger to the President."[1] At the last minute, the plan was again altered, and Mary Lincoln and her younger sons did not accompany her husband when the train left Springfield.

The switch in arrangements may have had something to do with Mary's bizarre conduct the morning of February 11. She had been unsuccessfully lobbying her husband to give Isaac Henderson, part owner of a leading New York newspaper, a juicy patronage plum. To improve his chances, Henderson had sent diamond jewelry to a Springfield merchant with instructions to present it to Mrs. Lincoln if she persuaded her husband to appoint him to a leadership post in the New York

Custom House. Lincoln resisted her appeals until finally on the morning of the planned departure for Washington she threw a tantrum, causing a delay. To inquire about it, Herman Kreismann called at the room of the hotel where the Lincolns had been spending their final days in Springfield. As he told a reporter years later, Kreismann "found Mrs. Lincoln had thrown herself upon the floor and was crying and saying: 'I will not go. I will not go—I will not go.'" Lincoln explained to his startled visitor: "Kreismann, she will not let me go until I promise her an office for one of her friends."

The president-elect managed to calm his spouse "by agreeing to what had apparently been a subject of controversy. Mrs. Lincoln then stopped crying, got up cheerfully, shook out her skirts, gave a push or two to her hair, and went to the station with Mr. Lincoln."[2] After capitulating to his spouse, Lincoln joined his son Robert and an entourage of journalists, secretaries, friends, bodyguards, and a servant aboard the presidential train. Mrs. Lincoln and her younger sons did not accompany them; the following day she and the two boys caught up with Lincoln in Indianapolis.

On his journey from the Illinois capital to the U.S. capital, Lincoln ended months of public silence with speeches foreshadowing his eagerly awaited inaugural address. But as his train zigged and zagged its way eastward over two dozen different railroads, his rhetoric seemed to zig and zag between confrontation and conciliation.

Farewell Speech

Lincoln began his oratorical marathon with a brief farewell to Springfield, one of his most affecting prose masterpieces. On the morning of February 11, he spent half an hour at the small, dingy depot shaking hands with innumerable friends and neighbors. As he did so, he was hardly able to speak, for he was deeply moved. The mood was solemn and anxious as he mounted the platform of the train's rear car. For a few seconds he surveyed the crowd of a thousand well-wishers, Republicans and Democrats alike, as the cold wind blew a combination of snow and rain into their faces. Only the locomotive's steady hissing broke the silence.

Finally, in a sad voice, he slowly expressed his profound feelings: "My friends—No one, not in my situation, can appreciate my feeling of sadness at this parting. To this place, and the kindness of these people, I owe every thing. Here I have lived a quarter of a century, and have passed from a young to an old man. Here my children have been born, and one is buried. I now leave, not knowing when, or whether ever, I may return, with a task before me greater than that which rested upon Washington. Without the assistance of that Divine Being, who ever attended him, I cannot succeed. With that assistance I cannot fail. Trusting in Him, who can go with me, and remain with you and be every where for good, let us confidently hope that all will yet be well. To His care commending you, as I hope in your prayers you will commend me, I bid you an affectionate farewell."[3]

"We will do it; we will do it," responded the crowd, who, like the speaker, had tears in their eyes.[4] An editor of the *Illinois State Journal* called it "a most impressive scene. We have known Mr. Lincoln for many years; we have heard him speak upon a hundred different occasions; but we never saw him so profoundly affected, nor did he ever utter an address which seemed to us so full of simple and touching eloquence, so exactly adapted to the occasion, so worthy of the man and the hour. Although it was raining fast when he began to speak, every hat was lifted, and every head bent forward to catch the last words of the departing chief."[5] After Lincoln took leave of his wife and younger sons and entered the car, the crowd gave three cheers and then stood silently as the train, made up of three ordinary coaches and a baggage car, slowly pulled away from the depot.

The entourage included his eldest son and his two secretaries, as well as journalists, political allies, and friends. For protection, a military escort was arranged, but to avoid a bellicose appearance, some of its members joined the party later. Among those guarding the president-elect were army officers who volunteered for that duty while on leave, including Colonel Edwin V. Sumner, Captain John Pope, Major David Hunter, and Captain George Whitfield Hazzard. Assisting them were Ward Hill Lamon, Lincoln's burly colleague at the bar and close personal friend, and Elmer E. Ellsworth, a young militia leader who had achieved national renown and was a surrogate son to Lincoln.

While the train rolled eastward that morning, Lincoln took a pencil and on a large pad wrote a speech that he was to deliver in Indianapolis later that day. As he filled the sheets, his secretaries, John G. Nicolay and John Hay, took them and made copies. He seemed gloomy at first, but his spirits lifted briefly when people cheered the passing train. At Decatur, thousands had gathered to pay him honor. They insisted on shaking his hand, embracing him, and showering him with blessings. At the second stop, in Tolono, the crowd badgered him into giving a speech, which amounted to little more than a polite acknowledgment of their warm welcome. Their response was as intensely wild as if he had read them his inaugural address. And so it went for the next twelve days.

At each stop, enthusiastic committees greeted Lincoln on behalf of legislatures, governors, Wide Awakes, workingmen's clubs, and other organizations, all anxious to shake his hand, extend him invitations, deliver speeches to him, and exchange stories. Lincoln's friends, concerned for his safety and comfort, grew alarmed when he submitted himself to the mercy of these well-meaning but often inept committeemen. The resulting confusion was dangerous. The committees occasionally would "tumble pell-mell into a car and almost drag Mr. Lincoln out before the train had even stopped," Nicolay recalled. For a while Lincoln "could not resist the popular importunings." Only "after some days of experience and several incidents of discomfort" did he conquer that impulse, and he "would remain seated in his car until he received the notice agreed upon that preparations outside had been deliberately completed."[6]

At Indianapolis, Lincoln gratified stiff-backed opponents of appeasement with a startling preview of his inaugural address. He began his remarks, delivered from the balcony of the Bates House to an audience of twenty thousand, by analyzing the words *coercion* and *invasion*. "Would the marching of an army into South Carolina, for instance, without the consent of her people, and in hostility against them, be coercion or invasion?" he asked. Yes, he conceded, "it would be invasion, and it would be coercion too, if the people of that country were forced to submit." On the other hand, if the federal government "simply insists upon holding its own forts, or retaking those forts which belong to it—or the enforcement of the laws of the United States in the collection of duties upon foreign importations,—or even the withdrawal of the mails from those portions of the country where the mails themselves are habitually violated; would any or all of these things be coercion? Do the lovers of the Union contend that they will resist coercion or invasion of any State, understanding that any or all of these would be coercing or invading a State? If they do, then it occurs to me that the means for the preservation of the Union they so greatly love . . . is of a very thin and airy character." They regard the Union not "like a regular marriage at all, but only as a sort of free-love arrangement,—to be maintained on what that sect calls passional attraction."[7] This hardline speech, though couched in mild terms, thrilled the crowd. Congress and the public regarded it as a sign that he would strongly resist secession.

Things did not go smoothly at the Hoosier capital. Like many other committees in charge of arrangements, the Indianapolitans proved imperfect. Outsiders appropriated the carriages designated for the presidential party, compelling most of the entourage, clutching their luggage, to forge a path through the crowds to the hotel. Chaos reigned in the dining room, where Lincoln had to wait twenty minutes before being served. Waiters mishandled orders, spilled sugar down patrons' backs, brought biscuits to those ordering ham and pickles to those requesting tea. The mayhem amused Lincoln. He was emphatically not amused when his son misplaced a carpetbag containing the only copies of his inaugural address. Robert, not yet eighteen years old, had accepted an invitation by fellow adolescents to see the city's sights and carelessly left the bag with a hotel clerk. With great difficulty Lincoln retrieved it from a pile of similar luggage and took charge of it thereafter.

Robert Todd Lincoln was 18 years old when an unknown photographer took this portrait on July 24, 1861. That year a reporter wrote of Robert's "comparative elegance," which stood in "striking contrast to the loose, careless, awkward rigging of his Presidential father." Abraham Lincoln Presidential Library and Museum, Springfield, Illinois.

The next morning, Mrs. Lincoln and her younger sons arrived in Indianapolis a few moments before the presidential train departed for Cincinnati. As it sped along at thirty miles per hour, huge crowds at each station greeted it with wild cheering. At one stop, Lincoln indulged his well-wishers with some brief remarks in which he took his customary modesty to extreme lengths. "You call upon me for a speech," he told the residents of Lawrenceburg, Indiana. "I have been selected to fill an important office for a brief period, and am now, in your eyes, invested with an influence which will soon pass away; but should my administration prove to be a very wicked one, or what is more probable, a very foolish one, if you, the PEOPLE, are but true to yourselves and to the Constitution, there is but little harm I can do, thank God!"[8]

Approaching Cincinnati, the train was forced to halt by a crowd so large that it spilled onto the tracks. From the balcony of his hotel, Lincoln gave a much less confrontational speech than the one he had delivered at Indianapolis. He quoted the conciliatory words he had addressed to Kentuckians when he spoke at the Queen City two years earlier: "We mean to leave you alone, and in no way to interfere with your institution; to abide by all and every compromise of the constitution. . . . We mean to remember that you are as good as we; that there is no difference between us, other than the difference of circumstances."[9] These remarks pleased compromise enthusiasts. That evening Lincoln dodged an opportunity to address the secession crisis when he was serenaded by more than two thousand German workingmen who urged him to stand by his antislavery principles. Instead of focusing on that touchy subject, Lincoln addressed immigration, homestead laws, and the American dream.

On February 13, the train proceeded to Columbus, where Lincoln was scheduled to address the state legislature. Upon arrival, he found the city jammed with people swarming in from the countryside. At the depot many thousands boisterously welcomed the train with loud huzzahs. The legislature's solemn reception of Lincoln so moved him that he was, according to one observer, "hardly able to do himself justice in his reply to the address of the President of the Senate; but the earnestness and conscientiousness that plainly shone on his face effected more with the audience than words could."[10] The words he chose were unfortunate, for he clumsily tried to play down the seriousness of the crisis, saying that "there is nothing going wrong . . . there is nothing that really hurts anybody . . . nobody is suffering anything."[11] Critics jumped on these remarks. The president-elect was "a fool" for uttering "sheer nonsense," wrote a Philadelphian; "everybody about here is 'hurt,' and 'suffering,' and everything is 'wrong.'"[12] At the reception afterward, an immense crowd streamed into the recently completed state capitol. Ward Hill Lamon planted himself in front of Lincoln and stemmed the tide long enough for his friend to seek shelter behind a pilaster. There, overcome by heat, Lincoln stopped shaking hands and simply bowed to the passing public.

On Valentine's Day, as the party headed toward Pittsburgh, torrents of rain fell, inspiring hope in Lincoln that he might not have to address crowds along the way. Despite the bad weather, however, thousands of well-wishers turned out at each stopping point and insisted on a speech. He devised a clever stratagem for handling such crowds: he stayed inside the train until the conductor announced its imminent departure, at which point he emerged onto the platform of the car and bowed as the locomotive pulled out of the station.

To a crowd of twenty thousand at Steubenville, he offered a preview of an argument he would spell out more fully in his inaugural address: "If the majority does not control, the minority must—would that be right? Would that be just or generous? Assuredly not! Though the majority may be wrong, . . . yet we must adhere to the principle that the majority shall rule. By your Constitution you have another chance in four years. No great harm can be done by us in that time."[13]

The train arrived two hours late in Pittsburgh, where confusion reigned, for the presidential party's carriages had been stationed so close to the tracks that the horses took fright as the locomotive approached with its bell clanging and steam whistle screaming. In the resulting near stampede, Lincoln had to locate the carriage meant for him. His entourage, fearing for his safety, struggled to help him amid the panicky horses and the shouting committeemen, spectators, and drivers. When Lincoln finally reached the hotel, another crowd awaited him. Standing on a chair in the lobby, he made brief pro-Union remarks to his good-natured auditors.

In his address on February 15 at Pittsburgh, he sought to assure the five thousand people standing beneath a sea of umbrellas that he was sound on the tariff issue. But before dealing with that controversial topic, he explained that he was reluctant to discuss the secession crisis because it "would perhaps unnecessarily commit me upon matters which have not yet fully developed themselves. . . . My intention is to give this subject all the consideration which I possibly can before I speak fully and definitely in regard to it—so that, when I do speak, I may be as nearly right as possible." As he had done in Columbus, Lincoln played down the dangers of the secession movement, exclaiming that "there is really no crisis except an artificial one!" Somewhat lamely he addressed the tariff issue, which he admitted he did not fully comprehend.[14]

The train pulled out at 10:00 a.m., zigging westward toward the next stop, Cleveland. En route, he and his family rested quietly. Afflicted with a bad cold, the president-elect said little. The sentiments expressed by the crowds grew more hawkish as the train proceeded. Despite snow, rain, and mud, thirty thousand people lined the street connecting the depot with downtown Cleveland. From the balcony of the Weddell House, the president-elect assured his audience of ten thousand that the secession furor "is altogether an artificial crisis. . . . What is happening now will not hurt those who are farther away from here. Have they not all their rights now as they ever have had?"[15] At a reception that evening, Lincoln gave his weary arms and hands a rest by having the callers simply file past him at a safe distance. That manner of receiving guests was soon abandoned, for it made Lincoln feel "as if he were separated by an abyss from those with whom as fellow-citizens and constituents it was more than ever an imperative duty to be brought into closer relations and sympathy."[16] Departing Cleveland on February 16, the presidential cavalcade hugged the shore of Lake Erie en route to Buffalo. Lincoln, still fatigued from the exertion of the previous day, was subdued. Because of hoarseness, he spoke less than he had earlier in the trip.

At Westfield, New York, Lincoln asked if a little girl who had written him suggesting that he grow a beard were in the audience. The girl, 11-year-old Grace Bedell, had resented the hostile comments her schoolmates were making about the candidate's appearance, and so she had written to Lincoln: "All the ladies like whiskers and they would tease their husband's [*sic*] to vote for you and then you would be President." Lincoln had asked in reply, "As to the whiskers, having never worn any, do you not think people would call it a piece of silly affect[at]ion if I were to begin it now?"[17] But he had taken her advice anyway, and by February it was reported that "a vigorous growth of comely whiskers has entirely changed his facial appearance."[18] Grace's elderly father led her to the train, where Lincoln gave her a kiss and said, "You see, I let these whiskers grow for you, Grace."[19] At Dunkirk, New York, Lincoln electrified the crowd of twelve thousand with a brief, stirring declaration. On a platform adorned with a flagstaff, he concluded his remarks simply: "Standing as I do, with my hand upon this staff, and under the folds of the American flag, I ask you to stand by me so long as I stand by it."[20]

On February 16, the presidential party encountered chaos at Buffalo. As the train pulled into the station, the wildly cheering crowd of seventy-five thousand tried to compress itself to catch a glimpse of the president-elect. Soldiers cleared a path for Lincoln, who was greeted briefly by ex-president Millard Fillmore. No sooner had the former and future presidents reached their carriage than the frenzied crowd surged toward them, sweeping aside the soldiers protecting the honored visitor. In the crush, some men fainted and others were badly injured, including Major David Hunter, who suffered a dislocated collarbone. Only with aggressive, persistent elbowing were Nicolay and the rest of the entourage able to reach their coaches. After this experience, Lincoln's companions insisted that he refuse to attend such dangerous receptions unless he had better protection. At the hotel, the mayor welcomed Lincoln with a little speech, to which he responded with sentiments he had expressed many times earlier. His voice was starting to show signs of wear; during some passages he could scarcely be heard. Employing a firmer tone than he had been using, he urged the crowd to "stand up to your sober convictions of right, to your obligations to the Constitution, act in accordance with those sober convictions, and the clouds which now arise on the horizon will be dispelled."[21]

Tiring though it was, the journey had a salutary effect on Lincoln's spirits, which rose dramatically in the first week of the journey. The "encouragement he has received, [and] the hearty support he has been promised, have more than counterbalanced the fatigues of the way," noted a reporter.[22] And although his speeches received mixed reviews from Northern readers, they convinced people in the Deep South that they now had to deal with no weak-willed clone of James Buchanan but rather a firm leader resolved to maintain the Union. They assumed that his policies would lead to war, which they confidently assumed they would win.

The presidential party spent a quiet Sunday in Buffalo, where Lincoln seemed tired but in good spirits. He and his companions were glad for the much-needed respite. Lincoln had shaken hands for two hours at a reception Saturday night. With Millard Fillmore, he attended church services presided over by Father John Beason, a noted American Indian advocate. Afterwards Fillmore hosted Lincoln and his wife for lunch. The rest of that cold, damp day they spent quietly at their hotel. On Monday, February 18, in order to depart for Albany at 5:45 a.m., the entourage rose at 4:00. Lincoln was rested after his Sabbath in Buffalo, though still suffering from hoarseness and a sore chest. As the train sped through a snowstorm past Batavia, Rochester, Utica, Syracuse, and Schenectady, the recently resigned senator from Mississippi, Jefferson Davis, was being inaugurated in Alabama as provisional president of the Confederate States of America.

Lincoln's train reached Albany amid great confusion. Because the police and the military were late in arriving, the large crowd surged unimpeded against the cars. After the tardy soldiers finally cleared a path to the speakers' platform, Lincoln and the mayor emerged to faint cheering. On the platform, Lincoln responded briefly to the mayor's welcoming speech. As he proceeded to the capitol, the public showed less enthusiasm than Westerners had displayed. Standing before Governor Edwin D. Morgan, Lincoln appeared careworn. In the hall of the New York Assembly, Lincoln took his customary self-deprecation to unusual lengths, expressing gratitude to the legislature for its invitation: "It is with feelings of great diffidence, and I may say with feelings of awe, perhaps greater than I have recently experienced, that I meet you here in this place. . . . It is true that while I hold myself without mock modesty, the humblest of all individuals that have ever been elevated to the Presidency, I have a more difficult task to perform than any one of them."[23] After dining with Governor Morgan, Lincoln attended a reception at the Delavan House, where a thousand people shook his hand.

Lincoln felt relieved to depart Albany after a most disagreeable sojourn there. As the train sped toward New York City, he was so weary that he took little interest in the political discussions of his fellow passengers. He spoke at several stops, including Poughkeepsie, where he addressed a crowd of ten thousand. "It is with your aid, as the people, that I think we shall be able to preserve—not the country, for the country will preserve itself, but the institutions of the country; those institutions which have made us free, intelligent and happy—the most free, the most intelligent and the happiest people on the globe."[24]

Arriving in Manhattan, Lincoln was glad to find thirteen hundred police efficiently controlling the crowds (the largest of the entire journey) along the route from the train station to the Astor House. During the ride he occasionally stood to acknowledge cheers, but for the most part he remained seated, manifestly drained by the rigors of the trip. At the Astor House, Walt Whitman was impressed by Lincoln's "perfect composure and coolness."[25] During a reception, the president-elect warmly greeted Superintendent of Police John A. Kennedy: "I am happy to express my thanks and acknowledgements to you, Sir, for the admirable arrangements for the preservation of order." When Kennedy replied that he was merely doing his duty, Lincoln said: "Yes; but a man should be thanked for doing his duty right well."[26] Importuned by the crowd outside, he stepped to the balcony and made his customary non-speech. When complimented on his brief statement, he replied: "There was not much harm in it at any rate."[27]

The Lincolns dined with Hannibal Hamlin and his wife, who were also en route to Washington. Afterward Lincoln consulted with leading politicians and businessmen. When queried about his plans to deal with secession, he said he never crossed a river until he reached it. Thurlow Weed and others eager to placate the South were "much crosser than bears" at Lincoln's unwillingness to endorse a compromise.[28] Disappointed at his interview with the president-elect, Weed told Seward: "The conversation was confined to a single point, in relation to which I have no reason to suppose that he listened with profit."[29]

The next morning, Lincoln breakfasted with thirty business leaders, who urged the appointment of Cameron as secretary of the treasury. The stock market rose because the president-elect hobnobbed with conservative Wall Streeters rather than with Radicals. Further raising the hopes of compromisers was Lincoln's response to the official welcome extended by Mayor Fernando Wood, who sought to appease secessionists by openly calling for New York to declare itself a "free city." At 11:00 a.m., Lincoln visited City Hall, where Wood delivered a jeremiad about the woeful condition of business in the city. Observers murmured disapproval of

Wood's rudeness, but Lincoln took no offense. Seemingly preoccupied, he listened to the mayor's remarks with a dreamy look in his eye, smiled pleasantly when Wood finished, drew himself up to his full height, and responded in a voice weakened by a cold. His reply was unscripted: "I agree with the sentiments expressed by the Mayor," he began. "In my devotion to the Union, I hope I am behind no man in the nation."[30]

When the doors opened to admit the public, they tumbled in pell-mell, reminding onlookers of the onrush of a breached reservoir. As these well-wishers pressed toward him, Lincoln punned, "They are members of the Press." When a gentleman suggested that he might be unanimously reelected, Lincoln replied: "I think when the clouds look as dark as they do now, one term might satisfy any man." Said another, "I must shake hands with you, because they say I look like you," which prompted Lincoln to quip, "I take it that that settles that you are a good looking man." Upon leaving City Hall, Lincoln reportedly told the mayor "that, without intending any disparagement of others, he considered his (Mr. Wood's) speech the most appropriate and statesmanlike yet made on a like occasion, and that he (Mr. Lincoln) indorsed every word of it."[31] Among political leaders of the city, this well-publicized comment was viewed as one of his most meaningful statements, for in conjunction with his formal reply to the mayor, it indicated that the president-elect might support compromise. Lincoln seemed to be further distancing himself from his hardline Indianapolis speech.

When one of the mayor's staff suggested to Lincoln that he might don a mask and participate incognito in the party scene from Verdi's new opera *Un Ballo in Maschera*, then playing in town, the president-elect replied: "No, I thank you. The papers say I wear a mask already." That evening the president-elect attended a performance of Verdi's work, ironically the only opera in the standard repertory about the assassination of an American political leader ("the Governor of Boston"). Arriving after the overture had begun, he quietly slipped unnoticed into his seat. As time went by, however, his presence was detected, and all eyes turned from the stage to his box, where he sat stroking his newly grown whiskers. At the end of the opening act, the large audience cheered him lustily, waving hats and handkerchiefs. Calm and collected, he stood and bowed. When the curtain rose on act 2, the cast and chorus interpolated a spirited rendition of "The Star-Spangled Banner," at the close of which a huge American flag descended from the flies, touching off a frenzy of patriotic enthusiasm. Lincoln was deeply moved. Back at the Astor House, he was treated to more music by Verdi when a band serenaded him with selections from *Nabucco* and *Il Trovatore*. Too fatigued and unwell to respond, Lincoln asked Hannibal Hamlin, who had joined him that afternoon, to do the honors. In the morning, he appeared quite tired, saying "he had slept scarcely at all."[32]

On February 21, the presidential party entered New Jersey, where Lincoln dashed the hopes of soft-liners who had found encouragement in his previous day's remarks to Mayor Wood. In Newark, he took note of the effigy of a black-bearded man with a whip in his hand hanging from a beam and bearing the label "The Doom of Traitors."[33] At the Garden State's capitol, he addressed the General Assembly, emphasizing a theme he had hinted at in his Indianapolis speech ten days earlier. Speaking in a soft, conversational voice, he said: "I shall do all that may be in my power to promote a peaceful settlement of all our difficulties. The man does not live who is more devoted to peace than I am. None who would do more to preserve it. But it may be necessary to put the foot down firmly." John Hay reported that while delivering that last sentence, "with great deliberation and with a subdued intensity of tone," Lincoln "lifted his foot lightly, and pressed it with a quick, but not violent, gesture upon the floor." Hay wrote that he "evidently meant it. The hall rang long and loud with acclamations. It was some minutes before Mr. Lincoln was able to proceed."[34]

This extraordinary response may have helped persuade Lincoln that the North ached for a president who would deal firmly with secessionists. When the cheering died down, Lincoln leaned forward and with a smile asked the legislators, "If I do my duty, and do right, you will sustain me, will you not?"[35] Hay reported that there "was a peculiar naiveté in his manner and voice, which produced a strange effect upon the audience. It was hushed for a moment to a silence which was like that of the dead. I have never seen an assemblage more thoroughly captivated and entranced by a speaker than were his listeners."[36] These bold remarks seemed to clash with the more moderate tone Lincoln had adopted since his Indianapolis address. He apparently thought that if troops were dispatched to restore federal authority in the Lower South, the Upper South and the Border States would not resist.

Before the New Jersey Senate, Lincoln reminisced about reading Mason Weems's *Life of Washington* as a child. He recalled how the struggles of the Continental army crossing the Delaware River and fighting in New Jersey "fixed themselves upon my imagination so deeply," and he recollected "thinking then, boy even though I was, that there must have been something more than common that those men struggled for. I am exceedingly anxious that that thing which they struggled for; . . . that this Union, the Constitution, and the liberties of the people shall be perpetuated in accordance with the original idea for which that struggle was made, and I shall be most happy indeed if I shall be an humble instrument in the hands of the Almighty, and of this, his almost chosen people, for perpetuating the object of that great struggle."[37]

As he prepared to leave the capitol, Lincoln was mobbed and "set upon as if by a pack of good natured bears, pawed, caressed, punched, jostled, crushed, cheered, and placed in imminent danger of leaving the chamber of the assembly in his shirt sleeves, and unceremoniously at that."[38] After lunch, the entourage left for Philadelphia, where it arrived at 4:00 p.m. to find a crowd of one hundred thousand exuberant people braving the extreme cold and disregarding the threat of a snowstorm. Upon arrival, Lincoln and his party quickly became caught up in great confusion, for the local committee, like so many of its counterparts in other cities, proved inept. Chaos reigned as the party tried to enter the waiting carriages. At the Continental Hotel, he reiterated his earlier remarks about the artificiality of the crisis, though he carefully added that "I do not mean to say that this artificial panic has not done harm."[39]

Assassination Threat

That night, after the customary reception, which exhausted him, Lincoln received the alarming news that assassins planned to kill him as he passed through Baltimore on February 23. The bearer of this warning, Allan Pinkerton, a well-known Chicago detective and friend of Norman B. Judd's, had been hired by a railroad executive, Samuel Felton, to investigate rumors that his line would be sabotaged as Lincoln's train sped along its tracks to Washington. Felton and others had been alerted by an unnamed Baltimorean that a group in the Monumental City planned to set fire to a bridge as Lincoln's train approached, then attack the cars and kill the president-elect.

While in Baltimore, Pinkerton inadvertently learned of serious plots to assassinate the president-elect during a change of trains. (The entourage was scheduled to arrive at the depot of the Philadelphia, Wilmington, and Baltimore line and depart from the depot of the Baltimore and Ohio Railroad, over a mile distant. As it made its way between the two stations, conspirators planned to create a disturbance drawing off the police and then, as a crowd surged around the carriages, kill Lincoln.) On February 12 Pinkerton wrote to Judd informing him of the danger and recommending a change in itinerary. At Philadelphia, Judd met with Pinkerton and Felton, who laid out substantial evidence of the plot.

Convinced by their presentation, Judd summoned Lincoln to hear Pinkerton's case. He listened attentively and then quizzed the detective about the details of the plot and asked his opinion. Referring to the murderous expressions of reckless men who were prepared to sacrifice their lives to kill a supposed tyrant; to the disloyalty of police superintendent George P. Kane; and to the dangers presented by large crowds, Pinkerton warned that a deadly assault would be made. Lincoln remained silent for a while. When Judd and Pinkerton urged him to take the train to Washington that very night, the president-elect insisted that he must fulfill his obligation to raise a flag over Independence Hall the next morning and then address the Pennsylvania state legislature in Harrisburg.

Later that night, William Henry Seward's son Frederick reported a similar tale to Lincoln. Winfield Scott had learned from the newly appointed inspector general of the District of Columbia, Colonel Charles P. Stone, that conspirators planned to assassinate the president-elect as he passed through Baltimore. Stone's informant was a New York detective who had been snooping about the Monumental City for three weeks. General Scott had reported this information to Seward, who wrote Lincoln urging him to change his travel plans. When the senator's son handed him that letter, the president-elect inquired about the sources of Stone's information. That warning, based on sources different from Pinkerton's, persuaded Lincoln to take the threat seriously.[40] Authorizing Pinkerton to make all necessary arrangements, Lincoln agreed to return to Philadelphia that evening and take the late train to Washington surreptitiously. Cool and calm, Lincoln predicted that he would face no danger once he reached Washington. Later he explained to Isaac N. Arnold: "I did not then, nor do I now, believe I should have been assassinated, had I gone through Baltimore, as first contemplated; but I thought it wise to run no risk, where no risk was necessary."[41]

On February 22, Lincoln stood at Independence Hall, where he was to hoist a new American flag containing thirty-four stars (Kansas had been admitted to the Union the preceding month). Clearly, the warnings of Pinkerton and the others were on his mind, for in an impromptu address inside the historic building he alluded to assassination as well as to the Declaration of Independence. The Declaration, he said, promised "liberty, not alone to the people of this country, but hope to the world for all future time." He then concluded that if the nation "cannot be saved without giving up that principle—I was about to say I would rather be assassinated on this spot than to surrender it."

He assured the crowd that he sought to avoid war but warned that if the South attacked Northern facilities, his administration would retaliate: "There is no need of bloodshed and war . . . there will be no blood shed unless it be forced upon the federal Government." He closed with another allusion to his possible death: "I have said nothing but what I am willing to live by, and, in the pleasure of Almighty God, die by."[42] Outside, before a vast assemblage braving the winter chill, he removed his coat and firmly tugged the halyards, sending a large flag up the pole to unfurl and float majestically in the breeze as the newly risen sun illuminated it. The crowd of thirty thousand cheered wildly.

At 8:30 a.m. Lincoln departed for Harrisburg. En route, Judd spelled out the details of the altered itinerary: in the evening, he would return to Philadelphia on a special train and board the 10:50 p.m. regular train for Washington, accompanied only by Lamon, Pinkerton, and one of Pinkerton's agents; they would arrive in the nation's capital at 6:00 a.m.; telegraph wires from Harrisburg would be cut. In the Pennsylvania capital, Lincoln discussed the plan with a few members of his entourage, emphasizing the need for secrecy. Yet he insisted that his wife be informed, for, he said, "otherwise she would be very much excited at his absence."[43] He was right. When told of the changed plans, Mrs. Lincoln "became very unmanageable," according to Alexander K. McClure, who observed the scene. She demanded that she be allowed to accompany her husband on the new route and, McClure recalled, "spoke publicly about it in disregard of the earnest appeals to her for silence. Prompt action was required in such an emergency, and several of us simply hustled her into her room with Col. Sumner and Norman Judd . . . and locked the door on the outside. The men with her explained what was to be done and forced her to silence as she could not get out of the door." McClure "thought Mrs. Lincoln was simply a hopeless fool and was so disgusted with her conduct that evening" that he never spoke to her again.[44]

The trip to Harrisburg that morning was ominous. "All along the route from Philadelphia," John Hay reported, "receptions seemed more the result of curiosity than enthusiasm. Even at Harrisburg, not one man in a hundred cheered. The crowd everywhere were uniformly rough, unruly, and ill bred." Lincoln "was so unwell he could hardly be persuaded to show himself." At the state capital, the "arrangements were unprecedentedly bad." The "crowd, and the fatiguing ceremonies of the day, and the annoyances and vexation at the badly conducted hotel, proved too much for the patience of the party, who vented their disgust loudly."[45]

Also ominous were Lincoln's remarks in response to a welcoming speech by Governor Andrew G. Curtin. Alluding to a review he had recently witnessed, the president-elect declared: "I have been proud to see to-day the finest military array, . . . they give hope of what may be done when war is inevitable." He did not say *if* war was inevitable, but *when* it was inevitable. To offset the apparent belligerence of this remark, he expressed the hope that no blood would be shed. He took pains in his later address to the state legislature to underscore his peaceable intentions.[46] Even more ominously, a man on the street asked Lincoln: "How soon are you going to send us down South?" He replied "that there would be no occasion for such a course, but that he was glad to see that there was one ready to act, if the cause of his country should demand him. At this a number cried out, 'we will all go, if you want us.'"[47]

At the hotel that afternoon, Lincoln had Judd summon Governor Curtin and the most prominent members of the entourage: "I reckon they will laugh at us, Judd, but you had better get them together." When they were assembled, the president-elect said: "The appearance of Mr. Frederick Seward, with warning from another source, confirms my belief in Mr. Pinkerton's statement. Unless there are some other reasons, besides fear of ridicule, I am disposed to carry out Judd's plan."[48] Colonel Sumner indignantly declared, "I'll get a Squad of cavalry, Sir, and cut our way to Washington." Judd replied, "Probably before that day comes, the inauguration day will have passed."[49] The president-elect named the flamboyant Lamon to be his sole bodyguard on the trip, for in the East, Lamon—unlike Hunter and Sumner—was little known; as a native Virginian, he had a Southern accent; he was six feet, two inches tall, muscular, courageous, devoted to Lincoln, and heavily armed. They boarded the special train around 7:00 p.m., at which time all telegraph lines from Harrisburg were severed.

At 10:00 Lamon and Lincoln, accompanied by two railroad officials, reached West Philadelphia, where they were met by Pinkerton and another railroad executive. The men rode about in a carriage to kill time before the 10:50 departure of the regularly scheduled train to Washington. When it pulled into the station, Lincoln, stooping over to disguise his great height, climbed aboard through the sleeping car's rear door, accompanied by Lamon and Pinkerton. The president-elect, who was described to the conductor as an invalid, entered his berth and drew the curtains. During the ride to Baltimore, Lincoln told a joke sotto voce, but otherwise the three men remained silent. At 3:30 a.m. they reached the Monumental City; after a long layover, they departed for the capital, arriving at 6:00 a.m. As Lincoln and his two companions strode through the depot, Elihu B. Washburne emerged from behind a huge pillar and said, "Abe you can't play that on me." When Pinkerton raised his fist, Lincoln exclaimed: "Don't strike him Allan, don't strike him—that is my friend Washburne."[50] All four men took a hack to the Willard Hotel, where a few minutes after their arrival they were met by Seward, who had overslept and thus been unable to greet the party at the station.

Newspaper descriptions of the "undignified and ridiculous flight by night" proved most embarrassing, and caricaturists ridiculed Lincoln mercilessly.[51] Joseph Howard Jr. of the New York *Times* wrote a highly colored account, describing Lincoln's garb as a cowardly disguise: "He wore a Scotch plaid cap and a very long military cloak, so that he was entirely unrecognizable."[52] In fact, the president-elect had on an old overcoat and a new soft wool hat that he had been given in New York. George Templeton Strong rightly feared that "this surreptitious nocturnal dodging or sneaking of the President-elect into his capital city, under cloud of night, will be used to damage his moral position and throw ridicule on his Administration."[53] Some Republicans defended Lincoln's action. The Cincinnati *Gazette* speculated that if he had been killed, "civil war would have broken out immediately, for an enraged North would have blamed the South for the crime and taken swift revenge." If Seward, Scott, Pinkerton, Judd, and the others had entertained any doubts about Lincoln's safety, "it was their imperative duty to urge upon him to forego the Baltimore reception."[54]

Lincoln may have overreacted to a threat that was perhaps exaggerated, but given the bloody history of Baltimore mobs and the fatal attack they were to make on Union troops passing through that city on April 19, his decision seems in retrospect a reasonable precaution, especially since two independent sources had issued the warnings. Yet he came to rue that decision, telling friends that he considered it one of the worst mistakes he ever made. His embarrassment at appearing weak and fearful may have disposed him in the momentous coming weeks to avoid steps that might deepen that unfortunate impression.

20.

"I Am Now Going to Be Master"

Inauguration (February 23–March 4, 1861)

Lincoln's arrival in Washington cheered up the city, which had been in despair as the South girded for war and the Buchanan administration dithered. Yet people were unsure just what the president-elect's policy would be, for his speeches en route to the capital had oscillated between hard-line and conciliatory approaches to secession. Lincoln, suffering from fatigue, relaxed before breakfasting with Seward, who at 11:00 a.m. escorted him to the White House. After a brief chat with President Buchanan, Lincoln was introduced to the members of the cabinet. That afternoon, the president-elect was besieged by importunate visitors, as he would be for the rest of his stay there. In the evening, after dining with Seward, Lincoln held an informal reception for members of the Washington Peace Conference. Lucius E. Chittenden, a delegate from Vermont, admired his great aplomb in dealing with a group that included some political opponents: "He could not have appeared more natural or unstudied in his manner if he had been entertaining a company of neighbors in his Western home."[1] Lincoln impressed them with his uncanny memory. As he was introduced to the delegates by their last names, he recalled most of their first names and middle initials. To several he mentioned their family histories. Betraying no anxiety, he conversed with them warmly, candidly, and with animation. He paid special attention to the Southern delegates, particularly the Virginia Unionist William C. Rives, a former senator and minister to France. Massachusetts delegate John Z. Goodrich held a brief conversation with Lincoln and reported: "I cannot doubt he is firm & desires no compromise."[2]

On February 26, the peace conference session adjourned earlier than usual so that delegates could meet with the president-elect. That night, Stephen A. Douglas warned Lincoln that if the conference failed to agree on some compromise plan, the Upper South and the Border States might well secede. Lincoln "listened respectfully and kindly, and assured Mr. Douglas that his mind was engrossed with the great theme which they had been discussing, and expressed his gratification at the interview."[3] In fact, he worked behind the scenes to enable the conference to propose a solution to the sectional crisis.

That same night several commissioners, including Rives, also urged the president-elect to support a compromise. Lincoln reminded them of Aesop's fable about the lion in love with the beautiful damsel, "and how the lion who desired to pay his addresses, solicited permission from the bride's father, and how the father consented, but with the advice that as the lion's teeth were sharp and the claws long, and not at all handsome, he advised the King of Beasts to pull out the one and cut off the other, which being done, the good father easily knocked the lion in the head. So when we have surrendered Fort Sumter, South Carolina will do this with us." When Rives and others insisted that Sumter "could not be relieved without the loss of thousands of lives, and to hold it was but a barren honor," Lincoln replied with a dramatic proposal to solve the Sumter crisis: "You, gentlemen, are members of the Convention. Go to Richmond. Pass a resolution that Virginia will not in any event secede, and I may then agree with you in the fact a State any day is worth more than a Fort!"[4]

The following day, the conference adopted a version of the Crittenden Compromise and disbanded. In response, Lincoln told Washington city leaders "that though the plan of settlement adopted by the Peace Convention was not the one he would have suggested, he regarded it as very fortunate for the country that its labors had thus eventuated harmoniously."[5] While adoption of that scheme by the delegates helped postpone the secession of the Upper South, it went nowhere in Congress. Threatening to go somewhere was a force bill authorizing the president to call up the militia to suppress an insurrection, which Lincoln helped scuttle. He was "extremely anxious to see these sectional troubles settled peaceably and satisfactorily to all concerned." In order to accomplish that, he said, "I am willing to make almost any sacrifice, and to do anything in reason consistent with my sense of duty."[6] But he would not allow his opposition to the force bill to be publicized. That very night the House adjourned before voting on the measure, thus killing it.

Like some oversized, bipedal border collie, Seward shepherded Lincoln around Washington. The president-elect met congressmen and senators on February 25 when Seward escorted him to the Capitol. The Illinoisan's speeches on the train journey caused the secretary of state designate to remark that the prospect of having to educate Lincoln made him "more depressed than he has been during the whole winter."[7] That education was pursued earnestly in the hectic days of late February and early March, when Lincoln proved an attentive pupil under Seward's tutelage, submitting his inaugural address to him for comment. He had already shown it to Carl Schurz, who approved of its hardline tone, and to Orville H. Browning, who thought it too bellicose.

In Washington, Seward suggested many alterations. Like Browning, the senator tried to make the document less belligerent. He boasted to Lincoln, "I . . . have devoted myself singly to the study of the case here, with advantages of access and free communication with all parties of all sections. . . . Only the soothing words which I have spoken have saved us and carried us along thus far."[8] The modest Lincoln may well have recoiled at this display of raw egotism, but he took the advice of the New Yorker to drop an allusion to the Chicago platform, which might seem too partisan; to soften his discussion of reclaiming government property and references to exercising power; and to add a conciliatory final paragraph. On March 1, Lincoln read a draft of the inaugural to other cabinet appointees. Reportedly, he also submitted that document to the scrutiny of Senators Trumbull, Wade, and Fessenden, as well as to Norman B. Judd. Seward also lobbied intently for pro-compromise cabinet aspirants. Five of the seven posts had yet to be filled, including the office of treasury secretary. The struggle over that important position raged for days, with hard-liners supporting Salmon P. Chase and soft-liners, led by Seward and Weed, favoring Simon Cameron. That the Pennsylvanian would have a seat in the cabinet had been virtually settled during Lincoln's February 21 stopover in Philadelphia, where he met with James Milliken, a leading industrialist, and several other Cameron supporters. Milliken said that he was authorized to speak for McClure, Curtin, and other opponents of the Chief; that they had withdrawn their objections to Cameron and now supported his candidacy; and that the leading iron and coal men of the Keystone State desired his appointment. Lincoln replied "that it relieved him greatly" but that he was not "prepared to decide the matter and would not until he should reach Washington."[9]

At the capital, opponents of Cameron besieged Lincoln, who asked Thaddeus Stevens, "You don't mean to say you think Cameron would steal?"

"No, I don't think he would steal a red-hot stove."

When Lincoln repeated this quip to Cameron, the Chief was so incensed that he refused to speak to Stevens.

The Lancaster congressman asked why Lincoln had repeated his hostile remark to Cameron. "I thought it was a good joke and didn't think it would make him mad," replied the president-elect.

"Well, he is very mad and made me promise to retract. I will now do so. I believe I told you he would not steal a red-hot stove. I will now take that back."[10]

On February 28 and March 1, Lincoln met with Cameron, who later recalled that "I told him I was no lawyer; I didn't want anything if he couldn't give me what he had offered [in Springfield]."[11] Since Lincoln had already decided to name Chase secretary of the treasury, he gave Cameron the War Department post. As it turned out, that appointment was, as Horace White put it, "the most colossal blunder of

Lincoln's public life."[12] Cameron's selection pleased Seward, though that was not enough for the senator, who wanted as colleagues former Whigs like Charles Francis Adams, Caleb B. Smith, and Henry Winter Davis, all soft-liners on secession. As secretary of the interior Lincoln did name Smith, who proved to be a mediocrity, but Indiana had been promised a seat in the cabinet and no other Hoosier enjoyed so much home support. Seward was not pleased with the choices of former Democrats Gideon Welles as secretary of the navy, Montgomery Blair as postmaster general, and most especially Salmon P. Chase as treasury secretary. Lincoln favored Blair in part because of the influence of his family, especially his father, Francis P. Blair Sr. The president-elect read to that old Jacksonian his inaugural address and asked for suggestions. Lincoln explained that "it was necessary to have Southern men & men of Democratic anticedents" and that the Marylander Blair "fulfilled both requirements."[13] To placate Blair's chief rival, Henry Winter Davis, Lincoln gave him control of the Maryland patronage.

Gideon Welles, a newspaper editor and leader of the Connecticut Republican Party, proved to be a good choice, though his peculiar appearance made him the object of ridicule. Charles A. Dana noted that Welles "was a very wise, strong man. There was nothing decorative about him; there was no noise in the street when he went along; but he understood his duty, and did it efficiently, continually, and unvaryingly."[14] He was familiar with the Navy Department, in which he had served as chief of the Bureau of Provisions and Clothing during the Mexican War. In deciding between Cameron and Chase for the Treasury Department, Lincoln polled the Republican senators, who favored the latter.

Lincoln found the long struggle over the cabinet annoying and depressing. It culminated on the night of March 2, when in an agitated voice he told his numerous callers that "it is evident that some one must take the responsibility of these appointments, and I will do it. My Cabinet is completed."[15] To Marylanders protesting against Blair, Lincoln was emphatic: "I have weighed the matter—I have been pulled this way and that way—I have poised the scales, and it is my province to determine, and I am now going to be master."[16]

Seward was furious at Lincoln's choices and complained "that he had not been consulted as was usual in the formation of the Cabinet" and "that there were differences between himself and Chase which rendered it impossible for them to act in harmony." He therefore insisted that the Ohioan be kept out of the cabinet or else he would withdraw his acceptance of the State Department portfolio. Lincoln expressed surprise "that he should be met with such a demand" at that late hour and asked Seward to reconsider.[17] The next day, the New Yorker formalized his refusal in a letter to Lincoln.

Seward overplayed his hand. Realizing that the senator meant to dominate him, Lincoln decided to call his bluff by letting it be known that he might appoint someone else to head the State Department and name the New Yorker minister to Great Britain. Rumors spread quickly, including speculation that Chase was to be dropped. When Norman B. Judd heard that Henry Winter Davis rather than Montgomery Blair would become postmaster general, he asked Lincoln about this alteration in the reported cabinet slate. "Judd," came the reply, which clearly referred to Seward, "I told a man at eleven o'clock last night that if this slate broke again it would break at the head."[18] The man he took into his confidence was doubtless George G. Fogg, to whom Lincoln said: "We must give up both Seward and Chase, I reckon; and I have drawn up here a list of the cabinet, leaving them both out." The new slate included William L. Dayton as secretary of state, John C. Frémont as secretary of war, and a New York opponent of Seward as secretary of the treasury. "I am sending this to Mr. Weed," Lincoln remarked.[19] To Seward he submitted a different message, written as he was leaving the hotel to deliver his inaugural address: "Your note of the 2nd. inst. asking to withdraw your acceptance of my invitation to take charge of the State Department, was duly received. It is the subject of most painful solicitude with me; and I feel constrained to beg that you will countermand the withdrawal. The public interest, I think, demands that you should; and my personal feelings are deeply inlisted in the same direction. Please consider, and answer by 9 o'clock, A.M. to-morrow."[20] Seward, aware that he had lost his gamble, capitulated. After conferring with Lincoln on the night of inauguration day, he withdrew his resignation. Lincoln gave him "to understand that whatever others might say or do, they two would not disagree but were friends."[21]

Lincoln had to call Chase's bluff as well as Seward's. Assuming that the Ohioan would accept the Treasury portfolio, he had not consulted him about the matter since arriving in Washington. On March 6, when the names of all cabinet members were submitted to the Senate, the hypersensitive Chase explained to Lincoln his reluctance to accept the post. As Chase later recalled, the president "referred to the embarrassment my declination would occasion him," leading him to promise to reconsider. When word of this conversation leaked out, Chase "was immediately pressed by the most urgent remonstrances not to decline."[22] After Lincoln had Frank Blair sound out Congressman John Sherman about becoming treasury secretary and rumors spread that Chase would be named minister to England, Ohioans opposed to Chase reversed course and urged Lincoln to name him. Finally Chase yielded.

Lincoln's "compound cabinet" did not please all Republicans. Thaddeus Stevens said it consisted "of an assortment of rivals whom the President appointed from courtesy, one stump-speaker from Indiana, and two representatives of the Blair family."[23] In fact, Lincoln chose his four competitors for the presidential nomination not as an act of courtesy but to strengthen his administration by having the most prominent leaders of the party's factions, as well as the most important regions, represented. Lincoln was careful to balance the cabinet with former Whigs and former Democrats. When ex-congressman David K. Cartter of Ohio asked Lincoln, "Do you not think the elements of the Cabinet are too strong and in some respects too conflicting?," he replied: "It may be so, but I think they will neutralize each other."[24]

Meanwhile Congress, after debating compromise measures for three months, finally passed one designed to placate the South: the Adams-Corwin-Seward amendment to the Constitution guaranteeing slavery in the states where it already existed. Lincoln reportedly intervened to win support for that measure by both houses of Congress. In preliminary drafts of his inaugural address, he had expressed no enthusiasm for changes to the Constitution. In his final revision, however, he alluded to the newly passed amendment and also endorsed the suggestion made by Trumbull and Seward that a national convention be held to consider other alterations to the document. Lincoln's willingness to support such an amendment was yet another example of his desire to appear accommodating to both the South and moderate Republicans like Seward, as well as to show that he was not inflexible (except with regard to slavery expansion and secession). He probably thought that the amendment merely reaffirmed what was already guaranteed in the Constitution. Moreover, he doubtless assumed that the amendment had little chance of ratification by three-quarters of the states.

Other revisions to the inaugural, made largely at Seward's suggestion, added to the conciliatory tone created by his endorsement of a thirteenth amendment. A good example is Lincoln's reference to secession ordinances as "revolutionary" rather than "treasonable." More striking was Seward's recommendation about the conclusion of the address, which in its original form posed a bellicose challenge to the secessionists. Lincoln took Seward's advice to omit the phrase "unless you first assail it" and to replace the ominous final sentence ("Shall it be peace or the sword?") with a lyrical appeal to sectional fraternity. The senator proposed several rather leaden lines, which Lincoln, like a verbal alchemist, transformed into a golden prose poem: "I am loth to close. We are not enemies, but friends. We must not be enemies. Though passion may have strained, it must not break our bonds of affection. The mystic chords of memory, stretching from every battlefield, and patriot grave, to every living heart and hearthstone, all over this broad land, will yet swell the chorus of the Union, when again touched, as surely they will be, by the better angels of our nature."

Although not as conciliatory as Seward would have liked, Lincoln's address was tough but not bellicose. He would not try to repossess forts and other federal facilities, nor would he permit the seizure of any more, such as Fort Sumter in Charleston harbor and Fort Pickens off Pensacola. Lincoln's pledge to enforce the laws was softened by his declaration that "where hostility to the United States, in any interior locality, shall be so great and so universal, as to prevent competent resident citizens from holding the Federal offices, there will be no attempt to force obnoxious strangers among the people for that object." In a similar gesture of forbearance, he said that the "mails, unless repelled, will continue to be furnished in all parts of the Union." Also conciliatory were Lincoln's reiteration of his oft-stated pledge not to interfere with slavery in the states where it already existed and his failure to stress the inflammatory issue of slavery in the territories. In dealing with the Fugitive Slave Act, Lincoln was seemingly conciliatory but actually quite radical. He said that while the statute was constitutional and should be enforced, he suggested that it might be advisable to amend it to provide accused runaways the same due process accorded all citizens charged with violating criminal statutes. (Though couched in mild language, this endorsement of personal liberty laws was a startling call for Black civil and legal rights.)

While Lincoln had clearly followed Seward's advice and softened the hard-line approach taken in early drafts of his inaugural, he emphatically rejected the doctrine of secession, holding that "the Union of these States is perpetual." And so no state "upon its own mere motion" could legally secede. "I therefore consider that, in view of the constitution and the laws, the Union is unbroken; and, to the extent of my ability, I shall take care, as the constitution itself expressly enjoins upon me, that the laws of the Union be faithfully executed in all the states." Moreover, he maintained that "there needs to be no bloodshed or violence; and there shall be none, unless it be forced upon the national authority."

Lincoln offered practical as well as constitutional and historical objections to secession. If states were allowed to withdraw whenever they felt so inclined, chaos would result, leading to anarchy or tyranny. He pointed out the obvious economic, geographical, and political drawbacks to secession. "Physically speaking, we cannot separate. We cannot remove our respective sections from each other, nor build an impassable wall between them. A husband and wife may be divorced, and go out of the presence, and beyond the reach of each other; but the different parts of our country cannot do this. They cannot but remain face to face; and intercourse, either amicable or hostile, must continue between them." Such "intercourse" would be "more advantageous," he argued, if the states remained united. "Can aliens make treaties easier than friends can make laws?" he asked rhetorically.

On the cloudy morning of March 4, Lincoln rose at 5:00 a.m. After eating breakfast and conferring with Seward, he put the finishing touches on his address, which his son Robert read aloud to him. Until 11:00 a.m., he consulted with various other callers, including Bates, Welles, Cameron, Trumbull, and David Davis. At dawn, crowds began gathering before the Capitol, where the Senate was about to take a three-hour break after its all-night session. Colonel Charles P. Stone, acting on General Scott's orders, deployed 2,000 volunteer soldiers to their posts. Supplementing them were 653 regular troops summoned from distant forts and marines based at Washington's Navy Yard. Sharpshooters clambered to the roofs of the taller buildings lining Pennsylvania Avenue, along which police took up positions. Cavalry patrolled the side streets. Plainclothes detectives circulated among the crowd with instructions to arrest for "disorderly conduct" anyone speaking disrespectfully of the new president. The sound of fife and drum filled the air. Flags and banners fluttered in the chill wind. Rumors of bloody doings were bruited about, though the heavy military presence made it unlikely that anyone would disturb the day's ceremony. Colorfully attired marshals assembled, ready to lead the procession. Gradually the streets became choked with humanity, eagerly awaiting the appearance of the president-elect. Good humor, decorum, order, and enthusiasm prevailed among the people who turned out to witness the event. Ominously, however, the parade lacked the customary civic groups and political clubs, a sure sign that many Washingtonians did not sympathize with the new president or his party.

A handsome open barouche bore President Buchanan to the Willard Hotel, where Lincoln climbed aboard. The president-elect's bearing was "calm, easy, bland, self-possessed, yet grave and sedate."[25] Accompanying them were Lincoln's good friend Oregon senator Edward D. Baker and Maryland senator James A. Pearce. As the carriage, surrounded by a double row of cavalry and led by sappers and miners from West Point, rolled over the dusty cobblestones of Pennsylvania Avenue, cheers rang out from the dense crowds lining the sidewalks. In response to the sociable and animated observations made by Lincoln, who seemed calm and oblivious of the excited crowd, the nerve-wracked Buchanan had little to say and gave the impression that he would have preferred to be elsewhere. Unable to engage the lame duck president in conversation, Lincoln stared at the floor of the carriage absently.

Arriving at the capitol at 1:15 p.m., Lincoln and Buchanan descended from their carriage. The weary, sad-faced, white-haired incumbent aroused pity, for he seemed friendless and abandoned. By contrast, the black-haired, younger Lincoln, though looking somewhat awkward, radiated confidence and energy. The party repaired to the President's Room, where the two men chatted amicably. "I think you will find the water of the right-hand well at the White-House better than that at the

The president-elect and outgoing chief executive James Buchanan pass the northwestern base of Capitol Hill en route to Lincoln's inauguration. *Harper's Weekly*, March 16, 1861. Library of Congress.

left," said Buchanan, who "went on with many intimate details of the kitchen and pantry." The president-elect "listened with that weary, introverted look of his, not answering," observed John Hay. The following day, when Hay mentioned this colloquy, Lincoln "admitted he had not heard a word of it."[26]

Arm in arm the two presidents entered the Senate chamber, where diplomats, congressmen, senators, military officers, governors, justices of the Supreme Court, cabinet members, and other officials had foregathered. Preternaturally calm and impassive, Lincoln sat still, heedless of the gaze directed at him by all onlookers. The nervous, discouraged, and tired Buchanan, on the other hand, fidgeted and sighed gently. After the swearing in of Vice President Hamlin, the assembled dignitaries proceeded to a temporary platform erected over the steps of the east portico of the Capitol, which had for almost a decade been undergoing a major extension. Above the ramshackle scaffolding loomed the skeletal, half-finished, new cast-iron dome, flanked by a crane. Before it stood thousands of cheering spectators of all ages. The clouds, which had seemed so threatening that morning, had lifted, giving way to bright sunshine. In his famously sonorous voice, Senator Baker announced: "Fellow Citizens: I introduce to you Abraham Lincoln, the President elect of the United States of America." Before rising, Lincoln sought a place to put his hat. Observing his awkwardness, Stephen A. Douglas held it during the entire reading of the inaugural address. When Lincoln stood up, he was calm, cool, and self-possessed. The crowd cheered, but not vociferously.

After surveying the vast assemblage, Lincoln began deliberately and solemnly reading his address, which lasted thirty-five minutes. He seemed very much at ease as he recited the carefully prepared text. His clear, high, firm voice carried to the outer edge of the vast crowd, faltering only in the final paragraph, whose reference to "the better angels of our nature" brought tears to many eyes. The crowd often applauded Lincoln's remarks, most fervently when he alluded to the Union. As the ancient, shriveled Chief Justice Taney rose to administer the oath of office, he was agitated. After Lincoln swore to "faithfully execute the office of President" and to "preserve, protect, and defend the Constitution," he kissed the Bible. The crowd tossed their hats into the air, wiped their eyes, and shouted till they grew hoarse. Lincoln shook hands with Taney and the other dignitaries on the platform, then rode with Buchanan back down Pennsylvania Avenue to the White House for a public reception. There the ex-president shook his successor's hand and cordially wished him success, then returned to his Pennsylvania home to write a defense of his administration.

That evening at the inaugural ball, Mrs. Lincoln entered on the arm of Senator Douglas, which some regarded as an indication that the Little Giant and the Rail-splitter had "buried the hatchet." Relieved to be safely installed, and drained by the ordeal of preparing and delivering his momentous address, the new president appeared tired. After fifteen minutes of exchanging pleasantries in the receiving line, Lincoln remarked: "This hand-shaking is harder work than rail-splitting." But when the journalist Gail Hamilton offered to spare him the necessity of shaking her hand, he exclaimed: "Ah! Your hand doesn't hurt me."[27] When a correspondent of the New York *Herald* asked the president if he had any message to convey to that paper's editor, James Gordon Bennett, Lincoln replied: "Yes, you may tell him that Thurlow Weed has found out that Seward was not nominated at Chicago!"[28] The president stayed for only thirty minutes; his wife remained for another two hours.

People throughout the country eagerly read the inaugural, which many Northerners viewed positively. Benjamin Brown French, a New Hampshire Democrat whom Lincoln was to appoint commissioner of public buildings, wrote that it "is conciliatory—peaceable—but firm in its tone, and is exactly what we, Union men, want."[29] Charles Sumner likened the inaugural to a "hand of iron in [a] velvet glove."[30] Some, however, feared the consequences of Lincoln's pledge to hold the forts and to collect the revenues. "Either measure will result in Civil War which I am compelled to look upon as almost certain," Edward Everett speculated presciently.[31] Most Southerners were of the same mind. The Charleston *Mercury* grimly proclaimed that "the declaration of war has been spoken."[32]

Some abolitionists disapproved of the inaugural, which they scorned as too conservative. Alluding to the slaves, Frederick Douglass lamented that Lincoln "has avowed himself ready to catch them if they run away, to shoot them down if they rise against their oppressors, and to prohibit the Federal Government irrevocably from interfering for their deliverance."[33] But other abolitionists thought that Lincoln "met the trying emergency with rare self possession and equanimity" and called his address "a very manly sensible document" that "must inspire the respect and confidence of all who are not blinded by jealousy or partizan zeal."[34]

The inaugural received mixed reviews in the Upper South and the Border States, where voters could not determine whether it meant peace or war. Many thought it bellicose, among them North Carolina senator Thomas Clingman, who warned that if the president "intends to use the power in his hands as he states in his inaugural, we must have war."[35] But others read it differently. The Baltimore *Clipper* maintained that the inaugural "means only peace and nothing but peace, as far as is possibly consistent with our national honor and the public welfare."[36] In the nation's capital, John C. Rives, the slave-owning editor of the Washington *Daily Globe*, tellingly asked critics of the inaugural "what position . . . the President of the United States could possibly take, other than that taken by President Lincoln, without a palpable, open violation of his inaugural oath, and an utter abnegation and abdication of all the powers of government?"[37]

Lincoln could breathe a sigh of relief and look forward to a peaceable solution to the secession crisis. He had delivered a firm but conciliatory address that seemed likely to strengthen the hand of Southern Unionists. Now time could work its healing wonders. "Nothing valuable can be lost by taking time," he had said in his inaugural. Southerners would eventually realize that Lincoln was no wild-eyed abolitionist; the Upper South would probably remain in the Union; the Deep South would eventually come to understand that it was too small to survive as a viable nation and would therefore return to the fold. The nation would be restored without bloodshed.

On March 6 and 7, Congressmen Horace Maynard and Thomas A. R. Nelson of Tennessee asked Lincoln how his inaugural should be interpreted. He told them "that he was for peace, and would use every exertion in his power to maintain it; that he was then inclined to the opinion that it would be better to forego the collection of the revenue for a season, so as to allow the people of the seceding States time for reflection, and that regarding them as children of a common family, he was not disposed to take away their bread by withholding even their mail facilities."[38]

The time for reflection would be far shorter than Lincoln anticipated, however. The day after his inauguration, the new president received a letter shattering that rosy scenario. From Charleston, Major Robert Anderson wrote that his Fort Sumter garrison would run out of food within six weeks. The fort, sitting on an island in the harbor and ringed by hostile South Carolina batteries, must be either resupplied or surrendered. The former course would probably lead to war, the latter to "national destruction."[39] Lincoln had to choose between them.

21.

"A Man So Busy in Letting Rooms in One End of His House, That He Can't Stop to Put Out the Fire That Is Burning in the Other"

Distributing Patronage (March–April 1861)

His first six weeks in office taxed Lincoln so severely that he told his friend Orville H. Browning in July 1861: "Of all the trials I have had since I came here, none begin to compare with those I had between the inauguration and the fall of Fort Sumter. They were so great that could I have anticipated them, I would not have believed it possible to survive them."[1] He was compelled to make fateful decisions regarding war and peace while dealing with hordes of mendicant office seekers. Two days after the inauguration, more than a thousand place hunters thronged the White House. Less than a month into his administration, the president told Henry J. Raymond that "he wished he could get time to attend to the Southern question . . . but the office-seekers demanded all his time. 'I am,' he said, 'like a man so busy in letting rooms in one end of his house, that he can't stop to put out the fire that is burning in the other.'"[2] Varying the image, he said he "was so badgered with applications for appointments that he thought sometimes that the only way that he could escape from them would be to take a rope and hang himself on one of the trees in the lawn south of the Presidents House."[3]

Lincoln devoted much time to patronage because he wished to unite his party, and by extension the entire North. Judicious distribution of offices could help cement the many factions of the Republican organization (former Whigs, Free Soilers, Know Nothings, and anti-Nebraska Democrats) into a harmonious whole. Many thought it an unattainable goal, given the party's heterogeneity, but somehow Lincoln managed to do it. Moreover, as Gideon Welles noted, extensive "removals and appointments were not only expected, but absolutely necessary."[4] Lincoln believed "that all the departments are so penetrated with corruption, that a clean sweep will become necessary."[5] When one of his favorite journalists, Simon P. Hanson, wrote that the Lincoln administration would be "a reign of steel," the pun-loving president asked, "Why not add that Buchanan's was the reign of *stealing*?"[6] Disloyalty as well as corruption had to be rooted out. On March 22, the president's

"Gulliver Abe, in the White House, Attacked by the Lilliputian Office-Seekers" appeared on the front page of *Frank Leslie's Budget of Fun*, March 15, 1861, with the caption "Well, this is orful! Who'd a' ever believed such diminutivorous varmints could have had such impudence! Why, they're creeping all over me! I feel a kinder goosefleshy. Scratch himself couldn't get rid of 'em!" Abraham Lincoln Presidential Library and Museum, Springfield, Illinois.

longtime friend Hawkins Taylor observed that "Mr Lincoln is now more to be pitied than any man living; he is literally run down day and night."[7] When a journalist expressed sympathy for the president, Lincoln replied: "Yes, it was bad enough in Springfield, but it was child's play compared with the tussle here. I hardly have a chance to eat or sleep. I am fair game for everybody of that hungry lot."[8]

The "hungry lot" was made up primarily of brazen self-promoters. The would-be civil servants evidently imagined that Lincoln had little better to do than tend to their needs. One day on the street, when an office seeker thrust a letter into the president's hand, he snapped: "No, sir! I am not going to open shop here."[9] John Hay reported that office seekers "come at daybreak and still are coming at midnight."[10]

Lincoln asked one supplicant, "So you think you made me President?"

"Yes, Mr. President, under Providence, I think I did."

"Well," said he puckishly, "it's a pretty mess you've got me into. But I forgive you."[11] In Washington, men from all sections of the country expressed indignation and disappointment that Lincoln "mixes himself up with all the small appointments, & fritters away valuable time in talking about tide waiterships."[12] A successful applicant said "the practice seems to be with Lincoln that he yields to the man that bores [i.e., pesters] him the most."[13] The president rose early and spent at least twelve hours a day meeting with callers. He was "profoundly disgusted with the importunate herd of office beggars" and complained about being cooped up all day dealing with them.[14] One corrective was to have each caller screened by the sober, dignified, blunt John G. Nicolay, who did not hesitate to tell people his opinion of them. Nicolay's principal assistant, John Hay, also helped breast the surging tide, a task that he found disagreeable. But Lincoln objected to pushy lawmakers lobbying on behalf of their clamorous constituents. William O. Stoddard, assistant to Nicolay and Hay, recalled that the president listened to office seekers and their congressional patrons "with a degree of patience and good temper truly astonishing. At times, however, even his equanimity gave way, and more than one public man finally lost the President's good will by his pertinacity in demanding provision for his personal satellites."[15]

Hay described himself to a friend as the conscience of the president, but in fact he was more like a surrogate son, resembling Lincoln in temperament and interests more than did Robert Todd Lincoln. Hay's humor, intelligence, love of wordplay, fondness for literature, and devotion to his boss made him a source of comfort to the beleaguered president in the loneliness of the White House. Hay became as much a friend and confidant to the president as their age difference (nineteen years) permitted. In late March, Nicolay persuaded his boss to set business hours from 10:00 a.m. until 3:00 p.m.; soon thereafter he shortened them by two hours and eliminated Saturday visits. Nevertheless, by April, according to Edwin M. Stanton,

The two principal White House secretaries, John G. Nicolay (*seated*) and John Hay (*standing*), flank the president at Alexander Gardner's studio, November 8, 1863. Hay recorded in his diary that "Nico & I immortalized ourselves by having ourselves done in group with the Presdt." Abraham Lincoln Presidential Library and Museum, Springfield, Illinois.

the president was "said to be very much broken down with the pressure in respect to appointments."[16]

At first, Lincoln planned to examine applications closely in order to keep patient merit from being eclipsed by the unworthy. Among the worthy party workers to be rewarded were campaign biographers. John Locke Scripps received the Chicago post office; William Dean Howells became consul at Venice; James Quay Howard held that same post in Saint John, New Brunswick; Joseph H. Barrett was named commissioner of pensions; and in 1862 Jesse W. Fell won a coveted paymastership in the army. Lincoln intended to call on his cabinet and Congress to help select applicants, but as he told a friend, he "found to his Surprise, that members of his Cabinet, who were equally interested with himself, in the success of his administration, had been recommending parties to be appointed to responsible positions who were often physically, morally, and intellectually unfit for the place."[17] Indeed, congressmen, senators, and cabinet members were less concerned with the success of the administration than with their own short-term political gain. Patronage greased the gears of political machines; party service counted for more than honesty and competence when government jobs were being filled. Friendship or family ties with the powerful also weighed heavily in the balance.

Cabinet secretaries quarreled over patronage. On March 26, Attorney General Edward Bates reported that his colleagues "are squabbling around me" about "the distribution of loaves and fishes."[18] Seward in particular aroused anger by meddling outside his department. Chase too poached on others' turf. Upset by the treasury secretary's attempt to dictate post office appointments, Samuel Galloway warned that if the president "permits his judgment to be swayed by the dictation of Chase he will soon draw upon himself universal contempt & condemnation. Chase has already alienated by his selfishness some of his warmest adherents in Ohio."[19] The treasury secretary protested both to Lincoln and to Seward that Ohio was not receiving its fair share of diplomatic appointments. Others groused that consulates were given disproportionally to Easterners and to ex-Whigs. (The president eventually ruled that the 262 diplomatic and consular posts should be distributed among the states based on their population.)

Lincoln displayed exceptional tact and preternatural skill as a party leader. Thurlow Weed, who worked hard on behalf of his own faction, was widely regarded as a master wire-puller, but the president was shrewder. To Seward, Lincoln explained his guiding principle: "In regard to the patronage, sought with so much eagerness and jealousy, I have prescribed for myself the maxim, 'Justice to all.'"[20] No one faction of the party was allowed to hog the best jobs. As a participant in the 1849 patronage lottery, Lincoln had observed Zachary Taylor undermine his presidency by mishandling the distribution of offices. More recently, Franklin Pierce and James Buchanan had badly divided the Democratic Party not only with unwise policies regarding slavery but also with ill-advised use of the patronage power. Unlike Buchanan, Lincoln fully appreciated the significance of patronage and through its careful distribution was able to keep Congress relatively happy and his party intact.

The president estimated "with some disgust" that 30,000 office seekers had flocked to Washington, but he quickly added, "There are some 30,000,000 who ask for no offices."[21] He predicted that "if ever this government is overthrown, utterly demoralized, it will come from this struggle and wriggle for office, for a way to live without work; from which nature I am not free myself."[22] In July, just after the Union defeat at Bull Run, he asked a friend: "What do you think has annoyed me more than any one thing? . . . the fight over two post offices—one at our Bloomington, and the other at——[Bloomington], in Pennsylvania."[23]

Lincoln gave offices to many of his wife's relatives, but he did little to accommodate his mother's family, though he rewarded many of his Illinois friends. Uncle Jimmy Short, his benefactor in New Salem, became an Indian agent. Oliver G. Abell, son of a New Salem woman who had acted as a surrogate mother to Lincoln, was appointed messenger in the General Land Office. Ethelbert P. Oliphant, who had served with Lincoln in the Black Hawk War, became a judge in the Washington Territory. His good friends and fellow clerks from New Salem days, William G. Greene and Charles Maltby, were named collectors of internal revenue.

One of Lincoln's first appointments was Norman B. Judd as minister to Berlin. The president explained that although Judd was not his oldest friend, he was yet "so devoted and self-sacrificing a friend as to make the distinction of an early nomination to that mission a well due tribute."[24] To assist Judd, Herman Kreismann was named secretary of the legation. This irritated Seward, who complained about Lincoln's "utter absence of any acquaintance" with foreign affairs, "and as to men he was more blind and unsettled than as to measures." The nominations of Judd and Kreismann, he said, "were made without consultation, merely in fulfillment of a promise to give the former a Cabinet appointment, which he had been compelled to give up," largely because of the First Lady's intervention.[25] She never forgave Judd for opposing her husband's Senate bid in 1855.

Other Illinois friends fared well in the patronage lottery. The lucrative job of marshal of the District of Columbia went to Ward Hill Lamon; Anson G. Henry was named surveyor general of the Washington Territory; Simeon Francis became a paymaster in the army; Allen Francis received a consulate in Canada; and Theodore Canisius served as consul in Vienna. The pastor of Springfield's First Presbyterian Church, James Smith, whom Lincoln described as "an intimate personal friend of mine," represented U.S. interests as a consul in his native Scotland.[26] Jackson Grimshaw became a collector of internal revenue, and Gustave Koerner minister to Spain. William Jayne, Lincoln's personal physician and a brother-in-law of Lyman Trumbull, was appointed governor of the Dakota Territory. Other Illinoisans won coveted places in the federal bureaucracy, including Charles L. Wilson, editor of the Chicago *Journal*, who was named secretary of the U.S. legation in London, despite the objections of the minister-designate to Great Britain, Charles Francis Adams. David Davis helped procure the appointment of Congressman William Pitt Kellogg as chief justice of the Nebraska Territory.

Illinois congressmen and senators objected to some of these appointments, which were made without their input. When Congressman William Kellogg sourly protested about the treatment of a friend, Lincoln found his ingratitude dismaying. In a memo composed around April 3, the president gave vent to his wounded feelings: "Mr. Kellogg does me great injustice to write in this strain. He has had more favors than any other Illinois member. . . . Is it really in his heart to add to my perplexities now?"[27]

Not all of Lincoln's Illinois friends succeeded in their quest for government positions. Herndon was denied a patronage post because, Lincoln allegedly said, "he would be charged with paying the debts of personal friendship with public patronage."[28] David Davis irritated the president with numerous patronage requests. His longtime friend, said Lincoln, "has forced me to appoint Archy Williams Judge in Kansas right off and Jno. Jones to a place in the State department: and I have got a bushel of dispatches from Kansas wanting to know if I'm going to fill up *all* the offices from Illinois." In naming Williams, Lincoln had not consulted with members of the Illinois congressional delegation, who were understandably angry. Lincoln often used patronage to attract new allies rather than to reward old ones. Leonard Swett observed that the president would "give more to his enemies than he would to his friends" because "he never had anything to spare, and in the close calculation of attaching the faction to him, he counted upon the abstract affection of his friends as an element to be offset against some gift with which he must appease his enemies."[29]

David Davis was hurt that Lincoln gave him no office. The president had wanted to name him commissary-general of the army, but when Winfield Scott objected to placing a civilian in that post, Lincoln deferred to the general. Davis was also miffed when his recommendations for clerkships were ignored by Secretaries Smith and Cameron, whom he had championed for cabinet posts. Davis's good friend Leonard Swett also met with frustration in his quest for a government job. He wished to serve as consul in Liverpool, a lucrative post, but he lost out to Thomas H. Dudley of New Jersey. Swett was "deeply wounded" but eventually said that if David Davis were named to the U.S. Supreme Court, he would regard that as enough for both of them.[30] In 1862, Lincoln did nominate Davis to the high court.

Most of the friends Lincoln appointed reflected credit on his administration, but two did not: Mark Delahay and Ward Hill Lamon. Lincoln's affection for the bibulous Delahay, whom Henry Villard described as "an empty-headed, self-puffing, vainglorious strut," was curious.[31] He may have felt sorry for the Kansas politico, who had little money and a large family, had at one time been a law partner of Lincoln's close friend Edward D. Baker, and was married to Louisiana Hicks, the daughter of a cousin of Lincoln's. His later appointment as a judge aroused strong opposition from Kansans who insisted that he lacked any qualifications for the post. When Congress launched an impeachment investigation, Delahay was revealed to be a corrupt drunkard whose behavior had disgraced the court.

Lamon's appointment as marshal of the District of Columbia was highly controversial and created friction between Lincoln and Congress. The president evidently took pity on Lamon and sought to help him out of desperate financial straits by giving him that remunerative post. Like Delahay, Lamon came under investigation by a congressional committee, which in 1861 found him guilty of an "unwarranted and a scandalous assumption of authority" in detaching a regiment from

Missouri, bringing it east, and putting himself in charge of it as a brigadier general. For this misconduct, he was fined $20,000.[32] The following year, Lamon again antagonized Congress, this time over the issue of fugitive slaves. As marshal of the District of Columbia, he was in charge of the Washington jail, where he held Blacks accused of being runaway slaves. Overcrowding became a scandal as the prison became packed with four times as many inmates as it was designed to hold. Lamon collected 21¢ per day per prisoner, which yielded him a handsome profit. Despite demands that he fire Lamon, Lincoln stood by his old friend, who served as an informal presidential bodyguard and companion not only on the train ride from Harrisburg to Washington but throughout the Civil War. Lincoln valued his humor, charm, high spirits, conviviality, and exceptional loyalty.

Another ethically challenged friend whom Lincoln sought to oblige was Edward D. Baker, newly elected senator from Oregon, who wished to control all West Coast patronage. (As a law partner of Stephen T. Logan, he had mishandled clients' money. During the Civil War, he received substantial sums to raise a regiment; upon his death in October 1861, it was discovered that he had left $10,000 unaccounted for. His closest political adviser was the notoriously corrupt Andrew J. Butler, brother of Massachusetts politico Benjamin F. Butler.) Baker felt entitled to command the patronage because he was the only Republican senator from the Pacific Northwest. Prominent California Republicans resented Baker's presumption and complained to Lincoln. On March 30, the antagonistic factions met at the White House to discuss offices in the Far West. Baker's opponents were particularly upset that Democrat Robert J. Stevens, a son-in-law of Baker's, was being put forward for superintendent of the San Francisco mint. When they called at the Executive Mansion, they were surprised to discover Baker and his henchman Butler there. The meeting began with Joseph A. Nunes, president of the California Republican conventions of 1856 and 1860, delivering a temperate appeal, after which he handed the president a slate of suggested nominees for California posts and mildly remonstrated against Baker's interference. James W. Simonton, editor of the San Francisco *Evening Bulletin*, followed by reading a bitter attack on the Oregon senator, who, he said (perhaps alluding to Butler), had "presented to the President, as a most substantial and respectable man, a person whose antecedents and reputation Mr. Simonton denounced severely."[33] Simonton characterized other men endorsed by Baker as gamblers and blackguards.

Lincoln asked if he could keep the papers, including Simonton's speech. The editor said he would "like to make some emendations" to his remarks. "Never mind the emendations," replied Lincoln, "if it is mine, I want it as is." Then, "in a withering tone of indignation," he said that Nunes's paper, "being *somewhat* respectful in its tone, I *think* I will keep; but this one," he said holding Simonton's text aloft,

"I will show you what I will do with it." He stepped to the fireplace and flung the offending document into the flames.[34] Returning to his desk, Lincoln erupted in anger so vehemently that, as one observer put it, "everybody present quailed before it. His wrath was simply terrible."[35] He declared: "I have known Colonel Baker longer and better than any of you here, and these attacks upon him I know to be outrageous. I will hear no more of them. If you wish to do so, present your recommendations for office, and I will give them a respectful hearing, but no more of this kind of proceeding."[36] Simonton "looked as though he had been struck by a thunderbolt," but he finally recovered enough to say, "I have simply done my duty: I have nothing to expect from the Executive, and in doing what I did, I merely meant to protect the interests of my State."[37] As the delegation left, one of Baker's friends threatened to shoot Simonton on the spot. Soon thereafter the president called them back, but Simonton did not reappear. On being told that the editor felt insulted, Lincoln sent a special messenger to fetch him, and they reached an *entente cordiale*, though patronage matters were not settled then and there. Later the president explained that Simonton's paper "was an unjust attack upon my dearest personal friend. . . . The delegation did not know what they were talking about when they made him responsible, almost abusively, for what I had done, or proposed to do. They told me that that was my paper, to do with as I liked. I could not trust myself to reply in words: I was so angry."[38] It seems that Lincoln had implicitly promised Baker's daughter that her husband would receive a federal job. Stevens did win his appointment, only to be unceremoniously removed two years later on charges of fraud leveled by the president's old friend from New Salem days, Charles Maltby.

For all his politically shrewd use of the patronage power, Lincoln found it difficult to reject applicants who told sob stories. "If I have one vice," he confessed, "and I can call it nothing else, it is not to be able to say no! Thank God for not making me a woman, but if He had, I suppose He would have made me just as ugly as He did, and no one would ever have tempted me."[39] California senator John Conness complained that Lincoln had a "too kindly heart" and thus "would yield to the pressure for place."[40] Occasionally, Lincoln could avoid saying no and still turn aside friends importuning him for office. When Indiana chums William Jones and Nat Grigsby called in quest of jobs, the president skillfully finessed them before they could make their wishes known. He greeted them warmly and took them to the White House living quarters, where he introduced them to his wife: "Mary, here are two of my old Jonesboro friends who have journeyed all the way up here just to see their old friend. You know the office seekers are pestering the life out of me and I tell you it is a comfort to me to have these boys here especially when I know they do not come to bother me about some position or office. I must hurry back to the office and

I want you to take good care of these boys till I can pull loose." Acting on this hint, Jones and Grigsby returned home without asking for anything.[41]

If Lincoln had a hard time saying no to some office seekers, on occasion he could do so most emphatically. Hay recalled an occasion when the president's patience with an insolent and persistent caller wore out: "He looked at the man steadily for a half-minute or more, then slowly began to lift his long figure from its slouching position in the chair. He rose without haste, went over to where the man was sitting, took him by the coat-collar, carried him bodily to the door, threw him in a heap outside, closed the door, and returned to his chair."[42]

Occasionally Lincoln used humor in turning down pestiferous office seekers and their congressional patrons. When a delegation asked him to name an ill friend of theirs as commissioner of the Hawaiian Islands, where the salubrious climate might improve his health, the president replied: "I am sorry to say that there are eight other applicants for that place, and they are all sicker than your man."[43] A Philadelphia office seeker who repeatedly boasted of his services to the party was told by the president: "I had in my pig sty a little bit of a pig, that made a terrible commotion—do you know why? Because the old sow had just one more little pig than she had teats, and the little porker that got no teat made a terrible squealing." Lincoln's caller took the hint and returned to Pennsylvania.[44] When trying to balance competing claims, Lincoln sometimes had to take into account religion as well as ideology, region, and friendship. Dismayed by sectarian lobbying, he once quipped "that he preferred the Episcopalians to every other sect, because they are equally indifferent to a man's religion and his politics."[45] He tried to bolster Southern Unionists by giving patronage to non-Republicans in the Upper South and the Border States. To John A. Gilmer he explained that in Slave States with few Republicans "I do not expect to inquire for the politics of the appointee, or whether he does or does not own slaves. I intend in that matter to accommodate the people in the several localities, if they themselves will allow me to accommodate them. In one word, I never have been, am not now, and probably never shall be in a mood of harassing the people either north or south."[46] To show that he was reaching out to Democrats and Constitutional Unionists, he cited the example of Louisville, where he had appointed a Bell supporter as postmaster rather than a Republican aspirant. Lincoln told a group of Baltimoreans who urged him to name only Republicans to office that "he was aware that the republicans who lived in Southern States were brave men, and fond of taking a tilt, but he doubted whether that would be the correct principle upon which he should settle the question, as to who should be Collector and Postmaster of Baltimore."[47]

The president encouraged supporters of John J. Crittenden's candidacy for a seat on the Supreme Court. Upon assuming command of the State Department, Seward (presumably with Lincoln's approval) immediately asked Edwin M. Stanton to draw up papers nominating the Kentuckian to the high court. The secretary of state confidently predicted that Crittenden would become a justice, but Radical Republicans, including Chase and Trumbull, objected so vehemently that the plan was scrapped. Lincoln stated "that he will not make any appointment which will be calculated to divide the Republicans in the Senate, as he desires to so act as to consolidate and strengthen the party."[48] Lincoln's willingness to support Crittenden's candidacy was a tribute to the president's magnanimity, for Crittenden had played a key role in defeating Lincoln's bid for the Senate in 1858.

As promised in his inaugural, Lincoln strove to appoint men to posts in the South who were unobjectionable to local residents. He urged his cabinet secretaries to make no removals on political grounds in that region, especially Virginia. When Montgomery Blair selected a postal agent for the Old Dominion who proved so unpopular that after his first run he was threatened with death should he return, Lincoln "expressed his regret that any obnoxious person was appointed mail agent on any mail route" in Virginia.[49]

One particularly insistent group of office seekers, the German Americans, gave Lincoln more trouble than most. "About one-third of the German population of the West are applicants for consulships," the New York *World* reported humorously.[50] At the center of the storm was Carl Schurz, the Wisconsin orator and indefatigable campaigner, who shamelessly lobbied for a first-class diplomatic appointment in Europe. Lincoln had encouraged the young would-be diplomat, whom he liked and admired, but Seward, responding to pressure from the Catholic leadership of New York, raised objections. The secretary of state urged Schurz to accept a post in Latin America or a territorial governorship rather than a European mission. Schurz balked, insisting that he be named minister to Sardinia (i.e., Italy). He managed to persuade one competitor, Anson Burlingame, to withdraw from the field. When Schurz complained to Lincoln about Seward's opposition, the president told him: "I would have appointed you at once, but I deemed it my duty to consult my Secretary of State, with whom I should not like to quarrel right after the organization of the Cabinet. I appreciate your pride and I like it, and I shall be just to you."[51] Schurz believed that his struggle for the Sardinian mission would cause Lincoln to confront his domineering secretary of state. As time passed, Schurz came to regard his case as part of the larger struggle waged by Seward and other compromisers to dominate the administration.

When George Perkins Marsh won the Sardinian post, Lincoln offered to appoint Schurz minister to Portugal, Brazil, Chile, or Peru. "I gave him my mind without reserve," the disgruntled Schurz wrote his wife. He told Lincoln "that he and the republicans had been heretofore supposed to have elected a President, and not a sub-Secretary of State" and "that two thirds of the republican Senators would be before long hostilely arrayed against the administration."[52] He neither accepted nor rejected the proposed alternatives. On March 19, the New York *Herald* reported that the question of Schurz's appointment "seems to bother the administration more than anything else [except] the difficulty about Fort Sumter." That day the matter appeared to be resolved when Schurz agreed to accept the position as minister to Lisbon provided that its status would be elevated to a first-class mission (with a pay increase of $4,500). Seward, however, inexplicably refused to support that change.

On March 21, the president, the secretary of state, and Schurz held a stormy meeting during which the young German refused to back down despite Seward's entreaties. "Lincoln grew quite pale, but I stood firm," Schurz told his wife. Though he was "fed up" with politics and Washington, Schurz felt obliged to stay because of "the possibility of breaking Seward's power over Lincoln, which would ruin the whole Administration." Schurz lamented that in "all things, including for example the Fort Sumter affair, Seward's fatal influence makes itself felt." With characteristic immodesty, he crowed: "I have done more than all the others to keep Lincoln on the right track." The president asked Montgomery Blair to act as an intermediary and persuade Schurz to accept the mission to Russia or Spain. Schurz agreed to the latter post, which had already been assigned to Cassius M. Clay. "Seward's hostility against me is so sharp and his influence over Lincoln is so great, that I am not sanguine enough to expect a favorable result," Schurz wrote. After mulling over the matter, Lincoln authorized Blair to ask Clay to give up the Spanish post. To Schurz it seemed that "Lincoln has finally made up his mind to act independently." On March 28, the three-week contest ended when Clay agreed to accept the mission to Russia rather than the one to Spain. The president thanked the Kentuckian, saying: "Clay, you have relieved me from great embarrassment."[53] Thus "Seward's influence is conquered, and I am master of the battlefield," Schurz bragged. By stiffening Lincoln's backbone, he may have made it easier for the president to stand up to Seward when the Fort Sumter crisis reached a climax. A strong critic of appeasement reported that it "is a matter of congratulation today *among Seward's opponents* that he has suffered the first serious defeat wh[ich] he has yet experienced in respect to any app[ointmen]t—in the instance of Schurz, against whom for a European Mission he had made an especial point."[54]

Although Seward opposed Schurz's appointment in part because of the young German American's radical antislavery views, several of the ministers sent abroad were staunch critics of the peculiar institution. In addition to Schurz, Marsh, and Clay, they included George G. Fogg (Switzerland), Norman B. Judd (Prussia), Rufus King (Papal States), Anson Burlingame (China), and James Shepherd Pike

(Holland). Many consuls were also militant opponents of slavery, among them Zebina Eastman (Bristol), Joshua R. Giddings (Montreal), John Bigelow (Paris), and Hinton Rowan Helper (Buenos Aires). They helped educate their hosts about the fundamental issues of the Civil War. The South reacted to these appointments indignantly, while Northern abolitionists applauded them. The assignment of Helper to Argentina may have given Lincoln special pleasure, for he had read the North Carolinian's controversial 1857 antislavery tract, *The Impending Crisis of the South*, and marked passages in it.

Other distractions prevented Lincoln from focusing on the Fort Sumter crisis, including White House social events and ceremonies. On March 8, he hosted his first White House reception, which Edward Bates described laconically as a "motley crowd and terrible squeeze."[55] The president, according to one report, "with his towering figure and commanding presence, stood like a hero, putting the foot down firmly, and breasting the stream of humanity as it swept by." By one estimate, he shook three thousand hands. On March 22, Herman Melville attended the second public reception at the White House. The president, he said, "shook hands like a good fellow—working hard at it like a man sawing wood at so much per cord."[56]

During an official visit with foreign representatives on March 7, Lincoln "was polite and engaging toward all." The Russian minister, Edouard de Stoeckl, a sarcastic, witty put-down artist who thought the president's "manners are those of a man who has spent all his life in a small Western town," reported that generally speaking "the diplomatic corps has only praise for the reception."[57] Two days later, Lincoln received the officers of the navy, among them David D. Porter, who wrote that the president "was much confused at meeting such an imposing looking set of men. Such was his embarrassment that he could not answer the little speech made to him by Commodore [Joseph] Smith." When the officers asked to meet his wife, Lincoln went off to fetch her and "returned half dragging in the apparently confused lady." After "a few commonplace remarks," the visitors left. "The interview," said Porter, "was not at all calculated to impress us favorably, and there were many remarks made about the President's gaucherie."[58]

As Lincoln dealt with patronage squabbles and hosted White House receptions, he was oppressed by the Fort Sumter crisis. Should he reinforce the garrison, merely resupply it, or surrender it in hopes of avoiding civil war?

22.

"You Can Have No Conflict Without Being Yourselves the Aggressors"

The Fort Sumter Crisis (March–April 1861)

One of Lincoln's greatest challenges was taming his imperious secretary of state. "I can't afford to let Seward take the first trick," he told his chief personal secretary in early March.[1] While struggling with the Fort Sumter dilemma, Lincoln had to keep the wily New Yorker, who presumed he would serve as the Grand Vizier of the administration, from taking not just the first trick but the entire rubber. Seward hoped to dominate Lincoln just as he had President Zachary Taylor. Charles Francis Adams Jr. said that Seward "thought Lincoln a clown, a clod, and planned to steer him by . . . indirection, subtle maneuvering, astute wriggling and plotting, crooked paths. He would be Prime Minister."[2] The Sage of Auburn considered himself, not Lincoln, the "leader of the ruling party." In his own eyes, he was a veteran statesman who must guide the inexperienced Illinoisan. Unlike the president, he did not believe that the new administration had to implement the Chicago platform. Taming the meddlesome, headstrong, mercurial Seward was a Herculean task.

The day after the inauguration, Lincoln was astounded not only by the news that Major Robert J. Anderson, commander of the Fort Sumter garrison, had only six weeks' worth of supplies left but also by a letter from General Scott stating that Anderson believed that the fort must be either surrendered or overrun. The obese, vain, aged general in chief was retreating from his hard-line position of October, when he had urged the reinforcement of forts throughout the South. On March 6, at Lincoln's request, Scott briefed Welles, Cameron, Seward, and other officials, who were dumbfounded when the general reiterated what he had told the president. Welles and Cameron urged that the administration "take immediate and efficient measures to relieve and reinforce the garrison." Scott did not express an opinion but pointed out that the earlier attempt by the Buchanan administration to provision the fort had miscarried. The following day, Lincoln again met with this group. Scott and his chief engineer, Joseph G. Totten, agreed that it would be impracticable to reinforce Sumter. Welles and his adviser, Captain Silas Stringham, insisted that the navy could do so. Seward offered many suggestions and raised several questions, but no conclusions were reached.

On March 9, the full cabinet convened to hear the bad news about Fort Sumter. That same day, Lincoln asked Scott how long the garrison could hold out, whether he could supply or reinforce it within that time, and what additional means might be needed to accomplish that goal. He asked the general to put his answers in writing and to "exercise all possible vigilance for the maintenance of all the places within the military department of the United States; and to promptly call upon all the departments of the government for the means necessary to that end."[3] Incredibly, Scott ignored that directive and simply replied that in order to save Sumter, he would need a large fleet, 25,000 more troops, and several months to train them.

On March 11, Scott drafted an order instructing Anderson to evacuate the fort. Lincoln gave serious thought to issuing it but hesitated. Based on leaks, probably from Seward, newspapers reported that the administration would remove the Sumter garrison, thereby touching off a firestorm of indignant protest. Montgomery Blair was so angry at the prospect of surrendering the fort that he prepared a letter of resignation. He described the cabinet discussions to his father, who, at the urging of some senators, called on the president to stiffen his backbone. The old man, with vivid memories of Andrew Jackson's forceful crushing of South Carolina's nullifiers in 1832–33, condemned Scott and Seward and warned that the president might be impeached if he followed their counsel.

Montgomery Blair sought to persuade Lincoln that Sumter could be held. On March 12, he summoned his brother-in-law Gustavus Fox, a 34-year-old former naval officer. Fox proposed that troops and supplies be carried to the bar of Charleston harbor by a large commercial vessel, then transferred to light, fast tugboats that would convey them to the fort under cover of darkness, all to be done while being protected by an accompanying warship. The next day, Blair took the energetic, industrious, and self-assured Fox to the White House, where he outlined his scheme to the president. Lincoln came to like and admire Fox, a cheerful, buoyant raconteur whose wife's sister was married to Montgomery Blair. (In August 1861 Fox became assistant secretary of the navy and in effect served as chief of naval operations, working smoothly with Gideon Welles.)

On the Ides of March, Fox briefed the cabinet. At that meeting, Generals Totten and Scott reiterated their objections. The president asked the cabinet secretaries to answer in writing a simple question: "Assuming it to be possible to now provision Fort-Sumpter, under all the circumstances, is it wise to attempt it?"[4] In a lengthy reply, Seward argued that such an effort would needlessly trigger a civil war, that it was militarily impracticable, that it would accomplish nothing worthwhile, that it would drive the Upper South and the Border States into the Confederacy, that the nation could never be made whole again, that a policy of conciliation should be pursued, and that Sumter was strategically unimportant. But he would insist that import duties be collected by ships stationed outside Southern ports, even if it might provoke hostilities.

Bates argued that provisioning the fort would be legal as well as physically possible, but imprudent. He feared that if war resulted, it would seem to the world as if the North had provoked it and would lead to unimaginably horrid slave uprisings. He recommended adopting a tough stand against any attempt to block the mouth of the Mississippi River and making a show of resolve at the other forts remaining in Union hands, most notably Pickens in Florida. Similarly, Welles argued that even though a relief expedition like the one being contemplated might work, the North could be compelled to fire the opening shot and thereby become guilty of shedding the first blood. Cameron said the administration should defer to the military men who denied the feasibility of resupplying the fort. Smith maintained that an expedition should be sent to Charleston only if it were able to bring overwhelming force to bear. Chase waffled, saying he would recommend provisioning the fort as long as it would not touch off a war, which the nation could ill afford. But such a war seemed to him unlikely. Montgomery Blair was the only cabinet secretary to favor the relief effort unconditionally. Secessionists were taking heart from Northern timidity and vacillation, he asserted; to continue an appeasement policy would only encourage them further. On the other hand, to provision the fort, which was militarily possible, would demoralize them and spark a Southern movement to reunite the country.

While mulling over his options, Lincoln urged the cabinet to avoid offending the South. Despite the advice he was receiving from prominent military and civilian leaders, Lincoln hesitated to abandon Sumter. He knew that step would outrage the North, for as March dragged on, public opinion grew ever more discontented with the president's "namby pamby course."[5] Letters poured into the Capitol and the White House insisting that if Sumter were surrendered, something else must be done to prove that the nation still had a government. One obvious way to offset the evacuation of Sumter was to reinforce the only other major Deep South fort still in Union hands, Pickens, off Pensacola, Florida. Bates had suggested that strategy privately, and some newspapers did so publicly. To implement that plan, Lincoln on March 5 verbally instructed Scott to hold Pickens and the other Southern forts. When a week later the president discovered that nothing had been done to carry out this order, he put it in writing. On March 12, in obedience to the president's instructions, Scott ordered the two hundred troops aboard the USS *Brooklyn*, then in Florida, to occupy the fort.

To obtain more information before making up his mind, Lincoln asked the wife of an officer stationed at Fort Sumter, Abner Doubleday, if she would show him her husband's letters. In addition, he dispatched troubleshooters to Charleston. Fox volunteered to visit that city and ascertain the feasibility of his plan after consulting with Major Anderson; on March 19 he departed for South Carolina. Two days later Lincoln asked his Illinois friend Stephen A. Hurlbut, a bibulous native of Charleston, to return to his hometown and sample public opinion. The president dispatched Ward Hill Lamon to accompany him as an informal bodyguard.

After interviewing many lawyers, merchants, workingmen, and transplanted Northerners, Hurlbut reported "that Separate Nationality is a fixed fact . . . there is no attachment to the Union." He expressed serious doubt "that any policy which may be adopted by this Government will prevent the possibility of armed collision," and he was sure that "a ship known to contain *only provisions* for Sumpter would be stopped & refused admittance." He did not predict that such a ship would be fired upon or that its dispatch would provoke an attack on Sumter. Lincoln had Hurlbut repeat his findings to Seward, who continued to insist that Southern Unionists would thwart the secessionists. Hurlbut replied that Sumter "was commanded by batteries which had been erected without molestation" and "that it was the intention to reduce the fort at all hazards." After Hurlbut wrote up his report, Lincoln read it to the cabinet.[6]

That document clearly destroyed whatever hope Lincoln may have entertained that the Deep South would voluntarily return to the fold. Seward's faith in a peaceful reconstruction seemed more and more chimerical; war appeared to be the only means to restore the Union. Hurlbut's report may well have convinced Lincoln that since war was inevitable no matter what he did, it therefore made sense to relieve Sumter and thus placate Northern hard-liners. Meanwhile, Fox consulted with Major Anderson, who predicted that his supplies would run out by April 15, that any attempt to provision or reinforce the garrison would precipitate a war, that it was too late, and that no relief vessels could slip past the South Carolina artillery. Fox did not argue, but he closely observed the fort and the surrounding waters. What he saw convinced him that his plan would work, and he so informed Lincoln.

While the missions of Hurlbut and Fox yielded useful information, Lamon's provided harmful disinformation. The egotistical cavalier misled South Carolina governor Francis Pickens and Major Anderson by assuring them, without authorization, that the Sumter garrison would soon be withdrawn. He explained to the governor that his mission was to facilitate the evacuation of the fort. More misleading still was the conduct of Seward, who virtually told Upper South Unionists (as well as the three commissioners sent by the Confederate government to demand formal recognition) that Sumter would be evacuated. Forbidden by the president to receive the commissioners officially, Seward employed go-betweens to negotiate with them. At first, former senator William M. Gwin of California played that role, but he grew suspicious of Seward, dropped out, and wrote Jefferson Davis a telegram stating that the appointment of Chase to the cabinet meant war. When Seward was shown the telegram, he revised the text to read, "Notwithstanding Mr. Chase's appointment, the policy of the Administration will be for peace and the amicable settlement of all questions between the sections." Gwin sent the revised message to Montgomery, capital of the newly formed Confederacy, then departed Washington. Seward was thus communicating almost directly with the Confederate president without his own president's authorization.

U.S. Supreme Court Justice John A. Campbell of Alabama replaced Gwin as Seward's intermediary. On March 13, when the commissioners demanded that the Confederacy be acknowledged as an independent nation, Seward, fearing that a blunt refusal might precipitate war, desperately tried to stall them. Two days later the secretary of state told Campbell that the administration would withdraw the Sumter garrison within a week. When Campbell asked what he could write to Jefferson Davis, Seward replied: "You may say to him that before that letter reaches him, the telegraph will have informed him that Sumter will have been evacuated." It is possible but highly unlikely that Lincoln authorized his secretary of state to make such a statement. He strongly denied having done so. More probably, Seward was gambling that the president would go along with the majority of the cabinet, who opposed relieving Sumter.

So Campbell assured both Davis and the Confederate commissioners that he had "perfect confidence in the fact that Fort Sumter will be evacuated in the next five days." He sent a copy of this letter to Seward, who did not correct him. When five days had passed and the Sumter garrison still remained in place, the commissioners asked Campbell what was causing the delay. The judge consulted Seward, who assured him that everything was all right and told him to return the following day. When Campbell did so, the secretary "said he did not know why the evacuation order had not been executed" but that "there was nothing in the delay that affected the integrity of the promise or denoted any intention not to comply." Seward also reassured Campbell that the administration would not alter the situation at Fort Pickens. Campbell reported back to the commissioners that Sumter would be evacuated soon and that "no prejudicial movement to the South is contemplated as respects Fort Pickens."[7]

Lincoln concluded that if he removed the Sumter garrison, he could justify it as a matter of practical necessity while simultaneously asserting federal authority by reinforcing Fort Pickens. To take a hard line at Pickens would immunize him against charges that he had abandoned his inaugural pledge "to hold, occupy, and possess the property, and places belonging to the government." If, however, Pickens were not available as an offset to the surrender of Sumter, the evacuation of the Charleston fort would be tantamount to a formal recognition of the Confederacy's independence. In late March, he informed some congressmen, "in unmistakable terms," that even if Sumter were abandoned, "the other forts yet in possession of federal troops will be held to the last."[8]

The situation changed dramatically on March 28 when Scott recommended that Sumter *and* Pickens be abandoned. "Our Southern friends," the general wrote, "are clear that the evacuation of both the forts would instantly soothe and give confidence to the eight remaining slaveholding States, and render their cordial adherence to this Union perpetual."[9] Scott's recommendation shocked Lincoln, who convened his cabinet the following day. "I never shall forget the President's excitement," Montgomery Blair wrote. In an "agitated manner," Lincoln read Scott's letter. A "very oppressive silence" prevailed, broken only when Blair remarked: "Mr President you can now see, that Gen[era]l Scott in advising the surrender of Fort Sumpter is playing the part of a politician not of a General, for as no one pretends that there is any military necessity for the surrender of Fort Pickens which he now says it is equally necessary to surrender, it is plain that he is governed by political reasons in both recommendations." As Blair recalled, "No answer could be made to this point & the President saw that he was being misled."[10]

That night Lincoln did not sleep. The next day he confessed that he was "in the dumps," and according to his wife, he "keeled over with [a] sick headache for the first time in years."[11] At a noon cabinet meeting, he took Edward Bates's advice and had each department head write out yet another opinion about Sumter. Evidently it had occurred to Lincoln that Fort Sumter could perhaps be relieved after all. But if it were to be resupplied, that would damage Lincoln's credibility in the South, where newspapers as well as the commissioners proclaimed that his administration would abandon the fort.

The drama of the preceding night changed Welles's mind; he now recommended sending both provisions and troops to Sumter and notifying South Carolina authorities of the decision. He also urged that "Fort Pickens and other places retained should be strengthened by additional troops, and, if possible made impregnable." Similarly, Chase abandoned his earlier position and expressed himself in favor "of maintaining Fort Pickens and just as clearly in favor of provisioning Fort Sumter. If that attempt be resisted by military force Fort Sumter should, in my judgment, be reinforced." Blair stated that he had no confidence in Scott's judgment and that supplies ought to be sent to Sumter without reference to Fort Pickens. Bates favored reinforcing Pickens but straddled the Sumter issue: "As to fort Sumter—I think the time is come either to evacuate or relieve it."[12] Seward had no allies except Smith, who recommended the surrender of Sumter but not of Pickens. (Remarkably, Cameron was out of town.) So three cabinet secretaries favored relieving Sumter, two opposed it, one waffled, and one was absent.

When the press, evidently aware of Scott's proposal, reported that Fort Pickens would be evacuated, Congress and the public were outraged. Republican lawmakers called on Lincoln and protested, as did many correspondents. "We (the people of the West) have accepted the evacuation of Fort Sumter as a military necessity," wrote an Illinoisan. "But you & your Cabinet cannot imagine our chagrin at the report of the probable evacuation of Fort Pickins and that a portion of your Cabinet with the Sec. of State at their head is in favour of peace and evacuation on almost any terms. It has taken us all aback."[13]

In late March, when Lincoln received word that the USS *Brooklyn* had sailed from Pensacola to Key West for supplies, he wrongly assumed that she had taken with her the soldiers designated to reinforce Fort Pickens. In fact, those troops had been transferred to the USS *Sabine*, which remained on station at Pensacola. Unaware of this important information, the president concluded that his March 12 order had "fizzled out."[14] Therefore it was imperative to launch a new expedition to reinforce Pickens. In case that was not effected before the Sumter garrison ran out of food, it was also essential to prepare a relief expedition for the Charleston fort. So on March 29 the president ordered Fox to make ready a squadron for relieving Sumter but to enter into no binding agreements. By mid-April the garrison would be starved out; in order to get provisions to Charleston before then, an expedition would have to be organized immediately. If it turned out that Scott's March 12 order to reinforce Pickens actually had been obeyed, or if the new Pickens expedition reached Pensacola before the Sumter garrison exhausted its food supply, then Fox's mission—which might precipitate war—could be scrubbed.

That afternoon, Lincoln summoned Scott to the White House. In the course of their long conversation about the forts, Lincoln said that "*Anderson had played us false*" and predicted that the administration "would be broken up unless a more decided policy was adopted, and if General Scott could not carry out his views, some other person might." He chided the Hero of Chapultepec for not promptly carrying out his directive of March 5 to reinforce Pickens.[15] The ever-resourceful Seward, observing his plans crumble, frantically tried to salvage the situation. While maintaining his opposition to the relief of Sumter, he now recommended that Lincoln "at once and at every cost prepare for a war at Pensacola and Texas, to be taken however only as a consequence of maintaining the possession and authority of the United States."[16]

Seward's sudden concern for Fort Pickens was puzzling, since he had earlier shown little interest in that bastion; at the forefront of his mind on March 29 was the Sumter expedition. How could he explain to the Confederate commissioners and to Justice Campbell that his assurances about the evacuation of the Charleston fort had proved false? How could he maintain leadership in the administration now that the president had overruled him, with the support of a plurality of the cabinet? How could he prevent the outbreak of civil war? One way was to sabotage the Sumter expedition by stripping it of its key component, the warship *Powhatan*. That vessel, it was understood, was the only one in the navy capable of carrying out the mission. Perhaps Lincoln could be persuaded to send her to Pensacola rather than to Charleston. But Welles would probably want the *Powhatan* for the Sumter expedition. So the relief of Pickens, including the *Powhatan*, must be undertaken without Welles's knowledge. But how? Seward could argue that the mission must be kept secret, lest word of it leak out and impel the Confederates to attack Pickens before ships arrived to protect it. Therefore only Seward, the president, and officers in charge of the ships and troops should be informed. This highly irregular proceeding would certainly offend the secretaries of war and the navy, but Seward regarded them as ciphers. So the Sage of Auburn, desperately seeking a way to preserve his honor, his leadership position, and the peace, scrambled to implement this devious scheme. He would also try to persuade the president to let him take charge of the administration.

On March 29, Seward summoned his friend Captain Montgomery C. Meigs, an ambitious, vain, 45-year-old army engineer who had recently visited Fort Pickens. Alluding to General Scott, the secretary explained to Meigs "that he thought the President ought to see some of the younger officers, and not consult only with men who, if war broke out, could not mount a horse."[17] (All along Seward had been using Scott as his authority in arguing that Sumter should be abandoned. Now, with Scott discredited, the secretary needed some other military man to lend credibility to his strategizing.) At the White House, Meigs confidently asserted that both Sumter and Pickens could be held. The danger in reinforcing the Florida fort was that Confederates might intercept boats ferrying troops across Pensacola Bay. But, he said, if a swift warship were sent there immediately, it could protect those boats from rebel attackers. Thus Seward's new plan would be supported: send the *Powhatan* to Florida and thus make it unavailable for a mission to Sumter.

Lincoln ordered that an expedition sail to Florida as soon as possible. The next morning Seward informed Scott of the president's directive. The general then consulted with his military secretary, Colonel E. D. Keyes, who argued that it would be extremely difficult to reinforce Fort Pickens. Scott directed him to share his thoughts with Seward. When the colonel pointed out the problems he had mentioned to

Scott, Seward interrupted saying, "I don't care about the difficulties," and ordered him to fetch Meigs forthwith. Ten minutes later the captain and the colonel stood before the secretary of state, who commanded them to devise a plan for reinforcing Pickens and present it at the White House no later than 3:00 that afternoon. The two officers hurriedly carried out their assignment but had insufficient time to consult with Scott. At the Executive Mansion, Meigs and Keyes read their proposals to Lincoln, who approved them despite his puzzlement at references to scarps, terreplains, barbettes, and the like. To command the ships involved, Meigs recommended Lieutenant David Dixon Porter, an ambitious, bold young officer. "Gentlemen," the president directed, "see General Scott, and carry your plans into execution without delay."[18] When they did so later that day, the general approved their scheme and wrote orders implementing it.

Meanwhile, that same day the Confederate commissioners called Justice Campbell's attention to a telegram from Governor Pickens complaining that Lamon had failed to honor his promise to arrange for the evacuation of Sumter. Two days later, Seward told Campbell that Lamon had no authorization to make promises. He handed the judge a note stating that Lincoln "may desire to supply Fort Sumter, but will not undertake to do so without first giving notice to Governor Pickens." This represented a dramatic change from his earlier assurances to Campbell, who protested that if such a message were conveyed to Charleston, the authorities there would bombard Sumter immediately. Seward then consulted with Lincoln and returned with a modified version of a message for the South Carolina governor: "I am satisfied the Government will not undertake to supply Fort Sumter without giving notice to Governor Pickens." This was still a far cry from what Campbell had been told previously. Clearly the secretary was deceiving the commissioners, unless he believed that he could sabotage the Sumter expedition and thereby thwart Lincoln.

On April 1, Lieutenant Porter and Seward reviewed the secret plans to reinforce Pickens. Porter suggested that Lincoln, not the secretary of the navy, issue a direct order to ready the *Powhatan*. At a conference with Porter, Meigs, and Seward, Lincoln approved these arrangements, though he felt uneasy about bypassing normal channels and having his secretary of state act as de facto secretary of the navy. The formal order instructed Porter to sail the *Powhatan* into Pensacola harbor and cover the reinforcement of the fort. The order had been, as Meigs put it, "extracted" from the president, who may well have been confused about three different warships with Indian names beginning with the letter *P*. (The other two "P" vessels were the Pocahontas and the Pawnee, all part of Fox's squadron.) While signing the various documents, Lincoln said: "Gentlemen I don't know anything of your army and navy rules only don't let me burn my fingers."[19]

Because of the secrecy and haste involved, the plan quickly created a bureaucratic nightmare. The *Powhatan* was under the command of Captain Samuel Mercer, who received an order written by Porter and signed by Lincoln instructing him to turn the ship over to the lieutenant. On April 1, Welles, unaware of the Seward-Porter-Meigs-Lincoln scheme, ordered the *Powhatan* to be readied for duty as soon as possible. As if this were not sufficiently perplexing, another problem immediately arose: how was the Pickens expedition to be paid for? Congress, now adjourned, had appropriated no money for such purposes that could be spent without going through normal channels. The only recourse was the secret-service fund of the State Department, which could be tapped with the approval of the president alone. So Lincoln authorized this unconventional funding arrangement, and Seward gave ten thousand dollars to Meigs, who distributed it to both Porter and Keyes. Porter was responsible for hiring a steamer in New York and overseeing the preparation of the other ships for the Pickens expedition. Armed with orders freshly signed by Lincoln, Porter left for New York on April 1. The next day the acting commandant of the Brooklyn Navy Yard, Andrew H. Foote, hesitated to let the lieutenant have the *Powhatan*, for the previous afternoon Welles's order assigning that vessel to Fox had arrived. After some cajoling, the lieutenant persuaded Foote to honor Lincoln's directive and to maintain secrecy. The *Powhatan* was ready to sail by April 6.

On April 1, Lincoln sent Welles copies of some of the documents he had that day approved, one of which seemed to undercut the secretary's authority. Indignantly, Welles called at the White House to protest. Lincoln, sensing his anger, plaintively asked: "What have I done wrong?" In addition to the orders regarding the Pickens expedition, he had signed instructions to Welles to send most of the navy to Mexico; to reassign the secretary's trusted assistant, Captain Stringham, to Pensacola; and to replace Stringham with Captain Samuel Barron. Welles explained that Barron's loyalty was suspect and he could not work with such a man as his principal subordinate. (In fact, Barron soon thereafter joined the Confederate navy.) The restructuring of the department specified in Lincoln's directive would have put Barron virtually in charge of naval operations. The president explained that Seward "with two or three young men had been there through the day, on a matter which Mr. Seward had much at heart; that he had yielded to the project of Mr. Seward, but as it had involved considerable detail and he had his hands full, and more too, he had left Mr. Seward to prepare the necessary papers. These papers he had signed, some without reading, trusting entirely to Mr. Seward, for he could not undertake to read all the papers presented to him; and if he could not trust the Secretary of State, whom could he rely upon in a public matter that concerned us all?" Lincoln told Welles that "he never would have signed that paper had he been aware of its contents, much of which had no connection with Mr. Seward's scheme."[20] The president countermanded the order reassigning Stringham and Barron, but he still did not fully inform Welles about the Pickens relief mission.

Four days later Seward and his son Frederick called on the navy secretary late at night with a telegram from Meigs and Porter asking for clarification of orders regarding the *Powhatan*, since confusion reigned at the Brooklyn Navy Yard. Seward demanded that Welles retract his order assigning that warship to Fox. Puzzled, Welles insisted that they consult the president immediately despite the lateness of the hour. Around midnight they arrived at the Executive Mansion, where Lincoln was still up. Surprised by the telegram from Meigs and Porter, the president suggested that he might have misunderstood which vessel would serve as flagship for the Sumter squadron, confusing the *Pocahontas* with the *Powhatan*.

The navy secretary quickly retrieved documents from his office indicating that Lincoln had authorized the assignment of the *Powhatan* to Fox. To set things aright, Lincoln told Seward "that the Powhatan must be restored" to the Sumter expedition, which must "on no account" be allowed to fail. Seward said he "thought it was now too late to correct the mistake" and that "he considered the other [Fort Pickens] project the most important, and asked whether that would not be injured if the Powhatan was now withdrawn." Lincoln "would not discuss the subject, but was peremptory—said there was not the pressing necessity in the other case. . . . As regarded Sumter, however, not a day was to be lost—that the orders of the Secretary of the Navy must be carried out." When Seward opined that it might be too late to send a telegram to New York, Lincoln insisted that it be done.[21] Reluctantly the secretary of state obeyed, sending a telegram to Porter ordering him to do as the president had instructed. Amazingly, it did not arrive until 3:00 p.m. the next day. Seward signed the message with his own name, not the president's. The frigate, which had already set sail, was overtaken and the message handed to Porter, who refused to obey it because it bore the signature of the secretary of state and he was operating on orders signed by the president.

Whether Seward deliberately sabotaged the change in plans by signing his own name rather than the president's is not known for certain, but it seems probable. He was trying to thwart the Sumter expedition, which he opposed fiercely. Calling Seward "that timid traitor" who "paralizes every movement from abject fear," Fox accused him of "treachery" by "interfering with the other dep[artment]s as the last hope of preventing the reinforcing of Sumpter."[22] Gideon Welles always believed that "to save himself" Seward had "detached the Powhatan from the expedition and sent her to Pensacola."[23] Without the *Powhatan*, Fox might not be able to carry out his orders.

Welles recalled that Lincoln "took upon himself the whole blame—said it was carelessness, heedlessness on his part—he ought to have been more careful and attentive" and that "we were all new in the administration; that he permitted himself, with the best intentions, to be drawn into an impropriety without sufficient examination and reflection." He assured the navy secretary that "he was confident no similar error would again occur." This willingness to accept blame was characteristic of Lincoln. As Welles put it, the president "never shunned any responsibility and often declared that he, and not his Cabinet, was in fault for errors imputed to them, when I sometimes thought otherwise."[24] Magnanimity was one of Lincoln's most extraordinary qualities, one that would serve him well in trying times to come.

Meanwhile, Seward overplayed his hand once again. On April 1 he virtually offered to take over the administration. In a memorandum entitled "Some Thoughts for the President's Consideration," he rashly told Lincoln that the administration, now four weeks old, had no foreign or domestic policy. The latter should be to "change the question before the public from one upon slavery, or about slavery, for a question upon union or disunion." This could be achieved by shifting the country's focus from Sumter (which the public associated with the issue of slavery) to Pickens (associated in the public mind with the issue of union) by abandoning the former and reinforcing the latter.

This may not have surprised Lincoln, but he was doubtless amazed by Seward's foreign policy recommendations. Alluding to recent events on the island of Hispaniola, where Spain and France appeared to be maneuvering to reestablish colonial rule, the secretary urged Lincoln to "demand explanations" from those two European powers, "categorical at once." If they provided unsatisfactory answers, the president should "convene Congress and declare war against them." On top of that eccentric counsel, Seward then hinted broadly that he would be glad to run the country: "whatever policy we adopt, there must be an energetic prosecution of it. . . . Either the President must do it himself, and be all the while active in it, or devolve it on some member of his cabinet. Once adopted, all debates must end, and all agree and abide." In case Lincoln did not catch his drift, Seward added: "It is not my special province, but I neither seek to evade nor to assume responsibility."[25]

The president sought to calm Seward down, responding gently but firmly to this bizarre memorandum. He assured his secretary of state that the administration did indeed have a domestic policy, which had been spelled out in the inaugural: "to hold, occupy and possess the forts, and all other property and places belonging to the government, and to collect the duties on imports." Seward had approved that policy, and the two leaders were still in agreement except with regard to Fort Sumter. Lincoln denied that the relief of Pickens would be viewed as a pro-Union gesture and the relief of Sumter as a pro-abolitionist gesture; both were attempts to uphold the government's authority. He dismissed the suggestion that war should be declared on European powers. Finally, Lincoln tactfully handled Seward's bid to assume responsibility for making and implementing policy: "If this must be done, I must do it. . . . still upon points arising in its progress I wish, and I suppose I am entitled to have, the advice of all the Cabinet."[26] Seward had originally planned to have his memorandum and Lincoln's response published in the New York *Times*. When the president rejected his proposal, the secretary of state inspired attacks on Lincoln in friendly journals. On April 3, the *Times* published a blistering editorial, "Wanted—A Policy," containing the arguments in Seward's April 1 memo.

While the Sumter expedition was being mounted in early April, Seward continued trying to control events. There was still time, for the point of no return had not yet been reached. Neither the governor of South Carolina nor Major Anderson had been notified, and Fox's ships had not left New York. Perhaps something at the last minute might prevent the outbreak of war. To that end, Seward urged the president to summon the leader of Virginia's Unionists, George W. Summers, who was spearheading the fight against secession at the Richmond convention. When Summers demurred, a caucus of Unionist leaders agreed that John B. Baldwin should meet with Lincoln. He left immediately for Washington. On April 4, as the Virginia convention was voting 89–45 against secession, Baldwin reported to Seward, who escorted him to the White House. Although the substance of their conversation is a matter of some dispute, much evidence suggests that Lincoln offered to remove the Sumter garrison if the Virginia convention would adjourn *sine die*. Three years later Fox recalled that Lincoln had sent for a Unionist member of the Virginia convention "and assured him that if that convention would adjourn, instead of staying in session menacing the Gov't. that he would immediately direct Major Anderson to evacuate Fort Sumter." When that offer proved unavailing, the president on April 4 "sent for me and told me that the expedition [to relieve Sumter] might go forward."[27]

That same day, Lincoln notified Anderson that a relief expedition was under way, but he did not inform Governor Pickens, for that would represent the point of no return, and the president still wished to keep his options open as he awaited word from Florida. Two days later, he learned to his consternation that Scott's order of March 12—to have the troops aboard the *Brooklyn* transferred to Fort Pickens—had been refused by navy captain Henry A. Adams, in command of the Union squadron off Pensacola. Adams, who had three sons serving in the Confederate military, told Welles that he was unwilling to obey orders from an army officer—especially orders that would violate the truce that had been in effect since January—and requested further instructions. The secretary, in consultation with

Lincoln, immediately dispatched navy lieutenant John L. Worden to Pensacola with orders directing Adams to carry out Scott's March 12 instruction. Worden delivered the message on April 12, and the troops accordingly occupied Fort Pickens. There was insufficient time for the administration to learn this good news and call off Fox's mission. On April 17, Porter's ships, including the *Powhatan*, arrived at Pensacola and significantly reinforced Pickens, which remained in Union hands throughout the war.

A month earlier, Major Anderson's message about his dwindling supplies had ruined Lincoln's original plan for dealing with secession. Now Captain Adams's refusal to obey orders wrecked his strategy for solving the Sumter dilemma. At 6:00 p.m. on April 6, hours after learning of Captain Adams's refusal to allow the reinforcement of Fort Pickens, Lincoln reluctantly sent the South Carolina governor word of Fox's expedition, stating that "an attempt will be made to supply Fort Sumpter with provisions only, and that, if such attempt be not resisted, no effort to throw in men, arms, or supplies will be made, without further notice, or in case of an attack upon the Fort."[28] The next day, elements of Fox's squadron left New York for Charleston. The die was finally cast.

When Lincoln issued the order to Fox and sent the fateful message to Governor Pickens, he did so after consulting only with Welles, Fox, and Montgomery Blair. Upon learning of this action later that evening, Seward expressed astonishment. "I want no more at this time of the Administration," he told George Harrington of the Treasury Department. "We are not yet in a position to go to war."[29] Meanwhile, the Confederate commissioners in Washington were growing ever more restive. On April 7, when Campbell relayed their concern to Seward, the secretary blandly reassured them: "Faith as to Sumter fully kept; wait and see." After he formally turned down their renewed demand for recognition, they sent him a blistering letter and departed Washington.

Lincoln could not be sure that his decision to launch the Sumter expedition would precipitate a war, though he had good reason to believe that it might well do so. But there was a remote chance that the Confederates would hesitate to fire on a ship conveying food to hungry men. By announcing that he was sending food rather than troops, Lincoln had masterfully put his opponents on the horns of a dilemma; both options were unpalatable. In the apt words of Lincoln's private secretaries, when he "finally gave the order that the fleet should sail he was master of the situation; master of his Cabinet; master of the moral attitude and issues of the struggle; master of the public opinion which must arise out of the impending conflict; master if the rebels hesitated or repented, because they would thereby forfeit their prestige with the South; master if they persisted, for he would then command a united North."[30]

A Democratic newspaper in Ohio argued that by ordering the fleet to Charleston, Lincoln was "shrewdly inviting the secessionists to open the ball."[31] In fact, Lincoln hoped to avoid, not provoke, bloodshed. If the Fort Pickens strategy had worked, he might have been able to do so; but it failed. By April 6, when he sent his message to the governor of South Carolina, he had exhausted every peaceful option short of acknowledging the legitimacy of secession or surrendering the basic principles of the Republican Party. He probably believed that war might well come as a result of the attempt to provision Fort Sumter, though he did not want war. But if war were to come, he naturally wanted the odium for starting it to fall on the Confederates.

As Porter and Fox began steaming southward on April 8, many Northerners took heart. A Connecticut Republican reported that "we all feel that Mr Lincoln has something of the Old Hickory about him. I hear on every hand . . . 'Give the South (the rebels) a *good thrashing*.'"[32] If war did result from Lincoln's decision, he was assured of military assistance from several Northern leaders. On April 6, he met with the governors of Indiana, Maine, Illinois, Wisconsin, Michigan, Ohio, and Pennsylvania. He asked them to call up their militias and be prepared to defend the capital on a moment's notice, predicting "that when the ball opened," Washington "will be the first [city] that will be attacked."[33]

In the midst of all the excitement and anxiety, office seekers continued to pester Lincoln, who jocularly remarked on the morning of April 10 "that he would henceforth require all applicants to demonstrate their patriotism by serving three months at Forts Sumter and Pickens."[34] That evening he more soberly told a caller that soon it would become clear "whether the revolutionists dare to fire upon an unarmed vessel sent to the rescue of our starving soldiers."[35]

"I hope it may do some good," he told a congressman.[36]

Jefferson Davis authorized the attack on Fort Sumter, which began on April 12 and was over the following day. It proved to be a major blunder, for it outraged and unified the North while dampening pro-Confederate sympathy in the Border States. Remarkably, though thousands of rounds were fired, no one was killed during the bombardment, which touched off the bloodiest war in American history. Gustavus Fox's squadron, shorn of the *Powhatan*, arrived at Charleston too late to affect the outcome. As he transported the Sumter garrison to New York, he told Anderson "how anxious the Prest was that they (S[outh]C[arolina]) should stand before the civilized world as having fired upon bread."[37] Alluding to this important point, Lincoln wrote Fox on May 1: "You and I both anticipated that the cause of the country would be advanced by making the attempt to provision Fort Sumter, even if it should fail; and it is no small consolation now to feel that our anticipation is justified by the result."[38]

In a draft of his July 4 message to Congress, Lincoln summarized the reasoning behind his decision: "I believed . . . that to [withdraw the Sumter garrison] . . . would be utterly ruinous—that the *necessity* under which it was to be done, would not be fully understood—that, by many, it would be construed as a part of a *voluntary* policy—that, at home, it would discourage the friends of the Union, embolden it's foes, and insure to the latter a recognition abroad—that, in fact, it would be our national destruction consummated."[39] Lincoln had not permitted Seward to take the first trick, nor had he let the Confederates corner him. It was a masterful exercise of leadership. In June, Seward told his wife, "Executive skill and vigor are rare qualities. The President is the best of us."[40] Months later, the secretary called Lincoln's decision to relieve Sumter "the central and crowning act of the Administration," the one "which determined . . . that Republican institutions were worth fighting for." It meant "the preservation of the Union and in that, the saving of popular government for the world."[41]

In March 1865, Lincoln succinctly analyzed the outbreak of hostilities: "Both parties deprecated war, but one of them would *make* war rather than let the nation survive, and the other would *accept* war rather than let it perish, and the war came."[42] Lincoln was willing to accept war because he believed, as he told Orville H. Browning, that "far less evil & bloodshed would result from an effort to maintain the Union and the Constitution, than from disruption and the formation of two confederacies."[43]

23.

"I Intend to Give *Blows*"

The Hundred Days (April–July 1861)

"I have desired as sincerely as any man—I sometimes think more than any other man—that our present difficulties might be settled without the shedding of blood," Lincoln told a group of ersatz soldiers in late April. "But if I have to choose between the maintenance of the union of these states, and of the liberties of this nation, on the one hand, and the shedding of fraternal blood on the other, you need not be at a loss which course I shall take."[1] Little did he and most of his contemporaries realize how much fraternal blood would flow in order to save that union and preserve those liberties; some 750,000 soldiers and sailors would die over the next four years. In the fourteen weeks after the bombardment of Sumter, Lincoln acted decisively to meet the emergency. The challenge was daunting, for as he himself put it, the war "began on very unequal terms between the parties. The insurgents had been preparing for it more than thirty years, while the government had taken no steps to resist them. . . . Their sympathizers pervaded all departments of the government, and nearly all communities of the people."[2] In that hectic time, Lincoln took firm hold of the government. In his initial hundred days in office, he raised and supplied an army, sent it into battle, held the Border States in the Union, helped thwart Confederate attempts to win European diplomatic recognition, declared a blockade, asserted leadership over his cabinet, dealt effectively with Congress, averted a potential crisis with Great Britain, and eloquently articulated the nature and purpose of the war. He proved forceful without being obstinate or autocratic, and in doing so, he started to infuse his own iron will into the North as it struggled to preserve what he was to call "the last, best hope of earth."[3]

On the evening of Friday, April 12, word of the attack on Fort Sumter reached Washington, where Lincoln calmly remarked that "he did not expect it so soon," for he had anticipated that the secessionists would wait until the arrival of Gustavus Fox's fleet.[4] When a congressional delegation asked his reaction to the news, he replied laconically, "I do not like it."[5] That day Lincoln met twice with Benjamin

Brown French, who told his son that the president "is as firm as a rock, & means to show the world that there is a United States of America left yet."[6]

The following day, Lincoln remained outwardly unperturbed as he inquired about reports from South Carolina, commented on their probable accuracy, signed routine documents, and received callers. When suspicion was voiced that Anderson had behaved traitorously, Lincoln denied it, insisting that the major had acted in accordance with instructions. The president was glad that no one had been killed during the bombardment.

Upon receiving word of Sumter's surrender, Lincoln met with General Scott, Pennsylvania governor Andrew G. Curtin, and Alexander K. McClure, chairman of the military committee of the Pennsylvania state senate. When Scott insisted that Washington could not be captured by the Confederate army, then in South Carolina under the command of General Pierre G. T. Beauregard, Lincoln observed: "It does seem to me, general, that if I were Beauregard I would take Washington."

"Mr. President," said Scott, "the capital can't be taken, sir; it can't be taken."[7]

When Lincoln asked how Pennsylvania would respond to a proclamation calling up the militia, Curtin pledged to send a hundred thousand men within a week. The president responded: "Give me your hand, Andy. Thank God for that reply."[8] The governor promptly telegraphed word of the forthcoming proclamation to agents in the Keystone State, which on April 18 dispatched the first militiamen to arrive at the capital.

The press on Monday would carry a proclamation summoning all state militias to put down the rebellion. Drafting that document consumed much of Lincoln's time that Sunday. As he and the cabinet worked on it, they faced a dilemma: prompt action must be taken, but could the army and navy be expanded, unappropriated money be spent, Southern ports be blockaded, and the privilege of the writ of habeas corpus be suspended, all without congressional approval? Would it be wise to call Congress into session immediately? Would Washington, nestled between Virginia and Maryland—two Slave States that might well secede—be a safe place for senators and representatives to gather? Lincoln had been resisting appeals by businessmen and New York newspapers to convene a special session of Congress, in part because elections for U.S. representatives had not yet taken place in several states. (In that era, not all states held congressional elections in November of even-numbered years.)

The president also feared that a reconvened Congress might again try to pass compromise measures permitting slavery to expand. The Republican majority in the House would be small, and if some of its members joined the Democrats to insist on abandoning basic Republican Party principles, the result might be unfortunate. Lincoln and his cabinet also favored delaying a special session of Congress lest a deliberative body prove unable to act decisively. So it was decided that Congress would not convene until July 4, allowing enough time to determine whether Washington would be a safe place to meet. It also meant that some emergency measures would have to be taken without prior congressional approval, measures that might be of questionable constitutionality.

The cabinet also considered the size of a militia force to call up. Some favored 50,000; Seward and others recommended double that number. Lincoln split the difference and decided to ask the states to provide 75,000 men for three months' service, which the Militia Act of 1795 authorized. Once that decision was made, action was swift: the president drafted a proclamation, Cameron figured the quotas for each state, Nicolay had the document copied, and Seward readied it to distribute to the press in time for Monday's papers. In the proclamation, Lincoln stated that the purpose of the war was not just to preserve the Union but also to assure "the perpetuity of popular government." The mission of the troops, he explained, would "probably be to repossess the forts, places and property, which have been seized from the Union; and, in every event, the utmost care will be observed, consistently with the objects aforesaid, to avoid any devastation; any destruction of, or interference with, property, or any disturbance of peaceful citizens, in any part of the country."[9]

In North Carolina, Virginia, Arkansas, and Tennessee the Unionist sentiment, which had been waxing, abruptly waned. Those states withdrew from the Union after their governors indignantly refused to provide militia to invade their sister states. They might have resisted secession, at least temporarily, if Lincoln had announced that the troops would be used solely to protect Washington. The president had committed a "wicked blunder," John Pendleton Kennedy protested from Baltimore. Half of the adult males in Maryland, he said, would have gladly rallied to defend the capital, but they would not consent to attack the South. "We are driven into extremities by a series of the most extraordinary blunders at Washington, which I think must convince everybody that there is no ability in the Administration to meet the crisis."[10] Lincoln soon regretted that he had not justified the militia call-up as a defensive measure to protect Washington. He exclaimed to the mayor of Baltimore on April 21, "I am not a learned man!" and insisted "that his proclamation had not been correctly understood; that he had no intention of bringing on war, but that his purpose was to defend the capital, which was in danger of being bombarded from the heights across the Potomac."[11]

If unpopular in the Upper South and the Border States, Lincoln's proclamation was enthusiastically received in the North, where the bombardment of Sumter triggered a passionate uprising. For too long had White Southerners played the bully; now Northerners would stand up for themselves and their rights. On April 16,

John Hay noted that there "is something splendid, yet terrible, about this roused anger of the North."[12] Mass meetings testified to the deep devotion felt for the Union. Thousands flocked to join the army. Seward's fear of divisiveness within the North proved illusory. Indeed, the Free States rallied around the flag with virtual unanimity.

While the North erupted in wrath, Washington sat vulnerable to Confederate attack. Anxiously Lincoln awaited the arrival of troops. On April 20, a member of an informal military force that was hastily thrown together to protect Washington confided to his diary: "A universal gloom and anxiety sits upon every countenance." The city was "rife with *treason*, and the street full of traitors." Anxiously he asked: "When will reinforcements come? Will it be too late?"[13] On April 23, the president exclaimed in anguish, "Why don't they come! Why don't they come!"[14] Compounding Lincoln's woes was the resignation of about one-third of the officers in the army and the navy. Especially disconcerting was the case of Colonel Robert E. Lee, who spurned an offer that Lincoln unofficially conveyed through Francis P. Blair Sr. to command the Union army. On April 23, Lee accepted command of the Old Dominion's military forces.

Immediately after the fall of Fort Sumter, Northern anxiety mounted steadily as one disaster followed another. On April 17 the Virginia convention voted to secede; on the eighteenth, federal troops abandoned Harpers Ferry, torching the armory as they left; on the twentieth, Union forces set fire to the Gosport Navy Yard in Norfolk before evacuating it. Relieving tension slightly was the arrival of five unarmed companies of Pennsylvania militiamen on April 18. Accompanied by Cameron and Seward, Lincoln visited them at the Capitol to express hearty thanks for their promptitude.

Patronage Headaches

Patronage squabbles continued apace, with Seward and Cameron leading the way as they lobbied on behalf of friends. On April 13, when the slate of Philadelphia appointments was announced, the president told a Pennsylvania congressman that he was greatly relieved to have that chore out of the way. He "hoped now to be able to devote his attention exclusively to the condition of the country."[15] But no sooner had civilian patronage been distributed than a great clamor arose for military positions. Especially coveted were paymasterships, which carried the rank of major, provided good pay, and presented little danger to life and limb. In the evening of April 18, when informed that some daredevil Virginia guerillas planned to swoop into the city and either capture or assassinate him, the president merely grinned. Mary Lincoln, however, was not so insouciant, and John Hay did "some very dexterous lying" to calm her fears.[16]

On April 19, the anniversary of the 1775 Battle of Lexington, in which Massachusetts men had been the first to be killed in the Revolutionary War, members of the Sixth Massachusetts Regiment were the first to die in the Civil War when a mob attacked them as they passed through Baltimore. Shots were exchanged, killing four soldiers and wounding thirty-six of their comrades; in addition, twelve civilians were killed and scores injured. The North howled in outrage, causing residents of the Monumental City to dread possible retaliation.

When informed of the attack on the Massachusetts Sixth, Lincoln was quite astounded, for he said that Maryland governor Thomas H. Hicks "had assured him . . . that the troops would have no trouble in passing through Baltimore, and that if they wanted any troops from Washington he (Gov. Hicks) would telegraph." When Hicks wired saying "Send no more troops," Lincoln assumed that the governor meant that he wanted no help from the administration and would "take care and see that the troops passed safely."[17] In fact, on April 18 Governor Hicks and Baltimore mayor George W. Brown had telegraphed Lincoln ambiguously: "send no troops here."[18] They meant to say "send no troops *through* here." When the Massachusetts Sixth arrived in Washington, Lincoln shook hands with every member of the regiment and greeted its commander warmly: "Thank God, you have come; for if you had not, Washington would have been in the hands of the rebels before morning. Your brave boys have saved the capital. God bless them."[19]

After midnight, when a delegation from Baltimore arrived at the White House to make an appeal like Hicks's, Nicolay refused to waken the president but instead called on the secretary of war, who indicated no interest in complying with their request. The next morning Lincoln encountered the Baltimoreans, who urged that reinforcements be sent around rather than through the Monumental City. Temperamentally disposed to believe everyone fair and sincere, Lincoln agreed to this compromise solution, thus satisfying the committee. Half in jest, he told them that "if I grant you this, you will come to-morrow demanding that no troops shall pass around."[20] Lincoln wired Hicks and Brown, summoning them to Washington for a consultation. Around midnight, a telegram arrived from Brown stating that Hicks was unavailable and asking if he should come alone. At 1:00 a.m., Nicolay woke Lincoln, who had his secretary reply to the mayor: "Come."[21]

On April 20, Lincoln also met with Maryland congressmen Anthony Kennedy and J. Morrison Harris, who repeated the message of previous Baltimore callers. Impatiently, Lincoln declared: "My God, Mr. Harris, I don't know what to make of your people. You have sent me one committee already, and they seemed to be perfectly satisfied with what I said to them." When Harris insisted that no more troops pass through his state, the president answered: "My God, Sir, what am I to do? I had better go out and hang myself on the first tree I come to, than to give up the power of the Federal Government in this way. I don't want to go through your town, or near it, if I can help it; but we must have the troops here to relieve ourselves, or we shall die like rats in a heap."[22]

Sunday, April 21, was an especially anxious day at the White House. That morning, Brown and several of his fellow townsmen fulfilled Lincoln's prediction by earnestly insisting that no troops pass through their state at all. The president at first balked, asserting emphatically that protection of Washington "was the sole object of concentrating troops there, and he protested that none of the troops brought through Maryland were intended for any purposes hostile to the State, or aggressive as against Southern States." The delegation left, reassured of the president's desire to avoid further bloodshed. But upon reaching the depot, they received word that Pennsylvania reinforcements had recently arrived in Cockeysville, fourteen miles north of Baltimore, throwing the Monumental City into a panic. Indignantly the delegation returned to the White House to insist that those troops be sent back to the Keystone State. Fearing that renewed hostilities between troops and civilians might play into the hands of Maryland's secessionists and that a pitched battle in Baltimore would delay the arrival of troops, Lincoln "at once, in the most decided way, urged the recall of the troops, saying he had no idea they would be there today, and, lest there should be the slightest suspicion of bad faith on his part in summoning the Mayor to Washington and allowing troops to march on the city during his absence, he desired that the troops should, if it were practicable, be sent back at once."[23] This order outraged many Unionists, including some cabinet members.

To those protesting his decision to detour troops around Baltimore, Lincoln explained that he had gone out of his way, "as an exhaustion of the means of conciliation & kindness," to accommodate the municipal authorities, who assured him that they had insufficient power to guarantee the safety of Union troops passing through their city but could ensure undisturbed passage elsewhere in Maryland. He added "that this was the last time he was going to interfere in matters of strictly military concernment" and that "he would leave them hereafter wholly to military men."[24] (Eventually he would change his mind about relying entirely on such men.) He also argued that it had been imperative to maintain the goodwill of the Maryland authorities lest they hinder troop movements via the alternate route through Perryville and Annapolis.

On April 22, when yet another group from Baltimore called to demand that troops be forbidden to pass through Maryland and that the Confederacy be recognized, the president lost his customary patience. With some asperity he scolded them: "You, gentlemen, come here to me and ask for peace on any terms, and yet have no word of condemnation for those who are making war on us. You express great horror of bloodshed, and yet would not lay a straw in the way of those who are organizing in Virginia and elsewhere to capture this city. The rebels attack Fort Sumter, and your citizens attack troops sent to the defense of the Government, and the lives and property in Washington, and yet you would have me break my oath and surrender the Government without a blow. There is no Washington in that—no Jackson in that—no manhood nor honor in that." Lincoln insisted that he had "no desire to invade the South; but I must have the troops, and mathematically the necessity exists that they should come through Maryland. They can't crawl under the earth, and they can't fly over it. Why, sir, those Carolinians are now crossing Virginia to come here to hang me, and what can I do?" He added that "he must run the machine as he found it." There would be no need for a clash as Union soldiers crossed Maryland: "Now, sir, if you won't hit me, I won't hit you!" But if those troops were forcibly resisted, "*I will lay Baltimore in ashes*."[25]

On April 27, Lincoln explained to an old friend that he could "easily have destroyed Baltimore, but that it would have been visiting vengeance upon a large body of loyal citizens, who were the property-holders, for the sake of punishing the mob who had committed the outrage upon the Massachusetts troops, but which mob, as to property, had little or nothing to lose."[26] When a leading Maryland Unionist, Reverdy Johnson, warned that the people of both his state and Virginia feared the troops headed for Washington would invade the South, Lincoln denied any such intent. On April 24, he assured the former senator that "the sole purpose of bringing troops *here* is to defend this capital. . . . I have no purpose to *invade* Virginia, with them or any other troops, as I understand the word *invasion*." But Lincoln insisted that he must strike back if Virginia attacked Washington or allowed other Rebels to pass though her territory to do so.[27]

Anxiety Grows

Meanwhile, Washington had become isolated. On April 20, Maryland officials ordered the destruction of railroad bridges on lines connecting the capital with Baltimore. In addition, telegraph wires were cut, and mail service to the District ceased. Troops heading thither were held up for several days as they sought alternate routes. One day, while nervously awaiting the arrival of reinforcements, Lincoln thought he heard a cannon boom in the distance, signaling what he thought was a Confederate attack. Nonplussed by his aides' insistence that they heard nothing, the president walked over to the arsenal, which he found unguarded, much to his surprise and dismay. All was quite still both there and along his route back to the White House. As he returned, he asked passers-by if they had heard cannonading earlier. When they said that they had not, he assumed that his imagination was playing tricks on him.

In Washington on April 24, gloom and doubt seemed to infect everyone. In despair, Lincoln told some of the Massachusetts soldiers who had survived the Baltimore attack, "I don't believe there is any North. The [New York] Seventh Regiment is a myth. R[hode] Island is not known in our geography any longer. *You* are the only Northern realities."[28] Washingtonians not only feared a Confederate attack but also worried that the anxiety of the populace had become so intense that a minor episode could touch off rioting or panic.

Relief at Last

A day later the thick gloom that had blanketed the capital for more than a week suddenly lifted as the crack New York Seventh arrived to thunderous cheers. Even more encouraging was word that several more regiments were on their way from Annapolis via train, having skirted Baltimore by a water route. Those units came pouring into Washington during the last week of April, ensuring the safety of the city. Lincoln's decision to have those reinforcements avoid Baltimore, despite severe criticism from many Republicans, helped prevent Maryland from seceding. Also keeping Maryland loyal was Lincoln's refusal to honor the request of Massachusetts general Benjamin F. Butler "to bag the whole nest of traitorous Maryland Legislators and bring them in triumph" to Washington. On April 25, the president, who desired to observe punctiliously the rights of all states, told Winfield Scott that the Maryland legislature "have a clearly legal right to assemble; and, we can not know in advance, that their action will not be lawful, and peaceful." So Scott should "watch, and await their action, which, if it shall be to arm their people against the United States, he is to adopt the most prompt, and efficient means to counteract, even, if necessary, to the bombardment of their cities—and in the *extremest* necessity, the suspension of the writ of habeas corpus."[29]

At the last minute, the Maryland legislature decided to convene in Frederick, a Unionist stronghold, instead of Annapolis. The secessionist tide that had flowed so strongly in eastern Maryland was now ebbing. Federal soldiers occupied strong positions near Baltimore and the state capital. On May 9, troops once again began passing through the City of Monuments en route to Washington. Rather than calling for a secession convention, the General Assembly sent a deputation to Lincoln to learn what military action he planned in their state and to protest various measures taken by the administration. On May 4, he bluntly told them "that while the Government had no intention to retaliate for Baltimore outrages by force of arms, it had determined upon measures to secure the unobstructed passage of troops through their State, and would carry them out at all hazards." He also assured them that "the public interest and not any spirit of revenge should actuate his measures."[30] Nine days later, General Butler marched a thousand troops by night into Baltimore and occupied Federal Hill, thus ensuring that the city would remain pacified. After the legislature's adjournment on May 14, Governor Hicks complied with Lincoln's proclamation by issuing a call for four militia regiments. In mid-June, Unionist candidates won elections in sixteen of the state's twenty-one counties, signifying that less than two months after the Baltimore riots, Maryland had recovered its loyalty to the Union.

As Lincoln struggled to nurture Unionism in Maryland, he was assisted by Governor Hicks, who during the secession winter had supported the formation of a border state nation as a buffer between North and South. Bucking strong pressure, Hicks refused to call a secession convention. In September, however, the administration feared that the Maryland legislature, scheduled to meet at Frederick on September 17, might yet adopt an ordinance of secession. It was rumored that disunionists planned a *coup de main*, joining forces with Virginia rebels. To counter that possibility, Lincoln and Seward arranged with Generals George B. McClellan, John A. Dix, and Nathaniel P. Banks to have pro-secession legislators detained before they could reach Frederick, even in cases when no hard evidence had been produced against them. This controversial decision, carried out primarily by Allan Pinkerton, led to the arrest of fourteen legislators and guaranteed that the state would remain in the Union. In November, the election of a pro-Union governor, Augustus Bradford, along with a lopsided Unionist majority in the legislature, sealed the state's loyalty.

Bending the Constitution

In the ten weeks between Sumter's fall and the convening of Congress in July, Lincoln acted unilaterally in the belief that such emergency measures would be endorsed retrospectively by Congress and thus made constitutional. On April 19, he declared his intention to blockade ports in the seven seceded states; a week later he extended the blockade to cover Virginia and North Carolina. This he justified as a response to the Confederacy's announcement on April 17 that it would issue letters of marque, authorizing privateers to seize Union shipping. Recognizing that the 75,000 militia called up on April 15 would be insufficient, Lincoln two weeks later ordered the expansion of the armed forces far beyond what Congress had authorized. On May 3, an official proclamation specified that 42,034 volunteers would be recruited to serve three years; 22,714 soldiers were to be added to the Regular Army and 18,000 sailors to the navy. Here Lincoln violated the explicit provision of the Constitution empowering Congress to raise armies.

Lincoln's most controversial act was authorizing General Scott to suspend the privilege of the writ of habeas corpus, thus allowing the military to arrest and detain persons without charges. When Seward recommended that step, Lincoln at first demurred, but after the secretary argued that "perdition was the sure penalty for further hesitation," the president acquiesced.[31] The initial suspension, limited to military lines between Washington and Philadelphia, was authorized on April 27. Two weeks later Lincoln suspended the writ in Florida. In early July, he authorized Scott to suspend the writ along the military lines between Washington and New York. In response to several arrests in the capital, he counseled restraint in using the power thus granted: "Unless the *necessity* for . . . arbitrary arrests is *manifest*, and *urgent*, I prefer that they should cease."[32]

In May, one John Merryman, a wealthy Marylander serving as a lieutenant in a pro-secession cavalry troop that had helped cut telegraph wires and burn bridges, was apprehended for preparing men to serve in the Confederate army. He sued for his freedom, arguing that the suspension of the writ was illegal. Roger B. Taney, the octogenarian chief justice of the Supreme Court, heard the case in his capacity as a circuit court judge. Taney ruled that Lincoln had acted unconstitutionally, for only Congress, not the president, was authorized to suspend the writ of habeas corpus. Referring to the chief executive, he added that it was "up to that high officer, in fulfillment of his constitutional obligation to 'take care that the laws be faithfully executed,' to determine what measures he will take to cause the civil process of the United States to be respected and enforced."[33] Lincoln ignored the order, and Merryman remained in prison for weeks.

In his July 4 message to Congress, Lincoln responded to Taney's arguments. "Are all the laws, *but one*, to go unexecuted, and the government itself go to pieces, lest that one be violated?" he asked rhetorically. Yet, Lincoln maintained, "In my opinion I violated no law," for the Constitution provided that "such previlege may be suspended when, in cases of rebellion, or invasion, the public safety *does* require it. I decided that we have a case of rebellion, and that the public safety does require the qualified suspension of the previlege of the writ of habeas corpus." Moreover, the Constitution was silent as to "who, is to exercise the power; and as the provision plainly was made for a dangerous emergency, I can not bring myself to believe that the framers of that instrument intended that in every case the danger should run it's course until Congress could be called together, the very assembling of which might be prevented, as was intended in this case, by the rebellion."[34] Lincoln had a good argument, for Congress in that era was often out of session, and an invasion or rebellion might well take place during one of its long recesses, just as had occurred in April. Clearly, in the case of Maryland that spring, emergency conditions prevailed. In August, Congress by a near-unanimous vote approved a resolution approving all Lincoln's actions since the outbreak of war, with the exception of the suspension of habeas corpus. (Congress approved that measure in March 1863.) Two years later, the Supreme Court upheld this unorthodox procedure in the Prize Cases, involving a plaintiff who argued that the blockade was illegal from the time Lincoln announced it in April until July 1861, when Congress in effect declared war. Upholding the blockade and all other emergency measures taken by Lincoln in the first weeks of the war, a bare five-man majority of the court ruled in the administration's favor.

Despite his early foray into extraconstitutionality, Lincoln for the rest of the war generally respected constitutional restraints. In fact, political opponents for the most part were allowed free rein to criticize the administration; the press was rarely censored, even when editors called for the president's assassination; elections were conducted freely and fairly, with some bending of the rules in the Border States; courts remained open; and with one exception (Maryland, briefly), legislatures met unimpeded. When urged to confiscate Southern property in the North, he replied: "No, gentleman, never." To rejoinders that the Confederates seized Northern property, he said: "They can afford to do a wrong—I cannot."[35]

Keeping Kentucky Loyal

Lincoln worried a great deal about Kentucky. During the first year and a half of the war, some of his most important decisions were designed to help keep her loyal. "I think to lose Kentucky, is nearly the same as to lose the whole game," he told his good friend Orville H. Browning.[36] He allegedly said that to win the war he "wanted God on his side, but he must have Kentucky."[37] His concern was understandable, for the Bluegrass State ranked ninth in the nation in terms of population, seventh in terms of farm value, and fifth in terms of livestock value. Her men, horses, mules, grain, fruit, hay, hemp, and flax would all be valuable assets to whichever side Kentucky favored. Geographically she occupied a crucial location: Northern armies would have to pass through her to get at Tennessee, Mississippi, and Alabama; and from Kentucky, Southern troops could establish a formidable defensive barrier along the Ohio and even penetrate the Midwest.

To retain his native state in the Union, Lincoln exercised preternatural tact, especially in dealing with slavery. Soon after the firing on Fort Sumter, that state's legislature and governor, the pro-secession Beriah Magoffin, expressed their wish that the state remain neutral. Lincoln recommended to a group of Southern Unionists that young Kentuckians must be organized to resist the governor, whose views were unrepresentative of most of his constituents.

In late April, the president assured Kentucky senator Garrett Davis, a strong Unionist, that the administration's intentions were not aggressive. Alluding to slavery, he said that he "intended to make no attack, direct or indirect, upon the institutions or property of any State; but, on the contrary, would defend them to the full extent with which the Constitution and laws of Congress have vested the President with the power. And that he did not intend to invade with an armed force, or make any military or naval movement against any State, unless she or her people should make it necessary by a formidable resistance of the authority and laws of the United States. . . . That if Kentucky made no demonstration of force against the United States he would not molest her."[38] To placate Kentuckians, Lincoln allowed them to trade with the Confederacy until mid-August, by which time the state's Unionists had gained the upper hand. He honored Kentucky's neutrality, though he regarded it as unrealistic, calling it "treason in effect."[39]

Although he refrained from sending troops into Kentucky, Lincoln did establish a military presence there (at Newport) under the command of Robert Anderson, who was empowered to recruit volunteer regiments from both the Bluegrass State and western Virginia. In July, the president authorized navy lieutenant William "Bull" Nelson, then on loan to the army, to enlist Kentuckians. Lincoln also arranged with Joshua Speed to smuggle weapons into the state, including twenty thousand rifles, which became known as "Lincoln guns." General George B. McClellan, in charge of the Department of the Ohio, told the president that according to leading Kentucky Unionists, "the effect [of distributing arms] has been extremely beneficial, not only in giving strength to the Union party & discouraging the secessionists, but that it has proved to the minds of all reasonable men that the Genl. Govt has confidence in their loyalty & entertains no intention of subjugating them."[40] On June 20, Lincoln's delicate cultivation of Kentucky paid off when Unionist candidates captured nine of the state's ten congressional seats. Seven weeks later, Unionists scored another triumph, winning 103 of the 138 seats in the General Assembly.

Kentucky's neutrality abruptly ended on September 3, when the willful Confederate general Leonidas Polk rashly ordered the occupation of Columbus, prompting Union troops under Ulysses S. Grant to seize Paducah. Polk's action resembled the blunder the Confederates had made by attacking Fort Sumter; just as that bombardment had solidified the North and reduced the chances that the Border States would secede, the Confederate invasion of Kentucky helped secure that state to the Union. The General Assembly demanded the withdrawal of Polk's troops but not Grant's.

Keeping Missouri Loyal

In his effort to prevent Missouri from seceding, Lincoln faced severe obstacles. With a population of approximately 1,200,000, it was the largest state in the Trans-Mississippi West. Its proximity to Kansas, Kentucky, and southern Illinois made it strategically important. Secessionist governor Claiborne F. Jackson plotted to seize the St. Louis arsenal and distribute its muskets, powder, and cartridges to Confederate volunteers. Opposing him were two impetuous Unionists, Congressman Frank Blair and Captain Nathaniel Lyon, both of whom needed assistance. At the end of April, the president authorized Lyon to enroll 10,000 Missourians into the army and to declare martial law in St. Louis. This action was highly irregular, but General Scott endorsed it because the times were "revolutionary."[41] On May 10, the headstrong Lyon, acting without authorization from Washington, thwarted Governor Jackson's plans by capturing the pro-secession militia before they could aid the Confederacy. That captain then led his troops westward toward Jefferson City, where Governor Jackson and General Sterling Price had assembled a pro-Confederate militia. As Lyon approached, Jackson and Price retreated, leaving the state's capital in Union hands. In July, a new provisional government was formed, with the conservative Unionist Hamilton R. Gamble as its governor. He proclaimed Missouri loyal to the Union and won the acquiescence of much of the state as well as official recognition from the Lincoln administration.

Nonetheless, in August, regular Confederate forces won the battle of Wilson's Creek, where Lyon was killed. But in March 1862, at the battle of Pea Ridge, Arkansas, the Rebels were defeated; thereafter armed resistance to federal authority in Missouri took the form of guerilla warfare and savage bushwhacking. Missouri remained in the Union throughout the war.

Helping Unionists in Western Virginia

When Unionists in western Virginia, a region culturally and economically distinct from the eastern portion of the state, appealed to Lincoln for help, he complied promptly. Federal control of that area was important, for through it passed the main rail line connecting the Eastern Seaboard with the Midwest (the Baltimore and Ohio). In addition, it shielded eastern Ohio, western Pennsylvania, and eastern Kentucky. Unionists planned to move the seat of government from Richmond west of the Alleghenies or else cut themselves off from the eastern portion of the state and become a separate entity. On May 1, at Lincoln's invitation, a committee from Butler County called at the White House and asked for a hundred thousand dollars and five thousand rifles. Influential Republicans urged the president to grant the request. Edwin M. Stanton wrote a legal brief justifying the transfer of federal arms to private parties in Virginia, then pledged all his personal assets as bond to guarantee that the weapons would be used properly. Cameron saw to it that they were dispatched to the trans-Appalachian Virginia Unionists.

After Virginia voters ratified an ordinance of secession on May 23, more forceful measures were called for. The following day, when Congressman John S. Carlile of Clarksburg demanded that troops be sent into the Kanawha and Monongahela valleys, Lincoln replied that "we will help you."[42] Indeed, Ohio and Indiana troops promptly crossed the Ohio River and marched toward Wheeling. In June, Unionists held a convention and formed "the Reorganized Government of Virginia," purporting to represent the entire Old Dominion, with Francis Pierpont as its governor. The following month, Lincoln recognized the new government's legitimacy; he had worked behind the scenes to come up with this plan instead of acceding to the Unionists' wish to establish a new state, a move he considered premature. Eighteen months later he did approve that proposal.

Dealing with Europe

While laboring to retain the Border States, Lincoln did not lose sight of another danger: the possible intervention of European nations, especially Great Britain, on behalf of the Confederacy. Even before Fort Sumter fell, the British and French governments warned that if the administration cut off trade with the South, their major supplier of cotton, they might well recognize the Confederacy. Such a step would enable the South to negotiate military and commercial treaties and gain access to European ports, and thus win the war. The matter came up almost immediately with the commencement of hostilities. In response to Lincoln's April 19 and 27 proclamations of intent to blockade Southern ports, Queen Victoria on May 13 issued a proclamation of neutrality, granting the Confederacy belligerent status (but not official recognition), entitling it to employ privateers and take prizes to British ports, to borrow money from Great Britain, to obtain weapons from her, and to have commerce raiders built in British shipyards. Prime Minister Palmerston, likewise eager to avoid entanglement in the American Civil War, stated that the way to avoid strife was to declare neutrality. Charles Francis Adams, who arrived in London the very day that the queen's proclamation appeared in the press, objected that the document indicated partiality toward the Confederates, giving them hope that they might well be recognized as an independent nation. The outraged North shared his understandable but mistaken interpretation of the neutrality proclamation. The misunderstanding helped poison diplomatic relations between the two countries.

Mobilizing for War

Thanks to Northern outrage at the bombardment of Fort Sumter and to the energetic leadership of some governors, raising an army proved easy; training, equipping, arming, feeding, and supplying it, however, did not. For decades, Congress and state governments had neglected the military so badly that the North had great difficulty mobilizing its vast resources swiftly. Compounding the problem was the general lack of organizational sophistication throughout the economy and society.

The United States, still an immature country in many ways, had few men and institutions experienced in creating and managing large-scale enterprises of any kind. Nowhere was such backwardness more evident than in the War Department, with its aged and small staff, antiquated rules, and stifling bureaucracy. As men eagerly enlisted, their requests for weapons, uniforms, and equipment overwhelmed Secretary Cameron and his bureau chiefs. They responded to urgent appeals so slowly that some energetic governors took matters into their own hands, purchasing necessary paraphernalia at home and abroad. Other civilians did yeoman work in helping to compensate for the War Department's inadequacy. From one area of American life with significant organizational savvy—railroad corporations—came Thomas A. Scott to assist the beleaguered Cameron. Assuming the post of assistant secretary of war, this vice president of the Pennsylvania Railroad efficiently reformed procedures, got rid of dead wood, and dramatically improved the functioning of the department, especially its handling of railroads.

Some military men also stepped forward to fill the vacuum created by the War Department's ineptitude. A conspicuous example was the elderly General John E. Wool, who seized the initiative without waiting for department approval. His meritorious efforts in procuring arms and ammunition came to a halt when Cameron, allegedly at the behest of corrupt contractors, ordered him to resume his routine duties. Also efficient was Montgomery C. Meigs, who became quartermaster general in mid-June over the objections of Cameron, who was clearly not up to his job. A political wheeler-dealer, Cameron reveled in distributing patronage and awarding contracts to allies; in fact he devoted more attention to those congenial chores than to readying the nation to fight. By late summer, public opinion had soured on Cameron more because of his unsuitable appointments than because of his questionable contracts.

Lincoln also made some blunders as the mobilization effort got under way. He exasperated governors by allowing ambitious politicos to raise regiments independently and having them accepted into the army while Cameron was turning away units recruited in accordance with state regulations. In matters military, the president said he relied on General Scott, but the poor health and advanced years of that septuagenarian hero unfitted him to meet the challenge posed by a conflict far vaster than he had known during the War of 1812 or the Mexican War. So Lincoln gradually began to depend more on his own judgment. In August 1861, to facilitate the enlistment of volunteers, he issued an order eliminating much red tape. That summer the president acknowledged that his administration had "stumbled along" but said he thought that on the whole it had done so "in the right direction."[43]

Message to Congress

As July 4 approached, Lincoln put the finishing touches on his message to Congress, one of his most significant and eloquent state papers. For weeks he had been considering carefully what to say. On July 5, his message was read to Congress, as was the custom for such documents.

His principal goal was to define the stakes of the war. "Our popular government," he wrote, "has often been called an experiment." It remained to be seen whether that government could be maintained "against a formidable attempt to overthrow it. . . . And this issue embraces more than the fate of these United States. It presents to the whole family of man the question, whether a Constitutional republic, or a democracy—a government of the people, by the same people—can, or cannot, maintain its territorial integrity against its own domestic foes." In the most eloquent passage of the address, Lincoln called the war "essentially a People's contest." For Unionists, "it is a struggle for maintaining in the world, that form and substance of government, whose leading object is, to elevate the condition of men—to lift artificial weights from all shoulders; to clear the paths of laudable pursuit for all; to afford all, an unfettered start, and a fair chance, in the race of life." These words had a special resonance coming from a man who had made his way up from frontier poverty and ignorance.

Lincoln recounted the events leading to war, explaining why he had decided to relieve Fort Sumter. A dangerous precedent would be set if the public were to accept secession: "by allowing the seceders to go in peace, it is difficult to see what we can do, if others choose to go, or to extort terms upon which they will promise to remain." He pointed out that the Confederates had recently adopted a constitution that failed to include the right of secession. "The principle itself," he wryly observed, "is one of disintegration, and upon which no government can possibly endure." Moreover, Lincoln denied that a majority of voters in any Confederate state, except perhaps South Carolina, truly favored secession.

Apologetically, Lincoln asked Congress retrospectively to endorse the emergency measures he had taken since the bombardment of Fort Sumter. "It was with the deepest regret that the Executive found the duty of employing the war-power, in defence of the government, forced upon him. He could but perform this duty, or surrender the existence of the government. . . . In full view of his great responsibility, he has, so far, done what he has deemed his duty. You will now, according to your own judgment, perform yours." To supplement what he had already done, Lincoln urged Congress to authorize the creation of a huge army and to appropriate enormous sums of money. "One of the greatest perplexities of the government," he said, "is to avoid receiving troops faster than it can provide for them. In a word, the people will save their government, if the government itself, will do its part, only indifferently well."[44]

Congress Acts

Missing from the new Congress were members from the seceded states, with the notable exception of Tennessee senator Andrew Johnson. Thus the Republicans dominated both houses by substantial majorities. Their party was divided into radicals, moderates, and conservatives, who in time would clash, but not at this special session. Indeed, Congress agreed to deal with only military, financial, judicial, and naval matters and to postpone all other business until the regular session in December. As noted above, Congress obliged Lincoln by retroactively approving all his emergency measures except the suspension of the writ of habeas corpus. In addition, it authorized the enlistment of five hundred thousand volunteers for three years as well as the expansion of both the Regular Army and the navy; provided military leaders with larger staffs; enlarged the War Department; and empowered the Treasury Department to borrow $250 million, which would supplement the money raised by increased import duties and taxes.

In late July, Congress overwhelmingly approved John J. Crittenden's resolution stating that the war "forced upon the country by the disunionists of the southern States" was not being waged "in any spirit of oppression, or for any purpose of conquest or subjugation, or purpose of overthrowing or interfering with the rights or established institutions of those States."[45] By a much narrower margin, Congress also passed a confiscation act, seizing property (including slaves) employed by Confederates in direct support of military operations. It did not fully liberate bondsmen, but represented a huge step on the path to emancipation, for the administration was to implement it in such a way that tens of thousands of slaves were liberated well before the Emancipation Proclamation was issued seventeen months later. On paper, the law was a modest measure; as enforced in the field, it was a radical measure indeed.

The legislators also established a pair of special investigating committees. One, under the chairmanship of Wisconsin congressman John F. Potter, looked into reported disloyalty among government employees. Many Southerners had been appointed to office during the previous two administrations, and legitimate concerns were raised about their devotion to the Union. Unfortunately, Potter's committee pursued its mission clumsily, violating due process in denouncing men who were then fired. Charges were often falsely made by those who hungered for the jobs held by the accused. Another committee was set up under the leadership of Charles H. Van Wyck of New York to scrutinize government contracts. Although it did uncover fraud, the committee was highly controversial. When it criticized Ward Hill Lamon, Simon Cameron, and Gideon Welles, among others, John Hay denounced it as "an absurd fiasco" employed "chiefly as an engine to ventilate personal animosities and prejudices existing in the minds of the incorruptible committeemen against better people."[46] Lincoln complained that its most active member, Henry L. Dawes of Massachusetts, had "done more to break down the administration than any other man in the country."[47] Leading Radicals in Congress shared the president's dim view of Dawes and the contracts committee. That body may have embarrassed the administration, but it conscientiously investigated misfeasance and malfeasance in raising and equipping a five-hundred-thousand-man army and navy.

Giving Blows

As Congress debated, legislated, and investigated, the administration made and executed war plans. A week after Sumter fell, James A. Hamilton asked Lincoln if he proposed to launch an offensive soon. "I intend to give *blows*," he replied. "The only question at present is, whether I should first retake Fort Sumter or Harpers Ferry."[48] Fort Monroe, located at the mouth of the James River in Tidewater Virginia, was quickly reinforced with fifteen thousand men. But Lincoln withheld military action against Virginia until that state's electorate officially ratified the ordinance of secession on May 23.

Montgomery Blair urged an immediate attack on the Confederates, but Scott and Montgomery Meigs argued against a precipitate offensive with woefully ill-prepared troops. Lincoln accepted their advice, though he did authorize a mission to secure Alexandria. On May 24, federal troops crossed the Potomac and occupied the town largely without opposition, though one of Lincoln's favorite surrogate sons, Colonel Elmer E. Ellsworth, took umbrage at the Confederate flag atop a hotel. Impetuously the young officer dashed into the offending hostelry, clambered up the stairs to the roof, and hauled down the secessionist ensign. As he descended, Ellsworth encountered the hotel proprietor, who shot him dead. News of his murder shocked Northerners and devastated Lincoln, who mourned him as if he had been his own child. Upon learning of Ellsworth's death, the president burst into tears, telling some White House callers, "Excuse me, but I cannot talk." After regaining his composure, he said: "I will make no apology, gentlemen, for my weakness; but I knew poor Ellsworth well, and held him in great regard."[49] Ellsworth's body was taken to the Navy Yard, where the president and his wife for a long while looked tearfully upon the face of their dead friend. Finally Lincoln exclaimed: "My boy! My boy! Was it necessary that this sacrifice should be made?"[50] The body was removed to the White House, where a funeral service was held the following day. To Ellsworth's parents Lincoln wrote a heartfelt letter of condolence.

Indignation at Ellsworth's assassination helped swell the enlistment rolls. Although Lincoln had called for only 42,000 volunteers, by July 1 more than 200,000 had joined up.

In addition to occupying Alexandria, federal troops seized Arlington Heights, overlooking Washington, where Robert E. Lee's mansion stood. Attention then shifted to Harpers Ferry, where fewer than 10,000 Confederates under General Joseph E. Johnston had assembled. General Robert Patterson was selected to lead an expedition against them. With a force of 17,000, Patterson approached the town in mid-June, causing Johnston to retreat to Winchester. When urged to pursue the Confederates, the indecisive, fearful, 69-year-old Patterson, whose troops called him "Granny," balked. Further west in Virginia, Union forces under General George B. McClellan proved more aggressive, routing Confederates at Phillipi in a relatively minor skirmish that June. These small-scale engagements whetted the appetite of the Northern public, which desired its legions to attack the Confederate capital. "Forward to Richmond! Forward to Richmond!" trumpeted Horace Greeley's influential New York *Tribune*. Vexed by the paper's hectoring, Lincoln asked its Washington bureau chief: "What in the world is the matter with Uncle Horace? Why can't he restrain himself and wait a little?"[51]

Meanwhile, the general in chief had been formulating strategy without consulting the president. Nicknamed Old Fuss and Feathers, Scott had outlined to General McClellan a scheme that became known as the "Anaconda Plan." The Confederacy, he recommended, should be encircled and crushed through the combined effects of a stringent blockade and a movement down the Mississippi River by an eighty-thousand-man army, whose goal would be the capture of New Orleans; thus girdled, the rebellion could be squeezed to death. Before marching southward, troops should receive at least four months' training.

Many army officers doubted that Scott's policy was energetic enough and thought he was wasting time in making excessive preparations. Agreeing with those officers, the impatient Lincoln rejected Scott's advice. Calculating that the 50,000 Union troops in northern Virginia should be able to defeat the 30,000 Confederates there, the president decided to launch an offensive. Because many Union soldiers were ninety-day militiamen whose enlistments would soon expire, he understandably wished to have them fight before they were discharged. He may also have thought that to postpone an attack would dispirit the North and perhaps even lead to European recognition of the Confederacy. He was therefore enthusiastic about a plan drawn up at Scott's request by General Irvin McDowell, an abrasive, hypercritical, 42-year-old gourmand and West Pointer in charge of the Department of Northeastern Virginia. McDowell proposed to attack enemy forces concentrating near Manassas, an important rail junction some thirty miles southwest of Washington. When it was objected that the men needed more training, Lincoln replied that the enemy suffered from the same problem: "You are green, it is true; but they are green, also; you are all green alike."[52] Although that was an accurate statement, it was misleading, for the Union forces would have to maneuver in the presence of an entrenched enemy, a much more complicated challenge than the one the Confederates would face.

On June 25, Lincoln convened a council of war with Scott, Meigs, and the cabinet. There the president voiced his strong desire to trap Confederate forces under Thomas J. Jackson near Harpers Ferry, but Scott thought it unfeasible. Four days later, at a second council of war, McDowell's fundamentally sound plan was discussed at length, with Meigs countering Scott's vigorous objections. It was agreed to endorse McDowell's plan, which appeared likely to succeed if the Confederate forces under Johnston at Winchester were unable to join Beauregard. To prevent the two Rebel commands from uniting, Scott ordered Patterson to hold Johnston in check. After many delays, McDowell began lurching toward Manassas on July 16, eight days later than the date agreed upon at the council of war. General Beauregard, learning of McDowell's glacial advance, appealed for help to Johnston, who easily slipped away from the cautious Patterson and hastened to reinforce his threatened colleague. Upon receiving word of this development, Lincoln asked Scott if it might be advisable to postpone McDowell's attack until Patterson could join him; the general in chief did not think that would be necessary.

On the morning of Sunday, July 21, McDowell's troops splashed across Bull Run and so successfully drove the Confederates that victory seemed imminent. At noon, John G. Nicolay reported from the White House that "everybody is in great suspense. General Scott talked confidently this morning of success, and very calmly and quietly went to church." Every fifteen minutes or so, Lincoln received dispatches from a telegrapher near the battlefield—young Andrew Carnegie—describing what he was able to observe. Uneasy because those bulletins implied that Union forces were retreating, the president shortly after lunch called at Scott's quarters, where the general was napping. Lincoln wakened him and offered a pessimistic interpretation of the dispatches. Scott insisted that they were poor indicators of the battle's progress, for shifting winds, echoes, and the like so affected sounds that no conclusions could be drawn from them. The general was certain that McDowell would prevail. Back at the War Department, Lincoln joined Seward, who puffed confidently on a cigar, and Cameron, who forcefully expressed optimism. The president, according to a telegraph operator, was "deeply impressed with the responsibilities of the occasion" and made only a few measured observations.[53] Lincoln became more hopeful when dispatches arriving in midafternoon suggested that the Confederates were falling back. The general in chief believed this report and predicted that the Union forces would soon capture Manassas.

The president left to take his customary afternoon ride, visiting the Navy Yard, where he told its commander, John A. Dahlgren, "that the armies were hotly engaged and the other side [was] getting the worst of it."[54] At 6:00 p.m., an excited, frightened-looking Seward rushed into the Executive Mansion and asked Nicolay in a hoarse voice, "Where is the President?"

"Gone to ride."

"Have you any late news?"

Nicolay read a fresh dispatch: "General McDowell wishes all the troops that can be sent from Washington to come here without delay. He has ordered the reserve now here under Colonel Miles to advance to the bridge over Bull Run, on the Warrenton road, having driven the enemy before him."[55]

"Tell no one," enjoined Seward. "That is not so. The battle is lost. The telegraph says that McDowell is in full retreat, and calls on General Scott to save the Capitol. Find the President and tell him to come immediately to Gen. Scotts."[56] (In fact, late that afternoon the last of the Confederate reinforcements had arrived from Winchester and helped turn the tide. In pell-mell fashion, McDowell's men retreated ignominiously to Washington.) Thirty minutes later, Lincoln returned, heard the bad news with no outward sign of alarm, and promptly strode next door to the War Department. There he read a dispatch from a captain reporting that "General McDowell's army in full retreat through Centreville. The day is lost. Save Washington and the remnants of this army. All available troops ought to be thrown forward in one body. General McDowell is doing all he can to cover the retreat. Colonel Miles is forming for that purpose. He was in reserve at Centreville. The routed troops will not reform."[57]

Lincoln and his cabinet gathered in Scott's office to follow the latest developments. The captain's dismal report was soon confirmed by McDowell's telegram stating that his men, "having thrown away their haversacks in the battle and left them behind," were "without food" and "have eaten nothing since breakfast. We are without artillery ammunition. The larger part of the men are a confused mob, entirely demoralized. It was the opinion of all the commanders that no stand could be made this side of the Potomac. We will, however, make the attempt at Fairfax Court-House."[58] Scott was so dumbfounded by contradictory reports of success and failure that he scarcely credited the latter. Immediately all available troops were sent to McDowell's aid. Lincoln remained at the War Department until after 2:00 a.m. Back at the White House, he stayed up throughout the moonlit night, listening to reports from noncombatant eyewitnesses. The next morning, as a drizzling rain heightened the atmosphere of gloom pervading the capital, footsore, discouraged soldiers straggled into town.

During a postmortem meeting, Lincoln took umbrage at Scott's suggestion that he had been compelled to approve the Manassas plan. "Your conversation seems to imply that I forced you to fight this battle," Lincoln remarked. Scott denied any such implication, saying: "I have never served a President who has been kinder to me than you have been."[59] The day after the battle, Lincoln admitted that if Scott had been allowed to conduct the campaign as he wished, "this would not have happened."[60] Others were quick to blame Lincoln for the debacle. In Washington, it was widely believed "that Scott's policy was interfered with by the President in obedience to what he calls the popular will."[61]

The defeat profoundly affected Lincoln, who with intense emotion told John D. Defrees that "if Hell is [not] any worse than this, it has no terror for me."[62] On August 8, Orville Browning found the president "a little despondent, and not at all hopeful."[63] But Lincoln did not allow himself to wallow in self-pity. The morning after the battle, he said: "There is nothing in this except the lives lost and the lives which must be lost to make it good." Remarking on this statement, John Hay wrote that there "was probably no one who regretted bloodshed and disaster more than he, and no one who estimated the consequences of defeat more lightly. He was often for a moment impatient at the loss of time, and yet he was not always sure that this was not a part of the necessary scheme."[64]

Two days after the battle, Lincoln visited some troops in the field, accompanied by Seward. En route they encountered Colonel William T. Sherman, commander of a brigade that had taken three hundred casualties in the battle. When the colonel asked if they intended to inspect his camps, Lincoln said: "Yes; we heard that you had got over the big scare, and we thought we would come over and see the 'boys.'" He invited Sherman to join them, and as they rode along, the colonel "discovered that Mr. Lincoln was full of feeling, and wanted to encourage our men." Sherman asked "if he intended to speak to them, and he said he would like to." The colonel requested that he "please discourage all cheering, noise, or any sort of confusion," for they had had "enough of it before Bull Run to ruin any set of men"; what they needed was "cool, thoughtful, hard-fighting soldiers—no more hurrahing, no more humbug." Lincoln good-naturedly took the suggestion.

Upon reaching one of the camps, the president, according to Sherman, "made one of the neatest, best, and most feeling addresses I ever listened to, referring to our late disaster at Bull Run, the high duties that still devolved on us, and the brighter days yet to come. At one or two points the soldiers began to cheer, but he promptly checked them, saying: 'Don't cheer, boys. I confess I rather like it myself, but Colonel Sherman here says it is not military; and I guess we had better defer to his opinion.'" In concluding, "he explained that, as President, he was commander-in-chief; that he was resolved that the soldiers should have every thing that the law allowed; and he called on one and all to appeal to him personally in case they were wronged. The effect of this speech was excellent." As they passed by more camps, the president complimented Sherman "for the order, cleanliness, and discipline, that he observed." Seward and Lincoln remarked "that it was the first bright moment they had experienced since the battle."[65]

That same day, Lincoln sketched a new military plan, calling for swift implementation of the blockade; further drilling and instruction of troops at Fort Monroe; holding on to Baltimore; bolstering Patterson's forces in the Shenandoah Valley; leaving the troops farther west in Virginia under the command of McClellan; making Missouri a higher priority and encouraging Frémont to be more active there; reorganizing the forces that had retreated from Manassas; discharging swiftly the ninety-day enlistees who were unwilling to serve longer; and bringing forward the new volunteer forces rapidly and stationing them along the Potomac. Once these goals were reached, Union forces should advance on three fronts: in Virginia, take Strasburg and Manassas Junction and keep open lines from Washington to Manassas and from Harpers Ferry to Strasburg, then launch simultaneous campaigns against Memphis and eastern Tennessee. To carry out his grand strategy, Lincoln summoned George B. McClellan from western Virginia, where his successes, though minor, had cheered the North.

On July 27, McClellan officially took command of the Division of the Potomac, raising high Northern hopes. His presence in Washington "seems to inspire all with new courage and energy," reported William O. Stoddard from the White House.[66] The Young Napoleon, as the general was called, would redeem the shameful defeat at Bull Run, whip the demoralized army into shape, and soon bring the war to a victorious close.

Or so it was thought.

24.

Sitzkrieg

The Phony War (August 1861–January 1862)

The ignominious defeat at Bull Run disheartened the North and undermined support for the Lincoln administration. In early December, when Benjamin Brown French asked Lincoln why the army had made no serious advance since July, he replied: "If I were *sure* of victory we would have one at once, but we cannot stand a defeat, & we must be certain of victory before we strike."[1] Equally convinced that no attack should be made until victory seemed certain was the commander Lincoln had placed in charge of the army, George B. McClellan. Known as Little Mac and the Young Napoleon (though he lacked his namesake's boldness, among other things), he hesitated to commit his forces, which he had splendidly trained and equipped. For half a year the Civil War resembled what World War II in Europe would become during the fall and winter of 1939–40: a *sitzkrieg* (sitting war) instead of a *blitzkrieg* (lightning war). While the North grew exasperated with McClellan, the president bore with his timidity month after month after month. Lincoln's patience was legendary but, as McClellan would eventually discover, finite.

From August 1861 to March 1862 the press regularly reported "all quiet on the Potomac." At first, it was a simple statement of fact; eventually it came to express derision for McClellan's inactivity. In September, Lincoln asked a telegraph operator at the War Department, "What news?" When the reply came, "Good news, because none," the president remarked: "Ah! my young friend, that rule don't always hold good, for a fisherman don't consider it good luck when he can't get a bite."[2] McClellan was getting no bites.

The vain, arrogant, 34-year-old McClellan shared the Northern public's view that he was a savior. Shortly after arriving in Washington, he told his wife: "I find myself in a new & strange position here—Presdt, Cabinet, Genl Scott & all deferring to me—by some strange operation of magic I seem to have become *the* power of the land. I almost think that were I to win some small success now I could become

Dictator or anything else that might please me—but nothing of that kind would please me—*therefore* I *won't* be Dictator. Admirable self denial!"[3]

The general's cockiness was understandable, for he had been a high-achieving wunderkind, finishing second in the class of 1846 at West Point, serving creditably in the Mexican War, leading a prestigious commission to observe the Crimean War, inventing a saddle that became standard cavalry issue, becoming the president of a railroad after leaving the service in 1857, receiving command of Ohio's militia shortly after the fall of Sumter, attaining the rank of major general in the Regular Army (second behind Scott) in May 1861, and leading the only Union forces that won victories in the early months of the war. Failure was unknown to the Young Napoleon, which was unfortunate, for he could have profited from that painful experience, as Lincoln, U. S. Grant, and other successful leaders in the war had done; instead, his head swelled all too easily, creating a paradoxical amalgam of timidity and overconfidence.

While Lincoln and his constituents rejoiced at the triumph of Union arms in western Virginia, in fact McClellan had exhibited qualities during that campaign that boded ill. He ungenerously took credit due others, unfairly chastised subordinates, showed indecisiveness at key points, failed to follow up on his victories, made repeated promises that he did not honor, was tardy and irresolute on the battlefield, exhibited a lack of initiative, and tended to whine unjustly about a lack of support. These shortcomings were overlooked partly because he won and partly because he was a skillful self-promoter, writing vainglorious dispatches that exaggerated his accomplishments.

On August 2, in response to the president's request, McClellan submitted "a carefully considered plan for conducting the war on a large scale" that would end the war "at one blow." With 273,000 troops in his own army and an unspecified number in others, Little Mac proposed to take Richmond (the Confederate capital as of May 21), New Orleans, Charleston, Savannah, Montgomery, Pensacola, and Mobile and thus "crush out this rebellion in its very heart."[4] This impractical scheme resembled the "Kanawha plan," which Little Mac had months earlier submitted to General Scott, who rightly dismissed it as unfeasible.

If McClellan showed weakness as a strategist, he proved an exceptionally able organizer and administrator. In the late summer and throughout the fall he industriously drilled, trained, supervised, and inspired the troops under his command and replaced unfit officers, creating a disciplined, well-equipped army. He renamed his force, which had been called the Division of the Potomac, the Army of the Potomac. The soldiers loved him, for he seemed to care deeply about their well-being, even if he did not live among them in camp but rather in a comfortable house near the Executive Mansion. McClellan enjoyed showing off his troops at reviews, which Lincoln gladly attended. Frequently the president also visited army camps ringing the capital. At hospitals, he shook hands with sick and wounded troops, who were cheered by his warm cordiality.

Also cheering up the soldiers was Lincoln's merciful treatment of those condemned to death by courts-martial. On September 4, Private William Scott, an unsophisticated Vermont country boy who had fallen asleep on sentry duty, was sentenced to die before a firing squad. When Lincoln received appeals for clemency from officers in Scott's regiment as well as leading Washington clergymen, he assured them that he would consider the matter carefully. The day before the scheduled execution, McClellan, who had approved the sentence, issued an order announcing that "the President of the United States has expressed a wish that as this is the first condemnation to death in this army for this crime, mercy may be extended to the criminal. This fact, viewed in connection with the inexperience of the condemned as a soldier, his previous good conduct and general good character, and the urgent entreaties made in his behalf, have determined the Major General commanding to grant the pardon so earnestly prayed for."[5]

Lincoln's willingness to reprieve death sentences for sleeping sentinels, deserters, and others became legendary, and for good reason. When Congressman Henry L. Dawes asked him to spare the life of a 19-year-old constituent found guilty of desertion, the president replied "that the War Department insisted that the severest punishment for desertion was absolutely necessary to save the army from demoralization." He added: "But when I think of these mere lads, who had never before left their homes, enlisting in the enthusiasm of the moment for a war of which they had no conception and then in the camp or on the battle field a thousand miles from home, longing for its rest and safety, I have so much sympathy for him that I cannot condemn him to die for forgetting the obligations of the soldier in the longing for home life. There is death and woe enough in this war without such a sacrifice."[6] Despite his reluctance to do so, Lincoln approved 267 death sentences over the course of the war.

Rather than fighting the nearby Confederates, Little Mac defiantly campaigned against Winfield Scott, whom he wished to supplant as general in chief. Offended by McClellan's presumptuous tone, and feeling undermined by him, Scott in August asked to be retired. When the president tried to smooth things over and urged Old Fuss and Feathers to retract his letter of resignation, Scott agreed to stay on, at least for a while. Lincoln was, however, unable to stop the feuding between the two men, who continued to squabble for the next three months. Little Mac ignored Scott's requests for information about his command, bypassed him in communicating with the administration, and flouted his chief's orders. In October, when some impatient Radical Republican senators urged McClellan to advance, he replied that he could do nothing as long as Scott remained in overall command. Those senators then implored Lincoln to remove Old Fuss and Feathers. In fact, the president on October 18 had read to the cabinet the draft of a tactful letter accepting Scott's resignation. The aged general had become too ill and was too unfamiliar with war on so vast a scale to be effective.

Two weeks later the general in chief renewed his request that he be placed on the retired list. On November 1, Lincoln agreed, and along with the cabinet, he paid a visit to Scott, who was too weak to sit up. The president read him a statement expressing gratitude for his years of military service. The aged hero wept as he listened to Lincoln's words, replied graciously, and shook hands with his visitors as he bade them a sad farewell. Upon emerging from the room, Lincoln too had tears in his eyes. That evening, the president called on McClellan, who rejoiced in his triumph over Scott. Old Fuss and Feathers had magnanimously recommended Little Mac as his successor. After hearing McClellan read his order concerning Scott's retirement, the president said: "I should be perfectly satisfied if I thought that this vast increase of responsibility would not embarrass you."

"It is a great relief, sir. I feel as if several tons were taken from my shoulders today. I am now in contact with you, and the Secretary."

"Draw on me for all the sense I have, and all the information. In addition to your present command, the supreme command of the army will entail a vast labor upon you."

"I can do it all," McClellan replied quietly.[7]

Around that same time, Little Mac told the president: "I think we shall succeed entirely if our friends will be patient, and not hurry us."

"I promise you, you shall have your own way," Lincoln said.[8]

The quarrelsome Young Napoleon, who never could get along with superiors, implied that Scott alone had hindered him and that now that Old Fuss and Feathers was out of the way, he could take the offensive. But in fact he complained about the president as much as he ever had about Scott. To his wife, McClellan described Lincoln as "an idiot," "the original gorilla," a "baboon," and "'an old stick'—& pretty poor timber at that." He denounced "the cowardice of the Presdt," a man whom he could "never regard" with anything other than "thorough contempt—for his mind, heart & morality."[9]

McClellan manifested his contempt in deeds as well as words. Less than two weeks after his elevation to the supreme command, the Young Napoleon returned home from a wedding to discover the president, John Hay, and Seward waiting for him. According to Hay, the general "without paying any particular attention to the porter who told him the President was waiting to see him, went up stairs, passing the door of the room where the President and Secretary of State were seated. They waited about half-an-hour, and sent once more a servant to tell the General they were there, and the answer came that the General had gone to bed." As they returned to the White House, Hay bemoaned "this unparalleled insolence of epaulettes," but Lincoln "seemed not to have noticed it specially, saying it was better at this time not to be making points of etiquette & personal dignity."[10] On another of the numerous occasions when Lincoln called on McClellan, the general said, "Let the Commander-in-chief wait, he has no business to know what is going on."[11]

Little Mac's contempt for the president was partially rooted in snobbery. The scion of a prominent Philadelphia family, McClellan regarded many people as his social inferiors, among them Lincoln's cabinet, which he scorned as "a most despicable set of men."[12] He also denounced Radicals in Congress for their principles as well as their meddlesome ways. A partisan Democrat, he had little sympathy for the antislavery cause or for Blacks. He confided that he had "a prejudice in favor of my own race" and that he could not "learn to like the odor of either Billy goats or niggers." He told his wife, "I will not fight for the abolitionists." Tactlessly he made these views known to leading Radicals, including the influential senator Charles Sumner, with whom he had an interview soon after arriving in Washington.[13] When Radicals clamored for action, McClellan appealed to a Democratic leader in New York: "Help me to dodge the nigger—we want nothing to do with him. *I* am fighting to preserve the integrity of the Union & the power of the Govt—on no other issue."[14]

The self-aggrandizing McClellan may have conquered Scott, but the Confederates in Virginia went virtually unmolested. At the end of September, when the enemy abandoned Munson's Hill (within sight of the Capitol), Unionists were mortified to learn that the artillery posted there, which had intimidated McClellan, turned out to be "Quaker guns"—logs painted black to resemble cannon. Confederates laughed while Northerners fumed. This humiliating revelation did not deter McClellan from continuing to exaggerate Confederate strength, a mistake that affected all his decisions. A month later he submitted to Cameron a report (drafted by Edwin M. Stanton) stating that "all the information we have from spies, prisoners, &c., agrees in showing that the enemy have a force on the Potomac not less than 150,000 strong, well drilled and equipped, ably commanded, and strongly entrenched. It is plain, therefore, that to insure success, or to render it reasonably certain, the active army should not number less than 150,000 efficient troops, with 400 guns, unless some material change occurs in the force in front of us." By his peculiar accounting methods, his own force was so much smaller that he could not launch an offensive without significant reinforcements. If they were provided, he would attack no later than November 25.[15]

In actual fact, McClellan had between 85,000 and 100,000 effectives, while Joseph E. Johnston at Centerville and Manassas had only 30,000 to 35,000. The Young Napoleon could have assaulted Johnston or Confederate positions on the south bank of the Potomac, or Winchester, or Leesburg, or Norfolk, all of which were vulnerable to a force as large as the Army of the Potomac. There was no excuse for the inactivity, which demoralized the North and encouraged Confederates' hopes.

McClellan's overestimation of enemy strength stemmed in part, but only in part, from faulty information supplied by Allan Pinkerton, the detective who had warned Lincoln about the Baltimore plot in February. Little Mac hired him as his chief of intelligence well after the general had grossly overestimated Confederate forces in August. McClellan's central problem was not so much bad intelligence but paranoia, which led him not only to see enemies everywhere but also to quarrel with superiors, mistrust most people, indulge in extreme secrecy, judge others harshly, cling to preconceived notions in the face of overwhelming evidence discrediting them, and refuse to acknowledge his own faults. Compounding his paranoia was a streak of narcissism, predisposing him to envy, arrogance, grandiosity, vanity, and hypersensitivity to criticism.

Public pressure for action led to a humiliating fiasco on October 21 at Ball's Bluff, Virginia, forty miles from the capital, where Union forces under General Charles P. Stone, acting on vague orders from McClellan, crossed the Potomac to conduct a reconnaissance in force. During the Union repulse, the president's close friend Colonel Edward D. Baker was killed, along with dozens of others. Awaiting reports from the front, Lincoln prophetically said of Baker, "I am afraid his impetuous daring will endanger his life."[16] When this fear proved justified, the president was devastated. Emerging from the telegraph office with his head bowed down in grief and his ashen face streaked with tears, he failed to return the salute of the sentinel guarding the door. Occurring three months to the day after Bull Run, the disaster at Ball's Bluff demoralized the North badly. A few days later, several senators called on Lincoln demanding to know who was responsible for the army's failure to move on Richmond. Benjamin Wade declared: "Something, Mr. President, must be done. War must be made on the secessionists, or we will make war on the Administration."[17]

Developments on the western front also frustrated Lincoln. In Missouri, Union general John C. Frémont's impetuosity, tactlessness, poor judgment, egomania, ethical insensitivity, and administrative and military incompetence unfitted him for his heavy responsibilities. As commander of the Department of the West, his most pressing task was to thwart Confederate attempts to conquer Missouri. Shortly after his belated arrival at St. Louis on July 25, he had to decide whether to reinforce the threatened Union position at Cairo, Illinois, or Nathaniel Lyon's small army in southwestern Missouri. When he sensibly chose the former course, the impulsive, willful Lyon recklessly hurled his troops against a much larger Confederate force at Wilson's Creek on August 10 and suffered a predictable defeat, during which he was killed. This setback, a scant three weeks after Bull Run, further demoralized the public. Making matters worse still, in September Confederates captured the thirty-five-hundred-man Union garrison at Lexington, Missouri. Thus, in his first two months at St. Louis, Frémont lost almost half the state.

More than the general's military ineptitude, his political blundering upset Lincoln. On August 30, Frémont issued a proclamation establishing martial law throughout Missouri, condemning to death civilians caught with weapons behind Union lines, and seizing the property (including slaves) of rebels. Before issuing this decree, he had consulted his wife and a Quaker abolitionist but no one in the administration. While the Northern press generally lauded the Pathfinder's emancipation edict, Kentuckians indignantly denounced it. Robert Anderson, military commander in the Bluegrass State, warned Lincoln that Frémont's proclamation "is producing most disastrous results" and "that it is the opinion of many of our wisest and soundest men that if this is not immediately disavowed, and annulled, Kentucky will be lost to the Union."[18] The public there seemed to agree with the English newspaper that termed Frémont's proclamation a call for "negro insurrection, servile war, outrages and horrors without number and without name."[19]

Lincoln gently but firmly urged Frémont to rescind the emancipation order, which went beyond the Confiscation Act, freeing only those slaves directly supporting Confederate military efforts. The president advised Frémont that "liberating slaves of traiterous owners, will alarm our Southern Union friends, and turn them against us—perhaps ruin our rather fair prospect for Kentucky." Tactfully, "in a spirit of caution and not of censure," Lincoln asked the general to modify his order to conform to the new statute; he should do so as if it were his own idea, not as a grudging capitulation to a superior's order.[20] The president also instructed him to execute no one without his approval. The quarrelsome Frémont, who was temperamentally reluctant to follow orders and predisposed to ignore others' feelings, rashly declined to modify his decree without being instructed to do so. Defiantly, he ordered thousands of copies of the original proclamation distributed after the president had called for its modification.

Lincoln reluctantly complied with Frémont's request for a direct order and thus ignited a firestorm of protest. The White House mailbag overflowed with letters denouncing the revocation. On September 10, Jessie Benton Frémont, the general's headstrong wife, called on Lincoln and tongue-lashed him. He later recalled that "she taxed me so violently with many things that I had to exercise all the awkward tact I have to avoid quarrelling with her."[21] But Lincoln was not always decorous in handling Frémont's champions. To one friend of the Pathfinder he was abrupt: "Sir, I believe General Fremont to be a thoroughly honest man, but he has unfortunately surrounded himself with some of the greatest scoundrels on this continent; you are one of them and the worst of them."[22] To another defender of Frémont's proclamation Lincoln replied, "We didn't go into the war to put *down* Slavery, but to put the flag *back*; and to act differently at this moment, would, I have no doubt, not only weaken our cause but smack of bad faith; for I never should have had votes enough to send me here, if the people had supposed I should try to use my power to upset Slavery. Why, the first thing you'd see, would be a mutiny in the army. No! We must wait until every other means had been exhausted. *This thunderbolt will keep*."[23]

Lincoln's fear was justified, for the public was not yet ready for emancipation. Moreover, to allow Frémont's proclamation to stand would be to authorize every department commander to set policy without consulting elected officials. In addition, Lincoln felt obliged by his oath of office to modify the Pathfinder's edict. The Springfield, Massachusetts, *Republican* sympathized with Frémont but found it "gratifying to know that we have a president who is as loyal to law—when that is made to meet an emergency—as he is ready to meet an emergency for which no law is provided. The president is right."[24] Lincoln was also dismayed to learn from Frank Blair that Frémont let out contracts carelessly, secluded himself in his expensive mansion-headquarters, busied himself with trivial matters, and refused to draw up action plans. On September 19, the president had General Scott draft an order instructing Frémont to turn over his command and report to Washington immediately. At Seward's suggestion, however, Lincoln did not send it, for he feared that the popularity of Frémont and his proclamation, along with the difficulty of finding an adequate replacement, made his removal inadvisable at that time. As complaints continued to pour in, however, Lincoln finally issued an order dismissing Frémont on October 24. Nine days later it was handed to the Pathfinder, who grudgingly turned over his command to David Hunter. Hopefully Lincoln predicted that before spring arrived, "the people of Missouri will be in no favorable mood to renew, for next year, the troubles which have so much afflicted, and impoverished them during this."[25]

On November 9, Lincoln broke up the gigantic Department of the West, placing Henry W. Halleck, a pedantic, goggle-eyed, indecisive West Point graduate, in command of the new Department of Missouri (which also encompassed Arkansas and western Kentucky). Halleck had earned the sobriquet "Old Brains" for writing several books, most notably *Elements of Military Art and Science*, which made him the country's premier military theorist. Hunter was assigned to the Department of Kansas, and Don Carlos Buell was to head the Department of the Ohio, with responsibility for eastern Kentucky. Buell and Halleck were supposed to coordinate their efforts; the latter was to move south along the Mississippi toward Memphis, while the former was to slice the critically important rail line connecting Virginia with the Confederate West and to liberate eastern Tennessee, where Unionists were suffering persecution. In the West, Lincoln emphasized seizing territory; in the East, destruction of the enemy's army.

A stern martinet who like Halleck suffered from indecisiveness, Buell understandably thought Lincoln's plan infeasible, for his army faced daunting logistical problems in marching across four mountain chains in winter, then occupying eastern Tennessee, with no rail line to supply it. McClellan, however, counted on Buell to cut the railroad from Virginia to Chattanooga, isolating the Confederate forces that he planned to attack in the Old Dominion; Little Mac said he would be unable to advance until Buell accomplished his mission. Buell, however, favored moving against Nashville, in central Tennessee, following the line of the Cumberland River, as a more practicable alternative to Lincoln's strategy. Impertinently he told the president that he would move with reluctance to carry out that strategy. Meanwhile in Missouri, Halleck reported that "everything here is in complete chaos."[26] Swiftly he canceled fraudulent contracts, suppressed guerillas, brought order to the administrative rat's nest left behind by Frémont, fired do-nothing staffers, suspended the construction of needless fortifications around St. Louis, and restored order to the state, all the while complaining about a shortage of troops and weapons. From Kansas, David Hunter protested bitterly that his new command was too small for a man of his rank. Gently Lincoln chided him and offered sound paternal advice: "I am constrained to say it is difficult to answer so ugly a letter in good temper. . . . You constantly speak of being placed in command of only 3000. Now tell me, is not this mere impatience? Have you not known all the while that you are to command four or five times that many? I have been, and am sincerely your friend; and if, as such, I dare to make a suggestion, I would say you are adopting the best possible way to ruin yourself." Quoting one of his favorite poets, Alexander Pope, Lincoln counseled: "Act well your part, there all the honor lies." An officer "who does *something* at the head of one Regiment, will eclipse him who does *nothing* at the head of a hundred."[27]

Amid the gloomy aftermath of Bull Run, the Union navy provided the only bright spots. In August, with the help of troops under Ben Butler, it seized control of Hatteras Inlet on North Carolina's Outer Banks. The small-scale operation, which deprived the Confederates of a privateer haven, required only seven ships. Minor though it was, this victory just after McDowell's ignominious defeat at Bull Run cheered up Lincoln, his constituents, and the army. The navy achieved a far more important victory in November, when seventy vessels and twelve thousand troops captured Port Royal, South Carolina. That town then became a vital link in the chain enforcing the blockade. Northerners rejoiced at the "glorious achievement" and "our first great victory."[28] At Lincoln's suggestion, Congress expressed its thanks to the leader of that expedition, Captain Samuel Francis Du Pont, "for the decisive and splendid victory achieved at Port Royal."[29]

At the time when Frémont was removed, he was belatedly pursuing the enemy. Meanwhile in the East, the conservative Democrat McClellan presided over the disaster at Ball's Bluff and then refused to undertake even a modest offensive. When Congress reassembled in early December, the Radicals demanded an investigation of the army and established a body to carry it out, the Joint Committee on the Conduct of the War, which was authorized to examine all aspects of the conflict. It vindicated Frémont, whom the Radicals regarded as a martyr to emancipation. The naiveté of the committee members, mostly Radical Republicans, led them to support men like Frémont, whose antislavery ardor was matched only by their military incompetence. While the committee was critical of the president, it provided him with a tool to help spur his generals to fight, for Lincoln was just as eager as the Radicals to have the war conducted vigorously. He wanted aggressive, effective commanders. McClellan did not fit that description. The Radicals, along with the rest of the North, grew increasingly impatient with the Young Napoleon as winter approached. Ideal fighting weather persisted into December, but the Army of the Potomac failed to take advantage of it. Instead, it concentrated on ringing Washington with dozens of forts. Soon after being named general in chief, Little Mac promised to launch an offensive within weeks, but he did not do so. In early December, Lincoln asked him about the feasibility of attacking the Confederates' supply lines to Manassas. If the Union army managed to cut their rail link, Johnston would be forced out of his entrenched position. It was a sensible suggestion, but predictably Little Mac asserted that since the enemy forces were nearly as large as his own, no such advance should be risked. Yet, he said, he had a plan "that I do not think at all anticipated by the enemy nor by any of our own people." He did not deign to share its details.[30] On December 20, McClellan came down with typhoid fever and was indisposed for three weeks.

Despair overspread the North as the army entered winter quarters; some feared that its inaction would lead European nations to recognize the Confederacy. Bankers told Chase that unless the army advanced or there was a cabinet shake-up, they would not lend the government more money, for the administration had nothing to show for the funds already lent. Lincoln grew as frustrated and discouraged as the Joint Committee on the Conduct of the War. On January 2, he spoke to John A. Dahlgren "of the bare possibility of our being two nations."[31] When Ben Wade's committee visited him at the White House on December 31, the Ohio senator said bluntly: "Mr. President, you are murdering your country by inches in consequence of the inactivity of the military and the want of a distinct policy in regard to slavery."[32] Lincoln offered no reply, but he did write McClellan about it the next day: "I hear that the doings of an Investigating Committee, give you some uneasiness. You may be entirely relieved on this point. The gentlemen of the Committee were with me an hour and a half last night; and I found them in a perfectly good mood. As their investigation brings them acquainted with facts, they are rapidly coming to think of the whole case as all sensible men would."[33] Thus Lincoln hinted that the Army of the Potomac must attack.

On January 6, Wade's committee met with Lincoln and the cabinet. They earnestly recommended that Irvin McDowell be given command of the Army of the Potomac and insisted that the war be prosecuted with vigor. According to one committee member, "Neither the President nor his advisers seemed to have any definite information respecting the management of the war, or the failure of our forces to make any forward movement. Not a man of them pretended to know anything of General McClellan's plans." The committee was "greatly surprised to learn that Mr. Lincoln himself did not think he had any *right* to know, but that, as he was not a military man, it was his duty to defer to General McClellan."[34]

Meanwhile, Union commanders in the West seemed as inert as Little Mac. Both Halleck and Buell offered abundant excuses for postponing offensives. When Buell opposed forwarding arms to eastern Tennessee, Lincoln urged that general to name a date when he could begin a campaign: "Delay is ruining us; and it is indispensable for me to have something definite."[35] The president sent a similar request to Halleck, who was unwilling to commit troops to Kentucky while he was preparing for an advance in southwestern Missouri. For Lincoln, January 10 was one of the worst days of the war. He dejectedly wrote to Simon Cameron apropos of the negative responses from Halleck and Buell: "It is exceedingly discouraging. As everywhere else, nothing can be done."[36] In despair, he turned to Montgomery Meigs, whose counsel he valued. "General," Lincoln asked, "what shall I do? The people are impatient; Chase has no money, and he tells me he can raise no more; the general of the army [McClellan] has typhoid fever. The bottom is out of the tub. What shall I do?"[37]

When Meigs suggested a consultation with Little Mac's division commanders, Lincoln called a meeting for January 10 with Generals McDowell and William B. Franklin, along with Seward and Assistant Secretary of War Thomas A. Scott. According to McDowell, the president told them that he "was in great distress, and, as he had been to General McClellan's house, and the General did not ask to see him, and as he must talk to somebody, he had sent for General Franklin and myself, to obtain our opinion as to the possibility of soon commencing active operations with the

Army of the Potomac." He added that "if something was not done soon, the bottom would be out of the whole affair; and if General McClellan did not want to use the army, he would like to '*borrow it*.'"[38] When Lincoln asked for recommendations, McDowell suggested an attack on the Confederates' supply line to Manassas, a plan the president had been urging on McClellan. Franklin proposed a campaign against Richmond via the York River. Lincoln asked that they reflect on the matter and convene again the next day, which they did.

Word that two of his division commanders had met with the president acted as a tonic, restoring McClellan's health. On Sunday morning, January 12, the Young Napoleon unexpectedly called at the White House and laid out a plan to attack Richmond by sailing his army down Chesapeake Bay to Urbanna, on the Rappahannock River. Early that afternoon the president met with Chase, Seward, Montgomery Blair, McDowell, Franklin, and Meigs. After Meigs endorsed McDowell's proposal to attack the Confederate supply lines to Manassas, Lincoln suggested that since McClellan had recovered, they meet with him the next day.

On January 13 at 3:00 p.m. they did so. Lincoln asked McDowell and Franklin to go over their proposals. The former restated his plan to attack enemy supply lines, prompting the sullen general in chief "coldly, if not curtly" to exclaim: "You are entitled to have any opinion you please!"[39] As the discussion continued, McClellan ominously remained silent. Into Little Mac's ear, Meigs whispered that Lincoln expected him to participate. The general in chief replied that the Confederates had at least 175,000 men at Manassas (a gross exaggeration). Moreover, he sneered: "If I tell him my plans they will be in the New York Herald tomorrow morning. He can't keep a secret, he will tell them to Tadd." Meigs responded: "That is a pity, but he is the President,—the Commander-in-Chief; he has a right to know; it is not respectful to sit mute when he so clearly requires you to speak." (Meigs thought McClellan's conduct a "spectacle to make gods and men ashamed!")[40] Chase told Franklin, "If that is Mac's decision, he is a ruined man."[41] Responding to pressure from the treasury secretary, McClellan deigned to say that he would prod Buell to launch an offensive in Kentucky but was reluctant to discuss his plans further. Lincoln asked Little Mac "if he had counted upon any particular time" for that movement to begin. When McClellan replied affirmatively, the president said: "Well, on this assurance of the General that he will press the advance in Kentucky, I will be satisfied, and will adjourn this Council."[42] Incredibly, McClellan the next day spelled out to a New York *Herald* reporter the plan he had refused to describe to Lincoln because he did not want it revealed to that very newspaper! Little Mac began a three-hour conversation with correspondent Malcolm Ives by saying, "What I declined communicating to them [Lincoln and the others] I am now going to convey through you to Mr. [James Gordon] Bennett . . . *all* the knowledge I possess myself, with no reserve."[43]

McClellan's stubborn unwillingness to confide in Lincoln would prove a grave mistake and lead to his undoing. The president's tendency to defer to Little Mac was also unwise; if he had been more assertive, the general might have been more compliant. Edward Bates realized this; at a cabinet meeting on January 10 he emphatically urged the president to "take and act out the power of his place, to command the commanders," and if they balked, to fire them.[44]

The *Trent* Crisis

Lincoln found it even more frustrating to cope with a diplomatic crisis that nearly led to war with Great Britain. That autumn, the Confederate government decided to replace its three roving commissioners to Europe with two ministers plenipotentiary, former senators James M. Mason of Virginia (to England) and John Slidell of Louisiana (to France). In mid-October, the two men boarded a blockade runner that whisked them to Havana, where they transferred to the British mail packet *Trent*, bound for St. Thomas. There they intended to book passage for Europe. On November 8, Union captain Charles Wilkes, commanding the *San Jacinto*, rashly stopped the *Trent*, boarded her, seized Mason and Slidell as contraband, and shipped the would-be diplomats to Fort Warren in Boston harbor.

The North rejoiced, for Mason and Slidell were particularly loathed as extreme fire-eaters. Congress voted a resolution of thanks to Wilkes. Many prominent observers, including Charles Sumner, chairman of the Senate Foreign Relations Committee, did not celebrate, however; they quite rightly thought Wilkes had violated international law by seizing men from a neutral ship in transit from one neutral port to another. The envoys should have been released as soon as the administration ascertained the facts. Lincoln may have briefly shared his constituents' glee, but within hours of receiving the news he realized that Mason and Slidell had to be surrendered. To Gideon Welles he expressed "anxiety" about "the disposition of the prisoners." The public's "indignation was so overwhelming against the chief conspirators, that he feared it would be difficult to prevent severe and exemplary punishment, which he always deprecated."[45]

At a cabinet meeting early in the crisis, Lincoln, according to a press account, "expressed himself in favor of restoring them [Mason and Slidell] to the protection of the British flag, if it should be demanded. He said it was doubtful if the course of Captain Wilkes could be justified by international law, and that, at all events, he could not afford to have two wars upon his hands at the same time." (More succinctly, he cautioned: "one war at a time.") Only Montgomery Blair agreed. Chase "argued forcibly and with warmth that the course recommended by the President would be dishonorable." Bates believed that "it was lawful to seize the men."[46]

When the British first learned of Wilkes's act, their indignation knew no bounds. The Union Jack had been insulted! The outraged prime minister, Lord Palmerston, allegedly exclaimed to his cabinet: "I don't know whether you are going to stand for this, but I'll be damned if I do!" He instructed his foreign minister, Lord John Russell, to compose a belligerent, curt message, which Queen Victoria and her mortally ill husband, Prince Albert, toned down. The revised document stated that British authorities would accept an American explanation that Wilkes had acted without instructions, but the United States must within seven days agree to offer an apology, pay indemnities, and forthwith release Mason and Slidell. If the Lincoln administration refused, the British minister to the United States, Richard Lyons, must return home. He was to give Seward informal notice of this message in order to allow the administration sufficient time to consider its response. Ominously, eleven thousand British troops set sail for Canada; Great Britain refused to sell the United States any more saltpeter (then the principal ingredient of gunpowder, imported from India); and several warships were ordered to the North American station.

Russell's dispatch did not reach Washington until December 19. Meanwhile, Lincoln took comfort from mistaken reports that British legal authorities had declared Wilkes's action justified. On December 10 the president told his old friend Orville H. Browning "that there would probably be no trouble about it."[47] Three days later he was jolted out of his complacency when English newspapers arrived with blaring headlines about the indignation sweeping the British Isles. Two days thereafter, Lincoln was astounded when informal word came that Her Majesty's government would demand the release of the Confederate emissaries and an apology. On December 16, Seward exclaimed to a British journalist and some diplomats: "We will wrap the whole world in flames! No power so remote that she will not feel the fire of our battle and be burned by our conflagration."[48] That day he and his fellow cabinet members decided to keep Mason and Slidell because it was believed that Her Majesty's government would not go to war over their capture; instead it would probably demand that they be released, and a prolonged diplomatic correspondence would then resolve the issue.

But lengthy negotiations no longer seemed possible after December 19, when Lord Lyons informally showed Seward the dispatch from Russell. Four days later, the British envoy officially submitted Russell's document, giving the administration until December 30 to reply. The president thus confronted a dilemma: if the Confederate envoys were released, it would outrage public opinion in the North;

if they were not, Britain might declare war and break the blockade. On December 20 and 21, Lincoln drafted a dispatch for Seward's signature. He tactfully wrote: "This government has intended no affront to the British flag, or to the British nation; nor has it intended to force into discussion, an embarrassing question, all which is evident by the fact, hereby asserted, that the act complained of was done by the officer, without orders from, or expectation of, the government."[49] Seward meanwhile drafted his own response to the British government, which Lincoln promised to examine carefully. The secretary endorsed the release of Mason and Slidell, even though he maintained that they were in fact contraband of war. Wilkes had acted without instructions, Seward explained, and though justified in seizing the Confederate emissaries, the captain should have taken the *Trent* to a prize court. But because he had voluntarily let the *Trent* sail away, Wilkes had vitiated America's case for holding Mason and Slidell.

On December 25 and 26, the cabinet discussed Seward's draft at length. According to Edward Bates, everyone understood "the magnitude of the subject, and believed that upon our decision depended the dearest interest, probably the existence, of the nation." The attorney general, waiving the question of legal right, "urged the necessity of the case; that to go to war with England now is to abandon all hope of suppressing the rebellion."[50] Chase said, "It is gall and wormwood to me. Rather than consent to the liberation of these men, I would sacrifice everything I possess." But even he agreed to their release, explaining that as long as "the matter hangs in uncertainty, the public mind will remain disquieted, our commerce will suffer serious harm, our action against the rebels must be greatly hindered, and the restoration of our prosperity . . . must be delayed."[51] The next day, after making several changes, the cabinet endorsed Seward's dispatch, which was submitted to Lord Lyons on December 27. It made a clever, face-saving argument, designed to mollify the British government without offending the American public. Seward read it to several members of Congress, who agreed that Mason and Slidell must be released. When the secretary of state asked Lincoln why he had not submitted a paper justifying retention of the Confederate diplomats, he replied: "I found I could not make an argument that would satisfy my own mind, and that proved to me your ground was the right one."[52]

The Palmerston government withdrew the demands for reparations and an apology, viewing the release of Mason and Slidell as a gesture sufficiently conciliatory to end the crisis. Lincoln called that surrender "a pretty bitter pill to swallow" but told Horace Porter that "I contented myself with believing that England's triumph in the matter would be short-lived, and that after ending our war successfully, we would be so powerful that we could call her to account for all the embarrassments she had inflicted upon us."[53]

At the conclusion of the *Trent* crisis, Sumner twitted Lincoln about his reluctance to liberate the slaves. If he had publicly announced an emancipation plan, the United States would have enjoyed far more support in Europe, the senator claimed, and the *Trent* affair "would have come and gone and would have given you no anxiety."[54] In fact, the president had been working on a scheme to free slaves in Delaware, a plan he hoped would serve as a model for other Border States. With a mere 1,798 enslaved residents, Delaware would experience less economic and social upheaval as a result of emancipation than any other Slave State. On November 4, Lincoln consulted with Delaware congressman George P. Fisher, who agreed to draft an emancipation bill that would be submitted after Lincoln had revised it. When the president suggested that owners receive $300 for each slave, Fisher held out for $500; Lincoln agreed. The president believed that gradual, compensated emancipation was not only constitutional but also the cheapest and most humane way to end the war, and Delaware was the ideal place to start implementing the plan. To compensate slaveowners, the federal government would provide the state with $719,200 in bonds. In order to carry out the scheme, it was necessary that Congress appropriate the money and that the Delaware legislature accept the offer.

On December 3, Lincoln submitted to the newly reconvened Congress his annual message, which did not mention the Delaware plan directly but did address the matter of compensated emancipation in a roundabout way. Moreover, any slaves who might in the future be liberated by state action—and free Blacks as well—should be offered the opportunity to resettle at government expense "at some place, or places, in a climate congenial to them." Lest his modest remarks be construed as rank abolitionism, Lincoln stressed that he would treat the slavery issue cautiously: "In considering the policy to be adopted for suppressing the insurrection, I have been anxious and careful that the inevitable conflict for this purpose shall not degenerate into a violent and remorseless revolutionary struggle." (By that he probably meant a slave rebellion.) "I have, therefore, in every case, thought it proper to keep the integrity of the Union prominent as the primary object of the contest on our part, leaving all questions which are not of vital military importance to the more deliberate action of the legislature." But he hinted that emancipation might be necessary in time, for the "Union must be preserved, and hence, all indispensable means must be employed."[55]

Just before the message was submitted to Congress, Lincoln told his cabinet why he had soft-pedaled the slavery issue: "Gentlemen, you are not a unit on this question, and as it is a very important one, in fact the most important which has come before us since the war commenced, I will float on with the tide till you are more nearly united than at present. Perhaps we shall yet *drift* into the right position."[56]

In early 1862, the Delaware plan fizzled when the legislature refused by a one-vote margin to endorse it.

The proposal to resettle freedmen outraged many abolitionists, including Frederick Douglass, who denounced it and bitterly remarked that the president "is quite a genuine representative of American prejudice and negro hatred" and "shows himself to be about as destitute of any anti-slavery principle or feeling as did James Buchanan."[57] (Two of Douglass's three sons, however, disagreed and signed up for a colonization scheme in Panama that the administration almost implemented in the latter part of 1862.) To place Lincoln's remarks in context, it should be noted that some of his cabinet members (Montgomery Blair, Caleb B. Smith, and Edward Bates) and congressional Republicans (notably Frank Blair, Lyman Trumbull, James R. Doolittle, and Preston King) were colonizationists and that during the antebellum era many Whites who strongly opposed slavery had also supported colonization, among them Theodore Parker, Horace Greeley, Gerrit Smith, Salmon P. Chase, Leonard Bacon, Harriet Beecher Stowe, Thaddeus Stevens, James G. Birney, Eli Thayer, Benjamin Lundy, and James Lane. So too did several Black antislavery champions, including such luminaries as John Russwurm, Samuel Cornish, Alexander Crummell, James McCune Smith, James T. Holly, Martin Delany, Henry McNeal Turner, Henry Highland Garnet, and Paul Cuffee. Moreover, in the 1850s, delegates to Black emigration conventions had endorsed a large-scale exodus. Douglass himself in early 1861 had urged African Americans to consider immigrating to Haiti.

Lincoln's support of colonization was not rooted in "negro hatred" but in hard political realities. Border States simply would not voluntarily emancipate slaves unless the freedpeople left the country, and many Whites in the Lower North would not support emancipation unless it was coupled with colonization. Frederick Milnes Edge, a correspondent for the London *Star*, interpreted the 1862 statute emancipating slaves in the District of Columbia for his readers. One clause, he said, "is likely to meet with misconstruction in Europe—namely, the appropriation for colonising the freed slaves. This was adopted to silence the weak-nerved, whose name is legion, and to enable any of the slaves who see fit to migrate to more congenial climes."[58]

Indeed, Lincoln was covering his flank against attacks that would inevitably attend emancipation and also trying to sugar-coat it to make it a less bitter pill for "weak-nerved" conservatives to swallow. In addition, he evidently believed that anti-Black prejudice was so deeply rooted and so widespread that it was reasonable for some African Americans to fear that they would never achieve anything like first-class citizenship in the United States and that the government owed it to them to provide a haven overseas where they could enjoy full citizenship rights. Moreover, practical considerations made colonization seem like a humane program. Thousands of slaves in Virginia, South Carolina, and elsewhere were in the custody of the Union army, which did not wish to continue feeding and housing them. Neither the North nor the Border States wanted them; the public disapproved of allowing them to serve in the army; in "contraband camps" being established to care for refugee slaves conditions were truly deplorable. And so colonization seemed the only viable option, especially since practical steps had already been taken to find sites abroad where freedpeople might resettle.

Radicals were further disenchanted with Lincoln's insistence that Simon Cameron revise a paragraph in his annual report that called for emancipating and arming slaves. On December 1, immediately after reading it, the president exclaimed: "This will never do! General Cameron must take no such responsibility. This is a question that belongs exclusively to me!"[59] Lincoln told the secretary of war that his recommendation would hurt the Union cause in Kentucky and demanded that he delete the controversial paragraphs. The president was working on his proposal to abolish slavery in Delaware and did not want Cameron to rile up the public on that sensitive subject. The impertinent war secretary refused. At a cabinet meeting the next day, Welles and Chase backed Cameron, but Bates, Blair, Seward, and Smith did not. The secretary of state was especially alarmed. According to the Philadelphia *Inquirer*, Lincoln "finally settled it by going to General Cameron and insisting upon his confining his report to a statement of the past, and not dictate to Congress what they should do! Cameron insisted that his policy was correct, and must be carried out at once." The president assured the secretary that "if he changed his report or left out any of it," it did not necessarily mean that he was changing his policy, only that he was letting "Congress take hold of the matter first."[60] Cameron reluctantly agreed to comply with Lincoln's directive.

Tension had been building between the president and his war secretary for some time. In October, Lincoln complained that Cameron was "utterly ignorant and regardless of the course of things, and the probable result," "selfish and openly discourteous," "obnoxious to the country," and "incapable of organizing details or conceiving and advising general plans."[61] In September 1861, Lincoln told Hiram Barney that he wished to remove Cameron because the Chief "was unequal to the duties of the place" and "his public affiliation with army contractors was a scandal."[62]

The president had long been planning to replace Cameron. In September, he allegedly hinted to Edwin M. Stanton that soon he would probably be named to an important position. In October, the president let his war secretary know he would be dismissed sooner or later. But what to do with him? Because he remained a powerful a force in Pennsylvania politics, the Chief had to be given a consolation prize, such as a diplomatic post. As it developed, Cassius M. Clay wished to return home from Russia, where he had been serving as U.S. minister. From Thurlow Weed, the president learned that Cameron would be willing to take Clay's place. (When informed of this move, Thaddeus Stevens quipped: "Send word to the Czar to bring in his things of nights.")[63] On January 11, Lincoln sent the secretary of war an uncharacteristically curt note: "As you have, more than once, expressed a desire for a change of position, I can now gratify you, consistently with my view of the public interest. I therefore propose nominating you to the Senate, next monday, as minister to Russia."[64] Because Lincoln's note contained no expression of regret or gratitude, Cameron felt so deeply wounded that he tearfully said it "meant personal degradation."[65] So the president sent Cameron another missive, backdated to January 11, paying tribute to his services.

Cameron's dismissal electrified both the public and Congress. In the spring of 1862, when the House of Representatives censured Cameron, Lincoln defended him, much to the surprise of the legislators. With characteristic magnanimity, he assumed much of the blame for mistakes made at the beginning of the war, when contracts were let without the usual precautions. While Lincoln's defense of Cameron antagonized many Republicans, the president's gesture won him Cameron's unflagging gratitude, which would prove vital later on.

When Lincoln asked Cameron about potential successors, the Chief recommended Edwin Stanton, whom Lincoln regarded as politically attractive, for he lived in Pennsylvania and had been a Democrat. In addition, his service in Buchanan's cabinet had made him famous as a staunch Unionist. And so the president chose the man who had humiliated him at the McCormick reaper trial in 1855. Stanton's appointment was one of the most magnanimous acts of a remarkably magnanimous president. When informed that he would be offered the War Department portfolio, Stanton said: "Tell the President I will accept if no other pledge than to throttle treason shall be exacted."[66]

Although he consulted many men before selecting Stanton, Lincoln had not spoken with McClellan. On the day after the appointment, he told the general in chief that he knew Stanton was a friend of McClellan's, that the general would probably be happy to have Stanton at the helm of the War Department, and that he had been afraid that if he informed Little Mac ahead of time, Radical Republicans would allege that the general had inveigled him into making that choice. In early January, Stanton said that "he regarded McClellan as the greatest military genius upon the continent."[67] That opinion would soon change.

News of Stanton's appointment exploded like an artillery round among the Republicans, including Senator William P. Fessenden, who reported that it "astounded every body."[68] When some protested against the selection of a prominent Democrat as secretary of war, Lincoln replied: "If I could find four more democrats just like Stanton, I would appoint them."[69] He said that he knew Stanton was "a true and loyal man, and that he possessed the greatest energy of character and systematic method in the discharge of public business."[70]

Stanton proved to be a remarkably capable war secretary who worked well with the president. Whereas the selection of his first secretary of war was one of Lincoln's greatest mistakes, the choice of a successor turned out to be one of his most inspired appointments. Shortly after Stanton assumed control of the War Department, Joshua Speed praised the way he transformed it: "Instead of that loose shackeling way of doing business in the war office, with which I have been so much disgusted & which I have had so good an opportunity of seeing—there is now order regularity and precision. . . . I shall be much mistaken if he does not infuse into the whole army an energy & activity which we have not seen heretofore."[71]

Unlike the president, Stanton had little trouble saying no. When Judge Joseph G. Baldwin asked for a pass to visit his brother in Virginia, Lincoln suggested that he see Stanton. The judge replied that he had done so and had been refused. With a smile Lincoln observed, "I can do nothing; for you must know that I have very little influence with this administration."[72] By performing the unpleasant but necessary duty of denying requests, Stanton helped the president seem accommodating. With Stanton's assistance, Lincoln began to assert himself more forcefully in dealings with his generals. The new secretary's first directive to McClellan was signed by order of "the President, Commander-in-Chief of the Army and Navy," a not very subtle message to the Young Napoleon.

Lincoln had been studying military literature and acquired a better understanding of overall strategy than most of his generals. He spelled it out in a letter to Buell on January 13, 1862: "I state my general idea of this war to be that we have the *greater* numbers, and the enemy has the *greater* facility of concentrating forces upon points of collision; that we must fail, unless we can find some way of making *our* advantage an over-match for *his*; and that this can only be done by menacing him with superior forces at *different* points, at the *same* time; so that we can safely attack, one, or both, if he makes no change; and if he *weakens* one to *strengthen* the other, forbear to attack the strengthened one, but seize, and hold the weakened one, gaining so much."[73]

Lincoln was right: the North's advantages in manpower and economic strength would produce victory only if its military forces applied pressure on all fronts simultaneously. Buell, Halleck, McClellan, and numerous others failed to grasp this elementary point. Eventually the president would find generals to implement that approach, but it would take time, lots of time.

25.

"This Damned Old House"

The Lincoln Family in the Executive Mansion

During the Civil War, the atmosphere in the White House was usually sober, for as John Hay recalled, it was a time "of a seriousness too intense to leave room for much mirth."[1] The death of Lincoln's favorite son and the misbehavior of the First Lady significantly intensified that mood.

Daily Routine

Lincoln usually rose early, for he slept lightly and fitfully. Before consuming his modest breakfast of an egg, toast, and coffee, he spent a couple of hours glancing at newspapers, writing letters, signing documents, or studying the subjects most pressing at the time. After eating, he would read telegrams at the dingy War Department building next to the White House. For Lincoln's convenience, the telegraph operators routinely kept copies there of all messages received at military headquarters, which he regularly read. Upon his return, he would inspect the mail. At around 10:00 visitors were admitted. Cabinet members had precedence, then senators, then congressmen, and finally the general public. On Tuesdays and Fridays, cabinet meetings were usually held, so visiting hours ended at noon.

When the public's turn to enter came, Lincoln had the doors opened, and in surged a crowd, filling his small office. Those who simply wished to shake his hand or to wish him well were quickly accommodated. Others seeking mercy or assistance told their tales of woe, unconcerned about who might overhear them. All kinds of people sought presidential assistance, including army officers longing for promotion, foreign diplomats concerned about their country's interests, autograph seekers, inventors touting their creations, cabinet members and congressmen soliciting favors for friends, women appealing on behalf of their sons or husbands or fathers, and businessmen in quest of contracts. Seated at his table, Lincoln greeted visitors kindly, saying to those he was not acquainted with, "Well?" and to those he did know, "And how are you to-day, Mr.——?" He usually called old friends by their first names. Patiently he listened to callers' requests, asked them a few questions, then informed them what he would do.

To Lincoln's annoyance, many callers insisted that he solve minor disputes and address private grievances, misfortunes, and wishes, leading him to remark that "it seemed as if he was regarded as a police justice, before whom all the petty troubles of men were brought for adjustment."[2] An enlisted man once pestered Lincoln with a matter that the president said should be handled by the soldier's superior officer. When his advice was ignored, Lincoln peremptorily barked: "Now, my man, go away! I cannot attend to all these details. I could as easily bail out the Potomac with a spoon."[3] Sometimes Lincoln resorted to gentle sarcasm. When a delegation once appealed to him to help the Washington fire department obtain new equipment, he interrupted their presentation: "It is a mistake to think that I am at the head of the fire department of Washington. I am simply the President of the United States."[4]

At lunchtime, Lincoln ran a gauntlet formed by would-be callers lining the hallway between his office and the family quarters. Late in the day he would usually take a carriage ride, often with the First Lady. Dinner was served at 6:00 p.m. He liked simple food, especially cornpone, cabbage, and chicken fricassee. After the evening meal, he would usually return to his office and continue working. Sometimes at dinner he enjoyed the company of friends, who joined him for coffee and a postprandial chat. He went to bed between ten and eleven, but if he was expecting important news, he would stay up as late as one or two in the morning, closeted with the telegraph operators at the War Department. Tad usually slept with him after the death of Willie.

On Sundays, Lincoln often attended services at the nearby New York Avenue Presbyterian Church, where the Reverend Dr. Phineas Gurley presided. Upon arriving in Washington, Lincoln had asked friends and allies to recommend a house of worship. "I wish to find a church," he had said, "whose clergyman holds himself aloof from politics."[5]

Receptions

Like their predecessors, the Lincolns hosted receptions, levees, open houses, and state dinners. William O. Stoddard recalled that Lincoln's "manner at receptions" was "that of a man who performs an irksome but unavoidable duty, though he was never lacking in cordial hospitality."[6] When asked if he found shaking so many hands tiresome, he replied: "Oh—it's hard work, but it is a relief, every way; *for here nobody asks me for what I cannot give*."[7] At a typical reception, as fancifully described by Noah Brooks, the marshal of the District of Columbia (Ward Hill Lamon) would announce the names of callers, for example, "Mr. Snifkins of California." Lincoln would greet him: "I am glad to see you, Mr. Snifkins—you come from a noble State—God bless her." Snifkins "murmurs his thanks, is as warmly pressed by the hand as though the President had just begun his day's work on the pump handle, and he is replaced by Mr. Biffkins, of New York, who is reminded by the Father of the Faithful that the Empire State has some noble men in the Army of the Union."[8]

The Lincolns' Children

During Lincoln's first year in office, the solemn atmosphere in the White House was somewhat relieved by his two sons, the studious and lovable Willie, born in 1850, and the irrepressible and equally lovable Tad, born in 1853. Their older brother, Robert, was attending Harvard and spent little time in Washington. The young boys, John Hay recorded, "kept the house in an uproar." Willie, "with all his boyish frolic," was nonetheless "a child of great promise, capable of close application and study." Tad, on the other hand, "was a merry, warm-blooded, kindly little boy, perfectly lawless, and full of odd fancies and inventions, the 'chartered libertine' of the Executive Mansion. He ran continually in and out of his father's cabinet, interrupting his gravest labors and conversations with his bright, rapid, and very imperfect speech—for he had an impediment which made his articulation almost unintelligible until he was nearly grown. He would perch upon his father's knee, and sometimes even on his shoulder, while the most weighty conferences were going on. Sometimes escaping from the domestic authorities, he would take refuge in that sanctuary for the whole evening, dropping to sleep at last on the floor, when the President would pick him up and carry him tenderly to bed."[9]

The children had ponies, which they loved to ride. In February 1864, a fire burned down the stables, killing those steeds. Upon observing the flames, Lincoln ran toward them, nimbly vaulted over a hedge, and asked the guards if the horses had been removed. When told they had not, he asked impatiently why and threw open the doors. Then he realized that none of the animals within could survive. Concerned for his safety, the guards hustled him back into the White House, where he wept, for Willie's pony was among the animals killed.

Among the White House menagerie on the large south lawn were donkeys, horses, and a pair of goats, Nanny and Nanko. Tad hitched the latter to a chair, which he used as a cart, and drove pell-mell through the White House during a reception, to the consternation of the guests. Lincoln was fond of the cats that Seward gave to the boys. In April 1862, a dinner guest observed one of the felines perched on a chair next to the president. As he fed it with Executive Mansion cutlery, the First Lady asked: "Don't you think it is shameful for Mr. Lincoln to feed tabby with a gold fork?" Her husband replied: "If the gold fork was good enough for Buchanan I think it is good enough for Tabby" and continued feeding the cat.[10]

This photograph of Willie Lincoln was taken in 1861, when the lad was 10 years old. After his death the following year, his mother wrote to a friend: "You have doubtless heard, how very handsome a boy, he was considered—with a pure, gentle nature, always unearthly, & in intellect far, far beyond his years." John Hay noted that Willie was "a child of great promise, capable of close application and study. He had a fancy for drawing up railway time-tables, and would conduct an imaginary train from Chicago to New York with perfect precision. He wrote childish verses, which sometimes attained the unmerited honors of print." Abraham Lincoln Presidential Library and Museum, Springfield, Illinois.

Willie and Tad were prankish. One day they commandeered the spring-bell system used to summon servants. Discovering in the attic the node where the cords to the various bells were gathered, they pulled all of them, sending servants scurrying madly from room to room. On another occasion Tad, dressed in a lieutenant's uniform (Stanton had appointed him to that rank), dismissed the regular guards and assigned the White House staff to protect the house. When his stuffy brother Robert observed this, he indignantly protested to Lincoln, who laughed it off and refused to take any disciplinary action.

The Lincoln boys had two playmates, the young sons of a Patent Office examiner, Horatio Nelson Taft. Eight-year-old "Holly" (Halsey Cook) and 11-year-old "Bud" (Horatio Nelson Jr.) frequently visited the White House, escorted by their 16-year-old sister, Julia. Lincoln told stories to the four boys, who especially relished tales of bloody conflict between Indians and frontiersmen. He also played on the floor with them. One day Julia Taft found Lincoln pinned down by the lads; when she entered the room, Tad instructed her to sit on the presidential stomach.

Tad once enraged John Watt, the White House gardener, by eating all the strawberries he was growing for a formal dinner party. Watt, who called the boy a "wildcat," doubtless was perturbed when Tad dug up the rose garden to make a grave for a Zouave doll named Jack who had fallen asleep on sentry duty and been executed by a firing squad armed with the lad's toy cannon. The boys performed this funeral several times until Watt suggested that the president might pardon Jack. Inspired by the suggestion, Tad appealed to his father for mercy. After a formal hearing, Lincoln granted the request.

The boys' fun came to an end with the death of Willie Lincoln in February 1862. Thereafter, his mother forbade the Tafts' sons to enter the White House, for their presence conjured up memories too painful for her to bear.

The First Lady

Mary Lincoln was a constant source of anxiety and embarrassment to her husband.[11] Among other things, she meddled in patronage matters, forcing Lincoln to do things that he knew were inappropriate in order "to keep quiet in his house" and keep his wife's "fingers out of his hair," as William Herndon put it.[12] According to journalist Murat Halstead, some of Lincoln's "most unfortunate appointments have been made to please his wife who is anxious to be thought the power behind the throne and who is vulgar and pestiferous beyond description." He added that the First Lady was "a fool—the laughing stock of the town, her vulgarity only the more conspicuous in consequence of her fine carriage and horses and servants in livery and fine dresses, and her damnable airs."[13] Indeed, she thought of herself as

Lincoln and his youngest son, Tad, examine a photograph album (not a Bible, as is sometimes alleged). This image, taken by Anthony Berger on February 9, 1864, was reproduced by the thousands and became a great popular favorite. Library of Congress.

a kind of assistant president and as such even tried to influence cabinet selections. She did not like Seward and let her feelings be known to visitors. When her spouse indicated to a caller that he would appoint the New Yorker secretary of state, she interrupted: "Never! Never! . . . Seward in the Cabinet! *Never*!"[14] As time passed, she grew ever more hostile to the secretary of state; she even instructed the White House coachman never to drive by Seward's nearby residence.

In 1861, Mary Lincoln championed William S. Wood, the impresario of the Lincolns' train journey from Springfield, for the post of commissioner of public buildings. On that trip, Wood's "attentions were devoted exclusively to the whims and caprices of Mrs. Lincoln."[15] She reportedly "became smitten with his handsome features, luxuriant whiskers and graceful carriage." Wood "saw how well he 'took' with my lady, and resolved to cultivate her favor as much as possible." On

This little-known vignette of Mary Todd Lincoln was evidently taken in 1861. Both William H. Mumler of Boston and the New York Photographic Company issued it as a *carte-de-visite.* Abraham Lincoln Presidential Library and Museum, Springfield, Illinois.

March 6, Wood presented the First Lady with a pair of fine horses, a gift from some anonymous New Yorkers, and she in turn lobbied furiously on behalf of Wood. But when he applied for the post of commissioner of public buildings, he was told that it had already been promised. At that point, the First Lady "stormed and scolded," demanding that Wood be appointed. The president resisted at first, "but there was such a tempest made about his ears" day after day that he eventually yielded, and Wood was nominated on May 31.[16]

Lincoln told friends that he thought it would be ruinous to appoint Wood. He did not explain why, but it was perhaps because of rumors that his wife was committing adultery with Wood. In June 1861, the president received a pseudonymous letter about a "scandal" involving Mary Lincoln and Wood, who went on shopping trips together to New York. The writer warned that if the gossip about that scandal were published, it would "stab you in the most vital part."[17] Lincoln finally agreed to appoint Wood only after the First Lady shut herself in her room. Wood did not last long as commissioner, however. After learning from a congressional delegation that he was corrupt, Lincoln obtained his resignation.

Mary Lincoln boasted that she significantly influenced the president's appointments, and her relatives fared well in the patronage lottery. Indeed, the largesse enjoyed by her family created bad blood in Illinois. Lincoln was clearly embarrassed by the extensive patronage given to the Todds. To one of his wife's importunate cousins, he asked: "Will it do for me to go on and justify the declaration that Trumbull and I have divided out all the offices among our relatives?"[18]

The First Lady's sartorial taste also scandalized polite society. She shocked many people at Edward D. Baker's funeral by appearing in a lilac outfit. Some members of her circle, thinking she should be made aware of that breach of etiquette, dispatched one of her closest friends to convey the message. That emissary was greeted by Mary Lincoln with an exclamation: "I am so glad you have come, I am just as mad as I can be. Mrs. Crittenden has just been here to remonstrate with me for wearing my lilac suit to Colonel Baker's funeral. I wonder if the women of Washington expect me to muffle myself up in mourning for every soldier killed in this great war?"

"But Mrs. Lincoln," came the reply, "do you not think black more suitable to wear at a funeral because there is a great war in the nation?"

"No, I don't. I want the women to mind their own business; I intend to wear what I please."[19]

In August 1861, a New York politico expressed disapproval of Mary Lincoln because at a time when "the country was in the throes of revolutionary travail she was coolly buying china and dresses in New York."[20] Journalist Laura Redden Searing thought Mrs. Lincoln found herself "in a situation for which her natural want of tact, and her deficiencies in the sense of the fitness of things, and her blundering outspokenness, and impolitic disregard of diplomatic considerations unfitted her."[21]

Mary Lincoln evidently sold state secrets to newspapermen. She also padded invoices, made false bills to defraud the government, used government funds for personal use, engaged in extortion, overspent her congressional budget for refurbishing the White House, and became entangled in a blackmail scheme. According to Alexander K. McClure, the First Lady "was the easy prey of adventurers, of which the war developed an unusual crop, and many times they gained such influence over her as to compromise her very seriously."[22]

Lincoln was exasperated by his wife's overspending on White House redecoration. When told of this, he exclaimed: "It never can have my approval—I'll pay for it out of my own pocket first—it would stink in the nostrils of the American people to have it said that the President of the United States had approved a bill overrunning an appropriation of $20,000 for *flub dubs* for this damned old house, when the poor freezing soldiers cannot have blankets!"[23] In February 1862, Congress passed a supplemental appropriation of $14,000 for White House "extras," over the objections of some leading Republican senators.

William H. Russell noted that Mary Lincoln "is accessible to the influence of flattery, and has permitted her society to be infested by men who would not be

This photo of Mary Todd Lincoln was probably taken at the Mathew Brady Studio in January 1862. She loved flowers and often plastered down her hair in order to wear a floral arrangement on her head. She did not like to pose for photographs because, as she put it, "my hands are always made in them, very large, and I look too stern." Library of Congress.

received in any respectable private house in New York."[24] The Cincinnati *Commercial* thought it "unfortunate that Mrs. Lincoln has so poor an understanding of the true dignity of her position, and the duties devolving upon her. It is not becoming her to be assuming the airs of a fine lady and attempting to shine as the bright star of 'the Republican court,' as shameless and designing flatterers call the White House circle." The editors disapproved of her "rich dresses and glittering equipage, her adornment of the President's House with costly upholstery," and her penchant for "crowding it with gay assemblages."[25] It is no wonder that Alexander K. McClure concluded that the First Lady "was a consuming sorrow to Mr. Lincoln." Yet, McClure recalled, the president "bore it all with unflagging patience. She was sufficiently unbalanced to make any error possible and many probable, but not sufficiently so as to dethrone her as mistress of the White House."[26] Lincoln almost never discussed his wife with anyone except his old friend Orrville H. Browning, who recalled that the president often talked to him "about his domestic troubles." As Browning reported, the president "several times told me there [in the White House] that he was constantly under great apprehension lest his wife should do something which would bring him into disgrace."[27]

And so she did.

26.

"I Expect to Maintain This Contest until Successful, or till I Die, or Am Conquered, or My Term Expires, or Congress or the Country Forsakes Me"

From the Slough of Despond to the Gates of Richmond (January–July 1862)

Stanton's ascension represented a key turning point in the war. As William O. Stoddard aptly noted, it ended "the first scene in the great tragedy," after which "changes were gradual, but the old order of things passed away." The Northern public was transformed "from a peaceful into a military people, to whom the army was all in all."[1]

In January 1862, Lincoln began to assert himself in dealing with generals as he had earlier done with cabinet members. He followed the sound advice of Edward Bates, who "insisted that, being 'Commander in chief' by law," Lincoln "*must* command—especially in such a war as this."[2] Lyman Trumbull noted that Lincoln "at last seems to be waking up to the fact " that "the responsibility is upon *him*."[3] As Lincoln took charge of his administration more forcefully, he won increased respect from Trumbull's colleagues in Congress. By the spring of 1862, the public too had come to share that feeling. "The confidence felt by all loyal men in the integrity and wisdom of President Lincoln forms one of the most marked and hopeful features of the existing political condition of our country," observed the Philadelphia *Press*. "Even those who do not approve all his acts accord to him perfect rectitude of purpose and fervent patriotism."[4]

Lincoln did not burn with a desire to wield power, but his keen sense of responsibility led him to perform his duties conscientiously, onerous though he found them to be. He told an Illinois friend, "This getting the nomination for President, and being elected, is all very pleasant to a man's ambition; but to be the President, and to meet the responsibilities and discharge the duties of the office in times like these is anything but pleasant. I would gladly if I could, take my neck from the yoke, and go home with you to Springfield, and live, as I used [to do], in peace with my friends, than to endure this harassing kind of life."[5]

In exercising his new-found assertiveness, Lincoln continued to face a daunting challenge in McClellan; persuading him to move proved as difficult as ever.

Among Little Mac's chief defects were the ones that he mistakenly ascribed to Robert E. Lee, who he alleged "is *too* cautious & weak under grave responsibility" and "wanting in moral firmness when pressed by heavy responsibility & is likely to be timid & irresolute in action."[6]

Lincoln seemed to William O. Stoddard like "a man who carried a load too great for human strength; and, as the years went on and the load grew heavier, it bowed him into premature old age. He was the American Atlas."[7] Signs of this aging process were obvious in the winter of 1861–62, when the president looked especially haggard and careworn. In mid-January, a dinner guest said that it "was evident that he was harassed by haunting cares; the obligation of politeness to his guests made him endeavor to be agreeable; he would tell a funny story to my mother who sat next to him, or make some amusing remark to his other neighbor, then when the attention of these ladies was called away, Mr. Lincoln's thoughts lapsed into their 'sea of troubles' and flew far away."[8] The president, wrote D. W. Bartlett on New Year's Day 1862, "is not so cheerful as he used to be, is a little more grave in his demeanor, and is somewhat worn."[9] This news caused alarm, for it was widely believed that Lincoln's face unerringly indicated the state of public affairs.

As his anxiety grew, Lincoln's temper shortened. To increasingly vehement criticism of McClellan's tardiness in attacking the Confederates, he responded that "there was probably but one man in the country more anxious for a battle than himself, and that man was McClellan." He "repudiated in words of withering rebuke those who make the charge that he or Mr. Seward or General McClellan were temporizing or delaying out of any consideration for rebels or rebel institutions, or that they indulged any thought of ending the war by any means other than by conquest on the battlefield."[10] He insisted that "McClellan is not a traitor; his difficulty is that he always prefers to-morrow to to-day. He never is ready to move. I think the immense importance of the interests at stake affects him thus. In this he is very much like myself. When I was practicing law at Springfield, I sometimes had a case involving a man's life or death, and I never could feel that I was ready to go on with the trial; I always wished to postpone it; and when the next court came round I felt a similar impression that I was not ready, whatever preparations I had made."[11]

Union army victories in early 1862 caused Lincoln to remark "that he felt more confidence now than ever in the power of the Government to suppress the rebellion."[12] On January 19, 1862, bluejackets under the exceptionally capable Virginian George H. Thomas won a battle at Mill Springs, Kentucky, killing 148 of the enemy, including General Felix K. Zollicoffer, while losing only 55 men. Three weeks later, cheering news arrived from North Carolina, where General Ambrose E. Burnside defeated the Confederates at Roanoke Island. At the same time, U. S. Grant, with the help of gunboats under the command of navy captain Andrew Hull Foote, took Fort Henry on the Tennessee River, a victory Lincoln deemed "of the utmost importance."[13] A few days later, when Grant amazingly captured a Rebel army at nearby Fort Donelson on the Cumberland River, Washingtonians became wildly excited. Grant's operation represented the first major Northern victory in the war; it opened the South to invasion along two rivers and led the Confederates to forsake their positions in Kentucky and much of Tennessee.

Lincoln rejoiced at the triumph of Grant and Foote. When the good news arrived and someone jubilantly suggested "Let's have a drink," the teetotaling president drolly responded: "All right bring in some water."[14] Informed that the victory had been achieved with the help of many Illinois troops, he remarked: "I cannot speak so confidently about the fighting qualities of the Eastern men, but this I do know—if the southerners think that man for man they are better than our Illinois men, or western men generally, they will discover themselves in a grievous mistake."[15]

Lincoln had been working behind the scenes to provide Grant and Foote with floating mortars, the brainchild of Gustavus Fox. While still in charge of the Department of the West, Frémont, to his credit, had ordered the construction of a mortar fleet at Cairo. It was to assist the army in a thrust led by Grant, who had won authorization to launch an offensive down the Tennessee. Special beds had to be manufactured to accommodate the gigantic thirteen-inch mortars. This was successfully accomplished for a flotilla being constructed in New Jersey at the behest of David Dixon Porter, who was planning to attack New Orleans, but Lincoln grew anxious as the work on a similar fleet in Cairo had evidently stalled. On January 10, the cabinet learned that nobody knew anything about those vessels. Lincoln became infuriated when he discovered that no mortars had been constructed for Foote's armada. He instructed navy lieutenant Henry A. Wise "to put it through." With fierce determination, he told Wise on January 23, "I am going to devote a part of every day to these mortars and I wont leave off until it fairly rains Bombs."[16] He wanted "to rain the Rebels out" and "treat them to a refreshing shower of sulphur and brimstone."[17]

Wise turned to the firm of Cooper and Hewitt, which with remarkable dispatch completed the mortar beds by mid-February and sent them westward in boxcars plainly labeled "U.S. GRANT, CAIRO. NOT TO BE SWITCHED UNDER PENALTY OF DEATH."[18] A similar feat was accomplished by a Cincinnati foundry. Lincoln supervised all these efforts closely. Despite his best endeavors, however, the mortar flotilla was not ready in time for Foote and Grant's campaign. Happy as he was with the news from Tennessee, Lincoln was "mad about mortars." He remarked that "he must take these army matters into his own hands. The Navy have built their ships and mortars for N[ew] O[rleans] and are ready to go."[19]

Lincoln Promotes Military Research and Development

Lincoln's attempt to expedite the creation of a mortar fleet was emblematic of his desire to provide the military with the latest, most lethal weapons. During the first two years of his administration he became, in effect, a one-man research and development branch of the War Department as well its main strategist. But the chief of army ordnance, General James W. Ripley (known as "Ripley Van Winkle"), proved obstinate and recalcitrant. Trying to get the unimaginative, cantankerous Ripley to adopt technological innovations was as difficult as it was to get McClellan or Buell to attack the enemy.

Lincoln concerned himself with a wide variety of weapons: small arms, artillery, flamethrowers, rockets, submarines, mines, ironclad ships, and explosives. Often he tested new-fangled rifles himself. An inventor with a patent of his own, he encouraged all sorts of innovations, most notably the breech-loading rifle and the machine gun. His interest in the latter began in June 1861, when he observed tests of "the Union Repeating Gun," modestly described by its salesman as "an army in six feet square." Lincoln dubbed it the "coffee-mill gun" because its hopper, into which bullets were poured, resembled that culinary apparatus. Impressed by what he saw, Lincoln ordered all ten guns then available; later he ordered forty more, which were used sparingly. More significantly, Lincoln championed the introduction of breech-loading rifles, which allowed a soldier to avoid the cumbersome, time-consuming, and dangerous procedures necessary to reload single-shot muzzleloaders. Had breechloaders been widely adopted by the North early in the war, that conflict might have been significantly shortened.

Getting McClellan to Move

Lincoln agreed with Stanton's insistence that "while men are striving nobly in the West, the champagne & oysters on the Potomac must be stopped."[20] The new secretary of war said that if Little Mac did not move soon, he (Stanton) "should move *him*."[21] The president had waited patiently—and in vain—for McClellan's plan of operations, and like the electorate, he was growing restless. To smoke the general out, Lincoln on January 27 issued President's General War Order No. 1, commanding all land and naval forces to begin a "general movement" against the enemy on George Washington's birthday, February 22.[22] As Hay observed, this marked a turning point: "He wrote it without any consultation and read it to the Cabinet, not for their sanction but for their information. From that time he influenced actively the operations of the Campaign. He stopped going to McClellan's and sent for the general to come to him. Every thing grew busy and animated after this order."[23] When it was made public in March, the Cincinnati *Gazette* called the order "the stroke that cut the cords which kept our great armies tied up in a state of inactivity."[24] On January 31, Lincoln followed up with President's Special War Order No. 1, directing the Army of the Potomac to attack Confederate supply lines at Manassas. The New York *Tribune* predicted that Lincoln, as de facto commander in chief of the army, along with the "prodigiously energetic" Stanton, "will now lift this war out of mud and delay, and carry it to victory."[25]

Goaded into action by these presidential war orders, Little Mac hastened to the Executive Mansion to register objections and ask permission to submit in writing an alternative plan. Lincoln may well have exclaimed to himself, "At last!" The general wrote a twenty-two-page document proposing an attack on Richmond from the lower Chesapeake. He would move the Army of the Potomac by water to the hamlet of Urbanna, on the Rappahannock River, then drive toward the Confederate capital, forty miles to the west, before Johnston's force at Manassas could shift to protect it. McClellan argued that while it was "by no means certain" that victory could be achieved following the Manassas plan, an attack via Urbanna would provide "the most brilliant result" (as "certain by all the chances of war") partly because the roads in the lower Chesapeake region "are passable at all seasons of the year."[26] (To his dismay, he was to learn that was untrue. How he reached such an erroneous conclusion is hard to understand.)

The president offered to defer to the general if Little Mac could satisfactorily answer five questions: "1st. Does not your plan involve a greatly larger expenditure of *time*, and *money* than mine? 2nd. Wherein is a victory *more certain* by your plan than mine? 3rd. Wherein is a victory *more valuable* by your plan than mine? 4th. In fact, would it not be *less* valuable, in this, that it would break no great line of the enemie's communications, while mine would? 5th. In case of disaster, would not a safe retreat be more difficult by your plan than by mine?"[27] Inexplicably, McClellan did not deign to respond. Now Lincoln faced a dilemma: he must acquiesce in the Urbanna strategy or order McClellan to carry out the Manassas plan. A further alternative was to replace the Young Napoleon. But with whom? There was no obvious alternative. Lincoln confided to Charles Sumner that Little Mac's scheme "was very much against his judgment, but that he did not feel disposed to take the responsibility of overruling him."[28]

So the president reluctantly consented to the Young Napoleon's plan, but only with the understanding that enough troops would be left behind to defend Washington in case the Confederates attacked it while the Army of the Potomac was eighty miles away. McClellan promised to leave a sufficient force to protect the capital, the number to be determined by all twelve division commanders. They recommended a force of forty to fifty thousand, which seemed reasonable since McClellan insisted that the enemy at Manassas and Centerville numbered over a hundred thousand. Unfortunately, Lincoln and McClellan did not agree on a specific number, nor did they identify which troops would be assigned to protect Washington.

Meanwhile, critics demanded that the Young Napoleon break the Confederate hold on the upper and lower Potomac. The blockade of that river below Washington cut the capital off from all seafaring traffic save warships; control of the river above the city obstructed a main rail line between the Atlantic seaboard and the Ohio Valley (the Baltimore and Ohio). An exasperated Lincoln impatiently asked Gideon Welles if the enemy batteries along the river could not be destroyed. The navy secretary said that it could be easily done by ten thousand troops but that McClellan would never agree to it. Little Mac wishfully assumed that the lower Potomac would be opened when his Urbanna offensive got under way.

As for the upper Potomac, McClellan took action to keep Confederates from disrupting the Baltimore and Ohio rail line. In late February, he ordered troops under General Nathaniel P. Banks to move toward Winchester, Virginia. To facilitate that offensive, a light pontoon bridge was thrown across the Potomac at Harpers Ferry; it was to be supplanted by a permanent bridge of heavy timbers resting upon canal boats anchored in the river. On February 27, when those boats tried to enter a lift lock in order to move from the Chesapeake and Ohio Canal to the Potomac, they proved six inches too wide. The entire operation had to be called off, prompting Chase to quip that the Winchester expedition had died of lockjaw. Upon learning this, Lincoln banged his fist on a table and exclaimed: "Why in hell didn't he measure first!" This was the only time Nicolay heard his boss swear, and William O. Stoddard said he "never knew Mr. Lincoln so really angry, so out of all patience."[29]

The public was beginning to regard the Army of the Potomac, whose delays and blunders contrasted sharply with the success of Grant's army in the West, as "a gigantic joke."[30] Lincoln seemed ready to fire Little Mac. On March 3, when a Pennsylvania congressman complained that he and his colleagues felt "humiliated at the long siege of the Capital, and the blockade of the Potomac," Lincoln replied that "if Gen. Washington, or Napoleon, or Gen Jackson were in command on the Potomac they would be obliged to move or resign the position." Emphatically he added that "the army will move, either under General McClellan or some other man and that very soon."[31]

Death of Willie Lincoln

Lincoln's despair at the canal boat fiasco was doubtless intensified by the crushing blow he had sustained a week earlier when his beloved 11-year-old son Willie died. In early February, the boy contracted a fever that laid him low. At the same time, Tad grew sick. For days the president was so attentive to the boys, spending night after night at their bedsides, that he hardly tended to public business. On February 18, Edward Bates noted that Lincoln was "nearly worn out, with grief and watching."[32] White House receptions were canceled.

As time passed, Willie became so weak that he resembled a shadow. The disease finally took him on February 20. When he died, his father chokingly told his principal White House secretary, "Well, Nicolay, my boy is gone—he is actually gone!" and burst into tears.[33] That day a journalist reported that "it would move the heart of his bitterest political enemy . . . to witness the marked change which grief has wrought upon him."[34] The next morning he appeared "completely prostrated with grief" when speaking with Elihu B. Washburne, who told his wife that Lincoln "is one of the most tender-hearted of men and devotedly attached to his children."[35] For the next two days he remained sunk in grief and took little interest in public affairs.

On February 23, Lincoln started to recover. The following day the Reverend Dr. Phineas D. Gurley conducted a funeral at the White House. There, as the president stood with tear-filled eyes gazing at his boy's corpse, a look of the utmost grief came over his face, and he exclaimed that Willie "was too good for this earth . . . but then we loved him so. It is hard, hard to have him die!"[36] Repeatedly he said, "This is the hardest trial of my life. Why is it? Oh, why is it?"[37] His body shook convulsively as he sobbed and buried his face in his hands. By the end of February, Lincoln had recovered enough to attend to his duties. Willie died on a Thursday, and for several weeks afterward Lincoln would take time out from work on Thursdays to mourn.

Willie's younger brother, Tad, had also contracted a fever and seemed near death. Dorothea Dix, who called at the White House to express her condolences, detailed a nurse, Rebecca Pomroy, to help tend the sick youngster and his distraught mother. Mrs. Pomroy, who had lost all her family except for one son then serving in the army, tried to console the president by assuring him that thousands of Northerners prayed for Tad every day. "I am glad of that," he replied, then hid his face in his hands and wept. On February 24, just before returning to his office, he looked at his youngest son and told Mrs. Pomroy: "I hope you will pray for him, that he may be spared, if it is God's will; and also for me, for I need the prayers of many."[38] The pious nurse explained how her faith in God had sustained her through the loss of her husband and two children. Lincoln, who called Mrs. Pomroy "one of the best women I ever knew," arranged to have her son promoted to lieutenant.[39] Her faith may well have strengthened Lincoln's own. Mrs. Lincoln said that her husband reflected more intently on the ways of God after Willie's death.

A month after the boy's funeral, William O. Stoddard reported that Lincoln had "recovered much of his old equanimity and cheerfulness; and certainly no one who saw his constant and eager application to his arduous duties, would imagine for a moment that the man carried so large a load of private grief, in addition to the cares of a nation."[40] But it was known by some, including Le Grand Cannon, who in May observed Lincoln weep convulsively after reciting from Shakespeare's *King John* the lament of Constance for her dead son. He had dreamed of Willie and wanted to believe that he had actually communed with him, though he understood that he had not really done so.

Like her husband, Mary Lincoln was wracked with grief. To Elihu Washburne she lamented that the White House seemed "like a tomb and that she could not bear to be in it." Willie, she said, "was the favorite child, so good, so obedient, so promising."[41] She wrapped herself profoundly in mourning, prompting Lincoln one day to lead her to a window, point to an insane asylum in the distance, and say: "Mother, do you see that large white building on the hill yonder? Try and control your grief, or it will drive you mad, and we may have to send you there."[42] For consolation, Mary Lincoln consulted spiritualists, who allegedly enabled her to communicate with her dead sons. On several occasions she participated in séances at the White House.

The death of Willie deprived Lincoln of an important source of comfort and relief from his official burdens. Springfield neighbors said he "was fonder of that boy than he was of anything else."[43] His sons Robert and Tad did not resemble Lincoln physically or temperamentally. The president's eldest son, with whom he shared little in common, was attending college in Massachusetts. His youngest son, the hyperactive, learning-disabled, effervescent Tad, was not a clone like Willie; he had inherited his mother's ungovernable temper and intense aversions.

In the wake of Willie's death, the president's love for Tad grew stronger as he displaced onto him the powerful feeling he had harbored for the older boy. He explained to a friend that he wished to give Tad "everything he could no longer give Willie." Lincoln derived great comfort from Tad's fun-loving, irrepressible nature and delighted in his common sense. Although Tad suffered from learning disabilities, his indulgent father was unconcerned and often said, "Let him run; he has time enough left to learn his letters and get poky." Occasionally Lincoln tried to tame the lad, but he was forced to acknowledge that the effort was futile. Late one night, when White House servants complained that they could not get the boy into bed, the president told his guests, "I must go and suppress Tad." On his return, he said: "I don't know but I may succeed in governing the nation, but I do believe I shall fail in ruling my own household." A White House guard thought that Tad was "the best companion Mr. Lincoln ever had—one who always understood him, and whom he always understood."[44] Thus Tad became, to some degree, another Willie for his grief-stricken father.

McClellan Finally Moves

On March 8, Lincoln called McClellan to the White House and evidently spoke plainly to him. The general declared that he would submit his Chesapeake plan to a vote of his division commanders. Eight of those twelve generals favored McClellan's Urbanna plan, and seven also supported his proposal to ignore the blockade of the lower Potomac. Only two recommended an immediate attack on the enemy batteries commanding the river, prompting Stanton to remark that "we saw ten generals afraid to fight." Lincoln was less critical, saying to them: "I don't care, gentlemen, what plan you have, all I ask is for you to just pitch in!"[45]

The same day, Lincoln issued General War Order No. 2, stipulating that the Army of the Potomac's dozen divisions be organized into four army corps, to be commanded by three of the dissenting generals plus Erasmus Keyes, who had supported the Urbanna plan only if the enemy were first cleared from the banks of the Potomac. (For three months Lincoln had been urged to undertake such a reorganization, for it was feared that the army's cumbersome structure made its defeat inevitable.) The following morning, the president reconvened the war council to announce his approval of the Urbanna scheme and urge all the generals to support it. Lincoln issued a third general war order, stating that the move to Urbanna must begin by March 18, that sufficient troops must be left behind to protect Washington, and that the blockade of the lower Potomac must be lifted. Finally, plans for the long-delayed advance seemed in place. McClellan would sail his army down the Chesapeake, move swiftly overland to Richmond, and capture the city before Johnston could hasten to its rescue.

On March 11, Lincoln issued yet another war order, this time removing the Young Napoleon from his post as general in chief of all armies. At a cabinet meeting that day, McClellan became the target of sharp criticism. In his diary, Bates wrote that "I think Stanton believes, as I do, that McC. has no plans but is fumbling and plunging in confusion and darkness."[46] The president said "that though the duty of relieving Gen McC. was a most painful one, he yet thought he was doing Gen McC. a very great kindness in permitting him to retain command of the Army of the Potomac, and giving him an opportunity to retrieve his errors."[47] Once McClellan had left for the Chesapeake, Lincoln told a journalist "that though he had relieved him from the general command, in part because he was not satisfied with his course, he had confidence that now he had taken the field at the head of his especial division of the army, he would push forward the campaign as rapidly as possible, and prove worthy of the position."[48] In that same War Order, Lincoln created a new military district in eastern Tennessee and western Virginia, the Mountain Department, and placed Frémont in charge. Yet another presidential war order stipulated that enough troops must be left behind to render Washington secure in the judgment of both McClellan and his division commanders; that the advance must begin no later than March 18; and that no more than two of the four corps could depart before the enemy batteries along the Potomac were eliminated.

Commenting on the president's war orders, the New York *Herald* said: "Lincoln holds the reins, and is handling them . . . with the skill and discretion of an old campaigner."[49] McClellan, however, resented them, even though some accorded with his own views. He had, for instance, planned to organize the divisions into corps after a major battle revealed his generals' strengths and weaknesses; he had agreed to leave sufficient troops behind to protect the capital; and the March 18 deadline fell within the time frame he had established in his own mind. He did not like the choice of corps commanders, but they were the most senior generals, and army tradition dictated that seniority must be taken seriously.

Suddenly word arrived that the Confederates had abandoned their entrenchments at both Manassas and Centerville and were heading south toward the Rappahannock. (General Johnston feared an attack like the one recommended by Lincoln, which his inferior numbers could not withstand.) The incredulous McClellan, for unknown reasons, sent 112,000 troops arrayed for battle toward Centerville and Manassas, where he discovered that the artillery that had so intimidated him was the same sort that he had earlier feared on Munson's Hill: Quaker cannon (logs painted black). The news saddened and angered Lincoln, who had hoped the Army of the Potomac would win a smashing victory at Manassas. It was not an unreasonable expectation, for if McClellan had moved against Johnston on February 22, as Lincoln had ordered him to do, he might well have whipped the Confederates badly.

Once again the general stood embarrassed before the disgusted people of the North. The Washington bureau chief of the New York *Tribune* asked rhetorically, "How long can the country afford to worship this do-nothing, this moral coward?"[50] The spectacle of "an army of 200,000 allowing an enemy encamped within 27 miles, to go quietly away" struck Adam Gurowski as "something like treason."[51] In executive session on March 14, the Senate considered a resolution calling for McClellan's removal. Three days later a congressional delegation visited the White House to urge that a new commander be named for the Army of the Potomac. Senator Fessenden bemoaned Lincoln's reluctance to dismiss McClellan: "Every movement has been a failure. And yet the President will keep him in command, and leave our destiny in his hands. I am, at times, almost in despair. Well, it cannot be helped. We went in for a rail-splitter, and we have got one."[52] The New York *Herald* denounced Little Mac as a "Quaker general."[53] The president wanted to replace McClellan with a senior officer, Ethan Allen Hitchcock, whom Winfield

Scott recommended highly. On March 15, Stanton amazed that 63-year-old general by offering him command of the Army of the Potomac. According to Hitchcock, the war secretary "spoke of the pressure on the President against McClellan, saying that the President and himself had had the greatest difficulty in standing against it." Hitchcock declined on the grounds of poor health.[54]

With the Confederates under Johnston heading for the Rappahannock, McClellan had to alter his plans, for the Army of the Potomac could not be safely landed at Urbanna. His fallback strategy was to use Fort Monroe, at the tip of the Virginia Peninsula (bounded by Hampton Roads, Chesapeake Bay, and the James and York Rivers).

The Epochal Battle of the *Monitor* and the *Merrimack*

On March 8, the Confederate ironclad ram *Virginia*, better known as the *Merrimack*, further upset McClellan's plans by destroying two Union frigates in Hampton Roads and driving others aground. When word of this naval disaster reached Washington, panic quickly spread. Would that powerful warship sail up the Potomac and destroy the capital and sink McClellan's transports, thus wrecking the planned offensive? On the morning of March 9, Lincoln sent for Gideon Welles, who joined other alarmed cabinet members at the White House. Lincoln, according to the navy secretary, "was so deeply interested and excited, that he could not deliberate or be satisfied with the opinions of non-professional men." So, accompanied by Orville H. Browning, the president left the White House to fetch John A. Dahlgren, commander of the Washington Navy Yard. Lincoln told Dahlgren that he had "frightful news." As they rode back to the White House, the president indicated that he "did not know whether we might not have a visit [from the *Merrimack*] here." Dahlgren "could give but little comfort," saying only that "such a thing might be *prevented*, but not met. If the 'Merrimac' entered the river it must be blocked; that was about all which could be done at present." He explained that since the Confederate ironclad drew less than twenty-two feet of water, it could attack Washington or even "go to New York, lie off the City, and levy contributions at will." In his diary, Dahlgren noted that "the President was not at all stunned by the news, but was in his usual suggestive mood."[55]

Back at the White House, Dahlgren's inability to recommend a means to stop the *Merrimack* intensified the cabinet's anxiety. Stanton was nearly frantic, predicting that the Confederates would destroy the blockading fleet, capture Fort Monroe, and arrive by nightfall in Washington, where it would demolish the Capitol and other public buildings, or perhaps it would sail further north and level New York and Boston or exact tribute from those cities. The secretary of war scurried frantically from room to room, then sat down only to leap up after scribbling a bit, then swing his arms about while raving and scolding. He wired instructions to New York that an ironclad counterpart to the *Merrimack* be constructed immediately. Welles calmly informed him that the previous night a new Union ironclad, the *Monitor*, had reached Hampton Roads and would challenge the Confederate vessel that very day. Lincoln had endorsed the construction of ironclad ships months earlier, when it seemed as if the Confederates would build one. Responding to plans for the unusual craft, he remarked: "All I have to say is what the girl said, when she put her foot into the stocking, 'It strikes me there's something in it.'"[56]

When Stanton learned that the *Monitor* mounted only two guns, he expressed incredulity and contempt, which intensified the anxiety of Lincoln and the others. Again and again the president and the secretary of war strode to the window to peer down the river to see whether the *Merrimack* was steaming their way. Lincoln was relieved when Welles, contradicting Dahlgren, assured him that the heavily armored Confederate ship drew so much water that she could only be effective in Hampton Roads and the Chesapeake. The historic battle at Hampton Roads resulted in a draw, with the *Merrimack* forced to retreat to its base. There it remained, held in check by the doughty *Monitor*. On March 10, Lieutenant Henry A. Wise described the epic battle to the cabinet, emphasizing the bravery of the *Monitor*'s captain, John L. Worden. When he concluded, Lincoln arose and said: "Well, gentlemen, I am going to shake hands with that man," and he proceeded to Wise's house, where Worden lay abed, his scorched eyes covered with bandages.

As he shook Lincoln's hand, Worden remarked: "You do me great honor, Mr. President, and I am only sorry that I can't see you."

Lincoln burst into tears and replied: "No, sir, you have done me and your country honor and I shall promote you. We owe to you, sir, the preservation of our navy. I can not thank you enough." He then "expressed the warmest sympathy with his suffering, and admiration of his bravery and skill."[57]

The Peninsula Campaign

With the *Merrimack* thus neutralized, the Army of the Potomac began sailing for the Peninsula on March 17. Lincoln was not optimistic about its prospects. On April 2, he told Orville Browning that he had studied McClellan "and taken his measure as well as he could—that he thought he had the capacity to make arrangements properly for a great conflict, but as the hour for action approached he became nervous and oppressed with the responsibility and hesitated to meet the crisis, but that he had given him peremptory orders to move now, and he must do it."[58]

On April 4, after the first 58,000 Union troops had reached their destination (Fort Monroe), Little Mac began his march toward Richmond, seventy-five miles distant. He abruptly halted upon encountering a weakly held Confederate line stretching across the Peninsula from Yorktown to the James River. The flamboyant Confederate commander John Magruder skillfully deployed his 17,000 troops, marching and countermarching them in a successful attempt to fool McClellan into thinking his force was much larger than it actually was. In fact, the Army of the Potomac could easily have swept it aside, but the hypercautious McClellan decided to besiege Yorktown, devoting a month to preparing for a massive bombardment.

In reply to Little Mac's pleas for more men, Lincoln wired him on April 6: "You now have over one hundred thousand troops, with you. . . . I think you better break the enemies' line from York-town to Warwick River, at once. They will probably use *time*, as advantageously as you can."[59] Three days later, disturbed by McClellan's lack of self-confidence and losing patience with his sluggish progress, Lincoln again bluntly implored him to move: "Your despatches complaining that you are not properly sustained, while they do not offend me, do pain me very much. . . . I think it is the precise time for you to strike a blow. By delay the enemy will relatively gain upon you—that is, he will gain faster, by *fortifications* and *re-inforcements*, than you can by re-inforcements alone. And, once more let me tell you, it is indispensable to *you* that you strike a blow. *I* am powerless to help this. . . . *But you must act*."[60] On May 1, the president similarly responded to McClellan's request for more artillery: "Your call for Parrott guns from Washington alarms me—chiefly because it argues indefinite procrastination. Is anything to be done?"[61]

Lincoln was understandably puzzled at McClellan's audit of his troops. The general counted only the enlisted men present for duty, whereas the president counted all those being fed and equipped by the War Department, which in addition to the ones on McClellan's list included officers, men on sick call, denizens of the guardhouse, and noncombatants. Disingenuously, Little Mac used the latter method to calculate the size of the enemy forces. In exasperation, the commander in chief declared that getting troops to McClellan was like trying to gather fleas in a barn: "the more you shovel them up in the corner the more they get away from you."[62] But he wanted to give Little Mac no cause for complaint, so over the objections of Stanton and Generals Ethan Allen Hitchcock, Montgomery C. Meigs, James W. Ripley, and Lorenzo Thomas, Lincoln shipped McClellan two brigades of engineers plus William B. Franklin's division from McDowell's corps, even though he acknowledged "that the force was not needed by General McClellan," who deeply resented presidential prodding.[63] He said that he felt like telling his commander in chief that if he wished the Confederate line broken, "he had better come & do it himself."[64]

While the Young Napoleon wasted time preparing to besiege Yorktown, Joseph E. Johnston reinforced Magruder. McClellan had squandered a glittering opportunity to advance swiftly to the gates of Richmond. Upon seeing the weakness of Magruder's forces, Johnston remarked: "No one but McClellan could have hesitated to attack."[65] Lincoln said "there was no reason why he should have been detained a single day at Yorktown, but he waited and gave the enemy time to gather his forces and strengthen his position."[66] One excuse McClellan gave for his timidity was the president's decision to withhold Irvin McDowell's corps, which had originally been slated to sail to the Peninsula. Lincoln changed that plan at the last minute when he discovered that Little Mac, in violation of orders, had not left enough men behind to guarantee the safety of Washington.

Meanwhile, in the western theater the combined forces of Grant and Buell fought an exceptionally bloody battle against Confederates under the gifted commander Albert Sidney Johnston, who was killed in the fighting near Shiloh, Tennessee. Johnston had at first seemed victorious, catching Grant off guard, but on the battle's second day Buell's reinforcements allowed the Federals to drive the enemy from the field. The victory paved the way for the capture of Memphis in June.

Impatient with McClellan's delays, Lincoln felt impelled to visit the army and actually helped direct the capture of Norfolk and the destruction of the *Merrimack*. On May 3, just as McClellan was finally ready to begin shelling Yorktown, the 56,000-man Confederate army there, under Joseph E. Johnston, pulled back toward Richmond. Little Mac, surprised by that retreat, had made no plans to pursue. On May 5, when some elements of the Army of the Potomac engaged the rearguard of the enemy at Williamsburg, they suffered serious losses.

Lincoln Campaigns against Norfolk

That same day, eager to infuse some energy into McClellan and to persuade the army and navy to cooperate more effectively, Lincoln sailed for the front, accompanied by Stanton, Chase, General Egbert Viele, and several others. Upon their arrival, McClellan announced that he was too busy to see the president, thus unwisely passing up an opportunity to repair his frayed relationship with the commander in chief. Lincoln then decided to take charge of an effort to capture Norfolk. He consulted with John E. Wool, the general in charge at Fort Monroe, and with the chief naval commander in the area, Louis M. Goldsborough. He asked Wool: "Why don't you take Norfolk?" and speculated that "it may be easier taken than the Merrimac; and, once [Norfolk is] in our possession, the Merrimac, too, is captured, not, perhaps, actually, but virtually she is ours." "Pooh," replied the general, "you don't understand military necessity."[67] Soon thereafter, Lincoln learned that Norfolk was nearly deserted, and he resolved to spur the military to capture it. He ordered Goldsborough to attack Rebel forts commanding the James, which were promptly knocked out of commission.

With those threats removed, the next question was where to land Wool's troops. On May 9, Lincoln, along with Wool, Stanton, and Chase, scouted the waters of Hampton Roads. When their ship, the revenue cutter *Miami*, came under enemy fire, Lincoln was told that he should seek safety in another part of the vessel. He replied: "Although I have no feeling of danger myself, perhaps for the benefit of our country, it would be well to step aside."[68] Eventually they selected a spot at Willoughby's Point, eight miles from Norfolk. Union sailors dubbed it "Lincoln's Choice." The president was rowed to shore and inspected the terrain. Upon his return to Fort Monroe, the troops who were to seize the town cheered him enthusiastically. It was determined to launch an assault immediately.

That night, Union troops were dispatched, and Norfolk soon surrendered, though delays allowed the Confederates to destroy shipping and burn the navy yard at Portsmouth. Fearing that the *Merrimack* might be captured, the Rebels set it afire and watched it explode spectacularly. Lincoln ranked the destruction of the *Merrimack* and the occupation of Norfolk "among the most important successes of the present war."[69] On May 11, as he sailed back to Washington, he believed that the Union cause was making as much progress as could reasonably be expected. He took pride in his own handiwork, explaining: "I knew that Saturday night that the next morning the Merrimac would either be in the James river or at the bottom."[70] Others shared Lincoln's estimate of his role. En route back to Washington, Chase wrote his daughter: "So has ended a brilliant week's campaign of the President; for I think it quite certain that, if he had not come down, Norfolk would still have been in possession of the enemy, and the 'Merrimac' as grim and defiant and as much a terror as ever."[71]

Lincoln's trip to the front revitalized him. He was cheered not only by the success of the Norfolk campaign but also by several other recent Union triumphs, including the capture of New Orleans in late April. He also rejoiced at the surrender of Fort Pulaski, outside Savannah, Georgia, and at John Pope's capture of both Island No. 10 in the Mississippi and the town of New Madrid, Missouri. In late April, a journalist reported that Lincoln "is looking better than he did the day of his inauguration. He has gained steadily in health, strength, and even in weight."[72]

The Valley Campaign

In mid-May, McClellan clamored once again for reinforcements, alleging that he had only eighty thousand effective troops and the enemy had double that number (a characteristically gross overestimate of Confederate forces). Earlier, when Lincoln offered to send McDowell's corps to him from Fredericksburg with the understanding that McDowell would remain in charge of those troops, Little Mac had refused to accept them on those terms. Now he backed down and expressed willingness to take reinforcements under any arrangement, though he wanted them shipped via water. Lincoln agreed to send McDowell to McClellan, but overland in order to screen Washington. On May 22–23, Lincoln again visited the troops, this time McDowell's corps at Fredericksburg. Now that it had been decided to forward those forces to McClellan, the president wanted to expedite that transfer. He reviewed them and consulted their commander, who declared he could be ready to march south on Sunday, May 25. But Lincoln suggested that he "take a *good ready*" that Sabbath and start out on Monday.[73]

When the president returned to Washington, he became quite agitated upon being informed that on the previous day, May 23, Stonewall Jackson had captured Colonel John R. Kenly, cut his regiment at Front Royal to pieces, routed Nathaniel P. Banks's other forces, and begun driving them down the Shenandoah Valley toward the Potomac. The Confederates captured so much material that General Jeb Stuart deemed Banks the best supply officer in Jackson's corps. Word that Banks had managed to escape across the Potomac greatly relieved Lincoln, who then spent long hours at the War Department firing off telegrams in an attempt to bag Jackson. Instead of marching south from the Rappahannock with all his men to join McClellan, McDowell was ordered to send twenty thousand troops west to block Jackson's line of retreat. McDowell assigned James Shields's division to carry out that order. The president directed Frémont's seventeen thousand men to move thirty miles east from Franklin to Harrisonburg, on the Valley Turnpike, Jackson's escape route. "Do not lose a minute," Lincoln urged the Pathfinder.[74] He told McClellan to support the portion of McDowell's corps that was to keep marching south. In addition, the battered remnants of Banks's army were to regroup and pursue Jackson from the north, a directive they were slow to obey. To prevent the Confederates from entering Maryland, the president ordered a force from Baltimore to occupy Harpers Ferry. With significant help from Stanton, Lincoln was now acting as general in chief as well as commander in chief. To assist those two civilians, General Hitchcock reluctantly agreed to come out of retirement. Between them, Frémont and McDowell just might be able to cut off Jackson's retreat. Lincoln knew that the Confederates intended "by constant alarms to keep three or four times as many of our troops away from Richmond as his own force amounts to."[75] Even so, he decided to take a gamble: if McDowell, Frémont, and Banks moved quickly and cooperated with one another, their forty thousand combined troops could cut off Jackson's seventeen thousand. There was a reasonable chance that the plan would work.

For the next month, Lincoln continued to supervise Union forces in the Valley. On May 28, he spurred McDowell on, telling him that "it is, for you a question of legs. Put in all the speed you can."[76] As McDowell and Frémont converged on Strasburg, it looked as if they might close the pincers on Jackson. But that wily Confederate slithered between them and escaped up the Valley, burning bridges behind him to slow the pursuers. On June 8, he wheeled about and bloodied Frémont in a rearguard action at Cross Keys. The following day he did the same thing to Shields at Port Republic. Soon thereafter he left the Valley and returned to Lee unmolested, for Lincoln directed Frémont to stay at Harrisonburg, sent Banks to protect Front Royal, and had Shields return to Fredericksburg. The administration was so anxious about any future attacks by Stonewall Jackson's men that two of McDowell's divisions were left in or near the Valley. Thus Jackson had succeeded in keeping some of McDowell's force from linking up with McClellan. It was a masterful campaign.

As the Confederates evaded the trap Lincoln had set, the president lamented the failure to bag them. He reportedly "felt certain that Jackson should have been captured" and could not "comprehend the excuses made by the generals who should have taken him."[77] Critics chastised Lincoln for his decision to send part of McDowell's corps to the Valley rather than to McClellan, but his thinking seems sound. Jackson might have been bagged if the amateur Union generals had been more capable.

Climax of the Peninsula Campaign

Meanwhile, on May 31 and June 1 Little Mac had fought Joseph E. Johnston in a bloody, indecisive battle at Fair Oaks, five miles from the Confederate capital. During that action, the Rebel commander was wounded and replaced by Robert E. Lee. McClellan, horrified by the severe losses his army sustained, grew increasingly reluctant to assault the enemy directly. Lincoln viewed the fighting "as the last desperate effort of the rebels in which they had thrown their whole strength. Their defeat he regarded as final."[78] It was not. As time passed, Lincoln grew impatient to know why the Army of the Potomac remained idle after the battle of Fair Oaks. On June 5, Nicolay reported from the White House that "McClellan's extreme caution, or tardiness, or something, is utterly exhaustive of all hope and patience, and leaves one in that feverish apprehension that as something *may* go wrong, something most likely *will* go wrong."[79] Anxious about the fate of the army, Lincoln on June 23 slipped out of Washington to consult with Winfield Scott at West Point. The only formal record of their five-hour conversation that survives is a memo by the general approving Lincoln's decision to send McDowell's corps to McClellan. The retired general also assured the president that the forces of Frémont and Banks were properly deployed. In all likelihood, the president and

Scott discussed a plan to unite the corps of Frémont, Banks, and McDowell under one commander.

That new commander was to be John Pope, who was summoned from the West. On June 26, the general met with Lincoln, who persuaded him to accept the newly created Army of Virginia, comprising the forty-five thousand troops of the three corps in the Shenandoah Valley. Pope's selection was dictated more by politics than by considerations of military merit. Chase and Stanton pressed Lincoln to name him, for they were tired of McClellan's everlasting delays and suspicious of his political conservatism. They wanted a fighting general to replace the Young Napoleon, and Pope had proved aggressive in the West. Warned that Pope bragged and lied, Lincoln remarked that "a liar might be as brave and have [as much] skill as any officer."[80] Pope's tasks were to shield Washington, defend the Shenandoah Valley, and move south up the Valley and then turn to assault Richmond from the west as McClellan did so from the east.

But Lee thwarted that strategy by attacking on the very day of Pope's appointment. The Confederate general had resolved to act boldly in the face of superior forces instead of waiting for McClellan to besiege Richmond. (Lee had managed to scrape together 92,000 troops. McClellan had 115,000 present for duty.) Attack, attack, attack was Lee's motto. He took a gamble, concentrating most of his army north of the Chickahominy River. If McClellan had been at all bold, he could have easily brushed aside the remaining Confederate forces south of the river and marched into Richmond. In the final week of June, Lee, counting on Little Mac's timidity, launched a series of battles that became known as the Seven Days.

When Lee began his offensive, McClellan retreated; but instead of returning to his base on the Pamunkey River, he moved south to Harrison's Landing, on the James, thirty-five miles from Richmond, where Union gunboats could fend off pursuers. In the final battle of the Seven Days, at Malvern Hill, Lee rashly hurled his men against an exceptionally strong Union position from which artillery cut the attackers down; their bodies covered the field like windrows. Instead of following up with a counterattack that might well have carried Richmond, McClellan retreated to Harrison's Landing, where he established a new base. In doing so, he abandoned twenty-five hundred wounded men and destroyed tons of precious material.

Sidling toward the James, Little Mac telegraphed to Stanton complaining bitterly about the administration's failure to reinforce him. He closed with a remarkably insubordinate blast: "If I save this army now, I tell you plainly that I owe no thanks to you or to any other persons in Washington. You have done your best to sacrifice this army."[81] Before passing this message on to his boss, the scandalized telegrapher omitted these last two sentences. Even in its bowdlerized version, the telegram angered Stanton, who took it to Lincoln and said "with much feeling 'You know—Mr President that all I have done was by your authority.'"[82] Lincoln magnanimously overlooked McClellan's insolence and tried to calm him. "Save your Army at all events," he wired in response to Little Mac's frantic appeals. "Will send reinforcements as fast as we can." The president ordered Dix, Burnside, Halleck, Hunter, and Goldsborough to rush to McClellan's assistance. But as he told the Young Napoleon on July 1, there was little hope that they could make a difference: "It is impossible to reenforce you for your present emergency. . . . Maintain your ground if you can, but save the army at all events."[83]

Though polite in his correspondence with McClellan, the president felt bitter about the general's wildly unrealistic demands. When asked the size of the Confederate army, Lincoln replied sarcastically: "*Twelve hundred thousand, according to best authority*. . . . no doubt of it. You see, all of our Generals, when they get whipped, say the enemy outnumbers them from three to five to one, and I must believe them. We have four hundred thousand men in the field, and three times four make twelve."[84]

On July 2, when the magnitude of the Union defeat became apparent, Lincoln understandably despaired, telling a congressman that when "the Peninsular campaign terminated suddenly at Harrison's Landing, I was as nearly inconsolable as I could be and live."[85] As McClellan fell back, Lincoln responded to the defeat on the Peninsula by arranging to expand the army. When Seward offered to arouse Northern governors, the president gave him a strongly worded letter to show them. It closed with a sentence of iron: "I expect to maintain this contest until successful, or till I die, or am conquered, or my term expires, or Congress or the country forsakes me."[86] Seward recommended that the governors band together and request that Lincoln ask them for a fresh levy. They did so, and in response the president called on the governors for three hundred thousand new troops. When volunteering did not pick up that summer, a draft seemed necessary. On July 17, Congress passed a militia act authorizing the secretary of war to call on states for nine-month militiamen above and beyond the regular three-year recruits. If the quotas were not met, the administration could institute a draft. The governors eventually raised more men than the administration had requested. Helping the recruitment effort was a new song written by a fighting Quaker abolitionist, James S. Gibbons: "We Are Coming, Father Abraham, Three Hundred Thousand More."

Fearing that McClellan might surrender the army, Lincoln hastened to confer with him. Before departing the capital, he assured congressional supporters that "henceforth the war shall be conducted on war principles." They were sure that he had finally "convinced himself of the folly of rose-water warfare."[87] Upon the president's arrival at Harrison's Landing, nearby soldiers cheered him repeatedly. In his diary, a lieutenant described the reaction: "Long and hearty was the applause and welcome which greeted him. His presence after the late disaster . . . seemed to infuse new ardor into the dispirited army."[88] To help achieve that goal, the president scaled the outer line of an artillery battery and made a brief, informal address to the troops: "Be of good cheer; all is well. The country owes you an inextinguishable debt for your services. I am under immeasurable obligations to you. You have, like heroes, endured, and fought, and conquered. Yes, I say conquered; for though apparently checked once you conquered afterwards and secured the position of your choice. You shall be strengthened and rewarded. God bless you all." These remarks were greeted with hearty cheers.[89]

But while Lincoln's spirits were buoyed by the army's relatively good condition, they were depressed by a long letter that McClellan handed him upon his arrival. In that remarkable document, which became known as the Harrison's Landing letter, the Young Napoleon offered detailed advice about "civil and military policy, covering the whole ground of our national trouble." Patronizingly, he lectured the president on his responsibilities: "Our cause must never be abandoned; it is the cause of free institutions and self-government. The Constitution and the Union must be preserved, whatever may be the cost in time, treasure, and blood." McClellan presumptuously urged that the war be conducted "upon the highest principles known to Christian civilization," with all the property rights of the Confederates, including the right to own slaves, scrupulously protected. "Neither confiscation of property, political executions of persons, territorial organization of States, or forcible abolition of slavery should be contemplated for a moment. . . . Military power should not be allowed to interfere with the relations of servitude, either by supporting or impairing the authority of the master, except for repressing disorder." Such a conservative policy, the Young Napoleon predicted, "would receive the support of almost all truly loyal men" and "would deeply impress the rebel masses and all foreign nations." Ominously he warned that if such a policy were not adopted, "the effort to obtain requisite forces will be almost hopeless. A declaration of radical views, especially upon slavery, will rapidly disintegrate our present armies."[90] Here McClellan meddled with slavery policy almost as blatantly as Frémont, Hunter, and Cameron had done.

It is hard to know how Lincoln felt about McClellan's brazen letter. After receiving it from the general's hand, he read it, thanked its author, and then said nothing about it to him. He jestingly told Frank Blair that Little Mac's advice reminded him "of the man who got on a horse, and the horse stuck his hind foot into a stirrup. The man said, 'If you're going to get on I'll get off.'"[91] Although he joked about it, the letter, according to Gideon Welles, "struck the President painfully." He may have regarded it as a veiled threat to march on Washington and overthrow the government. The navy secretary wrote that within the Army of the Potomac "there was a belief, hardly a design perhaps, among a few of their indiscreet partisans, that these generals, better than the Administration, could prescribe the course of governmental action."[92] Two years later Lincoln told a political ally that McClellan's letter convinced him that the general intended to run for president in 1864.

By the time Lincoln returned to the White House, his morale seemed to be much improved. He may have been cheered to discover that the number of troops in the Army of the Potomac was greater than he had anticipated; nevertheless, he worried about the enormous number of absentees. On July 13, he asked McClellan what had happened to the more than 160,000 men who had been sent to the Peninsula: "When I was with you the other day we made out 86,500 remaining, leaving 73,500 to be accounted for."[93]

Lincoln's suggestion that McClellan go on the offensive amused the general. "It is so easy," the general exclaimed to his wife, "for people to give advice—it costs nothing!" It would be impossible for him with only 75,000 combat-ready men to attack 150,000 to 170,000 entrenched Confederates.[94] When he told Lincoln the same thing, the president abandoned hope for a renewed assault on the enemy capital, predicting to Orville H. Browning that if he could somehow by magic send McClellan 100,000 more troops, Little Mac "would be in an ecstasy over it, thank him for it, and tell him that he would go to Richmond tomorrow, but then when tomorrow came he could telegraph that he had certain information that the enemy had 400,000 men, and that he could not advance without reinforcements."[95]

In August, Lincoln spoke at a huge war rally in Washington. The atmosphere was electric with anticipation. On the east portico of the Capitol, he addressed a wildly enthusiastic crowd of ten thousand, which greeted him with several minutes of deafening cheers. Modestly he acknowledged that he had little of interest to say that others on the platform could not better express than he might. "The only thing I think of just now not likely to be better said by some one else, is a matter in which we have heard some other persons blamed for what I did myself. There has been a very wide-spread attempt to have a quarrel between Gen. McClellan and the Secretary of War." But Lincoln assured the crowd "that these two gentlemen are not nearly so deep in the quarrel as some pretending to be their friends. . . . I know Gen. McClellan wishes to be successful, and I know he does not wish it any more than the Secretary of War for him, and both of them together no more than I wish it. . . . Gen. McClellan has sometimes asked for things that the Secretary of War did not give him. Gen. McClellan is not to blame for asking for what he wanted and needed, and the Secretary of War is not to blame for not giving when he had none to give. And I say here, so far as I know, the Secretary of War has withheld no one thing at any time in my power to give him. I have no accusation against him. I believe he is a brave and able man, and I stand here, as justice requires me to do, to take upon myself what has been charged upon the Secretary of War as withholding from him."[96]

Journalist Whitelaw Reid praised Lincoln's impromptu speech extravagantly, calling it "remarkable, alike for the courageous assumption of unpopular responsibility, and for the characteristic honesty with which he refrained from boastful promises and stirring declarations that the war should now soon be ended."[97] Erastus Brooks, a partisan Democratic journalist, noted that by such "frank confessions, which are often more generous to others than just to himself, the President draws friends around him, and makes many friends of those, who have been warm opponents of his policy, principles and his election."[98]

Lincoln's profound magnanimity would continue to win him vital respect and affection.

27.

"The Hour Comes for Dealing with Slavery"

Playing the Last Trump Card (January–July 1862)

The failure of the Peninsular campaign marked a key turning point in the war. If McClellan had won, his triumph, combined with other successes of Union arms that spring, might well have ended the war with slavery virtually untouched. But in the wake of such a serious Union defeat, Lincoln concluded that the peculiar institution must no longer be treated gently.

Promoting Gradual, Compensated Emancipation

Ever since the beginning of the war, Lincoln had been urged to attack slavery. Most appeals rested on moral grounds, but some emphasized practical considerations, such as the need to prevent European nations from intervening on behalf of the Confederates. In early 1862, when Carl Schurz made that argument, Lincoln agreed, though he doubted that the public "was yet sufficiently prepared for it." He wanted "to unite, and keep united, all the forces of Northern society and of the Union element in the South, especially the Border States." With good reason he feared that "the cry of 'abolition war,'" which an open antislavery policy would elicit, might well "tend to disunite those forces and thus weaken the Union cause."[1] In January, Lincoln voiced similar doubts to abolitionists who pressed him to emancipate the slaves and compensate their masters. "We grow in this direction daily," he said, "and I am not without hope that some great thing is to be accomplished. When the hour comes for dealing with slavery, I trust I shall be willing to act."[2] But that hour had not yet arrived.

Lincoln also fended off emancipationists by protesting that he did not cross rivers until reaching them. On January 28, 1862, George Templeton Strong recorded a presidential interview, providing a record of what Lincoln sounded like in conversation: "Wa-al, that reminds me of a party of Methodist parsons that was travelling in Illinois when I was a boy thar, and had a branch to cross that was pretty bad—ugly to cross, ye know, because the waters was up. And they got considerin' and discussin' how they should git across it, and they talked about it for two hours, and one on 'em thought they had ought to cross one way when they got there, and another another way, and they got quarrelin' about it, till at last an old brother put in, and he says, says he, 'Brethren, this here talk ain't no use. I never cross a river until I come to it.'"[3]

Pressure had grown intense after September 1861, when Lincoln overruled Frémont's proclamation liberating the slaves of disloyal Missourians. Some Radicals lost all patience. On March 6, 1862, George B. Cheever exclaimed to a fellow abolitionist, "How black the prospect looks before us!" He feared that "we are under a military pro-slavery despotism, and the President is at length taking the active command, in behalf of slavery and against freedom."[4] When Charles Sumner lobbied him to endorse gradual emancipation, Lincoln replied that the Massachusetts senator was "ahead of him only a month or six weeks."[5] As it turned out, Sumner was three months in front of the president.

At a cabinet meeting in March, Lincoln proposed sending a message to Congress urging it to fund a plan of gradual, compensated emancipation underwritten by the federal government. He showed a draft of the message to Sumner, who expressed approval. In vain, Montgomery Blair urged the president to include a colonization provision. On March 6, Lincoln submitted the proposal to Congress suggesting that it give states willing to abolish slavery "pecuniary aid" to "compensate for the inconveniences, public and private, produced by such change of system." Lincoln justified the recommendation "as one of the most efficient means of self-preservation." If Maryland, Delaware, Missouri, and Kentucky could be induced to abolish slavery on their own initiative, with federal help, then the Confederacy might well despair of winning the war. Although the government would have to pay a large sum to the states, the cost would be more than offset by the early termination of the war. Moreover, the plan, Lincoln argued, would be constitutional, for under its provisions the government "sets up no claim of a right, by federal authority, to interfere with slavery within state limits." In conclusion, the president intimated that if his plan were not adopted, the war might produce sudden rather than gradual emancipation. If Border State slave owners wanted to avoid losing the money they had invested in slaves, they should support his plan.[6]

Most Radical Republicans agreed with the New York *Tribune*, which praised "the message of freedom" as "the day-star of a new national dawn" and "one of those few great scriptures that live in history and mark an epoch in the lives of nations and of races." Enthusiastically the paper predicted that March 6 "will yet be celebrated as a day which initiated the Nation's deliverance from the most stupendous wrong, curse and shame of the Nineteenth Century."[7] When the New York *Times* called the plan too expensive, Lincoln asked editor Henry J. Raymond if he had considered "that eighty-seven days cost of this war would pay for all in Delaware, Maryland, District of Columbia, Kentucky, and Missouri" at the price of four hundred dollars per slave? Thus his plan would "be an actual saving of expense."[8] In response, the *Times* hailed Lincoln's message as one whose "words will echo round the globe," for the president "has hit the happy mean upon which all parties in the North and all loyalists in the South can unite."[9]

On March 9, the president asked Frank Blair to invite Border State congressmen and senators to the White House for a candid talk. The Missourian promptly urged Maryland congressman John W. Crisfield to round up fellow Border State colleagues for a White House meeting. The following day, Crisfield and a few other members of Congress from Missouri and Kentucky gathered at the Executive Mansion, where, according to Crisfield, Lincoln "disclaimed any intent to injure the interests or wound the sensibilities of the slave States." The president observed "that we were engaged in a terrible, wasting and tedious war" and that the "armies must, of necessity, be brought into contact with slaves in the States we represented, and in other States as they advanced; that slaves would come to the camps, and continual irritation was kept up." Some people "complained if the slave was not protected by the army," while "slaveholders complained that their rights were interfered with, their slaves induced to abscond and protected within the [Union] lines. These complaints were numerous, loud and deep; were a serious annoyance to him and embarrassing to the progress of the war; that it kept alive a spirit hostile to the government in the States we represented; strengthened the hopes of the Confederates that at some day the border States would unite with them, and thus tend to prolong the war." Lincoln believed that if Congress adopted his resolution and the Border States accepted it, then "these causes of irritation and these hopes would be removed, and more would be accomplished towards shortening the war than could be hoped from the greatest victory achieved by Union armies."[10]

When Crisfield observed that his constituents thought the administration was coercing them indirectly, Lincoln replied that as long as he remained in office "Maryland had nothing to fear, either for her institutions or her interests, on the points referred to." The congressman asked permission to make this pledge public, but Lincoln demurred, saying "it would force me into a quarrel before the proper time." Asked about his own attitude toward slavery, Lincoln "said he did not pretend to disguise his anti-slavery feeling; that he thought it was wrong, and should continue to think so; but that was not the question we had to deal with now." He believed the North as well as the South was "morally bound to do its full and equal share" to get rid of slavery, but "the rights of property . . . must be respected." He therefore proposed to "get rid of" slavery, "not by violating the right" but rather by "offering inducements to give it up."[11]

As Lincoln feared, the Border State delegations found his arguments unpersuasive. They balked at the modest sum to be paid for slaves, raised constitutional objections, predicted that a race war would ensue, warned that the president's scheme would cause taxes to rise dramatically, protested that their economies would be ruined, and feared that if adopted, the scheme would make life harder for Unionists in Virginia and Tennessee. On March 12, the Border State delegations held a caucus at which they angrily rejected emancipation. Congress nevertheless passed Lincoln's resolution by a wide margin.

Abolishing Slavery in Washington

Lincoln thanked Horace Greeley for his paper's approval of the emancipation plan and suggested that "as the North are already for the measure, we should urge it *persuasively*, and not *menacingly*, upon the South." The place to start might well be Washington, where slavery could be abolished legally, for the Constitution gave the federal government control of the capital. Lincoln, however, told Greeley that "I am a little uneasy about the abolishment of slavery in this District, not but I would be glad to see it abolished, but as to the time and manner of doing it. If some one or more of the border-states would move fast, I should greatly prefer it; but if this can not be [done] in a reasonable time, I would like the bill [abolishing slavery in the District] to have the three main features—gradual—compensation—and vote of the people."[12] He did not include colonization in that list.

In December 1861, Massachusetts senator Henry Wilson had introduced a bill abolishing slavery in the District immediately and providing compensation for slave owners. Four months later, Congress heatedly debated the measure, adding a provision for voluntary colonization to be funded by the government. Maryland Unionists denounced the statute as "an act of bad faith."[13] When Congressman Crisfield called at the White House to protest, Lincoln "said he greatly objected to the time, and terms of the bill, and saw the trouble it would cause, and would gladly have avoided any action upon it," but "he also saw the troubles to arise on its rejection." He "could not say it was unconstitutional, and he had come to the conclusion, after full consideration of all the pros & cons, that he would do less mischief by approving than by rejecting it; and he hoped that the people of Maryland, would see the difficulties of his position, and treat him with forbearance." Crisfield told his wife that he was "really sympathetic" with the president, "surrounded with immense difficulties" as he was.[14]

Lincoln's March 6 message recommending compensated emancipation helped pave the way for the bill's passage. Four days after that bombshell landed at the Capitol, the *National Anti-Slavery Standard* reported that "several members who before it was delivered were on the fence have since leaped headlong over on the emancipation side." The "hint at the close of his message, that a time *may* come when a decree of emancipation must be made, has worked wonders in Congress. Men who, a week ago, looked with horror upon any proposition to touch slavery in any manner, begin to shift position."[15]

On April 16, Lincoln signed the legislation even though it called for immediate rather than gradual emancipation and did not allow for a local referendum. Black Washingtonians were jubilant, and Frederick Douglass hailed the new law as "that first great step towards that righteousness which exalts a nation."[16] Most other Radicals rejoiced and thought that Lincoln's approval of the bill represented "the turning-point in the policy of the Administration upon the slavery question."[17] Conservatives in Congress, however, were gravely disappointed. When advised that the Maryland congressional delegation would protest that their constituents' slaves might escape to Washington, Lincoln remarked: "Well, I shall say to them, 'I am engaged in putting down a great rebellion, in which I can only succeed by the help of the North, which will not tolerate my returning your slaves, and I cannot try experiments. You cannot have them.'"[18]

Overruling Yet Another General's Emancipation Order

While he was willing to sign what he regarded as an imperfect emancipation measure for the District, Lincoln would not condone formal emancipation by military commanders. Just as he had overruled Frémont's proclamation in September 1861, he struck down General David Hunter's similar decree in the spring of 1862. On May 9, Hunter, in charge of the Department of the South (made up primarily of the Sea Islands off the coast of Georgia, Florida, and South Carolina), cited military necessity as a justification for liberating slaves there. Two days later he pressed hundreds of them into military service and gave them weapons, prompting Border State delegations to demand that Hunter be repudiated. Some Republicans argued that the general had acted within the scope of his authority as a department commander. When Salmon Chase counseled the president to support the general, Lincoln curtly replied: "No commanding general shall do such a thing, upon *my* responsibility, without consulting me."[19] He explained that Hunter "was specially enjoined not to meddle with matters political" and had been forbidden to issue proclamations.[20] Although Secretary of War Stanton approved of Hunter's act, he deplored his lack of discretion: "Damn him, why didn't he do it and say nothing about it?"[21] Similarly, Lincoln remarked that he wished the general "to *do* it, not say it."[22] On May 19, Lincoln formally revoked the controversial order, averring that "neither General Hunter, nor any other commander, or person, has been authorized by the Government of the United States, to make proclamations declaring the slaves of any State free."[23]

Having taken away with one hand, Lincoln then gave with the other. Significantly, he hinted that soon he himself might issue a proclamation like Hunter's: "I further make known that whether it be competent for me, as Commander-in-Chief of the Army and Navy, to declare the Slaves of any state or states, free, and whether at any time, in any case, it shall have become a necessity indispensable to the maintainance of the government, to exercise such supposed power, are questions which, under my responsibility, I reserve to myself, and which I can not feel justified in leaving to the decision of commanders in the field."[24] When a friend reminded the president that he had let stand Henry Halleck's notorious order of the previous November forbidding slaves admittance to Union lines, Lincoln replied: "D——n General order No 3."[25] To a commander who congratulated Lincoln on his decision, he remarked: "I am trying to do my duty, but no one can imagine what influences are brought to bear on me."[26]

Lincoln used the occasion to warn Border State senators and congressmen that they should approve the compensated emancipation plan he had submitted to Congress two months earlier. In his proclamation revoking Hunter's order, he issued an earnest appeal: "You can not if you would, be blind to the signs of the times. I beg of you a calm and enlarged consideration of them, ranging, if it may be, far above personal and partizan politics. This proposal makes common cause for a common object, casting no reproaches upon any. . . . May the vast future not have to lament that you have neglected it."[27] While Lincoln's revocation of Hunter's proclamation pleased moderates, most Radicals were disgruntled. In the House of Representatives, Thaddeus Stevens said that the president "is as honest a man as there is in the world, but I believe him too easy and amiable, and to be misled by the malign influence of Kentucky counselors."[28] Carl Schurz suggested to Lincoln that some true friends of freedom needed to be reassured by other actions, and he urged him to make gestures to placate them. Lincoln took that advice, mollifying Radicals by signing legislation to extend diplomatic recognition to Haiti and Liberia and by approving a treaty with Great Britain strictly enforcing the ban on the African slave trade. He further insisted that "no slave freed by the advance of our army would be returned" and approved an article of war enforcing that policy.[29]

On July 1, Lincoln showed Orville H. Browning a paper he had drafted stating that while no slaves "necessarily taken or escaping during the war are ever to be returned to slavery," on the other hand "no inducements are to be held out to them to come into our lines for they come now faster than we can provide for them and are becoming an embarrassment to the government."[30] Two days later, Stanton informed General Benjamin Butler that the president "is of the opinion" that runaway slaves "cannot be sent back to their masters; that, in common humanity, they must not be permitted to suffer for want of food, shelter or other necessaries of life; that, to this end, they should be provided for by the quartermaster and commissary departments, and that those who are capable of labor should be set to work and paid reasonable wages."[31] When a leading Kentucky Unionist protested that federal troops refused to turn over his runaway slave, Lincoln offered to pay five hundred dollars out of his own pocket to settle the matter.

Diplomatic recognition of Haiti and Liberia had long been resisted on the grounds that those nations might send Blacks to represent them at Washington. Lincoln, however, did not object to that possibility. In December 1860, he discussed the matter with a Radical abolitionist and John Brown ally, Richard J. Hinton, who recalled "very distinctly a remark" of the president-elect "which showed how little the prejudice against color affected his own conclusions." It stuck in Hinton's memory "because other Republican statesmen, to whom the same view was presented, expressed a different conclusion from that given by Mr. Lincoln." Hinton, who had been lobbying on behalf of the Haitian government, "suggested, as a matter of policy, that President [Fabre Nicolas] Geffrard would send, in the event of [diplomatic] recognition, as [the] representative of the republic at Washington, some one of the educated men of mixed blood, of whom there were many who would pass muster for Creole or Spanish American whites." Lincoln "remarked, in an animated manner, 'I don't see the necessity for that. An educated black man would be as dignified, I have no doubt, as a ginger-colored one.'"[32]

Especially pleasing to Radicals was Lincoln's decision in early 1862 to approve the execution of Nathaniel Gordon, the only American ever hanged for slave trading. When the prosecutor in the case, E. Delafield Smith, visited Washington to urge the president to uphold the death sentence, Lincoln said: "You do not know how hard it is to have a human being die when you know that a stroke of your pen may save him."[33] He explained that while he did not want to execute slave traders, he also "did not wish to be announced as having pardoned them, lest it might be thought at Richmond that he feared the consequences of such action and then he might be compelled to hang fifty such men."[34] Ultimately he refused to commute Gordon's sentence, telling the prisoner's intercessors that the "slave-trade will never be put down till our laws are executed, and the penalty of death has once been enforced upon the offenders."[35] Gordon's beautiful young wife also traveled to the capital, where she won the sympathy of Mary Lincoln. But it did her no good, for Lincoln would not allow the First Lady to raise the subject. When Gordon's lawyer sent Lincoln a last-minute appeal for mercy, the president allowed a brief postponement of Gordon's execution, but nothing more.

On July 12, Lincoln made his third and final appeal to Border State lawmakers, urging them to support his gradual emancipation plan and gently chiding them for their failure to do so: "If you all had voted for the resolution in the gradual emancipation message of last March, the war would now be substantially ended. And the plan therein proposed is yet one of the most potent, and swift means of ending it. Let the states which are in rebellion see, definitely and certainly, that, in no event, will the states you represent ever join their proposed Confederacy, and they can not, much longer maintain the contest." The president begged them to view things from his perspective, to realize how much pressure he was under to abolish slavery by decree, especially after he had overruled David Hunter. In closing, he appealed to their idealism: "As you would perpetuate popular government for the best people in the world, I beseech you that you do in no wise omit this. Our common country is in great peril, demanding the loftiest views, and boldest action to bring it speedy relief. Once relieved, it's form of government is saved to the world; it's beloved history, and cherished memories, are vindicated; and it's happy future fully assured, and rendered inconceivably grand. To you, more than to any others, the previlege is given, to assure that happiness, and swell that grandeur, and to link your own names therewith forever."[36]

A day later the president submitted to Congress a bill compensating any state that would abolish slavery voluntarily. Most legislators agreed with Vermont senator Jacob Collamer, who called the plan "ridiculous" and noted that it was received with "considerable disappointment," for Free State members were "about sick of this dickering, bargaining business. The feeling is, that inasmuch as a fair offer had been made, and the border states show no signs of accepting it, that they had better be left alone until great events shall terrify them into compliance."[37] They were unterrified. On July 14, twenty of the twenty-eight members of the Border State delegations rejected Lincoln's appeal.

That negative response depressed Lincoln badly. The following day, Orville H. Browning found him looking "weary, care-worn, and troubled." Alarmed by his appearance, Browning said: "Your fortunes Mr President are bound up with those of the Country, and disaster to one would be disaster to the other, and I hope you will do all you can to preserve your health and life." Lincoln "looked very sad" as he replied that he felt "tolerably well" and added "in a very tender and touching tone, 'I must die sometime.'" As Browning bade him goodbye, both men had tears in their eyes.[38] To Illinois congressmen Owen Lovejoy and Isaac Arnold, Lincoln vented his disappointment: "Oh, how I wish the border states would accept my proposition. Then, you, Lovejoy, and you, Arnold, and all of us, would not have lived in vain! The labor of your life, Lovejoy, would be crowned with success."[39]

Radicals also exasperated Lincoln. In December 1861, Lyman Trumbull introduced legislation embodying their demands for stronger action to liberate slaves and punish Rebels. Known as the Second Confiscation Act, it reflected the mood of the Northern public, which wanted stern measures to be taken against the Confederates. On July 12, after months of heated debate, Congress passed a watered-down version of Trumbull's bill providing that slaves of disloyal masters were free and that the property of Rebels could be confiscated. An additional provision authorized the enlistment of freedmen as soldiers.

Moderate and conservative Republicans urged Lincoln to veto the Second Confiscation Act, which seemed to violate the Constitution's ban on bills of attainder and ex post facto legislation. Senator Browning told the president that "he had reached the culminating point in his administration, and his course upon this bill was to determine whether he was to control the abolitionists and radicals, or whether they were to control him," and that a veto would secure "unity of sentiment and purpose which . . . would at once bring to his support every loyal Democrat in the free states, and consolidate all truly loyal men into one party—whereas if approved it would form the basis upon which the democratic party would again rally, and reorganize an opposition to the administration." Lincoln promised to give this advice "his profound consideration."[40]

In response, he asked Congress to delay its planned adjournment. When told that the members were exceedingly reluctant to do so unless there was a true emergency, he somewhat testily remarked: "I am sorry Senators could not so far trust me as to believe I had some real cause for wishing them to remain. I am considering a bill which came to me only late in the day yesterday, and the subject of which has perplexed Congress for more than half a year. I may return it with objections; and if I should, I wish Congress to have the oppertunity of obviating the objections, or of passing it into a law notwithstanding them."[41] Secluding himself, he hurriedly prepared a veto message dealing with the confiscation of Rebel property beyond the life of the guilty parties. Such confiscation, he argued, violated the Constitution's ban on "corruption of blood." Moreover, slave owners accused of treasonous acts committed before the passage of the bill would be victims of ex post facto legislation. As for a general policy in dealing with the Confederates, he counseled that the "severest justice may not always be the best policy." But he was careful to acknowledge his agreement with many provisions of the bill and with its ultimate aim. "That those who make a causeless war should be compelled to pay the cost of it, is too obviously just, to be called in question. To give governmental protection to the property of persons who have abandoned it, and gone on a crusade to overthrow that same government, is absurd."[42]

Indignant Radicals stormed into the White House and told Lincoln's principal secretary that if the president vetoed the bill "he destroys the Republican party and ruins his Administration."[43] They insisted that they would not compromise and threatened to denounce the administration publicly. Senators Wade, Wilkinson, Trumbull, and other Radicals predicted that "if the confiscation bill is not signed, & the policy of the government in prosecuting the war is not changed, the Union is gone."[44] Ultimately, Lincoln considered it an imperative duty to hold the party—and the North—together. To avoid a confrontation with Congress, he met secretly with some members to hammer out a compromise. On July 15, Tennessee representative Horace Maynard, evidently at the president's suggestion, introduced a "joint resolution for the purpose of correcting the confiscation act" that refined the language so as to meet Lincoln's desire for a more "justly discriminating application" of the measure.[45] That night, Senators William P. Fessenden of Maine and Daniel Clark of New Hampshire met with Lincoln, who warned them that he would veto the bill unless it was modified to conform to the Constitution. The following day, Clark offered another amendment, stating that no property would be confiscated beyond the lifetime of any offender. Despite the objections of Benjamin Wade and other Radical senators, who thought the president's tactics "monstrous" (as Preston King put it), these provisos passed, and Lincoln signed the bill and the joint explanatory resolution. The ban on the forfeiture of property beyond the owners' lifetime severely weakened the government's ability to restructure the society and economy of the South. Some Radicals expressed profound disgust for what they considered Lincoln's lack of backbone.

Curiously, Lincoln sent copies of his veto message to the House and the Senate, even though he now agreed to sign the modified bill. This uncharacteristically tactless gesture annoyed many members of Congress. Lincoln's motive was unclear. Perhaps he intended to show Congress that on matters of slavery and reconstruction, he was master. On other legislative matters—such as taxation, public lands, and internal improvements—he generally followed traditional Whig doctrine that the executive branch should defer to the legislature.

On July 25, Lincoln issued a proclamation warning all Rebels that if they did not "cease participating in, aiding, countenancing, or abetting the existing rebellion," they would suffer "the forfeitures and seizures" spelled out in the Second Confiscation Act.[46] But because the statute provided no mechanism for enforcement or for oversight of its implementation (thus giving Lincoln wide discretionary power to carry it out as he saw fit), he virtually ignored it. Although almost no Confederate property was seized under the provisions of the Second Confiscation Act, its passage was significant, for it helped pave the way for the Emancipation Proclamation. It showed Lincoln that such a document would not be as politically risky as it had earlier seemed, and the lengthy congressional debates helped undermine the notion that Blacks were property. As John Sherman noted, the statute "was more useful as a declaration of policy than as an act to be enforced."[47]

Emancipation Proclamation

On July 13, Lincoln took a fateful carriage ride with two of the more conservative members of his cabinet, Welles and Seward. A day earlier he had unsuccessfully attempted to persuade the Border States to accept his gradual emancipation plan; their negative reaction persuaded him that it was time for more drastic steps. As he rode with his secretaries of state and the navy to attend the funeral of Stanton's infant son, Lincoln discussed issuing an emancipation proclamation. According to Welles, he "dwelt earnestly on the gravity, importance, and delicacy of the movement, said he had given it much thought and had about come to the conclusion that it was a military necessity absolutely essential for the salvation of the Union, that we must free the slaves or be ourselves subdued." This was "the first occasion when he had mentioned the subject to any one, and wished us to frankly state how the proposition struck us. Mr. Seward said the subject involved consequences so vast and momentous that he should wish to bestow on it mature reflection before giving a decisive answer, but his present opinion inclined to the measure as justifiable, and perhaps he might say expedient and necessary." Welles agreed. "It was a new departure for the President, for until this time, in all our previous interviews, whenever the question of emancipation or the mitigation of slavery had been in any way alluded to, he had been prompt and emphatic in denouncing any interference by the General Government with the subject. This was, I think, the sentiment of every member of the Cabinet, all of whom, including the President, considered it a local, domestic question appertaining to the States respectively, who had never parted with their authority over it. But the reverses before Richmond, and the formidable power and dimensions of the insurrection, which extended through all the Slave States, and had combined most of them in a confederacy to destroy the Union, impelled the Administration to adopt extraordinary measures to preserve the national existence."[48]

Although disappointed by the negative response of the Border State lawmakers, Lincoln took heart from the positive response he received from Welles and Seward. He assumed that he could rely on the support of the more radical Chase and Stanton. Therefore he began drafting an emancipation proclamation that would be far more effective than the Confiscation Acts, which required a trial for disloyal slaveholders before their slaves would become legally free, and even then it was doubtful that the forfeiture of property could last beyond the lifetime of the convicted traitors.

To justify so momentous a step, Lincoln decided not to appeal to the idealism of the North; he had already done that eloquently and repeatedly between 1854 and 1860. Instead, he chose to rely on practical and constitutional arguments, which he assumed would be more palatable to Democrats and conservative Republicans, especially in the Border States. He knew full well that those elements would object to sudden, uncompensated emancipation and that many men who were willing to fight for the Union would be reluctant to do so for the liberation of slaves. To minimize their discontent, he would argue that emancipation facilitated the war effort by depriving Confederates of valuable workers. Slaves might not be fighting in the Rebel army, but they grew the food and fiber that nourished and clothed it. If those slaves could be induced to abandon the plantations and head for Union lines, the Confederates' ability to wage war would be significantly undermined. Military necessity, therefore, required the president to liberate the slaves, but not all of them. Residents of Slave States still loyal to the Union would have to be exempted, as well as those in areas of the Confederacy that the Union army had already pacified. Such restrictions might disappoint Radicals, but Lincoln was less worried about them than he was about moderates and conservatives.

Lincoln also feared that Roger Taney's Supreme Court might object. The constitutional basis for such a bold decree would have to be the war powers of the president, a somewhat vague concept implied in the chief executive's status as "Commander-in-Chief of the Army and Navy of the United States" and his oath to support, protect, and defend the Constitution. On July 20, John Hay told a friend that the president "has been, out of pure devotion to what he considers the best interests of humanity, the bulwark of the institution he abhors, for a year. But he will not conserve slavery much longer. When next he speaks in relation to this defiant and ungrateful villainy it will be with no uncertain sound."[49]

The following day, the president summoned his cabinet for an unusual Monday meeting. Chase recorded that Lincoln "had been profoundly concerned at the present aspect of affairs, and had determined to take some definitive steps in respect to military action and slavery."[50] But instead of springing his proclamation on them, Lincoln merely announced that he had prepared orders allowing commanders in the field to subsist their troops off the land in Confederate territory; authorizing the employment of Blacks within Union lines as laborers; and providing for colonization. These measures were discussed at length. When the use of Blacks as troops came up, Lincoln expressed reservations and proposed to discuss that matter, along with the others, on the morrow.

That fateful day, July 22, the cabinet reconvened to continue discussion of the arming of Blacks, which Chase heartily supported. The president demurred but added that he planned to issue a proclamation, based on the Second Confiscation Act, warning that all slaveholders who continued rebelling against the Union would have their property confiscated; declaring that he would once again urge Congress to renew its endorsement of his earlier offer of gradual, compensated emancipa-

The First Reading of the Emancipation Proclamation before the Cabinet (July 22, 1862), a steel engraving by Alexander Hay Ritchie of Francis B. Carpenter's enormous painting, completed in 1864. It depicts (*seated, left to right*), Secretary of War Edwin M. Stanton, the president, Navy Secretary Gideon Welles, Secretary of State William H. Seward, and Attorney General Edward Bates as well as (*standing, left to right*) Treasury Secretary Salmon P. Chase, Interior Secretary Caleb B. Smith, and Postmaster General Montgomery Blair. The painting hangs in the U.S. Capitol. The engraving offers a better image of Lincoln, for Carpenter kept tinkering with his canvas even after Ritchie completed the engraving, and the more Carpenter revised, the weaker Lincoln's portrait became. Library of Congress.

tion; and reaffirming that the war was being fought to restore the Union. The final sentence of this brief document stated that "as a fit and necessary military measure for effecting this object [i.e., restoration of the Union] I, as Commander-in-Chief of the Army and Navy of the United States, do order and declare that on the first day of January in the year of Our Lord one thousand, eight hundred and sixtythree, all persons held as slaves within any state or states, wherein the constitutional authority of the United States shall not then be practically recognized, shall then, thenceforward and forever, be free."[51] Lincoln explained that he "had resolved upon this step, and had not called them together to ask their advice, but to lay the subject-matter of a proclamation before them" and solicit suggestions.[52]

Surprisingly, the conservative Edward Bates agreed heartily. But he wanted colonization linked with emancipation. Chase approved Lincoln's proclamation in general but stated "that no new expression on the subject of compensation should be made, and I thought that the measure of Emancipation could be much better and more quietly accomplished by allowing Generals to organize and arm the slaves (thus avoiding depredation and massacre on the one hand, and support to the insurrection on the other)."[53] Stanton favored prompt issuance of Lincoln's decree. Blair, who arrived late, objected that such a move would cost the Republicans the fall elections. Caleb B. Smith did not voice an opinion at the meeting, but immediately afterward he told the assistant secretary of the interior that if Lincoln did issue an emancipation proclamation, "I will resign and go home and attack the administration."[54]

When no one else seemed willing to make suggestions, Seward offered what Stanton called "a long speech against its immediate promulgation."[55] To the artist Francis B. Carpenter, Lincoln recalled Seward's argument: "I approve of the proclamation, but I question the expediency of its issue at this juncture. The depression of the public mind, consequent upon our repeated reverses, is so great that I fear the effect of so important a step. It may be viewed as a last measure of an exhausted government, a cry for help; the government stretching forth its hands to Ethiopia, instead of Ethiopia stretching forth her hands to the government." So, the Sage of Auburn argued, "while I approve the measure, I suggest, sir, that you postpone its issue, until you can give it to the country supported by military success, instead of issuing it, as would be the case now, upon the greatest disasters of the war!" Lincoln told Carpenter that Seward's analysis "struck me with very great force. It was an aspect of the case that, in all my thought upon the subject, I had entirely overlooked. The result was that I put the draft of the proclamation aside, as you do your sketch for a picture, waiting for a victory. From time to time I added or changed a line, touching it up here and there, anxiously watching the progress of events."[56] For the next two months, those events would be unpropitious.

As July drew to a close, Charles Eliot Norton voiced questions preying on the minds of many in the North: "Will Lincoln be master of the opportunities, or will they escape him? Is he great enough for the time?"[57]

28.

"Would You Prosecute the War with Elder-Stalk Squirts, Charged with Rose Water?"

The Soft War Turns Hard (July–September 1862)

In the summer of 1862, as Northern disenchantment with the lack of progress grew ever more intense, Lincoln announced: "I have got done throwing grass." From now on, he "proposed trying stones."[1] Sarcastically he asked proponents of a conciliatory policy if they intended to prosecute the war "with elder-stalk squirts, charged with rose water?"[2] Solicitude for the rights of slaveholders as well as for civil liberties in the North had to be modified. Lincoln would prove that his reputation for tenderheartedness did not prevent him from employing stern measures to win the war. His principal secretary, John G. Nicolay, wrote an editorial (probably at the instigation of his boss) stating that the "people are for the war; for earnest, unrelenting war; for war now and war to the bitter end, until our outraged and insulted flag shall have been everywhere triumphantly vindicated and restored."[3] In carrying out this new strategy, Lincoln emancipated slaves, further suspended the writ of habeas corpus, drafted men into the army, confiscated Confederate civilian property, and tried to find more aggressive, capable military leaders. The administration's new toughness led a journalist to remark in August that recently "the Jacksonian qualities of Abraham Lincoln have been more than ever apparent."[4] This cheered the public, which, though discouraged by the failure of McClellan's Peninsula campaign, found reassurance in the president's leadership.

The military setback in Virginia prompted Lincoln to restructure the army command, seeking to appoint a general in chief empowered both to issue commands and give advice. The aged, infirm Ethan Allen Hitchcock had quit after a brief stint as military adviser to the president and the secretary of war. To replace him, Lincoln appointed Henry W. Halleck, the brusque, rigid, testy commander of armies in the West, known as Old Brains. The president was favorably disposed toward him, for the general's book *Elements of Military Art and Science* had impressed him. Lincoln realized that he needed a West Pointer to fill that post and approved of Halleck's conduct in St. Louis. On July 11, the day after returning from the Virginia

Peninsula, he issued an order naming Old Brains as general in chief of the Union army. Leaving Grant in charge of the forces around Corinth, Mississippi, Halleck repaired to Washington, arriving on July 23.

Lincoln's choice of Halleck proved to be a blunder. The president was evidently unaware that Old Brains had demonstrated the selfishness, hypercaution, reluctance to assume responsibility, deceitfulness, incompetence, and pettiness that would render him an ineffective general in chief. In keeping with the new spirit animating Lincoln, on August 25 Halleck reported that the administration "seems determined to apply the guillotine to all unsuccessful generals. It seems rather hard to do this where the general is not at fault, but perhaps . . . some harsh measures are justified."[5] Halleck criticized General Horatio G. Wright for "pursuing 'too milk and water a policy towards rebels in Kentucky.'" Sternly he lectured Wright: "Domestic traitors, who seek the overthrow of our Government, are not entitled to its protection and should be made to feel its power. . . . Let the guilty feel that you have an iron hand."[6]

Halleck's first assignment was to help determine what to do with the Army of the Potomac. Lincoln instructed the general in chief to visit the front, learn McClellan's views, and inform Little Mac that only twenty thousand reinforcements could be supplied and that he must either attack Richmond with those additional forces or withdraw and join John Pope. Lincoln told Halleck "that he was satisfied McClellan would not fight" and authorized him to remove the Young Napoleon if he saw fit.[7] The president also wanted Halleck to formulate strategic plans and coordinate the movement of all Union armies. When someone asked what would be done with McClellan's army, Lincoln replied: "You forget we have a general who commands all the armies and makes all the plans to suit himself—ask him!"[8] With some justification, Halleck complained that because the president and his cabinet had approved everything he proposed, "it only increases my responsibility, for if any disaster happens they can say we did for you all you asked."[9]

When Halleck delivered the presidential ultimatum to McClellan, Little Mac said he had a "good chance" of taking Richmond with 30,000 more troops but not with only 20,000 more. He soon changed his mind, however, and reluctantly agreed to try with 20,000. A day after Halleck left, the Young Napoleon reversed course yet again: he would need 50,000 more men, not 20,000! Upon Halleck's return to Washington, the administration debated whether to remove the Army of the Potomac from the Peninsula. When McClellan claimed that he had only 80,000 troops while Lee commanded 200,000, it became obvious to Halleck that the army could not safely remain on the Peninsula. And so on August 3 Old Brains ordered McClellan to transfer to Aquia Creek, where he would be near Pope. Little Mac objected heatedly but to no avail.[10] Ever so slowly the Army of the Potomac withdrew from Harrison's Landing, thus formally concluding the Peninsular Campaign, during which 25,000 Union soldiers and 30,000 Confederates were killed, wounded, or missing.

Second Battle of Bull Run

When Lee realized that the Army of the Potomac was pulling back, he began driving north toward Pope's 45,000-man Army of Virginia. If he could reach it before McClellan did, the Confederates might achieve a smashing triumph. Anxiously Lincoln wondered whether Little Mac would move fast enough to prevent such a calamity. In fact, the first units of the Young Napoleon's army did not join Pope until August 23. During those weeks, Halleck complained to his wife, "I cant get Genl McClellan to do what I wish."[11]

In July, while awaiting Halleck's arrival, Pope had made mistakes. Shortly after the retreat of the Army of the Potomac from the Peninsula, he had issued a boastful address to his men: "I have come to you from the West, where we have always seen the backs of our enemies; from an army whose business it has been to seek the adversary and to beat him when he was found; whose policy has been to attack, and not defense."[12] This message was widely ridiculed by the public and resented by the Army of the Potomac. Pope made matters worse by dictating that civilians should be treated harshly: property would be seized, disloyal residents deported south, violators of loyalty oaths executed, and guerilla attacks punished by reprisals. This policy sharply clashed with that adopted by McClellan, who responded coldly to Pope's friendly overtures. For good reason, Pope feared that Little Mac would not readily cooperate with him.

As the Army of Northern Virginia closed in on Pope, he retreated from the Rapidan to the north bank of the Rappahannock, where for several days he parried the Confederates' attempts to cross. On August 9 at Cedar Mountain, Stonewall Jackson whipped a much smaller force under N. P. Banks, who managed to inflict severe casualties before withdrawing. Pope and Banks bought enough time for McClellan's forces to join them, but Little Mac as usual moved at a glacial pace. Taking advantage of such tardiness, Lee boldly divided his 54,000-man force, sending half of it under Jackson on a wide flanking movement. On August 27, Stonewall's men astounded Pope by getting into his rear, sacking his supply depot at Manassas Junction, and severing his communications. When news of that calamity reached the capital, Lincoln felt mortified, depressed, angry, and alarmed. Jackson now stood between him and Pope, who sought to defeat Stonewall before the rest of Lee's forces could join him. But his failure to block Thoroughfare Gap allowed James Longstreet's corps to reinforce Jackson. On August 29 and 30, while the Second Battle of Bull Run raged, Lincoln anxiously followed events.

The president worried most about McClellan, who was supposedly hastening to Pope's assistance. Of the Army of the Potomac's 90,000 men, amazingly only 20,000 managed to connect with Pope's Army of Virginia. On August 29, Little Mac shocked the president by recommending that he "leave Pope to get out of his scrape."[13] Curbing his anger, the president replied: "I wish not to control. That I now leave to General Halleck, aided by your counsels."[14] On August 30, in conversation with John Hay, Lincoln "was very outspoken in regard to McClellan's present conduct. He said it really seemed to him that McC wanted Pope defeated." When Hay asked if the general in chief "had any prejudices," Lincoln exclaimed: "No! Halleck is wholly for the service. He does not care who succeeds or who fails so [long as] the service is benefited."[15] In fact, Halleck had misinformed Lincoln about the orders to McClellan. Old Brains had been too timid to confront the Young Napoleon.

With uncharacteristic promptitude, Little Mac responded, recommending that Pope immediately fall back to Washington, which was, he thought, in grave danger. On August 30, Hay and the president met with Stanton, who "said that nothing but foul play could lose us the battle & that it rested with McC. and his friends," who deserved to be court-martialed. According to Hay, Stanton "seemed to believe very strongly in Pope. So did the President." That night, Hay recorded in his diary, "Every thing seemed to be going well . . . & we went to bed expecting glad tidings at sunrise." But the next morning Lincoln told his young secretary: "Well John we are whipped again, I am afraid." He did not despair, however. Hay noted that Lincoln "was in a singularly defiant tone of mind. He often repeated, 'We must hurt this enemy before it gets away.'" The following day, when Hay remarked that things looked bad, Lincoln demurred: "We must whip these people now. Pope must fight them, if they are too strong for him he can gradually retire to these fortifications." Hay thought that it was owing largely to Lincoln's "indomitable will, that army movements have been characterized by such energy and celerity for the last few days."[16]

The president told Gideon Welles that "there has been a design, a purpose in breaking down Pope, without regard of consequences to the country. It is shocking to see and know this." He said that on August 30 "we had the enemy in the hollow of our hands" and would have destroyed him "if our generals, who are vexed with Pope, had done their duty. All of our present difficulties and reverses have been brought upon us by these quarrels of the generals."[17] The cabinet shared that view. Smith, Stanton, Bates, and Chase signed a round-robin declaring that it was their "deliberate opinion that, at this time, it is not safe to entrust to Major General McClellan the command of any of the armies of the United States."[18]

On September 1, McClellan met with Halleck and Lincoln, who explained that they were alarmed by Pope's dispatch complaining of the "unsoldierly and dangerous conduct of many brigade and some division commanders of the forces sent here from the Peninsula." The demoralization of the army seemed "calculated to break down the spirits of the men and produce disaster."[19] To avert that possibility, Lincoln asked Little Mac to command the defenses of Washington and to urge officers in the Army of the Potomac to cooperate with Pope. McClellan reluctantly agreed.

Lincoln was understandably perplexed. His friend Mark Skinner reported that he "wanders about wringing his hands and wondering whom he can trust and what he'd better do."[20] On September 2, at a heated cabinet meeting, he appeared to be suffering bitter anguish, saying "he felt almost ready to hang himself."[21] He astounded the secretaries by announcing that he had put McClellan in charge of Washington's defenses. When Stanton and Chase protested, Lincoln replied that "it distressed him exceedingly to find himself differing on such a point from the Secretary of War and the Secretary of the Treasury; that he would gladly resign his place; but he could not see who could do the work wanted as well as McClellan." The president would not budge. He insisted that Little Mac was the best man to protect the capital, for he "knows this whole ground—his specialty is to defend—he is a good engineer, all admit—there is no better organizer—he can be trusted to act on the defensive."[22]

The president said that he understood why cabinet members opposed McClellan and that he "was so distressed, precisely because he knew" they "were earnestly sincere. He was manifestly alarmed for the safety of the City. He had been talking with Gen Halleck . . . & had gotten the idea that Pope's army was utterly demoralized—saying that 'if Pope's army came within the lines (of the forts) as *a mob*, the City w[oul]d be overrun by the enemy in 48 hours!!'" Bates argued that "if Halleck doubted his ability to defend the City, he ought to be instantly broke."[23] The meeting adjourned without any discussion of the anti-McClellan round-robin, which the president never saw.

Two days thereafter, Lincoln concluded that McClellan was at that moment indispensable because of his popularity with the army. "Unquestionably he has acted badly toward Pope," the president acknowledged. "He really wanted him to fail. That is unpardonable, but he is too useful just now to sacrifice." In the present emergency, "we must use what tools we have."[24] Lincoln felt humiliated by the necessity of restoring McClellan, but he insisted that considerations merely personal to himself "must be sacrificed for the public good."[25] The president told Congressman William D. Kelley that reappointing Little Mac was "the greatest trial and most painful duty of his official life. Yet, situated as he was, it seemed to him to be his duty."[26]

Lincoln sought to comfort Pope, whom the cabinet viewed as a boastful liar unfit for high command. On September 3, he met with the general and "assured him of his entire satisfaction with his conduct; assured him that McClellan's command was only temporary; and gave him reason to expect that another army of active operations would be organized at once" for Pope to lead.[27] Although he thought of Pope "as brave, patriotic, and as having done his whole duty in every respect in Virginia," he nonetheless felt that the general must be sacrificed because the army was prejudiced against him.[28] A Dakota Sioux Indian uprising in Minnesota needed attention, and on September 6 Pope was sent to quell it. The exiled general called the president's treatment of him "dastardly & atrocious."[29]

Although Pope became the principal scapegoat for the defeat at Second Bull Run, sharp criticism was also directed at Lincoln and Stanton. The president tried to deflect it by stating "that he was 'under bonds' to let Halleck have his own way in everything in regard to the army."[30] While Stanton resumed his earlier status as a co-planner of the war effort after Second Bull Run, Old Brains "broke down—nerve and pluck all gone" and became "little more" than "a first-rate clerk."[31] Lincoln kept Halleck on as a technical adviser, a translator of presidential wishes into military parlance, a shield against criticism, and an administrator. In these roles he proved useful.

The Antietam Campaign

On September 3, Lee's army entered Maryland. For Lincoln, the vexing question of command arose once again: who should lead the Union forces pursuing Lee? Halleck declined the job, as did Burnside; by default, McClellan was chosen. On September 5, Old Brains and the president asked Little Mac to take charge of the army in the field. That same day, Lincoln observed that the Young Napoleon "is working like a beaver." Although "he can't fight himself," the president observed, "he excels in making others ready to fight."[32]

Restoring the soldiers' morale seemed vitally important to Lincoln, who told Welles that he "was shocked to find that of 140,000 whom we were paying for in Pope's army, only 60,000 could be found. McClellan brought away 93,000 from the Peninsula, but could not to-day count on over 45,000." The president believed "that some of our men permitted themselves to be captured in order that they might leave on parole, get discharged, and go home." Plaintively he asked, "Where there is such rottenness, is there not reason to fear for the country?"[33]

As he led the army into Maryland, McClellan wrote his wife that the "feeling of the Govt towards me is kind & trusting. I hope with God's blessing, to justify the great confidence they now repose in me, & will bury the past in oblivion."[34] Lincoln shared that hope, predicting that if the general did not win a victory, both of them "would be in a bad row of stumps."[35] But he was not sanguine. In early August, he ruefully told a group who criticized Little Mac that the general "*never em-*

braces his opportunities,—that's where the trouble is—he always puts off the hour for embracing his opportunities."[36] McClellan's leisurely progress in Maryland confirmed Lincoln's fears. He "can't go ahead—he can't strike a blow. He got to Rockville for instance on Sunday night [September 8], and in four days he advanced to Middlebrook, ten miles in pursuit of an invading enemy. This was rapid movement for him."[37] Lincoln seriously considered meeting with McClellan but was warned that it would be too risky. Characteristically overestimating the enemy's numbers, McClellan appealed for reinforcements. (In fact, the Army of the Potomac comprised 75,000 effective troops to Lee's 38,000.) Lincoln ordered Fitz John Porter's corps to join Little Mac. When Lee seemed to be retreating, Lincoln urged McClellan: "Please do not let him get off without being hurt."[38]

Alarm spread as the Confederates marched northward. When Pennsylvania governor Andrew G. Curtin appealed for 80,000 troops, Lincoln replied: "We have not to exceed eighty thousand disciplined troops, properly so called, this side of the mountains." The "best possible security for Pennsylvania is putting the strongest force possible into the enemies rear."[39] On September 15, Lincoln rejoiced to hear that the Army of the Potomac had the previous day beaten the enemy at South Mountain, though he could not know that Little Mac's dispatch announcing victory exaggerated its significance. The Rebels, McClellan had crowed, were retreating "in a perfect panic," and "Lee last night stated publicly that he must admit they had been shockingly whipped."[40] Lincoln sent congratulations: "God bless you, and all with you. Destroy the rebel army, if possible."[41] He told a friend, "I now consider it safe to say that Gen. McClellan has gained a great victory over the great rebel army in Maryland. He is now pursuing the flying foe."[42]

In fact, however, the Confederates were not flying but consolidating their scattered forces after capturing the 11,500-man Union garrison at Harpers Ferry on September 15. (Lincoln deplored this calamity, saying that McClellan "could and ought to have prevented the loss of Harper's Ferry, but was six days marching 40 miles, and it was surrendered.")[43] Little Mac, having fortuitously obtained a copy of Lee's orders on September 13 in a document known as the Lost Order, knew that the Confederate commander had divided his army. McClellan could have scored a smashing victory if he had acted swiftly to take advantage of that news, but his habitually slow movement permitted the enemy to regroup. Having won what he assumed was a major victory at South Mountain, he ignored the president's injunction to destroy the Army of Northern Virginia; instead he was content to let it recross the Potomac, which he mistakenly thought it was doing. He was startled to learn that the Rebels were in reality forming a line of battle near Antietam Creek. During the three and a half days following the discovery of the Lost Order, Lee's army had been in grave danger; now its components were reunited and ready to fight the Army of the Potomac. Little Mac had forfeited what he properly deemed the "opportunity of a lifetime."[44]

On September 17, the bloodiest single day's battle of the war was fought at Antietam, where the Army of the Potomac suffered 12,000 casualties and the Army of Northern Virginia, 14,000. The result was in effect a draw, though Lee abandoned the field. Lincoln believed that the Confederate army could be annihilated before it crossed the Potomac if only McClellan would act promptly. Little Mac committed only two-thirds of his men to battle; the remainder, reinforced by 12,000 freshly arrived troops, could have attacked effectively the following day, but the passive general allowed Lee to slip back into Virginia unharmed, much to the chagrin of the president.

The Greeley Letter

Well before the battle of Antietam, pressure on Lincoln to issue an emancipation edict had been building. The most dramatic and widely circulated appeal came from Horace Greeley, whose New York *Tribune* on August 20 published "The Prayer of Twenty Millions," an editorial scolding the president for dragging his feet on emancipation. Greeley demanded that Lincoln enforce the Confiscation Acts, ignore the counsels of "fossil politicians hailing from the Border States," stop deferring to slaveholders, adopt some consistent policy with regard to slavery, and employ runaway bondsmen as "scouts, guides, spies, cooks, teamsters, diggers and choppers."[45]

Lincoln responded swiftly with a public letter that soon became famous. He had been looking for an occasion to explain his thoughts about emancipation and thus smooth the way for his proclamation. Addressing the charge that he only *seemed* to have a policy dealing with slavery, the president tersely described the course he had been pursuing all along: "I would save the Union. I would save it the shortest way under the Constitution. The sooner the national authority can be restored; the nearer the Union will be 'the Union as it was.' If there be those who would not save the Union, unless they could at the same time *save* slavery, I do not agree with them. If there be those who would not save the Union unless they could at the same time *destroy* slavery, I do not agree with them. My paramount object in this struggle *is* to save the Union, and is *not* either to save or to destroy slavery. If I could save the Union without freeing *any* slave I would do it, and if I could save it by freeing *all* the slaves I would do it; and if I could save it by freeing some and leaving others alone I would also do that. What I do about slavery, and the colored race, I do because I believe it helps to save the Union; and what I forbear, I forbear because I do *not* believe it would help to save the Union. . . . I have here stated my purpose according to my view of *official* duty; and I intend no modification of my oft-expressed *personal* wish that all men every where could be free."[46]

In this final sentence, he made clear that he hated slavery. Still, he emphasized that as a president bound by an oath to uphold the Constitution, he could not ignore legal and political constraints.

Lincoln's unprecedented public letter caused a sensation. Sydney Howard Gay wrote him: "Your letter to Mr. Greeley has infused new hope among us at the North who are anxiously awaiting that movement on your part which they beleive [*sic*] will end the rebellion by removing its cause. I think the general impression is that as you are determined to save the Union tho' Slavery perish, you mean presently to announce that the destruction of Slavery is the price of our salvation."[47] There was good reason for such optimism. Lincoln told his friend Isaac N. Arnold "that the meaning of his letter to Mr. Greeley was this: that he was ready to declare emancipation when he was convinced that it could be made effective, and that the people were with him."[48]

Lincoln's letter has been misunderstood by those who view it as a definitive statement of his innermost feelings about the aims of the war. Some deplored its insensitivity to the moral significance of emancipation. In fact, the document was a political utterance designed to pave the way for the proclamation that he intended to issue as soon as the Union army won a victory. He knew full well that millions of Northerners as well as Border State residents would object to transforming the war into an abolitionist crusade; they were willing to fight to preserve the Union but not to free the slaves. As president, Lincoln had to make the mighty act of emancipation palatable to them. By assuring conservatives that emancipation was simply a *means* to preserve the Union, Lincoln hoped to minimize the inevitable White backlash. The letter to Greeley announced that Lincoln might free some slaves and leave others in bondage, which is just what his Emancipation Proclamation did.

Meeting with Black Leaders of Washington

In mid-August Lincoln gave another hint of future developments when he urged some leaders of Washington's Black community to immigrate to Panama. The president realized that he must at least appear to support colonization if he wanted the public, especially in the Border States and the Lower North, to accept an emancipation proclamation. The timing of the White House meeting, which represented the first occasion that Blacks were invited there to consult on public policy, suggests that Lincoln was trotting out colonization in order to help grease the skids for emancipation. If he had been truly enthusiastic about colonization, he might well have acted more swiftly on the $100,000 appropriation that Congress had voted months earlier to fund emigration of some of Washington's Blacks. (As noted earlier, the English journalist Frederick Milnes Edge interpreted that statute for readers of the London *Star*, saying that it "was adopted to silence the weak-nerved, whose name is legion, and to enable any of the slaves who see fit to migrate to more congenial climes.")[49]

Frederick Edge was not the only observer to suggest that Republican support for colonization was intended to prepare the public mind for emancipation. In late September 1862, a few days after the Emancipation Proclamation was announced, the Black abolitionist minister Henry McNeal Turner wrote: "Mr. Lincoln is not half such a stickler for colored expatriation as he has been pronounced." The president "loves freedom as well as any one on earth," and the colonization proposal he made was less a practical plan than a "strategetic [*sic*] move upon his part in contemplation of this emancipatory proclamation just delivered. He knows as well as any one, that it is a thing morally impracticable, ever to rid this country of colored people unless God does it miraculously, but it was [rather] a preparatory nucleus around which he intended to cluster the raid [rain?] of objections while the proclamation went forth." To assuage the fears of anxious voters, "the President stood in need of a place to *point to*," a place where Blacks could, with government support, resettle if they wished to do so.[50] Turner's analysis seems based on what the president told him.

Thus, when Lincoln in 1862 welcomed the Black delegation to the White House, along with a shorthand reporter to take down his words verbatim, he likely did so to silence the legions of "weak-nerved" voters who might object to the Emancipation Proclamation. His main audience was not those five African American guests but the millions of conservatives in the Lower North and Border Slave States. As historian David S. Reynolds observed, Lincoln's address to the deputation "was mainly a sop to conservatives," especially "of the Monty Blair stripe for whom colonization was *the* solution to slavery."[51] This is not to say that the president's endorsement of voluntary colonization was insincere or that he thought attempts to make African Americans first-class citizens were hopeless, but rather that he believed Negrophobia to be so deeply ingrained that at least some Blacks might reasonably agree with abolitionist John Russwurm, a Bowdoin College graduate and editor of the country's first African American newspaper, who considered it a "waste of words to talk of ever enjoying citizenship in this country; it is utterly impossible in the nature of things; all, therefore, who pant for this, must cast their eyes elsewhere."[52]

James Mitchell, a Methodist minister who had served as an agent for the American Colonization Society, set up the meeting. In 1862, Lincoln appointed him commissioner of emigration in the Interior Department. In July, he urged Lincoln to persuade Black Washingtonians to take the lead in colonization. Congressional pressure to do something about colonization also probably helped move Lincoln to summon the Black delegation that August. In April and July, Congress had appropriated a total of six hundred thousand dollars for colonizing Blacks.

The president's widely reported remarks to those men signaled his intention to emancipate at least some slaves. On August 14, he cordially shook the hands of each of the five Black leaders who gathered at the White House and explained that he wanted to consult with them about how the six hundred thousand dollars should be spent. In justifying colonization, he remarked: "You and we are different races. We have between us a broader difference than exists between almost any other two races. Whether it is right or wrong I need not discuss, but this physical difference is a great disadvantage to us both, as I think your race suffer very greatly, many of them by living among us, while ours suffer from your presence. In a word we suffer on each side. If this is admitted, it affords a reason at least why we should be separated." (The qualifier "whether it is right or wrong" implied that Lincoln thought discrimination against African Americans might well be wrong.)

Lincoln frankly acknowledged that American slaves "are suffering, in my judgment, the greatest wrong inflicted on any people" and "even when you cease to be slaves, you are yet far removed from being placed on an equality with the white race." He asked his guests to consider how best to deal with the harsh reality of slavery and discrimination, knowing "I cannot alter it if I would." (In so saying, he implied that he would alter the situation if he could.) Lincoln then added, "But for your race among us there could not be war, although many men engaged on either side do not care for you one way or the other. Nevertheless, I repeat, without the institution of Slavery and the colored race as a basis, the war could not have an existence." From these hard realities Lincoln concluded that it "is better for us both, therefore, to be separated." This was a blunt acknowledgment that the war was being fought by the South to protect slavery and White supremacy. If there had been no African Americans in the United States, the war would not have occurred.

Colonization, as he envisioned it, would not be compulsory. But how to persuade free Blacks to leave the country when they did not want to? Lincoln said that educated African Americans should take the lead in volunteering to be colonized, for they would serve as role models for slaves who might eventually be liberated. "If intelligent colored men, such as are before me, would move in this matter, much might be accomplished." To the practical question of just where American Blacks might move, Lincoln at first pointed to Africa. "The colony of Liberia has been in existence a long time." Another possible relocation site would be in the Chiriqui province of Panama, then part of Colombia (also known as New Grenada). That territory "is nearer to us than Liberia . . . and within seven days' run by steamers." Moreover, the mining of coal there "will afford an opportunity to the inhabitants for immediate employment till they get ready to settle permanently in their homes."

Lincoln warned the Black leaders that there was no guarantee that settlers would prosper in Chiriqui, but he expressed a keen desire to make sure that they would not become second-class citizens there. He pledged that he "would endeavor to have you made equals, and have the best assurance that you should be the equals of the best." Then he asked, "Could I get a hundred tolerably intelligent men, with their wives and children, to 'cut their own fodder,' so to speak? Can I have fifty? If I could find twenty-five able-bodied men, with a mixture of women and children, good things in the family relation, I think I could make a successful commencement. I want you to let me know whether this can be done or not."[53] The committee promised to consider Lincoln's request. Two days later its chairman, Edward M. Thomas, told the president that he had originally opposed colonization but had changed his mind and would like authorization to proselytize in New York, Boston, and Philadelphia on behalf of that scheme. Most Black leaders, however, were less enthusiastic. Frederick Douglass excoriated Lincoln for appearing "silly and ridiculous" by uttering remarks that revealed "his pride of race and blood, his contempt for negroes and his canting hypocrisy."[54] Hyperbolically, Douglass added that "the nation was never more completely in the hands of the Slave power."[55]

But some of Thomas's fellow Blacks, including well-known men like Henry Highland Garnet, Henry McNeal Turner, and Martin R. Delany, supported emigration, as did many rank-and-file Blacks. In late August, when Kansas senator Samuel Pomeroy, at Lincoln's behest, announced that he was organizing transportation to Chiriqui for African Americans who wished to emigrate, around four thousand quickly signed up. Of those, the senator chose five hundred to make the initial voyage, scheduled to depart in early October. (Pomeroy estimated that the total number of applicants eventually reached fourteen thousand.) Among them were two of Frederick Douglass's three sons, much to their father's chagrin. Douglass wrote Pomeroy: "To see my children usefully and happily settled in this, the land of their birth and ancestors, has been the hope and ambition of my manhood," but forces too powerful for him to overcome had persuaded his sons to join the colonization movement that he had so long and so fiercely denounced.[56] It was striking that emigration appealed to those sons, when their father was so vehemently opposed to it. They evidently did not share his view that Lincoln's appeal proved that he was "quite a genuine representative of American prejudice and negro hatred."[57]

Lincoln soon abandoned the Chiriqui proposal because it was tainted with corruption and because Central American governments objected. Seward wished to maintain good relations with that region, and in early October, Lincoln accepted his advice to shelve the project. Thus the Chiriqui scheme came to nothing.

Action Taken to Implement Colonization Plans

Something did come of a plan that Lincoln endorsed on December 31. Haitian authorities had long been encouraging Black emigration from the United States. To expedite matters, James Redpath, a radical abolitionist and devotee of John Brown, was appointed "general agent of emigration to Haiti." In 1861, he persuaded more than a thousand African Americans to settle in that Caribbean nation. Frederick Douglass's newspaper praised Redpath's efforts. Helping him were several Black recruiting agents, among them Douglass's assistant editor, William J. Watkins, the novelist William Wells Brown, the eminent divine Henry Highland Garnet, James Theodore Holly, and H. Ford Douglas. In October 1862, one Bernard Kock submitted a proposal to colonize the virtually uninhabited Cow Island (Ile à Vache) off the Haitian coast. Although Attorney General Bates rightly considered Kock "an arrant humbug" and a "Charleston adventurer," the president on New Year's Eve approved a contract offering him $250,000 to take five thousand African Americans to the island that he claimed he had leased from the Haitian government.[58]

Preoccupied with other matters that memorable New Year's Eve, Lincoln failed to note that Kock offered no reliable security to guarantee that he would fulfill his end of the bargain, nor did he provide evidence that the Haitian government had approved his scheme. Moreover, no one in the administration knew much about the self-styled "governor of Cow Island." When Kock asked the secretary of state to affix the great seal of the United States to the contract, the skeptical Seward refused, effectively scuttling the plan. In April 1863, the contract was cancelled.

The Cow Island scheme might have died aborning had it not been for Lincoln's humanitarian concern for fugitive slaves suffering in squalid, disease-ridden "contraband camps." The project was kept alive by New York capitalists, including Paul S. Forbes and Charles K. Tuckerman, who had advanced Kock money that was used to prepare the expedition. The new contract called for Tuckerman and Forbes to convey 500 American Blacks to Cow Island at fifty dollars per person. There they were to be given houses, land, education, and medical care, all under the supervision of Kock. A ship took 453 volunteers to that desolate spot, where nothing had been provided for them and where disease killed off many. The demoralized survivors, badly mistreated by Kock, longed to return to the United States. After an investigation revealed their plight, Kock was dismissed. In February 1864, Lincoln sent a transport to repatriate the 368 surviving emigrants, who were in wretched condition. Months later Congress repealed the laws appropriating money for colonization.

Lincoln was partly to blame for this fiasco, for his administration had been careless in negotiating the contract, then remiss in supervising its implementation.

The president's failure to examine closely the Cow Island contract stands in sharp contrast with the scrutiny he gave the Chiriqui contract a few months earlier. His motive seems clearly to have been a humanitarian desire to relive the suffering of Blacks in contraband camps.

Complicating the president's life in the summer of 1862 was a new patronage scramble created by the Internal Revenue Law, due to go into operation on September 1. The statute established for the first time in American history an income tax, which necessitated the appointment of many assessors and collectors. Candidates for these posts helped swell the flood of visitors to the White House.

Warnings of Backlash

As Lincoln struggled with colonization schemes and patronage distribution, he was cautioned about the backlash that emancipation would stir. Many warnings came from Border States and areas of the Confederacy now controlled by the Union. Most vocal in their opposition were some Louisiana conservative Unionists, to whom Lincoln explained that it was "a military necessity to have men and money; and we can get neither, in sufficient numbers, or amounts, if we keep from, or drive from, our lines, slaves coming to them." Lincoln refused to smooth "the rough angles of the war." The fighting would end only when the Rebels surrendered, and to achieve that end, stern measures must be taken. With some sarcasm, he asked: "What would you do in my position? Would you drop the war where it is? . . . Would you deal lighter blows rather than heavier ones? Would you give up the contest, leaving any available means unapplied?" He closed with an eloquent disclaimer: "I am in no boastful mood. I shall not do *more* than I can, and I shall do *all* I can to save the government, which is my sworn duty as well as my personal inclination. I shall do nothing in malice. What I deal with is too vast for malicious dealing."[59]

From the opposite end of the ideological spectrum, Radicals dogged Lincoln's heels. On July 4, when Charles Sumner urged that Independence Day be reconsecrated by issuing an emancipation decree, the president said it was "too big a lick," arguing that "half the army would lay down its arms, if emancipation were declared," and that Kentucky, Missouri, and Maryland "would rise."[60] The following month, when Sumner once more lobbied him on behalf of emancipation, Lincoln counseled patience: "Wait—time is essential."[61]

With emancipationists, Lincoln frequently played devil's advocate. The best-publicized episode of this sort occurred on September 13, when a delegation of clergy from Chicago presented a memorial calling on him to liberate the slaves. He told his visitors that he had long given the subject much thought and had "no objections against it on legal or constitutional grounds; for, as commander-in-chief of the army and navy, in time of war, I suppose I have a right to take any measure which may best subdue the enemy. Nor do I urge objections of a moral nature, in view of possible consequences of insurrection and massacre at the South. I view the matter as a practical war measure, to be decided upon according to the advantages or disadvantages it may offer to the suppression of the rebellion." The president asked, "What *good* would a proclamation of emancipation from me do, especially as we are now situated? I do not want to issue a document that the whole world will see must necessarily be inoperative, like the Pope's bull against the comet!"

Lincoln insisted that he lacked the power to free slaves in territory controlled by Confederates. "Would *my word* free the slaves," asked he, "when I cannot even enforce the Constitution in the rebel States?" Moreover, there was no evidence that the Second Confiscation Act "has caused a single slave to come over to us." Even if slaves could be induced to flee to Union lines, Lincoln was perplexed to know "*what should we do with them*?" The Blacks might, at least in theory, be accepted into the Union army, but Lincoln worried that they would be captured and re-enslaved. He agreed with his callers that "slavery is the root of the rebellion." He acknowledged "that emancipation would help us in Europe, and convince them that we are incited by something more than ambition." As for domestic opinion, emancipation "would help *somewhat* at the North, though not so much, I fear, as you and those you represent imagine." The greatest practical advantage to be gained by freeing the slaves was that it would undermine the Confederate war effort, for "unquestionably it would weaken the rebels by drawing off their laborers, which is of great importance." But that was offset by a grave disadvantage: soldiers from the Border States might "go over to the rebels."

Lincoln assured his callers that his questions merely "indicate the difficulties that have thus far prevented my action in some such way as you desire. I have not decided against a proclamation of liberty to the slaves, but hold the matter under advisement. And I can assure you that the subject is on my mind, by day and night, more than any other. Whatever shall appear to be God's will I will do."[62] At the close of the interview, he added that "there is a question of expediency as to time, should such a proclamation be issued. Matters look dark just now. I fear that a proclamation on the heels of defeat would be interpreted as a cry of despair. It would come better, if at all, immediately after a victory."[63]

Emancipation Proclamation Announced

The despair of many abolitionists turned to joy in September when Lincoln seized upon the result of Antietam and announced his intention to issue an emancipation proclamation. The battle took place on Wednesday, September 17, and three days passed before he felt sure that it could be considered a Union victory. That weekend he tinkered with the proclamation, which he presented to his cabinet on Monday the twenty-second. According to Welles, he said that "he had made a vow, a covenant, that if God gave us the victory in the approaching battle, he would consider it an indication of Divine will, and that it was his duty to move forward in the cause of emancipation.... God had decided this question in favor of the slaves. He was satisfied it was right, was confirmed and strengthened in his action by the vow and the results."[64]

After reading his draft, Lincoln asked for suggestions about the form but not the content of the proclamation, a four-page document, much longer than the one he had read to the cabinet two months earlier. That early version called for voluntary colonization of freedpeople, endorsed his gradual emancipation plan, and exempted both the Border States and some (but not all) areas occupied by the Union army. As Montgomery Blair remembered, the president said that "he had power to issue the proclamation only in virtue of his power to strike at the rebellion, and he could not include places within our own lines, because the reason upon which the power depended did not apply to them, and he could not include such places" because he personally opposed slavery.[65] Confederate slaveholders would have one hundred days to cease rebelling; if they would lay down their arms, they could keep their slaves. If they did not, then as of New Year's Day those slaves "shall be then, thenceforward, and forever free." Wherever the Union army penetrated, it would rigorously enforce the Proclamation.

A striking new feature of the Proclamation was its seeming hint that the administration would aid slave insurrections: "The executive government of the United States, including the military and naval authority thereof, will recognize the freedom of such persons [freed slaves], and will do no act or acts to repress such persons, or any of them, in any efforts they may make for their actual freedom." Lincoln probably meant that the Union army would not return runaways to bondage, though many would interpret his words to mean that the North would incite slave uprisings. Also noteworthy was the Proclamation's pledge that "all citizens of the United States who shall have remained loyal thereto throughout the rebellion, shall... be compensated for all losses by acts of the United States, including the loss of slaves." He was promising to compensate loyal slaveholders without congressional authorization!

After Lincoln finished reading the text, Seward suggested that it would be better to promise to "recognize *and maintain* the freedom" of the slaves rather than merely to "recognize" it. The secretary of state also objected that the document as written implied that emancipation would only be valid as long as Lincoln remained president. Lincoln took Seward's advice, adding "and maintain" and deleting the reference to "continuance in office of the present incumbent."

Chase expressed some reservations about the Proclamation, which "was going a step further than he had ever proposed," but he nevertheless pledged to "take it just as it is written, and to stand by it with all my heart." Stanton and Welles voiced strong approval, but Bates and Blair objected to the document's timing. The postmaster general, a strong emancipationist, feared that the Border States might be driven to secede. Lincoln acknowledged the validity of such criticism but replied that "the difficulty was as great not to act as to act. . . . For months he had labored to get those [Border] States to move in this matter," but "his labors were in vain." Blair also protested that the Proclamation put into the hands of Northern Democrats "a club to be used against us." Lincoln said that argument "had not much weight with him," for "their clubs would be used against us take what course we might."[66]

The language of the Proclamation disappointed some Radicals, including Frederick Douglass, who lamented that its words "touched neither justice nor mercy. Had there been one expression of sound moral feeling against Slavery, one word of regret and shame that this accursed system had remained so long the disgrace and scandal of the Republic, one word of satisfaction in the hope of burying slavery and the rebellion in one common grave, a thrill of joy would have run around the world."[67] Lincoln, however, carefully omitted any moral appeal in order to avoid antagonizing conservative opinion, especially in the Lower North and the Border States. He also wished to make sure that slaves liberated under the Proclamation had a sound legal basis to protect their freedom in court if necessary.

Months later, when the final Emancipation Proclamation was about to be issued, Lincoln told a journalist that he was "strongly pressed" to justify it "upon high moral grounds, and to introduce into the instrument unequivocal language testifying to the negroes' right to freedom upon the precise principles expounded by the Emancipationists of both Old and New-England." The president resisted this advice, for "policy requires that the Proclamation be issued as a war measure, and not a measure of morality; and that Law and Justice require that the slaves should be enabled to plead the Proclamation hereafter if necessary to establish judicially their title to freedom. They can do this, the President says, on a proclamation proceeding as a war measure from the Commander-in-Chief of the Army, but not on one issuing from the bosom of philanthropy."[68]

Lincoln gracefully expressed gratitude to a group of serenaders who called at the Executive Mansion on September 24. Whitelaw Reid reported that the crowd, which was "honoring the great act that shall make Abraham Lincoln immortal among men," cheered repeatedly as it listened to the leader whom "the people trust." When the cheering subsided, Lincoln said in a tone not triumphant or even confident that "what I did, I did after very full deliberation, and under a very heavy and solemn sense of responsibility." He added, "I can only trust in God I have made no mistake. . . . It is now for the country and the world to pass judgment on it, and, maybe, take action upon it."[69] When John Hay tried to speak to the president about hostile commentators, Lincoln cut him off, saying that "he had studied that matter so long that he knew more about it than they did."[70]

In the army, reaction to the Proclamation was mixed. Some officers and men disapproved emphatically. McClellan had intended to submit to the president a letter protesting against the Emancipation Proclamation "and saying that the Army would never sustain" it, but he had decided not to do so when General William F. Smith warned that Little Mac "would neither sustain himself with the army nor the country and that it would only array him in opposition" to the government "and result in disaster to him."[71] So McClellan belatedly issued a general order coolly hinting that the administration should be voted out of office. It counseled against criticism of the Proclamation and stated that the "remedy for political errors, if any are committed, is to be found only in the action of the people at the polls."[72] But most of the army supported the Proclamation. A partisan Democrat who as a medical commissioner visited the Peninsula reported that "with very few exceptions the *whole army* is in favor of the most stringent prosecution of the war, using every means in our power to stifle the rebellion, and it regards emancipation as one of our most potent weapons."[73]

Public response to emancipation did not encourage Lincoln. On September 28, he told his vice president that "while I hope something from the proclamation, my expectations are not as sanguine as are those of some friends. The time for its effect southward has not come; but northward the effect should be instantaneous. It is six days old, and while commendation in newspapers and by distinguished individuals is all that a vain man could wish, the stocks have declined, and troops come forward more slowly than ever. This, looked soberly in the face, is not very satisfactory. We have fewer troops in the field at the end of six days than we had at the beginning—the attrition among the old outnumbering the addition by the new. The North responds to the proclamation sufficiently in breath; but breath alone kills no rebels."[74]

Many more rebels would have to be killed before *de jure* emancipation became *de facto* emancipation.

29.

"The Great Event of the Nineteenth Century"

The Emancipation Proclamation (September–December 1862)

The Emancipation Proclamation, which some commentators dismissed as a political ploy to enhance Republican electoral prospects, in fact contributed to the party's severe losses in the fall of 1862. In October, opponents of the administration swept elections in Ohio, Indiana, and Pennsylvania and picked up governorships in New York and New Jersey. David Davis called the results "disastrous in the extreme" and remarked that the Emancipation Proclamation "has not worked the wonder that was anticipated."[1] The Democrats relentlessly employed their traditional appeal to what the New York *Tribune* aptly called "that cruel and ungenerous prejudice against color which still remains to disgrace our civilization."[2] Their race-baiting was especially virulent in Ohio and Indiana, which (like Pennsylvania) held elections in October. Democratic editors urged Buckeyes to vote for their party's candidates if they did "not desire their place occupied by negroes."[3] Playing on voters' fear that emancipated slaves might swarm across the Ohio River, Democrats adopted as their slogan "The Constitution as it is, the Union as it was, and the negroes where they are." In Ohio, Democrats captured fourteen House seats, the Republicans five; in Indiana, the Democrats won seven of the eleven House contests and gained a majority of the state legislature. The parties divided the Pennsylvania House seats evenly. Samuel Medary, editor of *The Crisis* in Columbus, spoke for many Ohio Democrats when he rejoiced that "free press and a white man's government is [*sic*] fully established by this vote."[4]

The defeats astounded Lincoln, who had not anticipated such a drubbing. The Democrats won the New York and New Jersey governorships and captured a majority of legislative seats in New Jersey and Illinois. The most telling result was New York gubernatorial candidate Horatio Seymour's eleven-thousand-vote triumph, which was widely regarded as a repudiation of "Old Lincompoop."[5] The president had good reason to lament the disastrous result in Illinois. Democrats elected their state ticket by fourteen thousand votes; their congressional candidates won nine of the fourteen seats; and they gained control of the legislature, thus assuring that Orville H. Browning would be ousted from the U.S. Senate. Most painful for Lincoln was the defeat of his dear friend Leonard Swett in a congressional race against John Todd Stuart. A War Department order issued in September resettling some newly liberated slaves in Illinois proved to be a blunder. It became the most significant issue in the campaign and helped swell the Democrats' vote. One consolation for Lincoln was the defeat of a proposed new Illinois constitution, which would have severely crippled the war effort. He also derived solace from the results in Missouri, where emancipationists gained a majority of the state's congressional seats. Providing further comfort was news that Republicans had retained control of the U.S. House of Representatives.

Lincoln had been warned that backlash against the Emancipation Proclamation would hurt the Republicans at the polls, but that did not deter him from announcing it a scant three weeks before crucial elections in Ohio, Indiana, and Pennsylvania. His willingness to run a grave political risk indicated the depth of his commitment to Black freedom. In light of the Republicans' dismal showing at the polls, it was widely speculated that Lincoln might renege on his commitment to issue the Proclamation. But he declared "that he would rather die than take back a word of the Proclamation of Freedom."[6] Alluding to the slaves, he said: "My word is out to these people, and I can't take it back."[7]

Firing McClellan

In addition to backlash against the Emancipation Proclamation, the absence of military success hurt the Republicans at the polls. After Antietam, McClellan dawdled in his usual fashion, allowing the Confederates to escape across the Potomac. When Little Mac boasted that he had achieved a great victory by driving the enemy from Union soil, the "hearts of 10 million people sank within them," according to Lincoln.[8] No one's heart sank deeper than his own. In early October, he visited the Army of the Potomac, hoping to goad it into action.

During his three days in Maryland, Lincoln toured hospitals, including one that housed some Confederates. To them he remarked "that if they had no objection he would be pleased to take them by the hand" and that "the solemn obligations which we owe to our country and posterity compel the prosecution of this war, and it followed that many were our enemies through uncontrollable circumstances, and he bore them no malice, and could take them by the hand with sympathy and good feeling." The Confederates, after a brief silence, "came forward, and each silently but fervently shook the hand of the President."[9] There was not a dry eye in the hospital. Lincoln inspected the troops, who were pleased to have him in their midst. One observed, "It was like an electric shock. It flew from elbow to elbow;

and, with one loud cheer which made the air ring, the suppressed feeling gave vent, conveying to the good President that his smile had gone home, and found a ready response."[10]

During his stay, Lincoln spoke often with McClellan, who reported that the president "was very kind personally—told me he was convinced I was the best general in the country. . . . I really think he does feel very kindly towards me personally."[11] Though pleasant in manner, Lincoln was stern in substance, asking tough questions and offering blunt criticism. He was puzzled to see most of the new recruits in Frederick, twenty miles from the veteran army units. Frankly, Lincoln told the general "that he w[oul]d be a ruined man if he did not move forward, move rapidly & effectively."[12] He instructed McClellan to launch an advance within two weeks. Unmoved by Lincoln's criticism, the general wrote his wife about the presidential entourage: "These people don't know what an army requires & therefore act stupidly."[13]

Although Lincoln "expressed himself eminently satisfied with the discipline and appearance of the troops," he was dismayed to learn that they numbered only

Detail of a photo by Alexander Gardner of the president and General George B. McClellan with some members of his staff on October 3, 1862. Lincoln then visited the Army of the Potomac in Maryland, near the site of the recent battle of Antietam, in an effort to urge it into action. *From left*, Colonel Alexander S. Webb, chief of staff, Fifth Corps; General McClellan; Scout Adams; Dr. Jonathan Letterman, army medical director; and an unidentified person. Behind the president stands General Henry J. Hunt, McClellan's chief of artillery. Library of Congress.

93,000, though 180,000 were on the muster rolls.[14] He cited similar figures to Samuel F. P. Du Pont as he bemoaned the "melting away" of the army. "These are the facts," he told the admiral; "how they are to be cured *I don't know*."[15] One way to deal with the problem was to crack down on deserters and bounty jumpers. After Commanding General Halleck and Secretary of War Stanton showed the president long lists of absentees, he "sternly pledged himself . . . to pursue the most rigorous policy with these offenders," including "executions, dismissals, ball-and-chain labor for the whole term of their enlistment, and other of the severest penalties."[16]

Shortly after his return to Washington on October 4, Lincoln had Halleck order McClellan to "cross the Potomac and give battle to the enemy or drive him south. Your army must move now while the roads are good."[17] But to no avail. Three days later, Old Brains lamented that "I cannot persuade him to advance an inch."[18] For the next month, Little Mac deluged Washington authorities with justifications for staying put. In response to McClellan's explanation that his horses were exhausted, Lincoln sent a tart reply: "I have just received your dispatch about sore tongued and fatiegued [*sic*] horses. Will you pardon me for asking what the horses of your army have done since the battle of Antietam that fatigue anything?"[19] While McClellan dithered, eighteen hundred Confederate cavalry under Jeb Stuart once again rode a circle around the Army of the Potomac. John G. Nicolay observed that Stuart's joyride was "a little thing, accomplishing not much actual harm, and yet infinitely vexatious and mischievous. The President has well-nigh lost his temper over it."[20]

The Congress, the cabinet, and the public shared Lincoln's impatience with McClellan. As the general moved south at a leisurely pace, Lee swiftly retreated toward Richmond. On November 4, the Confederates were positioned athwart the Union army's line of advance. Finally exasperated beyond endurance, Lincoln fired the Young Napoleon. He had been tempted to do so earlier but told a friend that "there was a question about the effect of [McClellan's] removal *before* the election."[21] He said he did not want "to estrange the affections of the Democratic party" or to make the general a martyr.[22] McClellan's dismissal was in part a response to the elections. Lincoln interpreted the negative results as the voters' demand for a more aggressive pursuit of victory. On November 13 he told Senator Zachariah Chandler of Michigan that the "war shall henceforth be prosecuted with tremendous energy."[23]

The McClellan of the West

McClellan was not the only important general lacking boldness; like the Young Napoleon, Don Carlos Buell had case of the "slows" and favored a "soft war" policy. He thought like a hidebound adjutant general rather than an aggressive field commander. When Confederates under Braxton Bragg invaded Kentucky in the summer of 1862, Buell abandoned his Chattanooga campaign in order to defend Louisville and Cincinnati. Panicky Ohio Republicans implored Lincoln to send reinforcements to protect the Queen City. "I have no regiments to put there. The fact is I do not carry any regiments in my trousers pocket," the president snapped.[24]

Buell had come within ten miles of Bragg's army at Munfordsville, Kentucky, but failed to attack. Goaded by the president, he stepped up his pursuit of Bragg and fought him at Perryville on October 8. When the Rebels withdrew into Tennessee, Buell failed to chase them vigorously and instead returned to Nashville. He could not follow the Confederates, he said, because they had entered an area where it would be difficult to supply his army. Remarking on Buell's inertia, Nicolay sarcastically observed that it "is rather a good thing to be a Major General and in command of a Department. One can take things so leisurely!"[25]

The exasperated president, always eager to aid the Unionists of eastern Tennessee, instructed Halleck to order Buell to move against Chattanooga once again. When Buell contended that his troops were not as highly motivated as the enemy's, the president on October 24 replaced him with hard-drinking, hot-tempered, excitable William S. "Old Rosy" Rosecrans of Ohio, who had recently shown vigor in battles at Iuka and Corinth, Mississippi. The appointment of Rosecrans came too late to affect the fall elections. After the November votes were in, the president expressed regret that he had not replaced Buell earlier. When Old Rosy tarried in Nashville, the president lost patience with him. Halleck informed the general that Lincoln was "greatly dissatisfied" and "has repeatedly told me time and again that there were imperative reasons why the enemy should be driven across the Tennessee River at the earliest possible moment."[26] The general in chief warned Rosecrans that twice already "I have been asked to designate someone else to command your army. If you remain one more week at Nashville, I cannot prevent your removal. . . . The Government demands action."[27] But the headstrong, argumentative Rosecrans stayed put until December 26, when he finally expelled Braxton Bragg's army from central Tennessee.

Lincoln also appointed another general to an important command in the West: John A. McClernand, an old political opponent from Illinois. In September, McClernand had proposed to recruit an army with which he would capture Vicksburg and thus seize control of the Mississippi River. Eager to have prominent Democrats support the war and raise troops, especially in his own state, Lincoln gave the scheme his blessing, for he believed that the Mississippi was "the backbone of the Rebellion" and "the key to the whole situation."[28] To facilitate that campaign, the president decided to replace Benjamin F. Butler, who had been in charge at New Orleans since its capture in April.

To take Butler's place, Lincoln chose Nathaniel P. Banks, who was informed by Halleck that the president "regards the opening of the Mississippi river as the first and most important of all our military & naval operations, and it is hoped that you will not lose a moment in accomplishing it."[29] Controlling the "Father of Waters," said the general in chief, "is worth to us forty Richmonds."[30] Confederate fortresses at Vicksburg, Mississippi, and Port Hudson, Louisiana, were the main obstacles to securing the Mississippi. Lincoln envisioned a three-pronged campaign: from New Orleans, Banks would move north toward Port Hudson; McClernand would move south toward Vicksburg; and a fleet of gunboats under Admiral David Dixon Porter would attack Confederate strongholds along the river. Where Grant would fit in was unclear. The failure of Lincoln and Stanton to consult with Halleck and Grant about this campaign laid the groundwork for later confusion; it was unclear just who would be in overall charge.

Explaining Electoral Setbacks

The voters, as the Cincinnati *Gazette* put it, "are depressed by the interminable nature of this war, as so far conducted, and by the rapid exhaustion of the national resources without progress."[31] Other factors aside from military stalemate contributed to the Republican reverses at the polls that fall, most notably the president's September 24 proclamation suspending the privilege of the writ of habeas corpus nationwide, thus empowering the military to arrest civilians who discouraged enlistments, resisted the militia draft, or were "guilty of any disloyal practice." Along with the Emancipation Proclamation, that suspension provided the Democrats with their most effective ammunition. Even some Republicans objected to the suspension; Henry Winter Davis said the administration was instituting "court martial despotism."[32]

Carl Schurz scolded the president, alleging that Democratic generals, unenthusiastic about the war's aims, had failed to deliver victories. "Let us be commanded by generals whose heart is in the war, and only by such," Schurz urged.[33] In reply, the president explained that he had distributed military patronage to Democrats because "very few of our friends had a military education or were of the profession of arms. . . . I received recommendations from the republican delegations in congress, and I believe every one of them recommended a majority of democrats."[34] When Schurz replied with a long, self-righteous lecture, Lincoln sent a crushing rebuke: "I certainly know that if the war fails, the administration fails, and that I *will* be blamed for it, whether I deserve it or not. And I ought to be blamed, if I could do better. You think I could do better; therefore you blame me already. I think I could not do better; therefore I blame you for blaming me. I understand you *now* to be willing to accept the help of men, who are not republicans, provided they have 'heart in it.' Agreed. I want no others. But who is to be the judge of hearts, or of 'heart in it'? If I must discard my own judgment, and take yours, I must also take that of others; and by the time I should reject all I should be advised to reject, I should have none left, republicans, or others—not even yourself. For, be assured, my dear sir, there are men who have 'heart in it' that think you are performing your part as poorly as you think I am performing mine."[35]

At the president's invitation, Schurz called at the White House to discuss matters further. "Now tell me, young man, whether you really think that I am as poor a fellow as you have made me out in your letter!" Lincoln exclaimed. After a friendly explanation of his policies, the president slapped Schurz's knee, laughed, and asked: "Didn't I give it to you hard in my letter? Didn't I? But it didn't hurt, did it? I did not mean to, and therefore I wanted you to come so quickly." He suggested that the general, whom Lincoln regarded as a kind of surrogate son, continue writing him. The brash Teuton often did so.[36]

The absence of many supporters serving in the military hurt the Republicans, as Lincoln argued. A defeated Ohio state legislator told the president that in his district 80 percent "of the forces sent into the field are from the Union ranks. . . . We could not induce the opposition to enlist, except an occasional one to keep up an appearance of Loyalty."[37] Ohio and other states that did not allow troops to vote in the field went Democratic; states like Iowa, which did allow such voting, went Republican. If all soldiers had voted and had cast their ballots in the same fashion that eligible soldiers did, Republicans would have won majorities in every Northern state save New Jersey.

In December, when the Thirty-seventh Congress reconvened for its lame-duck session, the mood was sour. In his annual message, Lincoln once again urged the legislators to adopt gradual, compensated emancipation. "Without slavery the rebellion could never have existed," he asserted; "without slavery it could not continue." Instead of passing statutes like the Confiscation Acts, which courts could overrule, he suggested that constitutional amendments be enacted providing federal aid to states abolishing slavery by 1900; guaranteeing freedom to slaves already liberated by the war, with compensation paid to loyal slave owners; and funding colonization efforts. In justifying compensation, he remarked that Northerners as well as Southerners were responsible for the introduction and continuance of slavery.

In an inspired conclusion, Lincoln supplied the soaring rhetoric so conspicuously absent from the legalistic Emancipation Proclamation: "The dogmas of the quiet past, are inadequate to the stormy present. The occasion is piled high with difficulty, and we must rise to the occasion. As our case is new, so we must think and act anew. We must disenthrall ourselves, and then we shall save our country.

Fellow citizens, *we* cannot escape history. We of this Congress and this administration, will be remembered in spite of ourselves. No personal significance, or insignificance, can spare one or another of us. The fiery trial through which we pass, will light us down, in honor or dishonor, to the latest generation. We *say* we are for the Union. The world will not forget that we say this. We know how to save the Union. The world knows we do know how to save it. We—even *we here*—hold the power, and bear the responsibility. In *giving* freedom to the *slave*, we *assure* freedom to the *free*—honorable alike in what we give, and what we preserve. We shall nobly save, or meanly lose, the last best hope of earth."[38]

It is not entirely clear why Lincoln once again trotted out his compensated-emancipation scheme. The electoral triumph by Missouri Republicans who supported gradual, compensated emancipation led the president to hope that the plan might be practicable there. If Missouri, Maryland, and Kentucky did free their slaves with financial help from Congress, backlash against emancipation would be reduced. If they did not, Lincoln at least wanted to appear magnanimous by demonstrating his willingness to go to great lengths in helping them avoid the shock of sudden, uncompensated emancipation. He had adopted a similar strategy during the secession crisis; he would later do so in dealing with Confederate peace feelers.

When a bill came before Congress to compensate Missouri slave owners, Lincoln appealed to that state's senators: "You and I must die but it will be enough for us to have done in our lives if we make Missouri free."[39] Each house of Congress passed a bill, but fierce resistance by Border State delegations blocked reconciliation of the two statutes, and the plan died with the expiration of the Thirty-seventh Congress in March. Lincoln was bitterly disappointed. In exasperation he declared that the "dissensions between Union men in Missouri are due solely to a factious spirit which is exceedingly reprehensible. The two parties ought to have their heads knocked together. Either would rather see the defeat of their adversary than that of Jefferson Davis."[40]

Burnside Replaces McClellan

Finding a replacement for McClellan proved a challenge. Lincoln did not consider appointing Halleck, for he thought Old Brains "would be an indifferent general in the field; that he shrank from responsibility in his present position; that he is a moral coward, worth but little except as a critic, though intelligent and educated."[41] So he turned once again to Ambrose E. Burnside, who had twice declined the job. This time the president insisted, and the personable, modest, 38-year-old corps commander from Rhode Island accepted after protesting that he "was not competent to command such a large army."[42] He rightly feared that if he turned it down yet again, Joseph Hooker, whom he despised, would be appointed. Burnside was chosen because he was next in rank behind McClellan and because none of the other corps commanders (with the possible exception of Hooker) seemed more capable. Moreover, he was a member of the pro-McClellan faction of the army, and the president felt constrained to choose someone from that circle.

Lincoln hoped the army would fight once again before cold weather made an offensive impracticable. Burnside promptly submitted a plan calling for an assault on Richmond via Fredericksburg. He would march the army to Falmouth, opposite Fredericksburg, and cross the Rappahannock River on pontoon bridges. On November 14, the president approved this scheme. Burnside moved quickly, but when his army arrived at Falmouth on November 17, it found no pontoons. Halleck and his subordinates had fumbled the assignment to deliver those essential items; during the fateful week that passed before they arrived, Lee occupied Fredericksburg.

Alarmed by the delay, Lincoln visited Falmouth and on November 26–27 conferred at length with Burnside, who said that "he could take into battle now any day, about, one hundred and ten thousand men, that his army is in good spirit, good condition, good moral[e], and that in all respects he is satisfied with officers and men; that he does not want more men with him, because he could not handle them to advantage; that he thinks he can cross the river in [the] face of the enemy and drive him away, but that, to use his own expression, it is somewhat risky."[43] The president suggested that instead of a frontal assault against Fredericksburg, the army wait till a twenty-five-thousand-man column could be assembled on the south bank of the Rappahannock far downstream from Fredericksburg; at the same time, a force of similar size would gather on the Pamunkey to launch a simultaneous assault in coordination with Burnside and thus drive Lee from Fredericksburg and prevent him from falling back to the Richmond entrenchments. Burnside argued that Lincoln's plan, though sound in principle, would postpone the operation too long. When Halleck concurred, the president shelved his scheme.

Meanwhile the Confederates dug into exceptionally strong positions behind Fredericksburg. Foul weather hindered Burnside's preparations for assault, but finally, on December 11, some of his men managed to lay down pontoons, cross the river, and drive the enemy from the town. Upon learning of this accomplishment, Lincoln rejoiced. "The rebellion is now virtually at an end," he exulted, predicting that Richmond would fall by year's end.[44] Two days later the president's elation turned to despair as the army stormed the heights overlooking the town and sustained a crushing defeat, taking more than twelve thousand casualties, over twice as many as the Confederates suffered.

While the battle raged, Lincoln visited the War Department and anxiously read telegrams from the front, which were quite vague. When General Herman Haupt arrived from Falmouth, the president eagerly quizzed him about the progress of the fighting. Once he understood the peril confronting Burnside, the president went to Halleck's residence and instructed him to command the general to withdraw across the Rappahannock. "I will do no such thing," the general in chief replied. "If such orders are issued, you must take the responsibility of issuing them yourself. I hold that an officer in command of an army in the field ought to be more familiar with the details of the situation than parties at a distance and should be allowed to exercise his own discretion." When Haupt predicted that Burnside would soon be able to retreat unmolested, the president sighed deeply and told him: "What you say gives me a great many grains of comfort."[45] After this interview, Haupt wrote his wife: "I pity the President very much. He is an honest and good man but never was poor mortal more harassed."[46]

Back at the White House, Lincoln received another eyewitness account of the slaughter from journalist Henry Villard, who described the grim battlefield and suggested that Burnside retreat. "I hope it is not so bad as all that," Lincoln sighed.[47] But it was, and so the president despaired. "I wonder if the damned in hell suffer less than I do," he said plaintively.[48] Similarly he declared that "if there is a worse place than hell I am in it."[49] When Pennsylvania governor Andrew G. Curtin depicted to him the carnage at Fredericksburg, Lincoln, his face "darkened with pain," "moaned and groaned in anguish," "showed great agony of spirit," and "walked the floor, wringing his hands and uttering exclamations of grief," repeatedly asking: "What has God put me in this place for?"[50] Curtin led a delegation of Pennsylvanians who warned Lincoln that unless there was a shake-up in the cabinet, "the people in forty days would *have his head*."[51]

Lincoln told a congressman that he would rather be a soldier in the ranks than president: "There is not a man in the army with whom I would not willingly change places."[52] He interrupted another congressman, freshly returned from Fredericksburg, who was recounting the battle: "I beg you not to tell me anything more of that kind. I have as much on me now as I can bear."[53] Lincoln's despair was so palpable that Noah Brooks expressed shock at his appearance. Comparing him with the vigorous campaigner he had known back in Illinois, Brooks wrote that the president's "hair is grizzled, his gait more stooping, his countenance sallow, and there is a sunken, deathly look about the large cavernous eyes." Philosophically Brooks remarked that it "is a lesson for human ambition to look upon that anxious and careworn face, prematurely aged by public labors and private griefs, and to remember that with the fleeting glory of his term of office have come responsibilities which make his life one long series of harassing care."[54]

The president did not blame Burnside for the defeat. "In my opinion Mr. Lee caused this trouble," he said.[55] He also compared Burnside favorably to his predecessor: "Had Burnside had the same chances of success that McClellan wantonly cast away, to-day he would have been hailed as the saviour of his country. A golden opportunity was lost by the latter General at Antietam."[56] Returning the favor, Burnside promised Lincoln that he would publish a letter accepting sole responsibility for the debacle. The grateful president told the general that he "was the first man he had found who was willing to relieve him of a particle of responsibility."[57] True to his word, Burnside wrote Halleck on December 17: "For the failure in the attack I am responsible. . . . The fact that I decided to move from Warrenton onto this line rather against the opinion of the President, Secretary, and yourself, and that you have left the whole management in my hands, without giving me orders, makes me the more responsible."[58] Burnside submitted this document to the newspapers, which circulated it widely.

In the wake of Fredericksburg, Lincoln's popularity sank. A Bostonian predicted that his resignation "would be received with *great satisfaction*" and might "avert what . . . will otherwise come viz a *violent and bloody revolution at the North*."[59] The president was aware of such threats against him. When told that a Pennsylvanian had expressed the hope that Lincoln would be hanged from a lamppost outside the White House, he remarked to Congressman William D. Kelley: "You need not be surprised to find that that suggestion has been executed any morning; the violent preliminaries to such an event would not surprise me. I have done things lately that must be incomprehensible to the people, and which cannot now be explained."[60]

Cabinet Putsch

Rather than attacking Lincoln directly, congressmen and senators upset by the defeat both at Fredericksburg and at the polls, made the cabinet, especially Seward, their scapegoat. Thirty-two Republican senators caucused secretly on December 16 and 17 "to ascertain whether any steps could be taken to quiet the public mind, and to produce a better condition of affairs." They denounced Seward bitterly "and charged him with all the disasters which had come upon our arms alleging that he was opposed to a vigorous prosecution of the war—controlled the President and thwarted the other members of the Cabinet." Lincoln too was criticized for failing "to consult his Cabinet councilors, as a body, upon important matters" and for appointing generals "who did not believe in the policy of the government, and had no sympathy with its purposes."[61]

The senators' chief informant was Salmon P. Chase, leader of the Radical faction in the cabinet. Seward, representing the opposite end of the ideological spectrum, had triumphed over the treasury secretary in the competition to win Lincoln's favor. The haughty Chase regarded both his cabinet colleagues and the president with lordly contempt and schemed to win the Republican presidential nomination in 1864. Lincoln said "he had no doubt that Chase was at the bottom of all the mischief, and was setting the radicals on to assail Seward."[62] The president believed that the putsch was rooted in personal hostility rather than a genuine concern for the country's welfare. Moreover, he disliked the senators' resort to a secret caucus rather than an open debate and vote of no confidence.

After twenty-eight senators agreed on a resolution stating that "the public confidence in the present administration would be increased by a change in and partial reconstruction of the Cabinet," they resolved to send a nine-man delegation to Lincoln.[63] Upon learning the results of the caucus, Seward said: "They may do as they please about me, but they shall not put the President in a false position on my account."[64] He promptly wrote a letter of resignation. Reading it, Lincoln appeared shaken, pained, and surprised. He urged Seward to reconsider. For the president, this was one of the darkest days of the war. He told Orville Browning: "Since I heard last night of the proceedings of the caucus I have been more distressed than by any event of my life." The Radical senators, he said, "wish to get rid of me, and I am sometimes half disposed to gratify them." In despair, he added, "We are now on the brink of destruction. It appears to me the Almighty is against us, and I can hardly see a ray of hope." Dismayed at the allegations against Seward, the president wondered, "Why will men believe a lie, an absurd lie, that could not impose upon a child, and cling to it and repeat it in defiance of all evidence to the contrary?" But he would not be bullied, insisting emphatically that "he was master."[65] On the evening of December 18, Lincoln met with the senatorial delegation. Jacob Collamer of Vermont began by reading a paper summarizing their grievances and suggestions. Among other things, it contained the startling implication that "all important public measures and appointments" should be made by presidents only after obtaining the consent of a cabinet majority. The senators then held a wide-ranging, frank conversation with the president, who listened respectfully and calmly to their complaints about the lack of unity in the cabinet, the failure of Lincoln to consult its members, and the need for a vigorous prosecution of the war by generals sympathetic to the administration. They charged Seward with "indifference, with want of earnestness in the War, with want of sympathy with the country in this great struggle, and with many things objectionable, and especially with a too great ascendancy and control of the President and measures of administration."

In reply, Lincoln "stated how this movement had shocked and grieved him; that the Cabinet he had selected in view of impending difficulties and of all the responsibilities upon himself; that he and the members had got on harmoniously, whatever had been their previous party feelings and associations; that there had never been serious disagreements, though there had been differences; that in the overwhelming troubles of the country, which had borne heavily upon him, he had been sustained and consoled by the good feeling and the mutual and unselfish confidence and zeal that pervaded the Cabinet."[66] "What the country wanted," Lincoln said, "was military success. Without that nothing could go right:—with that nothing could go wrong. He did not yet see how the measure proposed by the Committee would furnish the remedy required: if he had a Cabinet of angels they could not give the country military successes, and that was what was wanted and what must be had."[67]

When the dyspeptic Senator William P. Fessenden of Maine cited McClellan's complaint about the administration's failure to properly support the Army of the Potomac, Lincoln read several of his own letters to Little Mac showing how well that general had been sustained. Massachusetts senator Charles Sumner laced into Seward, denouncing his official correspondence, averring "that he had uttered sentiments offensive to Congress, and spoke of it repeatedly with disrespect, in the presence of foreign ministers—that he had written offensive despatches which the President could not have seen, or assented to." Lincoln replied that "it was Mr. Seward's habit to read his despatches to him before they were sent" and that "they were not usually submitted to a Cabinet Council." In conclusion, he "said he would carefully examine and consider the paper submitted" and "expressed his satisfaction with the tone & temper of the Committee."[68] As he ushered them out, he seemed cheerful and satisfied with the discussion. He invited them to return on the morrow.

Rumors swirled through the capital, causing people to fear that a coup d'état was in the making. The next morning, Lincoln summoned the cabinet, minus Seward, and recounted what had transpired. In obvious distress, he urged them not to quit and, according to Edward Bates, "said he could not afford to lose us" for he "did not see how he could get along with any new cabinet, made of new materials."[69] The president asked them to reconvene that evening, when the senators would again call. Chase, who realized that he would be put in an awkward position, tried to excuse himself from attending, but because all his colleagues agreed to be there, he felt compelled to join them. This proved to be an ingenious tactical stroke on Lincoln's part.

On the fateful night of December 19, the senators returned to the White House, where Lincoln opened the four-hour conference by stating "that he had invited the Cabinet, with the exception of Mr Seward, to meet the Committee for a free and friendly conversation, in which all, including the President, should be on equal terms—and he desired to know if the Committee had any objection to talk over matters with the Cabinet." Taken by surprise, the senators raised no objection, though it would be awkward for them to make their case in the presence of the treasury secretary, their main informant.[70] With some severity (and rather inaccurately), Lincoln spoke at length "of the unity of his Cabinet, and how, though they could not be expected to think and speak alike on all subjects, all had acquiesced in measures when once decided."[71] He said he "thought Mr Seward had been earnest in the prosecution of the war, and had not improperly interfered—had generally read him his official correspondence, and had sometimes consulted with Mr Chase." When Lincoln asked the cabinet "to say whether there had been any want of unity, or of sufficient consultation," Chase found himself on the spot.[72]

All eyes focused on the treasury secretary, who seemed to take offence and looked quite angry. He stated "that he should not have come here had he known that he was to be arraigned before a Committee of the Senate." Reluctantly acknowledging that "there had been no want of unity in the Cabinet, but a general *acquiescence* on public measures," he endorsed the president's statement "fully and entirely." Yet rather equivocally he said that he "regretted that there was not a more full and thorough consideration and canvass of every important measure in open Cabinet."[73] The senators, having often heard Chase bemoan the lack of unanimity and consultation, were astounded. The duplicitous treasury secretary felt humiliated. Replying to the charge that the committee was "arraigning" Chase, Fessenden "with much warmth" remarked: "It was no movement of ours, nor did we suspect that we came here for that purpose."[74]

Later, Orville Browning asked Collamer how Chase "could venture to make such a statement in the presence of Senators to whom he had said that Seward exercised a back stair and malign influence upon the President, and thwarted all the measures of the Cabinet." Bluntly Collamer responded: "He lied."[75] Disgusted with Chase, Stanton on December 20 told Fessenden that "what the Senators had said about the manner of doing business in the Cabinet was true, and *he* did not mean to lie about it." The war secretary added "that he was ashamed of Chase, for he knew better."[76]

As Stanton and Caleb Smith acknowledged, the senators were right in thinking that the cabinet lacked harmony and was often ignored when important decisions were made. Personal antagonisms were strong. Montgomery Blair called Seward an "unprincipled liar," and Bates and Welles held similarly dim views of the secretary of state.[77] Chase regarded him as an archenemy. They all resented Seward's toplofty condescension, his meddling in their affairs, and his intimacy with the president. But the senators' belief, nurtured by Chase, that the secretary of state dominated Lincoln was inaccurate. "Seward knows that I am his master," the president told an army chaplain.[78] Indeed, he was master of the entire cabinet. John Hay marveled at the "tyrannous authority" with which Lincoln "rules the Cabinet," for he decided the "most important things" and "there is no cavil."[79]

When Lincoln asked if he should accept Seward's resignation, the senators were divided. Chase's backpedaling led Collamer and Jacob Howard of Michigan to abstain and Ira Harris of New York to abandon his opposition to the secretary of state. Lincoln remarked "that he had reason to fear 'a general smash-up' if Mr Seward was removed, and he did not see how he could get along with an entire change in his Cabinet." He "thought Mr. Chase would seize the occasion to withdraw, and it had been intimated that Mr Stanton would do the same—and he could not dispense with Mr Chase's services in the Treasury just at this time."[80] At 1:00 a.m., the meeting broke up inconclusively. The next day, Welles, who thought "Seward's foibles" were "not serious failings," urged the president to reject the senatorial advice about the secretary of state and about compromising the independence of the executive branch. Lincoln, quite satisfied, responded that if the delegation's scheme were adopted, "the whole Government must cave in. It could not stand, could not hold water; the bottom would be out." The navy secretary, with Lincoln's blessing, hastened to Seward and urged him to withdraw his resignation. Seward agreed to stay on, though he was disappointed that Lincoln had not immediately rejected his resignation and that he had not refused to meet with the senators.

Meanwhile, Chase decided to quit, explaining to Fessenden that "Seward and he came into the Cabinet as representing two wings of the Republican party, and if he remained he might be accused of maneuvering to get Mr Seward out—and he thought he ought to relieve the President of any embarrassment, if he desired to reconstruct the Cabinet." He added that "Mr Seward's withdrawal would embarrass him so much that he could not get along with the Treasury. He found that very difficult as it was—and if he had to contend with the disaffection of Mr Seward's friends the load would be more than he could carry."[81] With his resignation letter in hand, Chase met with Lincoln, Stanton, and Welles. The treasury secretary "said he had been painfully affected by the meeting last evening, which was a total surprise to him, and, after some not very explicit remarks as to how he was affected, informed the President he had prepared his resignation."

Lincoln's eyes lit up as he asked, "Where is it?"

"I brought it with me," said Chase. "I wrote it this morning."

"Let me have it," said the president as he reached for the document, which its author hesitated to surrender.

Eagerly, Lincoln ripped open the envelope. "This cuts the Gordian knot," he said, laughing triumphantly. "I can dispose of this subject now without difficulty. I see my way clear."

Holding out Chase's letter, he said: "This is all I want; this relieves me; my way is clear; the trouble is ended. I will detain neither of you longer."[82] Soon thereafter,

Lincoln told a member of the senatorial committee: "Now I can ride: I have a pumpkin in each end of my bag."[83]

On December 20, Lincoln asked both Seward and Chase to withdraw their resignations. Seward agreed promptly, but Chase repeated the temporizing act he had engaged in two years earlier when Lincoln offered him the treasury portfolio. With a brilliant tactical stroke, Lincoln had successfully weathered one of the gravest political crises of the war and strengthened his control of the administration. Months later, reviewing these dramatic events, he told John Hay: "I do not now see how it could have been done better. I am sure it was right. If I had yielded to that storm & dismissed Seward the thing would all have slumped over one way & we should have been left with a scanty handful of supporters. When Chase sent in his resignation I saw that the game was in my own hands & I put it through."[84]

Amid the December cabinet imbroglio, one change was made, but not in response to congressional pressure. Secretary of the Interior Caleb B. Smith, in poor health and out of sympathy with the administration's emancipation policy, accepted a federal judgeship in his home state of Indiana. To fill Smith's place, the president chose another Hoosier, Assistant Secretary of the Interior John Palmer Usher, a longtime friend of Lincoln's from his days on the Eighth Judicial Circuit.

West Virginia Joins the Union

Lincoln worried about the constitutionality not only of the Emancipation Proclamation but also of a bill authorizing the creation of West Virginia. The northwesternmost counties of the Old Dominion had long been estranged from the eastern part of the state. Beyond the Allegheny mountains, Virginians owned few slaves and chafed at their high tax burden and their underrepresentation in the state legislature. They felt greater kinship with their neighbors in Ohio and Pennsylvania than with the residents of the tidewater region of their own state. In November 1861, delegates from thirty-four counties banded together at Wheeling and voted to secede from Confederate Virginia and establish a new state, to be called Kanawha. Six months later a Unionist legislature, in which only the northwestern portion of the state was represented, approved the creation of Kanawha and applied for admission to the Union.

The legality of this procedure was questionable. According to article 4 of the Constitution, new states can be carved from existing ones only with "the consent of the Legislatures of the States concerned, as well as of the Congress." The legislature of "the restored state of Virginia," which had representatives from counties containing roughly one-third of the state's population, did not appear sufficiently legitimate to authorize the division of the Old Dominion. Nevertheless, Congress voted on December 10 to admit West Virginia. Two days later, Lincoln told the cabinet that he thought "the creation of this new State at this time of doubtful expediency."[85] Proponents of West Virginia statehood greatly feared that Lincoln would veto the bill.

On New Year's Eve, leading champions of statehood from western Virginia (including Senator Waitman T. Willey and Congressmen Jacob B. Blair and William G. Brown) called on Lincoln by invitation. At his request, they rehearsed the various arguments in favor of statehood. They liked what Lincoln said but were disappointed that he would not definitely assure them he would sign the bill. He urged them to return the next morning to learn his decision. Jacob Blair recalled that on New Year's Day before 10:00 a.m., "I presented myself at the White House, but found the doors locked. I raised the sash of one of the large windows, gained an entrance, and went directly to the President's room. When I was ushered in I found Secretaries Seward and Stanton with him, but the President went directly to his desk and, taking out the West Virginia bill, held it up so that I read the signature, Approved: Abraham Lincoln." The president manifested "the simplicity and joyousness of a child, when it feels it has done its duty, and gratified a friend."[86] The bill admitted West Virginia, with the proviso that the voters of the new state would have to approve a clause in its constitution providing for compensated emancipation. They did so promptly, and the state was officially admitted to the Union in June 1863.

Consoler in Chief

In the midst of the turmoil created by the cabinet crisis, the defeat at Fredericksburg, the impending issuance of the Emancipation Proclamation, and the debate over statehood for West Virginia, Lincoln took time to pen a letter of condolence to Fanny McCullough, the grief-stricken daughter of his friend Lieutenant Colonel William McCullough. The colonel, who had served as sheriff and clerk of the courts in Bloomington, Illinois, was killed in action on December 5. His 21-year-old daughter suffered from a nervous condition and was shattered by the bad news. She spent her days either pacing back and forth violently or lethargically sitting without uttering a word.

When the president, who was warmly attached to McCullough and felt his loss keenly, learned of her condition, he offered her moving and revealing advice: "It is with deep grief that I learn of the death of your kind and brave Father, and, especially, that it is affecting your young heart beyond what is common in such cases. In this sad world of ours, sorrow comes to all; and, to the young, it comes with bitterest agony, because it takes them unawares. The older have learned to ever expect it. I am anxious to afford some alleviation of your present distress. Perfect relief is not possible, except with time. You can not now realize that you will ever feel better. Is not this so? And yet it is a mistake. You are sure to be happy again. To know this, which is certainly true, will make you some less miserable now. I have had experience enough to know what I say; and you need only to believe it, to feel better at once. The memory of your dear Father, instead of an agony, will yet be a sad sweet feeling in your heart, of a purer, and holier sort than you have known before." A friend of Fanny's reported that the "beautifully written" letter "had a very good effect in soothing her troubled mind."[87]

Emancipation Proclaimed

Lincoln had other things on his mind that busy New Year's Eve, notably the Emancipation Proclamation, due to be issued the following day. On December 29 and 31, the cabinet discussed a draft of the final version of the momentous document. The president had modified the preliminary version somewhat, toning down its pledge that the government "will recognize and maintain the freedom of such persons [freed slaves], and will do no act or acts to repress such persons, or any of them, in any efforts they may make for their actual freedom." Lincoln inserted the word *suitable* before *any efforts they may make for their actual freedom*. He had doubts about the word *maintain*. As he later told Governor Andrew G. Curtin, "It was Seward's persistence which resulted in the insertion of the word 'maintain,' which I feared under the circumstances was promising more than it was quite probable we could carry out."[88]

Chase argued that no areas of the Confederacy should be exempted save West Virginia, a suggestion that was not taken because the president understandably feared that slaveholders in territory under Union control might successfully argue in court that the government had no right to seize their slaves. Lincoln also hoped to placate Northern conservatives, Border State residents, and Southern Unionists. The treasury secretary further recommended a closing sentence with echoes of the Declaration of Independence: "And upon this act, sincerely believed to be an act of justice warranted by the Constitution, and of duty demanded by the circumstances of the country, I invoke the considerate judgement of Mankind and the gracious favor of Almighty God."[89] Lincoln included that sentence, substituting *upon military necessity* for *of duty demanded by the circumstances of the country*.

Montgomery Blair thought the freedpeople should be enjoined "to show themselves worthy of freedom by fidelity & diligence in the employments which may be given to them by the observance of order & by abstaining from all violence not required by duty or for self-defence. And whilst I appeal & & it is due to them to say that the conduct of large numbers of these people since the war began justifies confidence in their fidelity & humanity generally."[90] In keeping with this advice,

Lincoln altered his version to read: "I hereby enjoin upon the people so declared to be free to abstain from all violence, unless in necessary self-defence; and I recommend to them that, in all cases when allowed, they labor faithfully for reasonable wages." Curiously, Lincoln dropped the word *forever* from his earlier drafts, which stated that the slaves of disloyal masters "shall be then, thenceforward, and forever free." The final draft merely read that those slaves "are, and henceforward shall be free." He may have feared that courts would take a dim view of such language. Unlike the preliminary version announced in September, the final Emancipation Proclamation said nothing about colonization, a change that pleased Radicals.

A striking feature of the revised document was a provision that Blacks might serve in the military. This represented a reversal of Lincoln's earlier stand on the enlistment of African Americans. Politically, he had to contend with fierce popular resistance to recruiting Blacks, especially in the Midwest and the Border States. The way for the administration's new departure had been paved by Congress, which in July approved Senator Henry Wilson's amendment to the Militia Act authorizing the president "to receive into the service of the United States, for the purpose of constructing intrenchments, or performing camp service, or any other labor, or any military or naval service for which they may be found competent, persons of African descent."[91] The Second Confiscation Act contained a similar provision. Although authorized to enlist Blacks as combat troops, Lincoln decided to employ them only in support roles. He feared alienating the Border States and was aware that many in the army opposed using Blacks as fighters. On August 4, Lincoln refused the offer of two Black regiments recruited in the West, explaining to Senators James F. Harlan and Samuel C. Pomeroy that "he had made up his mind not to accept at present the service of armed negroes. He would use them as teamsters, cooks, laborers on entrenchments and in every capacity save fighting. He declared that to accept regiments of armed negroes would be to lose forty thousand white soldiers now in the army, and would drive some of the border States out of the Union." The employment of Black troops in combat was premature; he said "he should wait till such a course seemed to be a direct command of Providence before adopting it."[92] He concluded his remarks saying, "Gentlemen, you have my decision. I have made my mind up deliberately and mean to adhere to it. It embodies my best judgment, and if the people are dissatisfied, I will resign and let Mr. Hamlin try it." Pomeroy, laboring under the impression that the president was backing away from his earlier support of enlisting Blacks, snapped: "I hope in God's name, Mr. President, you will."[93]

Things began to change in August. An informal effort by General David Hunter to raise Black troops in the Sea Islands of South Carolina foundered because of that general's ineptitude. On August 10, Hunter reported that he was disbanding his Black regiment. Surprisingly, two weeks later the War Department authorized the enrollment of five thousand Blacks in the Sea Islands under Hunter's replacement, General Rufus Saxton. Without official sanction, a modest number of Black troops in Louisiana and Kansas had already been mustered in. Some Blacks had begun serving aboard Union warships as early as the fall of 1861. It was not clear that slaves thus employed would become free. Lincoln deliberately avoided an explicit policy statement for fear of antagonizing Border State sentiment.

The president evidently encouraged Kansas senator James H. Lane to enlist Blacks in his state and thereby induce slaves from neighboring Missouri to desert their plantations and farms, slip across the border, and join up. Missouri slave owners might then see merit in Lincoln's compensated-emancipation scheme and press their legislators to adopt it. In July, when Lane told the president and Stanton that he intended to raise two Black regiments in Kansas, he was not forbidden to do so. Six months earlier, Lane had planned to lead a column against Texas. According to one report, his instructions were, in effect, to "let slavery be disposed of by military necessities and the course of events. If slaves come within our lines from the plantations beyond the federal lines, use them. If they can work on fortifications use their services, clothe, feed and pay them. If absolutely necessary, arm them. If [they are] slaves of rebels, free them."[94] Lane's "Southern Expedition" was eventually scrubbed after he and David Hunter quarreled about who should command it.

After the Fredericksburg debacle, Maine governor Israel Washburn recommended that the president "now quietly commence organizing colored regiments—they will fight & will save him if he will let them." Why, Washburn asked, "are our leaders unwilling that Sambo should save white boys?"[95] In fact, Lincoln was no longer unwilling, as the Emancipation Proclamation made clear. At first he wanted Blacks to serve in capacities and areas where they were unlikely to be captured. Shortly after issuing the Proclamation, he suggested to General John A. Dix that Fort Monroe be manned by Blacks. Two months later, Lincoln encouraged Andrew Johnson, then serving as military governor of Tennessee, to recruit Blacks into the army. "The colored population is the great *available* and yet *unavailed* of, force for restoring the Union. The bare sight of fifty thousand armed, and drilled black soldiers on the banks of the Mississippi, would end the rebellion at once. And who doubts that we can present that sight, if we but take hold in earnest?"[96] He prodded General Banks to expedite the recruitment of Louisiana Blacks: "To now avail ourselves of this element of force is very important, if not indispensable. . . . I shall be very glad if you will take hold of the matter in earnest."[97] In the summer of 1863, Lincoln told U. S. Grant that Black troops constituted "a resource which, if vigorously applied now, will soon close the contest. It works doubly, weakening the enemy and strengthening us."[98]

Recruiting went too slowly for Lincoln's taste, but by war's end more than 170,000 Blacks soldiers and approximately 20,000 Black sailors served in the war, constituting about 9 percent of the total Union armed forces.

Emancipation Proclaimed

As New Year's Day approached, supporters and opponents of emancipation lobbied the president. On January 1, 1863, after a sleepless night, Lincoln made a fair copy of the revised Proclamation. As he was doing so, his wife, who according to her eldest son "was very much opposed to the signing of the Emancipation Proclamation," interrupted him, "inquiring in her sharp way, 'Well, what do you intend doing?'" He replied: "I am a man under orders, I cannot do otherwise."[99]

When Lincoln viewed the engrossed copy of the Proclamation prepared by the State Department, he noticed a technical error in the wording of the closing subscription and ordered that it be corrected. While that revision was taking place, he had to preside over the traditional New Year's reception at the White House. After three hours of greeting hordes of callers, the weary president returned to his office. When he began to sign the corrected copy of the Proclamation, his hand trembled. "I could not for a moment, control my arm," he later recalled. "I paused and a superstitious feeling came over me which made me hesitate." Had he made a mistake? he wondered.[100] But swiftly regaining his composure, he told Seward and his son Frederick: "I never, in my life, felt more certain that I was doing right, than I do in signing this paper." He added, "I have been receiving calls, and shaking hands since nine o'clock this morning, till my arm is stiff and numb." He feared that if his signature appeared shaky, some people would think "he had compunctions." So with renewed firmness he said: "Anyway, it is going to be done!" Slowly and carefully he wrote out his full name in a bold, clear hand. Smiling, he looked up and observed softly: "That will do."[101]

To Massachusetts senator Charles Sumner, a longtime champion of freedom, Lincoln gave the pen he used to sign the document. The president had been nettled by Sumner's brusque manner and impatient rhetoric, but as Carl Schurz observed, though "it required all his fortitude to bear Sumner's intractable insistence, Lincoln did not at all deprecate Sumner's agitation for an immediate emancipation policy, even though it did reflect upon the course of the administration." To the contrary, "he rather welcomed everything that would prepare the public mind for the approaching development."[102] Sumner's counterpart in the House, Thaddeus Stevens of Pennsylvania, often denounced the president, but in effect the two men worked in tandem. As Alexander K. McClure noted, "Stevens was ever clearing the underbrush and preparing the soil, while Lincoln followed to sow the seeds that were to ripen in a regenerated Union."[103]

Often portrayed as antagonists, in fact Lincoln and the Radicals were united in their desire for emancipation and for a vigorous prosecution of the war. They differed only in temperament and in tactics. Lincoln was no reluctant emancipator; he welcomed the liberation of slaves as enthusiastically as any abolitionist. In discussing the Emancipation Proclamation with Joshua Speed, he said: "I believe that in this measure my fondest hopes will be realized."[104] Constitutional and political constraints had forced him to delay issuing the document; if he had acted solely on his own convictions and inclinations, emancipation would have been declared much sooner. Lincoln was not forced by political considerations to issue the Proclamation; on the contrary, such considerations compelled him to *postpone* doing what he had long wanted to do.

Radicals rejoiced. William Lloyd Garrison saluted the Proclamation as "a great historic event, sublime in its magnitude, momentous and beneficent in its far-reaching consequences."[105] Blacks were especially jubilant. At mass rallies in New York, Philadelphia, Boston, and elsewhere in the North, speakers hailed the Proclamation, and cannon salvos honored the event. Henry Highland Garnet told a vast crowd that Lincoln was "the man of our choice and hope" and that the Proclamation was "one of the greatest acts in all of history."[106] When the news reached the capital of Massachusetts, thousands of Blacks there exulted passionately. "I never saw enthusiasm before," Frederick Douglass reported. "I never saw joy before. Men, women, young and old, were up; hats and bonnets were in the air, and we gave three cheers for Abraham Lincoln."[107]

Opinion in the Border States was, as Lincoln predicted, hostile. The Catholic archbishop of Baltimore indignantly exclaimed: "While our brethren are slaughtered in hecatombs, Abraham Lincoln coolly issues his Emancipation Proclamation, letting loose from three to four millions of half civilized Africans to murder their Masters and Mistresses! And all that under the pretense of philanthropy!!"[108] Many Democrats in the Free States also objected strenuously.

On January 12, Jefferson Davis expressed his outrage in a message to the Confederate Congress in which he called the Emancipation Proclamation "a measure by which several millions of human beings of an inferior race, peaceful and contented laborers in their sphere, are doomed to extermination, while at the same time they are encouraged to a general assassination of their masters by the insidious recommendation 'to abstain from violence unless in necessary self-defense.'"[109] Davis warned that White officers commanding Black units would be turned over to Confederate state governments for punishment as inciters of slave uprisings and that Black troops would be restored to their masters. When warned that the Proclamation "would rouse the South as one man and send a force into the field twice as great as then existed," Lincoln replied: "We'll double ours then."[110] The evening of New Year's Day, Lincoln confided to Indiana congressman Schuyler Colfax that the "South had fair warning, that if they did not return to their duty, I should strike at this pillar of their strength. The promise must now be kept, and I shall never recall one word."[111]

And he did not.

Lincoln said the issuance of the Emancipation Proclamation was "the central act of my administration" as well as "the great event of the nineteenth century" and speculated to Charles Sumner "that the name which is connected with this matter will never be forgotten."[112]

And it has not been.

30.

"Go Forward, and Give Us Victories"

From the Mud March to Gettysburg (January–July 1863)

The winter and early spring of 1863 found Lincoln and his constituents once again mired in the Slough of Despond. As 1862 drew to a close, George William Curtis remarked that "everything is very black."[1] From Washington, Richard Henry Dana wrote that the "lack of respect for the Prest, in all parties, is unconcealed."[2] Even allies in Illinois were becoming critical of the "imbecile Administration."[3] On January 25, when Wendell Phillips ascribed that discontent to the administration's lackluster enforcement of emancipation, Lincoln replied that "the masses of the country generally are only dissatisfied at our lack of military success. Defeat and failure in the field make everything seem wrong."[4]

At the same time, conservatives and moderates pressed Lincoln to rescind the Emancipation Proclamation. They were convinced, as Senator John Sherman of Ohio put it, that Negrophobia was causing significant backlash against emancipation. Democrats would "fight for the flag & the country," Sherman told his brother, "but they hate niggers."[5] Nonetheless, Lincoln rejected calls to withdraw the Proclamation, insisting that it was "a fixed thing" and "that he intended to adhere to it."[6]

Dakota Sioux Uprising

Discontent was especially strong in the West, where Lincoln's handling of an uprising by Dakota Sioux in the summer and fall of 1862 enraged the citizenry of Minnesota. The tribesmen, angry at White encroachment on their territory, at the failure of the government to deliver promised supplies and money, and at the notorious corruption of Indian agents and traders, launched savage attacks on White men, women, and children along the frontier, killing hundreds and driving more than thirty thousand from their homes. Settlers demanded protection, and Governor Alexander Ramsey appealed to Lincoln for troops.

John Pope, who was dispatched thither to restore order, issued a stern declaration: "It is my purpose utterly to exterminate the Sioux if I have the power to do so. . . . They are to be treated as maniacs or wild beasts, and by no means as people with whom treaties or compromises can be made." When the administration warned him to make no unreasonable demands for troops and supplies, Pope responded: "You have no idea of the wide, universal and uncontrollable pain everywhere in this country. Over 500 people have been murdered in Minnesota alone and 300 women and children are now in captivity. The most horrible massacres have been committed; children nailed alive to trees, women violated and then disemboweled—everything that horrible ingenuity could devise."[7] Under the leadership of Minnesota congressman Henry H. Sibley, militiamen and regular troops put down the Sioux rebellion by early October. As he conducted war crimes trials that led to the death sentence being imposed on 303 Sioux men, Sibley was urged by Pope not to "allow any false sympathy for the Indians to prevent you from acting with the utmost rigor." Sibley told his wife that "the press is very much concerned, lest I should prove too tender-hearted."[8]

Lincoln felt similar pressure to approve the death sentences. Pope warned that Minnesota settlers "are exasperated to the last degree, and if the guilty are not all executed I think it nearly impossible to prevent the indiscriminate massacre of all the Indians—old men, women, and children."[9] Governor Ramsey, abolitionist and feminist Jane Grey Swisshelm, and the Minnesota delegation in Congress joined the chorus demanding that the convicted Dakota be hanged, but as a pro-administration Washington paper announced, the president had "resolved that such an outrage, as the indiscriminate hanging of these Indians most certainly would be, shall not take place."[10] On November 10, he instructed Pope to forward the "full and complete record of these convictions."[11] As the president and two Interior Department lawyers scrutinized the record, they saw how badly due process had been violated. The attorneys recommended that many of the condemned men be pardoned. In the end, Lincoln authorized the execution of only 38 of the 303 condemned men. In making that decision, he sought to discriminate between those involved in massacres and those involved only in battles. In 1864, Governor Ramsey told him that if he had executed all 303 Indians, he would have won more support for his reelection. "I could not afford to hang men for votes," came the reply.[12]

Military Frustration

On the momentous first day of 1863, Lincoln had more on his mind than the Emancipation Proclamation; he must decide what to do about the demoralized Army of the Potomac. His anxiety for those troops was exacerbated by his fear that Union forces in the West might also suffer defeat. He had good reason, for on December 29 General William T. Sherman had led a disastrous assault at Chickasaw Bluffs, near Vicksburg, Mississippi, and two days later Confederates recaptured Galveston, Texas. The one positive development in the West occurred when Confederate general Braxton Bragg attacked the Army of the Cumberland, led by General William S. Rosecrans, at Stone's River, Tennessee. Although the outcome was hardly a resounding victory, the North could find some solace because by January 2 Bragg had withdrawn from the field. Greatly relieved, Lincoln congratulated Old Rosy: "God bless you and all with you!" Months later he wrote the general, "You gave us a hard earned victory which, had there been a defeat instead, the nation could scarcely have lived over." Rosecrans's success had checked "a dangerous sentiment which was spreading in the north."[13]

In the East, Burnside decided to launch yet another campaign and notified the administration of his plan; he also sent an undated letter of resignation to be used by the president whenever he saw fit. Lincoln urged him to be "cautious, and do not understand that the government, or country, is driving you."[14] As discontent welled up within the ranks, Burnside prepared to send them across the Rappahannock once again. When he did so on January 20, they promptly bogged down in a sea of mud created by a fierce rainstorm that persisted for days. The "Mud March" perforce halted, and the army fell back to its camps. Hooker, ever the malcontent, openly criticized his commander. Burnside, fed up with such insubordination, lashed out, dismissing Hooker and three other generals and relieving five others. On January 24, Burnside told the president he must support this astounding order, though Lincoln had not been consulted about the matter. The next day, Lincoln announced that Hooker was to be the new commander of the Army of the Potomac. Burnside offered to resign his commission, but the president instead granted Old Burn a one-month furlough and transferred him to the Department of the Ohio.

Hooker had behaved badly toward Burnside. Despite his reputation as a hard drinker, chronic intriguer, indiscreet talker, compulsive womanizer, and reckless gambler, Hooker was an obvious choice to command the Army of the Potomac. When the editor of the New York *Times* complained about attempts to undermine Burnside, Lincoln replied, "Hooker does talk badly, but the trouble is, he is stronger with the country today than any other man."[15] Known as "Fighting Joe," Hooker had earned a reputation for courage and skill. In naming him to the command, Lincoln read aloud to Hooker one of his most eloquent letters, a document illustrative of his deep paternal streak. Like a wise, benevolent father, he praised Hooker while gently chastising him for insubordination toward superior officers: "I think it best for you to know that there are some things in regard to which, I am not quite satisfied with you. I believe you to be a brave and a skilful soldier, which, of course, I like. I also believe you do not mix politics with your profession, in which you are right. "But, he added, "I think that during Gen. Burnside's command of the Army, you have taken counsel of your ambition, and thwarted him as much as you could, in which you did a great wrong to the country, and to a most meritorious and honorable brother officer. I have heard, in such way as to believe it, of your recently saying that both the Army and the Government needed a Dictator. Of course it was not *for* this, but in spite of it, that I have given you the command. Only those generals who gain successes, can set up dictators. What I now ask of you is military success, and I will risk the dictatorship." In closing, Lincoln urged Hooker to "beware of rashness, but with energy, and sleepless vigilance, go forward, and give us victories."[16]

Partially offsetting the dearth of success on the battlefield, New Hampshire and Connecticut voters provided two political victories in March and April, respectively. The Connecticut election was especially noteworthy, for the Democrats had nominated a virulent Peace Democrat, Thomas H. Seymour, who lost to the incumbent William A. Buckingham. But despite that good news, the bleak military situation continued to torment Lincoln. On April 1, he said to Schuyler Colfax: "How willingly would I exchange places to-day, with the soldier who sleeps on the ground in the Army of the Potomac!"[17]

The president was particularly exasperated by Admiral Samuel F. Du Pont's campaign against Charleston, the brainchild of Assistant Secretary of the Navy Gustavus V. Fox. Convinced that the ironclad monitors were invulnerable, he argued that a few of them could run past the forts guarding the entrance to Charleston harbor and compel the city to surrender. When he proposed to send an ironclad fleet against the storm center of secessionism, Lincoln responded enthusiastically. Under the impression that the army and navy would assault Charleston that winter, the president was dismayed by Du Pont's request for further plating of the ironclads. Suspecting that the admiral had lost faith in his chances of success, Lincoln insisted that Fox visit South Carolina to confer with Du Pont. Fox begged off, arguing that he did not wish to injure the admiral's hypersensitive pride, but he did implore Du Pont not to let the army's plans disrupt the navy's.

Lincoln instructed Du Pont either to attack Charleston or, if he doubted his ability to succeed there, to send his ironclads west to assist in the Vicksburg campaign. Before that telegram reached Du Pont, however, he had attacked Charleston on April 7 with eight monitors and a huge armored frigate, the *New Ironsides*. After a furious encounter of little more than half an hour, they withdrew. One monitor, the *Keokuk*, was sunk. As Lincoln awaited news of the assault, he was skeptical. "What will you wager that half our iron-clads are at the bottom of Charleston Harbor?" he asked Noah Brooks. "The people will expect big things when they hear of this; but it is too late—*too late*!" he exclaimed.[18]

On April 12, when he learned of the Union repulse, Lincoln appeared demoralized and unstrung as he told journalists that the news displeased him, for he had not supposed that the ironclads would quit after fighting for little more than half an hour, but rather assumed they would continue the campaign for days or weeks. The president conferred with Halleck about the army's ability to continue the Charleston campaign by seizing Morris Island and menacing Fort Sumter. Old Brains pooh-poohed the idea, insisting that troops "could do nothing once they got there." When Fox joined them and seconded Lincoln's proposal, Halleck continued to demur. According to Noah Brooks, "Though he treated the suggestions of Lincoln with respect," the general in chief "evidently entertained a profound contempt for his generalship."[19] Lincoln ordered Du Pont to hold his position inside the Charleston bar and prevent the Confederates from erecting more batteries at the harbor's entrance; both the admiral and General David Hunter were to renew the attack. By the time the presidential telegram reached Du Pont, the ironclads had already withdrawn. The thin-skinned admiral, unwilling to renew the assault, took offense at what he considered the president's implied censure and asked to be relieved. In June, Welles accepted his request. Summing up his disappointment, Lincoln observed that "the six months' preparation for Charleston was a very long grace for the thin plate of soup served in the two hours of fighting."[20]

Hooker's Campaign

Meanwhile, Hooker planned a spring offensive for the Army of the Potomac. In early April, Lincoln accompanied his wife and several others, including Noah Brooks, on a visit to the general. While at a grand infantry review near Falmouth, he returned the salute of officers by merely touching his hat but removed that item as he passed by enlisted men. One soldier was especially moved by Lincoln's appearance, writing that he "looks poorly . . . he is to all outward appearances much careworn, and anxiety is fast wearing him out, poor man; I could but pity as I looked at him, and remembered the weight of responsibility resting upon his burdened mind; *what* an ordeal he has passed through, and *what is yet before him!* All I can say is, *Poor Abe!*"[21] At hospitals Lincoln shook hands with many of the sick and wounded men. Although he had originally planned to stay for only a day, he enjoyed himself so much that he remained nearly a week in order to inspect each corps. He was relieved to escape from the capital and its clamorous politicians. Yet no matter what he did, he told Brooks, "nothing could touch the tired spot within, which was all tired."[22] He expressed to General Egbert Viele a wish that "George Washington or some of those old patriots were here in my place so that I could have a little rest."[23]

While Lincoln reviewed plans for the upcoming campaign, he was disturbed by the generals' discussion about whether to get to Richmond by going around Lee's right flank or his left. So he penned a memorandum noting that the presence of Lee's army on the opposite bank of the Rappahannock meant that there was "*no* eligible route for us into Richmond." Therefore, Hooker should consider that "our prime object is the enemies' army in front of us, and not with, or about, Richmond—at all."[24] Evidently fearing that Hooker might repeat McClellan's blunder at Antietam, he said to the general, "In your next fight put in all of your men."[25] Heavy rains led Hooker to revise his plans ingeniously, proposing to send some troops against Fredericksburg as a feint, throw most of his forces across the river well above the town, and menace Lee's communications, forcing the Confederates to abandon their strongly entrenched position and either retreat or fight in the open, where superior Union numbers and artillery could prevail. Upon receiving Hooker's dispatch about this new strategy, Lincoln replied with characteristic modesty: "While I am anxious, please do not suppose I am impatient, or waste a moment's thought on me, to your own hindrance, or discomfort."[26] Lincoln's hopes were soon dashed, for Lee did not cooperate with Hooker's plans. Instead of waiting on the defensive, he boldly attacked, dividing his numerically inferior force and smashing the Army of the Potomac between May 2 and May 6 at Chancellorsville. On the latter date, the Union army retreated back across the Rappahannock, having taken seventeen thousand casualties to Lee's thirteen thousand. The only consolation to Union forces was the death of Stonewall Jackson, who was accidentally shot by his own men.

When Lincoln received a dispatch reporting the defeat, he was stunned, turning pale as a corpse. "Had a thunderbolt fallen upon the President he could not have been more overwhelmed," Noah Brooks reported. "One newly risen from the dead could not have looked more ghostlike." At the president's request, Brooks read the fateful document aloud. With tears streaming down his ashen face, Lincoln paced about, exclaiming: "My God! my God! What will the country say? What will the country say?"[27] To Bishop Charles Gordon Ames, Lincoln sadly confessed, "I am the loneliest man in America. There is no one to whom I can go and unload my troubles, assured of sympathy and help."[28] Lincoln was particularly upset because Hooker had not committed all his men.

Immediately on hearing the bad news, the president hurried to the Army of the Potomac, where he was charitable to Hooker, saying "that the result was in his judgment unfortunate" but "that he did not blame anyone," for he "believed everyone had done all in his power" and "that the disaster was one that could not be helped." Yet he "thought its effect, both at home and abroad, would be more serious and injurious than any previous act of the war."[29] He asked the general: "What next? If possible I would be very glad of another movement early enough to give us some benefit from the fact of the enemies communications being broken, but neither for this reason or any other, do I wish anything done in desperation or rashness. An early movement would also help to supersede the bad moral effect of the recent one, which is sure to be considerably injurious."[30] Fighting Joe replied immediately that he wanted to stay on the Rappahannock and renew the campaign once his army was again prepared to advance.

Hooker wrote the president that even though the enemy now outnumbered him, he would attack on the morrow. Lincoln, doubtless reminded of McClellan's overestimate of Confederate troop strength, summoned the general to Washington, where he pointed out that the Confederates were no longer as vulnerable as they had been earlier and that therefore it "does not now appear probable to me that you can gain any thing by an early renewal of the attempt to cross the Rappahannock. I therefore shall not complain, if you do no more, for a time, than to keep the enemy at bay, and out of other mischief."[31]

Hooker Follows McDowell, McClellan, and Burnside to the Sidelines

On June 2, when asked if a Confederate raid was imminent, Lincoln replied "that all indications were that there would be nothing of the sort, and that an advance by the rebels could not possibly take place so as to put them on this side of the Rappahannock *unless Hooker was very much mistaken, and was to be again outgeneraled*."[32] But in fact, shortly thereafter Lee began his second invasion of the North. On June 5, when Hooker asked permission to attack the Confederate rear at Fredericksburg, Lincoln urged him to concentrate on the main body of the Army of Northern Virginia, not its tail. Using vivid rustic imagery, he warned against "any risk of being entangled upon the river, like an ox jumped half over a fence, and liable to be torn by dogs, front and rear, without a fair chance to gore one way or kick the other." If the Confederates crossed the river, Hooker should "keep on the same side & fight him, or act on the defence, according as might be my estimate of his strength relatively to my own." Modestly, the president closed by saying that "these are mere suggestions which I desire to be controlled by the judgment of yourself and Gen. Halleck."[33]

Ignoring this advice, Hooker on June 10 proposed to forget about Lee and march on Richmond. Lincoln, who thought "it would be a very poor exchange to give Washington for Richmond," immediately vetoed that suggestion.[34] Fighting Joe eventually decided to take Lincoln's advice and shadow Lee. As the Confederate army advanced, the president thought Hooker began to resemble McClellan more and more, complaining that he was outnumbered (he was not) and that the administration did not support him wholeheartedly (it did). The president said "that he had got rid of McC[lellan] because he let Lee get the better of him in the race to Richmond" and hinted "that if Hooker got beat in the present race—he would make short work of him."[35] On June 16, the general fired off a bitter telegram: "You have long been aware, Mr. President, that I have not enjoyed the confidence of the major-general commanding the army, and I can assure you so long as this continues we may look in vain for success."[36]

Lincoln replied with a blunt message: "To remove all misunderstanding, I now place you in the strict military relation to Gen. Halleck, of a commander of one of the armies, to the General-in-Chief of all the armies. I have not intended differently; but as it seems to be differently understood, I shall direct him to give you orders, and you to obey them."[37] To soften the blow, he sent a more conciliatory letter: "As it looks to me, Lee's now returning toward Harper's Ferry gives you back the chance that I thought McClellan lost last fall. Quite possibly I was wrong both then and now; but, in the great responsibility resting upon me, I cannot be entirely silent. Now, all I ask is that you will be in such mood that we can get into our action the best cordial judgment of yourself and General Halleck, with my poor mite added, if indeed he and you shall think it entitled to any consideration at all."[38]

When Hooker insisted that the ten thousand troops guarding Harpers Ferry be sent to join his army, Halleck vetoed the idea, prompting Hooker to quit in protest (and a huff) on June 27. Upon reading his dispatch, Lincoln's face turned leaden. To Stanton's query "What shall be done?" he replied: "Accept his resignation."[39] When Chase, who had strongly supported Hooker, protested, Lincoln cut him off abruptly: "The acceptance of an army resignation is not a matter for your department."[40]

Burnside Causes More Problems

While the Army of the Potomac was busy shadowing Lee, Burnside in his new position created yet another headache for Lincoln by arresting former congressman Clement L. Vallandigham of Dayton, Ohio, a prominent leader of the Peace Democrats. Dubbed by their opponents "Copperheads" after the poisonous snake that strikes without warning, Peace Democrats generally backed compromises that would bring about a negotiated restoration of the Union with slavery intact. War Democrats tended to support the administration's military policies. Each faction deplored arbitrary arrests and emancipation. During the winter of Northern discontent, the Emancipation Proclamation, the draft, and the suspension of the writ of habeas corpus greatly strengthened their appeal.

In April 1863, Burnside issued General Orders No. 38, stating that "the habit of declaring sympathy for the enemy will not be allowed in this department. Persons committing such offenses will be at once arrested," tried by military courts "as spies or traitors, and, if convicted, will suffer death" or will be "sent beyond our lines into the lines of their friends."[41] On May 1, Vallandigham delivered an inflammatory address denouncing the administration of "King Lincoln" in general and General Orders No. 38 in particular. Four days later, soldiers apprehended the Democratic firebrand, and soon thereafter a military commission found him guilty of disloyal speech and sentenced him to confinement for the rest of the war. Thus the obstreperous orator became a martyr whose treatment many Democrats deplored. Even some Republicans condemned what they called Burnside's "blunder" and "great mistake."[42]

Upon Vallandigham's arrival in Cincinnati, where he was incarcerated, he issued an address to his fellow Buckeyes: "I am here in a military bastille for no other offense than my political opinions, and the defense of them, and of the rights of the people, and of your constitutional liberties."[43] The Democrats of Ohio responded by unanimously nominating him for governor. In federal court, when Vallandigham's attorney asked for a writ of habeas corpus, Burnside emphatically defended his action, arguing that it was his duty "to stop license and intemperate discussion, which tend to weaken the authority of the Government and army."[44] Upholding the power of the president and his subordinates to arrest Vallandigham, the court denied the request.

Surprised and dismayed by Burnside's action, Lincoln sought to undo the damage. Fearing that he could not overrule the general without embarrassing him and simultaneously encouraging bitter dissenters, the president at first had Stanton send him a telegram approving his action. The cabinet, however, demurred; upon learning of their dissatisfaction, Burnside offered once again to resign. Lincoln replied that all cabinet members "regretted the necessity of arresting . . . Vallandigham, some, perhaps, doubting that there was a real necessity for it—but, being done, all were for seeing you through with it."[45] On May 19, Lincoln shrewdly undercut Vallandigham's martyr status by commuting his sentence, directing that he "be put beyond our military lines," and warning that if he returned to the North he would be "kept in close confinement for the term specified in his sentence."[46] Accordingly, Vallandigham was turned over to puzzled Confederates in Tennessee. After conferring with Jefferson Davis and other Southern leaders, he made his way to Canada, where he issued stirring if bootless addresses.

Lincoln's modification of Vallandigham's sentence represented one step in defusing the crisis caused by Burnside. Another was his prompt decision to revoke the general's June 1 order shutting down the vitriolic Chicago *Times*. That journal had fiercely denounced the administration, especially since the issuance of the Emancipation Proclamation. In February 1863, it declared that the "only way to compel the administration to withdraw its emancipation proclamation and kindred policies is for the democracy of the country to absolutely and unqualifiedly refuse to support the war for the enforcement of these policies."[47]

Upon learning of Burnside's highhanded act, Lincoln immediately had Stanton suggest to the general that he might want to rescind the order. The secretary of war explained that the president believed the "irritation produced by such acts is . . . likely to do more harm than the publication would do." Although he "approves of your motives and desires to give you cordial and efficient support," and "while military movements are left to your judgment," nevertheless "upon administration questions such as the arrest of civilians and the suppression of newspapers not requiring immediate action, the President desires to be previously consulted."[48] Because Lincoln acted so promptly, the *Times* was able to resume publication after an interruption of only one day.

Yet another step minimizing the effect of Burnside's blunders was Lincoln's public letter to the organizers of a protest meeting at Albany chaired by the industrialist Erastus Corning. In that important document, he defended the arrest of Vallandigham and the suspension of habeas corpus. Asserting that the government must execute deserters to maintain its armies intact, he argued that it was equally necessary to punish those who encouraged desertion. "Must I shoot a simple-minded soldier boy who deserts, while I must not touch a hair of a wily agitator who induces him to desert?" he asked rhetorically. Whoever "dissuades one man from volunteering, or induces one soldier to desert, weakens the Union cause as much as he who kills a union soldier in battle." To be sure, in peacetime the suspension of habeas corpus would be unconstitutional. But the Constitution provides that "the previlege of the writ of Habeas Corpus shall not be suspended, unless when in cases of Rebellion or Invasion, the public Safety may require it."

The secessionists, Lincoln argued, cynically expected constitutional scruples to hamper the government's attempt to preserve the Union. They planned to cry "Liberty of speech," "Liberty of the press," and "*Habeas corpus*" in order "to keep on foot amongst us a most efficient corps of spies, informers, supplyers, and aiders and abettors of their cause in a thousand ways." Fully aware that the Rebels would avail themselves of such tactics, Lincoln insisted that he nevertheless "was slow to adopt the strong measures." As the war progressed, however, he was forced to take steps "indispensable to the public Safety," steps that he believed were "within the exceptions of the constitution." Civilian courts were "utterly incompetent" to handle the vast number of cases that such a "clear, flagrant, and gigantic case of Rebellion" generated, and juries "too frequently have at least one member, more ready to hang the panel than to hang the traitor."

It would have been advisable, Lincoln argued, if at the outbreak of hostilities the government had arrested men like John C. Breckinridge, Robert E. Lee, Joseph E.

Johnston, and other high-ranking military leaders in the Confederacy. "Every one of them if arrested would have been discharged on Habeas Corpus, were the writ allowed to operate. In view of these and similar cases, I think the time not unlikely to come when I shall be blamed for having made too few arrests rather than too many."

Lincoln denied that any partisan motive underlay Vallandigham's arrest. After all, he pointed out, Burnside was a Democrat, as was the judge who refused to grant the Ohioan habeas corpus. The president suggested that if he had been in Burnside's position, he might not have arrested Vallandigham, but while he would not shirk the ultimate responsibility for the arrest, he believed that "as a general rule, the commander in the field is the better judge of the necessity in any particular case." He would gladly release Vallandigham as soon as he believed "the public safety will not suffer by it." In conclusion, Lincoln expressed the belief that as the war continued, the necessity for such strong measures would diminish. But, he insisted, "I must continue to do so much as may seem to be required by the public safety."[49]

Some of Lincoln's case was logically and constitutionally weak, especially his contention that anyone "who stands by and says nothing, when the peril of his government is discussed . . . is sure to help the enemy." The New York *World* with some justice asked: "Was anything so extraordinary ever before uttered by the chief magistrate of a free country? Men are torn from their home and immured in bastilles for the shocking crime of *silence*!"[50] Still, the homey rhetoric of this letter to Erastus Corning succeeded in allaying many public doubts. John G. Nicolay and John Hay would note that few of Lincoln's state papers "produced a stronger impression upon the public mind."[51] On June 30, Erastus Corning and the rest of the Albany committee issued a reply scorning Lincoln's "pretensions to more than regal authority." Vehemently they deplored the "gigantic and monstrous heresy" that the Constitution contained "a principle or germ of arbitrary power, which in time of war expands at once into an absolute sovereignty, wielded by one man; so that liberty perishes, or is dependent on his will, his discretion or his caprice."[52]

Lincoln did not offer a rejoinder to Corning, but when similar arguments were made by Ohio Democrats, he denied that he had said that "the constitution is different in time of insurrection or invasion from what it is in time of peace & public security." Rather he had "expressed the opinion that the constitution is different, *in its application* in cases of Rebellion or Invasion, involving the Public Safety, from what it is in times of profound peace and public security; and this opinion I adhere to, simply because, by the constitution itself, things may be done in the one case which may not be done in the other."[53] Lincoln failed to answer the telling objection raised by the Ohioans that Vallandigham was entitled to a civil trial

This portrait of Lincoln, which Anthony Berger of the Mathew Brady Gallery took in Washington on February 9, 1864, became the image that later appeared on the five-dollar bill. Robert Todd Lincoln thought it the best representation of his father as he actually looked. Library of Congress.

under the provisions of the Second Confiscation Act and the March 3, 1863, law authorizing the president to suspend habeas corpus.

Replacing Hooker

As Lincoln and Stanton discussed a replacement for Hooker, they rejected advice to choose McClellan. If not Little Mac, then who? By process of elimination, the choice settled on George Gordon Meade, who had distinguished himself in earlier campaigns. Although industrious and personally fearless, the reserved Meade lacked boldness.

That general accurately anticipated that Lee, who had divided his forces while entering Pennsylvania unopposed, would have to concentrate them as the Army of the Potomac drew nearer. From different directions the Confederates began streaming toward the small town of Gettysburg. There, during the first three days of July, the bloodiest battle of the war was fought. Lee lost fully a third of his men (28,000), while Meade lost a fifth of his (23,000). The Army of the Potomac, occupying high ground, fended off repeated attacks, including the fabled charge of George Pickett's division on July 3. The following day, Lee's shattered army began retreating toward the Potomac.

As he awaited news from the battlefield, Lincoln spent many anxious hours in the telegraph office. Word of the victory filled his heart with joy, though Meade's order congratulating his troops did not. The general said their job was now to "drive from our soil every vestige of the presence of the invader." When Lincoln read this proclamation, his heart sank. In anguish he exclaimed: "*Drive the invader from our soil! My God! Is that all?*"[54] Lincoln called it "a dreadful reminiscences of McClellan." Exasperated, he asked: "Will our Generals never get that idea out of their heads? The whole country is *our* soil."[55]

Halleck promptly notified Meade that if the Confederates were in fact crossing the Potomac, he should attack the portion still on the north bank. But with characteristic reluctance to give a direct command, Halleck added: "Do not be influenced by any dispatch from here against your own judgment. Regard them as suggestions only."[56] Lincoln believed that Meade could deliver the *coup de grâce* to the Army of Northern Virginia before it escaped to Virginia, for heavy rains delayed Lee's retreat. Thus, he thought, Meade could end the war, in conjunction with Grant's capture of Vicksburg on July 4. But Meade did not attack. On July 7 the deeply discouraged president, wearing a sad, almost desponding look, told his cabinet "that Meade still lingered at Gettysburg, when he should have been at Hagerstown or near the Potomac, to cut off the retreating army of Lee."[57]

Frustrated, Lincoln issued an unusual order directing Meade "to attack Lee's army with all his force immediately, and that if he was successful in the attack he might destroy the order but if he was unsuccessful he might preserve it for his vindication."[58] On July 12, Meade caught up with Lee at Williamsport, where he could have attacked that day or the next. When he said he would convene a council of war, Halleck warned him not to, for proverbially "councils of war never fight."[59] Meade ignored that advice, and as Old Brains had predicted, a majority of the corps commanders opposed an assault. The Confederates began crossing the river on the night of the thirteenth and finished doing so the next day. When Lee's escape was confirmed, Lincoln was overcome with grief and anger. Profoundly dismayed, he said: "We only had to stretch forth our hands & they were ours. And nothing I could say or do could make the Army move."[60] For the only time in his life, Robert saw tears in his father's eyes.

Aware of Lincoln's displeasure, Meade offered to resign. The president tried to comfort him with an extraordinary letter that began with an expression of sincere gratitude: "I am very—*very*—grateful to you for the magnificent success you gave the cause of the country at Gettysburg; and I am sorry now to be the author of the slightest pain to you." After this conciliatory opening, Lincoln became stern: "You fought and beat the enemy at Gettysburg; and, of course, to say the least, his loss was as great as yours. He retreated; and you did not, as it seemed to me, pressingly pursue him." In one of the harshest passages Lincoln ever penned, he told Meade how badly his failure to attack Lee had hurt the Union cause: "I do not believe you appreciate the magnitude of the misfortune involved in Lee's escape. He was within your easy grasp, and to have closed upon him would, in connection with our other late successes, have ended the war. As it is, the war will be prolonged indefinitely. . . . Your golden opportunity is gone, and I am distressed immeasureably because of it."[61] Lincoln never sent this stinging letter, but he did tell the general, "The fruit seemed so ripe, so ready for plucking, that it was very hard to lose it."[62]

While generals in the Army of the Potomac deeply disappointed Lincoln, their counterparts in the western theater, especially Ulysses S. Grant, gladdened his heart. He had not always been sanguine about Grant's campaign against Vicksburg, which had received a severe check in December. In March, the president complained that Union forces "were doing nothing at Vicksburg."[63] In late April, when Grant stopped making side expeditions and boldly threw his army across the Mississippi, he began a brilliant campaign. Upon learning that the general had moved south of Vicksburg and that David D. Porter had successfully run his fleet of gunboats past that city's batteries, Lincoln exclaimed: "This is more important than anything which is occurring in Virginia!"[64]

When Grant reached the east bank of the river below Vicksburg, he could have moved toward that citadel or headed south to link up with Banks, whose goal was to take Port Hudson. Lincoln hoped he would choose the latter course, but he did not, despite Halleck's urging. In May, as Grant daringly marched his army from triumph to triumph in Mississippi, defeating Confederate forces sent to relieve the threatened stronghold, Lincoln said: "I have had stronger influence brought against Grant, praying for his removal, since the battle of Pittsburg Landing [in April 1862], than for any other object, coming too from good men." But, the president added, "now look at his campaign since May 1. Where is anything like it in the Old World that equals it? It stamps him as the greatest general of the age, if not of the world."[65]

According to popular rumor, Lincoln asked critics of Grant's alleged drunkenness what brand of whiskey the general used so he could send some to his other generals. The president denied that he had made that witty remark, saying that it was probably ascribed to him "to give it currency." In fact, he pointed out, it was based on King George III's purported response to those who charged that General Wolfe was insane: "I wish he would bite some of my other generals then."[66]

(This anecdote appears in *Joe Miller's Complete Jest Book*, a favorite of Lincoln's.) Modestly, the president disclaimed credit for many other stories attributed to him, calling himself "only a retail dealer."[67]

On July 7, Gideon Welles rushed into the White House with a dispatch announcing the surrender of Vicksburg and in his great enthusiasm almost knocked Lincoln over. Hugging Welles tightly, the president exclaimed: "What can we do for the Secretary of the Navy for this glorious intelligence? He is always giving us good news. I cannot, in words, tell you my joy over this result. It is great, Mr. Welles, it is great!"[68]

Modestly, Lincoln congratulated Grant. "I do not remember that you and I ever met personally. I write this now as a grateful acknowledgment for the almost inestimable service you have done the country." Lincoln then added "a word further" about strategy: "I now wish to make the personal acknowledgment that you were right, and I was wrong."[69] When told that Grant should not have paroled the Confederate army he had captured, Lincoln replied: "Grant has done so well, and we are all so pleased at the taking of Vicksburg, let us not quarrel with him about that matter."[70]

Port Hudson Campaign

The Vicksburg campaign had not entirely opened the Mississippi, for two hundred miles south of that citadel Confederates at Port Hudson still threatened river traffic. The movement against the town was undertaken by General Nathaniel P. Banks, who in November 1862 had been appointed to command the Department of the Gulf, headquartered in New Orleans. Banks got off to a bad start in his new command. After receiving secret orders in late October to raise a force for an expedition to New Orleans, he went about organizing it poorly.

Banks finally got under way on December 4. When he reached Louisiana, he failed to understand that the administration wanted above all to secure the Mississippi. Throughout the spring, Halleck urged Banks to cooperate with Grant's Vicksburg campaign. Finally in May, Banks's Army of the Gulf began a siege of Port Hudson that dragged on into July. Five days after the surrender of Vicksburg, the Port Hudson garrison also capitulated, thus allowing the "Father of Waters" to flow "unvexed to the sea," as Lincoln would later put it.[71] The president gratefully told Banks that the "final stroke in opening the Mississippi never should, and I think never will, be forgotten."[72]

The North reveled in the victories at Port Hudson, Vicksburg, and Gettysburg. "How marvelously the clouds seem to part!" exclaimed George William Curtis. "Three armies under three true and skillful leaders and upon three points successful! I think that for the first time we have a *real* confidence in our Generals."[73]

Lincoln Meets with Frederick Douglass

A notable feature of Banks's campaign was his employment of Black combat troops. This represented a departure from Lincoln's plan to use African American soldiers only in support roles. On May 27, the First and Third Infantries of the Corps d'Afrique, which had been recruited by Butler, along with Banks's own First Engineers, distinguished themselves in an unsuccessful assault on the Confederate works at Port Hudson. Eleven days later at Milliken's Bend, Louisiana, Black troops heroically fended off Confederate attacks. Charles A. Dana, who visited the site shortly afterward, recalled that "the bravery of the blacks in the battle at Milliken's Bend completely revolutionized the sentiment of the army with regard to the employment of negro troops."[74] A week after the fall of Port Hudson, a Black regiment in South Carolina, the Fifty-fourth Massachusetts, covered itself with glory at the battle of Fort Wagner, part of the ongoing campaign against Charleston.

The conduct of those soldiers earned the respect of military leaders, including Grant. Lincoln too paid high tribute to Black troops. In one of his most eloquent public letters, he wrote: "Some of the commanders of our armies in the field who have given us our most important successes, believe the emancipation policy, and the use of colored troops, constitute the heaviest blow yet dealt to the rebellion." Rhetorically, he asked opponents of Black enlistment: "You say you will not fight to free negroes. Some of them seem willing to fight for you. . . . If they stake their lives for us, they must be prompted by the strongest motive—even the promise of freedom. And the promise being made, must be kept." When at last the North wins the war, "then, there will be some black men who can remember that, with silent tongue, and clenched teeth, and steady eye, and well-poised bayonet, they have helped mankind on to this great consummation; while, I fear, there will be some white ones, unable to forget that, with malignant heart, and deceitful speech, they have strove to hinder it."[75]

Confederates threatened to execute or enslave captured Black soldiers, prompting Lincoln to issue an order of retaliation. To Stanton he wrote: "It is the duty of every government to give protection to its citizens, of whatever class, color, or condition, and especially to those who are duly organized as soldiers in the public service. . . . To sell or enslave any captured person, on account of his color, and for no offence against the laws of war, is a relapse into barbarism and a crime against the civilization of the age. The government of the United States will give the same protection to all its soldiers, and if the enemy shall sell or enslave anyone because of his color, the offense shall be punished by retaliation upon the enemy's prisoners in our possession."[76]

Despite the prospect of being murdered in cold blood or enslaved if captured, Blacks joined the army in large numbers. Many, however, were understandably angry that they were paid less than White troops and that they could serve only as enlisted men, not officers. A prominent recruiter, Massachusetts abolitionist George Luther Stearns, suggested to Frederick Douglass that he lobby the administration to change those policies.

Taking that advice, the famed Black orator visited the White House on August 10, 1863. Douglass reported that he was "received cordially" by Lincoln, who rose and extended his hand. Hoping to get the president to talk in general terms about the administration's treatment of Blacks, including the pay differential and the refusal to allow African Americans to become officers, Douglass first thanked him for the recent order of retaliation. As Douglass recounted, Lincoln "instantly . . . proceeded with . . . an earnestness and fluency of which I had not suspected him, to vindicate his policy respecting the whole slavery question and especially that in reference to employing colored troops." In justifying his original hesitancy to endorse the recruitment of Black troops and to issue the order of retaliation, Lincoln "said that the country needed talking up to that point. He hesitated in regard to it when he felt that the country was not ready for it." He continued: "Remember this, Mr. Douglass; remember that Milliken's Bend, Port Hudson, and Fort Wagner are recent events; and that these were necessary to prepare the way for this very proclamation of mine." If he had issued it earlier, he said, "such was the state of public popular prejudice that an outcry would have been raised against the measure." Douglass found this argument "reasonable." In a letter describing this conversation, he wrote: "My whole interview with the President was gratifying and did much to assure me that slavery would not survive the War and that the country would survive both slavery and the War."[77] In December, Douglass told a Philadelphia audience that while in the White House, he "felt big."[78]

(Lincoln's order of retaliation was never implemented, even though Confederates did kill some Black prisoners in cold blood, most notoriously at Fort Pillow, Tennessee, in 1864. As Lincoln put it, the "difficulty is not in stating the principle, but in practically applying it." Blood, he said, "can not restore blood, and government should not act for revenge." [79] When Douglass called for the execution of Confederate prisoners, Lincoln replied that such retaliation "was a terrible remedy."[80] On May 17, 1864, after mulling over the matter, Lincoln ordered Stanton to notify Confederate authorities that if they did not abandon their policy, the Union would set aside a number of Rebel prisoners and "take such action as may then appear expedient and just."[81] That threat proved idle, however, for Grant's spring offensive distracted attention away from the subject of retaliation.)

Lincoln told Douglass that given the strong Negrophobia prevailing in the earlier stages of the war, "the fact that they [Black troops] were not to receive the same pay as white soldiers seemed a necessary concession to smooth the way to their employment at all as soldiers." But, the president added, "ultimately they would receive the same."[82] His prediction was more or less accurate. In June 1864, Congress mandated equal pay but made it retroactive only to the first of that year for those Blacks who had been freed during the war; for those who had been free as of April 19, 1861, no such limitation was applied.

The victories at Gettysburg, Vicksburg, and Port Hudson represented a major turning point. Gaining control of the Mississippi River, as Edward Bates observed, was "the crowning act of the war." He predicted that it "will go farther towards the suppression of the rebellion than twenty victories in the open field. It breaks the heart of the rebellion."[83] He accurately noted that "the rebellion *west* of the great river, will hardly need to be conquered in the field—it must die out, of mere inanition."[84] Indeed, three of the eleven Confederate states—Arkansas, Texas, and most of Louisiana—were cut off. In addition, one of the most gaping holes in the blockade was plugged. No longer could the Confederacy aspire to win independence on the battlefield. Its principal hope was that the Northern public would grow weary of the war and insist on a compromise peace.

31.

"The Signs Look Better"

Victory at the Polls and in the Field (July–November 1863)

Lincoln's popularity soared after the victories at Gettysburg, Vicksburg, and Port Hudson. Still, the Confederacy was not on the verge of collapse. White House secretary William O. Stoddard accurately predicted that even though the "tiger is wounded unto death," it "will die hard, and fight to the last." If "we slacken our efforts because of our successes, there is great danger that the hard-won fruit of them will be torn from us."[1] Lincoln fully realized the truth of this prophesy and worked hard to keep his generals from slackening their efforts. Simultaneously, he girded for the looming political struggle in the fall, when elections in Pennsylvania and Ohio would measure the public mood.

As the president did so, another White House secretary, John Hay, analyzed his leadership qualities. In the summer of 1863, Hay told John G. Nicolay that their boss "is in fine whack. I have rarely seen him more serene & busy. He is managing this war, the draft, foreign relations, and planning a reconstruction of the Union, all at once. . . . I am growing more and more firmly convinced that the good of the country absolutely demands that he should be kept where he is till this thing is over. There is no man in the country, so wise, so gentle and so firm."[2]

The Draft

In March 1863, Congress passed the Enrollment Act, which made most of the 3,115,000 Northern men between the ages of twenty and forty-five eligible for conscription. The provisions for commutation (allowing a man to buy his way out for $300, roughly an average worker's annual income) and substitution (allowing a man to hire a substitute to serve in his stead) aroused special ire, provoking widespread protests about "a rich man's war and a poor man's fight." Resistance to the draft became violent; by war's end, thirty-eight enrolling officers had been killed, sixty had been wounded, and a dozen had suffered damage to their property. In addition, anti-draft riots broke out in several cities, including New York. There, between July 13 and

15, 1863, a mob ran amok, venting its wrath primarily on Blacks. The rioters lynched African Americans and burned down the Colored Orphan Asylum. Other targets included the draft office, the New York *Tribune* building, police headquarters, homes of government officials and wealthy residents, tenements and boardinghouses occupied by Blacks, upscale stores like Brooks Brothers, and hotels denying liquor to the rioters. More than one hundred people were killed, and three hundred wounded. Lincoln reportedly said "that sooner than abandon the draft at the dictation of the mob, he will transfer Meade's entire army to the city of New York."[3]

During this bloody rampage Horatio Seymour, newly elected governor of New York, seemed to egg the rioters on by addressing them as "my friends."[4] Seymour, a Democrat, did not order them to disperse but gently suggested that they cease and desist. His speech seemed to please the mob. The indiscreet allusion to "friends" was widely criticized. He had been doing his best to obstruct the enrollment process by delay, neglect, and denunciation. After the riots, he bombarded Lincoln with acrimonious letters, arguing that the Empire State's draft quotas were disproportionate to its population. He also urged that no further conscription be undertaken until courts had ruled on the constitutionality of the Enrollment Act, ominously hinting that violent resistance might otherwise be renewed.

Ignoring the tone of menace in Seymour's appeal, Lincoln on August 7 tactfully refused to honor his request. The president explained that he did "not object to abide a decision of the United States Supreme Court" on "the constitutionality of the draft law," but he could "not consent to lose the *time* while it is being obtained." The Confederate government, which had instituted a draft in 1862, "drives every able bodied man [it] can reach, into [its] ranks, very much as a butcher drives bullocks into a slaughter-pen. No time is wasted, no argument is used." Thus the enemy "produces an army which will soon turn upon our now victorious soldiers already in the field, if they shall not be sustained by recruits."[5] To placate Seymour, Lincoln agreed to reduce the quotas in some New York districts.

The governor, however, was not satisfied; he angrily insisted that the draft was being conducted unfairly in his state. In response, Lincoln again reduced some New York quotas. When Seymour continued to behave uncooperatively, the administration dispatched ten thousand troops to New York to maintain order while the draft was renewed there on August 19. To repeated protests that the administration failed to properly credit volunteers against the draft quotas, Lincoln patiently explained to Seymour that when, "for any cause, a fair credit is not given at one time, it should be given as soon thereafter as practicable. My purpose is to be just and fair; and yet to not lose time."[6]

Seymour was not the only one protesting the alleged unfairness in the implementation of the draft. When several Chicagoans, led by Joseph Medill of the *Tribune*, called to lodge such a complaint, Lincoln listened patiently, then turned on them, saying: "It is you who are largely responsible for making blood flow as it has. You called for war until we had it. You called for Emancipation, and I have given it to you. Whatever you have asked you have had. Now you come here begging to be let off from the call for men which I have made to carry out the war which you have demanded. You ought to be ashamed of yourselves. I have a right to expect better things of you. Go home, and raise your 6,000 extra men." As Medill recalled, "I couldn't say anything. It was the first time I ever was whipped, and I didn't have an answer. We all got up and went out, and when the door closed one of my colleagues said: 'Well, gentlemen, the old man is right. We ought to be ashamed of ourselves. Let us never say anything about this, but go home and raise the men.' And we did."[7]

State courts that hindered enforcement of the draft through habeas corpus proceedings angered Lincoln. The problem became acute in Pennsylvania, where resistance to conscription was widespread. (That state's supreme court would eventually rule the Enrollment Act unconstitutional.) At a cabinet meeting on September 14, 1863, the president, according to Attorney General Bates, "was greatly moved—more angry than I ever saw him" by the action of judges who had been releasing civilians arrested for obstructing conscription. He "declared that it was a formed plan of the democratic copperheads, deliberately acted out to defeat the Govt., and aid the enemy" and that "no honest man did or could believe that the State Judges have any such power."[8] He was, he added, "determined to put a stop to these factious and mischievous proceedings." He even threatened to banish such jurists to Confederate lines, just as he had exiled Clement L. Vallandigham.[9] Pounding the table, he said emphatically: "I'll not permit my officers to be arrested while in the discharge of their public duties."[10]

The next day, Lincoln read to the cabinet a proposed order authorizing provost marshals to ignore habeas corpus injunctions in draft-related cases. If necessary, force could be used to resist the edict of state courts. Chase agreed that the president had the power to suspend the writ under the 1863 Habeas Corpus Act; but, he argued, Lincoln's order was too vague and might be challenged successfully. Better, said he, to issue a proclamation explicitly suspending the writ. Lincoln concurred, as did the rest of the cabinet. Seward then composed a document covering all cases involving military arrest of deserters, draft resisters, spies, aiders and abettors of the Confederacy, prisoners of war, "or [those guilty of] any other offense against the military or naval service," which, with slight modifications, was promulgated that day. It was officially announced on September 17, in the midst of the hotly contested Pennsylvania gubernatorial race. "The proclamation suspending the writ of *Habeas corpus* is a heavy blow but as it is right we can stand it," Governor Andrew G. Curtin (who was up for reelection) told the president.[11]

Around that time, Lincoln composed an angry message to draft protestors in which he explained the necessity for conscription and defended its constitutionality on the obvious grounds that Congress had the power to raise and support armies. After pointing out that some men had been drafted in the Revolutionary War and the War of 1812, he asked rhetorically: "Wherein is the peculiar hardship now? Shall we shrink from the necessary means to maintain our free government, which our grand-fathers employed to establish it, and our own fathers have already employed once to maintain it? Are we degenerate? Has the manhood of our race run out?"[12] Lincoln ultimately chose not to publish this message.

Although notoriously softhearted in issuing pardons, Lincoln had little sympathy for draft resistance. When the wives of two poor Irishmen who had been jailed for that crime asked the president to pardon them, he replied using their accent: "If yers hushbands had not been resisting the draft, they would not now be in prison; so they can stay in prison."[13]

Dealing with Missouri Radicals

Frustrating as problems associated with the draft might be, Lincoln found it even more vexatious to deal with political and military turmoil in the bitterly divided state of Missouri, where his generals clashed repeatedly with local authorities. Aside from being embroiled in controversies over control of the state militia, Lincoln also became entangled in questions related to confiscation, martial law, and the jailing or exiling of suspected disloyalists without due process. In December 1862, he intervened when General Samuel R. Curtis approved an order banishing the Reverend Dr. Samuel B. McPheeters, minister of the Pine Street Presbyterian Church in St. Louis. Although the pastor had taken a loyalty oath, his devotion to the Union cause appeared to some parishioners insufficiently fervent. He had offended many by baptizing an infant named after the Confederate general Sterling Price. McPheeters's case quickly became a cause célèbre. He hastened to Washington and appealed to Lincoln, who on December 27 suspended the banishment decree. When Curtis objected, the president explained that he saw no hard evidence of McPheeters's disloyalty but would rescind his order if the general insisted. Lincoln added, however, that the federal government "must not, as by this order, undertake to run the churches. When an individual, in a church or out of it, becomes dangerous to the public interest, he must be checked; but let the churches, as such take care of themselves."[14]

Guerilla warfare ravaged Missouri throughout the war, and during the summer of 1863 atrocities along the border with Kansas peaked. On August 21, the infamously cruel and brutal Confederate officer William Clarke Quantrill led a raid against Lawrence, Kansas, where his guerilla band, acting upon orders to "kill every man big enough to carry a gun" and to "burn every house," slaughtered 182 men and boys and torched a like number of buildings. This act of wanton terrorism shocked the North.

Shortly thereafter, General Thomas Ewing Jr., Union commander in the District of the Border, issued his controversial General Orders No. 11, banishing approximately twenty thousand residents of four Missouri counties bordering Kansas, causing immense hardship for the families of loyal Unionists as well as for guerilla supporters. Some evidence suggests that Lincoln tacitly authorized this stern measure, which was implemented four days after Quantrill's murderous raid. Union troops under the notorious Charles "Doc" Jennison carried out this assignment so harshly, pillaging and torching homes of the dispossessed residents, that the affected counties became known as the Burnt District. On October 1, Lincoln informed General John M. Schofield that he would not interfere with the deportations. His willingness to approve such a draconian measure reflected his awareness that dealing with guerillas required unorthodox tactics and that hard-and-fast rules like those laid out in General Order No. 100 (*Instructions for the Government of the Armies of the United States in the Field*, written by Francis Lieber at the behest of General Halleck) had to be applied flexibly. General Orders No. 11 aroused such vehement protests that it was suspended in November. Two months thereafter, deported loyalists were permitted to return to what was left of their homes, much to the dismay of Ewing. The policy failed to reduce guerilla violence in Missouri, though no more massacres were carried out in Kansas.

Missouri and Kansas Radicals, angry at Schofield's failure to protect them from outrages like Quantrill's raid and dismayed by that general's refusal to allow retaliatory action, decided to appeal directly to Lincoln. In September, a Radical Union Emancipation Convention in Jefferson City selected a delegation of seventy members to demand that Schofield be replaced by Benjamin F. Butler, a darling of antislavery militants. Further, they insisted that only loyal men be allowed to vote in state elections. Shortly before the Committee of Seventy arrived at the nation's capital, Lincoln said that "if they can show that Schofield has done anything wrong & has interfered to their disadvantage with State politics—or has so acted as to damage the cause of the Union and good order their case is made." But he suspected that "it will be found that Schofield is a firm competent energetic & eminently fair man, and that he has incurred their ill will by refusing to take sides with them in their local politics."[15]

The eyes of the North focused on the White House meeting, with Radicals regarding the Missourians as their surrogates. Not since the cabinet imbroglio of the previous December had factionalism so seriously threatened to rend the Republican coalition. The utmost tact was required to damp down Radical discontent without alienating moderates and conservatives. While willing to hear them out, the president was determined not to appease them.

On September 30, Lincoln spent more than two hours with the seventy angry Missourians and eighteen aggrieved Kansans, led by Charles D. Drake and Senator James Lane. Entering the spacious East Room at 10:30 a.m., Lincoln beheld a rather scruffy group. Some of the men were battle-scarred from guerilla warfare. The president offered no special greeting and shook no hands. Pompously and slowly, Drake delivered the committee's formal address. When the deep-voiced Missourian finished reading, Lincoln said he would consider the document "without prejudice, without pique, without resentment," and provide a written response soon.

There followed a long, desultory conversation. After several heated accusations, Lincoln replied: "I am aware that by many, by some even among this delegation [an allusion to Drake],—I shall not name them,—I have been in public speeches and in printed documents charged with 'tyranny' and willfulness, with a disposition to make my own personal will supreme. I do not intend to be a tyrant. At all events I shall take care that in my own eyes I do not become one. I shall always try and preserve one friend within me, whoever else fails me, to tell me that I have not been a tyrant, and that I have acted right. I have no right to act the tyrant to mere political opponents. If a man votes for supplies of men and money; encourages enlistments; discourages desertions; does all in his power to carry the war on to a successful issue,—I have no right to question him for his abstract political opinions. I must make a dividing line, somewhere between those who are the opponents of the Government and those who only oppose peculiar features of my administration while they sustain the Government." Lincoln also reiterated his support for gradual emancipation in Missouri and chided the Radicals for their unwillingness to compromise. "I had the highest hope that at last Missouri was on the right track. But I was disappointed by the immediate emancipation movement. It endangers the success of the whole advance towards freedom." He insisted that "the mode of emancipation in Missouri is not my business. That is a matter which belongs exclusively to the citizens of that state: I do not wish to interfere. I desire, if it pleases the people of Missouri, that they should adopt gradual emancipation. I think that a union of all anti-slavery men upon this point would have made emancipation a final fact forever. . . . I am sorry to see anti-slavery men opposing such a movement."[16]

Reflecting on the upcoming elections in Missouri, Lincoln told John Hay: "I believe, after all, those Radicals will carry the state & I do not object to it." They "are nearer to me than the other side, in thought and sentiment, though bitterly hostile personally. They are utterly lawless—the unhandiest devils in the world to deal with—but after all their faces are set Zionwards."[17] Nevertheless, the Radicals' intolerance offended Lincoln. While he and they shared much in common, he did object to what he deemed "the petulant and vicious fretfulness of many radicals" as well as "the self-righteousness of the Abolitionists."[18]

Eventually Lincoln did decide to reassign Schofield, who had not managed to stay above the factional fray in Missouri. To replace him, the president chose General William S. Rosecrans, who weeks earlier had been dismissed from his post as commander of the Army of the Cumberland.

Military Developments in the West

After his crucial victory at the battle of Stone's River in January 1863, Rosecrans did little for many months. In the summer, however, he maneuvered Braxton Bragg's army out of Shelbyville, then Tullahoma, and finally Chattanooga. But he incautiously pursued the Confederates into Georgia, where his army was routed on September 19 and 20 at the battle of Chickamauga and driven back into Chattanooga, which Bragg besieged.

Upon learning of that defeat, Lincoln told John Hay: "Well, Rosecrans has been whipped, as I feared. I have feared it for several days. I believe I feel trouble in the air before it comes."[19] He reportedly was "sober and anxious over it, but not in the least despondent."[20] He did severely criticize two of Rosecrans's corps commanders, Thomas L. Crittenden and Alexander McCook, who with their commander had skedaddled back to Chattanooga during the fight, leaving George H. Thomas to hold off the enemy. That Virginian did so effectively, earning the sobriquet "The Rock of Chickamauga."

Other distressing news arrived from the Georgia battlefield: the First Lady's brother-in-law, Confederate general Benjamin Hardin Helm, had been killed. Lincoln had befriended him and his wife before the war, and word of his death profoundly saddened the president. He invited Hardin's widow, Emilie (favorite half-sister of Mrs. Lincoln), to visit the White House, where he told her, "You know Little Sister I tried to have Ben come with me. I hope you do not feel any bitterness or that I am in any way to blame for all this sorrow."[21] She stayed for two weeks, much to the indignation of some, including Daniel Sickles. When that general chided Lincoln for hosting the widow of a Rebel commander, the president replied with quiet dignity: "Excuse me, General Sickles, my wife and I are in the habit of choosing our own guests. We do not need from our friends either advice or assistance in the matter."[22]

Responding to the defeat at Chickamauga, the excitable Stanton asked John Hay to summon the president from the Soldiers' Home to attend a council of war. The young secretary wakened his boss, who expressed concern, for this was the first time that Stanton had sent for him. At the War Department, Lincoln joined Halleck, Stanton, Seward, Chase, and others to consider ways to reinforce Rosecrans. When Stanton estimated that thirty thousand troops could be moved in five days from the Army of the Potomac to Chattanooga, Lincoln skeptically remarked: "I will bet that if the order is given tonight, the troops could not be got to Washington in five days."[23] Despite his reservations, it was agreed that the Eleventh and Twelfth Corps should be rushed to Rosecrans posthaste, with Hooker in charge. Though Fighting Joe would have a much smaller command than usual, and despite his reservations about the proposed strategy, he agreed to take on the new assignment. Stanton then organized the most successful and dramatic use of railroads in the war, dispatching twenty-three thousand men southwestward. They completed the 1,192-mile journey in record time.

Those reinforcements kept the Confederates from crushing Rosecrans's army, but Bragg might be able to starve it out. The tone of Old Rosy's dispatches convinced Lincoln that the general no longer felt able to hold the city. Those telegrams made Rosecrans seem, as Lincoln put it, "confused and stunned like a duck hit on the head."[24] So the president put all three Western armies under the command of U. S. Grant, who was told he could retain Rosecrans in charge of the Army of the Cumberland or remove him as he saw fit. Stating that Old Rosy "never would obey orders," Grant replaced him with George H. Thomas, who had heroically prevented the defeat at Chickamauga from becoming a total rout.[25] Lincoln had lavishly praised Thomas: "It is doubtful whether his heroism and skill . . . has ever been surpassed in the world."[26] Taking charge of the beefed-up combined Union forces, Grant swiftly opened a supply line to Chattanooga, then methodically planned a counteroffensive against Bragg. In the last week of November, Union troops at the battles of Lookout Mountain and Missionary Ridge trounced the Confederates, who fled to Georgia.

While Grant was reversing the tide in Tennessee, N. P. Banks bungled an attempt to secure a beachhead in Texas. After the surrender of Port Hudson, Banks wanted to move against Mobile, but Lincoln wished to establish a Union presence in the Lone Star State in order to send a message to Louis Napoleon, who had installed the Archduke Ferdinand Maximilian of Austria as head of a puppet government in Mexico. In September, Banks dispatched troops to Sabine Pass, where they were routed by a small contingent of Rebels. Weeks later, another Union advance toward Texas through western Louisiana was thwarted at the battle of Bayou Bourbeau. In November, Banks did manage to capture Brownsville, but that minor accomplishment hardly offset the earlier failures.

Vindication at the Polls

During the summer and fall of 1863, Lincoln worried about political as well as military developments. Eight gubernatorial elections were to be held and would prove a crucial turning point in the war. In June, he was optimistic, partly because of Republican successes that spring in New England's gubernatorial elections. As the summer progressed, military triumphs at Vicksburg, Gettysburg, and Port Hudson cheered up the public. Even Rosecrans's defeat at Chickamauga failed to persuade many voters that the war was a failure. Nor could the daring raid of Confederate partisan John Hunt Morgan, who in July led twenty-five hundred men across the Ohio River and rampaged through Indiana and Ohio before being driven off with huge losses. The raid backfired politically.

Further enhancing Republican chances was the blundering leadership of the Democrats. Their party sorely missed Stephen A. Douglas, whose unalloyed Unionism contrasted sharply with the negativism of so many other Democratic spokesmen. Even more embarrassing were Democratic legislatures in Indiana and Illinois, which brazenly refused to appropriate money or men for the war effort. To bolster Republican prospects, the administration furloughed thousands of soldiers and granted leave to government employees from Pennsylvania and Ohio, allowing them to return home to vote. Lincoln's most important contribution to the campaign was his response to an invitation to visit Springfield, where Republicans organized a huge rally in August and wanted the president to address it. He felt he could not leave Washington, so he wrote a public letter, one of his very best, to be read at the Springfield event.

The invitation had come from his old friend, James C. Conkling, who, like many Illinoisans, worried about the strength of antiwar Democrats capitalizing on opposition to emancipation and the recruitment of Black soldiers. Lincoln's letter masterfully defended the Emancipation Proclamation and the decision to enroll African American troops but avoided discussing the unpopular Enrollment Act. With iron logic, Lincoln bluntly challenged Peace Democrats to answer some tough questions: "You desire peace; and you blame me that we do not have it. But how can we attain it?" There were only "three conceivable ways. First, to suppress the rebellion by force of arms." This he was trying to do. "Are you for it? If you are, so far we are agreed. If you are not for it, a second way is, to give up the Union. I am against this. Are you for it? If you are, you should say so plainly. If you are not for *force*, nor yet for *dissolution*, there only remains some imaginable *compromise*." But, Lincoln averred, no compromise that restored the Union was possible, for neither the Confederate army nor its civilian leadership had demonstrated interest in such a solution. "In an effort at such compromise we should waste time, which the enemy would improve to our disadvantage; and that would be all."

Lincoln boldly addressed the race issue, challenging his critics: "You are dissatisfied with me about the negro. Quite likely there is a difference of opinion between you and myself upon that subject. I certainly wish that all men could be free, while I suppose you do not." Lincoln emphasized that he had issued the Emancipation Proclamation and approved the recruitment of Black troops as practical, Union-saving measures. He chided critics for their reluctance to avail themselves of his generous offer to pay for slaves. To those who objected that the Emancipation Proclamation violated the Constitution, Lincoln insisted that "the constitution invests its commander-in-chief, with the law of war, in time of war," which permitted the seizure of property. Was there any doubt, he asked rhetorically, "that by the law of war, property, both of enemies and friends, may be taken when needed? And is it not needed whenever taking it, helps us, or hurts the enemy?" Military leaders, the president assured his critics, had praised the issuance of the Emancipation Proclamation and the recruitment of Black troops as "the heaviest blow yet dealt to the rebellion."

Lincoln offered a brief report on the war's progress, rejoicing that the "signs look better." In an eloquent conclusion, he meditated on the larger significance of the contest. "Peace does not appear so distant as it did. I hope it will come soon, and come to stay; and so come as to be worth the keeping in all future time. It will then have been proved that, among free men, there can be no successful appeal from the ballot to the bullet; and that they who take such appeal are sure to lose their case, and pay the cost." With crushing force he put critics of Black recruitment in their place, as noted in the previous chapter.[27] With this powerful letter, Lincoln helped scotch the Copperhead snake. His insistence that emancipation would not be reversed pleased many Radicals. Democrats, however, protested that if "the proclamation cannot be retracted then every provision in the constitution pertaining to slavery is abrogated."[28]

The Democrats' most egregious blunder was nominating Clement L. Vallandigham instead of a more moderate candidate for governor of Ohio. The campaign became a referendum on the war rather than on alleged government violations of civil liberties. From exile in Canada, where Vallandigham had settled weeks after Lincoln banished him to the South, he was unable to mount a serious campaign against his opponent, John Brough, who warmly supported emancipation. Republicans denounced Vallandigham as a traitor for opposing the war effort. On October 13, as Ohio voters flocked to the polls, Lincoln said he felt nervous. When Brough triumphed by almost one hundred thousand votes, capturing 95 percent of the soldier vote, the president was vastly relieved and immensely delighted, regarding the outcome as a popular verdict on his leadership. Also gratifying was the outcome in Pennsylvania, where Governor Andrew G. Curtin won reelection despite suffering from such poor health that he could not campaign extensively. The Democrats had nominated George W. Woodward, the chief justice of the state supreme court, who would eventually hold that both the Enrollment Act and the Legal Tender Act were unconstitutional. In addition, Republicans won gubernatorial races in Iowa, Minnesota, Wisconsin, and Massachusetts.

"The Old Line State" Earns a New Title: "The Free State"

Lincoln tried to promote harmony between Unconditional and Conservative Unionists in Maryland. The army's practice of recruiting slaves rather arbitrarily, making little distinction between loyal and disloyal owners, had strained relations between the main Republican factions. When irate Unionist slaveholders complained, the president told them "that if the recruiting squads did not conduct themselves properly, their places should be supplied by others, but that the orders under which the enlistments were being made could not be revoked, since the country needed able-bodied soldiers, and was not squeamish as to their complexion."[29] He emphasized, however, that he wished to offend no Marylanders. In October, he issued a general order providing that loyal slaveholders would be paid up to three hundred dollars for any slave who enlisted, with the understanding that all such recruits would "forever thereafter be free."[30] Any loyal slave owners unwilling to let their slaves join the army must themselves enter its ranks.

Lincoln also sought to curb Robert C. Schenck's high-handed interference in elections. That general prescribed a stringent loyalty oath for voters and dispatched troops around the state to intimidate Democrats and Conservative Unionists. Although Lincoln upheld Schenck's test oath, he modified the general's order to arrest anyone near the polls who seemed disloyal. In an unapologetic letter to Governor Augustus W. Bradford, who protested against Schenck's procedures, the president insisted that loyal voters would be protected against violent attempts to intimidate them: "General Schenck is fully determined, and has my strict orders besides, that all loyal men may vote, and vote for whom they please."[31]

On election day, however, Schenck's forces actively intervened at the polls and helped depress the turnout. At the White House, the returns from Maryland were anxiously awaited. There was great relief when news arrived that Unconditional Unionists had won four congressional races, while Representative John W. Crisfield, a Conservative Unionist, had lost his reelection bid. Emancipationists also gained control of the legislature. The antislavery forces' triumph, which paved the way for emancipation the following year, would probably not have occurred without federal interference.

Lincoln's public letters, most notably the one to James C. Conkling, helped make the crucial electoral victories possible. That document, along with the two letters about the Vallandigham case and the correspondence with Seymour, was published in pamphlet form and widely distributed. Lincoln modestly disclaimed credit for the electoral victories, saying he was "very glad" that he had "not, by native depravity, or under evil influences, done anything bad enough to prevent the good result."[32] When congratulated on the outcome, he remarked: "The people are for this war. They want the rebellion crushed, and as quick as may be, too."[33]

Gettysburg Address

Shortly after the elections, Lincoln prepared a brief public utterance that would clinch his reputation as a writer: the Gettysburg Address. In the summer of 1863, when David Wills, a successful young attorney in Gettysburg, organized an effort to create a national cemetery for the Union soldiers killed there, he and his fellow planners decided to consecrate the site with a solemn ceremony. They agreed that the principal speaker should be Edward Everett and that Lincoln should also be invited to say a few words on November 19. Wills waited until November 2 to invite the president to deliver some "appropriate remarks."[34]

From the outset of the war, Lincoln had regarded the conflict as one to vindicate democracy, not simply to preserve the Union for its own sake or to liberate slaves. As he told John Hay in May 1861, "the central idea" of the war was to prove "that popular government is not an absurdity."[35] In his address, Lincoln made it clear that Union soldiers had died in the effort to demonstrate that self-government was viable for all nations, not just the United States. "Man's vast future" would be determined by the outcome of the war. In his speech he would also emphasize that the war would midwife "a new birth of freedom" by liberating slaves and thus move the country closer to realizing the Founders' vision of equality. Since the Peoria speech of 1854 he had been stressing the need to live up to the ideal expressed in the Declaration of Independence.

Lincoln told James Speed that "he was anxious to go" to Gettysburg, but as the ceremony date drew near, the president worried that he might not be able to do so, for he was reluctant to leave the bedside of his son Tad, ill with scarlatina. Despite that, the president departed for Pennsylvania on November 18. Arriving in Gettysburg in the late afternoon, Lincoln, flanked by a cheering crowd, proceeded to the home of David Wills, where he was to spend the night. At supper, Edward

Everett observed that the president was as gentlemanly in appearance, manners, and conversation as any of the diplomats, governors, and other *eminenti* dining there. After the meal, when serenaders regaled him at the Wills house, he asked to be excused from addressing them, saying, "I have no speech to make. In my position it is somewhat important that I should not say any foolish things." An irreverent voice rang out: "If you can help it." Lincoln replied good-naturedly: "It very often happens that the only way to help it is to say nothing at all."[36] The crowd cheered enthusiastically, then moved next door, where Seward was staying.

Later that evening, Lincoln greeted guests at a reception for an hour or so, then retired to work on his speech. Around 11:00 he stepped next door to confer with Seward, staying less than half an hour. It is not known what, if any, suggestions the secretary of state may have made. Lifting the president's spirits was a telegram announcing that his son was "slightly better."[37]

The next morning, as people swarmed into town, Lincoln rose early, toured the battlefield with Seward, and polished his address. At 10:00, upon emerging from the Wills house, Lincoln encountered a huge crowd whose deafening cheers made him blush. Benjamin Brown French was struck by the public's response to the president. "Abraham Lincoln is the idol of the American people at this moment," French confided to his journal. "Anyone who saw & heard as I did, the hurricane of applause that met his every movement at Gettysburg would know that he lived in every heart. . . . It was the spontaneous outburst of heartfelt confidence in *their own* President."[38]

At the cemetery, as Lincoln slowly approached the stage, the fifteen thousand spectators maintained a respectful silence. Opening the proceedings was a dirge, followed by a long prayer and then Everett's two-hour speech describing the battle, analyzing the causes and the nature of the war, rebutting secessionist arguments, predicting a quick postwar sectional reconciliation, citing ancient Greek funeral rites, and denouncing the enemy. When Everett alluded to the suffering of the dying troops, tears came to Lincoln's eyes.

After a musical interlude, the president slowly rose to speak. His words were taken down by reporters, whose accounts differ slightly. The following text is what he probably said, with bracketed italics representing revisions he made for the final version:

> Four score and seven years ago our fathers brought forth upon [*on*] this continent a new nation, conceived in liberty, and dedicated to the proposition that all men are created equal. [Applause.] Now we are engaged in a great civil war, testing whether that nation or any nation so conceived and so dedicated, can long endure. We are met on a great battle-field of that war. We are met [*have come*] to

> dedicate a portion of it [*that field*] as the [*a*] final resting place of [*for*] those who here gave their lives that that nation might live. It is altogether fitting and proper that we should do this. But, in a larger sense, we cannot dedicate, we cannot consecrate, we cannot hallow this ground. The brave men, living and dead, who struggled here have consecrated it far above our poor power to add or detract. [Applause.] The world will little note nor long remember what we say here, but it can never forget what they did here. [Applause.] It is for us, the living, rather to be dedicated here to the unfinished work that [*which*] they [*who fought here*] have thus far so nobly carried on [*advanced*]. [Applause.] It is rather for us to be here dedicated to the great task remaining before us, that from these honored dead we take increased devotion to that cause for which they here gave [*they gave*] the last full measure of devotion; that we here highly resolve that these dead shall not have died in vain [applause]; that the nation shall, under God, [*nation, under God, shall*] have a new birth of freedom; and that Government of the people, by the people, [*for the people*] and for the people, shall not perish from the earth. [Long-continued applause.]"[39]

The audience was profoundly moved. Isaac Jackson Allen of the Columbus *Ohio State Journal* reported that "when he had concluded, scarcely could an untearful eye be seen, while sobs of smothered emotion were heard on every hand."[40] Everett wrote with customary graciousness to Lincoln the day after the ceremony: "Permit me . . . to express my great admiration of the thoughts expressed by you, with such eloquent simplicity & appropriateness, at the consecration of the Cemetery. I should be glad, if I could flatter myself that I came as near to the central idea of the occasion, in two hours, as you did in two minutes."[41] Some Democrats criticized Lincoln for injecting politics into a solemn, nonpartisan occasion; they condemned most vehemently the implication that the war was being fought, at least in part, to free the slaves. (Although Lincoln did not say so explicitly, that was the evident meaning of his references to a "new birth of freedom" and to equality.) Although posterity has come to regard Lincoln's remarks as a succinct, sublime masterpiece and Everett's oration as a florid, diffuse history lecture, the contemporary press devoted more coverage to the latter than to the former. Several myths grew up around the Gettysburg Address, among them that the president composed it on the train, that he regarded it as a failure, that the crowd and other contemporaries did not appreciate it, and that it surreptitiously bootlegged the concept of equality into the Constitution. The speech was in effect another of Lincoln's highly successful public letters. His audience was the Northern public at large, whose morale he aimed to lift with a terse exposition of the war's significance. His words admirably served that function in his own day and have inspired the respect and admiration of subsequent generations.

Alexander Gardner took this memorable photograph of Lincoln on November 8, 1863, eleven days before he delivered the Gettysburg Address. The sculptor Daniel Chester French used it to model the statue of the seated Great Emancipator in the Lincoln Memorial. Indiana Historical Society, Indianapolis.

Presidential Smallpox

Back in Washington, Lincoln came down with a mild case of smallpox, known as varioloid, which persisted for several days. Part of that time he was quarantined. When told that his illness was contagious, he quipped that as president "he had always had a crowd of people asking him to give them something" and "*now he has something he can give them all.*" Alluding both to the scars that smallpox often caused and to his appearance, he told a physician: "There is one consolation about the matter, doctor. It cannot in the least disfigure me!"[42]

The varioloid did more than disfigure William H. Johnson, the young Black man who accompanied Lincoln from Illinois and served briefly in the White House until his fellow African American staffers there objected to his presence because his skin was too dark. Lincoln then obtained for him a job in the Treasury Department. Johnson contracted smallpox, which killed him in January 1864. Lincoln paid for Johnson's coffin, helped his family, and repaid the bank loans he had endorsed for Johnson.

Victories in Tennessee, Stalemate in Virginia

On November 21, Lincoln predicted that "the next two weeks would be the most momentous period of the rebellion."[43] Indeed, the war in the West was approaching a climax as Grant prepared to dislodge Bragg's forces from the heights above Chattanooga. On November 24 and 25, Union troops captured strong Confederate positions on Missionary Ridge and Lookout Mountain, forcing Bragg to retreat into Georgia.

Meanwhile, Lincoln grew quite anxious about Burnside's fate. That hapless general, ensconced in Knoxville, was menaced by James Longstreet's corps. On November 24, the president expressed great relief upon learning that firing had recently been heard in the vicinity of Knoxville. When asked why he had reacted so positively to news indicating that Union forces might be in serious danger, he replied: "I had a neighbor out West, a Sally Taggart, who had a great many unruly children whom she did not take very good care of. Whenever she heard one squall in some out-of-the-way place, she would say, 'Well, thank Goodness, there's one of my young ones not dead yet!' As long as we hear guns, Burnside is not captured."[44]

On November 29, Union forces repulsed Longstreet's attack. Soon thereafter, the Confederates pulled back. When the president learned the good news, he joyfully declared that it "is one of the most important gains of the war . . . it secures us East Tennessee." At the same time, he expressed dismay at the inactivity in the East, predicting that Meade probably would not move to intercept Longstreet's fleeing Confederates. In September, when Meade argued that it would be quite difficult to attack Richmond, the exasperated Lincoln told Halleck: "If our army can not fall upon the enemy and hurt him where he is, it is plain to me it can gain nothing by attempting to follow him over a succession of intrenched lines into a fortified city."[45] A month later, Lincoln tried to goad Meade into taking the offensive against Lee. "If Gen. Meade can now attack him on a field no worse than equal for us," he instructed the general through Halleck, "and will do so with all the skill and courage, which he, his officers and men possess, the honor will be his if he succeeds, and the blame may be mine if he fails."[46] Meade replied with a typical excuse for inaction.

Months later, Grant would be placed in charge of all Union forces, and the Army of the Potomac would move decisively against the enemy without such presidential inducements.

32.

"I Hope to Stand Firm Enough to Not Go Backward, and Yet Not Go Forward Fast Enough to Wreck the Country's Cause"

Reconstruction and Renomination (November 1863–June 1864)

In late 1863, as prospects for victory improved, Lincoln tried to devise a reconstruction policy that would protect the rights of the newly freed slaves while simultaneously restoring sectional harmony. To make emancipation more than a paper promise without alienating White Southerners was a daunting challenge, for every measure designed to guarantee the rights of Blacks was regarded as an insult by the region's Whites.

Lincoln was hard-pressed to keep the Republican coalition intact. Some Radicals, led by Charles Sumner, argued that each rebellious state had committed suicide, reverting to territorial status and therefore subject to congressional regulation. They also wished to emancipate all slaves, confiscate Rebel property, and deny political rights to most Confederates. Understandably fearing that such measures might alienate Unionists in the Border States and the Confederacy, along with Northern Democrats and conservative Republicans, Lincoln took charge of wartime reconstruction as Union forces occupied more and more Southern territory.

Early Experiments with Military Governors

Lincoln's initial ad hoc response was to appoint military governors and rely on Southern Unionists to rehabilitate their states, with some general guidance from the administration. In March 1862, he made Tennessee senator Andrew Johnson governor of the Volunteer State. Later that year he selected governors for North Carolina, Louisiana, Arkansas, and Texas. Congress acquiesced at first but eventually balked. Johnson was given a free hand to restore civilian government as soon as practicable. He undertook harsh measures, including the arrest of several clergymen, and used inflammatory rhetoric, telling a mass meeting that "treason must be crushed out and traitors must be punished."[1]

In July 1862, Lincoln urged Johnson to call an election. "If we could, somehow, get a vote of the people of Tennessee and have it result properly it would be worth more to us than a battle gained," he wrote.[2] The president hoped that a civilian government might be persuaded to abolish slavery and accord freedpeople some basic rights. If that could be done, the inevitable White backlash might be minimized, for the momentous changes would be the work of native Whites, not Yankees. Johnson disappointed the president by stating that it would be impossible to hold elections before eastern Tennessee was pacified. Conflict between Johnson and military commanders Buell, Halleck, and Rosecrans also chagrined Lincoln, who tactfully tried to reconcile their differences.

To placate Tennessee Unionists outraged by the Emancipation Proclamation, Lincoln agreed to exempt their state from its provisions, even though much of it remained under Confederate control. That drastic step illustrated the lengths to which the president was willing to go to accommodate beleaguered loyalists in eastern Tennessee. In September 1863, the president grew more optimistic. He told Johnson that "it is the nick of time for re-inaugerating a loyal State government. Not a moment should be lost." Lincoln warned that opponents of emancipation and the Union war effort should not be allowed to triumph: "Get emancipation into your new State government—Constitution—and there will be no such word as fail for your case."[3] Rosecrans's defeat at Chickamauga in September 1863 delayed implementation of the president's plan. When Lincoln summoned Johnson to Washington in October, the governor unwisely declined, pleading preoccupation with business. Lincoln's hopes to have Tennessee become the first Confederate state to reestablish loyal civilian government thus were not realized.

A similar attempt in North Carolina also fizzled. In early 1862, Union troops under Burnside had occupied coastal areas of the Tarheel State. To serve as military governor, Lincoln appointed an able, temperamental, and combative North Carolina native, Edward Stanly. Like Johnson, he received carte blanche from the administration, and when he pleaded for more explicit instructions, he was simply told to act as a dictator. Lincoln did, however, urge Stanly to call for congressional elections, but before that step could be undertaken, the governor committed blunders that outraged many Radicals. In 1862, he opposed the founding of schools for freedpeople, and he sought to stop fugitive slaves from escaping northward. In response, Lincoln insisted that "no slave who once comes within our lines a fugitive from a rebel, shall ever be returned to his master."[4] At the president's behest, Stanton commanded the governor to reopen the Black schools.

Stanly threatened to resign when the Preliminary Emancipation Proclamation was announced in September 1862. Lincoln dissuaded him by explaining that he had been forced to issue that document by intense Radical pressure. The president reminded Stanly that the Proclamation exempted all areas where elections for Congress had been held: "It is my sincere wish that North Carolina may again govern herself conformably to the constitution of the United States."[5] As he had done with the Border States, Lincoln used the looming prospect of emancipation as an inducement to encourage occupied Confederate regions to return to the Union, but the offer would expire on January 1. Fearing that unsuitable candidates might be elected and that very few voters would turn out, Stanly delayed calling an election; eventually he ordered one for New Year's Day, too late to qualify for the exemption. In the event, a small voter turnout made the election of congressmen seem illegitimate, and nothing came of it except Stanly's resignation on January 15, 1863. Lincoln appointed no successor.

The president enjoyed greater success in reconstructing Louisiana, where in June 1862 he appointed Colonel George S. Shepley military governor. Shepley proved a disappointment, for he regarded himself as the agent of Benjamin Butler rather than a policymaker in his own right. A massive influx of Blacks into New Orleans seriously challenged the new government. Butler and Shepley tried to staunch the flow, but General John W. Phelps of Vermont welcomed freed slaves into his camp. In July 1862, when informed that Phelps's policy was crushing Union sentiment in Louisiana, Lincoln tartly dismissed the complaint. Residents of Louisiana, he wrote, "know full well, that I never had a wish to touch the foundations of their society, or any right of theirs." If "they are annoyed by the presence of General Phelps," they could "remove the necessity of his presence" and "simply take their place in the Union upon the old terms." Hinting that he might issue an emancipation order, he said significantly: "I am a patient man—always willing to forgive on the Christian terms of repentance; and also to give ample *time* for repentance. Still I must save this government if possible. What I *cannot* do, of course I *will* not do; but it may as well be understood, once for all, that I shall not surrender this game leaving any available card unplayed."[6]

By late July 1862, Lincoln had grown exasperated with the slow pace of reconstruction efforts in Louisiana. When a local Unionist complained about the vagueness of the administration's policies, the president answered heatedly: "Broken eggs cannot be mended; but Louisiana has nothing to do now but to take her place in the Union as it was. . . . This government cannot much longer play a game in which it stakes all, and its enemies stake nothing. Those enemies must understand that they cannot experiment for ten years trying to destroy the government, and if they fail still come back into the Union unhurt. If they expect in any contingency to ever have the Union as it was, I join with the writer in saying, 'Now is the time.'"[7]

Impatient with Governor Shepley's failure to organize an election, Lincoln wrote him directly on November 21. "I wish elections for Congressmen to take place in Louisiana," he said, but added that "I wish it to be a movement of the people of the Districts, and not a movement of our military and quasi-military, authorities there.... Fix a day for an election in all the Districts, and have it held in as many places as you can."[8] In fact, unbeknownst to Lincoln, Shepley had arranged to hold congressional elections on December 3. That day, more than seventy-seven hundred voters turned out and chose the moderate Michael Hahn and the more radical Benjamin F. Flanders as U.S. representatives. In December, when those gentlemen arrived in Washington to take their seats, their appearance touched off a fierce debate. Radicals had come to regret giving Lincoln a free hand in the reconstruction process by admitting congressmen elected under his auspices in Virginia and Tennessee. As a result, those areas of the occupied South would be exempt from the impending Emancipation Proclamation.

Some Democrats joined the Radicals in objecting to presidential reconstruction. Lincoln was furious when told that Congress might refuse to seat Flanders and Hahn. Eventually the House accepted their credentials, which the president regarded as a major victory for his reconstruction policy; but it was a false dawn. Congress rejected the credentials of all other representatives elected from Confederate states, and little progress was made in 1863 toward restoring civil government in Louisiana, even though the politically experienced General Nathaniel P. Banks became military commander there in December 1862.

When word reached Washington in August 1863 that an effort was under way in Louisiana to hold a constitutional convention, Lincoln told Banks that he would be glad if the state would "make a new Constitution recognizing the emancipation proclamation, and adopting emancipation in those parts of the state to which the proclamation does not apply." He also desired to see Louisianans "adopt some practical system by which the two races could gradually live themselves out of their old relation to each other, and both come out better prepared for the new. Education for young blacks should be included in the plan." A contract system appeared to him best suited for that purpose. Lincoln strongly suggested that Louisiana form a new constitution and hold elections before Congress met in early December. Even if the voters did not provide for the abolition of slavery, the president said he would "not, in any event, retract the emancipation proclamation; nor, as executive, ever return to slavery any person who is free by the terms of that proclamation, or by any of the acts of Congress." Although he did not want his letter made public, he authorized Banks to show it to people who should understand the administration's wishes, presumably the convention delegates. He told the general that he was offering advice, not giving orders, but when he sent copies of the letter to the Free State Committee leaders, he added an endorsement: "Please observe my directions to him."[9] Significantly he did not say *suggestions* but rather *directions*. Banks replied that he would execute Lincoln's *orders*. He did not say *suggestions*. The emphasis on *directions* also appeared in orders that Stanton, speaking for the president, sent to Governor Shepley, instructing him clearly to arrange for a constitutional convention. Loyal citizens (presumably including Blacks) were to be registered and an election held within the month following the completion of that process.

With Banks distracted by military concerns, Shepley was left to carry out these presidential directives. Upon learning that the governor had not done so, Lincoln scolded Banks. The failure to register voters "disappoints me bitterly," he told the general, adding that he did not blame Banks or the Free State leaders. But he urged them to "lose no more time." Bluntly he stated his wish that they should, "without waiting for more territory" to be occupied, promptly "go to work and give me a tangible nucleus which the remainder of the State may rally around as fast as it can, and which I can at once recognize and sustain as the true State government. . . . Time is important. There is danger, even now, that the adverse element seeks insidiously to pre-occupy the ground. If a few professedly loyal men shall draw the disloyal about them, and colorably set up a State government, repudiating the emancipation proclamation, and re-establishing slavery, I can not recognize or sustain their work. I should fall powerless in the attempt. This government, in such an attitude, would be a house divided against itself."[10] Here Lincoln seemed to renege on his pledge to exempt part of Louisiana from the Emancipation Proclamation; the entire state, including the occupied areas, must abolish slavery if it wished to be restored.

The president grudgingly supported Banks's controversial system of halfway freedom, which provided that slaves in areas of Louisiana not exempted from the Emancipation Proclamation would contract with planters and farmers of their choice for wages, clothing, and housing in return for their labor but would not be allowed to leave the farm or plantation without the army's permission. Their children were authorized to attend schools that the army would establish. Physical punishment was forbidden, and employers were to set aside one acre for each Black family to grow its own produce. Contracts were to last one year.

Before Congress met in December 1863, Lincoln made yet another attempt to restart the sputtering reconstruction process in Louisiana. Ben Butler had suggested that as a preliminary measure, a referendum be conducted to determine whether voters would like to call a constitutional convention and repeal the ordinance of secession. On November 9, the president commended this proposal to Congressman Flanders, even though it meant tacitly acknowledging the legitimacy of secession. Nothing came of it. By December, hopes for the speedy restoration of Louisiana were fading fast. In nearby Arkansas and Texas, Lincoln's attempt to promote elections also foundered. It was time for a new approach.

Restructuring Reconstruction: The Ten Percent Plan

When Radicals urged Lincoln to ignore the advice of conservatives, he replied: "I hope to stand firm enough to not go backward, and yet not go forward fast enough to wreck the country's cause."[11] And so he offered a plan of reconstruction that he hoped would appeal to Radical and moderate Republicans, to War Democrats, and to Southern Unionists. Like his earlier effort, it was rooted in his sensible belief that Southern White backlash against emancipation would be reduced if voters in the Confederate states themselves organized loyal governments, applied for restoration, and abolished slavery. Some reports from the South indicated that if leaders of the Confederacy were held strictly accountable for the war and other Confederates granted amnesty, such a step would be hailed in the South and might well induce wavering Confederates to surrender, assured that they would receive lenient treatment.

The president's long-standing faith in Southern Unionism was strengthened during the fall of 1863, when a strong peace movement sprang up in North Carolina. Lincoln optimistically told John Hay that the rebellion was on the verge of collapse. Jefferson Davis's government depended completely on the army, he said, "not only against us, but against his own people. If that were crushed out, they would be ready to swing back to their old bearings."[12] This was wishful thinking, for Southern disaffection with the Richmond government was an expression not of Unionism but rather of anger at the failure of Confederate arms, at the Davis administration's inability to guarantee social order, and at its encroachment upon individual and states' rights.

Laboring under that misapprehension, the president devised a scheme known as the Ten Percent Plan. It allowed for the political restoration of rebellious states after a number of voters equal to one-tenth of those casting ballots in 1860 took an oath of future loyalty to the Union and of willingness to accept emancipation. (Some Confederates would be ineligible for this amnesty, including military and civilian leaders, those who resigned commissions in the U.S. military or federal legislative and judicial posts to join the rebellion, and those who mistreated captured Black troops or their White officers.) Once that threshold was reached, the state could hold elections and rejoin the Union, with all the rights and privileges it had enjoyed before the war. The oath-takers too would have all their former rights restored, except the right to own slaves.

Lincoln appended this Proclamation of Amnesty and Reconstruction to his annual message to Congress, which explained why the loyalty oath required acceptance of emancipation. Characteristically, he stressed its practical benefits. The wartime laws and proclamations regarding slavery and emancipation, he said, "were enacted and put forth for the purpose of aiding in the suppression of the rebellion. To give them their fullest effect, there had to be a pledge for their maintenance." To abandon those proclamations now would be "to relinquish a lever of power." But in addition to such pragmatic concerns, Lincoln forcefully stated moral objections to any backsliding on emancipation. Reneging would "be a cruel and astounding breach of faith." As long as he remained president, he promised, "I shall not attempt to retract or modify the emancipation proclamation; nor shall I return to slavery any person who is free by the terms of that proclamation, or by any of the acts of Congress."[13]

While Lincoln's proclamation did not allow ex-Confederate states to retain slavery, they could keep their antebellum political framework. The administration would not object if a restored state government were to provide a system of apprenticeship for freed slaves, so long as that government "shall recognize and declare their permanent freedom, provide for their education, and which [system] may yet be consistent, as a temporary arrangement, with their present condition as a laboring, landless, and homeless class." Lincoln justified this concession as a necessary expedient to reduce "the confusion and destitution which must, at best, attend all classes by a total revolution of labor throughout whole States." In addition, more Confederates might be inclined to surrender if "this vital matter be left to themselves." But ex-Confederates would not be allowed to mistreat the freedpeople: "no power of the national Executive to prevent an abuse is abridged by the proposition."

To counter objections that his proposal was premature, Lincoln stressed that Rebels might be more likely to surrender if they knew they would be treated leniently. He noted that in some occupied Confederate states "the elements for resumption seem ready for action, but remain inactive, apparently for want of a rallying point—a plan of action." The Proclamation provided such a plan. But he assured Congress that he was flexible. "Saying that, on certain terms, certain classes will be pardoned, with rights restored, it is not said that other classes, or other terms, will never be included. Saying that Reconstruction will be accepted if presented in a specified way, it is not said it will never be accepted in any other way." This concession, leaving the plan open to change, indicated Lincoln's willingness to have at least some Blacks vote, even though his proposal enfranchised only Whites. As he told Banks, the statement that other modes of reconstruction were acceptable had been added "on purpose that some conformity to circumstances should be admissible."[14] Cautiously Lincoln was laying the foundation for Black voting rights.

To justify his plan, Lincoln cited the provision of the Constitution authorizing the chief executive "to grant reprieves and pardons for offences against the United States," as well as the Second Confiscation Act, which stipulated that the president could "extend to persons who may have participated in the existing rebellion, in any State of party thereof, pardon and amnesty." Lincoln's citation of the pardoning power was strained, for the framers of the Constitution clearly meant it to apply to individuals, not whole classes of people.[15]

Congress was at first enthusiastic about this plan. For the time being, Lincoln had managed to accommodate all factions. Radicals in general were pleased because Lincoln agreed with their fundamental demand: the Union must be restored without slavery. They might differ with the president—and among themselves—about other matters, but not that. While Radicals seemed satisfied, conservative Republicans objected to making emancipation a requirement for reconstruction. Most of them, however, appreciated the conciliatory spirit of Lincoln's message as well as his willingness to leave the states and their governments intact (except with regard to slavery) and to let Southern Whites determine how the Blacks were to be treated.

The executive-legislative honeymoon was short lived, for Radicals quickly grew disenchanted. Even on December 9, the Chicago *Tribune* reported that "as they began to scan it more closely," Radicals "became more cautious in their praise." The "intense radicals" argued "that it owes its apparent popularity to its avoidance of points on which he knew that anything he would say would arouse differences among his supporters."[16]

Implementing the Ten Percent Plan: Florida and Louisiana

Implementation of Lincoln's plan got off to a rocky start. In January 1864, to bring Florida back into the Union, the president dispatched John Hay with instructions to enroll enough voters to meet the 10 percent threshold. Union military authorities in Florida had been planning a campaign to cut off the peninsula from the rest of the Confederacy. In January 1864, after authorizing General Quincy A. Gillmore to launch that offensive, Lincoln had Hay commissioned as a major and sent him to join it. At first, the young secretary was optimistic about his mission. "I think we will soon have the state back in the Union," he wrote on February 8. "If we get the 'President's Tithe' it will be fully half the voters in the state, as the poor old carcass of a neighborhood has been plucked to the bone, by North & South." Hay received "the best assurances that we will get the tenth required: although so large a portion of the rebel population is in the army & so many of the loyal people, refugees in the North, that the state is well-nigh depopulated. We will have almost a clean slate to begin with."[17]

A week later, however, Hay predicted that he would fail. On February 20, Gillmore's offensive was repulsed at the battle of Olustee, making that prediction a certainty. Hay explained that "we must wait for further developments in military operations before we can hope for a reorganization of the state under a loyal government. I find nearly everybody willing to take the oath of allegiance prescribed by the President, but I find scarcely anyone left in the country. Whole counties seem almost thoroughly depopulated. The few that remain seem heartily tired of the war, and willing to swear allegiance in any terms to the power that will protect them, but there are really not enough, as it seems to me, to justify a movement just at present, for rehabilitation."[18]

Criticism of the administration's plan grew more intense after Lincoln altered his policy in Louisiana. Frustrated by the endless delays in setting up a new government there, owing in part to the legalistic approach of Thomas J. Durant, he decided to stop relying on the Free State Committee and to count instead on Nathaniel P. Banks to get things moving. Thus he abandoned his earlier insistence that the formation of new state governments should "be a movement of the people of the Districts, and not a movement of our military and quasi-military, authorities there."

Banks had a plan that strongly appealed to Lincoln. The "*only speedy and certain* method of accomplishing your object," Banks told the president, would be to order an election "of a State Government, under the Constitution [of 1852] and Laws of Louisiana," except for the slavery provisions. Within two months, voters could be enrolled and an election held. Soon thereafter, a convention to revise the constitution could be launched. Such a strategy, Banks assured the president, "will be far more acceptable to the Citizens of Louisiana, than the submission of the question of slavery to the chances of an election. Their self-respect, their *Amour propre* will be appeased if they are not required to vote for or against it. Offer them a Government without slavery, and they will gladly accept it as a necessity resulting from the war." Banks explained that such an approach "carries moral, as well as physical power with it." Black suffrage could be considered later.[19] Delighted at the prospect of swift action, Lincoln wrote Banks on Christmas Eve 1863 endorsing his plan and authorizing him to carry it out: "You are master of all."[20]

True to his word, Banks delivered a Free State government in less than two months. Emboldened by his new authority as "master of all," he mandated that on February 22 elections be held for governor and other state officials based on the 1852 state constitution. To nullify provisions of that document sanctioning slavery, the general promulgated special orders. Michael Hahn, a moderate, won the governorship, defeating the Radical Benjamin Flanders and the conservative J. Q. A. Fellows. The turnout of more than eleven thousand voters far exceeded the 10 percent requirement. Lincoln congratulated Hahn for "having fixed your name in history as the first-free-state Governor of Louisiana."[21] Five weeks later, six thousand voters participated in the election of delegates to a constitutional convention, which met from April through July. In September, the resulting document won ratification by a handsome majority. Lincoln and Banks had transformed the sputtering reconstruction efforts of the Free State Committee and General Shepley into a successful movement restoring the Bayou State on the basis of liberty.

By all rights, Radicals should have been pleased, but they were not. A quarrel quickly broke out over Louisiana reconstruction as various factions argued about Black suffrage. When Lincoln received an appeal from a White Louisiana Unionist urging him to deny Blacks the right to vote for constitutional convention delegates, he endorsed it as follows: "On very full consideration I do not wish to say more than I have publicly said."[22] Just as he would not yet openly support Black voting, neither would he oppose it.

On March 13, 1864, Lincoln injected himself into the contest on the side of African American suffrage. Congratulating Hahn, he mentioned the upcoming constitutional convention, "which, among other things, will probably define the elective franchise. I barely suggest for your private consideration, whether some of the colored people may not be let in—as, for instance, the very intelligent, and especially those who have fought gallantly in our ranks. They would probably help, in some trying time to come, to keep the jewel of liberty within the family of freedom. But this is only a suggestion, not to the public, but to you alone."[23] Although phrased tentatively, the president's letter was really an order, similar to the earlier missive regarding emancipation that he had sent to Banks, with copies to Free State Committee leaders. Lincoln's letter to Hahn was prompted by a pair of New Orleans free Blacks who had recently submitted to the president a petition, ignored by Shepley and Banks, bearing the signatures of a thousand Blacks.

Acting on Lincoln's gently phrased letter, Governor Hahn threw his weight behind efforts to incorporate voting rights for at least some African Americans into the new state constitution. Banks, evidently at Lincoln's behest, worked behind the scenes to obtain the same result. The majority of delegates to the state constitutional convention, however, were unreceptive and went so far as to prohibit the legislature from ever granting Blacks the right to vote. Banks and Hahn worked hard to reverse that decision. The final version of the document authorized the legislature to allow Blacks to vote based on service in the army, intellectual merit, or payment of taxes. This did not satisfy Lincoln's desire for limited Black suffrage but did pave the way for its eventual adoption. The constitution also provided for the education of all children without distinction of race, allowed Blacks to serve in the militia, and guaranteed equal rights in court.

This was as much as White public opinion in Louisiana would abide. Chase's main informant about Louisiana affairs, George S. Denison (collector of the port of New Orleans), judged that the constitution's provision authorizing the legislature to enfranchise Blacks was "a great step in the right direction."[24] Lincoln's letter to Hahn had laid the groundwork for the adoption of that clause. The following year, Hahn said of that missive that "though marked 'private,'" it "was no doubt intended to be seen by other Union men in Louisiana beside myself, and was consequently shown to many members of our Constitutional Convention and leading free-State men." He added that the "letter, written in the mild and graceful tone which imparted so much weight to Mr. Lincoln's simple suggestions, no doubt had great effect on the action of the Louisiana Convention in all matters appertaining to the colored man."[25]

Lincoln also injected himself into the ratification contest. On August 9, he wrote to Banks that he had just seen a copy of the constitution and was "anxious that it shall be ratified by the people." To achieve that end he was willing to employ the patronage power, as he told the general: "I will thank you to let the civil officers in Louisiana, holding under me, know that this is my wish, and to let me know at once who of them openly declare for the constitution, and who of them, if any, decline to so declare."[26] Banks used this authorization effectively to enlist support for ratification and took other steps to assist the pro-constitution campaign, which proved successful. The new state legislature chose two U.S. senators and held elections for five representatives. But, Lincoln wondered, would Congress recognize them?

Chase Attempts to Supplant Lincoln

To attain congressional approval of the Louisiana experiment, Lincoln could have used the assistance of Chase, who had great influence with the Radical wing of the party, both in Louisiana and in Washington. The treasury secretary, however, was scheming to win the Republican presidential nomination—"at work night and day, laying pipe," as a Pennsylvania politician noted.[27] A rival for the nomination, Chase had little incentive to help Lincoln achieve a legislative victory, even though they shared similar views about reconstruction policy in the Bayou State. He also used patronage appointments to bolster his chances.

Radicals condemned Lincoln's purported conservatism, inconsistency, administrative incapacity, and reluctance to make difficult decisions. The president knew all about the discontent among congressional Radicals. In mid-February he indicated to Edward Bates that he understood "that they would strike at him at once, if they durst; but they fear that the blow would be ineffectual, and so, they would fall under his power as *beaten enemies*; and for that only reason the hypocrit[e]s try to occupy equivocal ground—so that, when they fail, as *enemies*, they may still pretend to be *friends*."[28] When Shelby Cullom warned him that everybody in Washington seemed to oppose his renomination, Lincoln replied: "Well, it is not quite so bad as that," and showed him a congressional directory in which he had marked the inclinations of all members.[29]

In letters and conversations throughout the fall and winter of 1863–64, Chase criticized the president repeatedly and expressed a willingness to replace him. Although Lincoln said he knew that Chase's head was "full of Presidential *maggots*," and while the president was "trying to keep the maggot out of his brain," he was "much amused" by the treasury secretary's "mad hunt after the Presidency."[30] When told about Chase's criticism of him, he replied that he did not care, for the secretary was "on the whole, a pretty good fellow and a very able man" whose "only trouble is that he has 'the White House fever.'"[31] To be sure, Lincoln thought Chase's maneuvering to win the nomination was in poor taste, but he said in October 1863 that he "shut his eyes to all these performances."[32] Because Chase did good work at the Treasury Department, he would be kept in the cabinet.

Such passivity dismayed Lincoln's supporters. But when David Davis described how Treasury Department employees were being forced to contribute to Chase's campaign fund, and how those who resisted were threatened with dismissal, Lincoln said with a grin that if such threats were carried out, "the head I guess would have to go with the tail."[33] Chase's candidacy was no secret to political observers, though he did not openly announce it until mid-January 1864. He insisted that he was motivated only by a desire to promote the public good and not by personal ambition. Few men have been as capable of self-deception as Chase.

In February, Chase's supporters, led by Kansas senator Samuel C. Pomeroy, organized a Chase-for-president committee in Washington and issued two documents that embarrassed the treasury secretary. The first, a pamphlet titled *The Next Presidential Election*, denounced the Lincoln administration. Without mentioning Chase, it called for the nomination of "a statesman profoundly versed in political and economic science, one who fully comprehends the spirit of the age in which we live" and criticized the president as inept.[34] The second document, known as the Pomeroy Circular, was not so coy. It asserted that Chase should be nominated because he had "more of the qualities needed in a President during the next four years than are combined in any other available candidate."[35] An ally had advised Chase that Lincoln's "integrity & apparent unselfishness entitle him to every courtesy," but these two documents were highly discourteous.[36] John Sherman mailed out copies of the pamphlet under his senatorial frank and received numerous complaints from offended constituents. The two documents did win Chase the endorsement of some New York newspapers, but in general the circular and the pamphlet backfired, alienating many who might have sympathized with Chase. When friends attempted to call the Pomeroy Circular to Lincoln's attention, he ignored their advice. On February 20, the press ran the document, impelling Chase to offer his resignation. But Lincoln replied that he had not read the circular and did not intend to. Moreover, he wished the treasury secretary to remain at his post.

The Chase boomlet ended with a whimper. Even among Radicals its support was weak, forcing the treasury secretary's supporters to grudgingly acknowledge that the president "is daily becoming more popular with the *unthinking* masses."[37] Chase withdrew from the race soon after Republicans in the Ohio legislature overwhelmingly resolved on February 26 that "the *People* of Ohio and her *Soldiers* in the field demand the renomination of Abraham Lincoln."[38]

A Big Fish: Chase's Resignation

Relations between Lincoln and Chase rapidly deteriorated over the following weeks. Throughout the winter and early spring, Frank Blair denounced the treasury secretary and other Radicals. The two most blistering philippics charged with some justification that Chase was improperly using patronage and trade regulations to help him win the Republican presidential nomination. "A more profligate administration of the Treasury Department never existed under any Government," the Missourian declared, adding that "the whole Mississippi valley is rank and fetid with the fraud and corruptions practiced there" by Chase's agents, who accepted bribes for trading permits.[39] Chase and the Radicals, livid with anger, believed that the president had encouraged Blair to launch those attacks. Lincoln, irritated and embarrassed by one of Blair's barnburners, summoned the congressman to the White House. When Blair volunteered to resign from the army, Lincoln said, "We must not back down" and handed him his commission. That reappointment without congressional approval rankled many lawmakers.

The steadily mounting tension between the president and his treasury secretary reached a climax in June, when Chase, to protest a patronage decision, submitted his resignation for the fourth time. The secretary had demanded exclusive control over the distribution of offices within his department, arguing that fitness alone, not political influence, should be the determining criterion. He failed to acknowledge that in order to placate Congress, the patronage wishes of senators and representatives had to be respected. In protest, Chase huffily offered his resignation on June 29, doubtless assuming that the president would back down as usual. But Lincoln shocked him by accepting it, for as he saw it, Chase in effect was saying: "You have been acting very badly. Unless you say you are sorry, & ask me to stay & agree that I shall be absolute and that you shall have nothing, no matter how you beg for it, I will go."[40] The president was in no mood to trifle, contending that Chase "is either determined to annoy me, or that I shall pat him on the shoulder and coax him to stay. I don't think I ought to do it. I will not do it. I will take him at his word."[41]

Having made up his mind to let Chase go, Lincoln summoned John Hay to take a message to Capitol Hill. "When does the Senate meet today?" the president asked.

"Eleven o'clock," replied the youthful secretary.

"I wish you to be there when they meet. It is a big fish. Mr. Chase has resigned and I have accepted his resignation. I thought I could not stand it any longer."

To succeed Chase, Lincoln picked another ex-governor of Ohio, David Tod, a Douglas Democrat turned Republican. Men in and out of Congress felt depressed and gloomy, regarding the abrupt change as a worrisome sign that the administration was breaking up. Indeed, Lincoln had blundered. Although his exasperation with Chase was entirely understandable, his decision to let the treasury secretary go at such a time showed poor judgment. As D. W. Bartlett remarked, the president "seems to have been deserted of his usual good sense" when he submitted Tod's name, for the "feeling was unanimous in Congress that for such a man to succeed Mr. Chase would be ruinous to the finances."[42]

That night, Tod wired his declination. In his stead, Lincoln the next morning decided to nominate William Pitt Fessenden, chairman of the Senate Finance Committee. As the Maine senator sat in the White House reception room (unaware of Lincoln's decision) awaiting an interview, the president dispatched Hay with the nomination to the Senate, where it was instantly ratified. When Lincoln told him of this move, the amazed senator, pleading poor health, said: "But it hasn't reached there—you must withdraw it—I can't accept." Lincoln protested, "If you decline, you must do it in open day: for I shall not recall the nomination."[43] The senator turned down the offer in a letter to Lincoln, who refused to receive it, "saying that Providence had pointed out the man for the crisis," that "none other could be found," and that he "had no right to decline." When Fessenden insisted that the job would kill him, Lincoln replied: "Very well, you cannot die better than in trying to save your country." In response to overwhelming pressure, the senator reluctantly acquiesced with what he called "all the feeling of a man being led to execution."[44] Lincoln, whose spirits had revived, exclaimed to Seward: "The Lord has never yet deserted me, and I did not believe he would this time!"[45]

The appointment of Fessenden undid much of the damage caused by Chase's resignation. Republican newspapers lauded the new secretary and even the Democratic New York *World* called Fessenden "unquestionably the fittest man in his party for that high trust."[46]

Renomination

With Chase out of the presidential race, Lincoln's chances for renomination, which he keenly desired, seemed excellent. "If the people think that I have managed their case for them well enough to trust me to carry up to the next term, I am sure that I shall be glad to take it," he remarked.[47]

The most serious potential rival for the nomination was Grant, whose popularity after the victories at Vicksburg and Chattanooga soared. Elihu B. Washburne, the general's chief sponsor in Congress, urged Grant not to challenge Lincoln. Recalling the president's support for the general after the battle of Shiloh, Washburne said Lincoln would "have my ever lasting gratitude."[48] Grant's close friend J. Russell Jones told the Illinois congressman that Lincoln would promote Grant to the exalted rank of lieutenant general if Grant would support the president's reelection. Washburne replied, "That is the programme I desire. Lincoln will then go in easy, and Grant must be made Lieut Genl."[49]

Grant discouraged talk of his candidacy, insisting that the only office he wanted was the mayoralty of Galena so that he could have a sidewalk laid from his house to the train station. But Lincoln was anxious about the general's intentions. Desiring reassurance from him, Lincoln, at the suggestion of Washburne, asked Jones about his friend's views on the presidency. When Jones showed him a letter from Grant denying any political aspirations and voicing strong support for Lincoln, the president replied: "You will never know how gratifying that is to me. No man knows, when that presidential grub gets to gnawing at him, just how deep it will get until he has tried it; and I didn't know but what there was one gnawing at Grant."[50] Grant did not publicly announce his unwillingness to run because, as his chief aide, John Rawlins, explained in March, if the general published a statement forswearing presidential ambition, it "would place him much in the position of the old maid who had never had an offer declaring she 'would never marry;' besides it would be by many construed into a modest way of getting his name before the country in connection with the office."[51]

Convinced that he would not have Grant as a rival, Lincoln threw his support behind the bill reviving the rank of lieutenant general, which passed Congress in late February. Soon after signing the legislation, he nominated Grant for that high honor. (Although Lincoln admired the general, he did find it necessary to overrule an infamous military order Grant had issued in December 1862 as commander of the Department of the Tennessee stipulating that the "Jews, as a class, violating every regulation of trade established by the Treasury Department, and also Department orders, are hereby expelled from the Department." The "Jews seem to be a privileged class," he told the War Department.[52] He hoped to discourage cotton traders, some of them Jewish, who frequently violated the complicated rules promulgated in Washington. Lincoln overruled the decision promptly.)

The president summoned Grant to Washington to receive his promotion and to consult about military strategy. The general arrived on March 8 and called that evening at the White House, where a public reception was being held. When Lincoln heard the crowd buzz, he knew Grant was on the premises and hurried to welcome him. The two men, who had not met before, greeted each other cordially but, as Nicolay recorded, "with that modest deference—felt rather than expressed by word or action—so appropriate to both." Lincoln dispatched Nicolay to notify Stanton and asked Seward to introduce the honored guest to Mrs. Lincoln.[53] In the East Room, the general was cheered lustily.

At the official commissioning ceremony next day, Lincoln addressed Grant formally: "The nation's appreciation of what you have done and its reliance upon you for what remains to do in the existing great struggle are now presented with this commission, constituting you lieutenant general in the Army of the United States. With this high honor devolves upon you also a corresponding responsibility. As the country herein trusts you, so under God it will sustain you. I scarcely need to add that with what I here speak for the nation goes my own hearty personal concurrence."[54] Grant replied with a few gracious sentences that he had so hastily scribbled down that he could barely read them.

With Chase and Grant out of the presidential race, Lincoln still faced potential challenges from Benjamin Butler and John C. Frémont, both darlings of the Radicals. To Lincoln's relief, Butler refused "to enter into a combination with other candidates against the President."[55] With Butler's declination, Radicals turned to Frémont, who deeply resented the way the administration had treated him. Most Republicans resisted the appeal of the Pathfinder, but his admirers could launch a third party and run him as their standard-bearer. On May 4, a self-styled "people's provisional committee" issued a call for a national convention to meet in Cleveland, one week before the Republicans gathered at Baltimore. Endorsing the movement were several prominent abolitionists.

Wendell Phillips was not among the four hundred who attended the Cleveland convention of the Radical Democratic Party, but he wrote a letter that was read to the wildly approving assemblage. In it he excoriated the Lincoln administration, calling it "a civil and military failure" and predicting that if the incumbent were reelected, "I do not expect to see the Union reconstructed in my day, unless on terms more disastrous to liberty than even Disunion would be." In stark contrast to Lincoln, Phillips asserted, stood Frémont, "whose first act was to use the freedom of the negro as his weapon . . . whose thorough loyalty to democratic institutions, without regard to race—whose earnest and decisive character, whose clear-sighted statesmanship and rare military ability, justify my confidence that in his hands all will be done to save the state that foresight, skill, decision and statesmanship can do."[56]

The delegates shared Phillips's enthusiasm for Frémont, but they ignored his advice regarding the platform; both Black suffrage and land redistribution to freedmen were glossed over in vague language about "equality before the law." The convention did, however, endorse a constitutional amendment abolishing slavery nationwide. That measure had been vigorously debated in Congress over the preceding months, easily passing the Senate in April but failing to gain the necessary two-thirds vote in the House. In his acceptance letter, Frémont attacked the administration: "The ordinary rights secured under the Constitution and extraordinary powers have been usurped by the Executive." Today, he averred, "we have in this country the abuses of a military dictation without its unity of action and vigor of execution."[57]

William Lloyd Garrison, who had repeatedly denounced Lincoln throughout the war, now disagreed with the president's critics and opposed the Frémont movement. Garrison insisted that Lincoln be judged on the basis "of his possibilities, rather than by our wishes, or by the highest abstract moral standard."[58] Two months later, in a widely reprinted editorial, Garrison called Lincoln's reelection essential for "the suppression of the rebellion, and the abolition of slavery." The editor declared that "a thousand incidental errors and blunders are easily to be borne with on the part of one who, at one blow, severed the chains of three millions three hundred thousand slaves,—thus virtually abolishing the whole slave system."[59]

The Baltimore Convention

To undercut Frémont's appeal, Lincoln bolstered the Republican Party's antislavery bona fides by endorsing the constitutional amendment outlawing slavery throughout the country. A few days before the convention met, party chairman Edwin D. Morgan called at the White House, where the president urged him to make support of the antislavery amendment the keynote of his opening speech at the convention. Morgan took the president's advice, admonishing delegates that the party would "fall far short of accomplishing its great mission, unless among its other resolves it shall declare for such an amendment of the Constitution as will positively prohibit African slavery in the United States."[60] In response, the platform committee wrote a plank declaring that "we are in favor" of "an amendment to the Constitution . . . as shall terminate and forever prohibit the existence of slavery within the limits or the jurisdiction of the United States." When introduced, this plank inspired wild enthusiasm.[61] Delegates leapt from their seats, waved their hats, applauded tumultuously, and adopted the resolution without dissent. This move stole some thunder from the Radical Democracy.

At the behest of the Missouri delegation, a plank was adopted indirectly calling for the resignation of conservative cabinet members, widely viewed as a demand for Montgomery Blair's dismissal. Although willing to intervene to shape the party platform, Lincoln refrained from expressing any preference for a running mate.

Shortly before Nicolay left to act as the president's eyes and ears at the convention, Lincoln told him "that privately and personally he would be best pleased if the convention would renominate the old ticket that had been so triumphantly elected in 1860 and which would show an unbroken faith . . . in the Republican party and an unbroken and undivided support of that party to the administration and in the prosecution of the war."[62] The delegates chose former Democrat Andrew Johnson of Tennessee to enhance the Republicans' new identity as the National Union Party. Johnson eventually turned out to be a disastrous choice, but Lincoln had nothing to do with his selection. Some Radicals expressed pleasure at Johnson's nomination, but Lincoln had reservations. When told of the convention's choice for his running mate, he said: "So they have chosen him—I thought perhaps he would be the man. He is a strong man. I hope he may be the best man. But—." He did not finish that sentence.[63] According to Noah Brooks, Lincoln at first "made an exclamation that emphatically indicated his disappointment" but shortly thereafter remarked, "Andy Johnson, I think, is a good man."[64]

On their way home from Baltimore, some delegates stopped at the White House to pay their respects. To Ohioans who serenaded him on June 9, he said that "the hardest of all speeches I have to answer is a serenade. I never know what to say on these occasions. I suppose that you have done me this kindness in connection with the action of the Baltimore convention, which has recently taken place, and with which, of course, I am very well satisfied. What we want, still more than Baltimore conventions or presidential elections, is success under Gen. Grant. I propose that you constantly bear in mind that the support you owe to the brave officers and soldiers in the field is of the very first importance, and we should therefore bend all our energies to that point."[65]

Lincoln expressed profound emotion in his response to the convention committee's formal notification of his candidacy. In his remarks, he laid special emphasis on the constitutional amendment abolishing slavery: "I approve the declaration in favor of so amending the Constitution as to prohibit slavery throughout the nation. . . . Such alone can meet and cover all cavils. Now, the unconditional Union men, North and South, perceive its importance, and embrace it. In the joint names of Liberty and Union, let us labor to give it legal form, and practical effect."[66]

Lincoln told a deputation from the Radical-dominated National Union League informing him of that body's endorsement, "I am very grateful for the renewed confidence which has been accorded to me, both by the convention and by the National League. I am not insensible at all to the personal compliment there is in this; yet I do not allow myself to believe that any but a small portion of it is to be appropriated as a personal compliment. . . . I have not permitted myself, gentlemen, to conclude that I am the best man in the country; but I am reminded, in this connection, of a story of an old Dutch farmer, who remarked to a companion once that 'it was not best to swap horses when crossing streams.'"[67] Lincoln was delighted, as he explained to A. K. McClure, that "his name would go down into history darkly shadowed by a fraternal war that he would be held responsible for inaugurating if he were unable to continue in office to conquer the Rebellion and restore the Union."[68]

But it was not clear that the country would in fact have the same administration for another quadrennium, since support for Lincoln might prove ephemeral. In late May, Theodore Tilton noted that there "is an insane popular sympathy for him [Lincoln] everywhere—very shallow, it is true—but salty & flavorsome, even though shallow."[69] The shallow lake of the president's popularity might evaporate in the fierce heat of summer if Grant did not promptly defeat Lee.

33.

"Hold On with a Bull-dog Grip, and Chew & Choke, as Much as Possible"

The Grand Offensive (May–August 1864)

That America would conduct a national election during a titanic civil war amazed German-born Francis Lieber, professor of history and political science at Columbia University. "If we come triumphantly out of this war, with a presidential election in the midst of it," he wrote in August 1864, "I shall call it the greatest miracle in all the historic course of events. It is a war for nationality at a period when the people were not yet fully nationalized."[1]

The military situation would determine the outcome of that election. As dismayed Confederates saw their chances of winning on the battlefield fade after the defeats at Gettysburg, Vicksburg, and Chattanooga, they pinned their hopes on Northern war weariness; they believed that if Lincoln could be defeated at the polls, their bid for independence just might succeed. Union military triumphs alone could prevent that, Lincoln realized, and so in the winter and spring of 1864 he and Grant devised a strategy to achieve final victory before the fall elections. The fate of the nation, and the cause of democracy throughout the world, hung in the balance.

Grand Strategy

General Grant later wrote that Lincoln gave him carte blanche, but in fact the president rejected parts of his initial proposal, including suggestions to launch a major thrust against Mobile and to attack Richmond's supply lines with an army landed in North Carolina. But both men agreed on the central principle that Union forces should attack on all fronts simultaneously. George Meade would strike southward against Lee's army; Franz Sigel would drive down the Shenandoah Valley, then swing eastward toward Richmond; Ben Butler would approach the Confederate capital from the opposite direction by moving up the Peninsula; Nathaniel Banks would push toward Mobile after taking Shreveport; and Sherman would capture Atlanta. Grant, in overall charge of operations, accompanied the Army of the Potomac, whose strategy he would supervise, while Meade controlled tactical moves. It was the sort of coordinated plan that Lincoln had been urging on his generals since early 1862. On the eve of the spring offensive, he told John Hay that Grant's strategy reminded him of his "old suggestion so constantly made and as constantly neglected, to Buell & Halleck et al to move at once upon the enemy's whole line so as to bring into action to our advantage our great superiority in numbers." Lincoln remarked, "Those not skinning can hold a leg."[2]

In addition to approving most of Grant's plan, Lincoln helped him reform the administration of the army. Congress had provided that staff departments report directly to the secretary of war, not the general in chief. When Grant asked that those departments be placed under him in the chain of command, the president explained that while he could not unilaterally alter the law, "there is no one but myself that can interfere with your orders, and you can rest assured that I will not."[3]

The president did intervene when Grant clashed with Stanton over force reductions in the Washington area. The general wanted to transfer many support troops to the front lines, but the war secretary overruled his order to send artillerymen from the defenses of the capital to the overland campaign in Virginia.

"I think I rank you in this matter, Mr. Secretary," Grant said.

"We shall have to see Mr. Lincoln about that," came the reply.

At the White House, the president ruled in favor of Grant. "You and I, Mr. Stanton, have been trying to boss this job, and we have not succeeded very well with it. We have sent across the mountains for *Mr.* Grant, as Mrs. Grant calls him, to relieve us, and I think we had better leave him alone to do as he pleases."[4] Lincoln did not, however, honor Grant's request to merge some of the twenty independent military departments, eliminate extraneous commands, and retire scores of generals. In an election year, such steps seemed politically dangerous. But he did agree to remove Banks from command of the Department of the Gulf and replace him with Edward R. S. Canby. (The failure of Banks's Red River campaign in April had sorely disappointed the president.)

Political considerations also affected the choice of Grant's principal subordinates in the East. While Meade, a professional soldier, would remain in command of the Army of the Potomac, the two men most responsible for assisting his campaign against Lee were political generals with limited military talent, Butler and Sigel. The former had been a prominent Democrat, and Lincoln considered it essential to retain the support of War Democrats; the latter was exceptionally popular with the Germans, an important voting bloc that had shown signs of disaffection.

On April 30, as Grant was about to launch his offensive, Lincoln wrote him: "Not expecting to see you again before the Spring campaign opens, I wish to express, in this way, my entire satisfaction with what you have done up to this time, so far as I understand it. The particulars of your plans I neither know, or seek to know.

You are vigilant and self-reliant; and, pleased with this, I wish not to obtrude any constraints or restraints upon you. While I am very anxious that any great disaster, or the capture of our men in great numbers, shall be avoided, I know these points are less likely to escape your attention than they would be mine. If there is anything wanting which is within my power to give, do not fail to let me know it. And now with a brave Army, and a just cause, may God sustain you."[5] Graciously the general replied: "The confidence you express for the future, and satisfaction with the past, in my military administration is acknowledged with pride. It will be my earnest endeavor that you, and the country, shall not be disappointed. . . . Should my success be less than I desire, and expect, the least I can say is, the fault is not with you."[6]

The North held its collective breath as Grant attacked Lee near Chancellorsville on May 5. The armies slugged it out in the dense, tangled wilderness, inflicting heavy casualties on each other. The first to bring Lincoln word of the bloody doings was a young New York *Tribune* reporter, Henry Wing, who briefed the president and cabinet on the morning of May 7. After he had delivered his news, Wing repeated to the president a message Grant had asked him to convey: "Whatever happens, there is to be no turning back."[7] Overjoyed at this declaration of steely resolve, the president kissed the youthful reporter on the forehead.

When, however, it became clear that the Army of the Potomac had taken especially heavy casualties, the anguished president asked Schuyler Colfax: "Could we have avoided this terrible, bloody war? Was it not forced upon us? Is it ever to end?"[8] As he observed the wounded in a long procession of ambulances, he said, "Look yonder at those poor fellows. I cannot bear it. This suffering, this loss of life is dreadful." When a friend tried to console him with the assurance that the North would eventually triumph, he replied, "Yes, victory will come, but it comes slowly."[9]

Grant did not win the Battle of the Wilderness, which was in effect a standoff, though the Army of Northern Virginia withdrew from the field. Unlike previous Union commanders, who retreated toward Washington after being bloodied by Lee, Grant swung around the Confederate right flank and drove toward Richmond. When Lincoln read a telegram from the general stating that "I intend to fight it out on this line if it takes all summer," he told John Hay: "I believe if any other General had been at the Head of that army it would have now been on this side of the Rapidan. It is the dogged pertinacity of Grant that wins."[10] On May 15, Nicolay reported that the "President is cheerful and hopeful—not unduly elated, but seeming confident; and now as ever watching every report and indication, with quiet, unwavering interest."[11]

A Bogus Proclamation

Three days thereafter, Lincoln was startled to read in two New York papers—the *World* and the *Journal of Commerce*—a bogus presidential proclamation calling for four hundred thousand more volunteers and designating May 26 as a day of fasting, humiliation, and prayer occasioned by "the situation in Virginia, the disaster at Red River, the delay at Charleston, and the general state of the country."[12] Such language profoundly disheartened a public anxiously awaiting word of Grant's progress. Panic spread throughout the North as the story radiated nationwide via wire services. Lincoln told a journalist that the announcement "was a fabrication" and "that he had decided to call for 300,000 in July, not before."[13] He may have suspected that the document he had drafted the previous night to that effect had been leaked. An eyewitness recalled that the publication of the fake proclamation "angered Lincoln more than almost any other occurrence of the war period."[14]

Not only did it threaten to depress Northern spirits but it also indicated that the administration harbored a disloyal mole. The forgery was written by journalist Joseph Howard, who sought to increase the price of gold, in which he had invested heavily. That the two newspapers running the forgery were bitter critics of the administration may have predisposed Lincoln to suspect treason. The editors of those journals had plenty of reason to doubt the genuineness of the phony proclamation, or at least to make inquiries before publishing it. Lincoln was understandably angry.

The backstory of this scandal is murky, but it seems likely that Howard learned about Lincoln's intention to issue a new draft call from someone in Washington to whom he might have paid money to divulge it. On May 20, Ohio congressman S. S. Cox reported to one of the jailed editors that Mrs. Lincoln may have been the source of Howard's tip: "The forged proclamation is based on a *fact*. . . . A proclamation *was written* and similar in impact to the base and damnable forgery for which you are under ban." Cox speculated that "it may come from Mrs. Mary Lincoln."[15]

Cox's guess about the First Lady's culpability is plausible. In 1861, she had sold Henry Wikoff access to at least one presidential document. Like Howard, Wikoff had shamelessly flattered her in a major New York newspaper. A knowledgeable reporter for another important New York paper described her in March 1864 as an insider who "sold state secrets" and was "one of the *leaky vessels* from which contraband army news, gets afloat."[16] Years later, Carl Schurz recalled that "it was commonly believed that she sold war secrets for large sums of money."[17] Moreover, she desperately needed cash to pay one of her major creditors by June 1.

To combat the dire effects of the bogus proclamation, Lincoln had Seward draft a clarification announcing that the proclamation "is an absolute forgery." The president agreed with Seward that the two newspapers should be suppressed, and through Stanton he ordered General John A. Dix to suspend the papers' publication and arrest their editors. It was the only time that Lincoln initiated such action. This order was carried out promptly but rescinded two days later when it became clear that the prisoners had been duped by Howard, the same journalist who in February 1861 had falsely reported that Lincoln had slunk into Washington wearing a scotch cap. Meanwhile, Stanton had ordered the apprehension of other journalists as well as some telegraphers, who were also released when the full story became known. Howard was jailed for three months, winning a reprieve only after his former employer, Henry Ward Beecher, appealed in person to Lincoln.

Democrats pointed to these arrests as further examples of the administration's alleged tyranny. Compounding the impression of arbitrariness was the arrest of an Ohio editor, Samuel Medary, editor of the ferociously anti-administration Columbus, Ohio, *Crisis*. Provost marshals, acting on a grand jury indictment for the crime of "conspiracy against the Union," apprehended him two days after the New York papers were shut down. The charges were eventually dropped, but meanwhile Democrats had yet more evidence of the administration's assault on freedom of the press.

Grant Moves South

As promised, Grant did fight it out all summer, constantly driving southward and battling Lee almost nonstop for six weeks. After the Battle of the Wilderness, the next collision took place at Spotsylvania Courthouse between May 8 and 20. Lee inflicted severe losses before falling back to Hanover Junction, where fighting raged from May 23 to May 27, then to Cold Harbor for more bloody work yet (June 1–12). The fighting finally came to a halt after a pitched battle at Petersburg (June 15–18), twenty miles south of Richmond. Lee's skillful maneuvering had kept Grant at bay, inflicting sixty-five thousand casualties and saving the Confederate capital.

Grant had little to show for the enormous sacrifice of blood and treasure. He was bogged down at Petersburg, which he besieged with no imminent prospect of victory. Meanwhile, Sigel had been repulsed in the Shenandoah Valley, Butler was helplessly bottled up on the Peninsula, and Sherman was making disappointingly slow progress in his campaign against Atlanta. The grand strategy that had seemed so promising in the spring had fizzled. As these developments unfolded, Lincoln occasionally found respite by attending the theater. "People may think strange of it," he remarked to Schuyler Colfax, "but I *must* have some relief from this terrible anxiety, or it will kill me."[18]

On July 18, to help fill the army's depleted ranks, Lincoln called for five hundred thousand men. When Ohio Republicans urged him to rescind the call lest it defeat the party in the fall, he asked: "What is the Presidency worth to me if I have no country?"[19] Logically, he argued that "we must either have men, or the war must stop; I shall issue the call, and if the old ship goes down, it will be with the colors flying. So whether they come by draft, or volunteering, the nation needs soldiers. These she must have, or else she dies, and then comes anarchy, and the frightful ruin of a dismembered country, or its final surrender to the slave power, against which it now struggles, and calls every freeman to the rescue. Peace! In this struggle that which comes by the sword will be the more lasting, and worthy as a legacy to posterity."[20] He wanted the people to realize that if they reelected him, it "will mean that the rebellion is to be crushed by force of arms."[21] In response, Democrats howled that "tens of thousands of white men must bite the dust to allay the negro mania of the president."[22]

In mid-September the administration began implementing the new draft call, which implied that the war would end within a year, for it stipulated that draftees would serve for only twelve months but volunteers would serve for three years. Democrats' attempts to make conscription a significant issue in the campaign failed to gain traction.

Lincoln had been encouraged when Grant crossed the James River in mid-June. "I begin to see it," he wired the general. "You will succeed. God bless you all."[23] The following day, the president told a Philadelphia audience that the North "accepted this war for an object, a worthy object, and the war will end when that object is attained. Under God, I hope it never will until that time. Speaking of the present campaign, General Grant is reported to have said, I am going through on this line if it takes all summer. [Cheers.] This war has taken three years; it was begun or accepted upon the line of restoring the national authority over the whole national domain, and for the American people, as far as my knowledge enables me to speak, I say we are going through on this line if it takes three years more."[24] Such candor illustrated Lincoln's iron determination, which helped strengthen Northern willingness to sustain the war effort. To help drive home the point that the war might not end quickly, Lincoln enlisted the aid of the press. He solemnly told Noah Brooks, "I wish, when you write or speak to people, you would do all you can to correct the impression that the war in Virginia will end right off and victoriously."[25]

When Lee drove back a nearly successful assault on Petersburg, the president became alarmed. On June 21 he made a two-day visit to the Army of the Potomac. "I just thought I would jump aboard a boat and come down and see you," he told Grant, modestly adding: "I don't expect I can do any good, and in fact I'm afraid I may do harm, but I'd put myself under your orders and if you find me doing anything wrong just send me right away."[26] After inspecting some units, Lincoln took Grant's suggestion that he "ride on and see the colored troops, who behaved so handsomely in [William F.] Smith's attack on the works of Petersburg last week."

The president expressed keen interest in doing so, for he had not reviewed any of the United States Colored Troops. He was delighted by reports of their gallantry, which vindicated his controversial decision to allow African Americans to enlist. When Lincoln reached the camp of the Eighteenth Corps, hundreds of excited Black troops rushed to see him, hurrahing and cheering. A journalist reported that it "was a spontaneous outburst of love and affection for the man they looked upon as their deliverer from bondage."[27]

The next day, Lincoln visited Butler's command. As the party sailed up the James River, men on every vessel they passed cheered him. A nervous Gustavus Fox, recognizing that the presidential boat had come within range of Confederate guns, wondered why the enemy did not fire on such an important target. Upon returning to City Point, Lincoln had an hour's conversation with Grant, during which the general assured the president he would eventually gain possession of the Confederate capital. Lincoln said: "I cannot pretend to advise, but I do hope sincerely that all may be accomplished with as little bloodshed as possible."[28] On the way back to Washington, he seemed cheerful and told Fox that he was pleased with what he had seen and heard. Gideon Welles thought the president's brief visit to the front had done "him good, physically, and strengthened him mentally."[29]

The friendship between Grant and Lincoln was growing stronger as each got to know and admire the strengths of the other. Murat Halstead reported Lincoln saying: "Grant is the first General I have had. You know how it has been with all the rest. As soon as I put a man in command of the Army, he'd come to me with a plan of campaign and about as much to say, 'Now, I don't believe I can do it, but if you say so, I'll try it on,' and so put the responsibility of success or failure on me. They all wanted me to be the General. Now, it isn't so with Grant. . . . I am glad to find a man that can go ahead without me. . . . He doesn't ask impossibilities of me."[30]

Jubal Early's Raid

Two weeks later, Lincoln's anxiety increased when Jubal Early's fifteen thousand Confederate troops swept down the Shenandoah Valley and seriously menaced Washington. After crossing the Potomac on July 5–6, they brushed aside a Union detachment along the Monocacy River and within days were a scant four miles from the Soldiers' Home, where the Lincolns were then in residence. On July 10, Stanton, alarmed for the president's safety, sent a carriage to convey the First Family back to the White House. Stanton himself arrived around 11:00 p.m. and insisted that Lincoln return. With some irritation the president "said he didn't think there was any danger," but he complied nonetheless.[31]

On July 11, eager to observe the fighting, Lincoln hastened to Fort Stevens, where he became the first and only sitting American president to come under serious enemy fire. As he gazed from the parapet at the skirmishing, a soldier rudely instructed him to get down lest he be shot. He did so. Excited, Lincoln returned to the War Department and vividly described the action. That evening he was in an exceptionally good mood. Hay recorded that he was "not in the least concerned about the safety of Washington. With him the only concern seems to be whether we can bag or destroy this force in our front."[32] The next day he revisited Fort Stevens, accompanied this time by his wife. As he again watched the action from the parapet, an army surgeon standing nearby was shot in the thigh. At the urging of General Horatio Wright, Lincoln descended from his exposed perch. As Early withdrew, the president thought that Union forces should "push right up the river road & cut off as many as possible of the retreating raiders."[33] Although he urged Halleck to see that it was done, the Confederates managed to slip across the Potomac unmolested, to his obvious disgust. On July 30, Northern spirits were further depressed by the disastrous Battle of the Crater at Petersburg. Pennsylvania miners had dug a long tunnel, placed kegs of gunpowder directly beneath enemy lines, and detonated a huge explosion, sending Confederate body parts and rifles pinwheeling skyward. Thousands of Union troops then blundered by pouring *into* the resulting crater rather than around it. The Rebels easily slaughtered them and stymied the attack. Like the country, Lincoln was deeply disturbed. The following day he met with Grant at Fort Monroe. They evidently discussed the need to find a new commander to deal with Jubal Early in the Shenandoah Valley, where Sigel and then David Hunter had conspicuously failed. Despite great pressure to restore McClellan, Lincoln passed over him and other senior generals in favor of the very junior Philip Sheridan, only 33 years old. From his conference with Grant, the president emerged optimistic, for the general had confidently predicted that he would capture Richmond after a few rebuffs. Following that meeting, Grant assigned Sheridan to pursue Early "to the death. Wherever the enemy goes let our troops go also."[34] A few days later, Grant told Lincoln that he was reluctant to break his hold on the Confederate army at Petersburg. The president replied in iron words that spoke volumes about his indomitable resolve: "Hold on with a bull-dog grip, and chew & choke, as much as possible."[35]

Public Disenchantment

Lincoln may have felt better after his July 31 visit with Grant, but the voters did not. As public morale sank, the president began to worry about his reelection chances. Gloomily he predicted to General Andrew J. Hamilton, provisional governor of Texas, that he would be "*badly beaten* unless some great change takes place." The people of the North, he told Hamilton, "promised themselves when Gen. Grant started out that he would take Richmond in June—he didn't take it, and they blame me, but I promised them no such thing, & yet they hold me responsible."[36]

Among those most disenchanted with Lincoln were congressional Radicals, who passed a bill written by Ohio senator Benjamin F. Wade and Maryland congressman Henry Winter Davis laying out a reconstruction program different in some ways from the president's. Both plans required Confederate states to emancipate their slaves, and both stipulated that the federal government would appoint governors to preside over the reconstruction process. Neither plan authorized Black voting. Unlike Lincoln's scheme, which called for military governors to be appointed by the president, the Wade-Davis Bill permitted the appointment of provisional civilian governors. Passed on July 2, the legislation provided that when armed resistance ended within a state, the provisional governor (named by the president) was to enroll adult White males and permit them to take an oath of allegiance to the Constitution. Once a *majority* of those registered (not 10 percent, as Lincoln's plan called for) had taken the oath of future loyalty, the governor would facilitate the election of a state constitutional convention. Only those taking an "iron-clad" oath that they had never fought against the Union could vote on the constitutions or serve as delegates to the constitutional conventions. (Lincoln's plan called for an oath of prospective, not retrospective, loyalty.) The new constitutions must repudiate all debt incurred in support of the war, disqualify from voting and officeholding all high-ranking members of the Confederate military or civilian governments, and abolish slavery. Once these requirements were met, the state could be readmitted to the Union, vote in presidential elections, choose members of Congress, and resume its normal operations. Under Lincoln's plan, Blacks were to be educated and their rights protected, but the states were to determine how these goals were to be met. Congress demanded that Blacks and Whites be treated equally before the law, that Blacks enjoy the privilege of the writ of habeas corpus, and that White kidnappers of Blacks be harshly punished.

The requirement that a *majority* had to take the oath of future loyalty effectively meant that reconstruction would be a postwar process; Lincoln wanted it implemented while the fighting still raged in order to help shorten the war. The retrospective oath dismayed him, for he objected in principle to "an oath which requires a man to swear he *has* not done wrong" because it "rejects the Christian principle of forgiveness on terms of repentance. I think it is enough if the man does no wrong *hereafter*."[37]

The Wade-Davis Bill did not satisfy many abolitionists, who objected to its failure to enfranchise African Americans. Wade explained that while he supported Black suffrage in principle, he opposed an amendment providing for it because he feared that "it will sacrifice the bill."[38] When rumors circulated that Lincoln might veto the bill, congressmen and senators expressed their dismay. On July 4, as Lincoln sat in the capitol affixing his signature to various pieces of legislation,

Michigan senator Zachariah Chandler accosted him, saying a veto "would make a terrible record for us to fight."

"Mr. Chandler, this bill was placed before me a few minutes before Congress adjourns," Lincoln replied. "It is a matter of too much importance to be swallowed in that way." (Lincoln was not being entirely candid, for the bill had been passed two days earlier and had been under discussion for months.)

"If it is vetoed it will damage us fearfully in the North West. It may not in Illinois, but it will in Michigan and Ohio. The important point is that one prohibiting slavery in the reconstructed states."

"That is the point on which I doubt the authority of Congress to act."

"It is no more than you have done yourself."

"I conceive that I may in an emergency do things on military grounds which cannot be done constitutionally by Congress."

When Chandler left, Lincoln told three of his cabinet members, "This bill and this position of these gentlemen seems to me to make the fatal admission (in asserting that the insurrectionary states are no longer states in the Union) that states whenever they please may of their own motion dissolve their connection with the Union. Now we cannot survive that admission I am convinced. If that be true I am not President, these gentlemen are not Congress. I have laboriously endeavored to avoid that question ever since it first began to be mooted & thus to avoid confusion and disturbance in our own counsels. It was to obviate this question that I earnestly favored the movement for an amendment to the Constitution abolishing slavery." When John Hay opined that the Radicals had lost touch with public opinion, Lincoln said: "If they choose to make a point upon this I do not doubt that they can do harm. They have never been friendly to me & I don[']t know that this will make any special difference as to that. At all events, I must keep some consciousness of being somewhere near right: I must keep some standard of principle fixed within myself."[39]

When they realized that the president was not going to sign the bill (thus killing it with a pocket veto), Radicals erupted in indignation. On the House floor, a wrathful Henry Winter Davis excoriated Lincoln. The president with characteristic magnanimity said of Davis's assault, "It appears to do him good, and as it does me no injury, (that is I don't feel that it does) what's the harm in letting him have his fling? If he did not pitch into me he would into some poor fellow whom he might hurt."[40]

Davis's anger resulted in part from Lincoln's unwillingness to help him gain control of the Maryland Republican Party, at that time dominated by the Blairs. But more than personal pique fueled the clash between the president and Congress. The central difference was rooted in conflicting interpretations of the Constitution's "guarantee clause," which states that "the United States shall guarantee to every State in this Union a Republican Form of Government" but does not specify which branch of the government is empowered to enforce the guarantee. Along with his allies, Davis, an Old Whig who strove to limit the power of the executive branch, argued that it rested with Congress to decide whether a state had a republican form of government. More extreme Radicals wanted to reconstruct the South on the basis of Charles Sumner's "state suicide" theory, which would allow Congress to treat the Rebel states as though they had reverted to the status of territories. But most Republicans rejected that approach in favor of relying on the guarantee clause.

A few days later, Lincoln released his veto message, which was superfluous since the Constitution does not require the president to justify a pocket veto. Lincoln explained that he was not ready "to declare, that the free-state constitutions and governments, already adopted and installed in Arkansas and Louisiana, shall be set aside and held for nought, thereby repelling and discouraging the loyal citizens who have set up the same, as to further effort." Although he doubted that there was "constitutional competency in Congress to abolish slavery in States," he was "at the same time sincerely hoping and expecting that a constitutional amendment, abolishing slavery throughout the nation, may be adopted." Notwithstanding these objections, Lincoln in a conciliatory vein added that he was "fully satisfied with the system for restoration contained in the Bill, as one very proper plan for the loyal people of any State choosing to adopt it" and was "prepared to give the Executive aid and assistance to any such people, so soon as the military resistance to the United States shall have been suppressed in any such State."[41]

The veto ignited an epic struggle between Lincoln and Congress. On August 5, Davis and Wade issued a scathing manifesto denouncing the president. They cynically ascribed his opposition to political expediency: he wanted to win reelection with the help of electoral votes from reconstructed Southern states like Arkansas and Louisiana, whose representatives Congress refused to seat. They declared that a "more studied outrage on the legislative authority of the people has never been perpetrated. Congress passed a bill; the President refused to approve it, and then by proclamation puts as much of it in force as he sees fit, and proposes to execute those parts by officers unknown to the laws of the United States and not subject to the confirmation of the Senate!" Darkly, they hinted at impeachment: "Let them consider the remedy for these usurpations, and, having found it, fearlessly execute it."[42]

The president told Gideon Welles that "he had no desire" to read the manifesto and "could himself take no part in such a controversy as they seemed to wish to provoke."[43] But Lincoln did allow Seward to read him the manifesto. After hearing it through, he wondered aloud "whether these men intend openly to oppose my election—the document looks that way."[44] After a White House interview, B.

Rush Plumly reported that Lincoln's "blood is up on the Wade & Winter Davis protest."[45] Hurt as well as angry, the president told Noah Brooks: "To be wounded in the house of one's friends is perhaps the most grievous affliction that can befall a man. I have tried my best to meet the wishes of this man [Davis], and to do my whole duty by the country."[46]

The Radical manifesto backfired, in part because Congress was out of session. It was designed to trigger a dump-Lincoln movement before the Democratic convention met in late August. In July, Davis proposed that abolitionists urge both Frémont and Lincoln to withdraw. Other Radicals favored that course. Chase said that his fears about Lincoln "arise from the manifestations I see of a purpose to compromise, if possible, by sacrificing all that has been done for freedom in the rebel states—to purchase peace for themselves—the whites—by the re-enslavement of the blacks."[47] Sumner thought the president should step down to make way for "any one of 100 names."[48]

Boston Radicals wrote Frémont a public letter endorsing the idea. On August 25, the Pathfinder replied that he would quit if Lincoln did also, but the president would not cooperate. As he told Carl Schurz, "They urge me with almost violent language to withdraw from the contest, although I have been unanimously nominated, in order to make room for a better man. I wish I could. Perhaps some other man might do this business better than I. That is possible. I do not deny it. But I am here, and that better man is not here."[49] In July, while discussing the clamor for peace, Lincoln told a visitor: "I have faith in the people. They will not consent to disunion. The danger is, they are misled. Let them know the truth, and the country is safe." Looking exhausted, he was asked if he worked too hard. "I can't work less, but it isn't that—work never troubled me. Things look badly, and I can't avoid anxiety. Personally I care nothing about a re-election; but if our divisions defeat us, I fear for the country."[50]

The lowest point in Lincoln's presidency arrived in August, when he and many party leaders became convinced that he would lose. His 1860 campaign manager, David Davis, noted that the public was "getting tired of the war." If the North did "not have military successes soon, & the democrats at Chicago act with wisdom, we are in danger of losing the Presidential election," he warned.[51] Henry J. Raymond, whom Lincoln called "my lieutenant general in politics," decided to call a meeting of the Republican National Committee in Washington with the understanding that Leonard Swett would prepare the way by visiting the president to see if he "understood his danger and would help to set things in motion."[52]

When Swett asked Lincoln if he expected to win reelection, the president responded gloomily: "Well, I don't think I ever heard of any man being elected to an office unless someone was for him."[53] In mid-August, Governor Francis Pierpont of loyal Virginia told Lincoln that the Democrats were waging "a very unfair campaign and it needed attention," to which he replied: "Yes, but we need military success more—and without it I doubt the result. . . . The people seem despondent, and our opponents are pressing the howl that the war is a failure and it has had its effect in the army and among the people. We must have military success."[54]

Peace Overtures

The despairing public had good reason to believe that Lincoln would not end the war before slavery was extirpated. In the summer of 1864, Confederate leaders, aiming to capitalize on Northern war weariness and fuel the growing demand for a negotiated peace, floated bogus peace overtures, which Horace Greeley took seriously. The *Tribune*'s gullible editor alerted Lincoln that he had received word from one William C. "Colorado" Jewett that two emissaries from Jefferson Davis were in Canada, fully authorized to parley for peace. In forwarding this information, Greeley told Lincoln: "I venture to remind you that our bleeding, bankrupt, almost dying country also longs for peace—shudders at the prospect of fresh conscriptions, of further wholesale devastations, and of new rivers of human blood. And a wide-spread conviction that the Government and its prominent supporters are not anxious for Peace, and do not improve proffered opportunities to achieve it, is doing great harm now, and is morally certain, unless removed, to do far greater in the approaching Elections."[55]

Although Lincoln assumed rightly that Jefferson Davis had given no authority to those emissaries in Canada, he knew that Greeley was correct in stating that the administration could not afford to seem indifferent to peace feelers, even if made by agents whose goal "was to inflame the peace sentiment of the North, to embarrass the administration, and to demoralize the army."[56] Because he personally was unwilling to treat the peace negotiators as representatives of a legitimate government, Lincoln asked Greeley to act as an unofficial mediator to deal with them. On July 9, he authorized the editor to bring to Washington for consultation "any person anywhere professing to have any proposition of Jefferson Davis in writing, for peace, embracing the restoration of the Union and abandonment of slavery." Six days later, the president told Greeley, who had averred that the Confederate agents seemed serious: "I not only intend a sincere effort for peace, but I intend that you shall be a personal witness that it is made."[57] When Ohio congressman James Ashley protested against Greeley's mission, Lincoln said: "Don't worry; nothing will come of it."[58] The *Tribune* editor "means right" but "makes me almost as much trouble as the whole southern confederacy," the president complained.[59]

When John Hay presented Lincoln's letter to Greeley, the editor described himself as "the worst man that could be taken for the purpose" and predicted that "as soon as he arrived there, the newspapers would be full of it" and that "he would be abused & blackguarded." Nonetheless, he accepted the mission and at Niagara Falls met with the Confederate spokesmen, James P. Holcombe, George N. Sanders, Clement C. Clay, and Jacob Thompson, whom he misled by failing to make clear that Lincoln insisted on "the restoration of the Union and abandonment of slavery." He thought the president should not propose terms but instead let Jefferson Davis do so.[60] When the Confederates told Greeley that they were not in fact officially accredited to negotiate, the editor requested further instructions. In reply, Lincoln sent John Hay with a document that was to shock Northern peace advocates, for it made abolition a prerequisite for peace: "To whom it may concern: Any proposition which embraces the restoration of peace, the integrity of the whole Union, and the abandonment of slavery, and which comes by and with an authority that can control the armies now at war against the United States will be received and considered by the Executive government of the United States, and will be met by liberal terms on other substantial and collateral points, and the bearer or bearers thereof shall have safe conduct both ways."[61] Democrats called this "the Niagara Manifesto."

Because Greeley had not informed the Confederate agents initially of the president's conditions for negotiations, they were surprised by this document. They erroneously concluded that Lincoln was acting in bad faith. To counteract that impression, the president asked Greeley to publish their correspondence, with minor omissions. Greeley refused to run anything but the entire text, with its melodramatic analysis of the state of the country. Lincoln decided to drop the matter rather than have the demoralizing parts of Greeley's letters appear in print and thus depress Northern spirits. Vexed by the editor's intransigence, Lincoln compared him to an old shoe. "In early life," he told the cabinet, "and with few mechanics and but little means in the West, we used to make our shoes last a great while with much mending, and sometimes, when far gone, we found the leather so rotten the stitches would not hold. Greeley is so rotten that nothing can be done with him. He is not truthful; the stitches all tear out."[62]

When some of their correspondence nonetheless appeared in newspapers, Greeley was made to look foolish as he tried to blame Lincoln for the misunderstanding. The abolitionist *Christian Advocate and Journal* praised the "to whom it may concern" letter as "one of the most dignified and appropriate acts in the records of the war."[63] Conservatives, by contrast, charged that Lincoln was transforming a war to preserve the Union into an abolitionist crusade. Despite the criticism, Lincoln thought that his involvement in the bungled affair had been worthwhile. At least, he said, it "will shut up Greeley, and satisfy the people who are clamoring for peace."[64] When some of those clamorers objected to making abolition a precondition for peace, he said: "There has never been a time since the war began when I was not willing to stop it if I could do so and preserve the Union, and earlier in the war I would have omitted some of the conditions of my note to the rebel Commissioners, but I had become satisfied that no lasting peace could be built up between the States in some of which there were free and in others slave institutions, and, therefore, I made the recognition of the abolition of slavery a *sine qua non*."[65]

John Brown Redivivus

On August 23, Lincoln wrote one of his most curious documents, a memorandum expressing the belief that a Democratic victory was likely: "This morning, as for some days past, it seems exceedingly probable that this Administration will not be re-elected. Then it will be my duty to so co-operate with the President elect, as to save the Union between the election and the inauguration; as he will have secured his election on such ground that he can not possibly save it afterwards."[66] He folded and sealed it and then, inexplicably, asked his cabinet to sign it without revealing its contents. It became known as the "blind memorandum."

Several weeks later, Lincoln read this document to the cabinet and explained its genesis: "You will remember that this was written at a time (6 days before the Chicago nominating convention) when as yet we had no adversary, and seemed to have no friends," he said. "I then solemnly resolved on the course of action indicated above. I resolved, in case of the election of General McClellan[,] being certain that he would be the Candidate, that I would see him and talk matters over with him. I would say, 'General, the election has demonstrated that you are stronger, have more influence with the American people than I. Now let us together, you with your influence and I with all the executive power of the Government, try to save the country. You raise as many troops as you possibly can for this final trial, and I will devote all my energies to assisting and finishing the war.'"

Seward remarked, "And the General would answer you '*Yes, Yes*'; and the next day when you saw him again & pressed these views upon him he would say, 'Yes—yes' & so on forever and would have done nothing at all."

"At least," Lincoln replied, "I should have done my duty and have stood clear before my own conscience."[67]

Because Lincoln quite rightly feared that a Democratic victory would end the emancipation process, he wanted to gather as many slaves as possible beneath the tent of freedom. Only those who were within Union lines by March 4, 1865, would be liberated by the Emancipation Proclamation. In August, he told Colonel John Eaton, superintendent of freedmen in the Department of the Tennessee and the state of Arkansas, "that he wished the 'grapevine telegraph,'" which informed slaves about the progress of the war, "could be utilized to call upon the Negroes of the interior peacefully to leave the plantations and seek the protection of our armies." When Eaton mentioned Frederick Douglass's recent criticism of administration policy, the president asked if Douglass might be persuaded to come to the White House for a discussion. Eaton, who knew Douglass well, facilitated the meeting.

On August 19, Lincoln and Douglass met for the second time. Among other things, they discussed a recent letter the president had drafted but had not yet not sent to the War Democrat Charles D. Robinson, who had written to Lincoln criticizing the "to whom it may concern" letter. Defending that missive, the president had composed a reply in which he appeared to withdraw his insistence on abolition as a prerequisite for peace: "If Jefferson Davis wishes, for himself, or for the benefit of his friends at the North, to know what I would do if he were to offer peace and re-union, saying nothing about slavery, let him try me."[68] Douglass emphatically objected to the letter's implicit backsliding on emancipation, and he urged the president not to send it. Lincoln took that advice.

Turning to the danger presented by a Democratic victory, Lincoln told Douglass that the "slaves are not coming so rapidly and so numerously to us as I had hoped." Douglass "replied that the slaveholders knew how to keep such things from their slaves, and probably very few knew of his Proclamation." Earnestly the president suggested a plan somewhat like John Brown's 1859 scheme, "that something should be speedily done to inform the slaves in the Rebel states of the true state of affairs in relation to them" and "to urge upon them the necessity of making their escape." Years later, Douglass recalled that Lincoln's words "showed a deeper moral conviction against slavery than I had ever seen before in anything spoken or written by him." The president said: "Douglass, I hate slavery as much as you do, and I want to see it abolished altogether."[69] The Black orator agreed to help recruit a band of African American scouts "whose business should be somewhat after the original plan of John Brown, to go into the rebel states, beyond the lines of our armies, and carry the news of emancipation, and urge the slaves to come within our boundaries."[70]

Douglass excitedly told Colonel Eaton that the president "treated me as a man; he did not let me feel for a moment that there was any difference in the color of our skins! The President is a most remarkable man. I am satisfied now that he is doing all that circumstances will permit him to do." The admiration was mutual, for Lincoln said "that considering the conditions from which Douglass rose, and the position to which he had attained he was, in his judgment, one of the most meritorious men in America."[71]

Demoralized Republicans

Along with the rest of the Republican National Executive Committee, Henry J. Raymond called at the White House on August 25. Nicolay reported: "Hell is to pay. The N.Y. politicians have got a stampede on that is about to swamp everything. . . . Everything is darkness and doubt and discouragement. Our men see giants in the airy and unsubstantial shadows of the opposition, and are about to surrender without a fight. I think that today and here is the turning-point in our crisis. If the President can infect R[aymond] and his committee with some of his own patience and pluck, we are saved."[72]

Lincoln did not show his visitors a letter to Raymond that he had drafted the previous day instructing him to "proceed forthwith and obtain, if possible, a conference for peace with Hon. Jefferson Davis, or any person by him authorized for that purpose," to "propose, on behalf of this government, that upon the restoration of the Union and the national authority, the war shall cease at once, all remaining questions to be left for adjustment by peaceful modes." If Davis rejected this offer, then Raymond was to "request to be informed what terms, if any embracing the restoration of the Union, would be accepted" and report back to Washington.[73] These instructions remained in the president's desk. Lincoln doubtless hoped to make Davis state unequivocally that he would accept no peace terms denying independence to the Confederacy.

Many Republicans shared Lincoln's view that an attempt to hold peace talks would be disastrous. Rumors that the administration might be willing to accept a compromise settlement were "paralyzing the Republican and the Union party," John Murray Forbes noted. It is not clear whether Lincoln seriously toyed with the idea of backsliding on emancipation. He probably had not meant to suggest that he would rescind the Proclamation; his "try me" dare was in all likelihood merely a ploy to smoke out Jefferson Davis and thus undo the harm done by the "to whom it may concern" letter, which the Democrats repeatedly attacked, calling it "The Republican Platform."[74] While a retraction of his antislavery pledge might gain him some support from conservatives, he said it would "lose ten times as much on the other side."[75]

In late August, John Murray Forbes, who had earlier favored postponing the Republican convention, warned that it was too late to field another standard-bearer. "We cannot change our Candidate," even though the Democrats might win, he told Charles Eliot Norton. If the Peace Democrats "keep in the background & let the opposition put up some one at Chicago who can catch the votes of the war & peace opposition men we shall have a hard time in electing Lincoln. Were we free today we could nominate Dix or Butler and elect him by a strong vote." But the time for such a change had passed.[76]

As August drew to a close, the future looked bleak indeed.

34.

"The Wisest Radical of All"

Reelection (September–November 1864)

The political tide began to turn on August 29, when the Democratic national convention met in Chicago. Lincoln accurately predicted that the delegates "must nominate a Peace Democrat on a war platform, or a War Democrat on a peace platform; and I personally can't say that I care much which they do."[1] In fact, the convention took the latter course, choosing George McClellan as the party's presidential candidate and adopting a platform that described the war as "four years of failure." It also called for the restoration of "the rights of the States unimpaired," which implied the preservation of slavery, as well as demanding that "immediate efforts be made for a cessation of hostilities, with a view to an ultimate convention of the states, or other peaceable means, to the end that, at the earliest practicable moment, peace may be restored on the basis of the Federal Union of the States." This "peace plank," the handiwork of Clement Vallandigham, rejected the terms of Lincoln's "to whom it may concern" letter; the Democrats would require as a prerequisite for peace only union, whereas the Republicans insisted on union and emancipation. For McClellan's running mate, the delegates chose Vallandigham's alter ego, Ohio congressman George Pendleton, a thoroughgoing opponent of the war who had voted against supplies for the army.

As the nation waited and waited to see how McClellan would react, Lincoln quipped that Little Mac "must be *intrenching*." More seriously, he added that the general "doesn't know yet whether he will accept or decline. And he never will know. Somebody must do it for him. For of all the men I have had to do with in my life, *indecision* is most strongly marked in General McClellan;—*if that can be said to be strong which is the essence of weakness*."[2] A week and a half after the Chicago convention, McClellan finally issued a temporizing letter formally accepting the nomination while implicitly disavowing the "peace plank." Yet he did indicate that he had no objection to a compromise settlement leaving slavery intact within a restored Union. It is highly unlikely that if he had won the election, McClellan could have brought the war to a successful close, with the nation reunited and slavery abolished. Throughout the campaign he never indicated that he approved of the Emancipation Proclamation or that he would make abolition a precondition for peace.

The news from Chicago restored Lincoln's flagging spirits. Along with Vallandigham's "peace plank," the defiant nomination of Pendleton estranged War Democrats and Conservative Unionists. Emphatically and confidently, Lincoln told a Pennsylvania Republican leader that "the danger was past" because "after the expenditure of blood and treasure that has been poured out for the maintenance of the government and the preservation of the Union, the American people were not prepared to vote the war a failure."[3] He was right.

Republican morale soared, for the Democrats' self-inflicted wounds seemed to fatally damage their electoral chances. As George Templeton Strong observed, the "general howl against the base policy offered for our endorsement at Chicago is refreshing. Bitter opponents of Lincoln join in it heartily."[4] One of those bitter opponents, Theodore Tilton, confided to a fellow abolitionist: "I was opposed to Mr. Lincoln's nomination: but now it becomes the duty of all Unionists to present a united front." While the incumbent might not be the best possible nominee, it would be "criminal" to desert the Republican Party, which was "the only one that can save the country."[5]

Other prominent Radical Republicans added their voices to the swelling pro-Lincoln chorus. Charles Sumner insisted that if the president would not withdraw, Republicans were duty-bound to unite behind him. The senator was as good as his word and delivered pro-Lincoln speeches in New York and Connecticut as well as the Bay State. Frederick Douglass, who had signed the call for the Radical Democracy convention, publicly endorsed Lincoln in September. "When there was any shadow of a hope that a man of a more decided anti-slavery conviction and policy could be elected, I was not for Mr. Lincoln," he told an abolitionist colleague. "But as soon as the Chicago convention [adjourned], my mind was made up."[6]

Other African Americans agreed. In Baltimore, a number of them raised money for an expensive Bible that they presented to Lincoln on September 7. It was, they told him, "a testimonial of their appreciation of your humane conduct towards the people of our race." The president replied that "it has always been a sentiment with me that all mankind should be free. So far as able, within my sphere, I have always acted as I believed to be right and just; and I have done all I could for the good of mankind generally."[7] The following month, Lincoln showed this volume to the Black abolitionist/feminist/grandmother Sojourner Truth, who complimented him as being "the best President" ever and later said that "I never was treated by any one with more kindness and cordiality than was shown me by that great and good man."[8]

Most Radicals, but not all, fell into line. Wendell Phillips declared, "I would cut off my right hand before doing anything to aid A.L.'s election."[9] Phillips's stance alienated other antislavery militants, including Congressman William D. Kelley of Pennsylvania, who spoke for many of them when he called Lincoln "the wisest radical of us all."[10]

Military Success

The Democrats' nomination of McClellan and adoption of a peace plank were not the only developments reviving Lincoln's chances. Four days after the Chicago convention, General Sherman captured Atlanta. On September 6, Nicolay predicted that the "Atlanta victory alone ought to win the Presidential contest for us," for it gave the lie to Democrats' charge that the war was a failure.[11] So too did Admiral Farragut's capture of Mobile Bay. Later in September, Philip Sheridan trounced Confederate forces under Jubal Early in the Shenandoah Valley, further discrediting the Democrats' allegation of failure. On September 23, as word of that general's victory at Fisher's Hill arrived, Lincoln was immensely cheered and told funny stories that made auditors laugh till they were sore. Grant further boosted Northern morale with a widely reprinted letter stating that "all we want now to insure an early restoration of the Union is a determined unity of sentiment [in the] North. The rebels have now in their ranks their last man. . . . A man lost by them can not be replaced. They have robbed the cradle and the grave equally to get their present force. . . . Their only hope now is in a divided North. . . . They hope [for] a counter revolution. They hope [for] the election of the peace candidate."[12]

Lincoln proclaimed Sunday, September 11, a day of thanksgiving for the good news from Atlanta and Mobile Bay, prompting the Reverend Dr. Joseph P. Thompson to commend his action. "I would be glad to give you such a proclamation every Sunday for a few weeks to come," the president replied."[13]

Frémont Withdraws

With the fall of Atlanta, the dump-Lincoln movement abruptly collapsed. Frémont withdrew from the race, largely thanks to the efforts of Michigan senator Zachariah Chandler, a self-appointed peacemaker who was working behind the scenes to unite the party. In August, he began extensive shuttle diplomacy with a visit to Ben Wade, who realized that he had made a mistake by signing Henry Winter Davis's manifesto. The Ohio senator was in a mood to reconcile with the president. When his good friend and ally Chandler asked him to stump for Lincoln, Wade agreed to do so if the president would dismiss Montgomery Blair from the cabinet.

When Chandler approached Lincoln with Wade's request, the president was reluctant to comply, even though Senator Henry Wilson advised him that "every one hates" the postmaster general and predicted that "tens of thousands of men will be lost to you or will give a reluctant vote on account of the Blairs."[14] When Thaddeus Stevens similarly warned that the Republicans of Pennsylvania would not "work with a good will" unless Blair were dismissed, Lincoln bristled. Expressing regret that he could not make such a promise, he told the influential congressman with some heat: "If I were even myself inclined to make it, I have no right to do so. What right have I to promise you to remove Mr. Blair, and not make a similar promise to any other gentleman of influence to remove any other member of my cabinet who he does not happen to like? The Republican party, wisely or unwisely has made me their nominee for President, without asking any such pledge at my hands. Is it proper that you should demand it, representing only a portion of that great party? Has it come to this that the voters of this country are asked to elect a man to be President—to be the Executive—to administer the government, and yet that this man is to have no will or discretion of his own? Am I to be the mere puppet of power—to have my constitutional advisers selected for me beforehand, to be told I must do this or leave that undone? It would be degrading to my manhood to consent to any such bargain—I was about to say it is equally degrading to your manhood to ask it."[15]

In August, Francis P. Blair Sr., recognizing that his controversial offspring might damage Lincoln's reelection chances, told the president "that he might rely on my sons to do all they could for him" and suggested that the president recall Frank Blair from the army "to heal party divisions in Missouri & Stump the States." He added that Montgomery "would go the rounds also—and would be very willing to be a martyr to the Radical phrenzy or jealousy, that would feed on the Blairs, if that would help." Lincoln replied that "nobody but enemies wanted Montg[omer]y out of the Cabinet" and that "he did not think it good policy to sacrifice a true friend to a false one or an avowed enemy." Still, he did appreciate Montgomery's generous offer to "cheerfully resign to conciliate the class of men who had made their war on the Blairs because they were his friends—and sought to injure him among the ignorant partizans of those seeking to supplant him."[16]

On September 3, Lincoln changed his tune when he met with Chandler, Elihu Washburne, Iowa senator James Harlan, and James M. Edmunds, head of the Union League. Those four men "intimated that the country thought well" of Lincoln but was unhappy with his earlier acceptance of Chase's resignation. If "he would remove Blair all might still be well." After the president defended his postmaster general in a lengthy rehearsal of events in Missouri, his callers replied that even if a strong case could be made for Blair, "still *all* who will vote for you think

Blair false and untrustworthy and you can't convince them; so you must remove him or be defeated."

"But I don't want to desert a friend!" Lincoln exclaimed.

"Very possibly, but you will go down with him. What you say about Blair may be true—but nobody thinks so and everybody wants to get rid of him. Won't you let him go?"

"Well I'll think of it."

Chandler then said: "I am going to New York to see Wade; and probably if I could say you will remove Blair I could secure *his* support and get Fremont out of the way."

Lincoln replied, "Well I think it may be done!"

The next morning Chandler told the president that "if Fremont could be induced to withdraw by giving up Blair he would do [arrange] it." To his wife, Chandler confided that Lincoln "was most reluctant to come to terms *but came*."[17] Chandler proceeded to New York on his mission. After some discussion and reflection, the Pathfinder said he would quit without conditioning his action on Blair's dismissal. Chandler hastened to inform Lincoln of Frémont's decision and to ask for the quid pro quo the senator had specified before undertaking his mission: Blair's head. When Chandler made that demand, Lincoln replied: "I must do it in my own way to soften it."

Frémont's letter of withdrawal understandably displeased Lincoln. Grudgingly the Pathfinder offered to support the Republican ticket: "In respect to Mr. Lincoln, I consider that his Administration has been politically, militarily, and financially a failure, and that its necessary continuance is a cause of regret for the country."[18] Lincoln was so put off that when Chandler called at the White House, the president "showed symptoms of flying from the bargain." But the senator argued that "the form of the withdrawal was not a condition; and offensive as it was, still it was a substantial advice to support L[incoln]."[19] The president agreed, and the next day he asked Blair to honor his pledge to step down when asked to do so: "You have generously said to me more than once, that whenever your resignation could be a relief to me, it was at my disposal. The time has come. You very well know that this proceeds from no dissatisfaction of mine with you personally or officially. Your uniform kindness has been unsurpassed by that of any friend."[20] Blair responded to the president's letter handsomely: "I can not take leave of you without renewing the expressions of my gratitude for the uniform kindness which has marked your course towards [me]."[21] He was pleased that Lincoln took Francis P. Blair's advice by appointing as the new postmaster general William Dennison, former governor of Ohio and a friend of the Blair family.

Lincoln's willingness to let Blair go was rooted in his fear that Frémont might siphon off essential votes. The Pathfinder was especially popular among Missouri

Germans, who scorned Lincoln as the "great violator of the Constitution," a "still greater butcher of men," one who "remains unmoved in the face of the greatest misery, and who can crack joke like a Nero while Rome is burning."[22] Lincoln was also eager to have Wade, Davis, and other Radicals rejoin the fold. Some administration critics hoped that Chase would publicly denounce Lincoln as he had done in private. But in September, Hugh McCulloch, comptroller of the currency, met with Lincoln to help reconcile Chase and the president. During their conversation, Lincoln "made a frank statement of his kind feelings for Mr. Chase," thus "removing all cause for estrangement between them."[23] Shortly thereafter, Chase, eager for the seat on the Supreme Court that seemed likely to open soon, returned to the Midwest to campaign for Lincoln. Reluctantly, other Radicals followed suit, for no other candidate seemed viable. Henry Winter Davis said he felt "so disgusted that he cannot talk" but pledged to make a pro-Lincoln speech if he could "get his disgust off sufficiently."[24] His support was far from warm. In late September, he told a Maryland audience "that neither McClellan nor Lincoln were leading men of vigor equal to the place & that the only difference was that . . . Lincoln would be compelled to wage the war & to execute the emancipation policy & [would be] firmly restrained from any ignominious or weak compromises."[25]

Democratic Demagoguery

As usual, Democrats appealed shamelessly to racial prejudice. A leading party newspaper alleged that Lincoln was descended from Blacks, and one editor summarized the Republican platform thus:

Hurrah for the nigger
The sweet-scented nigger,
And the paradise for the undertaker!
Hurrah for Old Abe![26]

The bogus issue of interracial sex, long a staple of Democratic campaign rhetoric, became more prominent than usual in 1864. The party's traditional appeal to anti-Black prejudice received a new twist in the campaign. David Goodman Croly and George Wakeman of the New York *World* coined a neologism for their anonymous anti-Republican pamphlet, *Miscegenation: The Theory of the Blending of the Races, Applied to the American White Man and Negro*, which was sent to leading antislavery spokesmen. (The common term for miscegenation before both Croly and Wakeman invented that term was *amalgamation*.) A fraud designed to trap its recipients into endorsing interracial marriage, the tract was purportedly written by an unnamed abolitionist advocating that policy. It was filled with bogus "facts" that shamelessly played on the North's deep-seated Negrophobia. The few gullible abolitionists who fell for the hoax became the butt of Democratic ridicule, but the attempt to inveigle a prominent Republican into supporting it failed. In some Democratic circles, Republicans were reviled as "nigger fuggers."[27] When asked if he supported miscegenation, Lincoln wryly answered: "That's a [D]emocratic mode of producing good Union men, & I don't propose to infringe the patent."[28]

The president could be sarcastic when confronting racist arguments. In August, an ungrammatical Pennsylvanian wrote him saying: "Equal Rights & Justice to all white men in the United States forever. White men is in class number one & black men is in class number two & must be governed by white men forever." Lincoln penned a biting reply over the signature of Nicolay: "The President has received yours of yesterday, and is kindly paying attention to it. As it is my business to assist him whenever I can, I will thank you to inform me, for his use, whether you are either a white man or black one, because in either case, you can not be regarded as an entirely impartial judge. It may be that you belong to a third or fourth class of *yellow* or *red* men, in which case the impartiality of your judgment would be more apparent."[29] Lincoln enjoyed the satirical journalism of David Ross Locke, who ridiculed Democrats' racism by having it spout from the mouth of his central character, the ignorant preacher Petroleum V. Nasby.

Democrats abused the president roundly, calling him "a miserable failure, a coarse filthy joker, a disgusting politician, a mean, cunning and cruel tyrant and the shame and disgrace of the nation."[30] Some newspapers suggested that Lincoln be killed. In late August, the La Crosse, Wisconsin, *Democrat* declared that if the president were reelected, it would be well if someone assassinated him: "Lincoln is a traitor and murderer," and so "if he is elected to misgovern for another four years, we trust some bold hand will pierce his heart with dagger point for the public good."[31]

False charges against Lincoln reached a peak when the New York *World* alleged that he had tastelessly requested Ward Hill Lamon to sing a popular ditty while they accompanied McClellan on a tour of the corpse-strewn Antietam battlefield. According to that flagship Democratic journal, the president said: "Come, Lamon, give us that song about Picayune Butler; McClellan has never heard it."

"Not now, if you please," McClellan allegedly remarked. "I would prefer to hear it some other place and time."[32]

When Lamon wrote a blistering denial, Lincoln advised him against releasing it: "I would not publish this; it is too belligerent in its tone. You are at times too fond of a fight. There is a heap of wickedness mixed up with your usual amiability. If I were you, I'd state the facts as they were. I would give the statement as you have it without the cussedness. Let me try my hand at it."[33] Lincoln then drafted a long letter for his friend's signature. After completing it, however, he told Lamon: "You know, Hill, that this is the truth and the whole truth about that affair; but I dislike to appear as an apologist for an act of my own which I know was right. Keep this paper, and we will see about it."[34] That document was not released to the press.

Democrats also attacked Mary Lincoln for her lavish spending sprees in New York and the corrupt actions she took to manage her debts. The First Lady observed the campaign uneasily. When a spiritualist told her that the president would be defeated, she returned to the White House inconsolably "crying *like a child*."[35] In response to such outbursts, Lincoln chided her gently: "Mary, I am afraid you will be punished for this overweening anxiety. If I am to be re-elected, it will be all right; if not, you must bear the disappointment."[36] (Her nervousness stemmed in part from a fear that if Lincoln were not reelected, her creditors would descend on her.)

When Democrats charged that Lincoln received his salary in gold, while other government employees got greenbacks, the U.S. treasurer, Francis E. Spinner, denied it, explaining that by law the president's salary was paid in monthly warrant drafts, minus income tax. Rather than drawing money on those drafts, Lincoln left them in his drawer for long periods without receiving any interest. Several times Spinner urged him to cash the warrants, pointing out that he was losing hundreds of dollars in interest. When Lincoln asked who gained thereby, Spinner said the Treasury. "I reckon the Treasury needs it more than I do," Lincoln replied.[37] By failing to cash his warrants, Lincoln had in effect contributed around $4,000 to the Treasury. Understandably, he resented the Democratic editor who had first published the false allegation. "See to what depths of infamy a Northern Copperhead can descend," he remarked. "If the scoundrel who wrote that don't boil hereafter, it will be because the devil hasn't got iron enough to make gridirons."[38]

Republican Tactics

Republicans countered Democratic rhetoric with exaggerated charges of treason, allegedly fomented by secret societies like the Sons of Liberty and the Order of American Knights. In October, Judge Advocate General Joseph Holt issued a report accusing such organizations of disloyalty. Lincoln charitably expressed skepticism about the Sons of Liberty, calling it "a mere political organization, with about as much of malice and as much of puerility as the Knights of the Golden Circle." In June, Vallandigham had returned from exile to serve as supreme grand commander of the Sons. Rather than having him rearrested, Lincoln thought it best to let him sow dissension within the Democratic ranks. To John Hay, Lincoln explained "that the question for the Government to decide is whether it can afford to disregard the contempt of authority & breach of discipline displayed in Vallandigham's unauthorized return: for the rest, it cannot but result in benefit to the

Union cause to have so violent and indiscreet a man go to Chicago as a firebrand to his own party." According to Hay, Lincoln had long beforehand "seriously thought of annulling the sentence of exile but had been too much occupied to do it."[39] In late June, he drafted instructions to watch Vallandigham closely, to report his activities to Washington, and to take him into custody only if he contributed to "any palpable injury" or presented a "danger to the military." But on second thought, he decided to withhold the order.[40]

Lincoln worried about his chances in New York, which he had carried with 54 percent of the vote in 1860. Thurlow Weed and his allies were, the president noted in June, on "the verge of open revolt."[41] Trouble had long been brewing as the Greeley wing of the party continued battling the Seward-Weed forces over patronage, especially in the customhouse. Weed was disgruntled when he heard that Lincoln regarded a controversy between Lord Thurlow and Greeley as a personal quarrel. The president tactfully apologized to the thin-skinned Weed: "I have been brought to fear recently that somehow, by commission or omission, I have caused you some degree of pain. I have never entertained an unkind feeling, or a disparaging thought towards you; and if I have said or done anything which has been construed into such unkindness or disparagement, it has been misconstrued. I am sure if we could meet we would not part with any unpleasant impression on either side."[42]

In a further attempt to pacify Weed, the president sent Nicolay to New York. There Lord Thurlow and Henry J. Raymond urged that immediate changes be made in the leadership of the customhouse. Nicolay found the assignment "very delicate, disagreeable and arduous" but derived satisfaction from his ability to help broker a deal. Hiram Barney, collector, and Rufus Andrews, surveyor, were replaced by Simeon Draper and Abram Wakeman, respectively. Those changes, along with others in several lesser customhouse posts, satisfied Weed. They displeased the Greeley faction of the party, however. "I am so disgusted with Lincoln's behavior that I cannot muster respectful terms in which to write him," grumbled William Cullen Bryant.[43]

Lincoln did not, however, make all the changes desired by New York politicos. To one of them, who demanded the removal of an official who opposed the president's renomination, Lincoln impatiently snapped: "You cannot think —— to be half as mean to me as I know him to be, but I can not run this thing upon the theory that every officeholder must think I am the greatest man in the nation, and I will not."[44] The offending critic kept his job. Similarly, Lincoln restored an officer to the army after Stanton had dismissed him for giving a pro-McClellan speech. "Supporting McClellan for the presidency is no violation of military regulations," said the president, adding puckishly that "as a question of taste of choosing between him and me, well, I'm the longest, but he's better looking."[45] Lincoln's remarkable ability to harmonize factions helped assure his reelection and Northern victory in the war. To Leonard Swett he stated: "I may not have made as great a President as some other men, but I believe I have kept these discordant elements together as well as anyone could."[46]

In addition to New York, Lincoln worried about the Border States, whose voters, like many conservatives throughout the North, disliked both the Emancipation Proclamation and the enlistment of Black troops. Hostility to Lincoln had grown especially acute in Kentucky. When a delegation from that state called at the White House in late March, the president made a brief speech to them, which he subsequently wrote out. It became one of his most masterful public letters, addressing head-on their complaints about his policies. In it, he sought to persuade them that circumstances beyond his control had forced him to liberate the slaves and enroll Blacks in the army. He began by frankly acknowledging his hostility to slavery: "I am naturally anti-slavery. If slavery is not wrong, nothing is wrong. I can not remember when I did not so think, and feel."

But he insisted that his hatred for slavery had not determined his policies, for he felt duty-bound to honor his oath of office: "I have never understood that the Presidency conferred upon me an unrestricted right to act officially upon this judgment and feeling. It was in the oath I took that I would, to the best of my ability, preserve, protect, and defend the Constitution of the United States. I could not take the office without taking the oath. Nor was it my view that I might take an oath to get power, and break the oath in using the power. . . . I did understand however, that my oath to preserve the constitution to the best of my ability, imposed upon me the duty of preserving, by every indispensable means, that government—that nation—of which that constitution was the organic law. Was it possible to lose the nation, and yet preserve the constitution? By general law life *and* limb must be protected; yet often a limb must be amputated to save a life; but a life is never wisely given to save a limb. I felt that measures, otherwise unconstitutional, might become lawful, by becoming indispensable to the preservation of the constitution, through the preservation of the nation. Right or wrong, I assumed this ground, and now avow it. I could not feel that, to the best of my ability, I had even tried to preserve the constitution, if, to save slavery, or any minor matter, I should permit the wreck of government, country, and Constitution all together."

Lincoln reminded his callers that he had overruled emancipation orders by John C. Frémont in 1861 and David Hunter in 1862 and had objected to Simon Cameron's 1861 call for arming African Americans. Back then, he thought there was no "indispensable necessity" for such measures. As a further indication of his essentially moderate approach, he cited his appeals in March, May, and July 1862 "to the border states to favor compensated emancipation," for, he said, he "believed the indispensable necessity for military emancipation, and arming the blacks would come, unless averted by that measure." After they rejected his advice, he said, he was "driven to the alternative of either surrendering the Union, and with it, the Constitution, or of laying strong hand upon the colored element. I chose the latter." That policy proved successful, and as a result the Union army had gained "a hundred and thirty thousand soldiers, seamen, and laborers. . . . We have the men; and we could not have had them without the measure."

In this letter, Lincoln supplemented his earlier verbal remarks. He wished the public to understand that the steps he had taken had to some extent been necessitated by the will of the Almighty: "In telling this tale I attempt no compliment to my own sagacity. I claim not to have controlled events, but confess plainly that events have controlled me. Now, at the end of three years struggle the nation's condition is not what either party, or any man devised, or expected. God alone can claim it. Whither it is tending seems plain. If God now wills the removal of a great wrong, and wills also that we of the North as well as you of the South, shall pay fairly for our complicity in that wrong, impartial history will find therein new cause to attest and revere the justice and goodness of God."[47]

Like the 1862 letter to Horace Greeley, this missive was a campaign document designed to reassure moderates and conservatives that he was scrupulously obeying the Constitution and not willfully imposing his own personal views on the public. Both letters have been misunderstood as profoundly revealing documents shedding light on Lincoln's innermost thoughts and feelings. To be sure, the frank acknowledgment of his long-standing hatred of slavery was candid. But the implication that he was essentially the plaything of forces beyond his control is misleading. Lincoln was a self-confident leader who used the power of his office tactfully but assertively, recognizing with characteristic fatalism that while he could shape events up to a point, forces larger than his own will were at work. His attitude toward fate resembled what the twentieth-century theologian Reinhold Niebuhr expressed in his "serenity prayer": "God grant me the serenity to accept the things I cannot change; the courage to change the things I can; and the wisdom to know the difference."[48]

In September, Lincoln shared with a Quaker leader his belief in the power of God to shape events: "The purposes of the Almighty are perfect, and must prevail, though we erring mortals may fail to accurately perceive them in advance. We hoped for a happy termination of this terrible war long before this; but God knows best, and has ruled otherwise. We shall yet acknowledge His wisdom and our own error therein. Meanwhile we must work earnestly in the best light He gives us, trusting that so working still conduces to the great ends He ordains. Surely He intends some great good to follow this mighty convulsion, which no mortal could make, and no mortal could stay."[49] (The previous year, he had told other Quakers that "if the Almighty be with us, we shall succeed; if He is against us, no human power can save us; but I cannot believe that He will suffer the enemies of our country to triumph and the great Christian principles we are contending for, to fall to the ground and be trampled under foot.")[50]

In a private memo to himself, probably written in the summer of 1864, Lincoln ruminated on the Lord's intentions. Distraught at the terrible bloodshed of the stalled military campaigns, he asked why a benevolent deity would allow it. "The will of God prevails. In great contests each party claims to act in accordance with the will of God. Both *may* be, and one *must* be wrong. God can not be *for*, and *against* the same thing at the same time. In the present civil war it is quite possible that God's purpose is something different from the purpose of either party—and yet the human instrumentalities, working just as they do, are of the best adaptation to effect His purpose. I am almost ready to say this is probably true—that God wills this contest, and wills that it shall not end yet. By his mere quiet power, on the minds of the now contestants, He could have either *saved* or *destroyed* the Union without a human contest. Yet the contest began. And having begun He could give the final victory to either side any day. Yet the contest proceeds."[51]

By March 1865, Lincoln had reached a conclusion about the will of God, a conclusion that he was to share with the public in his second inaugural address. But before he could be inaugurated once more, he must win reelection.

The Peace Issue

During the political campaign, Lincoln issued no other public letters, though he did draft one in which he addressed the problem of war weariness: "Much is being said about peace; and no man desires peace more ardently than I. Still I am yet unprepared to give up the Union for a peace which, so achieved, could not be of much duration. The preservation of our Union was *not* the sole avowed object for which the war was commenced. It was commenced for precisely the reverse object—*to destroy our Union.* The insurgents commenced it by firing upon the Star of the West, and on Fort Sumpter, and by other similar acts. It is true, however, that the administration accepted the war thus commenced, for the sole avowed object of preserving our Union; and it is not true that it has since been, or will be, prossecuted by this administration, for any other object." Turning to the employment of Black troops, he reiterated arguments he had made in his open letter—that it "is not a question of sentiment or taste, but one of physical force which may be measured and estimated as horse-power and Steam-power are measured and estimated. Keep it and you can save the Union. Throw it away, and the Union goes with it."

On second thought, Lincoln decided not to release this document. As he explained to the chief organizer of the event where it was to be read, "I believe it is not customary for one holding the office, and being a candidate for re-election, to do so." Moreover, "a public letter must be written with some care, and at some expense of time, so that having begun with your meeting, I could not well refuse others, and yet could not get through with all having equal claims."[52]

Although Lincoln generally avoided writing public letters and delivering formal speeches, he did speak informally to regiments calling at the White House. To those troops he pithily and eloquently summarized the Union cause. "We have, as all will agree, a free Government, where every man has a right to be equal with every other man," he told the 163rd Ohio in mid-August. "In this great struggle, this form of Government and every form of human right is endangered if our enemies succeed. There is more involved in this contest than is realized by every one. There is involved in this struggle the question whether your children and my children shall enjoy the privileges we have enjoyed."[53]

A few days thereafter, Lincoln told another Ohio regiment that it "is not merely for to-day, but for all time to come that we should perpetuate for our children's children this great and free government, which we have enjoyed all our lives. I beg you to remember this, not merely for my sake, but for yours. I happen temporarily to occupy this big White House. I am a living witness that any one of your children may look to come here as my father's child has. It is in order that each of you may have through this free government which we have enjoyed, an open field and a fair chance for your industry, enterprise and intelligence; that you may all have equal privileges in the race of life, with all its desirable human aspirations. It is for this the struggle should be maintained, that we may not lose our birthright—not only for one, but for two or three years. The nation is worth fighting for, to secure such an inestimable jewel."[54] These brief, informal addresses rank among the best of Lincoln's spontaneous utterances and give the lie to critics who disparaged his ability to speak extemporaneously.

Converting the Old Line State into the Free State

Throughout 1864, Lincoln strongly promoted emancipation in Maryland. In April, he helped open the Baltimore Sanitary Fair with a speech congratulating the people of the state for boosting the cause of freedom (they had just elected members to a constitutional convention that would abolish slavery). "The world has never had a good definition of the word liberty, and the American people, just now, are much in want of one," he said. "We all declare for liberty; but in using the same *word* we do not all mean the same *thing*. With some the word liberty may mean for each man to do as he pleases with himself, and the product of his labor; while with others the same word may mean for some men to do as they please with other men, and the product of other men's labor. Here are two, not only different, but incompatable things, called by the same name—liberty. And it follows that each of the things is, by the respective parties, called by two different and incompatable names—liberty and tyranny." Lincoln referred to the recent elections in the state, lauding the voters for "doing something to define liberty."[55]

In Maryland the president also assisted the emancipationist cause behind the scenes, for he believed that its success "would aid much to end the rebellion."[56] On the eve of the ratification vote in October, he wrote a letter to be read at a pro-constitution rally: "I presume the only feature of the instrument, about which there is serious controversy, is that which provides for the extinction of slavery. It needs not to be a secret, and I presume it is no secret, that I wish success to this provision. I desire it on every consideration. I wish all men to be free. I wish the material prosperity of the already free which I feel sure the extinction of slavery would bring. I wish to see, in process of disappearing, that only thing which ever could bring this nation to civil war."[57]

On October 12 and 13, Maryland voters ratified the proposed state constitution by the narrow margin of 30,174 to 29,799 (50.3% to 49.7%). Only the soldier vote (2,633 to 263) enabled it to win approval. The result delighted Lincoln as well as several hundred African Americans who descended on the White House to celebrate. Speaking off the cuff, he told them: "It is no secret that I have wished, and still do wish, mankind everywhere to be free. And in the State of Maryland how great an advance has been made in this direction." In closing, he urged those who had just been freed to "use this great boon which had been given you to improve yourselves, both morally and intellectually."[58]

That night, Lincoln addressed another issue when a group of Marylanders serenaded him. Democrats had been predicting that he would cling to power no matter how the election turned out. In response to such criticism, he declared that it was not his intention "to ruin the government." On the contrary, said he, "I am struggling to maintain government, not to overthrow it. I am struggling especially to prevent others from overthrowing it. I therefore say, that if I shall live, I shall remain President until the fourth of next March; and that whoever shall be constitutionally elected therefor in November, shall be duly installed as President on the fourth of March; and that in the interval I shall do my utmost [so] that whoever is to hold the helm for the next voyage, shall start with the best possible chance to save the ship. This is due to the people both on principle, and under the constitution. Their will, constitutionally expressed, is the ultimate law for all."[59]

Presidential Anger

Toward the end of the campaign Lincoln's anger burst forth when a delegation from Tennessee called to protest the strict loyalty oath that Governor Andrew Johnson had prescribed for would-be voters. The visiting Tennesseans submitted a petition implying that the president "was making a selfish and corrupt use of his power."[60]

In reply, Lincoln impatiently asked: "May I inquire how long it took you and the New-York politicians to concoct that paper?" (In fact, New York Democratic leaders complained with some justice that the oath virtually "commands every loyal citizen of Tennessee to vote for the Republican candidate or to abstain from the polls.")[61] The delegation's spokesman insisted that the document accurately represented the opinion of Volunteer State citizens. Lincoln snorted: "I expect to let the friends of George B. McClellan manage their side of this contest in their own way; and I will manage my side of it in my way."[62] Democrats denounced this "undignified and rude" response from "our coarse despot" as "an exhibition of party spite and petulance."[63] A few days thereafter, Lincoln sent the Tennesseans a far more civil response in which he asserted somewhat disingenuously that he had no control over the governor (Andrew Johnson) whom he had appointed.

Later that fall, Lincoln was beseeched to pardon a condemned soldier whose mother wanted to plead on her son's behalf. He "cried out angrily, 'There is no use of her coming here crying about me. I can't do anything for her.'" The chaplain escorting her then explained that he wished to represent the interests of the accused lad and some other young men. "Well," the president asked, "suppose they were old men, with families to support, would that make it any better?" He later relented.[64]

William O. Stoddard ascribed intemperate outbursts like these to stress and overwork. Lincoln's "absorbed devotion to business" created such a "perpetual strain upon his nervous system" that it "began to tell seriously upon his health and spirits."[65] Noah Brooks also observed that as the war progressed, Lincoln's "hearty, blithesome, genial, wiry" spirit changed: "The old, clear laugh never came back; the even temper was sometimes disturbed; and his natural charity for all was often turned into an unwonted suspicion of the motives of men."[66]

The Soldier Vote

Lincoln had blamed the Republicans' 1862 political reverses on the inability of many soldiers to vote. To prevent a recurrence of that electoral setback, nineteen states passed laws allowing troops to cast ballots in the field or by proxy. Indiana was not among them. Republicans there feared that the state would go Democratic in the October gubernatorial election unless the draft were delayed and fifteen thousand Hoosier soldiers could return to their home districts in time to vote. So in mid-September Lincoln appealed to General Sherman: "Any thing you can safely do" to permit Indiana troops to "go home and vote at the State election, will be greatly in point," he wrote, adding: "This is, in no sense, an order, but is merely intended to impress you with the importance, to the army itself, of your doing all you safely can, yourself being the judge of what you can safely do."[67] Sherman furloughed only sick and wounded troops, numbering around nine thousand.

Keenly aware of the importance of the soldier vote, Lincoln told a crowd at a White House rally that "no classes of people seem so nearly unanamous as the soldiers in the field and the seamen afloat" in their desire "to save the country and it's liberties." Let their devotion to the cause inspire others, he counseled. "Do they not have the hardest of it? Who should quail while they do not? God bless the soldiers and seamen, with all their brave commanders."[68]

The first electoral contest took place in Kentucky, where a judicial race on August 1 was regarded as a portent of things to come. On July 5, Lincoln had somewhat redundantly suspended the privilege of the writ of habeas corpus in the Bluegrass State; he had stipulated, however, that martial law must not "interfere with the holding of lawful elections." Nonetheless, General Stephen G. Burbridge struck the name of the incumbent judge from the ballot three days before the election. To avoid arrest, that jurist fled the state. Democrats hastily found a replacement, who won, an outcome that foreshadowed McClellan's decisive victory there in November.

For Republicans in other states, auguries were more propitious. In September, they handily won gubernatorial contests in Maine and Vermont. Far more significant elections took place on October 11, when voters trooped to the polls in Ohio, Indiana, and Pennsylvania. Shortly before that fateful day, a White House caller noted that the president "seemed careworn and not very well. He was thin in flesh and with sunken eyes and uncombed bristling straight hair which he wore short and stuck straight up, and a white woolen bandage around his neck."[69] He need not have worried about Ohio, where Republicans swept to victory, claiming seventeen of the nineteen congressional seats and carrying the state ticket by more than fifty thousand votes. Nor had he good reason to fear the outcome in Indiana, where Governor Morton received twenty thousand more votes than his Democratic challenger, and the Republicans took eight of the eleven congressional seats while gaining control of the legislature. In Pennsylvania, however, Republican/Union candidates barely eked out a victory with a 15,000-vote margin; their majority in the home vote was an exiguous 391.

As Lincoln sat at the War Department with Stanton and Charles A. Dana awaiting the election returns, he read aloud from one of his favorite humorists, David Ross Locke. The secretary of war had little patience for such levity, but the president paid him no mind, continuing to read with an occasional pause to glance at telegrams. Stanton pulled Dana into an adjoining room and erupted in indignation: "God damn it to hell. Was there ever such nonsense? Was there ever such inability to appreciate what is going on in an awful crisis? Here is the fate of this whole republic at stake, and here is the man around whom it all centers, on whom it all depends, turning aside from this monumental issue to read the God damned trash of a silly mountebank!!"[70]

The soldier vote seemed to being going heavily Republican save for the Ohio, Indiana, and Pennsylvania patients at Washington's Carver hospital, past which Lincoln and Stanton both rode daily. (The First Family was still residing at the Soldiers' Home at the time.) "That[']s hard on us Stanton," said the president; "they know us better than the others." Lincoln's own bodyguard unit, the 150th Pennsylvania, voted 63–11 in favor of the Republican ticket. As the evening wore on, Lincoln grew concerned, saying "he was anxious about Pennsylvania because of her enormous weight and influence which, cast definitely into the scale, wd. have closed the campaign & left the people free to look again with their whole hearts to the cause of the country."[71]

Two days after the gubernatorial elections, Lincoln appeared more tired and downcast than usual as he sat in the War Department telegraph office jotting down an estimate of the likely November results. He said he was not entirely sure that he would be reelected, for he anticipated losing New York, Pennsylvania, New Jersey, Delaware, Maryland, Kentucky, and Illinois, thus managing to defeat McClellan in the Electoral College by an extremely narrow margin (117–114).

Especially alarmed by the Democrats' strong showing in the Pennsylvania contest, Lincoln asked Alexander K. McClure to help strengthen the Republican state central committee. That was necessary, for McClure, who barely won his bid for a legislative seat in October, warned that the committee was "a miserable affair" and that McClellan might well carry the state in November.[72] When Lincoln urged Cameron to cooperate with McClure, from whom he had long been estranged, the Chief agreed, for he was mortified by the poor showing in his state compared with the impressive Republican victories in Ohio and Indiana. Despite the resulting improvement in party operations, the president continued to fear the result in the Keystone State. According to McClure, Lincoln knew that if he lost "Pennsylvania on the home vote, the moral effect of his triumph would be broken and his power to prosecute the war and make peace would be greatly impaired."[73] At McClure's suggestion, Lincoln arranged to have ten thousand Pennsylvania troops furloughed in order to be able to return home and vote.

The Republican victories in October foreshadowed the party's triumph the following month. On election day, November 8, Lincoln said of the campaign: "It is a little singular that I who am not a vindictive man, should always have been before the people for election in canvasses marked for their bitterness."[74] When a positive report arrived from Maryland that morning, he expressed surprise, for a month earlier the state had gone Republican by only a narrow margin. "I shall be glad if that holds," the president remarked somewhat skeptically.

That afternoon he found it difficult to concentrate on routine business. Tad relieved the tension somewhat when he raced into his father's office to announce that the soldiers guarding the White House were off to vote. Lincoln noticed that the boy's pet turkey was accompanying the troops to the polls. (They had made a mascot of it.) When the president asked if the turkey was also going to vote, Tad shot back: "Oh, no; he isn't of age yet!" The proud father thought that response far superior to many of the humorous "Lincoln stories" in circulation.[75]

With Lincoln was Noah Brooks, who reported that the president "took no pains to conceal his anxious interest in the result of the election." Lincoln confessed: "I am just enough of a politician to know that there was not much doubt about the result of the Baltimore Convention, but about this thing I am far from being certain; I wish I were certain." Around 6:30 p.m., word arrived from Indianapolis announcing a predictable Republican landslide. After dinner, the president and John Hay splashed over to the War Department through the rainy, dark, gloomy night. Passing a soaked sentry encased in his own vapor, they entered the building through a side door and climbed to the telegraph room, where Lincoln was handed a dispatch from John W. Forney predicting a ten-thousand-vote majority in Philadelphia. Laconically he remarked, "Forney is a little excitable." Around 9:00 p.m., a telegram from Baltimore announced a solid ten-thousand-vote Republican victory. Lincoln merely smiled and remarked, "That was a fair beginning."[76]

From Massachusetts came news that Congressman Alexander H. Rice was leading by four thousand votes. Incredulous, Lincoln said: "Rice has one of the closest districts in the country, and those figures are more likely to be 40 or perhaps 400." When subsequent reports confirmed the original estimate, he took heart: "If the doubtful districts come in in this shape, what may we expect from the certain ones?" Assistant Secretary of the Navy Gustavus Fox took special pleasure in Rice's victory, for the congressman was a friend of the navy. When Fox expressed joy that two of his department's congressional enemies had been defeated, Lincoln told him: "You have more of that feeling of personal resentment than I. Perhaps I may have too little of it, but I never thought it paid. A man has not time to spend half his life in quarrels. If any man ceases to attack me, I never remember the past against him."[77] When a dispatch announced that Pennsylvania was indeed going heavily Republican, Lincoln appeared unusually sober as if contemplating the prospect of another four years of heavy responsibility. He observed, "As goes Pennsylvania, so goes the Union, they say."[78] He had the news conveyed to his wife, explaining that she was more anxious than he was.

Returns from New York were slow to come in. A dispatch indicating that McClellan had carried it by forty thousand votes was regarded skeptically, for the state had been carefully canvassed, and a close result was expected. When another dispatch announced that the Republicans had won the state by ten thousand, Lincoln scoffed: "I don't believe that." More plausible to him was a midnight wire from Greeley predicting a four-thousand-vote Republican victory, which, combined with triumphs in Pennsylvania, Maryland, New England, Michigan, and Wisconsin, seemed to clinch the election. Lincoln responded calmly, saying "that he was free to confess that he felt relieved of suspense, and was glad that the verdict of the people was so likely to be clear, full and unmistakable, for it then appeared that his majority in the electoral college would be immense."[79] During a dinner break, he "went awkwardly and hospitably to work shoveling out the fried oysters." Hay recorded that the president "was most agreeable and genial all the evening."[80]

Lincoln still felt anxious about Illinois, which did not report good news until 1:00 a.m. An hour later, when a group of Pennsylvanians serenaded him, Lincoln replied with what Noah Brooks called "one of the happiest and noblest little speeches of his life."[81] He emphasized to his well-wishers the significance of the election: "I earnestly believe that the consequences of this day's work . . . will be to the lasting advantage, if not to the very salvation, of the country." All those "who have labored to-day in behalf of the Union organization, have wrought for the best interests of their country and the world, not only for the present, but for all future ages. I am thankful to God for this approval of the people." Yet Lincoln would not gloat: "It is no pleasure to me to triumph over any one; but I give thanks to the Almighty for this evidence of the people's resolution to stand by free government and the rights of humanity."[82]

On November 10, a huge crowd converged on the White House with banners, lanterns, transparencies, and bands blaring martial tunes. Approximately one-third of the serenaders were Black, prompting one aged citizen to observe: "The white men there would not have made up a very large assemblage."[83] Such a turnout of African Americans was unprecedented. Upon appearing at a second story window, the president was greeted with "a tremendous yell."[84] After the cheering finally died down, he began with a point he had made in his July 4, 1861, message to Congress: "It has long been a grave question whether any government, not *too* strong for the liberties of its people, can be strong *enough* to maintain its own existence, in great emergencies. On this point the present rebellion brought our republic to a

"Long Abraham Lincoln a Little Longer" appeared in *Harper's Weekly*, November 26, 1864, on the heels of Lincoln's landslide reelection victory. Cartoonists, both favorable and hostile, typically emphasized Lincoln's great height (6 feet, 4 inches). Abraham Lincoln Presidential Library and Museum, Springfield, Illinois.

severe test; and a presidential election occurring in regular course during the rebellion added not a little to the strain. If the loyal people, *united*, were put to the utmost [test] of their strength by the rebellion, must they not fail when *divided*, and partially paralized, by a political war among themselves?" Though the danger was great, it would not have justified suspending or canceling the election, which "was a necessity," for "we can not have free government without elections; and if the rebellion could force us to forego, or postpone a national election, it might fairly claim to have already conquered and ruined us."

Deplorable though the bitter canvass may have been, Lincoln insisted that it "has done good too," for it "demonstrated that a people's government can sustain a national election, in the midst of a great civil war. Until now it has not been known to the world that this was a possibility. It shows also how *sound*, and how *strong* we still are." In closing, Lincoln urged his supporters to show magnanimity toward their defeated opponents: "May I ask those who have not differed with me, to join with me, in this same spirit towards those who have?"[85] As Lincoln stepped away from the window while the crowd gave him three enthusiastic cheers, he remarked to John Hay: "Not very graceful, but I am growing old enough not to care much for the manner of doing things."[86] Hay thought more highly of the effort, calling it "one of the weightiest and wisest of all his discourses."[87]

Lincoln's annual message to Congress the following month eloquently summarized the lesson taught by the election: "The most reliable indication of public purpose in this country is derived through our popular elections. Judging by the recent canvass and its result, the purpose of the people, within the loyal States, to maintain the integrity of the Union, was never more firm, nor more nearly unanimous, than now. The extraordinary calmness and good order with which the millions of voters met and mingled at the polls, give strong assurance of this."[88]

Lincoln savored his victory, though the possibility of defeat held few terrors for him. As he told Noah Brooks the day after the election: "Being only mortal, after all, I should have been a little mortified if I had been beaten in the canvass before the people; but the sting would have been more than compensated by the thought that the people had notified me that my official responsibilities were soon to be lifted off my back."[89] To another journalist he said that the cares of his office were "so oppressive" that "he felt as though the moment when he could relinquish the burden and retire to private life would be the sweetest he could possibly experience."[90]

Lincoln won 55.4 percent of the popular vote and carried all the loyal states save Kentucky, Delaware, and New Jersey, receiving 212 electoral votes; McClellan won 21. The recorded soldier vote (6% of the total) was 78 percent for the president, as compared with 53 percent of the civilian vote. As a Vermont trooper wrote, "Soldiers don't generally believe in fighting to put down treason, and voting to let it live."[91] One high-ranking officer was especially pleased: "Congratulate the President for me for the double victory," Grant wired Stanton. "The election having passed off quietly, no bloodshed or riot throughout the land, is a victory worth more to the country than a battle won. Rebeldom and Europe will so construe it."[92] (In fact, Lincoln probably was supported by only 50 to 60 percent of the eligible soldiers, for voting in the field was not secret, and many pro-Democratic troops felt too intimidated to cast a ballot.) Gratified as he was to receive the soldier vote, Lincoln did not need it; in most states that he won, the civilian vote sufficed. In New York and Connecticut, however, where no separate record of soldier and home votes was kept, the former may have made the difference.

With Lincoln's reelection, antislavery forces heaved a sigh of relief. Gerrit Smith said he was "more thankful than joyful over the Election—too deeply thankful to be joyful."[93] Some Radicals, however, were less enthusiastic. Henry Winter Davis groused: "We must for four years more rely on the forcing process of Congress to *wring* from that old fool what can be gotten for the nation."[94]

In his formal reply to the congressional committee notifying him of his reelection, Lincoln was unusually eloquent: "Having served four years in the depths of a great, and yet unended national peril, I can view this call to a second term, in nowise more flatteringly to myself, than as an expression of the public judgment, that I may better finish a difficult work, in which I have labored from the first, than could any one less severely schooled to the task. In this view, and with assured reliance on that Almighty Ruler who has so graceously sustained us thus far; and with increased gratitude to the generous people for their continued confidence, I accept the renewed trust, with it's yet onerous and perplexing duties and responsibilities."[95] Thurlow Weed told the president that this document "is not only the *neatest* but the most pregnant and effective use to which the English Language was ever put."[96]

Democratic blunders and Union military success did not alone account for Lincoln's reelection, important though they were. It is hard to say precisely how significant a role his character and personality played, but it was a big one. The perceptive journalist E. L. Godkin informed readers of the London *Daily News* that rural Americans showed little concern about the president's sartorial taste or his manners. Instead, "his logic and his English, his jokes, his plain common sense, his shrewdness, his unbounded reliance on their honesty and straightforwardness, go right to their hearts." They "are in earnest in a way the like of which the world never saw before, silently, calmly, but deliberately in earnest; and they will fight on, in my opinion, as long as they have men, muskets, powder, and corn and wool, and would fight on, though the grass were growing in Wall Street, and there was not a gold dollar on this side of the Atlantic."[97] This iron resolve was partly inspired by Lincoln's own indomitable will.

Endearing him to the voters was his remarkable unselfishness. "Among the great civilians of the day," William O. Stoddard noted in 1862, "the greatest and strongest, our good Chief Magistrate, is great and strong chiefly because the people have perfect faith in him that he has no ambition, no selfish lust of power, nor any hope for the future unconnected with the welfare of his country." In addition, people identified with Lincoln. "He is the most perfect *representative* of the purely American character now in public life," Stoddard maintained. "This is why the mutual understanding between him and the people is so perfect. This it is which enables him to exercise powers which would never by any possibility be entrusted to another man, though his equal in other respects. The people know that they can trust their great chief, and so they bid him 'see to it that the Republic suffers no detriment.'"[98] In early 1864, Harriet Beecher Stowe noted that of all "the many accusations which in hours of ill-luck have been thrown out upon Lincoln, it is remarkable that he has never been called self-seeking, or selfish. When we were troubled and sat in darkness, and looked doubtfully towards the presidential chair, it was never that we doubted the good-will of our pilot—only the clearness of his eyesight. But Almighty God has granted to him that clearness of vision which he gives to the true-hearted, and enabled him to set his honest foot in that promised land of freedom which is to be the patrimony of all men, black and white—and from henceforth nations shall rise up to call him blessed."[99]

Lincoln's victory reminded him of an ominous vision that he had seen just after the election of 1860. He was reclining in his chamber, as he told Noah Brooks, when he looked across the room and saw his image in a mirror, "but my face, I noticed, had *two* separate and distinct images, the tip of the nose of one being about three inches from the tip of the other. I was a little bothered, perhaps startled, and got up and looked in the glass, but the illusion vanished. On lying down again, I saw it a second time—plainer, if possible, than before; and then I noticed that one of the faces was a little paler, say five shades, than the other. I got up, and the thing melted away, and I went off and, in the excitement of the hour, forgot all about it—nearly, but not quite, for the thing would once in a while come up, and give me a little pang as though something uncomfortable had happened. When I went home, I told my wife about it, and a few days after I tried the experiment again, when, sure enough, the thing came back again; but I never succeeded in bringing the ghost back after that, though I once tried very industriously to show it to my wife, who was worried about it somewhat. She thought it was 'a sign' that I was to be elected to a second term of office, and that the paleness of one of the faces was an omen that I should not see life through the last term."[100]

35.

"Let the *Thing* Be Pressed"

Victory at Last (November 1864–April 8, 1865)

On October 12, 1864, as Lincoln sought to unify his party, a special opportunity to conciliate Radicals presented itself with the death of Chief Justice Roger B. Taney. Upon hearing the news, the president said he would not nominate a replacement right away but would remain silent for a while. Preoccupied with the election and his annual message to Congress, he postponed consideration of the matter until Congress met in December.

Edward Bates personally asked Lincoln for the chief justiceship, which he thought would be a "crowning and retiring honor." The president told Isaac Newton he would gladly name Bates as Chief Justice "if not overborne by others" like Chase, who "was turning every stone, to get it."[1] (At the end of November, Bates stepped down as attorney general, to be replaced by Lincoln's Kentucky friend James Speed, brother of Joshua Speed.) Chase was indeed turning every stone. Mary Lincoln implored Francis P. Blair Sr. to help thwart the Ohioan's candidacy. The former treasury secretary and his allies, she told him, "are besieging my Husband for the Chief-Justiceship[.] I wish you could prevent them."[2] When a friendly letter from Chase arrived at the White House, the president laconically instructed that it be filed "with his other recommendations."[3] Those recommendations were especially numerous. Chase had strengthened his chances by actively campaigning for Lincoln in the fall. Coyly remaining in Cincinnati while the decision about the chief justiceship was pending, he urged friends to lobby the president on his behalf.

Lincoln worried that Chase's insatiable desire for the presidency would undermine his ability to be a good chief justice. "He has got the Presidential maggot in his head," he said, "and it will wriggle there as long as it is warm. If I were sure that he would go upon the bench and give up his aspirations to do anything but make himself a great judge, I would send in his name at once."[4] Nevertheless, Lincoln had evidently decided on Chase as early as the spring of 1864. Upon accepting the treasury secretary's resignation, Lincoln suggested that he "go home without making any fight and wait for a good thing hereafter, such as a vacancy on the Supreme Bench."[5] A week after Taney's death, the president told Treasury Secretary Fessenden that he planned to appoint Chase, "but as things were going on well he thought it best not to make any appointment or say anything about it, until after the election," when Congress would return from its five-month recess.[6]

Lincoln submitted Chase's name to the newly reconvened Senate on December 6, much to the Radicals' delight. "It is equal to a military victory" and shows "that Mr. Lincoln is in sympathy with the spirit of those who supported him at the last election," declared a colonel in the U.S. Colored Troops.[7] "Probably no other man than Lincoln," Nicolay told his fiancée, "would have had, in this age of the world, the degree of magnanimity to thus forgive and exalt a rival who had so deeply and so unjustifiably intrigued against him. It is however only another most marked illustration of the greatness of the President, in this age of little men."[8] Lincoln was magnanimous indeed, for Chase had deeply angered him. The president said that personally he would rather "swallow his buckhorn chair" or "eat flat irons" than appoint Chase.[9] Montgomery Blair speculated plausibly that Chase "was the only human being that I believe Lincoln actually hated."[10]

On the bench, Chase confirmed Lincoln's fears that he would continue intriguing to win the presidency. Lincoln explained that he had appointed Chase because the Ohioan would uphold both emancipation and the Legal Tender Act. Ironically, Chase's appointment proved unnecessary for protecting either; the Thirteenth Amendment took care of emancipation, and Chase voted with the majority to declare the Legal Tender Act unconstitutional.

The Bixby Letter

Immediately after the election, Lincoln was unusually preoccupied. When Massachusetts governor John A. Andrew requested a presidential acknowledgment of the heroic sacrifice purportedly made by one of his constituents (a widow named Lydia Bixby, who alleged that she had lost five sons in the war), a letter of condolence was sent to her from the White House: "I feel how weak and fruitless must be any words of mine which should attempt to beguile you from the grief of a loss so overwhelming. But I cannot refrain from tendering to you the consolation that may be found in the thanks of the Republic they died to save. I pray that our Heavenly Father may assuage the anguish of your bereavement, and leave you only the cherished memory of the loved and lost, and the solemn pride that must be yours, to have laid so costly a sacrifice upon the altar of Freedom."[11]

The Bixby letter, as Lincoln biographer James G. Randall noted, "has taken a pre-eminent place as a Lincoln gem and a classic in the language."[12] It is beautiful indeed, though it was written not by Lincoln but rather by John Hay; nor was its recipient the mother of five sons killed in the war. She lost two of her boys and tried to cheat the government by claiming the others had also been killed. Of the three survivors, one had deserted to the enemy, another may have done so, and the third was honorably discharged. She was born in Virginia, sympathized with the Confederacy, and disliked Lincoln so much that she apparently destroyed the letter in anger. Evidence suggests that she ran a whorehouse in Boston and was "perfectly untrustworthy."[13]

The adjutant general of Massachusetts, after hand-delivering the letter to Mrs. Bixby, provided copies to newspapers, which gave it wide circulation. One partisan Democratic journal sneeringly asked why "Mr. Lincoln's sons should be kept from the dangers of the field, while the sons of the laboring men are to be hurried into the harvest of death at the front? Are the sons of the rail-splitter porcelain, and these others common clay?"[14] Of course Tad was far too young to serve, but 21-year-old Robert was not. In fact, he was eager to drop out of Harvard and enlist, but his mother adamantly objected. "We have lost one son, and his loss is as much as I can bear, without being called upon to make another sacrifice," she told the president, who replied: "But many a poor mother has given up all her sons, and our son is not more dear to us than the sons of other people are to their mothers."

"That may be; but I cannot bear to have Robert exposed to danger. His services are not required in the field, and the sacrifice would be a needless one."

"The services of every man who loves his country are required in this war. You should take a liberal instead of a selfish view of the question, mother."[15]

In January 1865, when the First Lady finally yielded, Lincoln wrote Grant asking that Robert be placed on his staff: "Please read and answer this letter as though I was not President, but only a friend. . . . Could he, without embarrassment to you, or detriment to the service, go into your Military family with some nominal rank, I, and not the public, furnishing his necessary means? If no, say so without the least hesitation, because I am as anxious, and as deeply interested, that you shall not be encumbered as you can be yourself." Grant replied graciously: "I will be most happy to have him in my Military family in the manner you propose."[16] Robert entered the army as a captain on February 11 and served creditably on Grant's staff until he resigned five months later.

Annual Message

In late November, Lincoln was busy drafting his annual message. When it was read aloud to the House on December 6, some passages elicited cheers, notably the line that "Maryland is secure to liberty and Union for all the future. The genius of rebellion will no more claim Maryland. Like another foul spirit, being driven out, it may seek to tear her, but it will woo her no more."

The message dealt at length with foreign relations, especially developments in the country's immediate neighbors, Canada and Mexico. Confederates operating in Ontario (then known as Canada West) laid various schemes to undermine the Union war effort. Jacob Thompson, secretary of war in Buchanan's administration, helped to foment armed uprisings in the Northwest. One plan called for the liberation of thousands of Rebel prisoners of war held in Chicago's Camp Douglas. It was squelched when detectives got wind of it and arrested the leaders, among them John B. Castleman, whose life Lincoln mercifully spared by having him banished rather than tried as a spy. The president was not so merciful to John Yates Beall of the Confederate navy, who attempted to liberate Rebel prisoners held at Johnson's Island near Sandusky, Ohio. Tried and convicted as a spy and guerilla, Beall was hanged on February 24. Lincoln was equally stern with another terrorist, Robert C. Kennedy, one of eight conspirators operating out of Canada who attempted to burn down buildings in New York City. Following a military trial, he went to the gallows in late March.

American anger at the British for allowing Confederates to use Canada as a staging area for sabotage, terrorism, and sedition grew stronger after twenty raiders plundered St. Albans, Vermont. The public was outraged when the Canadian government refused to extradite them. In his annual message, Lincoln indicated that the United States might expand its navy on the Great Lakes, require Canadians to have passports to enter the country, and abrogate the reciprocity treaty of 1854. But he hoped that such steps might not have to be taken, for he expected that Canadian authorities would prevent any more such raids. When they in fact did so, Lincoln rescinded the passport order.

Patronage Matters

Lincoln was also busy dealing with importunate office seekers. Congressman Edwin Webster of Maryland advised job applicants that the only way to get the president to remove incumbent officeholders was to harass him. In March 1865, Lincoln told Colonel James Grant Wilson, who joined him for an opera, that he attended the performance "for the rest. I am being hounded to death by office-seekers, who pursue me early and late, and it is simply to get two or three hours' relief that I am here."[17]

Of all the would-be civil servants, none dismayed Lincoln more than the eminent Shakespearean actor James H. Hackett. After seeing Hackett play Falstaff, the president wrote him a fan letter, which the indiscreet thespian released to the New York *Herald*. The paper ridiculed Lincoln's taste in Shakespearian soliloquies as expressed in that missive. Abashed, Hackett apologized to the president, who replied: "Give yourself no uneasiness on the subject. . . . My note to you I certainly did not expect to see in print; yet I have not been much shocked by the newspaper comments upon it. Those comments constitute a fair specimen of what has occurred to me through life. I have endured a great deal of ridicule without much malice; and have received a great deal of kindness, not quite free from ridicule. I am used to it."[18] The friendly correspondence between them came to an end when Hackett asked to be named consul in London, a post that could not be given to him. John Hay recalled that a "hundred times this experience was repeated: a man would be introduced to the President whose disposition and talk were agreeable; he took pleasure in his conversation for two or three interviews, and then this congenial person would ask some favor impossible to grant, and go away in bitterness of spirit."[19]

In March, Chase's successor as treasury secretary, William P. Fessenden, resigned in order to accept a seat in the U.S. Senate. To replace him, Lincoln wanted Edwin D. Morgan, who refused. So the president turned to Hugh McCulloch, an Indiana banker then serving as comptroller of the currency.

Thirteenth Amendment

Lincoln's chief goal in the wake of the election was to secure passage of the Thirteenth Amendment, outlawing slavery throughout the country. After failing in June to win the requisite two-thirds majority of the House, that measure did not become a significant issue in the presidential campaign, for Republicans soft-pedaled it while Democrats focused on miscegenation, civil liberties, conscription, and the "Niagara Manifesto." Voters assumed that Congress would not deal with the amendment again until the members elected in 1864 took their seats in December 1865, and so they did not consider it a pressing matter. Thus the president's reelection could not legitimately be interpreted as a mandate for the amendment.

Yet in his annual message Lincoln did just that, boldly claiming that the public had endorsed the amendment: "It is the voice of the people now, for the first time, heard upon the question." And so he urged its immediate approval, noting that the "next Congress will pass the measure if this does not. Hence there is only a question of *time* as to when the proposed amendment will go to the States for their action. And as it is to so go, at all events, may we not agree that the sooner the better?" Emphatically he reiterated his commitment to emancipation: "If the people should, by whatever mode or means, make it an Executive duty to re-enslave such persons, another, and not I, must be their instrument to perform it."[20] Congress applauded this statement loud and long.

Lincoln's motives were partly political. He evidently calculated that the amendment might help heal the breach in the Republican ranks by rendering moot the thorny question of whether Congress had the power to abolish slavery by statute. Moreover, with the slavery issue solved, some Democrats might be willing to join the Republicans, who had won in 1860 and 1864 only because of highly unusual circumstances.

The president also argued that rapid adoption of the amendment might shorten the war. In December he lobbied the slaveholding Missouri congressman James S. Rollins, who had voted against the amendment in the spring. Lincoln told him that "if the members from the Border States would unite, at least enough of them to pass the 13th amendment to the Constitution, they [Confederates] would soon see they could not expect much help from that quarter, and be willing to give up their opposition, and quit their war upon the Government." Remarking that he had "never seen any one evince deeper interest and anxiety upon any subject than did Mr. Lincoln upon the passage of this amendment," Rollins agreed to lobby fellow representatives.[21]

In mid-January, when the amendment seemed doomed to fail yet again, Lincoln stepped up his lobbying effort, telling a representative who had lost a sibling in the war that "your brother died to save the Republic from death by the slaveholders rebellion. I wish you could see it to be your duty to vote for the Constitutional amendment ending slavery."[22] He explained to a pair of House members that two more votes were needed and that they were to be obtained by hook or by crook. He evidently implied that favors could be expected from the administration in return for such support.

No evidence survives indicating that Lincoln offered a specific quid pro quo for votes, but it seems that he authorized his lieutenants to bargain, particularly Seward and Congressman James Ashley, floor manager of the amendment. Ashley cut a deal with Democratic representative Anson Herrick of New York, assuring him that his brother would receive a federal job in return for the congressman's vote. After the amendment passed, Lincoln allegedly told Herrick "in person that whatever Ashley had promised should be performed, and he signified his good faith by sending the name to the Senate."[23] In March, Lincoln nominated Hugh Herrick as an assessor of internal revenue, but the Senate did not confirm him.

A Pennsylvania Democratic congressman whose election was being contested, Alexander Coffroth, voted for the amendment apparently in return for Republican pledges that the party would support his claim to the seat. Moses Odell, a Democrat representing Brooklyn, received the coveted post of naval agent in New York after supporting the amendment (in both 1864 and 1865). Lame-duck congressman George Yeaman of Kentucky, who had voted against the amendment in 1864, supported it in 1865. In August of that year, he was named minister to Denmark.

Seward's agents evidently offered cash in return for votes. In early January, one of the more prominent of them, Robert W. Latham, told the secretary of state that he had "no doubt about passing" the amendment, for "money will certainly do it, if patriotism fails."[24] Latham was a shady character who had worked closely with the notoriously corrupt John B. Floyd, Buchanan's secretary of war. Of the sixteen Democrats voting for the amendment, six represented New York districts. The Seward lobby evidently persuaded the Democrats' flagship newspaper, the New York *World*, to change its anti-amendment stance to quasi neutrality. Other important papers were cajoled into taking similar action.

Just how much corruption was involved in the passage of the amendment is hard to measure. According to Montgomery Blair, Seward "made Lincoln beleive [*sic*] that he had carried that Amendment by Corruption."[25] Blair denied Seward's contention, saying the only case resembling bribery was the position offered to Anson Herrick's brother. Ohio congressman Samuel Cox, however, alleged that a Radical who was boarding at the same house with him had acknowledged that the New Yorkers were offering substantial bribes to Democrats willing to vote for the amendment.

On January 31, as the hour for voting on the amendment drew near, rumors swept through the House that Confederate peace commissioners were en route to the capital. Ashley panicked, fearing that some Democrats might backslide and defeat the measure. To prevent that from happening, the congressman appealed to Lincoln, who was busy composing instructions for Seward's use in negotiations with Confederate emissaries. The president, confident that the amendment would pass, wrote a disingenuous message that calmed the storm: "So far as I know, there are no peace commissioners in the city, or likely to be in it."[26] This was a lawyer's quibble, for Lincoln knew that commissioners were on their way to Hampton Roads, Virginia, where they would meet with Seward to discuss peace terms. This "little secret piece of history" amused Lincoln, who told a caller several days later, "I *eased* it [the amendment] along—and concluded to send Seward down" to Fort Monroe. Recalling Ashley's fear that his Democratic "converts" might "have gone off in a tangent at the last moment had they smelt Peace," he laughed and repeated the phrase "as far as I know."[27]

With peace rumors thus denied, the amendment narrowly won the necessary two-thirds approval in the House by a margin of 119 to 56, with sixteen Democrats voting for it and eight absent and not paired. (If four of those absentees had voted no, the amendment would have failed.) Six representatives who had opposed it earlier were absent or not voting, and ten who had been absent for the June ballot now voted for it, as did every Republican. Women watching from the galleries fluttered their handkerchiefs while men cheered thunderously and threw their hats in the air. Black spectators in the galleries also cheered heartily. When Lincoln heard the news, it "filled his heart with joy," for he "saw in it the complete consummation of his own work, the emancipation proclamation."[28]

The president's active lobbying of congressmen was highly unusual, for he generally obeyed the Whig dictum that the executive should defer to the legislature when statutes were being framed. He seldom initiated or vetoed legislation. His willingness to intervene so vigorously for the Thirteenth Amendment indicated the depth of his commitment to Black freedom. The day after the House passed the amendment, Lincoln told serenaders that he "could not but congratulate all present, himself, the country and the whole world upon this great moral victory." It was essential "to remove all causes of disturbance in the future; and to attain this end it was necessary that the original disturbing cause should, if possible, be rooted out." The Emancipation Proclamation "falls far short of what the amendment will be when fully consummated." If the Proclamation were all that protected the freedom of the slaves, its legality might be questioned, but "this amendment is a King's cure for all the evils. It winds the whole thing up."[29]

Peacemaking

In his annual message that December, Lincoln explained how he hoped to end the war swiftly. While Jefferson Davis could not bring about peace because of his mulish insistence on independence, the people of the Confederacy "can, at any moment, have peace simply by laying down their arms and submitting to the national authority under the Constitution." Lincoln repeated his "declaration made a year ago" that "while I remain in my present position I shall not attempt to retract or modify the emancipation proclamation, nor shall I return to slavery any person who is free by the terms of that proclamation, or by any of the Acts of Congress." With these public statements, Lincoln may have been trying to make an end run around Jefferson Davis by indirectly appealing to Robert E. Lee, whose power in the Confederacy waxed as the Confederate president's waned.

Lee did make overtures to Grant, suggesting that they meet to discuss peace terms. When Grant forwarded the proposal to Washington, he received a blunt response from Stanton: "The President directs me to say that he wishes you to have no conference with General Lee, unless it be for the capitulation of General Lee's army, or on some minor or purely military matter. He instructs me to say that you are not to decide, discuss, or confer upon any political questions; such questions the President holds in his own hands and will submit them to no military conferences or conventions. Meanwhile, you are to press to the utmost your military advantages."[30]

Lincoln tactfully acknowledged that Congress had a role to play in setting peace terms. Furthermore, he conceded that his power "would be greatly diminished by the cessation of actual war. Pardons and remission of forfeitures, however, would still be within Executive control." He warned Southerners that the amnesty policy he had announced a year earlier might not remain in effect much longer.[31]

The peace initiative that nearly sidelined the Thirteenth Amendment had been undertaken by Francis P. Blair Sr., who entertained the delusive notion that the North and South might reconcile their differences by joining together to expel the French from Mexico. Without explaining his plan, Blair asked Lincoln for permission to confer with Jefferson Davis. The president replied: "Come to me after [the fall of] Savannah." When William T. Sherman took that Georgia port on December 22, Lincoln gave Blair the pass he had requested. In Richmond, Davis indicated a willingness to participate in a joint invasion of Mexico. In mid-January, upon receiving a report of this conversation, Lincoln authorized Blair to tell Davis "that I have constantly been, and am now, and shall continue ready to receive any agent whom he, or any other influential person now resisting the National authority, may informally send to me, with the view of securing peace to the people of our one common country."[32]

In this photo, taken by Alexander Gardner on February 5, 1865, Lincoln seems to radiate an inner peace, for he knew that the war would soon end. Library of Congress.

Davis should have realized that his cause was hopeless, for the Union had recently captured Fort Fisher at Wilmington, North Carolina, thus plugging the last hole in the blockade and cutting one of Lee's most important supply lines. General Sherman had spent December marching across Georgia en route to Savannah, a city he tendered to the president as a Christmas gift. That month George H. Thomas had obliterated John Bell Hood's army at Nashville. Sherman followed up his spectacular march by thrusting into the Carolinas as he headed toward a rendezvous with Grant.

Instead of taking Lincoln's offer seriously, Jefferson Davis defiantly sent a trio of peace commissioners with instructions to confer informally with Lincoln "for the purpose of securing peace to the two countries." Many members of the Confederate Congress, believing that the war was lost, had urged the appointment of ersatz diplomats to effect a surrender. They were surprised to learn much later of Davis's unyielding instructions, which doomed the conference to failure before it began. One Confederate emissary, Alexander H. Stephens, considered his mission a "humbug" from the outset.[33]

When word of Blair's mission leaked, Radicals expressed alarm, suspecting that Lincoln might offer universal amnesty to the Confederates, restore their confiscated property, allow their army to join with Union forces to attack Mexico, offer slaveholders enormous financial compensation for their escaped bondspeople, and leave those still outside Union lines in slavery. Such skepticism prompted Lincoln to remark: "Some of my friends in Congress act as if they were afraid to trust me with a dinner, yet I shall never compromise the principles upon which I was elected."[34] On February 1, when Henry Ward Beecher called at the White House to express concern about Blair's peace overtures, Lincoln explained that "Blair thinks something can be done, but I don't, but I have no objection to have him try his hand. He has no authority whatever but to go and see what he can do."[35]

On January 30, the Confederate commissioners (Vice President Stephens, Senator Robert M. T. Hunter, and Assistant Secretary of War John A. Campbell) arrived at Grant's lines and asked permission to proceed to Washington. Lincoln sent word that they would receive a safe-conduct pass only if they agreed to negotiate "with a view of securing peace to the people of our one common country." When they seemed to accept that condition, the president on January 31 dispatched Seward to parley with them informally at Hampton Roads. The secretary of state was to make clear "that three things are indispensable." First, "the national authority" must be restored "throughout all the States." Second, there was to be no "receding, by the Executive of the United States on the Slavery question." And finally, there was to be no "cessation of hostilities short of an end of the war, and the disbanding of all forces hostile to the government." Lincoln also instructed Grant to let "nothing which is transpiring change, hinder, or delay your military movements or plans."[36]

When the Confederates seemed to renege on their agreement to negotiate according to Lincoln's conditions, the talks nearly collapsed. The president was about to recall Seward when he received a dispatch from Grant that changed his mind. On February 1, sensing that such a denouement would "have a bad influence," the general urged Lincoln to meet with the commissioners.[37] Upon reading Grant's dispatch, Lincoln hastened to join Seward at Fort Monroe, and on February 3 they conferred with the Confederate delegation aboard the steamer *River Queen*. The president greeted the commissioners warmly, especially Stephens. As the diminutive vice president began to remove his heavy overcoat and large scarf, the president poked gentle fun at him: "Now, gentleman, you see what a large amount of 'shuck' Mr. Stephens has—just wait a minute and you will be surprised to find what a small 'nubbin' he is." During the informal conversation that preceded the negotiations, Lincoln "was very talkative and pleasant with all of the commissioners," Stephens recalled.[38] After these preliminaries, the five men got down to business. According to Stephens, Lincoln was "perfectly frank," submitting "his views, almost in the form of an argument." The only way to restore peace and harmony was "for those who were resisting the laws of the Union to cease that resistance." Ignoring this plain language, Stephens expatiated on a plan like the one suggested by Blair, involving an armistice and a joint expedition against the French in Mexico. Lincoln firmly rejected the idea of an armistice, which "would be a *quasi* recognition of the States then in arms against the National Government, as a separate power." That he "never could do."

Hunter urged "that the recognition of Mr. Davis's power to make a treaty, was the first and indispensable step to peace, and referring to the correspondence of King Charles the First, and his Parliament, as a reliable precedent, of a constitutional ruler, treating with rebels." Lincoln's face "then wore that indescribable expression which generally preceded his hardest hits," and he remarked drolly: "Upon questions of history, I must refer you to Mr. Seward, for he is posted in such things, and I don't profess to be bright. My only distinct recollection of that matter is, *that Charles lost his head*." That observation "settled Mr. Hunter for a while."[39]

Lincoln said the Confederate states could resume their place in the Union once they had laid down their arms and allowed the federal government to resume its traditional functions. Congress would determine who was legitimately elected to serve in it, Lincoln pointed out, but he believed "that when the resistance ceased and the National authority was recognized the States would be immediately restored to their practical relations to the Union." He added that "individuals subject to pains and penalties under the laws of the United States might rely upon a very liberal use of the powers confided to him to remit those pains and penalties if peace be restored." When Hunter remarked that he had no fear of harsh treatment, "Lincoln retorted, that he, also, had felt easy as to the rebels, but not always so easy about the lamp posts around Washington city—a hint that he had already done more favors for the rebels, than was exactly popular with the radical men of his own party."

As for emancipation, Lincoln said that he "never would change or modify the terms of the proclamation in the slightest particular." But that document had freed only about two hundred thousand slaves thus far; the status of the remaining three million-plus would be settled by the courts. (Lincoln underestimated the number of slaves already liberated, which probably amounted to half a million.) Seward interjected that if the Thirteenth Amendment, whose passage by Congress was unknown to the Confederates, were ratified by three-quarters of the states, all slaves would be free. Apropos of that amendment, Lincoln "suggested that there was a question as to the right of the insurgent States to return at once, and claim a right to vote upon the amendment." If slavery were abolished, Stephens asked, "what are we to do? I know that negroes will not work, unless forced to it, and I tell you that we shall all starve together." Southern Whites, Lincoln replied, "can go to work like honest people or starve."[40]

Lincoln renewed his proposal to compensate slaveholders, for he believed that "people of the North were as responsible for slavery as people of the South, and if the war should then cease, with the voluntary abolition of slavery by the States, he should be in favor, individually, of the Government paying a fair indemnity for the loss to their owners. . . . But on this subject he said he could give no assurance—enter into no stipulation."[41] When Seward objected to compensating slaveholders, Lincoln replied that "if it was wrong in the South to hold slaves, it was wrong in the North to carry on the slave trade and sell them to the South."

In frustration, Hunter protested that the Confederacy was being asked to surrender unconditionally. Denying that assertion, Seward said he did not "think that yielding to the execution of the laws under the Constitution of the United States, with all its guarantees and securities for personal and political rights, as they might be declared to be by the court, could be properly considered as unconditional submission to conquerors, or as having anything humiliating about it."[42] Seward was right. The terms Lincoln offered the South—reunion and emancipation—were far more limited and generous than the demands that the United States imposed on Germany and Japan in 1945.

As the meeting closed, Hunter asked about the U.S. Capitol expansion. Seward described how the dome had been completed and was now crowned by a large statue of Armed Liberty. (A few months earlier Lincoln had said "that there were

some people who thought the work on the Capitol ought to stop on account of the war, people who begrudged the expenditure, and the detention of the workmen from the army." But he believed that the completion of the Capitol would symbolize the preservation of the Union: "If people see the Capitol going on, it is a sign we intend the Union shall go on.")[43]

The only agreement to emerge from the conference dealt with prisoner exchanges. At Stephens's suggestion, Lincoln said he would recommend to Grant that a cartel for such exchanges be negotiated with the Confederates. The president also agreed to have Stephens's nephew released from a Northern prison camp in exchange for a Union soldier. The disappointed commissioners relayed Lincoln's terms to Jefferson Davis, who regarded them as an insult. With a sneer, he declared that rather than rejoin the Union, "he would be willing to yield up everything he had on earth—if it were possible he would sacrifice a thousand lives."[44] As it turned out, more than a thousand lives were sacrificed because of Davis's stubborn unwillingness to accept the plain reality of defeat.

Lincoln returned to Washington optimistic that the conference at Hampton Roads might lead to peace. On February 6, he introduced to the cabinet a resolution embodying the proposal he had made at the conference to offer $400 million as compensation to slaveholders if the Confederacy would surrender by April 1. The first half would be paid upon that surrender, and the other half if the Thirteenth Amendment were ratified by July 1. Lincoln pledged that should Congress pass this resolution, he would fully exercise the power granted him and "the war will cease, and armies be reduced to a basis of peace; that all political offences will be pardoned; that all property, except slaves, liable to confiscation or forfeiture, will be released therefrom, except in cases of intervening interests of third parties; and that liberality will be recommended to congress upon all points not lying within executive control."[45]

Lincoln may well have intended the $400 million to help revive the blighted economy of the South, an enlightened proposal to help restore sectional harmony. In justifying it, he asked the cabinet, "How long has this war lasted, and how long do you suppose it will last? We cannot hope that it will end in less than a hundred days. We are now spending three millions a day, and that will equal the full amount I propose to pay, to say nothing of the lives lost and property destroyed. I look

Opposite, "If people see the Capitol going on, it is a sign we intend the Union shall go on," Lincoln said when someone suggested suspending construction of the dome during the war. These photographs depict the building at the time of Lincoln's first and second inaugurations. Photos by Montgomery Meigs and Alexander Gardner, respectively. Abraham Lincoln Presidential Library and Museum, Springfield, Illinois.

upon it as a measure of strict and simple economy." The cabinet, however, unanimously rejected the proposal, causing him to remark sadly, "You are all against me" and to drop the matter.[46]

Lincoln's willingness to meet Confederate commissioners and offer generous peace terms was inspired by his wish to end the war swiftly, to restore goodwill between the sections, to reduce the chances of guerilla warfare breaking out after war's end, and to stave off impending anarchy and poverty in the South.

Second Inaugural

On March 4, Lincoln's desire for a true sectional reconciliation shone through his inaugural address, the greatest of his oratorical masterpieces. Although the morning was dark and rainy, well before 10:00 huge crowds lined Pennsylvania Avenue, hoping to catch a glimpse of the president as his carriage passed by. They were doomed to disappointment, for quite early he had gone to the Capitol to sign bills passed during the final hours of the Thirty-eighth Congress. The presidential carriage, however, did roll down the avenue, conveying the First Lady and Robert Lincoln as well as Iowa senator James Harlan, whose daughter would marry Robert in 1868.

Spectators filled the plaza in front of the Capitol's east portico. When the doors to the Senate gallery were finally opened, women rushed in, taking all the seats. Although the Senate was still in session, they made so much noise with their chatter that the presiding officer tried unsuccessfully to shush them. Finally they quieted down when admirals, generals, cabinet members, Supreme Court justices, and the president filed in and took their seats.

At noon, the outgoing vice president, Hannibal Hamlin, entered with his successor, Andrew Johnson. After the former delivered a brief valedictory, the latter embarrassed all present with a drunken harangue. The night before, Johnson and his friend John W. Forney had consumed several drinks, and the next morning, feeling unwell, he had taken three glasses of whiskey straight. (He had been recovering from a debilitating bout of typhoid.) In his weakened state, the liquor was more than he could handle. Obviously intoxicated, he spoke for twenty minutes. When Hamlin nudged him from behind and audibly reminded him that his time was up, Johnson paid no attention. After the new vice president had finished this incoherent tirade, Lincoln told a marshal: "Do not permit Johnson to speak a word during the exercises that are to follow."[47]

As the presidential party emerged from the Rotunda onto the platform erected for the occasion, many spectators followed, swarming over the stairs, the column bases, and every other vantage point. As Lincoln gazed out over the vast, surging throng, cheering broke out, bands blared away, and flags fluttered everywhere. As he stood to read his remarks, a thunderous outburst of applause greeted him. Just before he began speaking, the sun emerged from behind the clouds that had obscured it all morning. Lincoln's central aim was to prepare the public mind for a generous reconstruction policy. Rather than introducing a series of policy recommendations, he sought to exorcise feelings of vindictiveness and self-righteousness. He also wished to share his understanding of the nature of the war and the reasons for its long duration. His deep thinking on those questions led him to conclusions that he shared with the nation in this unusually brief address. Lincoln began by explaining that no lengthy account of recent events was necessary: "The progress of our arms, upon which all else chiefly depends, is as well known to the public as to myself; and it is, I trust, reasonably satisfactory and encouraging to all. With high hope for the future, no prediction in regard to it is ventured." After a succinct description of *how* the war had begun, Lincoln explained *why* it had occurred. The "peculiar and powerful interest" of slavery had "somehow" caused the war. He continued: "Neither party expected for the war, the magnitude, or the duration, which it has already attained. Neither anticipated that the *cause* of the conflict might cease with, or even before, the conflict itself should cease. Each looked for an easier triumph, and a result less fundamental and astounding." Invoking a theme that had long been at the core of his antislavery feeling, Lincoln said that it "may seem strange that any men should dare to ask a just God's assistance in wringing their bread from the sweat of other men's faces; but let us judge not that we be not judged."

At this point the inaugural took an abrupt turn as Lincoln analyzed why the war had dragged on and on: "The Almighty has His own purposes." He then quoted Jesus's words, "Woe unto the world because of offences! for it must needs be that offences come; but woe to that man by whom the offence cometh!" He continued: "If we shall suppose that American Slavery is one of those offences which, in the providence of God, must needs come, but which, having continued through His appointed time, He now wills to remove, and that He gives to both North and South, this terrible war, as the woe due to those by whom the offence came, shall we discern therein any departure from those divine attributes which the believers in a Living God always ascribe to Him? Fondly do we hope—fervently do we pray—that this mighty scourge of war may speedily pass away. Yet, if God wills that it continue, until all the wealth piled by the bond-man's two hundred and fifty years of unrequited toil shall be sunk, and until every drop of blood drawn with the lash, shall be paid by another drawn with the sword, as was said three thousand years ago, so still it must be said 'the judgments of the Lord, are true and righteous altogether.'"

This pronouncement might not have sounded out of place in the mouth of a pious abolitionist or a Christian minister preaching a sermon, but for a president to utter it on such an important state occasion was astonishing. It rested on a proposition that he had articulated earlier: that both North and South were complicit in the sin of slavery. But never before had he suggested that Whites of both sections must suffer death and destruction on a vast scale in order to atone for that sin, and that the war would not end until the scales were evenly balanced. Lincoln offered this as a hypothesis, not a firm conclusion, but if it were true, then the words of Psalm 19 would have to be recalled: "The judgments of the Lord, are true and righteous altogether."

Lincoln closed by shifting the emphasis from justice to mercy. His final paragraph honored the men who had served in the army and the navy and expressed his hope for the future: "With malice toward none; with charity for all; with firmness in the right, as God gives us to see the right, let us strive on to finish the work we are in; to bind up the nation's wounds; to care for him who shall have borne the battle, and for his widow, and his orphan—to do all which may achieve and cherish a just, and a lasting peace, among ourselves, and with all nations."[48]

Lincoln delivering his second inaugural address, March 4, 1865. Some close students of this image assert, a bit dubiously, that they can detect John Wilkes Booth and his co-conspirators in the crowd. Booth did attend the event and, according to Commissioner of Public Buildings Benjamin Brown French, was rebuffed when he attempted to get at the president. Photo by Alexander Gardner, Library of Congress.

After Chief Justice Chase administered the oath of office, Lincoln kissed the Bible and bowed to the audience, whose many cheers were punctuated by booming artillery salvos. During the speech the crowd had listened intently but for the most part had remained silent, save for the many Blacks who murmured "bress de Lord" at the close of most sentences.[49] The final paragraph brought tears to many eyes.

Frederick Douglass, who thought the address "sounded more like a sermon than like a state paper," admired above all its final two paragraphs. After hearing them, he applauded "in gladness and thanksgiving," for to him they seemed "to contain more vital substance than I have ever seen compressed into a space so narrow." Afterwards, Douglass joined the crowd moving toward the White House to attend the traditional post-inaugural reception. At the door, two policemen rudely blocked his way. Douglass asked a passer-by whom he recognized: "Be so kind as to say to Mr. Lincoln that Frederick Douglass is detained by officers at the door." That gentleman hastened to convey the message, and in less than a minute Douglass was admitted. When Lincoln saw him, he exclaimed, "Here comes my friend Douglass." After the two men shook hands, the president said, "Douglass, I saw you in the crowd today listening to my inaugural address. There is no man's opinion that I value more than yours; what do you think of it?" Douglass replied, "Mr. Lincoln, it was a sacred effort." Gratified, Lincoln said, "I am glad you liked it."[50]

When Thurlow Weed also praised the address, Lincoln said that he expected it "to wear as well as—perhaps better than—any thing I have produced; but I believe it is not immediately popular. Men are not flattered by being shown that there has been a difference of purpose between the Almighty and them. To deny it, however, in this case, is to deny that there is a God governing the world. It is a truth which I thought needed to be told; and as whatever of humiliation there is in it, falls most directly on myself, I thought others might afford for me to tell it."[51]

The inauguration had "passed off well," as General Halleck put it. "Thanks to abundant preventions we had no disturbances, no fires, no raids, or robberies," he noted.[52] A disturbance had been briefly created by one of the more sinister onlookers, a famous young actor, John Wilkes Booth, who seethed with hatred for African Americans and for the man they called the Great Emancipator.

Clashing with Congress

Lincoln was predisposed to meet Congress halfway on the contentious subject of reconstruction. In his annual message, he acknowledged that his power in that area would decline sharply with the end of the war. He also appointed two commissioners to investigate conditions in Louisiana and Arkansas, thus signaling his willingness to rethink the reconstruction policy that had been followed in those states. Congress was also predisposed to compromise with Lincoln. The two

Memorabilia celebrating the martyred president and the victorious side in the Civil War included this hand-colored lithograph produced by Anton Hoenstein and published by John Smith of Philadelphia in 1865. Entitled *Abraham Lincoln's Last Reception*, it fancifully brought together the president and Mrs. Lincoln, Vice President and Mrs. Andrew Johnson, cabinet members, and various high-ranking military officers—all gathered in timeless triumph. Library of Congress.

branches worked together to pass the Thirteenth Amendment, and a conciliatory House referred measures relating to reconstruction to the Judiciary Committee rather than to Henry Winter Davis's Select Committee on the Rebellious States. In mid-December, James Ashley introduced a bill stipulating that such recognition would be granted if Lincoln would agree that only "loyal male citizens" (presumably including African Americans) could vote and serve on juries.

On December 18, Lincoln told Nathaniel P. Banks, who since September had been in Washington lobbying Congress on behalf of the Louisiana government, that he had been reading the legislation with care and "liked it with the exception of one or two things which he thought rather calculated to conceal a feature which might be objectionable to some." The first feature "was that under the provisions of that bill negroes would be made jurors & voters under the temporary governments." The president was not voicing his own opposition to Black voting but expressing the fear that it might be so "objectionable to some" that the bill would be defeated. Just as with emancipation, on the issue of Black enfranchisement Lincoln did not wish to get very far ahead of public opinion. Banks agreed, saying: "Yes, that is to be stricken out and the qualification white male citizens of the U.S. is to be restored. What you refer to would be a fatal objection to the Bill."

Lincoln's second reservation concerned "the declaration that all persons heretofore held in slavery are declared free." That did not seem critical, for he said it was evidently "not a prohibition of slavery by Congress but a mere assurance of freedom to persons then [free] in accordance with the proclamation of Emancipation. In that point of view it is not objectionable though I think it would have been preferable to so express it."[53] Two days later, Ashley accepted amendments designed to meet the president's objections: slaves would be freed only in the areas already covered by the Emancipation Proclamation, and voting rights would be extended only to White males and to those African Americans serving in the military. In addition, Louisiana would be readmitted, but Congress would have the power to set terms for the admission of other Confederate states. Action on this compromise measure was postponed until after the Christmas recess.

During that time, Wendell Phillips visited Washington and reported that "the radical men feel that they are powerless and checkmated." Henry Winter Davis "told him the game was up—'Lincoln with his immense patronage can do what he pleases; the only hope is an appeal to the people.'"[54] In January, Phillips made such an appeal at a meeting of the Massachusetts Anti-Slavery Society. He warned that to admit Louisiana under the Banks-Hahn government would set a dangerous precedent. The "principle underlying Louisiana" was, he charged, "a brutal, domineering, infamous overseer spirit."[55] In response to Radical pressure, Ashley significantly modified the compromise bill, virtually eliminating the possibility of admitting Louisiana, Arkansas, and Tennessee under the Lincoln reconstruction plan. In effect, the measure was the Wade-Davis Bill redivivus with Black suffrage added. Moderate Republicans rebelled, and the measure was tabled. Partly in response to Lincoln's reelection, most Republican lawmakers were backing away from their earlier endorsement of the Wade-Davis approach to reconstruction and moving toward the president's plan. Noah Brooks reported that members who had voted in July for the Radical bill "are now willing to admit that the President's sagacity was greater than theirs."[56] Moderates agreed with Lincoln that no rigid formula should be applied to all eleven Confederate states.

Although the Thirty-eighth Congress would pass no reconstruction bill, few regarded a postponement of the issue as a misfortune. But in the meantime, would Congress admit Louisiana and Arkansas? Smarting from their defeat on the reconstruction bill, Radicals sought revenge. The opportunity arose when the senators and congressmen from Louisiana asked to be seated. As the Senate addressed that matter in January, Lincoln tried to frame the debate by suggesting to the chairman of the Judiciary Committee, Lyman Trumbull, that the most important question before that body was, "Can Louisiana be brought into proper practical relations with the Union *sooner* by *admitting* or by *rejecting* the proposed Senators?"[57] The committee, which had refused to seat Arkansas's senators a few months earlier, now recommended that Louisiana's be accepted. That necessarily entailed recognizing the Hahn government, which the committee said "fairly represented a majority of the loyal voters of the State."[58]

Although most senators favored acceptance of the committee's report, a few Radicals, led by Charles Sumner, demurred. They objected to the Louisiana constitution's failure to enfranchise at least some Black men and to the Lincoln administration's alleged usurpation of congressional prerogatives. Sumner vowed to employ "all the instruments . . . in the arsenal of parliamentary warfare" to block the will of the majority. The Hahn government, he charged, was "a mere seven-months' abortion, begotten by the bayonet in criminal conjunction with the spirit of caste, and born before its time, rickety, unformed, unfinished—whose continued existence will be a burden, a reproach, and a wrong."[59] Conservative Democrats like Kentuckians Garrett Davis and Lazarus Powell, fearing that Louisiana would ratify the Thirteenth Amendment, teamed up with Sumner and a few other Radicals to conduct a successful filibuster, thus preventing recognition of the Bayou State.

Lincoln was furious. He told James Ashley that Sumner "hopes to succeed in beating the President so as to change this government from its original form, and making it a strong centralized power."[60] It is not hard to understand Lincoln's aversion to the vain, haughty, pedantic senator. When the press began to speak of a personal rupture between Sumner and himself, however, Lincoln quickly moved to squelch the rumor by magnanimously inviting the senator to join him at the inaugural ball on March 6. Sumner accepted and escorted the First Lady into the festivities at the mammoth Patent Office building, following closely behind the president and his escort, House Speaker Schuyler Colfax. The New York *Herald* inferred that Lincoln had endorsed Sumner's approach to reconstruction, but in fact the president had not done so. He would postpone for five weeks his formal response to the Senate's action.

Lincoln was angry at the military in Louisiana as well as at Congress for failing to support the Hahn government. In September he had summoned Banks to Washington and directed him to lobby Congress on behalf of that government. Taking over Banks's role in New Orleans were Generals Stephen Hurlbut, Lincoln's friend from Illinois, and E. R. S. Canby. To Hurlbut the president wrote a blistering letter in November decrying the "bitter military opposition to the new State Government of Louisiana"—a government that had been established "under military protection, directed by me, in the belief, still sincerely entertained, that with such a nucleous [*sic*] around which to build, we could get the State into position again sooner than otherwise." After describing ways that the civil authorities had been interfered with, Lincoln concluded that the military must not "crush out the civil government."[61]

On November 29, Hurlbut replied: "I recognize as thoroughly as any man the advance toward the right made by the adoption of the Free Constitution of Louisiana, and have done and shall do all in my power to vindicate its declaration of freedom, and to protect and prepare the emancipated Bondsmen for their new status & condition. The fact has been withheld from you, Mr President, but it still exists that nothing has been done for this purpose since the adoption of the Constitution—*except by military authority*."[62] Dissatisfied with this response, Lincoln ordered Banks to return to Louisiana. He did not write out instructions for the general, but his intentions can be inferred from Banks's remarks upon arriving in New Orleans. There he told a mass meeting of African Americans "that the day is not far distant when they will be in the enjoyment of all rights. . . . Abraham Lincoln gave his word that you will be free, and enjoy all the rights invested to citizens."[63] Presumably that included voting rights.

By April, Lincoln doubtless sensed that Northern support for Black suffrage was waxing. To keep his party together, he understood that the time was growing ripe to support Black voting rights publicly. He had already done so privately. But when to announce his decision publicly?

Visit to the Front

As he mulled over that question, Lincoln was becoming ever more weary of the White House grind. So on March 20, when Grant invited him to visit the front, he gladly accepted and requested Assistant Secretary of the Navy Gustavus Fox to make travel arrangements. Fox asked Captain John S. Barnes, commander of the USS *Bat*, a swift, armed blockade enforcer, if his vessel might be made suitable for the president. Barnes said he thought it could, and Fox took him to the White House to receive instructions. "I'm only a fresh-water sailor and I guess I have to trust you salt-water folks when afloat," Lincoln said, adding that he "wanted no luxuries but only plain, simple food and ordinary comfort." Whatever was good enough for Barnes, he stressed, was sufficient for him.[64]

The following day, however, the president told Barnes that more luxurious accommodations would be necessary, for Mrs. Lincoln had decided to join him. The captain recalled that in modifying his request, Lincoln had "a certain look of embarrassment and a look of sadness which struck me forcibly and rather embarrassed me." Taken aback, Barnes observed that the *Bat* was unsuitable for female passengers. So Fox and Barnes arranged to charter the *River Queen*, the side-wheeled passenger ship on which the Hampton Roads conference had taken place. Fox warned Barnes to be cautious in protecting Lincoln and said he regretted "that the determination of Mrs. Lincoln to accompany the President had made the *Bat* an impossible home for him and his family party." Lincoln, however, felt no concern for his own safety. As for bombs disguised as coal lumps like the one that had sunk the *River Queen*'s sister ship, he "expressed great contempt for cowardly assaults of such nature." On March 23, the president, along with his wife and their son Tad, boarded the *River Queen* and sailed for City Point, escorted by the *Bat*. Accompanying them were Mrs. Lincoln's maidservant and army captain Charles B. Penrose, whom Stanton had assigned to act as a bodyguard.

The following day the *River Queen* arrived at City Point, an immense army supply base. When Grant and his wife called to pay their respects, he and the president retired to discuss military affairs. Coldly the First Lady received Mrs. Grant, who committed an act of lèse-majesté by sitting down next to her hostess. Mrs. Lincoln imperiously exclaimed: "How dare you be seated until I invite you!"[65] The First Lady would make other such scenes over the next several days. Her sense of entitlement led her to insist that the *River Queen* be berthed next to the dock, though Grant's headquarters boat, the *Carrie Martin*, had been assigned that location. The two vessels were placed side by side, but Mrs. Lincoln refused to cross what became known as "Mrs. Grant's boat" in order to reach the gangplank. So, despite Lincoln's protests, the *Martin* was regularly forced to move out in order to make way for the *Queen*, necessitating extra work for the crews and creating some confusion.

The journalist Sylvanus Cadwallader, whose wife was friendly with Mrs. Grant, reported that the First Lady "seemed insanely jealous of every person, and everything, which drew him [Lincoln] away from her and monopolized his attention for an hour." She regularly dispatched Tad to summon his father back to the *River Queen*. On one occasion the boy, after a vain attempt to deliver such instructions, interrupted the president in the midst of an animated conversation: "Come, come, come now, mama says you must come instantly." Lincoln's face fell, and he hesitated for a moment, then rose to leave, asking rhetorically, "My God, will that woman never understand me?" Submissively, he returned to the *River Queen* with Tad.[66]

On the morning of March 25, Lincoln's plans to review the troops were disrupted by Lee's desperate attempt to break through the ever-tightening noose around Petersburg. In a pre-dawn assault, the Confederates punched a hole in the Union line, capturing Fort Stedman and two nearby batteries, but were soon driven back. Lincoln had wanted to observe the action, but Grant thought it too dangerous. When the firing stopped, however, the general suggested that they inspect the battlefield. Around noon Grant, his staff, Lincoln, Barnes, and others boarded a train that took them seven miles to the front, where burial squads were digging graves for the many corpses scattered about as doctors tended to wounded Rebels. Lincoln showed great interest in the sixteen hundred ragged, dirty prisoners who had been taken earlier in the day. Although for the most part he remained silent, he did remark on their forlorn condition, showing compassion for the suffering he observed all around him. While frequently consulting a map, he indicated an awareness of the positions of various units. A member of General Meade's staff reported that as Lincoln "rode past the troops, he removed his hat gracefully by the hinder part of the brim, and the troops cheered quite loudly."[67] That afternoon, Meade took Lincoln to Fort Wadsworth, where they spent two hours observing the Sixth Corps attack enemy picket lines.

When Lincoln returned to the train, he noticed cars full of wounded men. Appearing fatigued, he said "that he had seen enough of the horrors of war, that he hoped this was the beginning of the end, and that there would be no more bloodshed or ruin of homes." During his visit, he repeated this hope earnestly and often. While comforting the wounded, he was told about a young boy in a Confederate uniform moaning "Mother! Mother!" When asked where he was hurt, the lad had turned his head, revealing a ghastly wound, and died. Hearing this sad tale, Lincoln wept and with an emotion-choked voice "repeated the well-known expression about 'robbing the cradle and the grave.'"[68]

Upon reaching City Point, Lincoln sat by a smoky campfire with Grant and his staff. Initially his demeanor was solemn as he "spoke of the appalling difficulties encountered by the administration, the losses in the field, the perplexing financial problems, and the foreign complications; but said they had all been overcome by the unswerving patriotism of the people, the devotion of the loyal North, and the superb fighting qualities of the troops." In time, he unwound and entertained his companions with amusing anecdotes about public men and measures. When Grant asked, "Mr. President, did you at any time doubt the final success of the cause?" he replied swiftly and emphatically: "Never for a moment."[69]

Worn out by the day's excitement, Lincoln declined the general's dinner invitation and returned to the *River Queen*, where he went to bed earlier than usual. After a good night's sleep, he arose to encouraging bulletins from the front. Although he lamented that so many lives had been lost and that the wounded had suffered so badly, he optimistically predicted that the war would soon end. He was especially pleased to learn that General Philip Sheridan, having whipped Jubal Early's army in the Shenandoah Valley, had reached the James River. At Grant's headquarters he found that diminutive cavalryman, along with Admiral David Dixon Porter and Generals Meade and E. O. C. Ord. It was suggested that since the president had been unable to review troops the previous day, he might like to watch Sheridan's army cross the river and then review both the naval flotilla and Ord's corps. He accepted the invitation.

Looking worn out, the president sailed downriver to the spot where Sheridan's men were to cross. En route he seemed gloomy and spoke earnestly about the possibility that the Confederates might suddenly move to capture City Point. Uncharacteristically, he told no anecdotes. But upon observing Sheridan's soldiers traverse the bridge, he perked up, showing great interest and asking several questions of the young general. He thoroughly enjoyed the bustling scene. Some cavalry on the banks cheered loudly on catching sight of him. He met the same reception when the ship passed Porter's flotilla, which he happily saluted by waving his tall hat. After lunch aboard Porter's flagship, the *Malvern*, Lincoln proceeded to Aiken's Landing, where Ord's officers were waiting to escort the presidential party to the review. The president rode with Grant and Ord, while the First Lady and Julia Grant, along with Grant's aides Adam Badeau and Horace Porter, followed in an ambulance. The president cheerfully laughed and chatted with the generals. When they arrived at their destination, he was dismayed to learn that the troops had been awaiting their arrival for hours and had missed lunch. He therefore urged that the review begin without further delay while the women caught up.

Meanwhile, Badeau tried to make polite conversation with the First Lady and Mrs. Grant. He predicted that a battle would soon take place, for Grant had ordered to the rear the wives of officers in the Army of the Potomac. The beautiful Mrs. Charles Griffin, who had received special permission from the president, was an exception. This news rasped Mary Lincoln. "What do you mean by that, sir?" she asked indignantly. "Do you mean to say that she saw the President alone? Do you know that I never allow the President to see any woman alone?"

Julia Grant tried to rescue poor Badeau, who balked when the First Lady instructed him to order the vehicle to halt so that she could leave it. She then took matters into her own hands by seizing the driver, but Mrs. Grant persuaded her to stay aboard until they had reached the reviewing ground. There General Meade, unaware of the delicacy of the situation, briefly replaced Badeau as the women's escort. When they returned to the carriage, the First Lady glared at Badeau and remarked, "General Meade is a gentleman, sir. He says it was not the President who gave Mrs. Griffin the permit, but the Secretary of War."

An even more embarrassing scene occurred as the party approached the reviewing site. General Ord's vivacious wife, like Mrs. Griffin, had been allowed to remain at the front. On a high-spirited horse she rode alongside Lincoln while the First Lady's vehicle was still catching up. According to Badeau, as "soon as Mrs. Lincoln discovered this her rage was beyond all bounds. 'What does the woman mean,' she exclaimed, 'by riding by the side of the President? and ahead of me? Does she suppose that *he* wants *her* by the side of *him*?' She was in a frenzy of excitement, and language and action both became more extravagant every moment."

She grew angry when Julia Grant once again attempted to soothe her. Haughtily, the First Lady asked, "I suppose you think you'll get to the White House yourself, don't you?" Mrs. Grant explained that she was quite content with her current situation, provoking a sharp retort: "Oh! you had better take it if you can get it. 'Tis very nice."

At this awkward moment an officer approached and innocently remarked, "The President's horse is very gallant, Mrs. Lincoln; he insists on riding by the side of Mrs. Ord."

"What do you mean by that, sir?" she exclaimed.

The astounded officer slunk away. When the carriage finally reached Ord's headquarters, that general's wife rode up. As Badeau remembered it, Mary Lincoln "positively insulted her, called her vile names in the presence of a crowd of officers, and asked what she meant by following up the President. The poor woman burst into tears and inquired what she had done, but Mrs. Lincoln refused to be appeased, and stormed till she was tired." All who saw this were "shocked and horrified." At dinner that evening, the First Lady vehemently condemned General Ord and urged the president to remove him, insisting that he was not fit for his command.

Badeau recalled that Mrs. Lincoln over the next few days "repeatedly attacked her husband in the presence of officers because of Mrs. Griffin and Mrs. Ord." That spectacle dismayed the colonel, who later wrote: "I never suffered greater humiliation and pain . . . than when I saw the Head of State, the man who carried all the cares of the nation at such a crisis—subjected to this inexpressible public mortification." Lincoln "pleaded with eyes and tones, and endeavored to explain or palliate the offenses of others, till she turned on him like a tigress; and then he walked away, hiding that noble, ugly face that we might not catch the full expression of its misery." Mary Lincoln returned to Washington on April 1, accompanied by Carl Schurz.

On the way back from reviewing Ord's corps, Lincoln felt his spirits revive. The next morning Captain Barnes as usual reported to the *River Queen*, where the president received him cordially and told him that Mrs. Lincoln was unwell. The two men then visited the headquarters of Grant, who sat rather silent while Lincoln and Admiral Porter discussed news from the front. That night General Sherman arrived from North Carolina, where his eighty-thousand-man army was being resupplied. Over the next two days he, along with Admiral Porter and Grant, conferred with Lincoln aboard the *River Queen*.

As the president listened anxiously, Grant explained how Sheridan's men would soon swing around Lee's flank and sever his supply lines. His only concern was that Lee might abandon Petersburg and Richmond and try to connect with Joseph E. Johnston. If the Confederates made such a move, they would be pursued hotly. The president took great interest in this scenario. Grant assured him that he could prevent Lee's breakout, for Sheridan's cavalry were just then moving on the Confederates' communications. Sherman remarked that even if the Army of Northern Virginia did break out, he could fend off both Johnston and Lee until Grant caught up and placed the Confederates in a fatal vise. When Lincoln expressed fear that in Sherman's absence Johnston might escape southward by rail, the general replied: "I have him where he cannot move without breaking up his army, which, once disbanded, can never again be got together."

In response to the president's questions about the march from Georgia to North Carolina, Sherman regaled him with amusing tales about his troops. According to the general, Lincoln's "face brightened wonderfully" in "lively conversation," but when the conversation flagged his face "assumed a sad, and sorrowful expression." The president exclaimed more than once: "Must more blood be shed! Cannot this last bloody battle be avoided!" The generals remarked that it was up to the Confederates.[70] Sherman returned to North Carolina that afternoon, and the following day, Grant left City Point to launch his final offensive. Before departing for the front, the commanding general bade farewell to Lincoln. The president cordially shook hands with Grant and his staff and said with heartfelt emotion, "Good-by, gentlemen. God bless you all! Remember, your success is my success."[71]

For the next few days, Lincoln spent much of his time in the telegraph office, reading and sending messages. He also toured hospitals. Sometimes he took excursions with Admiral Porter on the river or around the countryside by carriage. He carried a detailed map of the area showing the location of all the forces and would often explain to Porter how he would act if he were the commander in charge. One day they visited a deserted fort overlooking the Union army's works. After Porter described the troops' difficulties in constructing it under enemy fire and the hardships they had undergone throughout the harsh winter, Lincoln remarked, "The country can never repay these men for what they have suffered and endured."[72] On April 1, when journalist Sylvanus Cadwallader handed him battle flags captured earlier that day by Sheridan's men, Lincoln joyfully exclaimed: "Here is something material—something I can see, feel, and understand. This means victory. This *is* victory."[73]

The following day, Union forces broke through the Confederate lines, forcing Lee to abandon Petersburg. A jubilant Lincoln telegraphed Grant: "Allow me to tender to you, and all with you, the nations grateful thanks for this additional, and magnificent success."[74] On April 3, at the general's invitation, Lincoln hastened to inspect the fallen city. En route, his train halted as thousands of Rebel prisoners crossed the tracks. Mostly conscript youngsters in rags and lacking blankets, shoes, and headgear, their appearance moved the president to exclaim: "Poor boys! poor boys! If they only knew what we are trying to do for them they would not have fought us, and they would not look as they do."[75]

Upon arrival, Lincoln, his son Tad, and Admiral Porter quickly rode down the largely deserted streets to Grant's headquarters. The president's face radiated joy as he grabbed the general's hand, which he shook for a long time as he poured from his overflowing heart profound thanks and congratulations. It was one of the happiest moments of his life. As they discussed postwar political arrangements, the president emphasized, as he had done with Sherman, that he wished the Rebels to be treated leniently. After about an hour and a half, Grant returned to the front.

As Lincoln rode back to City Point, troops greeted him jocularly, shouting out, "How are you, Abe?" and "Hello, Abe!"[76] Lincoln was refreshed and energized, happily convinced that the war would soon end. That evening aboard the *Malvern*, he asked Admiral Porter: "Can't the navy do something at this particular moment to make history?"

"Not much," replied Porter; "the navy is doing its best just now holding in utter uselessness the rebel navy, consisting of four heavy ironclads. If those should get down to City Point they would commit great havoc."

"But can't we make a noise?" asked Lincoln. "That would be refreshing." Porter obligingly had broadsides from several ships fired rapidly for an hour, lighting up the night sky. Lincoln acknowledged "that the noise was a very respectable one." Suddenly, a distant huge explosion rocked the *Malvern*, prompting Lincoln to jump up and exclaim: "I hope to Heaven one of them [i.e., Union ships] has not blown up!" Porter assured him that no Union vessel had been harmed but rather that the Confederates were destroying their ironclads.

"Well," Lincoln remarked, "our noise has done some good; that's a cheap way of getting rid of ironclads. I am certain Richmond is being evacuated, and that Lee has surrendered, or those fellows would not blow up their ironclads." Shortly thereafter, three more such explosions announced the destruction of the remaining ironclads. To clear the river, Porter ordered the immediate removal of all obstructions. By morning that task had been accomplished, and boats began sweeping the James for mines.

April 4 was the most remarkable day of Lincoln's presidency. Learning that Union troops were entering Richmond, he exclaimed: "Thank God I have lived to see this! It seems to me that I have been dreaming a horrid dream for four years, and now the nightmare is gone. I want to see Richmond."[77] At 9:00 a.m. he and Tad, along with his bodyguard (army captain Charles B. Penrose) and several officers, set sail for the Virginia capital, landing near the notorious Libby Prison. As

Lincoln and his companions stepped ashore, the journalist Charles Carleton Coffin pointed them out to some nearby Blacks, who shouted "Hallelujah!" and "Glory! Glory! Glory!" Dozens raced to the landing, yelling and screaming "Hurrah! Hurrah! President Linkum hab come!"[78]

The presidential party was led by half a dozen sailors from the barge, armed with carbines; another six brought up the rear. Sandwiched between those two lines, Lincoln walked along holding Tad's hand. African Americans surrounded the little group, frantically shouting, clapping, dancing, throwing hats into the air, waving bonnets and handkerchiefs, and applauding loudly. They stirred up great clouds of dust, which, combined with smoke from smoldering buildings set ablaze by the retreating Confederates, made the warm atmosphere quite oppressive. Lincoln, wearing a long overcoat, was perspiring freely and fanning himself to cool off.

Because of the heat, and because Tad had trouble keeping up, the little party stopped to rest. At that point, according to Coffin, "an old negro, wearing a few rags, whose white, crisp hair appeared through his crownless straw hat, lifted the hat from his head, kneeled upon the ground, clasped his hands, and said, 'May de good Lord bress and keep you safe, Massa President Linkum.'"[79] The president raised his own hat and bowed, a gesture that, according to Coffin, "upset the forms, laws, customs, and ceremonies of centuries. It was a death-shock to chivalry, and a mortal wound to caste."[80]

As the procession made its way slowly up the street, it paused at Libby Prison, where captive Union officers had been incarcerated in especially grim conditions. When someone suggested that it be torn down, Lincoln objected, saying it should be preserved as a monument. A White man in shirtsleeves rushed from the sidewalk toward the president and shouted, "Abraham Lincoln, God bless you! You are the poor man's friend!"[81] Then a beautiful White teenaged girl pushed through the crowd to hand the president a bouquet of roses with a card bearing the simple message "From Eva to the Liberator of the slaves."[82] Eventually word reached headquarters that the president had arrived, and a squad of cavalry was dispatched to escort him to General Weitzel, who was ensconced in the Confederate White House.

There Lincoln, pallid and fatigued, sat down in Jefferson Davis's chair and quietly requested a glass of water. Captain Barnes, who had finally caught up with the presidential party, recalled that there "was no triumph in his gesture or attitude. He lay back in the chair like a tired man whose nerves had carried him beyond his strength."[83] So weary was he that when he stepped onto the balcony to acknowledge the cheering crowd in the street, he merely bowed.

Soon General Weitzel arrived, along with General George F. Shepley, military governor of Virginia. After congratulating them, Lincoln met privately with some

Thomas Nast, the eminent artist and political cartoonist, drew this image of Lincoln entering Richmond, April 4, 1865, based on an eyewitness account provided to him by the journalist Charles Carlton Coffin. A reversed image appeared in *Harper's Weekly*. In 1868, Nast painted a large version of this scene, which hangs in the Union League Club in New York. Lincoln supposedly referred to Nast as "our best recruiting sergeant. His emblematic cartoons have never failed to arouse enthusiasm and patriotism." John Hay Library, Brown University, Providence, Rhode Island.

Confederate leaders who had requested an interview. Among them were former associate justice of the U.S. Supreme Court John A. Campbell and General Joseph R. Anderson. The agitated Campbell gave Lincoln a very low bow. The president received him in a dignified yet cordial manner. After explaining that that he had no authorization to negotiate on behalf of the Confederacy or Virginia, Campbell recommended a lenient peace and stated that the war for all intents and purposes was over, that the Army of Northern Virginia could not be held together, and that leading Virginians would help restore the Union. Weitzel recalled that Lincoln "insisted that he could not treat with any Rebels until they had laid down their arms and surrendered, and that if this were first done he would go as far as he possibly could to prevent the shedding of another drop of blood, and that he and the good people of the North were surfeited with this thing and wanted it to end as soon as possible."[84]

After this conversation, Lincoln joined Weitzel and Shepley for a tour of Richmond in an ordinary two-seat buggy. As they rode along, hundreds of the city's African Americans in a frenzy of exultation shouted out expressions of gratitude and joy, sang songs of deliverance, wept, and threw their hands in the air. A Black correspondent told readers of the Philadelphia *Press* that there was "no describing the scene along the route. The colored population was wild with enthusiasm. Old men thanked God in a very boisterous manner, and old women shouted upon the pavement as high as they had ever done at religious revival."[85]

At Capitol Square, Lincoln addressed a huge crowd of ex-slaves: "My poor friends, you are free—free as air. You can cast off the name of slave and trample upon it; it will come to you no more. Liberty is your birthright. God gave it to you as he gave it to others, and it is a sin that you have been deprived of it for so many years. But you must try to deserve this priceless boon. Let the world see that you merit it, and are able to maintain it by your good works. Don't let your joy carry you into excesses. Learn the laws and obey them; obey God's commandments and thank him for giving you liberty, for to him you owe all things. There, now, let me pass on; I have but little time to spare."[86]

Lincoln toured the capitol, which legislators had precipitously abandoned two days earlier. Overturned desks, bundles of Confederate money, and random government documents were strewn about haphazardly. En route back to the landing site, the presidential entourage rolled past the notorious prisons, Libby and Castle Thunder, both overflowing with captured Rebels.

The next morning, Lincoln met again with Campbell and Richmond attorney Gustavus Myers. To encourage die-hards to surrender, the president offered a practical inducement: the remission of confiscated property, with the exception of slaves. He also suggested that "the Virginia Legislature might be brought to hold their meeting in the Capitol in Richmond,—for the purpose of seeing whether they desired to take any action on behalf of the State in view of the existing state of affairs, and informed Genl Weitzel that he would write to him from City point on that subject in a day or two." As the three men discussed loyalty oaths, Lincoln (according to Myers) "declared his disposition to be lenient towards all persons, however prominent, who had taken part in the struggle, and certainly no exhibition was made by him of any feeling of vindictiveness or exultation."[87] Campbell read a paper suggesting that Grant be authorized to establish an armistice that would lead to permanent peace; that no loyalty oaths be required; that no property be confiscated; and that modes for negotiating with Confederate officials be spelled out.

Around noon, Lincoln called at Weitzel's headquarters and told the general that he would consider the issues carefully and send instructions the following day. As they discussed the best way to treat the defeated enemy, Lincoln said that he was reluctant to issue orders on the matter, but he did advise the general: "If I were in your place I'd let 'em up easy—let 'em up easy."[88] Then he returned to the *Malvern* and steamed back to City Point.

When General Shepley, an accomplished lawyer, learned of Lincoln's authorizing the members of the Virginia legislature to reconvene, he predicted that it would be wildly unpopular in the North, that the cabinet would disapprove, and that Weitzel might well be blamed unless the president issued the order in writing. Anticipating that Weitzel might be unfairly censured for his own decision, Lincoln sent him a formal order confirming his earlier verbal instructions. Weitzel was to regard this document as private but could show it to Campbell.

"The drafting of that order, though so short, gave me more perplexity than any other paper I ever drew up," Lincoln told Francis H. Pierpont, governor of loyal Virginia. He worked on it for hours that night, trying to make clear that the men who had been serving in the legislature were to reassemble for the sole purpose of withdrawing the army from the field. "But if I had known that General Lee would surrender so soon I would not have issued the proclamation," he added. Lincoln assured Pierpont that "your government at Alexandria was fully in my mind, and I intended to recognize the restored government, of which you were head, as the rightful government of Virginia."[89]

The legislators remaining in Richmond did meet and, grossly overstepping the boundaries Lincoln had placed on their authority, acted as though they were the legitimate government of the commonwealth, empowered to negotiate peace terms. As Shepley had predicted, Lincoln's order sparked a firestorm of protest, and the cabinet disapproved of the plan. Lincoln was understandably indignant at the Virginians and three days later revoked the order to Weitzel. To the cabinet, he explained that he thought "the members of the legislature, being the prominent and influential men of their respective counties, had better come together and undo their own work [of secession]." He continued, "Civil government must be reestablished as soon as possible. There must be courts and law and order, or society would be broken up, the disbanded armies would turn into robber bands and guerrillas."[90]

Events were rapidly overtaking the peacemakers. As Union cavalry pursued the Confederates fleeing westward, Lincoln remarked that "Sheridan seemed to be getting Virginia soldiers out of the war faster than this legislature could think."[91] The Army of Northern Virginia was indeed dwindling, as more and more troops deserted. In desperation, the Confederate Congress had authorized the enlistment of slaves, and Jefferson Davis reluctantly assented. When told that the Rebels might resort to such a measure, Lincoln remarked that "when they had reached that stage the cause of the war would cease and hostilities with it. The evil would cure itself."[92]

On April 6, Mrs. Lincoln returned to City Point and once again engaged in hysterics. She came with an entourage comprising her confidante and dressmaker Elizabeth Keckly, Charles Sumner and his young French friend Charles Adolphe Pineton (the Marquis de Chambrun), James Speed, William T. Otto, and Iowa senator James Harlan with his wife and daughter Mary, who was the object of Robert Lincoln's affections. The First Lady, disappointed that she had not been able to accompany her husband on his entry into Richmond two days earlier, was eager to tour that city. So while Lincoln attended to business, she and her friends headed up the James for the Confederate capital.

Upon her return the following day, she expressed a desire to visit Petersburg, and Lincoln reluctantly agreed to join her. Some curious Black servants on board the *River Queen* wished to accompany them. Chambrun reported that Lincoln, who "was blinded by no prejudices against race or color" and who "had not what can be termed false dignity," invited them to sit with the presidential party.[93] That morning he also sent Grant a telegram succinctly expressing the iron determination that characterized his leadership throughout the war: "Gen. Sheridan says 'If the thing is pressed I think that Lee will surrender.' Let the *thing* be pressed."[94]

As the visitors toured the town, where most houses were closed and most shops either abandoned or vandalized, African Americans crowded the streets to cheer the man they regarded as their liberator, while Whites hastily sought refuge to avoid having to look upon him. Lincoln reported to his companions that "animosity in the town is abating, [for] the inhabitants now accept accomplished facts," including "the final downfall of the Confederacy, and the abolition of slavery. There still remains much for us to do, but every day brings new reason for confidence in the future."[95]

The next night, Lincoln returned to Washington, where Seward had recently been injured in a carriage accident. Before departing, he spent five hours visiting the hospitals of each corps, despite the doctors' warning that to try to greet thousands of men would be more than he could endure. When they spoke proudly of the hospital facilities, he replied: "Gentlemen, you know better than I *how* to *conduct* these hospitals, but I came here to take by the hand the men who have achieved our glorious victories."[96] And so he began shaking hands with the wounded. Private Wilbur Fisk noted that the president "appeared to take delight in it. I believe he had almost as much pleasure in honoring the boys, as the boys did in receiving the honor from him."[97]

After shaking the hands of all the Union soldiers, Lincoln turned to enter tents housing Confederate wounded.

"Mr. President, you do not want to go in there!" exclaimed a doctor.

"Why not, my boy?" he asked.

"Why, sir, they are sick rebel prisoners."

"That is just where I do want to go," he said and shook the hands of many surprised Confederates.[98]

Lincoln's mood in his final days at the front oscillated between hearty bonhomie and sad introspection. In discussing peace plans, he emphasized the need to show mercy to the defeated foe. When it was suggested that Jefferson Davis be hanged, he calmly replied: "Let us judge not, that we be not judged." Told that the suffering of Union soldiers in Libby Prison should trump the claims of mercy, he repeated that biblical injunction twice. When Chambrun alluded to the possibility of war between France and the United States over Napoleon III's intervention in Mexico, Lincoln remarked: "There has been war enough. I know what the American people want, but, thank God, I count for something, and during my second term there will be no more fighting."

In the afternoon, Lincoln asked a military band to play "La Marseillaise," saying "he had a great liking for that tune." To Chambrun he noted the irony of the situation: "You must come over to America to hear it." (Napoleon III had banned that revolutionary anthem from France.) Upon learning that Chambrun was unfamiliar with the song "Dixie," Lincoln requested the band to strike it up, much to the musicians' surprise. "That tune is now Federal property; it belongs to us, and, at any rate, it is good to show the rebels that with us they will be free to hear it again."[99]

At 10:00 p.m. the *River Queen* weighed anchor and headed for Washington. As it pulled away, Lincoln, lost in thought, stood at the rail gazing at the distant hills. It is hard to imagine the profound feelings that must have run through his mind that night. He may have reviewed the entire course of the war, from the shelling of Fort Sumter through the capture of Richmond. He perhaps thought of all the blood shed by the more than seven hundred thousand troops, North and South, who had died over the past four years, including friends like Elmer Ellsworth, Ben Hardin Helm, and Edward D. Baker; all the wounded, many of whom he had spoken

FROM OUR SPECIAL WAR CORRESPONDENT.

"CITY POINT, VA., *April* —, 8.30 A.M.

"All seems well with us."—A. LINCOLN.

On the day Lincoln died, this touching cartoon appeared, quoting the president's April 2 telegram from the front to Secretary of War Stanton. Grant had just broken through the Confederate lines at Petersburg and forced Lee to evacuate Richmond. *Harper's Weekly*, April 15, 1865. Abraham Lincoln Presidential Library and Museum, Springfield, Illinois.

to that day; all the mourning widows and orphans; and all the vast destruction of property, so vividly apparent amid the ruins of Petersburg and Richmond. Counterbalancing those grim reflections, he may have derived immense satisfaction recalling the joy of the liberated slaves who thronged about him in those two cities. How could justice for those people be secured while simultaneously granting mercy to their former masters? Long ago, while immersed in the study of geometry, he had tried to square the circle. Now he would, metaphorically speaking, try once again to do the same thing, this time politically.

Lincoln and Gongress both addressed the problem of reconstruction and had reached an impasse. He had stuck by his Ten Percent Plan, and the Radicals had countered with the Wade-Davis Bill. He had stymied them with his veto; they had thwarted him by refusing to recognize the Louisiana government and seat its congressmen and senators. His principal motive in framing reconstruction policy had been to induce the Confederates to surrender. Now that the war was virtually over, should he move to compromise with the Radicals? If so, how far?

36.

"This War Is Eating My Life Out; I Have a Strong Impression That I Shall Not Live to See the End"

The Final Days (April 9–15, 1865)

Lincoln sensed that he would not outlive the war. He had no doubt that the Union would ultimately triumph, "but I may not live to see it," he said in July 1864. "I feel a presentiment that I shall not outlast the rebellion. When it is over, my work will be done."[1] He even told his friend Owen Lovejoy that he might die before peace came: "This war is eating my life out; I have a strong impression that I shall not live to see the end."[2]

On April 9, as Lee was surrendering to Grant at Appomattox, the *River Queen* chugged up Chesapeake Bay and the Potomac River. To his companions Lincoln read for several hours, mostly from Shakespeare's *Macbeth*. After reciting the thane's guilty soliloquy following the murder of his cousin, King Duncan, the president remarked, "How true a description of the murderer that one was; when, the dark deed achieved, its tortured perpetrator came to envy the sleep of his victim." He read that scene several times.

While the ship was passing Mount Vernon, Adolphe de Chambrun predicted that Americans would one day revere his home in Springfield as much as they did Washington's home. "Springfield! How happy, four years hence, will I be to return there in peace and tranquility!" the president exclaimed. As they approached Washington, Mrs. Lincoln said: "That city is full of our enemies." Her husband impatiently rejoined, "Enemies! We must never speak of that."[3] Thomas Stackpole, a White House staffer, reported that en route to the capital, the First Lady struck her husband in the face, damned him, and cursed him; she was evidently still fuming over events at City Point.

Lincoln rejoiced greatly at Lee's surrender. "The very day after his return from Richmond," Stanton recalled, "I passed with him some of the happiest moments of my life; our hearts beat with exultation at the victories."[4] But the president did not long indulge in celebrating, for he had to deal with the thorny issues of reconstruction. On April 10, when Virginia governor Francis H. Pierpont congratulated him on the fall of Richmond, he replied: "I want it distinctly understood that I claim no part nor lot in the honor of the military movements in front of Richmond[.] All the honor belongs to the military." From Pierpont, Lincoln wanted information rather than kudos. What should be done in Virginia now that Lee had surrendered? Elements of the disloyal state legislature had reassembled in Richmond but had overstepped their mandate. Should Pierpont, as governor of loyal Virginia (based in Alexandria), proceed to the state capital? How would people there receive him? Lincoln enjoined Pierpont to be "industrious, and ascertain what Union sentiment there is in Virginia, and keep me advised."[5]

Virginia was a special case, for it had a Unionist government under Pierpont already in place. What about the other states lately in rebellion? Of them, Louisiana was furthest along the road to restoration. Lincoln wanted to continue nurturing the Michael Hahn government there and win congressional recognition for it. But to do so he must overcome the resistance of Radicals, many of whom shared Andrew Johnson's view that "treason must be made odious" and "traitors must be impoverished, their social power broken."[6] Other Radicals, concerned more about protecting former slaves than about punishing their erstwhile masters, championed Black suffrage. On April 11, Lincoln moved dramatically closer to those Radicals in a carefully prepared address. The day before, he had been twice serenaded by thousands of cheering Washingtonians, who clamored for a speech. To their disappointment, he replied that he would not deliver one then but would do so the next day. As a gesture to placate them, he instructed the Marine band to play "Dixie." In justifying that selection, he jocularly explained: "I have always thought 'Dixie' one of the best tunes I have ever heard. Our adversaries over the way attempted to appropriate it, but I insisted yesterday that we fairly captured it. . . . I now request the band to favor me with its performance."[7]

On the night of April 11, Lincoln, as promised, gave a formal speech to a crowd whose response to his appearance was unusually intense. Elizabeth Keckly wrote that she "never saw such a mass of heads before." Adding "to the weird, spectral beauty of the scene, was the confused hum of voices that rose above the sea of forms, sounding like the subdued, sullen roar of an ocean storm, or the wind soughing through the dark lonely forest. It was a grand and imposing scene."[8] When Noah Brooks expressed surprise that the president had a manuscript from which to read, Lincoln explained: "It is true that I don't usually read a speech, but I am going to say something to-night that may be important, I am going to talk about reconstruction."[9] As the president spoke from a window of the White House, his wife and Clara Harris, daughter of New York senator Ira Harris, stood at a nearby window chatting so loudly that they nearly drowned out the president. Initially, the crowd tolerated that unbecoming behavior, but in time some people emphatically told the two women to quiet down. Disconcerted by that shushing, Lincoln feared that something he said had given offense. But he soon realized that no disrespect was meant and continued reading his speech.

Instead of delivering the expected triumphal paean to the conquering Union army and navy, he dwelt at length on the problems of reconstruction, explaining how he and General Banks had labored to make Louisiana a model for the other seceded states. Frankly acknowledging that some Radical criticism of their handiwork was valid, he dismissed as "a merely pernicious abstraction" the question whether the seceded states were in or out of the Union. Some Radicals insisted that by seceding, the Confederate states had reverted to the status of territories and could therefore be governed by Congress. Lincoln resisted that line of argument, asserting that he and the Radicals "agree that the seceded States, so called, are out of their proper practical relation with the Union; and that the sole object of the government, civil and military, in regard to those States is to again get them into that proper practical relation. I believe it is not only possible, but in fact, easier, to do this, without deciding, or even considering, whether these states have even been out of the Union, than with it. Finding themselves safely at home, it would be utterly immaterial whether they had ever been abroad. Let us all join in doing the acts necessary to restoring the proper practical relations between these states and the Union."

To strengthen this appeal for Republican unity, Lincoln offered the Radicals an important substantive concession. Hitherto he had expressed support for Black suffrage only in private; this evening, fatefully—and fatally—he made it public: "I would myself prefer that it were now conferred on the very intelligent, and on those who serve our cause as soldiers." Months later, Frederick Douglass stated that while Lincoln's call for Black suffrage "seemed to mean but little," because of its limited scope, it actually "meant a great deal. It was just like Abraham Lincoln. He never shocked prejudices unnecessarily. Having learned statesmanship while splitting rails, he always used the thin edge of the wedge first—and the fact that he used it at all meant that he would if need be, use the thick as well as the thin."[10] One member of Lincoln's audience did not underestimate the importance of his call for limited Black suffrage. Upon hearing the president's words, a handsome, popular, impulsive 26-year-old actor named John Wilkes Booth turned to a friend and declared: "That means nigger citizenship. Now by God I'll put him through!"[11] He added: "That is the last speech he will ever make."[12]

Clearly Lincoln was moving toward the Radical position. Now that the war was over, there was no need to entice Confederates into surrendering by offering them exceptionally lenient peace terms. His proclaimed support for limited Black suffrage was but one sign of his willingness to meet Radical critics halfway. In March, he had without reservation signed the Freedmen's Bureau Act, which established a federal agency—the Bureau of Refugees, Freedmen and Abandoned Lands—to protect the interests of former slaves as well as White refugees. No longer would freedpeople work under the supervision of provost marshals and treasury agents; the legislation even held out the promise, somewhat vaguely, of land redistribution. Lincoln's concern all along, according to chaplain John Eaton, "was to illustrate the capacity of these people for the privileges, duties and rights of freedom."[13]

Moreover, Lincoln suggested that he was willing to compromise on reconstruction policy. On April 10, he told Pierpont "that he had no plan for reorganization, but must be guided by events."[14] While he hoped that Congress would seat the Louisiana senators and congressmen, in his April 11 speech he conceded that conditions varied from state to state and that "no exclusive, and inflexible plan can safely be prescribed as to details and colatterals. Such exclusive, and inflexible plan, would surely become a new entanglement. Important principles may, and must, be inflexible." As for the Louisiana government, he said that although he had promised to sustain it, "bad promises are better broken than kept" and he would "treat this as a bad promise, and break it, whenever I shall be convinced that keeping it is adverse to the public interest." He closed with a tantalizing hint: "It may be my duty to make some new announcement to the people of the South. I am considering, and shall not fail to act, when satisfied that action will be proper."[15] It is not clear what Lincoln meant, but three days later at a cabinet meeting he "said he thought [he] had made a mistake at Richmond in sanctioning the assembling of the Virginia Legislature and had perhaps been too fast in his desires for early reconstruction." Commenting on that cabinet session, the pro-Radical James Speed remarked to Salmon P. Chase that the president "never seemed so near our views."[16] Despite his ill-advised decision to let the Virginia legislature reconvene, Lincoln shared the Radicals' desire to keep the old leadership class of the South from returning to power. In Louisiana he had worked to block reactionaries' attempts to gain positions of authority, and presumably he would do so in other states. As Frederick Douglass plausibly speculated in December 1865, if Lincoln had lived, "no rebels would hold the reins of Government in any one of the late rebellious states."[17]

Lincoln, however, was not disposed to back down on amnesty. According to Gideon Welles, he "dreaded and deprecated violent and revengeful feelings, or any malevolent demonstrations toward those of our countrymen who were involved, voluntarily or involuntarily in the rebellion."[18] When criticized for being too lenient, he asked, "How many more lives of our citizen soldiers are the people willing to give up to insure the death penalty to Davis and his immediate coadjutors?"[19] But what should be done with those Confederate leaders? He told Grant and Sherman that he hoped they would leave the country without his knowledge. And if Confederate leaders did not emigrate? Lincoln confided to Schuyler Colfax "that he did not want their blood, but that we could not have peace or order in the South while they remained there with their great influence to poison public opinion." To encourage them to flee, he suggested that military authorities "inform them that if they stay, they will be punished for their crimes, but if they leave, no attempt will be made to hinder them. Then we can be magnanimous to all the rest and have peace and quiet in the whole land."[20]

The subject of amnesty came up at a cabinet meeting on April 14. According to Welles, Lincoln expressed the hope that "there would be no persecution, no bloody work, after the war was over. None need expect he would take any part in hanging or killing those men, even the worst of them. Frighten them out of the country, open the gates, let down the bars, scare them off," he said, gesturing as if he were shooing sheep. "Enough lives have been sacrificed. We must extinguish our resentments if we expect harmony and union."[21] Stanton reported that Lincoln "spoke very kindly of General Lee and others of the Confederacy" and showed "in marked degree the kindness and humanity of his disposition, and the tender and forgiving spirit that so eminently distinguished him."[22]

At that cabinet meeting, with Grant in attendance, Lincoln stressed that reconstruction "was the great question now before us, and we must soon begin to act."[23] At his request, Stanton had drafted an executive order establishing temporary military rule in Virginia and North Carolina, restoring the authority of federal laws, to be enforced by provost marshals. It did not deal with the sensitive issue of Black suffrage, for as Stanton later explained, "he thought it would be impolitic to press that question then for there were differences among our friends on that point, and it would be better to go forward on the great essentials wherein we agreed."[24] When Stanton read this *projet* to his colleagues, Welles objected to the provision combining Virginia and North Carolina in a single military district. The navy secretary noted that the Pierpont regime had been recognized by the administration as the legitimate government of the Old Dominion during the struggle over West Virginia statehood. Lincoln "said the point was well taken" and "that the same thing had occurred to him and the plan required maturing and perfecting." Therefore he instructed Stanton "to take the document, separate it, adapt one plan to Virginia and her loyal government—another to North Carolina which was destitute of legal State authority and submit copies of each to each member of the Cabinet."[25] He added that the federal government "can't undertake to run State governments in all these Southern States. Their people must do that,—though I reckon at first some of them may do it badly."[26] Lincoln expressed relief that Congress had adjourned

Often misidentified as the last photograph taken of Lincoln before his death, this Alexander Gardner portrait dates from February 5, 1865, a month before the final photograph of the president. In the developing process, the negative broke. Gardner simply placed the two pieces back together, made one print, and disposed of the negative. Abraham Lincoln Presidential Library and Museum, Springfield, Illinois.

until December. For several months, no more filibusters led by obstructionists like Charles Sumner, in league with Border State conservatives, could thwart the will of a congressional majority.

Regarding military matters, Lincoln predicted the imminent arrival of important news from Sherman, for the previous night he had experienced what he called "the usual dream which he had preceding nearly every great and important event of the war. Generally the news had been favorable that preceded this dream, and the dream itself was always the same." He explained that "he seemed to be in some singular, indescribable vessel, and that he was moving with great rapidity towards an indefinite shore; that he had this dream preceding Sumter, Bull Run, Antietam, Gettysburg, Stones River, Vicksburg, Wilmington, etc." Grant interrupted, observing that "Stones River was certainly no victory, and he knew of no great results which followed from it." Lincoln replied that "however that might be, his dream preceded that fight." He continued: "I had this strange dream again last night, and we shall, judging from the past, have great news very soon." It "must be from Sherman," he speculated, for "my thoughts have been in that direction, and I know of no other very important event which is likely just now to occur."[27]

The cabinet found Lincoln in exceptionally good spirits. Stanton remarked: "That's the most satisfactory Cabinet meeting I have attended in many a long day." He asked a colleague, "Didn't our chief look grand today?"[28] Similarly, the First Lady reported that her husband was "supremely cheerful" and that during their afternoon carriage ride his "manner was even playful." She had remarked to him, laughingly, "You almost startle me by your great cheerfulness." He had responded, "And well I may feel so, Mary; for I consider this day the war has come to a close. We must both be more cheerful in the future. Between the war and the loss of our darling Willie we have been very miserable."[29]

The previous evening, Lincoln had been too sick with a headache to take a carriage ride with his wife, who wished to see the brilliant illuminations celebrating Lee's surrender. Grant, at Lincoln's request, had agreed to accompany her. As she and the general entered their carriage, the crowd outside the White House had shouted "Grant!" Taking offense, she instructed the driver to let her out, but she changed her mind when the crowd also cheered for the president. This happened again and again as the carriage proceeded around town. The First Lady evidently thought it inappropriate that the general should be cheered before her husband was so honored. The next day, Grant declined the president's invitation to join him and the First Lady to attend a performance of *Our American Cousin*, for he feared incurring her displeasure again. Moreover, Mrs. Julia Grant informed her husband that she did not wish to be around the First Lady after the unpleasantness at City Point three weeks earlier.

After learning that the Grants would not attend the performance at Ford's Theatre, Lincoln felt inclined to follow suit, but the First Lady insisted that they go. The press had announced that he and the general would be in attendance, and the audience would be terribly disappointed if neither man showed up. The president had no adequate security detail. This was not unusual, for at his request bodyguards did not accompany him to theatrical performances. John F. Parker, one of four Metropolitan Police patrolmen who had been detailed to the Interior Department to protect the White House and its furnishings, not its occupants, was part of the entourage that night, as was Charles Forbes, a White House messenger. Neither of them was a true bodyguard, nor were they asked to protect Lincoln. The man who had been performing that duty zealously, Ward Hill Lamon, was in Richmond on a presidential mission. When John Wilkes Booth made his fatal way to the presidential box, Parker was either at an adjacent tavern or watching the play, which Lincoln may have urged him to do. The president was notoriously indifferent about his safety, even though he had received many death threats. In 1863, he told Noah Brooks: "I long ago made up my mind that if anybody wants to kill me, he will do it. If I wore a shirt of mail and kept myself surrounded by a bodyguard, it would be all the same. There are a thousand ways of getting at a man if it is desirable that he should be killed." He thought it impossible to obtain foolproof protection. To well-wishers concerned about assassins he commented that "I should have to lock myself up in a box" and that he simply could not "be shut up in an iron cage and guarded."[30]

Lincoln's insouciance about assassination was widely shared. With the exception of a crazed Briton who had pulled the triggers of two guns in a miraculously unsuccessful attempt to kill Andrew Jackson, no leading American public official had been the target of a murderer. Starting in 1862, Lincoln did have military escorts when he rode to and from the Soldiers' Home during the warmer months. At first he protested, saying half in jest that he and his wife could barely hear themselves talk "for the clatter of their sabres and spurs" and that he was "more afraid of being shot by the accidental discharge of one of their carbines or revolvers than of any attempt upon his life."[31] One August night in 1864, however, while Lincoln was riding alone from the White House back to the Soldiers' Home, a would-be assassin shot his hat off. Thereafter security precautions grew more stringent. Lamon started to sleep at the White House, where John Hay observed him one November night as he slumbered before the door to the president's bedroom in an "attitude of touching and dumb fidelity, with a small arsenal of pistols and Bowie knives around him."[32]

In the midafternoon, the Lincolns visited the Navy Yard and toured the monitor *Montauk*. The ship's doctor reported that they "seemed *very* happy—and so expressed themselves."[33] Later that afternoon, Illinois governor Richard J. Oglesby called at the White House with his state's adjutant general, Isham Nicholas Haynie of Springfield. Delighted to see old friends, the president chatted with them for a while, then read aloud from the latest book by humorist David Ross Locke. Ignoring repeated summonses to dinner, Lincoln continued to read, laughing and commenting as he went along.

After supper, the president met with Speaker of the House Schuyler Colfax. Earlier in the day, when that Indiana congressman had mentioned that he was about to visit California, the president said he wished that he could go too. Colfax told Lincoln that many people had feared for his safety while he was visiting the Virginia capital. He replied: "Why, if any one else had been President, and had gone to Richmond, I would have been alarmed too; but I was not scared about myself a bit."[34]

Around 8:30, as Lincoln prepared to leave the White House, he asked his elder son if he would like to come along. Robert declined, citing fatigue. So his parents climbed into their carriage and proceeded to pick up Major Henry R. Rathbone and his stepsister/fiancée, Clara Harris. (When the Grants announced that they could not join the presidential party, Mrs. Lincoln had invited the young couple to take their place.) The party reached Ford's Theatre about half an hour after the curtain had risen on Tom Taylor's light comedy, *Our American Cousin*. As they entered, the orchestra struck up "Hail to the Chief," and the audience rose to greet them with vociferous applause, which Lincoln acknowledged with a smile and bow.

John Wilkes Booth had spent the day plotting to assassinate Lincoln, Vice President Johnson, and Secretary of State Seward. The previous autumn Booth had begun hatching a scheme to kidnap the president, spirit him off to Richmond, and exchange him for Confederate prisoners of war. That enterprise had fizzled in mid-March, when the conspirators planned to intercept Lincoln on his way to a hospital. With the failure of the capture plot, some of the conspirators quit Booth's team.

Soon thereafter, when Lincoln toured Richmond, Booth was indignant. According to his sister, the president's "triumphant entry into the fallen city (which was not magnanimous), breathed fresh air upon the fire which consumed him."[35] Depressed, he began drinking more heavily than usual, consuming as much as a quart of brandy in less than two hours. When a friend offered him a drink, he said: "Yes, anything to drive away the blues."[36]

Booth was even more disconsolate at the news of Lee's surrender on April 9, for he had come to feel guilty about his failure to strike a blow for the Confederacy. When he expressed to Henry Clay Ford, treasurer of Ford's Theatre, disappointment that Lee had surrendered after having promised never to do so, Ford pointedly asked what he had done compared with Lee. Defensively he replied that he was as brave as the general. "Well," Ford sneered, "you have not got three stars yet to show it."[37] With the war virtually over, what could he do to redeem himself in his own eyes? Killing Lincoln might salve his troubled conscience. On April 14 (Good Friday), when he heard that Grant and the president would attend Ford's Theatre that night, he impulsively decided to kill Lincoln. Earlier he had mentioned the possibility of murdering the president, but not to his colleagues in the capture plot. At the inauguration six weeks earlier, he had tried to break through the line of guards protecting Lincoln.

Summoning the remnants of the kidnapping team (David Herold, George Atzerodt, and Lewis Powell), Booth assigned them various tasks: Powell was to kill Seward, Atzerodt was to kill Andrew Johnson, and Herold was to help Booth escape after he shot Lincoln. The murder of Johnson and Seward would heighten the effect of the presidential assassination, throwing the government into chaos.

Once in their box, the Lincolns and their guests sat back to enjoy the show. Around 10:30, as Booth made his way toward them, he encountered Charles Forbes outside the box and gained admission after showing him a card. Once in the anteroom, Booth barred the door behind him with an improvised jam. Through a tiny peephole he could see the president. Waiting until there was but a single actor on stage, he opened the inner door, stepped quickly toward the president's rocking chair, and shot him in the back of the head at point-blank range. Rathbone struggled with the assassin, who slashed the major's arm badly with a long dagger, then leaped to the stage. Upon landing he shouted, "Sic semper tyrannis" (Thus always to tyrants), the Virginia state motto. Striding across the stage, he escaped via the back door, mounted a horse, and rode toward southern Maryland, following the route he had earlier established as part of the kidnapping scheme.

Booth's motives are not entirely clear, but he was an avid White supremacist whose racist rage formed an important part of his psyche. Infuriated by the proposal that Blacks would become citizen-voters, he decided to act. Thus Lincoln was a martyr to Black civil rights, as much as Martin Luther King, who fell victim to racist violence a century later.

In Booth's view, Lincoln was also a tyrant like Caesar. "When Caesar had conquered the enemies of Rome and with the power that was his menaced the liberties of the people, Brutus arose and slew him," Booth wrote as he planned to assassinate Lincoln.[38] To kill the president would be to help the Confederacy as it was dying. It might also allow Booth to achieve lasting renown. In 1864 he declared, "What a glorious opportunity there is for a man to immortalize himself by killing Lincoln."[39] A week before the assassination, he remarked to a friend: "What an excellent chance I had to kill the President, if I had wished, on inauguration day!" When asked what good that would have done, he replied, "I could live in history."[40]

The evening he murdered Lincoln, Booth ominously said, "When I leave the stage for good, I will be the most famous man in America."[41]

The instant Lincoln was shot he lost consciousness, never to regain it in the remaining nine hours of his life. Amid the pandemonium in Ford's Theatre, three doctors made their way to the presidential box, removed Lincoln from his rocker, placed him on the floor, and inspected his body for wounds. Meanwhile, guards cleared the theater. Discovering the hole in the back of his head, which they realized was fatal, the physicians feared that he could not survive a trip back to the White House. So they had him carried across the street to the boardinghouse of William Petersen, where he was laid diagonally on a bed too short to accommodate his long body.

Once Mrs. Lincoln recovered from fainting, she crossed the street to the Petersen house, escorted by Clara Harris and the bleeding Major Rathbone. Upon entering, she frantically exclaimed, "Where is my husband? Where is my husband?" as she wrung her hands in extreme anguish. Upon reaching his bedside, she repeatedly kissed his head, which was slowly oozing blood and brain tissue. "How can it be so?" she asked. "Do speak to me!"[42] When he failed to respond, she suggested that Tad be sent for, saying "she knew he would speak to him because he loved him so well."[43] With his tutor, the boy had been attending a performance of *Aladdin* at nearby Grover's Theatre. But she had second thoughts about summoning him to the Petersen house. "O, my poor 'Taddy,'" she asked plaintively, "what *will* become of him? O do not send for him, his violent grief would disturb the House."[44]

Tad in fact had heard the dreadful news when the management of Grover's Theatre announced it to the audience. The boy became hysterical and was taken to the White House, where he burst out to the guard Thomas Pendel, "O Tom Pen! Tom Pen! they have killed papa dead! They've killed papa dead!"[45] Pendel informed Tad's brother Robert, who had been socializing with John Hay. They immediately rushed to the theater on Tenth Street, accompanied by Senator Sumner, who had come to the Executive Mansion under the impression that the president had been taken there.

At the Petersen house, Robert spoke briefly to his mother, then entered his father's room and took a position at the head of the bed, crying audibly. Soon he composed himself, but on two later occasions he sobbed aloud and leaned his head on Sumner's shoulder. He had the presence of mind to ask that his mother's good friend Elizabeth Dixon, wife of Connecticut senator James Dixon, be notified. She came quickly to help comfort the distraught First Lady. Andrew Johnson called but abruptly left when Stanton, who knew that Mrs. Lincoln disliked the vice president, advised him that his presence was unnecessary.

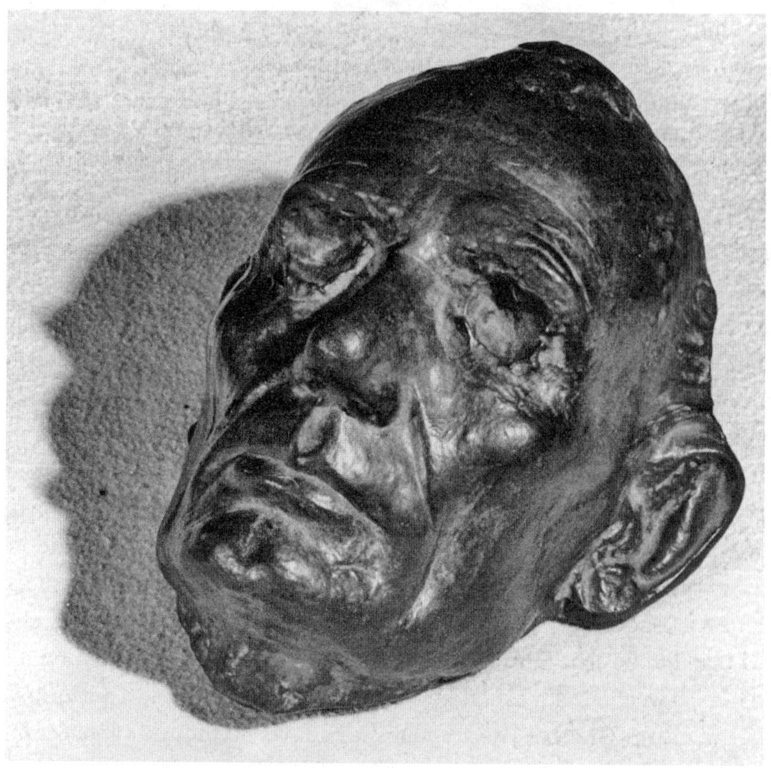

Lincoln's two life masks provide a remarkable study in contrasts. The first, which the sculptor Leonard Volk created in 1860, so impressed Lincoln that when he first saw it he declared: "There is the animal himself." According to the sculptor Avard T. Fairbanks, "Virtually every sculptor and artist uses the Volk mask for Lincoln. . . . It is the most reliable document of the Lincoln face, and far more valuable than photographs, for it is the actual form." Abraham Lincoln Presidential Library and Museum, Springfield, Illinois.

As the room in the Petersen house filled with cabinet members, doctors, generals, and others, Mary Lincoln occupied the front parlor, attended by some friends, including the family minister, Phineas T. Gurley, pastor of the New York Avenue Presbyterian Church. Clara Harris, whose dress was soaked with the blood of her fiancé, reported that "Mrs. Lincoln all through that dreadful night would look at me with horror & scream, oh! my husband's blood, my dear husband's blood!" In hysterics, she repeatedly asked, "Why didn't he shoot me?"[46] She made frequent visits to the bedroom. On one occasion she was so taken aback by Lincoln's distorted features that she passed out. Coming to, she pleaded with her dying spouse: "Love, live but for one moment to speak to me once, to speak to our children!"[47]

Clark Mills made this life mask in January 1865. Commenting on the difference between this one and the one made by Volk five years earlier, Lincoln's secretary John Hay wrote: "Under this frightful ordeal his demeanor and disposition changed, so gradually that it would be impossible to say when the change began; but he was in mind, body, and nerves a very different man at the second inauguration from the one who had taken the oath in 1861. He continued always the same kindly, genial, and cordial spirit he had been at first; but the boisterous laughter became less frequent year by year; the eye grew veiled by constant meditation on momentous subjects; the air of reserve and detachment from his surroundings increased. He aged with great rapidity." Library of Congress.

Around 7:00 a.m., as she sat by the bedside, her husband's breathing grew so stertorous that she jumped up shrieking, then fell to the floor. Hearing her, Stanton, who had in effect taken charge of the government, entered from an adjoining room and loudly snapped: "Take that woman out and do not let her in again."[48] As Mrs. Dixon helped her return to the front parlor, she moaned: "Oh, my God, and have I given my husband to die?" An observer remarked that he "never heard so much agony in so few words."[49] Lincoln's fitful breathing reminded Stanton of "an aeolian harp, now rising, now falling and almost dying away, and then reviving."[50]

At 7:22 a.m., the president finally stopped breathing. "Now he belongs to the ages," Stanton said tearfully.[51]

Lincoln was mourned as the savior of the Union, the liberator of the slaves, and the vindicator of democracy. In a eulogy delivered on June 1, 1865, Frederick Douglass would tell a large audience at Manhattan's Cooper Union that Lincoln was "in a sense hitherto without example, emphatically the black man's President: the first to show any respect for their rights as men." Although Douglass had been highly critical of Lincoln at various points during the war, he now eloquently concluded, "He was the first American President who . . . rose above the prejudice of his times, and country."[52]

Leo Tolstoy's tribute, given during an interview in 1909, provides moving testimony to the universality of Lincoln's fame. The Russian novelist admired the president's "peculiar moral power" and "the greatness of his character." Lincoln, he said, "was what Beethoven was in music, Dante in poetry, Raphael in painting, and Christ in the philosophy of life." No political leader matched Lincoln, in Tolstoy's judgment: "Of all the great national heroes and statesmen of history Lincoln is the only real giant. Alexander, Frederick the Great, Caesar, Napoleon, Gladstone and even Washington stand in greatness of character, in depth of feeling and in a certain moral power far behind Lincoln. Lincoln was a man of whom a nation has a right to be proud; he was a Christ in miniature, a saint of humanity, whose name will live thousands of years in the legends of future generations. We are still too near to his greatness, and so can hardly appreciate his divine power; but after a few centuries more our posterity will find him considerably bigger than we do. His genius is still too strong and too powerful for the common understanding, just as the sun is too hot when its light beams directly on us." Lincoln "lived and died a hero, and as a great character he will live as long as the world lives. May his life long bless humanity!"[53]

Lincoln speaks to us not only as a champion of freedom, democracy, and national unity but also as a source of inspiration. Few will achieve his world historical importance, but many can profit from his personal example, encouraged by the knowledge that despite a childhood of emotional malnutrition and grinding poverty, despite a lack of formal education, despite a series of career failures, despite a woe-filled marriage, despite a tendency to depression, despite a painful midlife crisis, despite the early death of his mother and his siblings as well as of his sweetheart and two of his four children, he became a model of psychological maturity, moral clarity, and unimpeachable integrity. His presence and his leadership inspired his contemporaries; his life story can do the same for generations to come.

Abbreviations

ALPL—Abraham Lincoln Presidential Library, Springfield

ALQ—Abraham Lincoln Quarterly

ALS—At Lincoln's Side: John Hay's Civil War Correspondence and Selected Writings, ed. Michael Burlingame (Carbondale: Southern Illinois University Press, 2000)

Barton MSS—William E. Barton Papers, University of Chicago

Bates Diary—The Diary of Edward Bates, 1859–1866, ed. Howard K. Beale (Annual Report of the American Historical Association for 1930, vol. 4; Washington, D.C.: U.S. Government Printing Office, 1933)

Beveridge MSS—Albert J. Beveridge Papers, Library of Congress

Brooks, *Lincoln and the Downfall of Slavery*—Noah Brooks, *Abraham Lincoln and the Downfall of American Slavery* (New York: G. P. Putnam's Sons, 1894)

Brooks, *Washington, D.C., in Lincoln's Time*—Noah Brooks, *Washington, D.C., in Lincoln's Time*, ed. Herbert Mitgang (1958; reprint with a new introduction, Chicago: Quadrangle Books, 1971)

Browne, *Every-Day Life of Lincoln*—Francis Fischer Browne, *The Every-Day Life of Abraham Lincoln* (Chicago: Browne & Howell, 1913)

Browning Diary—The Diary of Orville Hickman Browning, ed. Theodore Calvin Pease and James G. Randall (2 vols.; Springfield: Illinois State Historical Library, 1925–33)

Carpenter, *Six Months*—F. B. Carpenter, *Six Months at the White House with Abraham Lincoln* (New York: Hurd & Houghton, 1866)

CG—Congressional Globe

Chase Diary—The Salmon P. Chase Papers, ed. John Niven, vol. 1, *Journals, 1829–1872* (Kent, Ohio: Kent State University Press, 1993)

ChiTrib—Chicago *Tribune*

CHM—Chicago History Museum

Complete Hay Diary—Inside Lincoln's White House: The Complete Civil War Diary of John Hay, ed. Michael Burlingame and John R. Turner Ettlinger (Carbondale: Southern Illinois University Press, 1997)

CWL—The Collected Works of Abraham Lincoln, ed. Roy P. Basler, Marion Delores Pratt, and Lloyd A. Dunlap (8 vols. plus index; New Brunswick, N.J.: Rutgers University Press, 1953–55)

CWL, [First] Supplement—The Collected Works of Abraham Lincoln: Supplement, 1832–1865, ed. Roy P. Basler (Contributions in American Studies, no. 7; Westport, Conn.: Greenwood Press, 1974)

CWL, Second Supplement—*The Collected Works of Abraham Lincoln: Second Supplement, 1832–1865*, ed. Roy P. Basler and Christian Basler (New Brunswick, N.J.: Rutgers University Press, 1990)

Grant Papers—*The Papers of Ulysses S. Grant*, ed. John Y. Simon (32 vols.; Carbondale: Southern Illinois University Press, 1967–2012)

HI—*Herndon's Informants: Letters, Interviews, and Statements about Abraham Lincoln*, ed. Douglas L. Wilson and Rodney O. Davis (Urbana: University of Illinois Press for the Knox College Lincoln Studies Center, 1998)

HOLL—*Herndon on Lincoln, Letters*, ed. Douglas L. Wilson and Rodney O. Davis (Urbana: University of Illinois Press for the Knox College Lincoln Studies Center, 2016)

HWP—Herndon-Weik Papers, Library of Congress

ISJ—*Illinois State Journal* (Springfield)

ISR—*Illinois State Register* (Springfield)

IWAL—Michael Burlingame, *The Inner World of Abraham Lincoln* (Urbana: University of Illinois Press, 1994)

IWHWT—William O. Stoddard, *Inside the White House in War Times: Memoirs and Reports of Lincoln's Secretary*, ed. Michael Burlingame (1880; Lincoln: University of Nebraska Press, 2000)

JISHS—*Journal of the Illinois State Historical Society*

Keckley, *Behind the Scenes*—Elizabeth Keckley, *Behind the Scenes; or, Thirty Years a Slave and Four Years in the White House* (New York: G. W. Carleton, 1868)

LC—Library of Congress

LFFC—Lincoln Financial Foundation Collection, Allen County Public Library, Fort Wayne, Indiana

LJ—*Lincoln's Journalist: John Hay's Anonymous Writings for the Press, 1860–1864*, ed. Michael Burlingame (Carbondale: Southern Illinois University Press, 1998)

LO—*Lincoln Observed: Civil War Dispatches of Noah Brooks*, ed. Michael Burlingame (Baltimore: Johns Hopkins University Press, 1998)

LOC—Henry C. Whitney, *Life on the Circuit with Lincoln*, ed. Paul M. Angle (1892; reprint, Caldwell, Idaho: Caxton Printers, 1940)

LP-LC—Abraham Lincoln Papers, Library of Congress

LTC—Henry C. Whitney, *Lincoln the Citizen*, vol. 1 of Whitney, *A Life of Lincoln*, ed. Marion Mills Miller (2 vols.; New York: Baker & Taylor, 1908)

MaHS—Massachusetts Historical Society, Boston

Mary Lincoln Letters—*Mary Todd Lincoln: Her Life and Letters*, ed. Justin G. Turner and Linda Levitt Turner (New York: Knopf, 1972)

McClellan Papers—*The Civil War Papers of George B. McClellan*, ed. Stephen W. Sears (New York: Ticknor & Fields, 1989)

Nicolay and Hay, *Lincoln*—John G. Nicolay and John Hay, *Abraham Lincoln: A History* (10 vols.; New York: Century, 1890)

NYPL—New York Public Library
NYT—New York *Times*

OHAL—*An Oral History of Abraham Lincoln: John G. Nicolay's Interviews and Essays*, ed. Michael Burlingame (Carbondale: Southern Illinois University Press, 1996)
OR—*The War of the Rebellion: A Compilation of the Official Records of the Union and Confederate Armies* (128 vols.; Washington, D.C.: Government Printing Office, 1880–1901)

RAL—Allen Thorndike Rice, ed., *Reminiscences of Abraham Lincoln by Distinguished Men of His Time* (New York: North American Review, 1886)
RLAP—Jesse W. Weik, *The Real Lincoln: A Portrait*, ed. Michael Burlingame (Lincoln: University of Nebraska Press, 2002)
RW—*Recollected Words of Abraham Lincoln*, comp. and ed. Don E. Fehrenbacher and Virginia Fehrenbacher (Stanford: Stanford University Press, 1996)

Schurz, *Reminiscences*—*The Reminiscences of Carl Schurz* (3 vols.; New York: McClure, 1907–8)
Seward at Washington—Frederick W. Seward, *Seward at Washington as Senator and Secretary of State* (2 vols.; New York: Derby & Miller, 1891)
SJ—*Sangamo Journal*
SMDR—Springfield, Massachusetts, *Daily Republican*
Stevens, *Reporter's Lincoln*—Walter B. Stevens, *A Reporter's Lincoln*, ed. Michael Burlingame (Lincoln: University of Nebraska Press, 1998)

Tarbell, *Life of Lincoln*—Ida M. Tarbell, *The Life of Abraham Lincoln* (2 vols.; New York: McClure, Phillips, 1900)
Tarbell MSS—Ida M. Tarbell Collection of Lincolniana, Allegheny College, Meadville, Pennsylvania

UMi—William L. Clements Library, University of Michigan

Villard Dispatches—*Sixteenth President-In-Waiting: Abraham Lincoln and the Springfield Dispatches of Henry Villard, 1860–1861*, ed. Michael Burlingame (Carbondale: Southern Illinois University Press, 2018)

Welles, *Selected Essays*—Gideon Welles, *Selected Essays*, ed. Albert Mordell (New York: Twayne, 1959)
Welles Diary—*Diary of Gideon Welles, Secretary of the Navy under Lincoln and Johnson*, ed. Howard K. Beale and Alan W. Brownsword (3 vols.; New York: W. W. Norton, 1960)
WLWH—*With Lincoln in the White House: Letters, Memoranda, and Other Writings of John G. Nicolay, 1860–1865*, ed. Michael Burlingame (Carbondale: Southern Illinois University Press, 2000)

Notes

Chapter 1. "I Have Seen a Good Deal of the Back Side of This World"

1. *CWL*, 6:538.
2. *CWL*, 2:217.
3. *HOLL*, 100.
4. William H. Herndon, "Nancy Hanks," HWP.
5. Otis M. Mather, "Thomas Lincoln in Larue County, Kentucky," Otis M. Mather MSS, Filson Historical Society, Louisville.
6. *HI*, 67; Harvey H. Smith, *Lincoln and the Lincolns* (New York: Pioneer Publications, 1931), 168; Stevens, *Reporter's Lincoln*, 167; Janesville, Illinois, correspondence, 30 May 1880, Chicago *Chronicle*, n.d., copied in *La Porte (Ind.) Weekly Herald*, 27[?] October 1921, clipping, LFFC; George B. Balch, "The Father of Abraham Lincoln," manuscript pasted into a copy of Browne, *Every-Day Life of Lincoln*, Lilly Library, Indiana University, Bloomington.
7. Balch, "Father of Lincoln."
8. *HI*, 145; Chicago *Inter-Ocean*, 30 April 1881.
9. Eleanor Gridley, *The Story of Abraham Lincoln* (Chicago: M. A. Donohue, 1900), 62.
10. A. R. Simmons to William E. Barton, 7 March 1923, Barton MSS.
11. Ordway, Colorado, *New Era*, 9 February 1917.
12. *HI*, 240; Terre Haute, Indiana, *Star*, 11 February 1923; "Abraham Lincoln's Boyhood," anonymous manuscript, Francis Marion Van Natter MSS, Vincennes University; Louisville *Courier Journal*, n.d. [ca. 1886], clipping, Lincoln Scrapbook, Rare Book Room, LC.
13. *HI*, 37, 97.
14. *NYT*, 10 November 1860.
15. *HOLL*, 229.
16. Gridley, *Story of Lincoln*, 48, 45.
17. *HI*, 39.
18. Ida Tarbell to John S. Phillips, Louisville, Kentucky, 23 October 1922, Tarbell MSS.
19. *HI*, 113.
20. *CWL*, 4:65.
21. *ChiTrib*, 30 May 1885; *HI*, 176.
22. *HI*, 134.
23. *CWL*, 2:97.
24. Usher F. Linder, *Reminiscences of the Early Bench and Bar of Illinois* (Chicago: Chicago Legal News, 1879), 38.
25. *HOLL*, 84.
26. *HI*, 39; St. Louis *Post-Dispatch*, 26 May 1901.
27. Ward Hill Lamon, *The Life of Abraham Lincoln: From His Birth to His Inauguration as President* (Boston: J. R. Osgood, 1872), 40n.
28. "Notes on Arthur E. Morgan's first trip—Jasper [Arkansas, February 1909]," Arthur E. Morgan MSS, LC.
29. Dr. James LeGrande, undated questionnaire filled out for Arthur E. Morgan, Morgan MSS, LC.
30. *HI*, 48, 41.
31. *LTC*, 75; Browne, *Every-Day Life of Lincoln*, 88.
32. *HI*, 615, 598,113, 111, 97, 5, 84, 67, 403, 454, 113; Smith, *Lincoln and the Lincolns*, 11–12.

33. J. Edward Murr, "Some Pertinent Observations concerning '*Abe Lincoln—The Hoosier*,'" 5, Murr MSS, DePauw University, Greencastle, Indiana.

34. *HOLL*, 83; William H. Herndon to James W. Wartman, Springfield, 19 February 1870, copy, Southwestern Indiana Historical Society MSS, Evansville Central Library.

35. *HI*, 37.

36. *HI*, 113.

37. *HI*, 40.

38. *Indiana Herald* (Huntington), 18 March 1874; Murr, "Pertinent Observations," 5.

39. Smith, *Lincoln and the Lincolns*, 151; *HOLL*, 280.

40. Smith, *Lincoln and the Lincolns*, 76.

41. J. Edward Murr to Albert J. Beveridge, [New Albany, Indiana, 21 November 1924], Beveridge MSS, LC.

42. *HI*, 82, 86.

43. *HOLL*, 62.

44. *HOLL*, 204.

45. Ida N. Pendleton to Tarbell, Hartford, Kentucky, 17 June 1896, Tarbell MSS.

46. Smith, *Lincoln and the Lincolns*, 219, 71.

47. *HOLL*, 84; Herndon, "Nancy Hanks."

48. Herndon told this to Caroline Dall in 1866. Caroline Dall, "Journal of a tour through Illinois, Wisconsin and Ohio, Oct. & Nov. 1866," entry for 29 October 1866, Dall MSS, Bryn Mawr College.

49. *HOLL*, 62, 84.

50. *HI*, 122.

51. *HOLL*, 100.

52. *HOLL*, 68.

53. Quoted in William E. Wilson, "There I Grew Up," *American Heritage* 17 (October 1966): 102.

54. Smith, *Lincoln and the Lincolns*, 170–71.

55. *HI*, 57.

56. *RAL*, 457.

57. *CWL*, 1:384.

58. Browne, *Every-Day Life of Lincoln*, 322–23.

59. *HI*, 240; Washington, D.C., *Sunday Chronicle*, 23 April 1865.

60. Maude Jennings Cryderman to Mrs. Calder Ehrmann, 4 March 1928, John E. Iglehart MSS, Indiana Historical Society, Indianapolis.

61. Joseph D. Armstrong, "History of Spencer County," in *An Illustrated Historical Atlas of Spencer County, Indiana* (Philadelphia: D. J. Lake, 1879), 13.

62. *HI*, 185.

63. Noyes M. Miner, "Personal Reminiscences of Lincoln," MS, ALPL.

64. Thomas D. Clark, *The Kentucky Influence on the Life of Abraham Lincoln* (address at annual meeting of the Lincoln Fellowship of Wisconsin, Madison, 13 February 1961; Lincoln Fellowship Historical Bulletin No. 20, 1962), 4.

65. J. J. Wright to Tarbell, Emporia, Kansas, 18 April 1896, Tarbell MSS.

66. *HI*, 454, 241.

67. *LOC*, 36–37.

68. *LOC*, 22; Joseph H. Barrett, *The Life of Abraham Lincoln* (Cincinnati: Moore, Wilstach, Keys, 1860), 19.

69. *HI*, 67.

70. *CWL*, 3:511.

71. Barton to Robert Todd Lincoln, 15 March 1919, copy, Barton MSS.

72. John Locke Scripps, *Life of Abraham Lincoln*, ed. Roy P. Basler and Lloyd A. Dunlap (Bloomington: Indiana University Press, 1961), 37–38.

73. William Makepeace Thayer, *The Pioneer Boy and How He Became President* (Boston: Walker, Wise, 1863), 78–79.

74. *CWL*, 4:61–62.

75. *HI*, 36.

76. *HI*, 103–4.

77. New York *Herald*, 4 December 1860.

78. *HI*, 106.

Chapter 2. "I Used to Be a Slave"

1. J. Edward Murr, "The Wilderness Years of Abraham Lincoln," 125–26, MS, Murr MSS, DePauw University, Greencastle, Indiana.

2. *CWL*, 3:511, 4:62.

3. Murr, "Wilderness Years of Lincoln," 217.

4. *CWL*, 4:62.

5. *HI*, 40.

6. *CWL*, 6:16–17.

7. *RLAP*, 293.

8. Milton Lomask, *The Biographer's Craft* (New York: Harper & Row, 1986), 98.

9. Felix Brown, "Depression and Childhood Bereavement," *Journal of Mental Science* 107 (1962): 770.

10. Lerna, Illinois, *Eagle*, 27 February 1931.

11. Lerna, Illinois, *Eagle*, 27 February 1931; Paris, Illinois, *News*, 14 February 1922.

12. *HI*, 82.

13. *HOLL*, 203.

14. *HI*, 106, 41, 99.

15. *HI*, 108, 99.

16. *HI*, 108.

17. *HI*, 99, 136–37; *HOLL*, 66.

18. Bloomington, Illinois, *Pantagraph*, 17 December 1867.

19. *HI*, 137; *LOC*, 46; *LTC*, 37.

20. *HI*, 176.

21. *CWL*, 2:459.

22. *CWL*, 3:511.

23. *CWL*, 1:1.

24. *HOLL*, 157–58.

25. Henry J. Raymond, *The Life and Public Services of Abraham Lincoln* (New York: Derby & Miller, 1865), 21; Chauncey Hobart, *Recollections of My Life: Fifty Years of Itinerancy in the Northwest* (Red Wing, Minn.: Red Wing Printing, 1885), 71.

26. Grand Forks, North Dakota, *Daily Herald*, 1 November 1891.

27. *HI*, 109.

28. Benjamin Brown French to Mrs. Catherine J. Wells, 3 June 1862, French Family MSS, LC; Stevens, *Reporter's Lincoln*, 96; "Robert Livingston Stanton's Lincoln," ed. Dwight L. Smith, *Lincoln Herald* 76 (1974): 174; *HI*, 589.

29. *HI*, 25.

30. *HI*, 107, 104, 455, 79.

31. *HI*, 126, 151; *ISJ*, 22 June 1860.

32. *CWL*, 3:362–63.

33. John Locke Scripps, *Life of Abraham Lincoln*, ed. Roy P. Basler and Lloyd A. Dunlap (Bloomington: Indiana University Press, 1961), 29, 30–31.

34. *HI*, 7.

35. *RLAP*, 22.

36. *HI*, 107.

37. New York *Independent*, 1 September 1864; John P. Gulliver to Lincoln, 26 August 1864, LP-LC.

38. Joseph Nicholas Barker, "What I Remember of Abraham Lincoln," undated manuscript, Lincoln Collection, CHM.

39. John Langdon Kaine, "Lincoln as a Boy Knew Him," *Century Magazine*, February 1913, 557; *CWL*, 7:542.

40. Joshua F. Speed, *Reminiscences of Abraham Lincoln and Notes of a Visit to California. Two Lectures* (Louisville, Ky.: J. P. Morton, 1884), 32–33.

41. Noah Brooks, "Personal Recollections of Abraham Lincoln," *Harper's New Monthly Magazine*, XXXI (July 1865), 229.

42. *HI*, 106; *ChiTrib*, 30 May 1885.

43. *HI*, 107.

44. *HOLL*, 238.

45. Leonard W. Volk, "The Lincoln Life-Mask and How It Was Made," *Century Magazine* 23 (1881): 226.

46. *HI*, 108.

47. Clara Stillwell, "A Few Lincoln-in-Indiana Stories," typescript, 3, Lincoln MSS, Indiana University, Bloomington.

48. J. Edward Murr, "Lincoln in Indiana," *Indiana Magazine of History* 14 (1918): 57; Murr to Albert J. Beveridge, [21 November 1924], Beveridge MSS, LC.

49. Eli Grigsby, interview by Francis Marion Van Natter, 12 December 1935, Van Natter MSS, Vincennes University.

50. *HI*, 131.

51. Helena, Montana, *Independent*, 29 July 1891; Los Angeles *Times*, 12 February 1929.

52. Chicago *Times-Herald*, 25 August 1895.

53. *RAL*, 279–80.

54. E. Grant Gentry, recalling what his grandmother, Anna Caroline Roby Gentry, wife of Allen Gentry, had told him, in interviews by Francis Marion Van Natter, 21 January and 10 February 1936, and in an affidavit dated Rockport, 5 September 1936; Gentry's sisters Anna, Hannah, and Rose, interview by Van Natter, Rockport, 21 January 1936, Van Natter MSS, Vincennes University.

55. *HI*, 124.

56. *HI*, 56.

57. Francis Marion Van Natter, *Lincoln's Boyhood: A Chronicle of His Indiana Years* (Washington, D.C.: Public Affairs Press, 1963), 36; *HI*, 118.

58. Indianapolis *Star*, 11 February 1940.

59. Evansville (Ind.) *Journal*, 1 October 1902; Chicago *Times-Herald*, 22 December 1895.

60. *LTC*, 36, 56.

61. *HI*, 119–20, 645.

62. *HI*, 114.

63. *HI*, 127, 152, 118.

64. *HI*, 130, 114, 345.

65. Stillwell, "A Few Lincoln-in-Indiana Stories," 4–5.

66. *LTC*, 43, 47.

67. *RLAP*, 382.

68. *HI*, 112, 123.

69. *HI*, 147.

70. *HI*, 39.

71. George Close, interview by James Q. Howard, [May 1860], LP-LC.

72. *LTC*, manuscript version, 86, Lincoln Memorial University, Harrogate, Tennessee.

73. *OHAL*, 20.

74. Close, interview by Howard, [May 1860], LP-LC; William Dean Howells, *Life of Abraham Lincoln*, ed. Harry E. Pratt (Springfield: Abraham Lincoln Association, 1938), 28.

75. *HI*, 456.

76. *LTC*, 66–68.

77. Terre Haute, Indiana, *Star*, 11 February 1923.

78. *HI*, 359.

Chapter 3. "Separated from His Father, He Studied English Grammar"

1. *CWL*, 1:497.

2. *CWL*, 1:320.

3. *HI*, 73, 9, 13, 18, 456; Charles Maltby, *The Life and Public Services of Abraham Lincoln* (Stockton, Calif.: Daily Independent Steam Print, 1884), 25.

4. *HI*, 442–43.

5. *HI*, 174, 438.

6. *HOLL*, 116–17.

7. *HI*, 254.

8. *HI*, 457.

9. *CWL*, 4:63–64.

10. Cincinnati *Commercial*, 25 July 1867.

11. Charles James Fox Clarke to his mother, 3 August 1834, Clarke MSS, ALPL.

12. *CWL*, 1:274.

13. Robert D. Miller, *Past and Present of Menard County, Illinois* (Chicago: Clarke, 1905), 43.

14. *HI*, 80, 12.

15. *CWL*, 4:64.

16. Thomas P. Reep, *Lincoln at New Salem* (Chicago: Old Salem Lincoln League, 1927), 21.

17. *HI*, 89.

18. George Close, interview by James Q. Howard, [May 1860], LP-LC.

19. *HI*, 18.

20. Reep, *Lincoln at New Salem*, 55.

21. St. Louis *Globe-Democrat*, 20 December 1888; Douglas L. Wilson, *Honor's Voice: The Transformation of Abraham Lincoln* (New York: Knopf, 1998), 35–37.

22. John Todd Stuart, interview by James Q. Howard, [May 1860], John Hay MSS, Brown University.

23. *HI*, 10.

24. Brooks, *Lincoln and the Downfall of Slavery*, 186.

25. *HI*, 405; *LOC*, 183, 185, 405, 438.

26. Sue E. Onstot to James R. B. Van Cleave, 17 March 1909, Harry E. Pratt MSS, University of Illinois; Bloomington, Illinois, *Pantagraph*, 6 February 1909.

27. Carpenter, *Six Months*, 50–52; *CWL*, 6:392.

28. *HI*, 384–85, 539.

29. *ChiTrib*, 10 February 1895.

30. *LTC*, 96.

31. *CWL*, 3:512.

32. *HOLL*, 78.

33. [William Miller?], statement, September 1866, *HI*, 362; Royal Clary to Herndon, [October 1866?], *HI*, 371.

34. *HOLL*, 82.

35. Browne, *Every-Day Life of Lincoln*, 107.

36. *HI*, 481, 555.

37. *HI*, 6–9.

38. *HI*, 19.

39. *HI*, 18–19, 372.

40. *CWL*, 1:509–10.

41. *HI*, 385.

42. Michael F. Holt, *The Rise and Fall of the American Whig Party: Jacksonian Politics and the Onset of the Civil War* (New York: Oxford University Press, 1999), 67.

43. New York *Tribune*, 2 June 1848.

44. Daniel Walker Howe, "Why Abraham Lincoln Was a Whig," *Journal of the Abraham Lincoln Association* 16 (1995): 27–38; *CWL*, 2:220.

45. *CWL*, 1:5–9.

46. *ISJ*, 5 November 1864; *HI*, 16–17, 170.

47. *HI*, 7. I have modernized the spelling and punctuation in this quote.

48. *HI*, 7.

49. *CWL*, 3:512.

50. *LOC*, 56.

51. *OHAL*, 10–11.

52. *Petersburg (Ill.) Observer*, 23 August 1884; Chicago *Inter-Ocean*, 30 April 1881.

53. *CWL*, 4:65.

54. *RAL*, 465–66.

55. *CWL*, 4:65.

56. T. G. Onstot, *Pioneers of Menard and Mason Counties* (Forest City, Ill.: T. G. Onstot, 1902), 90.

57. *HI*, 715.

58. *HI*, 557, 450; Stevens, *Reporter's Lincoln*, 7; Reep, *Lincoln at New Salem*, 62.

59. *HI*, 74; Reep, *Lincoln at New Salem*, 65.

60. *OHAL*, 11.

61. *HOLL*, 103.

62. Maltby, *Lincoln*, 44–45.

63. Stevens, *Reporter's Lincoln*, 12.

64. *RAL*, 466.

65. *HI*, 446.

Chapter 4. "A Napoleon of Astuteness and Political Finesse"

1. *HI*, 501, 173.

2. *HI*, 173, spelling and punctuation modernized.

3. *SJ*, 14 May, 3 September, and 9 July 1841.

4. *ISJ*, 14 January 1886; Bloomington, Illinois, *Pantagraph*, 6 February 1886.

5. Alban Jasper Conant, "My Acquaintance with Abraham Lincoln" (New York: De Vinne, 1893), 172.

6. *CWL*, 4:121.

7. *HI*, 449.

8. Henry McHenry, interview by James Q. Howard, [May 1860], LP-LC.

9. *HI*, 160, 254.

10. Paul Simon, *Lincoln's Preparation for Greatness: The Illinois Legislative Years* (Norman: University of Oklahoma Press, 1965), 23.

11. John J. Hardin to Sarah Hardin, 14 December 1836, Hardin Family MSS, CHM; Joseph Duncan to Elizabeth Caldwell Smith Duncan, 18 December 1836, Duncan-Putnam Family MSS, Putnam Museum, Davenport, Iowa.

12. Frederick Hollman, "Autobiographical Sketch" (1870), 21, Evans Public Library, Vandalia.

13. *OHAL*, 3–4.

14. Andy Van Meter, *Always My Friend: A History of the State Journal-Register and Springfield* (Springfield: Copley Press, 1981), 109.

15. *HI*, 476.

16. Harry E. Pratt, "Lincoln and the Division of Sangamon County," *JISHS* 47 (1954): 400.

17. John Locke Scripps, *Life of Abraham Lincoln*, ed. Roy P. Basler and Lloyd A. Dunlap (Bloomington: Indiana University Press, 1961), 68–69.

18. H. Donald Winkler, *The Women in Lincoln's Life* (Nashville: Rutledge Hill, 2001), 47.

19. Belleville, Illinois, *Advocate*, 5 January 1866.

20. Chicago *Inter-Ocean*, 16 April 1881.

21. *OHAL*, 19; *HI*, 557.

22. Belleville, Illinois, *Advocate*, 5 January 1866.

23. E. J. Rutledge, Ottumwa, Iowa, *Courier*, n.d., clipping collection, LFFC.

24. *HOLL*, 131.

25. *HI*, 440.

26. *HOLL*, 108; Laura Isabelle Osborne Nance, *A Piece of Time (In Lincoln Country)*, ed. Georgia Goodwin Creager (n.p., [ca. 1967]), 26.

27. Nance, *Piece of Time*, 26.

28. Chicago *Inter-Ocean*, 12 February 1899.

29. Oakland, California, *Tribune*, 12 February 1922.

30. *HI*, 21.

31. New York *Mail and Express*, 15 February 1896.

32. *HI*, 556–57, 23.

33. *ChiTrib*, 25 December 1886.

34. *HI*, 243.

35. *HI*, 205.

36. *HI*, 440.

37. Matthew Marsh to George M. Marsh, 17 September 1835, LP-LC.

38. *CWL*, 1:269–70.

39. *CWL*, 1:48.

40. *RLAP*, 70.

41. *RLAP*, 70–71.

42. *LTC*, 127–28.

43. *CWL*, 1:48–49.

44. *CWL*, 8:429.

45. *SJ*, 7 November 1835, 3, 24 September 1836.

46. *SJ*, 2 and 16 January 1836.

47. *SJ*, 19 December 1835, 2 January 1836.

48. Herndon's recollection of a story he heard Lincoln tell often, n.d., HWP.

49. *HI*, 202–5.

50. *LTC*, 140.

51. *CWL*, 1:54–55.

52. *CWL*, 1:61–69.

53. *CWL*, 1:69.

54. *SJ*, 13 October 1838.

55. David Davis to William P. Walker, 26 January 1839, David Davis MSS, ALPL.

56. Alton *Telegraph*, 28 December 1839.

57. *CWL*, 1:488–89.

58. *OHAL*, 31.

59. *HI*, 204.

60. *LTC*, 131–32.

61. *House Journal*, 1836–37, 702.

62. *Peoria (Ill.) Register and North-Western Gazette*, 8 September 1838.

63. Thomas Ford, *History of Illinois from Its Commencement as a State in 1818 to 1847* (Chicago: Griggs, 1854), 222.

64. New York *Herald*, 4 December 1860.

65. *House Journal*, 1836–37, 241–44.

66. Julia Duncan Kirby, *Biographical Sketch of Joseph Duncan, Fifth Governor of Illinois* (Chicago: Fergus, 1888), 50–51.

67. *SJ*, 28 October 1837.

68. Van Meter, *Always My Friend*, 30.

69. *Our Constitution* (Urbana), 16 August 1856.

70. *ISJ*, 19 October 1854.

71. Robert H. Browne, *Abraham Lincoln and the Men of His Time* (2 vols.; Cincinnati: Jennings & Pye, 1901), 1:285.

72. John Linden Roll, "Sangamo Town," *JISHS* 19 (1926–27): 159.

73. *CWL*, 4:65.

74. *House Journal*, 1836–1837, 241–42 (12 January 1837).

75. Merton Dillon, *Elijah P. Lovejoy, Abolitionist Editor* (Urbana: University of Illinois Press, 1961), 47.

76. Gilbert Hobbs Barnes, *The Antislavery Impulse, 1830–1844* (1933; reprint, New York: Harcourt Brace & World, 1964), 25.

77. *The Liberator* (Boston), 1 January 1831.

78. *CWL*, 1:271–79.

Chapter 5. "We Must Fight the Devil with Fire"

1. *ISJ*, 13 February 1919, 12 February 1956.
2. Chicago *Daily Times*, 12 October 1858.
3. *ALS*, 68.
4. *CWL*, 1:78–79.
5. Allen F. Edgar to Ida Tarbell, 12 May 1927, Tarbell MSS.
6. *OHAL*, 22–23.
7. Osborn H. Oldroyd, ed., *The Lincoln Memorial: Album-Immortelles* (Chicago: Gem Publishing House, 1883), 145–46; Joshua F. Speed, *Reminiscences of Abraham Lincoln and Notes of a Visit to California. Two Lectures* (Louisville, Ky.: J. P. Morton, 1884), 21–22; *NYT*, 7 January 1884.
8. Complaint of plaintiff in the suit of *Hawthorn v. Woolridge*, 1 July 1836, in *The Law Practice of Abraham Lincoln: Complete Documentary Edition, Second Edition*, ed. Martha L. Benner et al., http://www.lawpracticeofabrahamlincoln.org/Search.aspx.
9. *CWL*, 2:81.
10. *SJ*, 26 May 1838.
11. Stephen A. Douglas, *Letters of Stephen A. Douglas*, ed. Robert W. Johannsen (Urbana: University of Illinois Press, 1961), 53–55.
12. *CWL*, 1:107, 113–14.
13. *CWL*, 1:108–15.
14. *HOLL*, 152; *LOC*, 12.
15. *CWL*, 1:108–15.
16. *CWL*, 1:108–15.
17. *CWL*, 1:120.
18. *SJ*, 21 July 1838.
19. "Lincoln in Fulton County," undated typescript, Tarbell MSS; *CWL*, 1:143.
20. John J. Hardin to his wife, 21 February 1839, Hardin Family MSS, CHM.
21. *CWL*, 1:123.
22. *CWL*, 1:147–48.
23. *SJ*, 16 February 1839.
24. *House Journal*, 1838–39, 171 (5 January 1839).
25. *CWL*, 1:126.
26. *House Journal*, 1838–39, 323 (1 February 1839).
27. *CWL*, 1:159, 184.
28. Clinton L. Conkling, "Movement for a Third Capital," in *Historical Encyclopedia of Illinois*, ed. Newton Bateman and Paul Selby, vol. 2, pt. 1 (Chicago: Munsell, 1912), 646–47.
29. Thomas Ford, *History of Illinois from Its Commencement as a State in 1818 to 1847* (Chicago: Griggs, 1854), 203.
30. David Davis to John J. Hardin, 1 June 1839, Hardin Family MSS, CHM.
31. Anthony Banning Norton, *The Great Revolution of 1840: Reminiscences of the Log Cabin and Hard Cider Campaign* (Mt. Vernon, Ohio: A. B. Norton, 1888), 10.
32. *Southern Review* 12 (April 1873): 360–61.
33. *ISR*, 23, 30 November 1839.
34. *HI*, 181.
35. *CWL*, 1:158.
36. *CWL*, 1:159.
37. *CWL*, 1:159–79.
38. Elihu B. Washburne, *Abraham Lincoln, His Personal History and Public Record, Speech delivered in the U.S. House of Representatives, May 29, 1860*, pamphlet ed. (1860), 2; *RAL*, 9–10.
39. *ISR*, 17 July and 25 January 1840.
40. *HI*, 471.
41. Belleville, Illinois, *Great Western*, 18 April 1840.
42. *HI*, 471.
43. *CWL*, 8:101.
44. *HI*, 472.
45. *HI*, 447, 472; Quincy, Illinois, *Whig*, 23 May 1840.
46. J. A. Powell to the editor of the *Century*, n.d., copy, and Powell to John G. Nicolay, 11 February 1889, both in Nicolay MSS, LC.
47. *CWL*, 1:211.
48. Davis to Walker, 16 November 1840, David Davis MSS, ALPL.
49. *HI*, 475.
50. *Christian Century*, 13 February 1909.
51. *CWL*,1:206.

52. *CWL*, 1:208.

53. *ChiTrib*, 12 February 1900.

54. *ISR*, 11 December 1840.

55. James Harvey Ralston to "Dear Sir," 30 January 1841, Ralston MSS, ALPL.

56. Davis, "Illinois Legislators and Jacksonian Democracy," 288–92; *SJ*, 5 February 1841.

57. *SJ*, 12, 19 February 1841.

58. *CWL*, 1:244–49.

59. *CWL*, 1:244n.

60. *CWL*, 1:237–38.

61. Quincy, Illinois, *Whig*, 9 January 1841.

62. *HOLL*, 88.

63. Horace White, *The Life of Lyman Trumbull* (Boston: Houghton Mifflin, 1913), 427.

64. Samuel C. Parks, *The Great Trial of the Nineteenth Century* (Kansas City, Mo.: Hudson-Kimberly, 1900), 141.

65. *Southern Review* 12 (April 1873): 364.

Chapter 6. "It Would Just Kill Me to Marry Mary Todd"

1. *HOLL*, 261; *ALQ* 1 (1941): 419. A full account of the Lincolns' marriage can be found in Michael Burlingame, *An American Marriage: The Untold Story of Abraham Lincoln and Mary Todd* (New York: Pegasus Books, 2021).

2. *HI*, 374, 250, 609–10, 256, 265, 530, 527, 175, 243.

3. *CWL*, 1:117.

4. *HI*, 263, 256.

5. *CWL*, 1:117.

6. *CWL*, 1:54–55.

7. *HI*, 256, 262.

8. *HI*, 531, 175, 599; Chicago *Inter-Ocean*, 23 April 1881.

9. *HI*, 81.

10. *CWL*, 1:78.

11. *CWL*, 1:94.

12. *HI*, 263.

13. Harold D. Lasswell, *Power and Personality* (New York: Norton, 1948), 38, 39, 50.

14. *HI*, 57.

15. G. Stanley Hall to William E. Barton, 3 October 1922, Barton MSS.

16. *CWL*, 1:8.

17. *CWL*, 1:281.

18. Elizabeth L. Norris to Emilie Todd Helm, 28 September 1895, Elizabeth L. Norris MSS, ALPL; Kansas City *Star*, 10 February 1907.

19. James C. Conkling to Mercy Levering, 21 September 1840, Conkling MSS, ALPL.

20. Mary Edwards Raymond, *Some Incidents in the Life of Mrs. Benjamin S. Edwards* (n.p., 1909), 11–12.

21. *HI*, 443; Stevens, *Reporter's Lincoln*, 114.

22. *HI*, 446; Katherine Helm, *The True Story of Mary, Wife of Lincoln* (New York: Harper, 1928), 62–63.

23. Donald G. Richter, *Lincoln: Twenty Years on the Eastern Prairie* (Mattoon, Ill.: United Graphics, 1999), 225.

24. Edwards Brown Jr., *Rewarding Years Recalled* (n.p.: privately published, 1973), 35–36.

25. Helm, *Mary, Wife of Lincoln*, 80–81, 83.

26. Bemidji, Minnesota, *Daily Pioneer*, 12 February 1920; *HI*, 612.

27. *HI*, 474.

28. *OHAL*, 2.

29. *Mary Lincoln Letters*, 588.

30. William H. Townsend, *Lincoln and His Wife's Home Town* (Indianapolis: Bobbs-Merrill, 1929), 46.

31. *HOLL*, 165; *HI*, 443.

32. *OHAL*, 1.

33. Samuel C. Parks, "Brief account of Lincoln's courtship & marriage," Carl Sandburg MSS, University of Illinois.

34. Allentown, Pennsylvania, *Morning Call*, 9 February 1936; Virginia Quigley to [Octavia Roberts] Corneau, 13 July [1939?], F. Lauriston Bullard MSS, Boston University; *OHAL*, 1; Stevens, *Reporter's Lincoln*, 113.

35. J. Bennett Nolan, "Of a Tomb in the Reading Cemetery and the Long Shadow of Abraham Lincoln," *Pennsylvania History* 19 (1952): 292.

36. Joshua Speed to Mary L. Speed, 2 February 1841, ALPL.

37. Carl Sandburg and Paul M. Angle, *Mary Lincoln: Wife and Widow* (New York: Harcourt, Brace, 1932), 180.

38. Jane Hamilton Daviess Bell to Anne Bell, 27 January 1841, Lincoln files, "Wife" folder, Lincoln Memorial University, Harrogate, Tennessee.

39. *HI*, 444.

40. Muncie, Indiana, *Evening Press*, 11 March 1895.

41. Kansas City *Star*, 10 February 1907.

42. *HI*, 474–75.

43. *HI*, 444.

44. *HI*, 133.

45. Jane D. Bell to Anne Bell, 27 January 1841, Lincoln files, "Wife" folder, Lincoln Memorial University, Harrogate, Tennessee.

46. *OHAL*, 1.

47. *HI*, 474–75.

48. *CWL*, 1:228–29.

49. *CWL*, 1:226–28.

50. Sarah Hardin to John J. Hardin, 26 January 1841, Hardin Family MSS, CHM.

51. *HI*, 464.

52. Sandburg and Angle, *Mary Lincoln*, 180.

53. *SJ*, 13 April 1843.

54. *Mary Lincoln Letters*, 27. The quote about "Richard" comes from Colley Ciber's adaptation of Shakespeare's *Richard III*.

55. Muncie, Indiana, *Evening Press*, 11 March 1895.

56. *HI*, 665.

57. *CWL*, 1:261.

58. Joshua Speed to Mary L. Speed, 31 October 1841, Speed Family MSS, Filson Historical Society, Louisville.

59. *CWL*, 1:268.

60. *CWL*, 1:266.

61. *CWL*, 1:268.

62. *CWL*, 1:269–70.

63. *CWL*, 1:280.

64. *CWL*, 1:282.

65. *CWL*, 1:289.

66. *CWL*, 1:295–96.

67. *CWL*, 1:299n.

68. *Century Magazine*, October 1887, 974.

69. *SJ*, 14 October 1842.

70. *CWL*, 1:299.

71. *CWL*, 1:299; *Alexandria (Va.) Gazette*, 8 November 1876.

72. *Alexandria (Va.) Gazette*, 8 November 1876; *Century Magazine*, March 1892, 796.

73. Linder, *Reminiscences*, 65–67.

74. New York *Ledger*, 23 June 1866.

75. *HOLL*, 201.

76. *CWL*, 1:301.

77. *ISR*, 4 November 1842, 30 June, 11 and 18 August, 20 October 1843.

78. Alton *Daily Telegraph & Democratic Review*, 1 October 1842.

79. *CWL*, 1:320.

80. Milton Hay to Thomas Venmun, 16 January 1892, Milton Hay MSS, ALPL.

81. Douglas L. Wilson, *Honor's Voice: The Transformation of Abraham Lincoln* (New York: Knopf, 1998), 283.

82. *HI*, 444.

83. *CWL*, 1:303.

84. W. H. McKnight to Ida M. Tarbell, 1 February 1909, in Louisville *Courier-Journal*, n.d., clipping collection, LFFC.

85. Brown, *Rewarding Years Recalled*, 34.

86. Octavia Roberts Corneau, "The Road of Remembrance," 120, Corneau MSS, ALPL.

87. Stevens, *Reporter's Lincoln*, 117.

88. Eugenia Jones Hunt, *My Personal Recollections of Abraham and Mary Todd Lincoln* (Peoria, Ill.: H. A. Moser, 1966), 8.

89. *HI*, 665.

90. *CWL*, 1:305.

91. *CWL*, 1:325.

92. Mrs. B. S. Edwards to Tarbell, 8 October 1895, Tarbell MSS.

93. *OHAL*, 2.

94. *HI*, 475.

95. *ISJ*, 28 February 1937.

96. *HOLL*, 55; *HI*, 251.

97. Caroline Dall, "Journal of a tour through Illinois, Wisconsin and Ohio, Oct. & Nov. 1866," entry for 29 October 1866, Dall MSS, Bryn Mawr College.

98. *HI*, 350.
99. *HOLL*, 311, 334.
100. *HOLL*, 296.
101. *HOLL*, 334.
102. *HOLL*, 202, 165.
103. *ALS*, 19–20; *WLWH*, 125.
104. Statement of Robert Williams, 9 February 1923, Barton MSS.
105. Dale Carnegie, *Lincoln the Unknown* (New York: Perma Giants, 1932), 71–72.
106. *HI*, 597.
107. *HI*, 722–23.
108. *RLAP*, 362–63.
109. Frank Edwards, "A Few Facts along the Lincoln Way," Barton MSS.
110. A. Longfellow Fiske, "A Neighbor of Lincoln," *Commonweal*, 2 March 1932.
111. Walter Graves to Tarbell, 18 August 1929, Tarbell MSS.
112. *HOLL*, 201–2.
113. *NYT*, 26 August 1934.
114. Fiske, "Neighbor of Lincoln," 494.
115. *HI*, 449.
116. *HOLL*, 189–90; Milton Hay to his wife, 6 April [1862], Stuart-Hay MSS, ALPL.
117. Preston H. Bailhache, "Recollections of a Springfield Doctor," *JISHS* 47 (1954): 60.
118. *HI*, 445.
119. George W. Murray, statement for William E. Barton, 21 April 1920, Barton MSS.
120. *HI*, 452.
121. *RLAP*, 123.
122. Elizabeth L. Capps, "My Early Recollections of Abraham Lincoln," Abraham Lincoln Association reference files, "Reminiscences," folder 1, ALPL.
123. *HOLL*, 185
124. *HI*, 63.
125. Ward Hill Lamon, *Recollections of Abraham Lincoln, 1847–1865*, ed. Dorothy Lamon Teillard (2nd ed.; Washington, D.C.: privately published, 1911), 21.
126. Cincinnati *Enquirer*, 26 August 1883.
127. *HOLL*, 349–50.
128. Carl Schurz, *Abraham Lincoln: An Essay* (Boston: Houghton Mifflin, 1891), 19.
129. Schurz, interview by Ida Tarbell, 6 November 1897, Tarbell MSS.

Chapter 7. "I Have Got the Preacher by the Balls"

1. *CWL*, 1:307.
2. *CWL*, 1:309–18.
3. *RLAP*, 328.
4. "Anecdotes of Mrs. Lincoln," quoted in *The News* (no city indicated), ca. 17 July 1882, unidentified clipping, LFFC.
5. Elizabeth Lushbaugh Capps, "Early Recollections of Abraham Lincoln," Abraham Lincoln Association reference files, "Reminiscences," folder 1, ALPL; Elizabeth Capps, interview by Hannah Hinsdale, clipping dated Yakima, Washington, 2 February [1929?], Lincoln Shrine, Redlands, California.
6. Esther Moreland Leithold, *And This Is Our Heritage* (Woodland, Calif., 1944), 80, 82.
7. *Central New Jersey Home News* (New Brunswick), 12 February 1920; Chicago *Tribune*, 4 February 1868.
8. Dale Carnegie, *Lincoln the Unknown* (New York: Perma Giants, 1932), 71.
9. *HOLL*, 154.
10. *HOLL*, 240.
11. Rufus Rockwell Wilson, *Intimate Memories of Lincoln* (Elmira, N.Y.: Primavera, 1945), 243.
12. *CWL*, 1:121, 123, 124, 130.
13. Chicago *Press and Tribune*, 23 February 1860.
14. *CWL*, 1:337–38.
15. Josiah G. Holland, *The Life of Abraham Lincoln* (Springfield, Mass.: Gurdon Bill, 1866), 94; Nicolay and Hay, *Lincoln*, 1:235.
16. *CWL*, 1:347.
17. William H. Herndon to Theodore Parker, 24 November 1858, Herndon-Parker MSS, University of Iowa.
18. Caroline Dall, "Journal of a tour through Illinois, Wisconsin and Ohio, Oct. & Nov. 1866," entry for 29 October 1866, Dall MSS, Bryn Mawr College.

19. William H. Herndon, "Analysis of the Character of Abraham Lincoln," *ALQ* 1 (1941): 417; *HOLL*, 54.

20. David Donald, *Lincoln's Herndon* (New York: Knopf, 1948), 13–14, 65–71, 129.

21. Washington *Evening Star*, 20 February 1889.

22. *ISJ*, 15 October 1874.

23. Dall, "Journal of a tour," 29 October 1866.

24. *HI*, 700.

25. *CWL*, 1:353.

26. Robert Boal to John J. Hardin, 10 January 1846, Hardin Family MSS, CHM.

27. *CWL*, 1:355–56.

28. *CWL*, 1:356–57.

29. Although Hardin's letter has not survived, passages from it are quoted in Lincoln's detailed response of 7 February 1846, *CWL*, 1:360–65.

30. *CWL, [First] Supplement*, 9.

31. *Woman's Home Companion*, December 1903, 15.

32. *Illinois Gazette* (Lacon), 25 July 1846.

33. *CWL*, 1:348.

34. Helen Nicolay, *Personal Traits of Abraham Lincoln* (New York: Century, 1912), 110–11.

35. Julian M. Sturtevant Jr. to William E. Barton, 2 August 1919, Barton MSS.

36. Lawrence B. Stringer's unpublished biography of Lincoln, ca. 1927, 92, ALPL.

37. *CWL*, 1:382.

38. *Illinois Gazette* (Lacon), 22 August 1846.

39. *HI*, 576.

40. *HI*, 506.

41. *HI*, 483.

42. *CWL*, 1:389–91.

43. *CWL*, 1:367–69, 378–79, 385–89, 392.

44. *CWL*, 1:392.

45. *CWL*, 1:378.

46. *CWL*, 1:378–79.

47. *CWL*, 1:385–86.

48. *HOLL*, 124.

49. *RAL*, 16.

50. *CWL*, 1:497.

51. *NYT*, 24 January 1909.

52. Matoon, Illinois, *Sunday Sun*, 24 August 1884; Jesse W. Weik, "Lincoln and the Matson Negroes: A Vista into the Fugitive-Slave Days," *Arena* 17 (April 1897): 753.

53. Oakland, Illinois, *Herald*, 17 July 1896.

54. *RLAP*, 372.

55. Paul M. Angle, "Aftermath of the Matson Slave Case," *ALQ* 3 (1944): 148.

56. Albert A. Woldman, *Lawyer Lincoln* (Boston: Houghton Mifflin, 1937), 56; John J. Duff, *A. Lincoln: Prairie Lawyer* (New York: Holt, Rinehart & Winston, 1960), 144; *LOC*, 315n4.

57. George Sharswood, *An Essay on Professional Ethics* (2nd ed.; Philadelphia: Johnson, 1860), 26.

58. *RLAP*, 198.

59. Katherine Helm, *The True Story of Mary, Wife of Lincoln* (New York: Harper, 1928), 101–2.

60. *HOLL*, 237.

61. *CWL*, 1:325.

62. Henry Clay, *The Papers of Henry Clay*, ed. Robert Seager and James F. Hopkins (10 vols.; Lexington: University of Kentucky Press, 1959–91), 10:364, 370–71, 372.

63. David Davis to his wife, 8 August 1847, David Davis MSS, CHM.

Chapter 8. "A Strong but Judicious Enemy to Slavery"

1. Marian Gouverneur, *As I Remember: Recollections of American Society during the Nineteenth Century* (New York: D. Appleton, 1911), 170.

2. Gilbert H. Barnes and Dwight L. Dumond, eds., *Letters of Theodore Dwight Weld, Angelina Grimke Weld, and Sarah Grimke, 1822–1844* (2 vols.; Washington, D.C.: American Historical Association, 1934), 2:883, 885, 914.

3. *CWL*, 4:391.

4. James Pollock, "Lincoln & Douglas," Lincoln MSS, Brown University.

5. *ISJ*, 22 June 1848.

6. New York *Tribune*, 15 December 1848.

7. Charles Henry Brainard, "Reminiscences of Abraham Lincoln," *Youth's Companion*, December 1880, 435–36.

8. *CWL*, 1:465.

9. New York *Tribune*, 4 September 1860.

10. *CG*, 30th Cong., 1st sess., appendix, 1 (1847).

11. *CWL*, 1:420–22.

12. Rockford, Illinois, *Forum*, 19 January 1848; *ISR*, 14 January 1848.

13. *ISR*, 14 January 1848, 26 June 1858.

14. *CG*, 30th Cong., 1st sess., 95 (1848).

15. *ISR*, 21 January 1848.

16. *CWL*, 1:493–94.

17. *CWL*, 1:431–42.

18. Boston *Atlas*, 15 January 1848.

19. *CG*, 30th Cong., 1st sess., appendix, 1 (1847), 246.

20. *ISR*, 10 March 1848.

21. *CWL*, 1:448.

22. *CWL*, 1:451–52.

23. *CWL*, 1:448.

24. *CWL*, 1:463, 474.

25. *CWL*, 1:476–77.

26. *CWL*, 1:475–76.

27. *CWL*, 1:501–5.

28. *CWL*, 1:491, 497.

29. *CWL*, 2:1–5.

30. New York *Tribune*, 25 September 1848.

31. *Seward at Washington*, 1:80.

32. New York *Evening Post*, 24 August 1848.

33. Don E. Fehrenbacher, *The Slaveholding Republic: An Account of the United States Government's Relations to Slavery* (New York: Oxford University Press, 2001), 67.

34. *CWL*, 2:253.

35. Horace Mann to Samuel Gridley Howe, 22 April 1848, Horace Mann MSS, MaHS.

36. *CWL*, 1:75.

37. John G. Palfrey to Charles Francis Adams, 13 December 1848, Adams Family MSS, MaHS.

38. Joshua Giddings to Charles Sumner, 22 December 1848, Sumner MSS, Harvard University; Joshua R. Giddings, *History of the Rebellion: Its Authors and Causes* (New York: Follett, Foster, 1864), 286–88.

39. Michael F. Holt, *The Rise and Fall of the American Whig Party: Jacksonian Politics and the Onset of the Civil War* (New York: Oxford University Press, 1999), 1046n4; *House Journal*, 30th Cong., 2nd sess., 132 (21 December 1848); Josiah G. Holland, *The Life of Abraham Lincoln* (Springfield, Mass.: Gurdon Bill, 1866), 120.

40. "Greeley's Estimate of Lincoln," *Century Magazine*, July 1891, 373–74; George W. Julian, *The Life of Joshua R. Giddings* (Chicago: A. C. McClurg, 1892), 261.

41. *CWL*, 2:20–22.

42. James Quay Howard's notes of an interview with Lincoln, [May 1860], LP-LC.

43. *The Liberator* (Boston), 13 July 1860.

44. Joshua Giddings diary, 8 and 11 January 1849, Giddings MSS, Ohio Historical Society, Columbus.

45. "Greeley's Estimate of Lincoln," 374.

46. New York *Herald*, 6 February 1849.

47. New York *Tribune*, 22 September 1849.

48. *The Liberator* (Boston), 30 June 1860.

49. *The Liberator* (Boston), 24 August 1860.

50. *HOLL*, 14.

51. Peter Menard to Lincoln, 4 April 1849, LP-LC.

52. *CWL*, 2:46.

53. *HOLL*, 100.

54. *CWL*, 2:28–29.

55. *CWL*, 2:41.

56. Cyrus Edwards to Justin Butterfield, 11 June 1849, Records of the Department of the Interior, Appointments Division, Central Office Appointment MSS, 1849–1907, box 32, RG 48, National Archives.

57. Josiah M. Lucas to Lincoln, 12 and 15 April 1849, LP-LC.

58. Anson G. Henry to Joseph Gillespie, 2 June 1849, Gillespie MSS, ALPL; Henry to David Davis, 2 June 1849, David Davis MSS, ALPL.

59. Lucas to Lincoln, 10 May 1849, LP-LC.

60. Lucas to Benjamin Edwards and Anson G. Henry, 22 May 1849, LP-LC.

61. Undated petition, Records of the Department of the Interior, Appointments Division, Central Office Appointment MSS, 1849–1907, box 32, RG 48, National Archives.

62. Peter J. Berry, *General James W. Singleton: Lincoln's Mysterious Copperhead Ally* (Mahomet, Ill.: Mayhaven, 2011), 37.

63. Nathaniel G. Wilcox to Lincoln, 6 June 1864, LP-LC; *CWL*, 2:54.

64. Lucas to Zachary Taylor, 6 June 1849, Small Manuscript Collections, LC.

65. Browne, *Every-Day Life of Lincoln*, 107.

66. *CWL*, 2:57–59.

67. Cyrus Edwards to Gillespie, 4 July 1860, Tarbell MSS.

68. *CWL, [First] Supplement*, 16.

69. Document headed "Applications" listing all letters in support of candidates for the commissionership of the General Land Office in 1849, National Archives; Lincoln to Thomas Ewing, Springfield, 9 July 1849, *CWL, Second Supplement*, 3–4.

70. *CWL*, 2:91–92.

71. *OHAL*, 15.

72. Brooks, *Lincoln and the Downfall of Slavery*, 116.

73. Joseph H. Barrett, *Lincoln and His Presidency* (2 vols.; Cincinnati: Robert Clarke, 1904), 1:108.

74. R. W. Thompson, "Abraham Lincoln," undated manuscript, 15, R. W. Thompson MSS, ALPL.

Chapter 9. "I Was Losing Interest in Politics and Went to the Practice of Law with Greater Earnestness Than Ever Before"

1. John M. Scott to Ida Tarbell, 14 August 1895, Tarbell MSS.

2. Robert H. Browne, *Abraham Lincoln and the Men of His Time* (2 vols.; Cincinnati: Jennings & Pye, 1901), 1:285.

3. *CWL*, 3:512, 4:67.

4. *CWL, [First] Supplement*, 19.

5. *HOLL*, 5.

6. William H. Herndon, "Lincoln's Ingratitude," HWP.

7. *RLAP*, 301.

8. *CWL*, 2:102.

9. William H. Herndon, "Analysis of the Character of Abraham Lincoln," *ALQ* 1 (1941): 427–28.

10. Los Angeles *Times*, 9 March 1902.

11. *CWL*, 2:76.

12. Lawrence Beaumont Stringer, "From the Sangamon to the Potomac: More Light on Abraham Lincoln," typescript of an unpublished manuscript, 95, Edgar Dewitt Jones MSS, Detroit Public Library.

13. William Hayes Ward, ed., *Abraham Lincoln, Tributes from His Associates: Reminiscences of Soldiers, Statesmen, and Citizens* (New York: Thomas Y. Crowell, 1895), 246.

14. *RAL*, 451.

15. Isaac N. Arnold, *Reminiscences of the Illinois-bar Forty Years Ago: Lincoln and Douglas as Orators and Lawyers* (Chicago: Fergus, 1881), 20, 22.

16. *ChiTrib*, 29 December 1895.

17. Charles Washington Moores, "Abraham Lincoln, Lawyer," *Indiana Historical Society Publications* 7 (1922): 509.

18. Chicago *Times*, 21 February 1876.

19. *HOLL*, 251

20. Anonymous undated manuscript, doubtless by James C. Robinson, Tarbell MSS.

21. *HI*, 239.

22. Frederick T. Hill, *Lincoln the Lawyer* (New York: Century, 1906), 181.

23. *HOLL*, 156.

24. *HI*, 350.

25. *HI*, 349.

26. Chicago *Times*, 21 February 1876.

27. Richard Yates to Schuyler Colfax, 9 February 1861, Lincoln Collection, Beinecke Library, Yale University; *Indiana Journal* (Indianapolis), 10 February 1879.

28. *CWL*, 2:33–33.

29. *CWL, [First] Supplement*, 20.

30. *CWL*, 2:106.

31. San Francisco *Call*, 9 April 1891.

32. John W. Starr, *Lincoln and the Railroads: A Biographical Study* (New York: Dodd, Mead, 1927), 61.

33. Hill, *Lincoln the Lawyer*, 260n.

34. Robert Henry Parkinson, "The Patent Case that Lifted Lincoln into a Presidential Candidate," *ALQ* 4 (1946): 115–16.

35. William B. H. Dowse to Albert J. Beveridge, 16 October 1925, Beveridge MSS, LC.

36. John J. Duff, *A. Lincoln: Prairie Lawyer* (New York: Holt, Rinehart & Winston, 1960), 323; Benjamin P. Thomas and Harold M. Hyman, *Stanton: The Life and Times of Lincoln's Secretary of War* (New York: Knopf, 1962), 66; Benjamin Rush Cowen, *Abraham Lincoln: An Appreciation by One Who Knew Him* (Cincinnati: Robert Clarke, 1909), 10–12.

37. Dowse to Beveridge, 10 October 1925, Beveridge MSS, LC.

38. Report of a statement by George Harding, Tarbell MSS.

39. W. M. Dickson, "Abraham Lincoln in Cincinnati," *Harper's New Monthly Magazine* 69 (June 1884): 62.

40. Colorado Springs *Gazette*, 16 August 1903.

41. J. N. Gridley, *Lincoln's Defense of Duff Armstrong: The Story of the Trial and the Celebrated Almanac* (pamphlet; Springfield: Illinois State Historical Society, 1910), 19.

42. Milton Logan, interview in a dispatch datelined Boone, Iowa, 5 September [1905], unidentified clipping, LFFC.

43. *HI*, 316, 333; Gridley, *Lincoln's Defense of Duff Armstrong*, 19–20.

44. *HI*, 526.

45. *Daily Illinoisan-Star* (Beardstown), 12 February 1916.

46. Lyman Lacey to James R. B. Van Cleave, 1 July 1908, copy, Abraham Lincoln Association reference files, ALPL.

47. Gibson William Harris, "My Recollections of Abraham Lincoln," *Woman's Home Companion*, November 1903, 11.

48. Hill, *Lincoln the Lawyer*, 186–87; *The People v. Hawley* (1851–52), in *The Law Practice of Abraham Lincoln: Complete Documentary Edition, Second Edition*, ed. Martha L. Benner et al., http://www.lawpracticeofabrahamlincoln.org/Search.aspx, case file 01119.

49. Chicago *Daily Inter-Ocean*, 30 January 1887.

50. Gibson William Harris, "My Recollections of Abraham Lincoln," *Woman's Home Companion*, December 1903, 15.

51. *Regnier v. Cabot and Taylor*, in Benner et al., *Law Practice of Abraham Lincoln*, case file 00158; *HI*, 239.

52. [John M. Scott], "Lincoln on the Stump and at the Bar," typescript, 9, Tarbell MSS.

53. *HI*, 350.

54. Herndon, "Analysis of the Character of Lincoln," 432–33.

55. Chicago *Times*, 21 February 1876.

56. Undated memo by J.S.S., Barton MSS.

57. *RAL*, 240, 333–34.

58. *CWL*, 2:132.

59. *CWL*, 4:67.

60. *CWL*, 2:150.

61. *Our Constitution* (Urbana), 4 July 1857.

62. *CWL*, 2:382–83.

63. *CWL, [First] Supplement*, 18.

64. William H. Herndon, "Facts Illustrative of Mr. Lincoln's Patriotism and Statesmanship," *ALQ* 3 (1944–45): 188–89.

65. *HI*, 197.

66. Lucy Harmon McPherson, *Life and Letters of Oscar Fitzalan Harmon* (Trenton, N.J: MacCrellish & Quigley, 1914), 11.

67. *Mary Lincoln Letters*, 567–68.

68. *CWL*, 2:97.

69. Louis P. Masur, ed., *The Real War Will Never Get in the Books: Selections from Writers during the Civil War* (New York: Oxford University Press, 1993), 127.

70. William H. Herndon, "Lincoln's Individuality," HWP.

71. Joshua F. Speed, *Reminiscences of Abraham Lincoln and Notes of a Visit to*

California. Two Lectures (Louisville, Ky.: J. P. Morton, 1884), 34.

72. *HI*, 499.

73. Nathan M. Knapp to O. M. Hatch, Winchester, Illinois, 12 May 1859, Hatch MSS, ALPL.

74. David Dixon Porter, *Incidents and Anecdotes of the Civil War* (New York: D. Appleton, 1885), 283.

75. Ward, *Lincoln Tributes*, 204–5.

76. Washington *Evening Star*, 27 June 1891.

77. *Transactions of the Illinois State Historical Society* 17 (1912): 108.

78. Henry C. Whitney, "Abraham Lincoln: A Study from Life," *Arena* 19 (1898): 466.

79. *RAL*, 413.

80. *NYT*, 24 January 1909.

81. *LO*, 211.

82. Undated statement by a Dr. Parker, Nicolay-Hay MSS, ALPL.

Chapter 10. "Aroused as He Had Never Been Before"

1. *CWL*, 4:67.

2. Mrs. Archibald Dixon, *A True History of Missouri Compromise and Slavery in American Politics* (2nd ed.; Cincinnati: Clarke, 1903), 445.

3. David M. Potter, *The Impending Crisis, 1848–1861* (New York: Harper & Row, 1976), 163.

4. Paul M. Angle, ed., *Created Equal? The Complete Lincoln-Douglas Debates of 1858* (Chicago: University of Chicago Press, 1958), 180.

5. *CWL*, 2:282.

6. Undated reminiscences of Amos French, Tarbell MSS.

7. New York *Tribune*, 10 May 1854.

8. Stephen L. Hansen, *The Making of the Third Party System: Voters and Parties in Illinois, 1850–1876* (Ann Arbor: UMI Research Press, 1980), 50.

9. Quincy *Herald*, 16 September 1854.

10. Arthur C. Cole, ed., *The Constitutional Debates of 1847* (Springfield: Illinois State Historical Library, 1919), 216–17.

11. New York *Tribune*, 13 January 1855.

12. Kenneth M. Stampp, *The Imperiled Union: Essays on the Background of the Civil War* (New York: Oxford University Press, 1980), 109.

13. John Russell Young's autobiography, Young MSS, LC; New York *Tribune*, 6 September 1866.

14. *SMDR*, 30 June 1860.

15. Schurz, *Reminiscences*, 2:30–32.

16. W. M. Dickson, "Abraham Lincoln in Cincinnati," *Harper's New Monthly Magazine* 69 (June 1884): 64.

17. *CWL*, 2:283.

18. Mrs. Archibald Dixon, *True History*, 445.

19. *CWL*, 2:228.

20. Los Angeles *Times*, 20 June 1894; *CWL*, 2:323.

21. *HI*, 266.

22. *LTC*, 150.

23. *CWL*, 2:289.

24. Isaac N. Phillips, *Abraham Lincoln, by Some Men Who Knew Him*, ed. Paul M. Angle (1910; Chicago: Americana House, 1950), 44.

25. Horace White, *The Life of Lyman Trumbull* (Boston: Houghton Mifflin, 1913), 40n.

26. Jacob Thompson to Albert J. Beveridge, 15 February 1927, Beveridge MSS, LC.

27. Chicago *Journal*, 9 October 1854.

28. *CG*, 35th Cong., 1st sess. (1857), 14–18; Stephen A. Douglas, *Letters of Stephen A. Douglas*, ed. Robert W. Johannsen (Urbana: University of Illinois Press, 1961), xxvi.

29. B. C. Bryner, *Abraham Lincoln in Peoria, Illinois* (2nd ed.; Peoria: Lincoln Historical Publishing Company, 1926), 155–56.

30. *ChiTrib*, 30 May 1857.

31. Chicago *Democrat*, 9 October 1854.

32. *CWL*, 2:247–76.

33. *CWL*, 4:67.

34. *ISR*, 28 September 1854.

35. Horace White, "Abraham Lincoln in 1854," *Transactions of the Illinois State Historical Society* 13 (1908): 10.

36. White, *Life of Lyman Trumbull*, 39.

37. San Francisco *Daily Evening Bulletin*, 22 April 1865; *ISR*, 6 October 1854; Chicago *Democrat*, 9 October 1854.

38. *ISR*, 16, 9 October 1854.

39. New York *Tribune*, 10 November 1854.

40. John M. Palmer to Lyman Trumbull, 11 January 1856, Trumbull MSS, LC.

41. Chicago *Journal*, 12 October 1854.

42. *CWL*, 2:290.

43. David Davis to Lincoln, 27 December 1854, LP-LC.

44. *CWL*, 2:288.

45. Chicago *Free West*, 30 November 1854.

46. *CWL*, 2:293.

47. Zebina Eastman to Elihu B. Washburne, 14 December 1854, Washburne MSS, LC.

48. Washburne to Eastman, 19 December 1854, Eastman MSS, CHM.

49. *HOLL*, 29.

50. *CWL*, 2:293–94.

51. Browne, *Every-Day Life of Lincoln*, 163.

52. Douglas, *Letters of Stephen A. Douglas*, 331, 333.

53. James W. Sheahan to Charles Lanphier, Chicago, 17 January 1855, Lanphier MSS, ALPL.

54. Charles H. Ray to Washburne, 12 January 1855, Washburne MSS, LC.

55. New York *Tribune*, 9 February 1855.

56. Chicago *Free West*, 15 February 1855.

57. *CWL*, 2:306.

58. Trumbull to Salmon P. Chase, 23 March 1855, Chase MSS, Historical Society of Pennsylvania, Philadelphia.

59. *CWL*, 2:306–7.

60. Elihu B. Washburne, "Abraham Lincoln in Illinois," *North American Review* 141 (1885): 316.

61. LeRoy H. Fischer, ed., "Samuel C. Parks' Reminiscences of Abraham Lincoln," *Lincoln Herald* 68 (Spring 1966): 11.

62. Joseph Gillespie to [M. D. Hardin], 22 April 1880, Hardin Family MSS, CHM.

63. White, *Life of Lyman Trumbull*, 45.

64. Chicago *Sunday Times-Herald*, 3 November 1895.

65. *LOC*, 150.

66. Jean Baker, *Mary Todd Lincoln: A Biography* (New York: Norton, 1987), 150; *Mary Lincoln Letters*, 406.

67. Julia Jayne Trumbull to Lyman Trumbull, 14 April and 5 May 1856, Trumbull Family MSS, ALPL.

68. *OHAL*, 45–46.

69. Cleveland *Leader*, 8 October 1893.

70. *HI*, 153.

Chapter 11. "Unite with Us, and Help Us to Triumph"

1. *CWL*, 2:322–23.

2. *CWL*, 2:316–17.

3. *CWL*, 2:317–18.

4. *CWL*, 2:320–22.

5. Frank I. Herriott to Albert J. Beveridge, 14 December 1922, Beveridge MSS, LC.

6. Ezra M. Prince, ed., *Meeting of May 29, 1900 Commemorative of the Convention of May 29, 1856 that Organized the Republican Party in the State of Illinois* (Bloomington: Pantagraph, 1900), 90.

7. Oliver P. Wharton, "Lincoln and the Beginning of the Republican Party in Illinois," *Transactions of the Illinois State Historical Society* 16 (1911): 62–63; Otto Kyle, *Abraham Lincoln in Decatur* (New York: Vantage Press, 1957), 141.

8. Tarbell, *Life of Lincoln*, 1:291.

9. John Wentworth to Lincoln, 21 October 1856, LP-LC.

10. *HOLL*, 3.

11. Joseph O. Cunningham, *Some Recollections of Abraham Lincoln* (Norwalk, Ohio: American Publishing Company, 1909), 6.

12. J. O. Cunningham, "The Bloomington Convention of 1856 and Those Who

Participated in It," *Transactions of the Illinois State Historical Society* 10 (1905): 104.

13. Prince, *Meeting of May 29, 1900*, 160–61.
14. *LTC*, 260–61.
15. Prince, *Meeting of May 29, 1900*, 160–62.
16. Prince, *Meeting of May 29, 1900*, 93–94.
17. *CWL*, 2:341.
18. Belleville, Illinois, *Weekly Advocate*, 4 June 1856.
19. Chicago *Democratic Press*, 31 May 1856.
20. Joseph Medill, Chicago, to the editor of *McClure's Magazine*, 15 May 1896, Tarbell MSS.
21. *CWL*, 2:342.
22. *LOC*, 96.
23. *CWL*, 2:349–53.
24. *CWL*, 2:354–55.
25. Newton Bateman and Paul Selby, eds., *Historical Encyclopedia of Illinois and History of Shelby County* (Chicago: Munsell, 1910), 786.
26. *CWL*, 2:361–66.
27. T. Lyle Dickey to Ward Hill Lamon, 5 June 1871, Jeremiah S. Black MSS, LC.
28. William H. Herndon to Lyman Trumbull, 11 August 1856, Trumbull MSS, LC.
29. *CWL*, 2:360.
30. *CWL*, 2:374; *CWL, Second Supplement*, 12.
31. *CWL*, 2:376.
32. C. C. Tisler and Aleita G. Tisler, *Lincoln Was Here for Another Go at Douglas* (pamphlet; Jackson, Tenn.: McCowat-Mercer Press, 1958), 21.
33. *CWL*, 2:380.
34. Herndon to Theodore Parker, 12 November 1856, Herndon-Parker MSS, University of Iowa.
35. *CWL*, 2:390–91.
36. *CWL*, 2:385.
37. *ISJ*, 13 December 1856.
38. Henry G. Little, "Personal Recollections of Abraham Lincoln," MS, J. G. Randall MSS, LC.
39. *ISJ*, 1 January 1857.
40. *ChiTrib*, 10 April 1857.
41. New York *Herald*, 3 July 1857.
42. *CWL*, 2:398–410.
43. Osborn H. Oldroyd, ed., *The Lincoln Memorial: Album-Immortelles* (Chicago: Gem Publishing House, 1883), 274.
44. *ISJ*, 16 July 1857.
45. *ChiTrib*, 29 June 1857.
46. Herndon to Wendell Phillips, 29 June 1857, Phillips MSS, Harvard University; Herndon to Parker, 29 June 1857, Herndon-Parker MSS, University of Iowa.
47. *CWL*, 2:382–83.

Chapter 12. "A House Divided"

1. *CWL*, 2:446.
2. *CWL*, 2:437–42, 3:356–63.
3. *CWL*, 2:427.
4. New York *Tribune*, 17 May 1858; Robert W. Johannsen, *Stephen A. Douglas* (New York: Oxford University Press, 1973), 632.
5. Horace Greeley to Schuyler Colfax, 5 February, 6, 17 May, 2 June 1858, Greeley MSS, NYPL; Greeley to Franklin Newhall, 8 January 1859, Greeley MSS, LC.
6. *CWL*, 2:430.
7. William H. Herndon to Elihu B. Washburne, 10 April 1858, Washburne MSS, LC.
8. *CWL*, 2:446.
9. *CWL, [First] Supplement*, 29.
10. *CWL*, 3:394.
11. *CWL*, 2:248–54.
12. New York *Tribune*, 27 May 1858.
13. *HOLL*, 177.
14. Herndon to Lincoln, 24 March 1858, HWP.
15. Herndon to Greeley, 8 April and 20 July 1858, Greeley MSS, NYPL.
16. Herndon to Charles Sumner, 24 April 1858, Sumner MSS, Harvard University; Herndon to Theodore Parker, 27 April 1858, Herndon-Parker MSS; Herndon to Lyman Trumbull, 24 April 1858, Trumbull MSS, LC.
17. *CWL*, 2:444.
18. *CWL*, 2:458.

19. Herndon to Trumbull, 19 February 1858, Trumbull MSS, LC; *HOLL*, 6–8.

20. *CWL*, 2:447.

21. *CWL*, 2:455.

22. *ISJ*, 17 June 1858; Tarbell, *Life of Lincoln*, 1:305.

23. Tarbell, *Life of Lincoln*, 1:304–5.

24. *CWL*, 2:461–69.

25. *ISJ*, 18 June 1858.

26. New York *Tribune*, 24 June and 12 July 1858.

27. LeRoy H. Fischer, ed., "Samuel C. Parks's Reminiscences of Abraham Lincoln," *Lincoln Herald* 68 (Spring 1966): 11–12.

28. *HI*, 163.

29. Lincoln, page proofs of an undated interview by Horace White, Horace White MSS, ALPL.

30. *CWL*, 2:471.

31. Chicago *Times*, 23 June 1858.

32. *CWL*, 2:473–81.

33. *ChiTrib*, 14 July 1858.

34. *HOLL*, 8.

35. Ezra Prince, "A Day and a Night with Abraham Lincoln," 10, HWP.

36. John W. Forney, *Anecdotes of Public Men* (2 vols.; New York: Harper & Brothers, 1881), 2:179.

37. Paul M. Angle, ed., *Created Equal? The Complete Lincoln-Douglas Debates of 1858* (Chicago: University of Chicago Press, 1958), 12–25.

38. *CWL*, 2:502.

39. *CWL*, 2:484–502.

40. *NYT*, 16 July 1858.

41. *ISR*, 8 October 1858.

42. Chicago *Journal*, 12 July 1858.

43. *ISR*, 14 July 1858.

44. *Political Debates between Abraham Lincoln and Stephen A. Douglas* (Cleveland, Ohio: O. S. Hubbell, 1895), 43, 55, 41.

45. Bloomington, Illinois, *Pantagraph*, 17 July 1858.

46. Angle, *Created Equal?*, 62–65.

47. *CWL*, 2:504–21.

48. *ChiTrib*, 16, 18, 19, 20 August 1858; *ISJ*, 19, 20, 21 August 1858.

49. C. D. Hay to Trumbull, 10 July 1857, Trumbull MSS, LC.

50. Cleveland *Plain Dealer*, 5 August 1858.

51. *ChiTrib*, 4 August 1858.

52. Horace White, introduction to *Abraham Lincoln: The True Story of a Great Life*, by William Herndon and Jesse W. Weik (2 vols.; New York: D. Appleton, 1896), 2:101–2, 96–97.

53. Isaac N. Arnold, *Reminiscences of the Illinois-bar Forty Years Ago: Lincoln and Douglas as Orators and Lawyers* (Chicago: Fergus, 1881), 26.

54. *CWL*, 2:546–47.

55. *CWL*, 3:84.

56. W. J. Usrey to Lincoln, 19 July 1858, LP-LC.

57. Chicago *Weekly Times*, 5 August 1858.

58. *OHAL*, 44–45.

59. Seattle *Post-Intelligencer*, 6 February 1916.

60. Henry T. Glover, undated interview by Ida Tarbell, Tarbell MSS.

61. Norman B. Judd to Lincoln, 27 July 1858, LP-LC.

62. *CWL*, 2:528–30.

63. Abraham Smith to Lincoln, 20 July 1858, LP-LC.

64. *NYT*, 13 July 1858.

Chapter 13. "A David Greater Than the Democratic Goliath"

1. *The Liberator* (Boston), 20 July 1860.

2. *CWL*, 2:506.

3. *ChiTrib*, 23 August 1858.

4. *CWL*, 3:12–30.

5. *CWL*, 3:30–37.

6. *Missouri Republican* (St. Louis), 31 August 1858.

7. R. R. Hitt to Horace White, 10 December 1892, White MSS, ALPL.

8. *ChiTrib*, 24, 26 August, 11, 13, 16, 18 October 1858.

9. Chicago *Weekly Times*, 26 August, 2 September 1858.

10. *ChiTrib*, 16 October 1858.

11. *CWL, [First] Supplement*, 32–33.

12. *OHAL*, 45.

13. Joseph Medill to Lincoln, [27 August 1858], LP-LC.

14. *CWL*, 2:530.

15. Gustave Koerner, *Memoirs of Gustave Koerner, 1809–1896*, ed. Thomas J. McCormack (2 vols.; Cedar Rapids, Iowa: Torch Press, 1909), 2:65.

16. *Missouri Democrat* (St. Louis), 11 September 1858.

17. W. M. Chambers to Lincoln and Thomas A. Marshall to Lincoln, both 22 July 1858, LP-LC.

18. *ISR*, 8 August 1858.

19. Chicago *Daily Times*, 9 October 1858.

20. Don E. Fehrenbacher, "Only His Stepchildren: Lincoln and the Negro," *Civil War History* 20 (1974): 304–5.

21. George M. Fredrickson, *Big Enough to be Inconsistent: Abraham Lincoln Confronts Slavery and Race* (Cambridge, Mass.: Harvard University Press, 2008), 41.

22. *RAL*, 446–47.

23. Julian M. Sturtevant, *An Autobiography* (New York: F. J. Revell, 1896), 292.

24. James Oakes, *The Radical and the Republican: Frederick Douglass, Abraham Lincoln, and the Triumph of Antislavery Politics* (New York: Norton, 2007), 125.

25. *CWL*, 3:245–57.

26. *CWL*, 3:283–325.

27. *CWL*, 2:484.

28. John J. Crittenden to Lincoln, 29 July 1858, LP-LC.

29. *ChiTrib*, 5, 17 November 1858.

30. Cincinnati *Commercial*, 12 January 1859.

31. *IWHWT*, 244.

32. Charles S. Zane, "Lincoln as I Knew Him," *JISHS* 14 (1921–22): 79–80.

33. *LOC*, 51, 411; *HI*, 622.

34. *CWL*, 3:339.

35. *ChiTrib*, 29 October, 10 November 1858.

36. Josiah M. Lucas to O. M. Hatch, July [1859], Hatch MSS, ALPL.

37. *CWL*, 3:339, 346, 351, 378.

Chapter 14. "That Presidential Grub Gnaws Deep"

1. J. Russell Jones, "Lincoln and Grant in 1863," Tarbell MSS.

2. Joseph Gillespie to [Martin Hardin], 22 April 1880, Hardin Family MSS, CHM.

3. Henry Villard, *Memoirs of Henry Villard, Journalist and Financier, 1835–1900* (2 vols.; Boston: Houghton Mifflin, 1904), 1:96.

4. Osborn H. Oldroyd, ed., *The Lincoln Memorial: Album-Immortelles* (Chicago: Gem Publishing House, 1883), 473–76.

5. Seth Eyland, *The Evolution of a Life* (New York: S. W. Green's Son, 1884), 293.

6. *CWL*, 3:337.

7. New York *Tribune*, 15 February 1867; William H. Herndon, "Analysis of the Character of Abraham Lincoln," *ALQ* 1 (1941): 429; *HOLL*, 170.

8. *CWL*, 3:345.

9. Lincoln to Thomas Corwin, 9 October 1859, https://www.americanheritage.com/lincoln-heard-and-seen.

10. *CWL*, 3:369–70.

11. *CWL*, 3:375–76.

12. *CWL*, 3:380.

13. *CWL*, 3:384.

14. *CWL*, 3:390–91.

15. *ALS*, 115–16.

16. *CWL*, 3:400–25.

17. *CWL, [First] Supplement*, 44–45; *CWL*, 3:438–62.

18. *CWL*, 3:470–71.

19. *CWL*, 3:471–82.

20. *CWL*, 3:511.

21. Joseph J. Lewis to Jesse W. Fell, 30 January 1860, Fell MSS, LC; West Chester, Pennsylvania, *Chester County Times*, 11 February 1860.

22. Lyman Trumbull to Lincoln, 23 November 1859, LP-LC.

23. William E. Frazer to Lincoln, 12 November 1859, LP-LC.

24. Elwood, Kansas, *Free Press*, 3 December 1859; *CWL*, 3:496; Kansas City *Star*, 11 February 1909.

25. *CWL*, 3:502.

26. *Daily Nebraska State Journal* (Lincoln), 10 July 1890.

27. New York *Tribune*, 30 August 1860.

28. *OHAL*, 46.

29. *Indiana Journal* (Indianapolis), 10 February 1879; *HI*, 247.

30. *Browning Diary*, 1:395.

31. *CWL*, 3:517.

32. Norman B. Judd to Trumbull, 2 April 1860, Trumbull MSS, LC.

33. *ChiTrib*, 27 February 1860.

34. Frederic Bancroft, *The Life of William H. Seward* (2 vols.; New York: Harper & Brothers, 1900), 1:531n.

35. *Nebraska State Journal* (Lincoln), 15 April 1881.

36. Harriet A. Weed and Thurlow Weed Barnes, eds., *Life of Thurlow Weed* (2 vols.; Boston: Houghton Mifflin, 1883–84), 2:269.

37. William Hayes Ward, ed., *Abraham Lincoln, Tributes from His Associates: Reminiscences of Soldiers, Statesmen, and Citizens* (New York: Thomas Y. Crowell, 1895), 28–29; "Lincoln at Plymouth," unidentified clipping, LFFC.

38. Truman H. Bartlett to Charles L. McLellan, 26 August 1908, Lincoln Collection, Brown University.

39. Roy Meredith, *Mr. Lincoln's Camera Man, Matthew B. Brady* (New York: Scribner's, 1946), 59.

40. New York *Evening Post*, 3 May 1865.

41. Brooks, *Lincoln and the Downfall of Slavery*, 186.

42. *CWL*, 3:522–50.

43. Brooks, *Lincoln and the Downfall of Slavery*, 186.

44. New York *Evening Post*, 3 May 1865.

45. John Bigelow to William Hargreaves, 30 July 1860, Bigelow MSS, NYPL; New York *Evening Post*, 28 February 1860.

46. "Greeley's Estimate of Lincoln," *Century Magazine*, July 1891, 373.

47. Charles T. Rodgers to Lincoln, 26 September 1864, LP-LC.

48. New York *Herald*, 19 May 1860.

49. *CWL, [First] Supplement*, 49.

50. *CWL*, 4:25.

51. New York *Independent*, 1 September 1864; *ChiTrib*, 12 February 1900.

52. John P. Bartlet to the editor, *Century Magazine*, July 1897, 475.

53. Patrick McCarty et al. to Lincoln, 16 October 1863, LP-LC.

54. *SMDR*, 3 March 1860.

55. "Lincolniana: The Problem of the Welcoming Speech," *JISHS* 54 (1951): 171.

56. Mark W. Delahay to Lincoln, 17 February, 7 April 1860, LP-LC; *CWL*, 4:32, 44.

57. *CWL*, 4:45.

58. *CWL*, 4:33–34.

59. *CWL*, 4:47–48.

60. Delahay to Lincoln, 26 March, 4 May 1860, LP-LC.

61. New York *Tribune*, 23 May 1860.

62. Charles A. Page, *Letters of a War Correspondent*, ed. James R. Gilmore (Boston: L. C. Page, 1899), 376; Mark A. Plummer, *Lincoln's Rail-Splitter: Governor Richard J. Oglesby* (Urbana: University of Illinois Press, 2001), 41–42; *HI*, 462–63; *ISJ*, 7 May 1860.

63. New York *Tribune*, n.d., reprinted in the Fremont, Ohio, *Journal*, 15 June 1860.

64. Ida Tarbell to John S. Phillips, 16 November 1922, Tarbell MSS; Nathaniel G. Wilcox to Lincoln, 6 June 1864, LP-LC.

65. J. M. Ruggles, "Reminiscences of the Pekin Convention and of Abraham Lincoln," Tarbell MSS.

66. Isaac N. Phillips, *Abraham Lincoln, by Some Men Who Knew Him*, ed. Paul M. Angle (1910; Chicago: Americana House, 1950), 65.

67. William Bross to John G. Nicolay, 25 January 1887, Nicolay MSS, LC.

Chapter 15. "The Most Available Presidential Candidate for Unadulterated Republicans"

1. Nathan M. Knapp to O. M. Hatch, Winchester, Illinois, 12 May 1859, Hatch MSS, ALPL.

2. *CWL*, 4:50.

3. *LTC*, 289.
4. New York *Sun*, 26 July 1891.
5. *NYT*, 21 May 1860.
6. Chicago *Herald*, 19 May 1860.
7. Cincinnati *Commercial*, 21 May 1860.
8. *ChiTrib*, 14 April 1895.
9. Murat Halsted, *The Caucuses of 1860: A History of the National Political Conventions* (Columbus: Follett, Foster, 1860), 149.
10. Cincinnati *Commercial*, 21 May 1860.
11. *ISJ*, 8 June 1865; *Central Illinois Gazette*, 23 May 1860; *HI*, 490–91; Charles S. Zane, "Lincoln As I Knew Him," *JISHS* 14 (1921–22): 82–83.
12. Paul M. Angle, *"Here I Have Lived": A History of Lincoln's Springfield* (Springfield: Abraham Lincoln Association, 1935), 237.

Chapter 16. "I Have Been Elected Mainly on the Cry 'Honest Old Abe'"

1. Joshua Giddings to Lincoln, 19 May 1860, LP-LC.
2. *OHAL*, 41.
3. *RLAP*, 319, 322.
4. *CWL*, 4:51.
5. Schurz, *Reminiscences*, 2:188.
6. *CWL, Second Supplement*, 20.
7. Thurlow Weed to William Henry Seward, 20 May 1860, Seward MSS, University of Rochester.
8. New York *Evening Post*, 8 September 1860.
9. *HI*, 57.
10. Carl Schurz, *Speeches, Correspondence and Political Papers of Carl Schurz*, ed. Frederic Bancroft (6 vols.; New York: G. P. Putnam's Sons, 1913), 1:120–21.
11. *North American and United States Gazette* (Philadelphia), 22 August 1860.
12. New York *Evening Post*, 3 May 1865.
13. *CWL*, 4:102.
14. Rufus Rockwell Wilson, *Lincoln in Portraiture* (New York: Press of the Pioneers, 1935), 109–10.
15. *CWL*, 4:109.
16. Steven Rowan, ed., *Germans for a Free Missouri: Translations from the St. Louis Radical Press, 1857–1862* (Columbia: University of Missouri Press, 1983), 130.
17. Rowan, *Germans for a Free Missouri*, 130–31.
18. *CWL*, 4:127.
19. David Davis to his wife, 15, 18 October 1860, David Davis MSS, ALPL.
20. *CWL*, 4:97–98.
21. New York *Herald*, 22, 23 May, 21 July 1860.
22. Joseph Medill to Lincoln, 5 July 1860, LP-LC.
23. *ChiTrib*, 17 October 1860.
24. New York *World*, 13 September 1860.
25. *Independent Democrat* (Concord, N.H.), 22 November 1860.
26. New York *Tribune*, 7, 10 November 1860.
27. Samuel R. Weed, "Hearing the Returns with Mr. Lincoln," *NYT Magazine*, 14 February 1932.
28. *Missouri Democrat* (St. Louis), 8 November 1860.
29. Weed, "Hearing the Returns."
30. Michael Burlingame, ed., *Abraham Lincoln: The Observations of John G. Nicolay and John Hay* (Carbondale: Southern Illinois University Press, 2007), 22.
31. New York *Tribune*, 8, 12 November 1860; Weed, "Hearing the Returns"; *Missouri Democrat* (St. Louis), 8 November 1860.
32. Weed, "Hearing the Returns."
33. Willard King, *Lincoln's Manager, David Davis* (Cambridge, Mass.: Harvard University Press, 1960), 161.
34. Medill to O. M. Hatch, 16 November 1860, Hatch MSS, ALPL.
35. New York *Tribune*, 9 July 1860.
36. *Douglass' Monthly*, December 1860, 370.
37. New York *Herald*, 30 June 1860.
38. Oliver R. Barrett to Albert J. Beveridge, 17 June 1926, Beveridge MSS, LC.
39. Gideon Welles, "Recollections in regard to the Formation of Mr. Lincoln's

Cabinet," Lincoln Collection, Beinecke Library, Yale University.

Chapter 17. "I Will Suffer Death before I Will Consent to Any Concession or Compromise"

1. George Sumner to John A. Andrew, 21 January 1861, Andrew MSS, MaHS.
2. *HOLL*, 15.
3. Sumner to Andrew, 21 January 1861.
4. *LJ*, 18.
5. Thomas D. Jones to [William Linn McMillen], 11 February 1861, Lincoln MSS, Indiana University, Bloomington.
6. *Villard Dispatches*, 49–51.
7. Henry Cleveland, *Alexander H. Stephens, in Public and Private* (Philadelphia: National, 1866), 721.
8. Donn Piatt, *Memories of the Men Who Saved the Union* (New York: Belford, Clarke, 1887), 30.
9. *CG*, 36th Cong., 2nd sess., 56 (1860).
10. George G. Fogg to Horace Greeley, 1 December 1860, Greeley MSS, LC.
11. *CWL*, 4:138–40.
12. *Villard Dispatches*, 33–34.
13. *CWL*, 4:141–42.
14. *Villard Dispatches*, 63–65.
15. John Thomas Hubbell, "The Northern Democracy and the Crisis of Disunion, 1860–1861" (Ph.D. diss., University of Illinois, 1969), 233–34.
16. *Missouri Democrat* (St. Louis), 8 January 1861.
17. *CWL*, 4:175–76.
18. Sumner to Andrew, 21 January 1861.
19. *Villard Dispatches*, 84, 127.
20. *CWL*, 4:160.
21. James D. Richardson, ed., *A Compilation of the Messages and Papers of the Presidents, 1789–1908* (Washington, D.C.: Bureau of National Literature and Art, 1909), 3157.
22. *Seward at Washington*, 1:480.
23. *CWL*, 4:149–53.
24. New York *Herald*, 15 December 1860.
25. *Villard Dispatches*, 368; *CWL*, 4:158.
26. Charles Francis Adams Jr. diary, 22 December 1861, Adams Family MSS, MaHS.
27. William S. Robinson, *"Warrington" Pen-Portraits: A Collection of Personal and Political Reminiscences* (Boston: Lee & Shepard, 1877), 93.
28. Carl Schurz, *Intimate Letters of Carl Schurz*, ed. Joseph Schaefer (Madison: State Historical Society of Wisconsin, 1928), 236, 237.
29. Joshua Giddings to George W. Julian, 14 December 1860, Giddings-Julian MSS, LC; Giddings to Gerrit Smith, 29 December 1860, Smith MSS, Syracuse University.
30. Charles Sumner to Joseph R. Hawley, 31 January 1861, Hawley MSS, LC.

Chapter 18. "What If I Appoint Cameron, Whose Very Name Stinks in the Nostrils of the People for His Corruption?"

1. Harriet A. Weed and Thurlow Weed Barnes, eds., *Life of Thurlow Weed* (2 vols.; Boston: Houghton Mifflin, 1883–84), 1:605–6.
2. Isaac N. Phillips, *Abraham Lincoln, by Some Men Who Knew Him*, ed. Paul M. Angle (1910; Chicago: Americana House, 1950), 114–15.
3. Montgomery Blair to Gideon Welles, 17 May 1873, Welles MSS, LC.
4. *WLWH*, 18.
5. Howard Carroll, *Twelve Americans: Their Lives and Times* (New York: Harper & Brothers, 1883), 154.
6. John A. Gilmer to Lincoln, 19 December 1860, LP-LC.
7. Frank Blair to Montgomery Blair, [15 December 1860], Blair and Lee Family MSS, Princeton University.
8. Joshua Speed to Welles, 8 August 1872, Lincoln Collection, Beinecke Library, Yale University.
9. *WLWH*, 17–19; Silas Noble to Elihu B. Washburne, 17 December 1860, Washburne MSS, LC.

10. Alexander K. McClure to Ward Hill Lamon, 8 May 1871, Jeremiah Black MSS, LC.

11. David Wilmot to Lincoln, 12 December 1860, LP-LC.

12. *OHAL*, 42; S. W. Crawford, memo of conversation with Simon Cameron, July 1883, S. W. Crawford MSS, ALPL.

13. *CWL*, 4:168.

14. *CWL*, 4:170.

15. Lyman Trumbull to Lincoln, 20 January 1861, LP-LC.

16. *CWL*, 4:174.

17. *OHAL*, 41.

18. *CWL*, 4:179–80.

19. William Butler to Trumbull, 7 February 1861, Trumbull MSS, LC; William Larimer to Cameron, 6 February 1861, Cameron MSS, LC.

20. Albany *Evening Journal*, 9 January 1861.

21. George G. Fogg to Lincoln, 5 February 1861, LP-LC.

22. William M. Wilson to Lincoln, 19 January 1861, and John D. Defrees to David Davis, 18 January 1861, LP-LC.

23. J. W. Schuckers, *The Life and Public Services of Salmon Portland Chase* (New York: D. Appleton, 1874), 201.

24. Salmon P. Chase, *The Salmon P. Chase Papers*, ed. John Niven (5 vols.; Kent, Ohio: Kent State University Press, 1993–98), 3:47.

25. Salmon P. Chase to John Jay, 16 January 1861, Jay Family MSS, Columbia University.

26. *WLWH*, 15.

27. *Nebraska State Journal* (Lincoln), 15 April 1881.

28. Weed and Barnes, *Life of Weed*, 1:611–12.

29. *CWL*, 4:161.

30. *CWL*, 4:162.

31. John Bigelow, *Retrospections of an Active Life* (5 vols.; New York: Baker & Taylor, 1909–13), 1:318.

32. Boston *Daily Advertiser*, 2 February 1861.

33. *Seward at Washington*, 1:491–97.

34. *RW*, 391.

35. William Henry Seward to Lincoln, 26 December 1860, LP-LC.

36. Fogg to Welles, 27 January 1861, Welles MSS, ALPL; *CWL*, 4:176; New York *Herald*, 23 January 1861.

37. Norman B. Judd to Chase, 16 January 1861, Chase MSS, LC.

38. Seward to Lincoln, 27 January 1861, LP-LC.

39. *CWL*, 4:183.

40. Henry Winter Davis to Samuel Francis du Pont, 14 February 1861, Du Pont MSS, Hagley Museum, Wilmington, Delaware.

41. *Seward at Washington*, 1:502, 505.

42. William Jayne to Trumbull, 28 January 1861, Trumbull MSS, LC.

43. *Browning Diary*, 1:453.

44. *CWL*, 4:137, 159.

45. New York *Herald*, 7 January 1861.

46. *HOLL*, 386.

47. *HOLL*, 390.

48. Nathan Allen, diary, entry for 1 February 1861, Missouri Historical Society, St. Louis.

49. Rufus Rockwell Wilson, *Lincoln in Portraiture* (New York: Press of the Pioneers, 1935), 149.

50. *WLWH*, 21.

51. J[ames] H. v[an] A[len] to Horace Greeley, 21 December 1860, Greeley MSS, NYPL.

52. New York *Tribune*, 5 February 1888.

Chapter 19. "The Man Does Not Live Who Is More Devoted to Peace Than I Am, but It May Be Necessary to Put the Foot Down Firmly"

1. *LJ*, 24.

2. Detroit *Free Press*, 2 January 1910.

3. *CWL*, 4:190.

4. Baltimore *Sun*, 13 February 1861.

5. *ISJ*, 12 February 1861.

6. *OHAL*, 113.

7. *CWL*, 4:195–96.

8. *CWL*, 4:199.

9. *CWL*, 4:199.

10. New York *Herald*, 14 February 1861.

11. *CWL*, 4:204.

12. C. Carter to William Overton Winston, 16 February 1861, Winston Family MSS, Virginia Historical Society.

13. *CWL*, 4:207.

14. *CWL*, 4:210–15.

15. *CWL*, 4:215–16.

16. *OHAL*, 112.

17. Grace Bedell to Lincoln, 18 October 1860, LP-LC; *CWL*, 4:129.

18. New York *Evening Post*, 1 February 1861.

19. *LJ*, 32; Westfield, New York, *Republican*, 14 May 1939.

20. *CWL*, 4:219–20.

21. *CWL*, 4:220–21.

22. New York *Tribune*, 19 February 1861.

23. *CWL*, 4:226.

24. *CWL*, 4:228.

25. Walt Whitman, *Prose Works* (Philadelphia: David McKay, 1892), 500–501.

26. *NYT*, 20 February 1861.

27. New York *Tribune*, 20 February 1861.

28. New York *Daily News*, 5 March 1861.

29. Thurlow Weed to William Henry Seward, 21 February 1861, Seward MSS, University of Rochester.

30. *CWL*, 4:223.

31. *NYT*, 21 February 1861; New York *Herald*, 22 February 1861.

32. Boston *Journal*, 26 February 1861.

33. Philadelphia *Press*, 22 February 1861.

34. *CWL*, 4:236–37; *LJ*, 40; Philadelphia *Press*, 22 February 1861.

35. New York *Herald*, 22 February 1861.

36. *LJ*, 40.

37. *CWL*, 4:235–36.

38. New York *World*, 25 February 1861.

39. *CWL*, 4:238–39.

40. Frederick W. Seward, *Reminiscences of a War-Time Statesman and Diplomat, 1830–1915* (New York: G. P. Putnam's Sons, 1916), 134–38.

41. Nicolay and Hay, *Lincoln*, 3:307.

42. *CWL*, 4:240–41.

43. Allan Pinkerton, *History and Evidence of the Passage of Abraham Lincoln from Harrisburg, Pa., to Washington, D.C.* (Chicago: Republican, 1868), 13–20.

44. Alexander K. McClure to Alonzo Rothschild, 9 May 1907, LFFC.

45. *LJ*, 41–42.

46. *CWL*, 4:243–45.

47. Philadelphia *Inquirer*, 23 February 1861.

48. Pinkerton, *History and Evidence*, 22.

49. Norma B. Cuthbert, ed., *Lincoln and the Baltimore Plot, 1861: From Pinkerton Records and Related Papers* (San Marino, Calif.: Huntington Library, 1949), 112.

50. *RAL*, 38.

51. New York *Daily News*, 26, 28 February 1861.

52. *NYT*, 25 February 1861.

53. George Templeton Strong, *The Diary of George Templeton Strong, 1835–1875*, ed. Allan Nevins and Milton Halsey Thomas (4 vols.; New York: Macmillan, 1952), 3:102 (entry for 18 February 1861).

54. Cincinnati *Gazette*, 26 February 1861.

Chapter 20. "I Am Now Going to Be Master"

1. Lucius E. Chittenden, *Recollections of President Lincoln and His Administration* (New York: Harper & Brothers, 1891), 71.

2. John Z. Goodrich to John A. Andrew, 23 February 1861, Andrew MSS, MaHS.

3. Philadelphia *Press*, 28 February 1861.

4. Philadelphia *Inquirer*, 9 March 1861.

5. Washington *Evening Star*, 28 February 1861.

6. Alexander K. McClure, ed., *The Annals of the War Written by Leading Participants North and South* (Philadelphia: Times Publishing Company, 1879), 220–27.

7. Charles Francis Adams Jr., *Charles Francis Adams, 1835–1915: An Autobiography* (Boston: Houghton Mifflin, 1916), 78.

8. *Seward at Washington*, 1:512.

9. James Milliken to Cameron, 22 February 1861, Cameron MSS, LC.

10. Fawn Brodie, *Thaddeus Stevens: Scourge of the South* (New York: Norton, 1959), 148.

11. *OHAL*, 42.

12. *RLAP*, 226.

13. Frank Blair to Montgomery Blair, [13 December 1860], Blair-Lee Family MSS, Princeton University.

14. Charles A. Dana, *Recollections of the Civil War: With the Leaders at Washington and in the Field in the Sixties* (New York: D. Appleton, 1898), 170; *LO*, 48.

15. *NYT*, 4 March 1861.

16. Philadelphia *Inquirer*, 4 March 1861.

17. *Welles Diary*, 3:391–92.

18. *OHAL*, 47.

19. F. B. Sanborn, *Recollections of Seventy Years* (2 vols.; Boston: R. G. Badger, 1909), 1:26–27.

20. *CWL*, 4:273.

21. John Bigelow diary, 27 March 1861, Bigelow MSS, NYPL.

22. J. W. Schuckers, *The Life and Public Services of Salmon Portland Chase* (New York: D. Appleton, 1874), 207.

23. James G. Blaine, *Twenty Years of Congress: From Lincoln to Garfield* (2 vols.; Norwich, Conn.: Henry Bill, 1884–86), 1:286.

24. New York *Tribune*, 9 August 1885.

25. *Missouri Democrat* (St. Louis), 9 March 1861.

26. *ALS*, 119.

27. Stephen Fiske, "When Lincoln Was First Inaugurated," *Ladies' Home Journal* 14 (March 1897): 8; [Mary Abigail Dodge], *Gail Hamilton's Life in Letters* (2 vols.; Boston: Lee & Shepard, 1901), 1:314.

28. Fiske, "When Lincoln Was First Inaugurated," 8.

29. Benjamin Brown French, *Witness to the Young Republic: A Yankee's Journal, 1828–1870*, ed. Donald B. Cole and John J. McDonough (Hanover, N.H.: University Press of New England, 1989), 348.

30. Charles Francis Adams Jr. diary, 4 March 1861, Adams Family MSS, MaHS.

31. Edward Everett diary, 4 March 1861, Everett MSS, MaHS.

32. Herbert Mitgang, ed., *Abraham Lincoln: A Press Portrait* (Chicago: Quadrangle Books, 1971), 242, 244.

33. *Douglass' Monthly*, April 1861, 475.

34. Diary of Samuel J. May, 4 March 1861, May MSS, Cornell University.

35. *CG*, 37th Cong., 4th sess., 1439.

36. Baltimore *Clipper*, 9 March 1861.

37. Washington *Daily Globe*, 6 March 1861.

38. Knoxville *Tri-Weekly Whig*, 16 March 1861.

39. *CWL*, 4:424.

Chapter 21. "A Man So Busy in Letting Rooms in One End of His House, That He Can't Stop to Put Out the Fire That Is Burning in the Other"

1. *WLWH*, 46.

2. Henry J. Raymond, *The Life and Public Services of Abraham Lincoln* (New York: Derby & Miller, 1865), 720.

3. *HI*, 206–7.

4. Harry J. Carman and Reinhard H. Luthin, *Lincoln and the Patronage* (New York: Columbia University Press, 1943), 336.

5. Cincinnati *Commercial*, 8 March 1861.

6. Ben: Perley Poore, "Reminiscences of the Great Northern Uprising," *Youth's Companion* 26 (July 1883): 301.

7. Hawkins Taylor to William Butler, 22 March 1861, Hatch MSS, ALPL.

8. Henry Villard, *Memoirs of Henry Villard, Journalist and Financier, 1835–1900* (2 vols.; Boston: Houghton Mifflin, 1904), 1:156.

9. Alexander Milton Ross, *Recollections and Experiences of an Abolitionist: From 1855 to 1865* (Toronto: Rowsell & Hutchinson, 1875), 138.

10. *ALS*, 5.

11. *ALS*, 126.

12. George Gibbs to John Austin Stevens, 16 March 1861, Stevens MSS, New-York Historical Society, New York.

13. Charles Washburn to Elihu B. Washburne, 23 May 1861, "The Early Life and Congressional Career of Elihu B. Washburne," by Russell K. Nelson (Ph.D. diss., University of North Dakota, 1954), 238.

14. Cincinnati *Commercial*, 11, 12, 13 March 1861.

15. *IWHWT*, 161.

16. Edwin M. Stanton to James Buchanan, 3 April 1861, Buchanan MSS, Historical Society of Pennsylvania, Philadelphia.

17. *HI*, 206–7.

18. Carman and Luthin, *Lincoln and the Patronage*, 54.

19. Samuel Galloway to Thurlow Weed, 23 March 1861, Weed MSS; Galloway to David Davis, 29 March 1861, David Davis MSS, ALPL.

20. *CWL*, 4:149.

21. *ALS*, 125.

22. William H. Herndon, "Lincoln's Individuality," HWP.

23. *LOC*, 439.

24. New York *Herald*, 8 March 1861.

25. Charles Francis Adams Jr. diary, 10 March 1861, Adams Family MSS, MaHS.

26. *CWL*, 6:51.

27. *CWL*, 4:321.

28. David Donald, *Lincoln's Herndon* (New York: Knopf, 1948), 153–55.

29. *HI*, 165.

30. Leonard Swett to Lincoln, 15 August 1861, LP-LC.

31. *HI*, 620; New York *Herald*, 9 December 1860.

32. Lavern Marshall Hamand, "Ward Hill Lamon: Lincoln's 'Particular Friend'" (Ph.D. diss., University of Illinois, 1949), 233–52; Clint Clay Tilton, *Lincoln and Lamon: Partners and Friends* (Springfield: Illinois State Historical Society, 1931), 27–29; *RLAP*, 218–21.

33. *NYT*, 1 April 1861.

34. Portland *Oregonian*, 29 April 1861.

35. *RAL*, 51.

36. Philadelphia *Press*, 1 April 1861.

37. Cincinnati *Commercial*, 1 April 1861.

38. Brooks, *Lincoln and the Downfall of Slavery*, 417.

39. Egbert L. Viele, "A Trip with Lincoln, Chase and Stanton," *Scribner's Monthly* 16 (October 1878): 818.

40. John Conness to Andrew Johnson, 31 May 1865, William H. Wallace file, NARA microfilm M650.

41. J. Edward Murr, "Some Pertinent Observations Concerning '*Abe Lincoln—The Hoosier*,'" 17–18, Murr MSS, DePauw University, Greencastle, Indiana.

42. Joseph Bucklin Bishop, *Notes and Anecdotes of Many Years* (New York: Scribner's, 1925), 65–66.

43. *RAL*, 239–40.

44. Herbert Mitgang, ed., *Abraham Lincoln: A Press Portrait* (Chicago: Quadrangle Books, 1971), 274.

45. Maunsell B. Field, *Memories of Many Men and of Some Women* (New York: Harper, 1874), 310.

46. *CWL*, 4:151.

47. New York *Herald*, 19 March 1861.

48. Boston *Journal*, 7 March 1861.

49. *SMDR*, 30 March 1861; Baltimore *Sun*, 26 March 1861.

50. New York *World*, 15 March 1861.

51. Michael Burlingame, "The Early Life of Carl Schurz, 1829–1865" (Ph.D. diss., Johns Hopkins University, 1971), 320–54.

52. New York *Herald*, 25 March 1861.

53. *RAL*, 300.

54. Albert G. Brown Jr. to John A. Andrew, [28 March 1861], Andrew MSS, MaHS.

55. *Bates Diary*, 177; *NYT*, 11 March 1861.

56. Herman Melville, *The Letters of Herman Melville*, ed. Merrell R. Davis and William H. Gilman (New Haven: Yale University Press, 1960), 210.

57. Betty John, *Libby: The Sketches, Letters & Journal of Libby Beaman* (Tulsa, Okla.: Council Oak Books, 1987), 23; Edouard de Stoeckl to Alexander Gortchakov, 12 March 1861, dispatch 15, Principal Archive of the Ministry of Foreign Affairs,

Russian Reproductions, MSS of the Foreign Copying Project, LC.

58. David Dixon Porter, "Journal of Occurrences during the War of the Rebellion," 1:56–58, Porter MSS, LC.

Chapter 22. "You Can Have No Conflict Without Being Yourselves the Aggressors"

1. Nicolay and Hay, *Lincoln*, 3:371.
2. Charles Francis Adams Jr. to Frederic Bancroft, 11 October 1911, Allan Nevins MSS, Columbia University.
3. *CWL*, 4:279; *WLWH*, 30.
4. *CWL*, 4:284.
5. New York *Morning Express*, 2 April 1861.
6. *OHAL*, 63–64; Stephen A. Hurlbut to Lincoln, 27 March 1861, LP-LC.
7. John A. Campbell, "Facts of History," *Southern Historical Society Papers* 42 (1917): 31–34.
8. Cincinnati *Commercial*, 2 April 1861.
9. *OR*, I, 1:200–201.
10. Montgomery Blair to Gideon Welles, 24 November 1870, Welles MSS, Connecticut Historical Society, Hartford; Blair to Welles, 17 May 1873, Welles MSS, LC; Blair to Welles, 22 January 1874, Lincoln Collection, Yale University; Blair to S. W. Crawford, 6 May 1882, Crawford MSS, LC.
11. Sam Ward to S. L. M. Barlow, 31 March 1861, Barlow MSS, Huntington Library, San Marino, California.
12. LP-LC; *Welles Diary*, 1:6.
13. Joseph Blanchard to Lincoln, 28 March 1861, LP-LC.
14. Montgomery C. Meigs diary, copy, 31 March 1861, Nicolay MSS, LC.
15. E. D. Keyes, *Fifty Years' Observations of Men and Events* (New York: Charles Scribner's Sons, 1884), 378.
16. William Henry Seward, memo on Fort Sumter, 29 March 1861, LP-LC.
17. Philadelphia *Press*, 18 September 1865.
18. Keyes, *Fifty Years' Observation*, 382–86; Meigs diary, 31 March 1861.
19. David Dixon Porter, *Incidents and Anecdotes of the Civil War* (New York: D. Appleton, 1885), 15; statement by Porter, 25 March 1873, Crawford MSS, LC; David Dixon Porter, "Journal of Occurrences during the War of the Rebellion," 1:52–68, Porter MSS, LC.
20. Gideon Welles, "Fort Sumter," *Galaxy*, November 1870, 57–61; *Welles Diary*, 1:16–21.
21. *Welles Diary*, 1:24–25; Welles, "Fort Sumter," 66–67.
22. Gustavus Vasa Fox, *Confidential Correspondence of Gustavus Vasa Fox*, ed. Robert Means Thompson and Richard Wainwright (2 vols.; New York: De Vinne, 1918–19), 1:33, 42–43; Fox to his wife, 2 May 1861, Fox MSS, New-York Historical Society, New York.
23. Welles to Blair, 30 April 1873, Blair Family MSS, LC.
24. *Welles Diary*, 1:25; Welles, "Fort Sumter," 68–69.
25. Seward to Lincoln, 1 April 1861, LP-LC.
26. *CWL*, 4:317.
27. *Army and Navy Register*, 31 May 1913; Fox, *Confidential Correspondence*, 1:39.
28. Simon Cameron to Robert S. Chew, 6 April 1861, LP-LC.
29. "Fort Sumpter," undated memo, George Harrington MSS, Missouri Historical Society, St. Louis.
30. Nicolay and Hay, *Lincoln*, 4:62.
31. Cleveland *Plain Dealer*, 9 April 1861.
32. George P. Bissell to Welles, 9 April 1861, Welles MSS, Huntington Library, San Marino, California.
33. New York *Herald*, 11 April 1861.
34. Cincinnati *Commercial*, 11 April 1861.
35. Cincinnati *Commercial*, 12 April 1861; New York *Herald*, 12 April 1861.
36. John A. Bingham, "Abraham Lincoln," *Current* (Chicago), 24 April 1886, 282.
37. Fox, *Confidential Correspondence*, 1:34–35.
38. Lincoln to Gustavus Fox, 1 May 1861, draft, LP-LC.
39. *CWL*, 4:424.

40. *Seward at Washington*, 2:590.
41. *Complete Hay Diary*, 211–12.
42. *CWL*, 8:332.
43. *Browning Diary*, 1:453.

Chapter 23. "*I Intend to Give* Blows"

1. *CWL*, 4:345.
2. *CWL*, 6:263.
3. *CWL*, 5:537.
4. New York *World*, 13 April 1861; *ISR*, 16 April 1861.
5. New York *World*, 13 April 1861.
6. Benjamin Brown French to Frank French, 14 April 1861, French Family MSS, LC.
7. Alexander K. McClure, *Abraham Lincoln and Men of War-Times* (Philadelphia: Times, 1892), 68–69.
8. New York *Evening Post*, 18 August 1863.
9. *OR*, III, 1:68.
10. John Pendleton Kennedy to Robert C. Winthrop, 25 April 1861, Winthrop Family MSS, MaHS.
11. George W. Brown, *Baltimore and the Nineteenth of April 1861* (Baltimore: N. Murray, 1887), 74.
12. *LJ*, 57–58.
13. Diary of Clifford Arrick, 20 April 1861, Frontier Guard Records, LC.
14. Nicolay and Hay, *Lincoln*, 4:152.
15. Philadelphia *Inquirer*, 19 April 1861.
16. *Complete Hay Diary*, 2–3.
17. *NYT*, 23 April 1861.
18. George W. Brown and Thomas H. Hicks to Lincoln, 18, 19 April 1861, LP-LC.
19. Benjamin F. Butler, *Butler's Book* (Boston: Thayer, 1892), 180.
20. *CWL*, 4:340; *WLWH*, 34–35; *Complete Hay Diary*, 5.
21. *WLWH*, 36, 37.
22. Cincinnati *Commercial*, 30 April 1861.
23. New York *World*, 24 April 1861.
24. *Complete Hay Diary*, 5, 6.
25. *CWL*, 4:341–42; Baltimore *Sun*, 23 April 1861; *NYT*, 27 April 1861; New York *Evening Post*, 24 April 1861.
26. John Austin Stevens, *The Union Defence Committee of the City of New York* (New York: Union Defence Committee, 1885), 154.
27. *CWL*, 4:342–43.
28. *Complete Hay Diary*, 11.
29. *Complete Hay Diary*, 12; *CWL*, 4:344.
30. *ChiTrib*, 7 May 1861; New York *Tribune*, 8 May 1861; *CWL*, 4:356; *Complete Hay Diary*, 17–18.
31. New York *Tribune*, 24 April 1861; Francis B. Carpenter, "A Day with Governor Seward at Auburn," July 1870, Seward MSS, University of Rochester.
32. *CWL*, 4:372.
33. James G. Randall, *Constitutional Problems under Lincoln* (rev. ed.; Urbana: University of Illinois Press, 1951), 121.
34. Lincoln, 4 July 1861 message to Congress, Lincoln MSS, LC (online edition, Douglas Wilson's version of the second printed draft with Lincoln's emendations).
35. New York *Tribune*, 17 May 1861.
36. *CWL*, 4:532.
37. *LOC*, 332.
38. New York *Tribune*, 5 May 1861.
39. *CWL*, 4:428.
40. *McClellan Papers*, 28–29.
41. *OR*, I, 1:675.
42. Reminiscences of Francis Pierpont, typescript, Pierpont MSS, West Virginia University.
43. Schurz, *Reminiscences*, 2:242.
44. *CWL*, 4:422–41.
45. Herman Belz, *Reconstructing the Union: Theory and Policy during the Civil War* (Ithaca: Cornell University Press, 1969), 24–28.
46. *LJ*, 188.
47. *SMDR*, 8 February 1862.
48. James A. Hamilton, *Reminiscences* (New York: C. Scribner, 1869), 477.
49. New York *Tribune*, 25 May 1861; New York *Herald*, 25 May 1861.
50. Los Angeles *Times*, 4 June 1887; St. Louis *Post-Dispatch*, 24 May 1901.
51. William A. Croffut, *An American Procession, 1855–1914* (Boston: Little, Brown, 1931), 123.

52. United States Congress, *Report of the Joint Committee on the Conduct of the War* (3 vols.; Washington, D.C., 1863), 2:38.

53. William B. Wilson, *A Leaf from the History of the Rebellion* (Harrisburg, Pa.: Meyers, 1888), 7–8.

54. John A. Dahlgren diary, copy, 21 July 1861, Nicolay MSS, LC.

55. *OR*, I, 2:747.

56. *WLWH*, 51.

57. *OR*, I, 2:747; Nicolay and Hay, *Lincoln*, 4:353–54.

58. *OR*, I, 2:316.

59. *CG*, 37th Cong., 1st sess., 246, 387.

60. *Browning Diary*, 1:485.

61. Worthington Chauncey Ford, ed., *A Cycle of Adams Letters, 1861–1865* (2 vols.; Boston: Houghton Mifflin, 1920), 1:22.

62. George P. Goff to John G. Nicolay, 9 February 1889, Nicolay MSS, LC.

63. Orville H. Browning to Lincoln, 19 August 1861, LP-LC.

64. *ALS*, 126.

65. William T. Sherman, *Memoirs of Gen. William T. Sherman* (2 vols.; New York: D. Appleton, 1875), 1:293.

66. William O. Stoddard, *Dispatches from Lincoln's White House: The Anonymous Civil War Journalism of Presidential Secretary William O. Stoddard*, ed. Michael Burlingame (Lincoln: University of Nebraska Press, 1998), 16.

Chapter 24. Sitzkrieg

1. Benjamin Brown French to Frank French, 8 December 1861, French Family MSS, LC.

2. William B. Wilson, *A Few Acts and Actors in the Tragedy of the Civil War in the United States* (Philadelphia: self-published, 1892), 111.

3. *McClellan Papers*, 70.

4. *McClellan Papers*, 71–75.

5. U.S. Army, *General Orders* (1862), 5.

6. Henry L. Dawes, "A Study of Abraham Lincoln," 53–57, Dawes MSS, LC.

7. *Complete Hay Diary*, 30.

8. *LJ*, 126; *Complete Hay Diary*, 25.

9. *IWAL*, 182.

10. *Complete Hay Diary*, 32.

11. David Dixon Porter, "Journal of Occurrences during the War of the Rebellion," 1:173–74, Porter MSS, LC.

12. *McClellan Papers*, 106–7.

13. *McClellan Papers*, 116–17.

14. *McClellan Papers*, 128.

15. *OR*, V, 1:9–11; Kenneth P. Williams, *Lincoln Finds a General: A Military Study of the Civil War* (5 vols.; New York: Macmillan, 1949–59), 1:127–30.

16. *LJ*, 122; *RAL*, 172.

17. New York *World*, 29 October 1861; Boston *Evening Journal*, 1 November 1861.

18. Robert Anderson to Lincoln, 13 September 1861, LP-LC.

19. *The Liberator* (Boston), 18 November 1861.

20. *CWL*, 4:506.

21. *Complete Hay Diary*, 123.

22. *IWAL*, 204.

23. Charles Edwards Lester, *Life and Public Services of Charles Sumner* (New York: United States Publishing Company, 1874), 359–60.

24. *SMDR*, 17 September 1861.

25. *CWL*, 5:1–2.

26. *OR*, I, 8:389–90.

27. *CWL*, 5:84–85.

28. Mark Howard to Gideon Welles, 14 November 1861, and Fanny Eames to Welles, 14 November 1861, Welles MSS, LC.

29. *Official Records of the Union and Confederate Navies in the War of the Rebellion* (30 vols.; Washington, D.C.: Government Printing Office, 1894–1922), 12:291.

30. George B. McClellan to Lincoln, 10 December 1861, LP-LC.

31. John A. Dahlgren diary, copy, Nicolay MSS, LC.

32. Hans L. Trefousse, *The Radical Republicans: Lincoln's Vanguard for Racial Justice* (New York: Knopf, 1969), 184.

33. *CWL*, 5:88.

34. George W. Julian, *Political Recollections, 1840 to 1872* (Chicago: Jansen, McClurg, 1884), 201–3.

35. *CWL*, 5:91–92.

36. *CWL*, 5:95.

37. M. C. Meigs, "The Relations of President Lincoln and Secretary Stanton to the Military Commanders in the Civil War," *American Historical Review* 26 (1921): 292.

38. Henry J. Raymond, *The Life of Abraham Lincoln* (New York: Derby & Miller, 1864), 773–76.

39. Raymond, *Life of Lincoln*, 776–77.

40. Meigs, "Relations of President Lincoln," 292–93.

41. Alexander K. McClure, ed., *The Annals of the War Written by Leading Participants North and South* (Philadelphia: Times Publishing Company, 1879), 78–79.

42. Raymond, *Life of Lincoln*, 777; Meigs, "Relations of President Lincoln," 293, 295.

43. Malcolm Ives to James G. Bennett, 15 January 1862 [misdated 1861], Bennett MSS, LC.

44. *Bates Diary*, 223–26.

45. Welles, *Selected Essays*, 270.

46. Cincinnati *Commercial*, 3 January 1862; New York *Tribune*, 31 December 1861; London *Times*, 3 December 1861.

47. *Browning Diary*, 1:513–14.

48. William Howard Russell, *My Diary North and South* (New York: Harper & Brothers, 1863), 587.

49. *CWL*, 5:63.

50. *Bates Diary*, 216.

51. *Chase Diary*, 319–20.

52. Frederick W. Seward, *Reminiscences of a War-Time Statesman and Diplomat, 1830–1915* (New York: G. P. Putnam's Sons, 1916), 190.

53. Horace Porter, *Campaigning with Grant* (New York: Century, 1897), 407–8.

54. Edward Everett Hale, *Memories of One Hundred Years* (2 vols.; New York: Macmillan, 1902), 2:191–92.

55. *CWL*, 5:48–49.

56. *SMDR*, 29 November 1861.

57. Frederick Douglass to Gerrit Smith, 22 December 1861, Smith MSS, Syracuse University; *Douglass' Monthly*, January 1862.

58. Frederick Milnes Edge, 16 April 1862, in London *Star*, n.d., reprinted in Edge, *Major-General McClellan and the Campaign on the Yorktown Peninsula* (London: Trubner, 1865), 61.

59. Carpenter, *Six Months*, 136.

60. Philadelphia *Inquirer*, 5 December 1861.

61. *WLWH*, 59.

62. Jacob W. Schuckers to Whitelaw Reid, 3 October 1872, Reid Family MSS, LC.

63. Fawn Brodie, *Thaddeus Stevens: Scourge of the South* (New York: Norton, 1959), 149.

64. *CWL*, 5:96.

65. Alexander K. McClure, *Abraham Lincoln and Men of War-Times* (Philadelphia: Times, 1892), 153.

66. Frank Abial Flower, *Edwin McMasters Stanton* (New York: Saalfield, 1905), 117.

67. *SMDR*, 18 January 1862.

68. William P. Fessenden to Elizabeth Warriner, 19 January 1862, Fessenden MSS, Bowdoin College.

69. Portland *Oregonian*, 20 May 1862.

70. Philadelphia *Inquirer*, 20 January 1862.

71. Joshua F. Speed to Joseph Holt, 4 February 1862, Holt MSS, LC.

72. *ChiTrib*, 26 March 1864.

73. *CWL*, 5:98–99.

Chapter 25. "This Damned Old House"

1. *ALS*, 134.

2. Josiah G. Holland, *The Life of Abraham Lincoln* (Springfield, Mass.: Gurdon Bill, 1866), 429.

3. *ALS*, 133.

4. William B. Wilson, *A Few Acts and Actors in the Tragedy of the Civil War in the*

United States (Philadelphia: self-published, 1892), 109–10.

5. Washington *Post*, 13 March 1893.

6. *IWHWT*, 150, 179.

7. Rochester, New York, *Daily Democrat*, 19 April 1865.

8. *LO*, 17.

9. *ALS*, 135–36.

10. Reminiscences of Mary Miner Hill, ALPL.

11. For a much fuller account of Mrs. Lincoln's misconduct as First Lady, see Michael Burlingame, *An American Marriage: The Untold Story of Abraham Lincoln and Mary Todd* (New York: Pegasus Books, 2021), 119–259.

12. *HOLL*, 335.

13. Sarah J. Day, *The Man on a Hill Top* (Philadelphia: Ware Brothers, 1931), 245, 243.

14. *Lincoln Lore*, no. 1718 (April 1981): 2–3.

15. Washington *Sunday Gazette*, 23 January 1887.

16. Sacramento *Daily Union*, 26 April 1861.

17. "Union" to Lincoln, Washington, D.C., 26 June 1861, copy, ALPL.

18. *CWL*, 4:303.

19. Omaha *Daily Bee*, 8 January 1867.

20. A. Oakey Hall to Thurlow Weed, 17 August 1861, Weed MSS.

21. New York *Independent*, 10 August 1882, 4–5.

22. A. K. McClure to Alonzo Rothschild, Philadelphia, 9 May 1907, LFFC.

23. Benjamin Brown French, *Witness to the Young Republic: A Yankee's Journal, 1828–1870*, ed. Donald B. Cole and John J. McDonough (Hanover, N.H.: University Press of New England, 1989), 382.

24. William Howard Russell, *My Diary North and South* (New York: Harper & Brothers, 1863), 567.

25. Cincinnati *Commercial*, 10 February 1862.

26. McClure to Rothschild, 9 May 1907.

27. *OHAL*, 3.

Chapter 26. "I Expect to Maintain This Contest until Successful, or till I Die, or Am Conquered, or My Term Expires, or Congress or the Country Forsakes Me"

1. *IWHWT*, 166.

2. *Bates Diary*, 218, 220.

3. Lyman Trumbull to Richard Yates, 6 February 1862, L. U. Reavis MSS, CHM.

4. Philadelphia *Press*, 21 April 1862.

5. *The Liberator* (Boston), 25 April 1862; *NYT*, 23 March 1872.

6. Stephen W. Sears, *George B. McClellan: The Young Napoleon* (New York: Ticknor & Fields, 1988), 180.

7. *IWHWT*, 149, 157.

8. Marie Caroline Post, *The Life and Mémoirs of Comte Régis de Trobriand* (New York: Dutton, 1910), 252.

9. *SMDR*, 4 January 1862.

10. *IWAL*, 183.

11. Boston *Commonwealth*, 6 September 1862.

12. New York *Tribune*, 7 February 1862.

13. New York *Evening Post*, 10 February 1862.

14. *HI*, 692.

15. *WLWH*, 69.

16. *CWL*, 5:108.

17. Henry A. Wise to Andrew Hull Foote, 31 January 1862, Western Reserve Historical Society, Cleveland.

18. Edwin Stanton, "In the Matter of Mortars," [25 January 1862], LP-LC.

19. Virginia Fox diary, [26?] January 1862, Levi Woodbury MSS, LC.

20. Edwin M. Stanton to Charles A. Dana, 24 January 1862, Dana MSS, LC.

21. *Iowa State Register* (Des Moines), 21 January 1862.

22. *CWL*, 5:111–12.

23. *Complete Hay Diary*, 35.

24. Cincinnati *Commercial*, 14 March 1862.

25. New York *Tribune*, 6 February 1862.

26. George B. McClellan to Lincoln, 31 January [3 February] 1862, LP-LC.

27. *CWL*, 5:118–19.

28. Charles Sumner, *The Selected Letters of Charles Sumner*, ed. Beverly Wilson Palmer (2 vols.; Boston: Northeastern University Press, 1990), 2:112.

29. *IWAL*, 183.

30. New York *Tribune*, 22 February 1862.

31. James H. Campbell to his wife, 4 March 1862, UMi.

32. *Bates Diary*, 233.

33. *WLWH*, 71.

34. Philadelphia *Inquirer*, 21 February 1862.

35. Elihu B. Washburne to his wife, 21 February [1862], Washburn Family MSS, Washburn Memorial Library, Norlands, Maine.

36. Keckley, *Behind the Scenes*, 103.

37. Anna L. Boyden, *Echoes from Hospital and White House: A Record of Mrs. Rebecca R. Pomroy's Experiences in War-Times* (Boston: Lothrop, 1884), 56.

38. Boyden, *Echoes from Hospital and White House*, 62.

39. *CWL*, 5:326.

40. *IWHWT*, 66.

41. Washburne to his wife, Tuesday [20 May 1862], Washburn Family MSS.

42. Keckley, *Behind the Scenes*, 104–5.

43. *IWHWT*, 66.

44. *IWAL*, 66–67.

45. New York *Herald*, 4 December 1864.

46. *Bates Diary*, 239.

47. *Complete Hay Diary*, 36.

48. *SMDR*, 27 March 1862.

49. New York *Herald*, 6 April 1862.

50. Adams S. Hill to Henry W. Bellows, 2 April [1862], Bellows MSS, MaHS.

51. Adam Gurowski to Zachariah Chandler, 12 March 1862, Chandler MSS, LC.

52. William P. Fessenden to Elizabeth Warriner, 15 March 1862, Fessenden MSS, Bowdoin College.

53. New York *Herald*, 18 March 1862.

54. Ethan Allen Hitchcock diary, 15 March 1862, William A. Croffut MSS, LC.

55. *Browning Diary*, 1:532–33; John A. Dahlgren diary, copy, Nicolay MSS, LC.

56. Cornelius S. Bushnell to Gideon Welles, [received 16 March 1877], Welles MSS, Huntington Library, San Marino, California.

57. Boston *Journal*, 20 March 1862; Worden's narrative, Worden MSS, Lincoln Memorial University, Harrogate, Tennessee.

58. *Browning Diary*, 1:537–38.

59. *CWL*, 5:182.

60. Montgomery Blair to McClellan, 9 April 1862, McClellan MSS, LC; *Browning Diary*, 1:540; *CWL*, 5:184–85.

61. *CWL*, 5:203.

62. New York *Evening Post*, 5 May 1865.

63. Stanton to Herman Dyer, 18 May 1862, Stanton MSS, LC.

64. *McClellan Papers*, 234.

65. Kenneth P. Williams, *Lincoln Finds a General: A Military Study of the Civil War* (5 vols.; New York: Macmillan, 1949–59), 1:166.

66. *Welles Diary*, 1:124.

67. New York *Tribune*, 13 May 1862; New York *Herald*, 13 May 1862.

68. *RW*, 387.

69. Stanton to John E. Wool, 16 May 1862, Wool MSS, New York State Library, Albany.

70. New York *Herald*, 26 June 1862.

71. Salmon P. Chase, *The Salmon P. Chase Papers*, ed. John Niven (5 vols.; Kent, Ohio: Kent State University Press, 1993–98), 3:197.

72. New York *Evening Post*, 29 April 1862.

73. Herman Haupt, *Reminiscences of General Herman Haupt* (Milwaukee: Wright & Joys, 1901), 49–50.

74. *CWL*, 5:230, 231.

75. *CWL*, 5:270–71.

76. *CWL*, 5:246.

77. *SMDR*, 7 June 1862.

78. Cincinnati *Commercial*, 3 June 1862.

79. *WLWH*, 80.

80. *Welles Diary*, 1:104, 126.

81. *OR*, I, 11 pt. 1: 61.

82. *Browning Diary*, 1:559.

83. *CWL*, 5:298.

84. Cincinnati *Commercial*, 12 September 1862.

85. New York *Evening Post*, 28 July 1862.

86. *CWL*, 5:292.

87. Cincinnati *Gazette*, 14 July 1862.

88. *Old Fort News* (Fort Wayne, Ind.) 28 (1965): 42.

89. New York *Evening Post*, 14 July 1862; New York *Herald*, 14 July 1862.

90. Sears, *Young Napoleon*, 227–28.

91. Carl Sandburg note, source unidentified, Sandburg-Barrett MSS, Newberry Library, Chicago.

92. Welles, *Selected Essays*, 235–36.

93. *CWL*, 5:322.

94. *McClellan Papers*, 358.

95. *Browning Diary*, 1:563.

96. New York *Tribune*, 7 August 1862.

97. New York *Tribune*, 7 August 1862; Cincinnati *Gazette*, 11 August 1862.

98. Providence, Rhode Island, *Journal*, 12 August 1862; New York *Evening Express*, 14 July 1862.

Chapter 27. "The Hour Comes for Dealing with Slavery"

1. Schurz, *Reminiscences*, 2:309–10.

2. Moncure D. Conway, *Autobiography: Memories and Experiences* (2 vols.; Boston: Houghton Mifflin, 1904), 1:161.

3. George Templeton Strong, *The Diary of George Templeton Strong, 1835–1875*, ed. Allan Nevins and Milton Halsey Thomas (4 vols.; New York: Macmillan, 1952), 3:204–5.

4. George B. Cheever to Gerrit Smith, 6 March 1861, Smith MSS, Syracuse University.

5. Edward Everett Hale, *Memories of One Hundred Years* (2 vols.; New York: Macmillan, 1902), 2:189–97; George Sumner to John A. Andrew, 27 December 1861, Andrew MSS, MaHS.

6. *CWL*, 5:144–45.

7. New York *Tribune*, 7, 8, 12 March 1862.

8. *CWL*, 5:153.

9. *NYT*, 8 March 1862.

10. New York *Herald*, 31 October 1862.

11. New York *Herald*, 31 October 1862.

12. *CWL*, 5:169.

13. Chicago *Times*, 18 April 1862.

14. John W. Crisfield to his wife, Washington, D.C., 25 April 1862, Crisfield MSS, Maryland Historical Society, Baltimore.

15. *National Anti-Slavery Standard* (New York), 15 March 1862.

16. *The Liberator* (Boston), 18 April 1862.

17. *National Anti-Slavery Standard*, 12 April 1862.

18. George W. Smalley to Sydney Howard Gay, 21 June 1862, Gay MSS, Columbia University.

19. *CWL*, 5:219.

20. Cincinnati *Commercial*, 17 May 1862.

21. Edward Atkinson to "Dear Ned," 10 June 1862, Atkinson MSS, MaHS.

22. Smalley to Gay, 21 June 1862, Gay MSS.

23. *CWL*, 5:222.

24. *CWL*, 5:222.

25. Adams S. Hill to Gay, [20 May 1862], Gay MSS.

26. George Meade, *The Life and Letters of George Gordon Meade* (2 vols.; New York: Charles Scribner's Sons, 1913), 1:267.

27. *CWL*, 5:222–23.

28. *CG*, 37th Cong., 2nd sess., 3125 (5 July 1862).

29. New York *Tribune*, 15 April 1862.

30. *Browning Diary*, 1:555.

31. *OR*, III, 2:200.

32. *For the People: A Newsletter of the Abraham Lincoln Association* 22 (March 2020): 1.

33. Ethan Allen, "Lincoln and the Slave Trader Gordon," in *Abraham Lincoln, Tributes from His Associates: Reminiscences of Soldiers, Statesmen, and Citizens*, ed. William Hayes Ward (New York: Thomas Y. Crowell, 1895), 168.

34. Lincoln told this to Dr. Robert K. Stone, who told it to Gordon's father, who in turn told it to the author of a letter dated Wednesday (probably written in January or February 1862 but misfiled August 1851) and signed "H." to "Dear Sir" (probably John W. Garrett), n.d., Garrett Family MSS, LC.

35. New York *Tribune*, 6 February 1862.

36. *CWL*, 5:317–19.

37. Hill to Gay, 14 July 1862, Gay MSS; New York *Evening Post*, 16 July 1862; *SMDR*, 19 July 1862.

38. *Browning Diary*, 1:559.

39. Isaac N. Arnold, *The History of Abraham Lincoln and the Overthrow of Slavery* (Chicago: Clarke, 1867), 251.

40. *Browning Diary*, 1:558.

41. *CWL*, 5:326.

42. *CWL*, 5:328–31.

43. Cincinnati *Gazette*, 19 July 1862.

44. Lyman Trumbull to Julia Jayne Trumbull, 16 July 1862, Trumbull Family MSS, ALPL.

45. Duke Frederick, "The Second Confiscation Act: A Chapter of Civil War Politics" (Ph.D. diss., University of Chicago, 1966), 211–14.

46. *CWL*, 5:341.

47. John Sherman, *John Sherman's Recollections of Forty Years in the House, Senate and Cabinet: An Autobiography* (2 vols.; Chicago: Werner, 1895), 1:316.

48. *Welles Diary*, 1:70–71.

49. *ALS*, 23.

50. *Chase Diary*, 348.

51. *CWL*, 5:336–37.

52. Carpenter, *Six Months*, 21.

53. *Chase Diary*, 351.

54. John Palmer Usher, *President Lincoln's Cabinet* (Omaha, 1925), 17.

55. Edwin M. Stanton, memo, 22 September 1862, Stanton MSS, LC.

56. Carpenter, *Six Months*, 21–22.

57. Charles Eliot Norton, *Letters of Charles Eliot Norton*, ed. Sara Norton and M. A. De Wolfe Howe (2 vols.; Boston: Houghton Mifflin, 1913), 1:255.

Chapter 28. "Would You Prosecute the War with Elder-Stalk Squirts, Charged with Rose Water?"

1. *SMDR*, 24 July 1862; Cincinnati *Gazette*, 22 July 1862; New York *Evening Post*, 23 July 1862.

2. *CWL*, 5:344–46.

3. *WLWH*, 91.

4. New York *Herald*, 5 August 1862.

5. *OR*, I, 20 pt. 2: 67–68.

6. John F. Marszalek, *Commander of All Lincoln's Armies: A Life of General Henry W. Halleck* (Cambridge, Mass.: Belknap Press of Harvard University Press, 2004), 168.

7. *OR*, I, 11 pt. 3: 337–38; *Browning Diary*, 1:563.

8. Providence, Rhode Island, *Journal*, 11 August 1862.

9. Henry W. Halleck to his wife, 9 August 1862, UMi.

10. Halleck to George B. McClellan, Washington, D.C., 6 August 1862, in *OR*, I, 11 pt. 1: 82–84.

11. Halleck to his wife, 9 August 1862.

12. *OR*, I, 12 pt. 3: 474.

13. McClellan to Lincoln, 20 August 1862, LP-LC.

14. *CWL*, 5:399.

15. *Complete Hay Diary*, 30.

16. *Complete Hay Diary*, 37–38.

17. *Welles Diary*, 1:113, 116.

18. Frank Abial Flower, *Edwin McMasters Stanton* (New York: Saalfield, 1905), 190–91.

19. Stephen W. Sears, *George B. McClellan: The Young Napoleon* (New York: Ticknor & Fields, 1988), 258–59.

20. George Templeton Strong, *The Diary of George Templeton Strong, 1835–1875*, ed. Allan Nevins and Milton Halsey Thomas (4 vols.; New York: Macmillan, 1952), 3:259.

21. New York *Tribune*, 3 September 1862; Edward Bates, memo, [2 September 1862], LP-LC; *Welles Diary*, 1:105.

22. *Welles Diary*, 1:105.

23. Bates memo, [2 September 1862].

24. *Complete Hay Diary*, 39.

25. Gideon Welles, *Lincoln and Seward* (New York: Sheldon, 1874), 197.

26. William D. Kelley, *Lincoln and Stanton* (New York: G. P. Putnam's Sons, 1885), 74–75.

27. *Chase Diary*, 370.

28. *Welles Diary*, 116; 126.

29. John Pope to Valentine B. Horton, 1 November 1862, Pope MSS, New-York Historical Society, New York.

30. Frederick Law Olmsted, *The Papers of Frederick Law Olmsted*, vol. 4, *Defending the Union: The Civil War and the U.S. Sanitary Commission, 1861–1863*, ed. Jane Turner Censer (Baltimore: Johns Hopkins University Press, 1986), 426.

31. *Complete Hay Diary*, 192, 183.

32. *Complete Hay Diary*, 38.

33. *Welles Diary*, 1:117.

34. *McClellan Papers*, 438.

35. Ward Hill Lamon, *Recollections of Abraham Lincoln, 1847–1865*, ed. Dorothy Lamon Teillard (2nd ed.; Washington, D.C.: privately published, 1911), 289.

36. Cincinnati *Gazette*, 11 August 1862.

37. *Welles Diary*, 1:124.

38. *CWL*, 5:418.

39. *CWL*, 5:417.

40. *McClellan Papers*, 462.

41. *CWL*, 5:426.

42. *CWL*, 5:425–26.

43. *Browning Diary*, 1:590.

44. Sears, *Young Napoleon*, 270.

45. New York *Tribune*, 20 August 1862.

46. *CWL*, 5:388–89.

47. Sydney Howard Gay to Lincoln, [August 1862], LP-LC.

48. Adams Hill to Gay, 1 September 1862, Gay MSS, Columbia University.

49. Frederick Milnes Edge, 16 April 1862, in London *Star*, n.d., reprinted in Edge, *Major-General McClellan and the Campaign on the Yorktown Peninsula* (London: Trubner, 1865), 61.

50. *Christian Recorder* (Philadelphia), 4 October 1862.

51. David S. Reynolds, *Abe: Abraham Lincoln in His Times* (New York: Penguin Press, 2020), 589, 770.

52. *African Repository* 37 (December 1851): 357.

53. *CWL*, 5:370–75.

54. *Douglass' Monthly*, September 1862.

55. Frederick Douglass to Gerrit Smith, 8 September 1862, Smith MSS, Syracuse University; *Douglass' Monthly*, January 1862.

56. Douglass to Samuel Pomeroy, 27 August 1862, in New York *World*, 3 September 1862.

57. *Douglass' Monthly*, September 1862.

58. *Bates Diary*, 268.

59. *CWL*, 5:344–46.

60. Hill to Gay, [9 July 1862], Gay MSS.

61. *RW*, 435.

62. *CWL*, 5:419–25.

63. William W. Patton, *President Lincoln and the Chicago Memorial on Emancipation* (Baltimore: J. Murphy, 1888), 32.

64. *Welles Diary*, 1:143.

65. Allen C. Guelzo, *Lincoln's Emancipation Proclamation: The End of Slavery in America* (New York: Simon & Schuster, 2004), 154–55.

66. Welles, *Selected Essays*, 247.

67. *Douglass' Monthly*, January 1863.

68. New York *Tribune*, 30 December 1862.

69. James G. Smart, ed., *A Radical View: The "Agate" Dispatches of Whitelaw Reid, 1861–1865* (2 vols.; Memphis: Memphis State University Press, 1976), 1:234–36; *CWL*, 5:438.

70. *Complete Hay Diary*, 41.

71. John Gregory Smith to Lincoln, 30 December 1864, Howe Library, University of Vermont, Burlington.

72. *OR*, I, 19 pt. 2: 396.

73. New York *Tribune*, 30 September 1862.

74. *CWL*, 5:444.

Chapter 29. "The Great Event of the Nineteenth Century"

1. David Davis to W.W. Orme, 20 October 1862, Orme MSS, ALPL.

2. New York *Tribune*, 16 October 1862.
3. *The Crisis* (Columbus, Ohio), 5 March 1862; Cincinnati *Enquirer*, 4 August 1862.
4. *The Crisis* (Columbus, Ohio), 29 October 1862.
5. George W. Towner to Albert G. Myrick, 9 November 1862, Myrick MSS, UMi.
6. New York *Tribune*, 24 November 1862.
7. George Boutwell, *Eulogy on the Death of Abraham Lincoln* (Lowell, Mass.: Stone & Huse, 1865), 9.
8. *Complete Hay Diary*, 62.
9. Cincinnati *Commercial*, 8 October 1862.
10. John L. Parker, *Henry Wilson's Regiment* (Boston: Rand Avery, 1887), 205.
11. *McClellan Papers*, 490.
12. Davis to Leonard Swett, 26 November 1862, David Davis MSS, ALPL.
13. *McClellan Papers*, 488.
14. *NYT*, 12 October 1862.
15. Samuel Francis Du Pont, *Samuel Francis Du Pont: A Selection from his Civil War Letters*, ed. John D. Hayes (3 vols.; Ithaca: Cornell University Press for the Eleutherian Mills Historical Library, 1969), 2:245–47, 251–53.
16. *NYT*, 19 November 1862.
17. *OR*, I, 19:6.
18. Henry W. Halleck to his wife, 7 October 1862, UMi.
19. *CWL*, 5:474.
20. *WLWH*, 89.
21. John A. Jones to Davis, 27 October 1862, David Davis MSS, ALPL.
22. New York *Tribune*, 9 November 1862.
23. New York *Evening Post*, 15 November 1862.
24. Chicago *Inter Ocean*, 26 December 1886.
25. *WLWH*, 89.
26. John F. Marszalek, *Commander of All Lincoln's Armies: A Life of General Henry W. Halleck* (Cambridge, Mass.: Belknap Press of Harvard University Press, 2004), 159.
27. *OR*, I, 1:20, 118.
28. William L. Shea and Terrence J. Winchel, *Vicksburg Is the Key: The Struggle for the Mississippi River* (Lincoln: University of Nebraska Press, 2003), 1.
29. Halleck to Nathaniel P. Banks, 8 November 1862, Banks MSS, LC.
30. Marszelek, *Halleck*, 172.
31. Cincinnati *Gazette* 17 October 1862.
32. Henry Winter Davis to Sophie Du Pont, 24 September 1862, Du Pont MSS, Hagley Museum, Wilmington, Delaware.
33. Carl Schurz to Lincoln, 8 November 1862, LP-LC.
34. *CWL*, 5:493–95.
35. *CWL*, 5:509–10.
36. Schurz, *Reminiscences*, 2:396
37. William H. West to Lincoln, 20 October 1862, LP-LC.
38. *CWL*, 5:537.
39. *Browning Diary*, 1:611–12.
40. *Missouri Democrat* (St. Louis), 9 June 1863.
41. *Welles Diary*, 1:180.
42. United States Congress, *Report of the Joint Committee on the Conduct of the War* (3 vols.; Washington, D.C., 1863), 1:650.
43. *CWL*, 5:514–15; David S. Sparks, ed., *Inside Lincoln's Army: The Diary of Marsena Rudolph Patrick* (New York: T. Yoseloff, 1964), 182–83.
44. *NYT*, 12 December 1862.
45. Philadelphia *Weekly Times*, 22 September 1884.
46. Herman Haupt to his wife, 15, 18 December 1862, Lewis Haupt MSS, LC.
47. Henry Villard, *Memoirs of Henry Villard, Journalist and Financier, 1835–1900* (2 vols.; Boston: Houghton Mifflin, 1904), 1:391.
48. J. T. Dorris, "President Lincoln's Clemency," *Lincoln Herald* 55 (1953): 6.
49. William Henry Wadsworth to S. L. M. Barlow, 16 December 1862, Barlow MSS, Huntington Library, San Marino, California.
50. *IWHWT*, 171.
51. Henry Winter Davis to Samuel Francis Du Pont, 2 January 1863, Du Pont MSS, Hagley Museum.
52. Peoria, Illinois, *Transcript*, 27 December 1862.

53. Herman Haupt to his wife, 18 December 1862, Lewis Haupt MSS, LC.

54. *LO*, 13.

55. Julia Lorrilard Butterfield, ed., *A Biographical Memorial of General Daniel Butterfield* (New York: Grafton Press, 1904), 159.

56. *NYT*, 26 December 1862.

57. "Excerpts from the Journal of Henry J. Raymond," *Scribner's Monthly* 19 (January 1880): 424.

58. *OR*, I, 21:66.

59. George F. Williams to Charles Sumner, 17 December 1862, Sumner MSS, Harvard University.

60. *RAL*, 276.

61. *Browning Diary*, 1:597–99.

62. *Browning Diary*, 1:602.

63. William P. Fessenden, manuscript account of the 1862 cabinet crisis, Fessenden MSS, Bowdoin College; hereafter cited as Fessenden, cabinet crisis.

64. *Seward at Washington*, 2:146.

65. *Browning Diary*, 1:600–601, 604.

66. *Welles Diary*, 1:195; Fessenden, cabinet crisis; New York *Tribune*, 22 December 1862.

67. *NYT*, 22 December 1862.

68. Fessenden, cabinet crisis.

69. *Bates Diary*, 269.

70. Fessenden, cabinet crisis.

71. *Bates Diary*, 270.

72. Fessenden, cabinet crisis.

73. Francis Fessenden, *Life and Public Services of William Pitt Fessenden* (2 vols.; Boston: Houghton, Mifflin, 1907), 2:236–38.

74. New York *Herald*, 22 December 1862; Fessenden, cabinet crisis; *Welles Diary*, 1:197.

75. *Browning Diary*, 1:603.

76. Fessenden, cabinet crisis.

77. *Bates Diary*, 291.

78. John Eaton, *Grant, Lincoln, and the Freedmen* (New York: Longmans, Green, 1907), 178.

79. *ALS*, 49–50.

80. *Welles Diary*, 1:196–98.

81. Fessenden, cabinet crisis.

82. *Welles Diary*, 1:201–2.

83. *OHAL*, 87.

84. *Complete Hay Diary*, 104.

85. *Welles Diary*, 1:191.

86. Wheeling, West Virginia, *Intelligencer*, 15 January 1876.

87. David Davis to Leonard Swett, 16 December 1862, and Orme to Davis, Bloomington, 2 January 1863, David Davis MSS, ALPL; *CWL*, 6:16.

88. Carpenter, *Six Months*, 83–84.

89. *CWL*, 6:25n.

90. *CWL*, 6:26n.

91. *U.S. Statutes at Large*, 12:599.

92. New York *Tribune*, 17 September 1862.

93. *IWAL*, 177.

94. New York *World*, 29 January 1862; Philadelphia *Inquirer*, 7 February 1862.

95. Israel Washburn to Hannibal Hamlin, 17, 20 December 1862, Israel Washburn MSS, LC.

96. *CWL*, 6:149–50.

97. *CWL*, 6:154.

98. *CWL*, 6:374.

99. *Christian Science Monitor*, 12 February 1935.

100. Isaac N. Arnold, *The History of Abraham Lincoln and the Overthrow of Slavery* (Chicago: Clarke, 1867), 304.

101. *Seward at Washington*, 2:151; Frederick W. Seward, *Reminiscences of a War-Time Statesman and Diplomat, 1830–1915* (New York: G. P. Putnam's Sons, 1916), 227.

102. Schurz, *Reminiscences*, 2:317.

103. Alexander K. McClure, *Abraham Lincoln and Men of War-Times* (Philadelphia: Times, 1892), 262.

104. *HI*, 197.

105. James M. McPherson, *The Struggle for Equality: Abolitionists and the Negro in the Civil War and Reconstruction* (Princeton, N.J.: Princeton University Press, 1964), 121.

106. New York *Weekly Anglo-African*, 10 January 1863.

107. Frederick Douglass, *The Frederick Douglass Papers, Series One, Speeches,*

Debates, and Interviews, ed. John W. Blassingame et al. (5 vols.; New Haven: Yale University Press, 1979–92), 3:568.

108. *Maryland Historical Magazine* 98 (2003): 94.

109. *OR*, II, 5:807–8.

110. Benjamin Moran diary, 11 December 1869, LC.

111. Carpenter, *Six Months*, 87.

112. Edward Everett Hale, *Memories of One Hundred Years* (2 vols.; New York: Macmillan, 1902), 2:193.

Chapter 30. "Go Forward, and Give Us Victories"

1. George William Curtis to Charles Eliot Norton, 28 December 1862, Curtis MSS, Harvard University.

2. Richard Henry Dana to [J. K. Schubert?], 23 February 1863, Dana MSS, MaHS.

3. Bradford R. Wood to George G. Fogg, 11 February 1863, Fogg MSS, New Hampshire State Historical Society, Concord.

4. Moncure Daniel Conway, *Autobiography: Memories and Experiences* (2 vols.; Boston: Houghton Mifflin, 1904), 1:379.

5. V. Jacque Voegeli, *Free but Not Equal: The Midwest and the Negro during the Civil War* (Chicago: University of Chicago Press, 1967), 82.

6. *Browning Diary*, 1:616.

7. *OR*, I, 13:686.

8. David A. Nichols, *Lincoln and the Indians: Civil War Policy and Politics* (Columbia: University of Missouri Press, 1978), 95–98.

9. John Pope to Lincoln, 11 November 1862, LP-LC.

10. Washington *Daily Morning Chronicle*, 12 November 1862.

11. *CWL*, 5:493.

12. *RW*, 372.

13. *CWL*, 6:39.

14. *CWL*, 6:49.

15. "Excerpts from the Journal of Henry J. Raymond," *Scribner's Monthly* 19 (January 1880): 705.

16. *CWL*, 6:78–79.

17. Schuyler Colfax, *Life and Principles of Abraham Lincoln* (Philadelphia: J. B. Rodgers, 1865), 14.

18. *LO*, 212–13.

19. *LO*, 100–101.

20. Adams S. Hill to Sydney Howard Gay, 14 April 1863, Gay MSS, Columbia University.

21. Robert G. Carter, *Four Brothers in Blue* (Washington, D.C.: Gibson bros., 1913), 237.

22. *LO*, 43.

23. *RW*, 454.

24. *CWL*, 6:164.

25. Robert Underwood Johnson, ed., *Battles and Leaders of the Civil War* (4 vols.; New York: Century, 1887–80), 3:155.

26. *CWL*, 6:189–90.

27. *LO*, 50; Brooks, *Lincoln and the Downfall of Slavery*, 358; Brooks, *Washington, D.C., in Lincoln's Time*, 60–61.

28. *National Labor Tribune* (Pittsburgh), 6 February 1937.

29. George Meade, *The Life and Letters of George Gordon Meade* (2 vols.; New York: Charles Scribner's Sons, 1913), 1:372.

30. *CWL*, 6:201.

31. *CWL*, 6:217.

32. *LO*, 56.

33. *CWL*, 6:249.

34. John F. Marszalek, *Commander of All Lincoln's Armies: A Life of General Henry W. Halleck* (Cambridge, Mass.: Belknap Press of Harvard University Press, 2004), 175.

35. Elizabeth Blair Lee, *Wartime Washington: The Civil War Letters of Elizabeth Blair Lee*, ed. Virginia Jeans Laas (Urbana: University of Illinois Press, 1991), 276.

36. Joseph Hooker to Lincoln, 16 June 1863, LP-LC.

37. *CWL*, 6:282.

38. *CWL*, 6:281.

39. *RAL*, 128.

40. Allan Nevins, *The War for the Union* (4 vols.; New York: Scribner, 1959–71), 3:95.

41. *OR*, I, 23 pt. 2: 237–38.

42. *The Crisis* (Columbus, Ohio), 27 May 1863.

43. Edward McPherson, *The Political History of the United States of America During the Great Rebellion* (Washington, D.C.: Philp & Solomons, 1865), 474.

44. *The Trial of Hon. Clement Vallandigham* (Cincinnati: Rickey & Carroll, 1863), 41.

45. *CWL*, 6:237.

46. McPherson, *United States During the Great Rebellion*, 162.

47. Chicago *Times*, 28 February 1863.

48. *OR*, II, 5:723–24.

49. *CWL*, 6:260–69.

50. New York *World*, 16 June 1863.

51. Nicolay and Hay, *Lincoln*, 7:349.

52. New York *World*, 4 July 1863.

53. *CWL*, 6:302.

54. *RAL*, 402.

55. *Complete Hay Diary*, 62.

56. Marszalek, *Halleck*, 179.

57. Nevins, *War for the Union*, 3:113; *Welles Diary*, 1:363–64.

58. *OHAL*, 88–89.

59. Marszalek, *Halleck*, 179.

60. *Complete Hay Diary*, 62.

61. *CWL*, 6:327–28.

62. *IWAL*, 189.

63. Marszalek, *Halleck*, 169.

64. New York *Independent*, 11 June 1863.

65. *RW*, 11.

66. *RW*, 92.

67. *LO*, 217.

68. *Welles Diary*, 1:364–65.

69. *CWL*, 6:326.

70. New York *Evening Post*, 14 June 1865.

71. *CWL*, 6:409.

72. *CWL*, 6:364.

73. Curtis to Norton, 12 July 1863, Curtis MSS, Harvard University.

74. Charles A. Dana, *Recollections of the Civil War: With the Leaders at Washington and in the Field in the Sixties* (New York: D. Appleton, 1898), 86.

75. *CWL*, 6:408–10.

76. *CWL*, 6:357.

77. Frederick Douglass, *The Frederick Douglass Papers, Series One, Speeches, Debates, and Interviews*, ed. John W. Blassingame et al. (5 vols.; New Haven: Yale University Press, 1979–92), 3:606–8.

78. Douglass, *Frederick Douglass Papers*, 3:606.

79. *CWL*, 7:302–3, 345.

80. Frederick Douglass, *Life and Times of Frederick Douglass* (Hartford, Conn.: Park, 1881), 348–49.

81. *CWL*, 7:345–46.

82. Douglass, *Life and Times*, 423.

83. Edward Bates to Salmon P. Chase, 19 July 1863, Chase MSS, Historical Society of Pennsylvania, Philadelphia.

84. Bates to Gideon Welles, 6 June 1863, Lincoln Collection, Yale University.

Chapter 31. "The Signs Look Better"

1. William O. Stoddard, *Dispatches from Lincoln's White House: The Anonymous Civil War Journalism of Presidential Secretary William O. Stoddard*, ed. Michael Burlingame (Lincoln: University of Nebraska Press, 1998), 162–63.

2. *ALS*, 49, 54.

3. New York *Independent*, 30 July 1863.

4. New York *Tribune*, 15 July 1863.

5. *CWL*, 6:369–70.

6. *CWL*, 6:391.

7. Tarbell, *Life of Lincoln*, 2:148–49.

8. *Bates Diary*, 306.

9. *Welles Diary*, 1:432.

10. Statement by the son of Robert B. Carnahan, May 1896, Tarbell MSS.

11. Andrew G. Curtin to Lincoln, 18 September 1863, LP-LC.

12. *CWL*, 6:444–49.

13. Thomas Pendel, *Thirty-Six Years in the White House* (Washington, D.C.: Neale, 1902), 17–18.

14. *CWL*, 6:33–34.

15. *Complete Hay Diary*, 88.

16. *Complete Hay Diary*, 125.

17. *Complete Hay Diary*, 101.

18. William D. Kelley, *Lincoln and Stanton* (New York: G. P. Putnam's Sons, 1885), 86; *Complete Hay Diary*, 216.

19. *Complete Hay Diary*, 86.

20. New York *Independent*, 1 October 1863.

21. Katherine Helm, *The True Story of Mary, Wife of Lincoln* (New York: Harper, 1928), 233.

22. *IWAL*, 162.

23. *Chase Diary*, 453–54.

24. *Complete Hay Diary*, 99.

25. *Complete Hay Diary*, 94, 107–8.

26. *CWL*, 6:475.

27. *CWL*, 6:406–11.

28. Chicago *Times*, n.d., reprinted in the Plymouth, Indiana, *Weekly Democrat*, 10 September 1863.

29. New York *Tribune*, 22 October 1863.

30. *OR*, III, 3:860–61.

31. *CWL*, 6:556–57.

32. *CWL*, 7:24.

33. New York *Evening Post*, 5 November 1863.

34. David Wills to Lincoln, 2 November 1863, LP-LC.

35. *Complete Hay Diary*, 20.

36. *CWL*, 7:17.

37. *Mary Lincoln Letters*, 158.

38. Benjamin Brown French, *Witness to the Young Republic: A Yankee's Journal, 1828–1870*, ed. Donald B. Cole and John J. McDonough (Hanover, N.H.: University Press of New England, 1989), 435–36.

39. *CWL*, 7:17–23.

40. *Ohio State Journal* (Columbus), 23 November 1863.

41. Edward Everett to Lincoln, 20 November 1863, LP-LC.

42. *ChiTrib*, 8 December 1863.

43. *NYT*, 23 November 1863.

44. *ALS*, 129; *Complete Hay Diary*, 118.

45. *CWL*, 6:457.

46. *CWL*, 6:518.

Chapter 32. "I Hope to Stand Firm Enough to Not Go Backward, and Yet Not Go Forward Fast Enough to Wreck the Country's Cause"

1. William C. Harris, *With Charity for All: Lincoln and the Restoration of the Union* (Lexington: University Press of Kentucky, 1997), 47.

2. *CWL*, 5:303.

3. *CWL*, 6:440.

4. *The Liberator* (Boston), 20 June 1862.

5. *CWL*, 5:445.

6. *CWL*, 5:342–43.

7. *CWL*, 5:350.

8. *CWL*, 5:504–5.

9. *CWL*, 6:364–66.

10. *CWL*, 7:1.

11. *CWL*, 7:24.

12. *Complete Hay Diary*, 71.

13. *CWL*, 7:51.

14. *CWL*, 7:162.

15. *CWL*, 7:50–53, 8:753.

16. *ChiTrib*, 10 December 1863.

17. *ALS*, 74–76.

18. *ALS*, 78–79.

19. Nathaniel P. Banks to Lincoln, 30 December 1863, LP-LC. This plan had been spelled out by Banks in a letter (no longer extant) to George Boutwell, who read it to the president on 21 December.

20. *CWL*, 7:89.

21. *CWL*, 7:243.

22. *CWL*, 7:71.

23. *CWL*, 7:243.

24. George S. Denison to Salmon P. Chase, 8 October 1864, Chase MSS, LC.

25. *NYT*, 23 June 1865.

26. *CWL*, 7:486.

27. *Complete Hay Diary*, 120.

28. *Bates Diary*, 333.

29. Shelby M. Cullom, *Fifty Years of Public Service: Personal Recollections* (Chicago: McClurg, 1911), 98.

30. [John B. Alley?] to Josiah G. Holland, 8 August 1865, J. G. Holland MSS, NYPL; John Bigelow, *Retrospections of an Active*

Life (5 vols.; New York: Baker & Taylor, 1909–13), 2:110; *Complete Hay Diary*, 103.

31. *RAL*, 581–82.

32. *Complete Hay Diary*, 103, 93, 78.

33. Sam Wilkeson to Sydney Howard Gay, [February 1864], Gay MSS, Columbia University.

34. Charles R. Wilson, ed., "The Original Chase Organization Meeting and The Next Presidential Election," *Mississippi Valley Historical Review* 23 (1936): 61–79.

35. Nicolay and Hay, *Lincoln*, 8:320.

36. Richard C. Parsons to Chase, 9 December 1863, Chase MSS, LC.

37. Thomas Brown to Chase, 4 January 1864, Chase MSS, LC.

38. *Ohio State Journal* (Columbus), 27 February 1864.

39. William Ernest Smith, *The Francis Preston Blair Family in Politics* (2 vols.; New York: Macmillan, 1933), 2:256–58.

40. *Complete Hay Diary*, 213.

41. Lucius E. Chittenden, *Recollections of President Lincoln and His Administration* (New York: Harper & Brothers, 1891), 379.

42. St. Paul, Minnesota, *Press*, 22 July 1864.

43. *Complete Hay Diary*, 216.

44. Francis Fessenden, *Life and Public Services of William Pitt Fessenden* (2 vols.; Boston: Houghton, Mifflin, 1907), 1:316–18.

45. *Complete Hay Diary*, 216.

46. Charles A. Jellison, *Fessenden of Maine, Civil War Senator* (Syracuse: Syracuse University Press, 1962), 182–83.

47. *LO*, 216.

48. *Grant Papers*, 9:522–23.

49. *Grant Papers*, 9:542.

50. Tarbell, *Life of Lincoln*, 2:188.

51. *Grant Papers*, 9:544.

52. *OR*, I, 17 pt. 2: 422.

53. *WLWH*, 239.

54. *CWL*, 7:234.

55. Benjamin F. Butler, *Private and Official Correspondence of Gen. Benjamin F. Butler, During the Period of the Civil War*, ed. Blanche Butler Ames (5 vols.; Norwood, Mass.: Plimpton Press, 1917), 4:66, 3:675–76.

56. Oscar Sherwin, *Prophet of Liberty: The Life and Times of Wendell Phillips* (New York: Bookman Associates, 1958), 493; Irving H. Bartlett, *Wendell Phillips: Brahmin Radical* (Boston: Beacon Press, 1961), 269; James M. McPherson, *The Struggle for Equality; Abolitionists and the Negro in the Civil War and Reconstruction* (Princeton, N.J.: Princeton University Press, 1964), 270.

57. *The American Annual Cyclopedia and Register of Important Events of the Year 1864* (New York: D. Appleton, 1865), 787.

58. Henry Mayer, *All on Fire: William Lloyd Garrison and the Abolition of Slavery* (New York: St. Martin's, 1998), 562, 563.

59. *The Liberator* (Boston), 18 March 1864.

60. U. F. Murphy, *Presidential Election, 1864* (New York: Baker & Godwin, 1864), 4.

61. *American Annual Cyclopedia and Register for 1864*, 788.

62. *RW*, 348.

63. William H. Crook, *Through Five Administrations: Reminiscences of Colonel William H. Crook, Body-guard to President Lincoln*, ed. Margarita Spalding Gerry (New York: Harper & Brothers, 1910), 45.

64. Brooks, *Washington, D.C., in Lincoln's Time*, 148, 142.

65. *CWL*, 7:384.

66. *CWL*, 7:380.

67. *CWL*, 7:383; New York *Evening Post*, 14 December 1863.

68. A. K. McClure, *Our Presidents and How We Make Them* (New York: Harper & Brothers, 1900), 184.

69. Theodore Tilton to Wendell Phillips, 31 May 1864, Phillips MSS, Harvard University.

Chapter 33. "Hold On with a Bull-dog Grip, and Chew & Choke, as Much as Possible"

1. Francis Lieber to Charles Sumner, 31 August 1864, Sumner MSS, Harvard University.

2. *Complete Hay Diary*, 193–94.
3. Brooks D. Simpson, *U. S. Grant: Triumph Over Adversity, 1822–1865* (Boston: Houghton Mifflin, 2000), 296.
4. William Conant Church, *Ulysses S. Grant and the Period of National Preservation and Reconstruction* (New York: G. P. Putnam's Sons, 1897), 248–49.
5. *CWL*, 7:324.
6. *Grant Papers*, 10:380.
7. Henry E. Wing, *When Lincoln Kissed Me* (New York: Eaton & Mains, 1913), 13, 36–39.
8. *RAL*, 337.
9. Isaac N. Arnold, *The Life of Abraham Lincoln* (Chicago: Jansen, McClurg, 1884), 375.
10. *Complete Hay Diary*, 195.
11. *WLWH*, 141.
12. John A. Dix to Edwin M. Stanton, 18 May 1864, Lincoln Collection, CHM.
13. James R. Gilmore to Sydney Howard Gay, 18 May 1864, Gay MSS, Columbia University.
14. James G. Randall and Richard N. Current, *Lincoln the President: Last Full Measure* (New York: Dodd, Mead, 1955), 156.
15. S. S. Cox to Manton Marble, Washington, D.C., 20 May 1864, Marble MSS, LC.
16. A[aron] H[omer] B[yington] to Sydney [Howard Gay], Washington, D.C., 23 March [1864], Gay MSS.
17. Carl Schurz, interview by Ida Tarbell, New York, 6 November 1897, Tarbell MSS.
18. Schuyler Colfax, *Life and Principles of Abraham Lincoln* (Philadelphia: J. B. Rodgers, 1865), 12.
19. Nicolay and Hay, *Lincoln*, 9:364.
20. Philadelphia *Inquirer*, 22 August 1864.
21. Tarbell, *Life of Lincoln*, 2:195.
22. *The Crisis* (Columbus, Ohio), 3 August 1864.
23. *CWL*, 7:393.
24. *CWL*, 7:395.
25. Brooks, *Washington, D.C., in Lincoln's Time*, 138.
26. Horace Porter to wife, 24 June 1864, Porter MSS, LC.
27. Sylvanus Cadwallader, *Three Years with Grant*, ed. Benjamin P. Thomas (New York: Knopf, 1955), 233.
28. Cadwallader, *Three Years with Grant*, 233.
29. *Welles Diary*, 258.
30. Church, *Ulysses S. Grant*, 231–32.
31. Matthew Pinsker, *Lincoln's Sanctuary: Abraham Lincoln and the Soldiers' Home* (New York: Oxford University Press, 2003), 136.
32. *Complete Hay Diary*, 221.
33. *Complete Hay Diary*, 222, 223.
34. *OR*, I, 37 pt. 2: 558.
35. *CWL*, 7:499.
36. Benjamin F. Butler, *Private and Official Correspondence of Gen. Benjamin F. Butler, During the Period of the Civil War*, ed. Blanche Butler Ames (5 vols.; Norwood, Mass.: Plimpton Press, 1917), 5:35.
37. *CWL*, 7:169.
38. *CG*, 38th Cong., 1st sess., 3449.
39. *Complete Hay Diary*, 218–19.
40. *ChiTrib*, 3 March 1864.
41. *CWL*, 7:434–35.
42. New York *Tribune*, 5 August 1864.
43. *Welles Diary*, 2:98.
44. Butler, *Private and Official Correspondence*, 5:8–9.
45. B. Rush Plumly to Nathaniel P. Banks, 9 August 1864, Banks MSS, LC.
46. Brooks, *Washington, D.C., in Lincoln's Time*, 156.
47. Salmon P. Chase, *The Salmon P. Chase Papers*, ed. John Niven (5 vols.; Kent, Ohio: Kent State University Press, 1993–98), 4:432.
48. Charles Sumner, *The Selected Letters of Charles Sumner*, ed. Beverly Wilson Palmer (2 vols.; Boston: Northeastern University Press, 1990), 2:253.
49. Schurz, *Reminiscences*, 3:103–4.
50. *SMDR*, 18 April 1865.
51. David Davis to Julius Rockwell, 4 August 1864, David Davis MSS, LC.
52. Tarbell, *Life of Lincoln*, 2:201–2.
53. *OHAL*, 58.

54. Undated memo by Francis Pierpont, Pierpont MSS, West Virginia University.

55. Horace Greeley to Lincoln, 7 July 1864, LP-LC.

56. Chauncey M. Depew, *My Memories of Eighty Years* (New York: C. Scribner's Sons, 1922), 61–62.

57. Greeley to Lincoln, 13 July 1864, LP-LC; *CWL*, 7:435, 442.

58. James Ashley, *Address of Hon. J. M. Ashley, at the Fourth Annual Banquet of the Ohio Republican League* (New York: Evening Post, 1891), 13.

59. Shelby M. Cullom, *Fifty Years of Public Service: Personal Recollections* (Chicago: McClurg, 1911), 101.

60. *Complete Hay Diary*, 224–25.

61. *CWL*, 8:63, emphasis added.

62. *Welles Diary*, 2:172.

63. Victor B. Howard, *Religion and the Radical Republican Movement, 1860–1870* (Lexington: University Press of Kentucky, 1990), 80.

64. Brooks, *Lincoln and the Downfall of Slavery*, 402.

65. *NYT*, 28 December 1882.

66. *CWL*, 7:514.

67. *Complete Hay Diary*, 248.

68. *CWL*, 7:501.

69. Washington *Daily Morning Chronicle*, 27 April 1865.

70. Philip S. Foner, ed., *The Life and Writings of Frederick Douglass* (4 vols.; New York: International Publishers, 1950), 3:422–24.

71. John Eaton, *Grant, Lincoln, and the Freedmen* (New York: Longmans, Green, 1907), 175–76.

72. *WLWH*, 152–54.

73. *CWL*, 7:517.

74. New York *World*, 29, 30 July, 25 August 1864.

75. *Complete Hay Diary*, 238.

76. John Murray Forbes to Charles Eliot Norton, 25 August 1864, Norton MSS, Harvard University.

Chapter 34. "The Wisest Radical of All"

1. Brooks, *Washington, D.C., in Lincoln's Time*, 164.

2. Joseph P. Thompson, "A Talk with President Lincoln," *Congregationalist and Boston Recorder*, 30 March 1866.

3. Washington *Post*, 16 August 1891.

4. George Templeton Strong, *The Diary of George Templeton Strong, 1835–1875*, ed. Allan Nevins and Milton Halsey Thomas (4 vols.; New York: Macmillan, 1952), 3:481.

5. TheodoreTilton to Anna E. Dickinson, 13 July, 3, 5 September 1864, Dickinson MSS, LC.

6. Philip S. Foner, ed., *The Life and Writings of Frederick Douglass* (4 vols.; New York: International Publishers, 1950), 3:424.

7. *CWL*, 7:542.

8. Carpenter, *Six Months*, 201–3; *National Anti-Slavery Standard*, 17 December 1864.

9. Wendell Phillips to Elizabeth Cady Stanton, 27 September 1864, in *The Selected Papers of Elizabeth Cady Stanton and Susan B. Anthony*, ed. Ann D. Gordon (6 vols.; New Brunswick, N.J. : Rutgers University Press, 1997–2013), 1:531.

10. William D. Kelley to J. Miller McKim, 1 May 1864, Garrison MSS, Boston Public Library.

11. John G. Nicolay to Tilton, 6 September 1864, Miscellaneous Manuscripts, New-York Historical Society, New York.

12. *Grant Papers*, 12:16–17.

13. Thompson, "Talk with President Lincoln"; *Our Martyr President, Abraham Lincoln* (New York: Tibbals & Whiting, 1865), 191.

14. Henry Wilson to Lincoln, 5 September 1864, LP-LC.

15. *OHAL*, 78–79.

16. Elizabeth Blair Lee, *Wartime Washington: The Civil War Letters of Elizabeth Blair Lee*, ed. Virginia Jeans Laas (Urbana: University of Illinois Press, 1991), 433.

17. Zachariah Chandler to his wife, 8 September 1864, Chandler MSS, LC.

18. Boston *Daily Advertiser*, 23 September 1864.

19. Samuel Francis Du Pont, *Samuel Francis Du Pont: A Selection from his Civil War Letters*, ed. John D. Hayes (3 vols.; Ithaca: Cornell University Press for the Eleutherian Mills Historical Library, 1969), 3:393–94.

20. *CWL*, 8:18.

21. Lee, *Wartime Washington*, 437n; William Ernest Smith, *The Francis Preston Blair Family in Politics* (2 vols.; New York: Macmillan, 1933), 2:290.

22. La Crosse, Wisconsin, *Daily Democrat*, 17 August 1864.

23. Hugh McCulloch to his wife, 25 September 1864, McCulloch MSS, LC.

24. Benjamin F. Butler, *Private and Official Correspondence of Gen. Benjamin F. Butler, During the Period of the Civil War*, ed. Blanche Butler Ames (5 vols.; Norwood, Mass.: Plimpton Press, 1917), 5:167.

25. Henry Winter Davis to Samuel Francis Du Pont, 25 September 1864, Du Pont MSS, Hagley Museum, Wilmington, Delaware.

26. Lacrosse, Wisconsin, *Daily Democrat*, 16 August 1864.

27. Arnold M. Shankman, *The Pennsylvania Antiwar Movement, 1861–1865* (Rutherford, N.J.: Farleigh Dickinson University Press, 1980), 196.

28. *CWL*, 7:508.

29. John McMahon to Lincoln, 5 August 1864, Nicolay MSS, LC; *CWL*, 7:483.

30. Elizabeth F. Yager, "The Presidential Campaign of 1864 in Ohio," *Ohio Archaeological and Historical Quarterly* 34 (1925): 571–72.

31. La Crosse, Wisconsin, *Daily Democrat*, 25 August 1864.

32. New York *World*, 9 September 1864.

33. Ward Hill Lamon, drafts and anecdotes (ca. 1887), folder 1, Lamon MSS; *RW*, 290.

34. Ward Hill Lamon, *Recollections of Abraham Lincoln, 1847–1865*, ed. Dorothy Lamon Teillard (2nd ed.; Washington, D.C.: privately published, 1911), 149.

35. A. H[omer] B[yington] to [Sydney Howard] Gay, 23 March [1864], and Sam Wilkeson to Gay, [23 March 1864], Gay MSS, Columbia University.

36. Keckley, *Behind the Scenes*, 149–50.

37. New York *Tribune*, 17 October 1864.

38. *IWAL*, 194.

39. *Complete Hay Diary*, 207–8.

40. *CWL*, 7:402.

41. *CWL*, 7:413–14.

42. *CWL*, 6:513–14.

43. John Murray Forbes, *Letters and Recollections of John Murray Forbes*, ed. Sarah Forbes Hughes (2 vols.; Boston: Houghton Mifflin, 1899), 2:101.

44. Chicago *Times*, 23 October 1880.

45. *RAL*, 518.

46. *HI*, 165n.

47. *CWL*, 7:281–82.

48. Fred R. Shapiro, "Who Wrote the Serenity Prayer?," *Chronicle of Higher Education*, 28 April 2014.

49. *CWL*, 7:535.

50. *The Friend: A Religious and Literary Journal* (Philadelphia), 25 January 1908.

51. *CWL*, 5:403–4.

52. *CWL*, 8:2.

53. *CWL*, 7:504–5.

54. *CWL*, 7:512.

55. *CWL*, 7:301–3.

56. *CWL*, 7:251.

57. *CWL*, 8:41

58. *LO*, 142.

59. *CWL*, 8:52–53.

60. Nicolay and Hay, *Lincoln*, 9:358.

61. David Black, *The King of Fifth Avenue: The Fortunes of August Belmont* (New York: Dial Press, 1981), 255.

62. *IWAL*, 205.

63. New York *Daily News*, 18, 25 October 1864.

64. E. S. Nadal, "Some Impressions of Lincoln," *Scribner's Magazine*, March 1906, 370.

65. *IWHWT*, 190.

66. *LO*, 211.

67. *CWL*, 8:11.

68. *CWL*, 8:52–53.

69. Margaret McKelvy Bird and Daniel W. Crofts, eds., "Soldier Voting in 1864: The David McKelvy Diary," *Pennsylvania Magazine of History & Biography* 115 (1991): 392 (6 October 1864).

70. Charles A. Dana, *Recollections of the Civil War: With the Leaders at Washington and in the Field in the Sixties* (New York: D. Appleton, 1898), 261–62.

71. *Complete Hay Diary*, 241.

72. Alexander K. McClure to Leonard Swett, 14 October 1864, LP-LC.

73. Alexander K. McClure, *Abraham Lincoln and Men of War-Times* (Philadelphia: Times, 1892), 200–203.

74. *Complete Hay Diary*, 243.

75. *LO*, 198–99.

76. *LO*, 142–43; Brooks, *Washington, D.C., in Lincoln's Time*, 195–96.

77. *Complete Hay Diary*, 245.

78. *LO*, 143.

79. *LO*, 143.

80. *Complete Hay Diary*, 246.

81. *LO*, 144.

82. *CWL*, 8:96.

83. *National Anti-Slavery Standard*, 19 November 1864.

84. *LO*, 145.

85. *CWL*, 8:100–101.

86. *Complete Hay Diary*, 248.

87. Nicolay and Hay, *Lincoln*, 9:379.

88. *CWL*, 8:149–50

89. Brooks, *Washington, D.C., in Lincoln's Time*, 198.

90. J. M. Winchell, "Three Interviews with President Lincoln," *Galaxy*, July 1873, 40.

91. Wilbur Fisk, *Anti-Rebel: The Civil War Letters of Wilbur Fisk*, ed. Emil Rosenblatt (Croton-on-Hudson, N.Y.: E. Rosenblatt, 1983), 276.

92. *OR*, I, 42 pt. 3: 541.

93. Ralph Volney Harlow, *Gerrit Smith, Philanthropist and Reformer* (New York: H. Holt, 1939), 441.

94. *Dupont Letters*, 3:392.

95. *CWL*, 8:326.

96. Thurlow Weed to Lincoln, 4 March 1865, LP-LC.

97. London *Daily News*, 27 September 1864.

98. William O. Stoddard, *Dispatches from Lincoln's White House: The Anonymous Civil War Journalism of Presidential Secretary William O. Stoddard*, ed. Michael Burlingame (Lincoln: University of Nebraska Press, 1998), 88.

99. Harriet Beecher Stowe, in *Littell's Living Age*, 6 February 1864.

100. *LO*, 205–6.

Chapter 35. "Let the Thing *Be Pressed"*

1. *Browning Diary*, 1:688.

2. Francis P. Blair to John A. Andrew, 19 November 1864, Andrew MSS, MaHS.

3. Nicolay and Hay, *Lincoln*, 9:391–92.

4. *OHAL*, 85.

5. *Complete Hay Diary*, 217.

6. William P. Fessenden to Salmon P. Chase, 20 October 1864, in James G. Randall and Richard N. Current, *Lincoln the President: Last Full Measure* (New York: Dodd, Mead, 1955), 271.

7. R. D. Musser to Chase, 8 December 1864, Chase MSS, LC.

8. *WLWH*, 166.

9. *RW*, 94, 163.

10. Samuel J. Tilden, *Letters and Literary Memorials of Samuel J. Tilden*, ed. John Bigelow (2 vols.; New York: Harper, 1908), 1:246.

11. *CWL*, 8:116–17; *ALS*, 169–84.

12. Randall and Current, *Lincoln the President: Last Full Measure*, 48.

13. *ALS*, 170–71.

14. *The Crisis* (Columbus Ohio), 12, 16 December 1864.

15. Keckley, *Behind the Scenes*, 121–22.

16. *CWL*, 8:224; Ulysses S. Grant to Lincoln, 21 January 1865, LP-LC.

17. James Grant Wilson, "Recollections of Lincoln," *Putnam's Magazine*, February 1909, 529.

18. *CWL*, 6:558.

19. *ALS*, 136.

20. *CWL*, 8:152.

21. Osborn H. Oldroyd, ed., *The Lincoln Memorial: Album-Immortelles* (Chicago: Gem Publishing House, 1883), 491–94.

22. Isaac N. Arnold, *The History of Abraham Lincoln and the Overthrow of Slavery* (Chicago: Clarke, 1867), 469.

23. Anson Herrick to William Henry Seward, 8 August 1865, Seward MSS, University of Rochester.

24. Robert W. Latham to Seward, 9 January 1865, Seward MSS.

25. Andrew Johnson, *The Papers of Andrew Johnson*, ed. LeRoy P. Graf and Ralph W. Haskins (16 vols.; Knoxville: University of Tennessee Press, 1967–2000), 8:247.

26. *CWL*, 8:248.

27. Arlin Turner, ed., "Elizabeth Peabody Visits Lincoln, February 1865," *New England Quarterly* 48 (1975): 119–20.

28. Isaac N. Arnold, *The Life of Abraham Lincoln* (Chicago: Jansen, McClurg, 1884), 366.

29. *CWL*, 8:244–45.

30. *Grant Papers*, 14:91.

31. *CWL*, 8:136–51.

32. William Ernest Smith, *The Francis Preston Blair Family in Politics* (2 vols.; New York: Macmillan, 1933), 2:363–67; *CWL*, 8:220–21.

33. Thomas E. Schott, *Alexander H. Stephens of Georgia: A Biography* (Baton Rouge: Louisiana State University Press, 1988), 442.

34. New York *World*, 11 February 1865.

35. *RAL*, 249–50.

36. *CWL*, 8:251–52.

37. Grant to Edwin M. Stanton, 1 February 1865, LP-LC.

38. *SMDR*, 25 February 1865; Wadesboro, North Carolina, *Messenger and Intelligencer*, 5 May 1895.

39. Augusta, Georgia, *Chronicle & Sentinel*, 7 June 1865; Alexander H. Stephens, *A Constitutional View of the Late War between the States* (2 vols.; Philadelphia: National Publishing Company, 1868–70), 2:604–8.

40. Stephens, *Constitutional View*, 2:604–8; Augusta, Georgia, *Chronicle & Sentinel*, 7 June 1865; *SMDR*, 25 February 1865.

41. Stephens, *Constitutional View*, 2:617.

42. Nicolay and Hay, *Lincoln*, 10:127.

43. John Eaton, *Grant, Lincoln, and the Freedmen* (New York: Longmans, Green, 1907), 89.

44. J. B. Jones, *A Rebel War Clerk's Diary at the Confederate States Capital* (2 vols.; New York: Old Hickory Bookshop, 1935), 2:411; Nicolay and Hay, *Lincoln*, 10:130.

45. *CWL*, 8:260–61.

46. *OHAL*, 65–66; Alexander K. McClure, *Abraham Lincoln and Men of War-Times* (Philadelphia: Times, 1892), 241.

47. *IWAL*, 168; *RW*, 235.

48. *CWL*, 8:332–33.

49. New York *Herald*, 5 March 1865.

50. Frederick Douglass, *Life and Times of Frederick Douglass* (Hartford, Conn.: Park, 1881), 372; *RAL*, 191–93.

51. *CWL*, 8:356.

52. Allan Nevins, *The War for the Union*, vol. 4, *The Organized War to Victory* (New York: Scribner's, 1971), 216.

53. *Complete Hay Diary*, 253–54.

54. Elizabeth Cady Stanton, *Elizabeth Cady Stanton as Revealed in Her Letters, Diary and Reminiscences*, ed. Theodore Stanton and Harriot Stanton Blatch (2 vols.; New York: Harper & Brothers, 1922), 2:104.

55. *The Liberator* (Boston), 10 February 1865.

56. *LO*, 184.

57. *CWL*, 8:206–7.

58. Herman Belz, *Reconstructing the Union: Theory and Policy during the Civil War* (Ithaca: Cornell University Press, 1969), 270.

59. Charles Sumner, *Charles Sumner: His Complete Works* (20 vols.; Boston: Lee & Shepard, 1900), 12:114.

60. *WLWH*, 171.

61. *CWL*, 8:106–8.

62. Stephen A. Hurlbut to Lincoln, 29 November 1864, LP-LC.

63. LaWanda Cox, *Lincoln and Black Freedom: A Study in Presidential Leadership* (Columbia: University of South Carolina Press, 1981), 117.

64. John S. Barnes, "With Lincoln from Washington to Richmond in 1865," *Appleton's Magazine* 9 (May 1907): 516–17.

65. Adam Badeau, *Grant in Peace, from Appomattox to Mount McGregor: A Personal Memoir* (Hartford, Conn.: S. S. Scranton, 1887), 362.

66. Sylvanus Cadwallader, *Three Years with Grant*, ed. Benjamin P. Thomas (New York: Knopf, 1955), 282–83.

67. George R. Agassiz, ed., *Meade's Headquarters, 1863–1865* (Boston: Atlantic Monthly Press, 1922), 325.

68. Barnes, "With Lincoln," 522.

69. Horace Porter, *Campaigning with Grant* (New York: Century, 1897), 406–8.

70. Porter, *Campaigning with Grant*, 423–24; William T. Sherman to Isaac Arnold, 28 November 1872, Arnold MSS, CHM; Sherman to John W. Draper, 27 November 1868, Draper MSS, LC; William T. Sherman, *Memoirs of Gen. William T. Sherman* (2 vols.; New York: D. Appleton, 1875), 2:325–27.

71. Porter, *Campaigning with Grant*, 423–25.

72. Frank Rauscher, *Music on the March, 1862–'65* (Philadelphia: W. F. Fell, 1892), 226.

73. Cadwallader, *Three Years with Grant*, 307.

74. *CWL*, 8:383.

75. Charles Carleton Coffin, *Abraham Lincoln* (New York: Harper & Brothers, 1893), 498–99.

76. David Dixon Porter, "Journal of Occurrences during the War of the Rebellion," 2:48, Porter MSS, LC.

77. David Dixon Porter, *Incidents and Anecdotes of the Civil War* (New York: D. Appleton, 1885), 294.

78. *RAL*, 179–81; Coffin, *Abraham Lincoln*, 193.

79. *RAL*, 182; Richmond correspondence by Coffin in the Boston *Journal*, n.d., in *Littell's Living Age*, 8 April 1865.

80. Charles Carleton Coffin, "Late Scenes in Richmond," *Atlantic Monthly*, June 1865, 755; Coffin, *Four Years of Fighting: A Volume of Personal Observation with the Army and Navy, from the First Battle of Bull Run to the Fall of Richmond* (Boston: Ticknor & Fields, 1866), 512.

81. Porter, *Incidents and Anecdotes*, 298–300.

82. Porter, *Incidents and Anecdotes*, 298–300.

83. Barnes, "With Lincoln," 748–49.

84. Philadelphia *Times*, 29 August 1881.

85. R. J. M. Blackett, ed., *Thomas Morris Chester, Black Civil War Correspondent: His Dispatches from the Virginia Front* (Baton Rouge: Louisiana State University Press, 1989), 295.

86. Porter, *Incidents and Anecdotes*, 295.

87. *Southern Historical Society Papers*, n.s., 4:68–69; *ChiTrib*, 12 July 1865.

88. Philadelphia *Times*, 29 August 1881.

89. Charles H. Ambler, *Francis H. Pierpont: Union War Governor of Virginia and Father of West Virginia* (Chapel Hill: University of North Carolina Press, 1937), 256–57.

90. *Welles Diary*, 2:279–80.

91. Charles A. Dana, *Recollections of the Civil War: With the Leaders at Washington and in the Field in the Sixties* (New York: D. Appleton, 1898), 267.

92. *Welles Diary*, 2:222.

93. Marquis de Chambrun, "Personal Recollections of Mr. Lincoln," *Scribner's Magazine*, January 1893, 28.

94. *CWL*, 8:359.

95. *RW*, 91.

96. Henrietta Stratton Jaquette, ed., *South after Gettysburg* (Philadelphia: University of Pennsylvania Press, 1937), 170.

97. Wilbur Fisk, *Hard Marching Every Day: The Civil War Letters of Private Wilbur

Fisk, 1861–1865, ed. Emil Rosenblatt and Ruth Rosenblatt (Lawrence: University Press of Kansas, 1992), 322–23.

98. Adelaide W. Smith, *Reminiscences of an Army Nurse during the Civil War* (New York: Greaves, 1911), 223–24.

99. Chambrun, "Personal Recollections of Mr. Lincoln," 32–34.

Chapter 36. "This War Is Eating My Life Out; I Have a Strong Impression That I Shall Not Live to See the End"

1. *SMDR*, 18 April 1865.

2. *IWAL*, 17.

3. Marquis de Chambrun, *Impressions of Lincoln and the Civil War: A Foreigner's Account* (New York: Random House, 1952), 83–86.

4. B. F. Morris, comp., *Memorial Record of the Nation's Tribute to Abraham Lincoln* (Washington, D.C.: W. H. & O. H. Morrison, 1865), 13.

5. Recollections of Francis Pierpont, typescript, Pierpont MSS, West Virginia University.

6. Washington *Daily Morning Chronicle*, 4 April 1865.

7. *CWL*, 8:393.

8. Keckley, *Behind the Scenes*, 176.

9. Noah Brooks, *Statesmen* (New York: C. Scribner's Sons, 1893), 214.

10. Frederick Douglass, manuscript of a speech, [ca. December 1865], Douglass MSS, LC.

11. George Alfred Townsend, *Katy of Catoctin* (New York: D. Appleton, 1886), 490n.

12. House Report no. 7, 40th Cong., 1st sess. (1867): 674.

13. LaWanda Cox, *Lincoln and Black Freedom: A Study in Presidential Leadership* (Columbia: University of South Carolina Press, 1981), 29.

14. Cox, *Lincoln and Black Freedom*, 142–43.

15. *CWL*, 8:399–405.

16. *Chase Diary*, 530; *Welles Diary*, 2:279–80.

17. Douglass, manuscript of a speech, [ca. December 1865].

18. Welles, *Selected Essays*, 184.

19. *RW*, 57.

20. *RW*, 114.

21. Welles, *Selected Essays*, 191.

22. *OR*, I, 46 pt. 3: 780, 785.

23. *Welles Diary*, 2:281.

24. Frank Abial Flower, *Edwin McMasters Stanton* (New York: Saalfield, 1905), 301–2; Seward, *Seward at Washington*, 2:274.

25. *Welles Diary*, 2:281–82; Welles, *Selected Essays*, 192.

26. Frederick W. Seward, *Reminiscences of a War-Time Statesman and Diplomat, 1830–1915* (New York: G. P. Putnam's Sons, 1916), 256.

27. *Welles Diary*, 2:282–83; Welles, *Selected Essays*, 188–89.

28. *OR*, I, 46 pt. 3: 785; W. Emerson Reck, *A. Lincoln: His Last 24 Hours* (Jefferson, N.C.: McFarland, 1987), 40.

29. Carpenter, *Six Months*, 293.

30. *RW*, 45, 349, 440.

31. *RW*, 194–95.

32. *Complete Hay Diary*, 246.

33. Timothy S. Good, ed., *We Saw Lincoln Shot: One Hundred Eyewitness Accounts* (Jackson: University Press of Mississippi, 1995), 71.

34. *RW*, 115.

35. Asia Booth Clarke, *The Unlocked Book: A Memoir of John Wilkes Booth by his Sister* (New York: G. P. Putnam's Sons, 1938), 139.

36. Mark A. Plummer, ed., "The Last Hours of Lincoln: The [Isham Nicholas] Haynie Diary," *Journal of Illinois History* 4 (2001): 36.

37. Michael W. Kauffman, *American Brutus: John Wilkes Booth and the Lincoln Conspiracies* (New York: Random House, 2004), 217–18.

38. John Wilkes Booth, *"Right or Wrong, God Judge Me": The Writings of John Wilkes*

Booth, ed. John Rhodehamel (Urbana: University of Illinois Press, 1997), 149.

39. Stanley Kimmel, *The Mad Booths of Maryland* (Indianapolis: Bobbs-Merrill, 1940), 175.

40. Kaufmann, *American Brutus*, 205.

41. Kimmel, *Mad Booths of Maryland*, 262.

42. George Francis to his niece Josephine, 5 May 1865, Lincoln Collection, CHM.

43. John Palmer Usher to his wife, 15 April 1865, copy, Usher MSS, LC.

44. Brooks, *Washington, D.C., in Lincoln's Time*, 251.

45. Thomas Pendel, *Thirty-Six Years in the White House* (Washington, D.C.: Neale, 1902), 42–44.

46. Kauffman, *American Brutus*, 37–38.

47. Charles Sabin Taft, "Abraham Lincoln's Last Hours," *Century Magazine*, February 1893, 635.

48. Charles A. Leale, "Lincoln's Last Hours," *Harper's Weekly*, 13 February 1909.

49. James Tanner to Henry F. Walch, 17 April 1865, UMi.

50. Moorfield Storey, "Dickens, Stanton, Sumner, and Storey," *Atlantic Monthly* 145 (1930): 463.

51. George S. Bryan, *The Great American Myth* (New York: Carrick & Evans, 1940), 189.

52. Frederick Douglass, eulogy for Lincoln, 1 June 1865, Douglass MSS, LC.

53. New York *World*, 7 February 1909.

Index

Page numbers in **bold** refer to illustrations.